THE CHANGING LAW OF NATIONS

THE CHANGING LAW OF NATIONS

Essays on International Law

By Josef L. Kunz

Ohio State University Press

To Hans Kelsen

Preface

CHANGE is the law of history. This book shows in a series of essays the tremendous change that the law of nations has undergone under the impact of world events since 1914. We are living in a period of world-wide, world-transforming, and most rapid change. But other periods of history have their change, too, even though they now appear to us relatively quiet; the difference is only in the magnitude and rapidity of change.

Change is the law of the life of man. Change could be the symbol of the life of the author. He is writing these lines as an old American citizen, but he was born in Vienna. He has changed continents; he has traveled the world; he knows every country in Europe and every country in the Americas. Educated in the Roman law, he has now, for over thirty years, studied the common law, too. He started his academic career in international law as an assistant professor at the Vienna University School of Law, and he came to America as a representative of the Vienna School of International Law. He has lectured at many universities in the United States, Latin America, and Europe, and has published in English, German, French, and Spanish. But with all this change there has to come the normal change involved in the growth from childhood to old age.

Change is the law of the universe. The stars eternally rotate; new stars constantly are born and old ones disappear; the universe itself is continuously expanding. This dynamic movement and change of which the destiny of men on this small planet is only a part was expressed two thousand years ago by a Greek philosopher of genius, Heraclitus of Ephesus, in two words: *Panta rhei* ("Everything flows").

It is the agreeable duty of the author to thank the Ohio State University Press for publishing this book. These thanks have to be made personally to two men: To the Director, Weldon A. Kefauver, who entered into negotiations with the author, completed the contract, and guided publication; and to the Editor, Thomas E. Sheahan, who has had the long and difficult task of preparing the manuscript for production.

JOSEF L. KUNZ

Toledo, Ohio
August 30, 1964

Acknowledgments

THE KIND PERMISSION of the original publishers to reprint the following essays is gratefully acknowledged.

"The Changing Law of Nations" was first published in the *American Journal of International Law*, Vol. LI. Copyright © 1957 by the American Society of International Law.

"The Distinctiveness of the International Legal Order: Comparison and Contrast" was first published in the *Ohio State Law Journal*, Vol. XXII. Copyright © 1961 by the *Ohio State Law Journal*.

"Pluralism of Legal and Value Systems and International Law" was first published in the *American Journal of International Law*, Vol. XLIX. Copyright © 1955 by the American Society of International Law.

"The 'Vienna School' and International Law" was first published in the *New York University Law Quarterly Review*, Vol. XI. Copyright © 1934 by the *New York University Law Review*.

"The Swing of the Pendulum" was first published in the *American Journal of International Law*, Vol. XLIV. Copyright © 1950 by the American Society of International Law.

"The Systematic Problem of the Science of International Law" was first published in the *American Journal of International Law*, Vol. LIII. Copyright © 1959 by the American Society of International Law.

"Natural-Law Thinking in the Modern Science of International Law" was first published in the *American Journal of International Law*, Vol. LV. Copyright © 1961 by the American Society of International Law.

"The Changing Science of International Law" was first published in the *American Journal of International Law*, Vol. LVI. Copyright © 1962 by the American Society of International Law.

"The Italo-Austrian Agreement on the Austrian South Tyrol" was first published in the *American Journal of International Law*, Vol. XLI. Copyright © 1947 by the American Society of International Law.

"Nationality and Option Clauses in the Italian Peace Treaty of 1947" was first published in the *American Journal of International Law*, Vol. XLI. Copyright © 1947 by the American Society of International Law.

"The Future of the International Law for the Protection of National Minorities" was first published in the *American Journal of International Law*, Vol. XXXIX. Copyright © 1945 by the American Society of International Law.

"The Free Territory of Trieste" was first published in the *Western Political Quarterly*, Vol. I. Copyright © 1948 by the *Western Political Quarterly*.

"The Status of Occupied Germany under International Law: A Legal Dilemma" was first published in the *Western Political Quarterly*, Vol. III. Copyright © 1950 by the *Western Political Quarterly*.

"The Status of the Holy See in International Law" was first published in the *American Journal of International Law*, Vol. XLIX. Copyright © 1955 by the American Society of International Law.

"Identity of States under International Law" was first published in the *American Journal of International Law*, Vol. XLIX. Copyright © 1955 by the American Society of International Law.

"The Present Status of the International Law for the Protection of Minorities" was first published in the *American Journal of International Law*, Vol. XLVIII. Copyright © 1954 by the American Society of International Law.

"The State Treaty with Austria" was first published in the *American Journal of International Law*, Vol. XLIX. Copyright © 1955 by the American Society of International Law.

"Austria's Permanent Neutrality" was first published in the *American Journal of International Law*, Vol. L. Copyright © 1956 by the American Society of International Law.

"The Nature of Customary International Law" was first published in the *American Journal of International Law*, Vol. XLVII. Copyright © 1953 by the American Society of International Law.

"The Meaning and the Range of the Norm *Pacta Sunt Servanda*" was first published in the *American Journal of International Law*, Vol. XXXIX. Copyright © 1945 by the American Society of International Law.

"Revolutionary Creation of Norms of International Law" was first published in the *American Journal of International Law*, Vol. XLI. Copyright © 1947 by the American Society of International Law.

"International Law by Analogy" was first published in the *American Journal of International Law*, Vol. XLV. Copyright © 1951 by the American Society of International Law.

"Roberto Ago's Theory of a 'Spontaneous' International Law" was first published in the *American Journal of International Law*, Vol. LII. Copyright © 1958 by the American Society of International Law.

"The Nottebohm Judgment (Second Phase)" was first published in the *American Journal of International Law*, Vol. LIV. Copyright © 1960 by the American Society of International Law.

"Experience and Techniques in International Administration" was first published in the *Iowa Law Review*, Vol. XXXI. Copyright © 1945 by the *Iowa Law Review*.

"General International Law and the Law of International Organizations" was first published in the *American Journal of International Law*, Vol. XLVII. Copyright © 1953 by the American Society of International Law.

"Privileges and Immunities of International Organizations" was first published in the *American Journal of International Law*, Vol. XLI. Copyright © 1947 by the American Society of International Law.

"The Legal Position of the Secretary General of the United Nations" was first published in the *American Journal of International Law*, Vol. XL. Copyright © 1946 by the American Society of International Law.

"Individual and Collective Self-defense in Article LI of the Charter of the United Nations" was first published in the *American Journal of International Law*, Vol. XL. Copyright © 1947 by the American Society of International Law.

"Bellum Justum and Bellum Legale" was first published in the *American Journal of International Law*, Vol. XLV. Copyright © 1951 by the American Society of International Law.

"Compulsory International Adjudication and Maintenance of Peace" was first published in the *American Journal of International Law*, Vol. XXXVIII. Copyright © 1944 by the American Society of International Law.

"The United Nations and the Rule of Law" was first published in the *American Journal of International Law*, Vol. XLVI. Copyright © 1952 by the American Society of International Law.

"Supranational Organs" was first published in the *American Journal of International Law*, Vol. XLVI. Copyright © 1952 by the American Society of International Law.

"The Secretary General on the Role of the United Nations" was first published in the *American Journal of International Law*, Vol. LII. Copyright © 1958 by the American Society of International Law.

"Sanctions in International Law" was first published in the *American Journal of International Law*, Vol. LIV. Copyright © 1961 by the American Society of International Law.

"International Arbitration in Pan-American Developments" was first published in the *Texas Law Review*, Vol. XXII. Copyright © 1948 by the *Texas Law Review*.

"The Idea of Collective Security in Pan-American Developments" was first published in the *Western Political Quarterly*, Vol. VI. Copyright © 1953 by the *Western Political Quarterly*.

"The Inter-American Treaty of Reciprocal Assistance" was first published in the *American Journal of International Law*, Vol. XLII. Copyright © 1948 by the American Society of International Law.

"The Bogotá Charter of the Organization of American States" was first published in the *American Journal of International Law*, Vol. XLII. Copyright © 1948 by the American Society of International Law.

"British Prize Cases, 1939–1941" was first published in the *American Journal of International Law*, Vol. XXXVI. Copyright © 1942 by the American Society of International Law.

"The Chaotic Status of the Laws of War and the Urgent Necessity for Their Revision" was first published in the *American Journal of International Law*, Vol. XLV. Copyright © 1951 by the American Society of International Law.

"The Laws of War" was first published in the *American Journal of International Law*, Vol. L. Copyright © 1956 by the American Society of International Law.

"The New U. S. Army Field Manual on the Law of Land Warfare" was first published in the *American Journal of International Law*, Vol. LI. Copyright © 1957 by the American Society of International Law.

"The 1956 Draft Rules of the International Committee of the Red Cross at the New Delhi Conference" was first published in the *American Journal of International Law*, Vol. LIII. Copyright © 1959 by the American Society of International Law.

Contents

PART VII: Laws of War

PART I

INTERNATIONAL LAW

CHAPTER 1: The Changing Law of Nations

IT HAS OFTEN BEEN STATED [1] that international law, although primitive as to structure and contents, has shown a remarkable stability as compared with more advanced legal orders. From its beginnings until 1914 it presents a clear continuity of development; no revolution as to its basic structure occurred. It remained based upon the same sociological foundations—the international community of sovereign states—and upon the same axiological foundation—the values of the Greek-Christian occidental culture.

True, international law during the nineteenth century saw an important, progressive development, including the beginnings of international organization. But the framework within which this progress developed remained essentially the same. The "classic" international law was, despite its world-wide expansion, a law based on occidental values: it was the law of a world in which Europe dominated Asia and Africa; it was the law of a pluralism of sovereign states, including a number of "Great Powers." But these states showed a more or less ideological conformity, as being mostly national states based on the values of the liberal, constitutional, democratic *Rechtsstaat*. Hence, the problem of keeping the peace was predominantly the problem of balance of power.

But in these last decades international law has been in a period of flux, restlessness, and profound change; recent developments are often full of contradictions. The year 1914 is the turning-point—a turning-point, but, as Max Huber points out, not a break. For, despite all changes, it has not been possible to "ban the spirit of sovereignty." Notwithstanding all new tendencies and changes, international law, even today, is still basically the law of a community of sovereign states.

It would, of course, be a mistake to identify change with progress, as some are inclined to do. Change can mean progress, but it can also mean retrogression. Newer developments have sometimes been strongly retrogressive. There is, further, the obvious ineffectiveness of some new rules and institutions such as the norms restricting or forbidding the use of force, the norms concerning collective security or international sanctions. Newer developments sometimes show a merely experimental character and are even ephemeral, such as mandates, international protection of minorities, the League of Nations. Hence, the changing law of nations is characterized by the uncertainty, insecurity, provisional nature of many rules or even of whole departments of that law. This present status makes any prophecy of the future of international law hazardous. Such future may lie between the extremes of an ethically higher and more effective law of one world and the possibility of a rapid fall of the whole law of nations, a return to ages of anarchy and barbarism; in the light of the terrible effect of modern weapons, even the vision of an end of civilization, of a possible suicide of humanity, cannot be wholly excluded. Only one thing is certain: a return to the shores of 1914 is impossible.

It is only natural that this changing and unsettled status of international law should have exercised a profound influence, not only on the minds of laymen, but also on the science of international law, that it should have led to often contradictory attitudes and bitter polemics between adherents of opposed opinions. That is why we see even among professional international lawyers such opposite attitudes as, on the one hand, the strong conservatives, passionately opposing any change in the "classic" law, or the "neo-realists," throwing that law away as "sterile," "insignificant," as a "naïve illusion," and proudly concentrating on the study of "naked power calculations"; and, on the other hand, the "wishful thinkers," confusing their dreams with reality, and the utopian preachers of the world federal state.

It is this unsettled and dynamic status of international law which, as far as methods are concerned, has led to an attack against analytical jurisprudence from two opposite sides: the adherents of "natural law," confusing, in extreme cases, law with ethics, and the pure sociologists, confusing law with fact, or, as in the case of the so-called policy science, confusing law with politics, confusing the law with the procedure of its making.

It is clear that the correct approach as to the attitude taken and the methods applied lies in the middle: sociological and axiological considerations are indispensable for a full understanding of the law; but it is, of course, equally indispensable to recognize the essentially normative character of law.[2]

II

This changing and insecure status of international law seems to stem from two different sets of phenomena which this writer has called the "crisis" and the "transformations" of the law of nations.[3] The "transformations" are the changes resulting from the change of general conditions, even if there were no crisis, although this change of general conditions contains also elements of the crisis. On top of these transformations there is a deep crisis which has its roots in earlier developments, but has become actual since the end of World War II. The change in the changing law of nations is, therefore, not along one line, or in one direction, but in many, sometimes contradictory, directions.

There is a transition from the law of a plurality of "Great Powers" to the law of a bi-polar world. There is the change from a law of a community of states with a certain ideological conformity to the law of two worlds, basically hostile to each other and with incompatible ideologies. Hence, the problem of peace is no longer so much a problem of balance of power, but a problem of what is now called "peaceful co-existence."

There is, further, a transition from the law of an international community of predominantly occidental character to the law of a community embracing also the very different legal and value systems of the non-occidental world.[4]

There is, finally, the transition from the "classic" to the "new" international law, from the law of a loose, unorganized society of sovereign states to a more organized, more centralized law; the transition from the traditional international law, limited in contents, dealing exclusively with the relations between sovereign states, to what Dr. Jenks [5] conceives as "an international law, expanded in scope, an international law representing the common law of mankind in an early stage of its development."

III

The changing character of international law is, first, a consequence of a transformation of general conditions, a transformation the impact of which is equally felt in the municipal legal orders. The "classic" international law presupposed the doctrines of democracy, capitalism, economic liberalism, "laissez faire," the principles of the sanctity of private property, the strict distinction between private enterprise and economic activities by states, the strict distinction between armed forces and the civilian population. All that has fundamentally changed. The coming of total war, of ever-expanding economic activities by states, the control by states of the economic life of the nation even in times of peace and more so in times of war, the appearance of totalitarian regimes, have profoundly influenced old and well-established rules of international law and brought about far-reaching uncertainty. These transformations, while particularly prominent in totalitarian states, are nevertheless more or less universal, to be seen also in the democracies of the free world. They have shaken the basis of many rules of the laws of war and of the law of neutrality. They have changed and made insecure the rules concerning immunity from jurisdiction of states in their economic activities, state instrumentalities, government-owned merchant vessels, government corporations; and the rules concerning state responsibility (political parties, subversive and terrorist activities, hostile propaganda), and finally the rules concerning nationalization, expropriation, confiscation.[6]

There are tendencies to weaken or to question old and well-established rules of international law: there is a tendency against conquest as a title of acquisition of sovereignty; there is uncertainty as to the so-called doctrine of contiguity; there is much confusion as to the recognition of states and governments; there are very doubtful areas as far as the law of international treaties is concerned, and a weakening of the requirement of effectivity by which sovereignty is acquired by occupation of a *terra nullius;* there is a complete lack of agreement as to the acquisition of sovereignty in the Arctic and in the Antarctic.

Technological developments have led to uncertainties in the laws of war, such as aerial war, chemical and bacterio-

logical warfare, magnetic mines, and so on, or have led to
completely new norms in fields which before had not been
of practical importance. The coming of aviation has led in
a short time to the new norm of general customary international law according to which the legal status of the airspace
is the same as the status of the subjacent space. We are at
the threshold of a completely new "international space
law."[7] The new interest in making use of the water of
streams for purposes of irrigation, hydroelectric power, and
so on, is transforming the laws of international rivers,
hitherto dominated by the interests of navigation.[8]

Other changes stem from technological (geological and
engineering) advances combined with economic considerations, neo-Malthusian fears of overpopulation, and an upsurge of sovereignty: the new norms *in fieri* concerning
the continental shelf, the disquieting developments with
regard to the limits of territorial waters, contiguous zones,
the law of high-seas fishing, developments which, in extreme
cases, threaten the survival of the fundamental principle
juris cogentis of the freedom of the high seas.

There is, further, the advent and enormous expansion of
international organizations, quasi-universal and regional,
general and specialized. They have brought many new developments: international organizations as subjects of international law; in the field of international treaties, privileges and immunities, responsibility, capacity to claim
indemnities. There is no doubt that the scope of international law, formerly restricted to relations between sovereign states, has expanded: stateless persons, refugees,
indigenous populations of trusteeship territories, solution
of economic, financial, social, health, cultural, educational
problems on a world-wide scale, development of, and technical aid and assistance to, underdeveloped countries. There
is no doubt that the law of international organizations, although based on particular international law, has also
deeply influenced general international law.[9]

The new quasi-universal general international organizations have not restricted themselves to international co-operation in the so-called non-political fields. They have attempted to regulate activities which the states hitherto have regarded as their exclusive domain. Hence new ideas and experiments have appeared which would have been unthinkable prior to 1914: the attempt to restrict or even abolish the use of force in international relations, the idea of "international concern" as expressed in Article XI of the League of Nations Covenant, the ideas of collective security and international sanctions, the attempts at an international criminal law and international protection of human rights. True, many of these attempts have hitherto been ineffective and have made whole departments of the law, like the laws of war and the law of neutrality, extremely insecure. These attempts have led scholars to question the whole philosophy on which the current concept of international organization is based.[10] Scholars have insisted that it is impossible to make revolutionary changes without changing the sociological foundations on which present-day international law is based. Charles De Visscher has written that any advance in this direction must start with a change in the distribution of power which, at this time, is in the hands of the sovereign states. Yet, on the other hand, it is unlikely that these new ideas, inspired by a deep concern with the consequences of modern war, will, despite their ineffectiveness so far, disappear completely.

IV

On top of all these elements of transformation there is an actual crisis, the elements of which can be only briefly enumerated here. There is, first, the decline of Europe, which prior to 1914 was the hub of international affairs, the creator of our occidental culture and of our international law based on the values of that culture. The center of gravity of occidental culture has definitively shifted from Europe to the United States of America.

There is, second, the emergence of the Soviet Union as the other of the only two Great Powers, a phenomenon which by itself has completely changed the power structure of the world. There is, third, the split between two antagonistic worlds, each led by one of the two Great Powers, the deep ideological abyss, the cold war. It is obvious that this split has the most far-reaching influence on general international law and the law and functions of international organizations.

There is, fourth, the "anti-colonial rebellion." The upsurge of Asia and Africa is a challenge, not only to Europe, but to the whole occidental world of the white man.

There is, fifth, the coming of the atomic age, a technological development to which a special place must be assigned, for in the last analysis it places humanity before the dilemma of a true peace or annihilation.

But all the transformations, all the elements hitherto mentioned, of the crisis do not yet fully explain the present crisis of the law of nations. For this is only a partial phenomenon of the total crisis of our whole occidental culture. This crisis produces many technical, including legal, problems; but, as every authentic and genuine crisis, it has its deepest and veritable roots in philosophy, ethics, and religion. It is the crisis of the ideals and values of our occidental culture which has produced in all realms of human life the uncertainty, insecurity, provisional nature, so characteristic of this epoch since 1914. Modern man has lost faith, has lost his connection with God. He has during the last centuries put all the emphasis on natural sciences and technology—and has done so with astonishing success. But the truly fundamental problems, which are not the technological problems dealing only with means but those dealing with the ends, have been neglected or ignored. Man has confused technological with ethical progress. The present crisis clearly shows that these fundamental problems cannot be ignored with impunity. That is why man today finds himself unprepared for his own scientific conquests, which tend to become a mortal danger rather than a benefit. Modern life has strongly contributed to bring about and to deepen this spiritual crisis: the de-personalization of man through the machine, the struggle, haste, and overburdening of modern life, the lack of time, energy, and the will to perfect oneself. There has been the emergence of the masses, dominating modern life, the serious crisis of the intellectual elites; hence the decline of great literature, art, and music, the monotony of modern "entertainment" by standardized mass media, productions which so often bring out the contrast between the technologically wonderful means and the inartistic, valueless contents. Hence the indifference to everything which is not "practical" in terms of money and power, the lack of interest in the higher things; hence also the declining respect for the rule of law, the "politicization" of everything, the unwillingness of men to think, the mass indoctrination, the preference given to security over freedom, the superficiality and spiritual emptiness of the life of the majority of mankind; as the president of Georgetown University formulated it a few years ago in a speech: The majority of men in the so-called backward countries have nothing to live on and the majority of men in the so-called advanced countries have nothing to live for. A true civilization is not a technological but an ethical phenomenon; where the ethical basis disappears, a civilization is bound to disappear. Who can look without the deepest concern at the horrible persecutions and tortures, at the growing inhumanity of men toward men, as shown by total war, at the prevalence of purely materialistic doctrines which necessarily imply nihilistic consequences? That is why a truly great man, Dr. Albert Schweitzer in his speech on the occasion of receiving the Nobel Peace Prize, could speak of the "horror and inhumanity of our present existence."

To overcome the crisis and to preserve our occidental culture more is needed than technical means, however important and indispensable they are. Thus also for a truly progressive international law, what is needed, in the deepest sense, is a spiritual, ethical regeneration: For man does *not* live by bread alone.

[1] Cf. Max Huber, *Die Wandlungen des Völkerrechts*, 52 DIE FRIEDENS-WARTE 297–310 (1955).

[2] This is the approach of CHARLES DE VISSCHER, THÉORIES ET RÉALITÉS EN DROIT INTERNATIONAL PUBLIC (1953).

[3] See this writer's lectures in French, "La Crise et les Transformations du Droit des Gens," to be published in the *Recueil des Cours* of the Hague Academy of International Law.

[4] See "Pluralism of Legal and Value Systems and International Law," below.

[5] C. W. Jenks, *The Scope of International Law*, 31 BRIT. YB. INT'L L. 1–48 (1956).

[6] These transformations are dealt with in the article of W. Friedmann, *Some Impacts of Social Organization on International Law*, 50 AM. J. INT'L L. 474–514 (1956).

[7] The strictly legal question has been asked: Who owns the universe? Cf. C. W. Jenks, *International Law and Activities in Space*, 5 INT'L & COMP. L. Q. 99–114 (1956); PROCEEDINGS OF THE AMERICAN SOCIETY OF INTERNATIONAL LAW 84–115 (1956). See also the attempts to frame principles of a new international law applicable to the realms of space at the International Astronautical Congress, held in Rome (N. Y. Times, September 20, 1956, p. 12).

[8] Cf., e.g., J. J. Lador-Lederer, *Vom Wasserweg zur internationalen Gemeinschaft*, 53 DIE FRIEDENS-WARTE 225–44 (1956).

[9] See this writer's editorial, *General International Law and the Law of International Organizations*, 47 AM. J. INT'L L. 456–62 (1953).

[10] See W. SCHIFFER, THE LEGAL COMMUNITY OF MANKIND (1954).

CHAPTER II: The Distinctiveness of the International Legal System: Comparison and Contrast

IN ORDER TO WRITE on the distinctiveness of the international legal order by comparison and contrast, it is, first of all, necessary to clarify the meaning of this problem. Such clarification again presupposes a firm theoretical basis from which to start. A sketch of this writer's views on these preliminary problems will be given here by way of introduction.

With which legal orders do we compare and contrast the international legal order? Most writers, such as John Austin, believe the comparison can only be made with advanced municipal legal orders, but that constitutes an unjustified narrowing of the concept of law. Primitive law is law, too. If we take into consideration also constitutional and administrative law, the distinctiveness of international law appears in a different light. It has correctly been stated that many problems of modern labor law can be analogized to problems of international law.

All that presupposes a basic concept of what law is. For this writer a legal order is a system of norms, prescriptive in nature—a coercive order which regulates human conduct in such a way that under certain conditions prescribed by law a legal sanction, as determined by law, ought to follow; the particularity of a legal sanction, as compared, *e.g.*, with a moral sanction, consists in the fact that the sanction, prescribed by law, ought to take place on this earth [1] without or against the will of the person against which it is applied and ought to be executed if necessary by the application of physical force.[2] This delimits a legal norm, not only against the "laws of natural science" which are statements of facts linking cause to effect, but also against norms of other normative systems, such as moral, religious, or conventional norms. Whatever the "realists" may tell us, it is obvious that the corresponding norm of criminal law does *not* predict that a murderer *will* be hanged—which is often not the case—but that he *ought* to be hanged. Laws of natural science, including sociology, can only be true or false; legal norms can only be valid or not. Nevertheless, the "oughtness" is not without links to "isness" and the norms of law are standards of valuation of the *real* conduct of men; a norm must be valid, but it must further be, by and large, effective. Mere paper rules are not legal norms.

This analytical definition of a legal norm does not overlook either the contents of the norm or the fact and values. The *making* of the law is, of course, a political, sociological, and historical problem; a problem in the realm of "isness." But the norm thus created is the objective meaning of the norm-creating act—a prescription in the realm of "oughtness." This writer has always insisted that a knowledge of all three elements—norms, facts, and values—is necessary in order to understand a given legal order fully. One must not only study the legal norms analytically; one must also know how they were made, the political and sociological environment from which they arose, the basic values on which they are based, the ultimate ends which they want to realize—all that is of particular importance with regard to international law.

One must further take the *whole* legal order into consideration. Continental lawyers restrict the "law" often to the constitution, statutes, and ordinances; whereas, contracts, judicial, and administrative decisions are for them not "law," but only "application" of law. American "realists," on the other hand, see only court decisions and sometimes deny even the existence of general legal norms. For Continental lawyers, there are only general legal norms, for "realists" there are only individual legal norms. This stand is certainly a consequence of the history of the two legal systems: the codified law, based on Roman law, in which the legal hero is the legislator (and, perhaps, the savant), whereas the judge remains in anonymous obscurity; and the "judge-made" common law. But both standpoints are theoretically untenable. A legal order is a dynamic system which itself regulates the creation of the law— a "pyramid" consisting of general as well as individual legal norms. It is not possible to strictly delimit "creation" and "application" of law. Just as the legislator creating a statute at the same time applies constitutional norms, thus a judge is never merely an automatic "applier" but always also a creator of law, creator of an individual legal norm, and, under some legal orders, also a creator of general legal norms.

We must, further, not only know with what we have to compare and contrast, but we must know also what is meant by the "international law" which is to be compared and contrasted. It is clear that such international law as may have existed earlier [3] has no historical connection with *our present-day* international law with which we are to deal. *Our* international law is strictly an historical creation of western Europe; it is, therefore, not necessarily *the* international law, but only one of the possible international laws. It came historically into being among the Christian states of western Europe. It presupposes in consequence a plurality of sovereign states having a certain community of culture and interests and being in contact *inter se*. There is already here a certain distinctiveness: there must not always be an international law in our sense, namely where these presuppositions do not exist; thus, there was no international law in the Imperium Romanum, nor between medieval Europe and the Inca Empire.

Nor is there any guarantee that our international law will continue to exist in the future. Like any historical creation, it may come to an end and be replaced by something else. There is a theoretical, although at this time no practical, possibility of a world state. Whether it would be created by one power or as a world federal state, it would mean that our international law has come to an end and been replaced by "world law," i.e., the municipal law of the world state.

There is a further distinctiveness. From the moment that our international law came into existence up to the present day, its legal character has been challenged, whereas ancient, primitive Germanic law, or the primitive law of African tribes has always been recognized as law. Now, if international law were not law, it would make no sense to compare and contrast it with other legal orders; one would only have to delimit it from law, as Austin did, who saw in international law not law, but only "positive morality." Naturally, this fundamental problem of whether international law is law at all cannot be investigated here. For this writer it *is* law, although primitive law. As our international law is based on the practice of states, it seems to us sufficient here to point out that the practice of states has treated international law at all times as law in the legal sense and carefully and sharply distinguishes it from other international normative systems, such as "international ethics" and "courtoisie internationale."

II

The international law to be compared and contrasted is the historical creation of western Europe. Although it has its roots in the Middle Ages of Catholic western Europe, in the "Communitas Christiana," [4] it is exactly through the decentralization of this medieval Christian community that both the single sovereign states and our international law came into being. It was a new law—a fresh start. A legal order must not only have a structure but also a content; legal norms must be created, and the creators of law cannot shape its contents *ex nihilo*. The creation of early international law was done by Catholic theologians, and later by lawyers based on the Roman law. That explains why many rules of international law,[5] some of them still valid today, are mere transplantations of norms of Roman private law into the international sphere. That explains also the great role of "natural law" in early international law, as this "natural law" came from Roman law—which itself was regarded on the Continent as "ratio scripta"—and the dogmas of Christianity. This early international law was valid only for the Christian states of western Europe and the Holy See.[6] This early international law was exclusively based on the values of the Greek - Christian, occidental culture.[7]

Now, this early international law has seen, from the fifteenth century to the end of World War I, a great development, both as to its contents and to the territorial sphere of its validity. In the latter respect, the United States and the Latin-American republics became members of the international community and, later, other states, like Australia and New Zealand, based primarily on the occidental culture. To this geographical expansion outside of Europe came an expansion outside of the occidental culture. In 1856, Turkey was admitted into the international community; from that time on to 1914, and in League of Nations times, international law, originally a "regional" law of Christian western Europe, became valid for nearly all states, regardless of continent, religion, culture, race, and so on; it had become universal. The worldwide expansion of our international law was strictly an historical phenomenon. Hence, just as there is no guarantee that our international law will be valid in all future times, there is no guarantee that it will retain its universal validity at all times.

Another fundamental remark has to be made. While international law, although primitive in structure and content, has seen this great development in its content and in its territorial validity up to 1914, this development of international law has shown, contrary to many advanced municipal legal orders, a remarkable stability and a clear continuity, and no revolutionary change as to its basic structure has occurred. It remained based on the same sociological foundations, on European legal systems—rather predominantly Roman law—anchored exclusively on the values of the occidental culture, notwithstanding its universal validity. It was the law of a world in which Europe and the United States, equally of the occidental culture, dominated in all fields; of a world in which Europe, through colonies, protectorates, and many other devices, dominated Asia and Africa. This period of hundreds of years, up to 1914, may be called, for reasons of brevity, the period of the "classic" law of nations.

But since the end of World War I, and particularly since 1945, international law has been in a period of uncertainty, constant flux, transformation, and crisis; we may speak, for reasons of brevity, of the "new" international law. But while 1914 constitutes a turning point in the development of our international law, it does not constitute a break; it is only a new phase of the development of *our* international law. This insight dictates the approach to writing on the distinctiveness of the international legal order by comparison and contrast: first, this distinctiveness of the classic international law must be briefly investigated; then, the difference between the "new" and the classic law of nations must be briefly stated, showing that, in spite of this difference, the distinctiveness of international law, whether before or after 1914, compared with other legal orders has only changed in degree, but not in kind.

III

If we compare classic international law with *all* other legal orders, it *is* law. If we compare it with the advanced municipal legal orders of sovereign states and, particularly, with private law, it is law, but a law of a different type. If we, finally, compare it with certain fields of advanced municipal law, such as constitutional law or modern labor law, this difference becomes somewhat *deminimis*. This difference between classic international law and advanced municipal legal orders has two different sources; the primitiveness of structure, and certain particularities of a sociological nature.

From its beginnings up to 1914, our international law was nearly exclusively [8] the law "between" sovereign states, first between those of Christian western Europe, then, by 1914, between nearly all sovereign states. Its definition as "the body of customary and treaty rules which are considered legally binding by States in their intercourse with each other" [9] was correct. Our international law came into being, as stated, together with the coming into existence of national, territorial, and sovereign states through the decentralization of the "Communitas Christiana." That explains that these sovereign states, as well as the international community, are primarily territorial communities. Modern municipal law, as well as international law, are legal orders on a territorial rather than on a personal basis. That explains that certain principles came into existence which, more or less, have remained basic up to the present day—the sovereignty of states, their equality and independ-

ence, their jurisdiction within the territorial limits of the
state. It was the claim to sovereignty, with which the "divi-
sio regnorum" started; Bartolus' definition of sovereign
states as "civitates superiorem non recognoscentes" led to
the definition of Bodin. The bearer of sovereignty has
changed—originally "the prince," since the French Revolution, "la nation," and since the nineteenth century, "the
State." But sovereignty has remained basic for international
law. In the sense of Bartolus' definition it has had and has
"no superior"; it is a law *inter pares*, a "law of co-ordination," not, as advanced municipal legal orders, a law of
subordination.

Primitiveness is not a feature of international law alone,
it is characteristic for all law, whether municipal or international, at a certain stage of its development. The primitiveness of any legal order is a consequence of its lack of
organization, of its lack of centralization. Classic international law was—and international law is still today—a
highly decentralized legal order. It is decentralized dynamically by its lack of special organs for the making, application, and execution of its norms. As in any primitive law, all
these functions must be exercised by the members of the legal community, hence by the sovereign states. There are no
special organs for the creation of norms of international
law, there was and is no international legislature; hence,
the sovereign states are not only the nearly exclusive subjects, but also the creators of the rules of international law;
the methods of creation—custom and treaty—are highly
decentralized. General international law, binding on all the
states of the international community, has been created only
by custom. Treaty law is always particular international
law, binding only on the states which have ratified the
treaty. To that extent the norms of general international
law created by custom are relatively few whereas the bulk
of modern international law consists of treaty law binding

only on certain states. The small range of international law, up to 1914, is not only to be explained by the lack of an international legislature, but also classic international law dealt nearly exclusively with the rights and duties of sovereign states and many problems, although of the highest international importance, were excluded by "sovereignty" and exclusive jurisdiction of the members of the international community.

International law was decentralized dynamically because its norms oblige only states, not individuals. An international norm prescribes what is or is not to be done by a "state," and delegates to the municipal legal orders the function to designate the persons who, as organs of the states, have to do it. The acts of these individuals are imputed by international law, not to them, but to the states on behalf of which they act. Treaties, granting certain advantages to the citizens of the contracting parties, must first be "transformed" into municipal law. International law is, therefore, not only a primitive, but also an *incomplete*, legal order which needs the municipal legal orders for the completion of its own norms.

There are no special organs for the application of international law. Thus, there are no special international organs to ascertain objectively whether a territorial community has fulfilled the conditions laid down by international law for the coming into existence of a new sovereign state; hence, the "recognition" of new states is left to the existing sovereign states. In consequence of the lack of special international organs, sovereign states, under general international law, have the right of auto-interpretation of the treaties which they have concluded, although this right ought to be exercised in good faith. For the same reason, sovereign states, under general international law, have a right of auto-determination of the existence of an international delinquency as well as of its legal consequences. As

there is, under general international law, a complete lack
of collective sanctions, neither special organs nor a monopoly of force are at the disposal of the international community. General international law, like any primitive law,
must rely on the principle of self-help under general international law, reprisals, and war.

General international law recognizes the validity of certain treaties, even if they are imposed by force upon the
other party; it does not distinguish delinquencies into torts
and crimes; it makes no distinction as to sanctions between
civil execution and criminal penalty; it does not know individual responsibility for fault, but only absolute, collective
responsibility. The primitiveness of classic international law
is emphasized by the great importance which the principle
of effectivity bears.

The tremendous disadvantages of classic international
law as a primitive law are obvious; it was, primarily, a
static law. It was impossible to state with legal authenticity
which state in an international conflict was legally right and
which legally wrong. In the case of the application of force,
it was again impossible to state objectively which state
acted legally. Custom, as the only way of creating norms of
general international law, often rendered classic international law inadequate for the needs of the times. The right
of auto-interpretation of treaties, of auto-determination of
international delinquencies, of responsibility for them, and
of the legal consequences—all gave great advantages to the
powerful states. The absence of international courts with
compulsory jurisdiction made the peaceful settlement of
international legal conflicts impossible except by agreement.
The absence of an international legislature rendered the
problem of "peaceful change" again only possible of solution
by agreement. Classic international law made the resort to
war never an international delinquency; war served not
only as a sanction by way of self-help but also as a revolu-

tionary means to change the law. The principle of effectivity emphasized the role of the *fait accompli*. The principle of sovereignty emphasized the "vital interests" of the members, regardless of law. Classic general international law was a primitive and a weak legal order.

Notwithstanding its primitiveness and its weakness, international law, if one accepts it to be law, is necessarily a law *above* the states—a law *inter pares*. A "law of co-ordination" is necessarily above the *pares*, otherwise it would not be law at all. All law is by nature heteronomous, or "vertical."

IV [10]

Classic international law had necessarily to delimit its own competence from that of the sovereign states. Whereas the sovereignty of states is limited by norms of international law, the spheres of validity of international law are, in principle, unlimited. It is international law which determines by its norms which entities are "persons in international law." The temporal sphere of validity is, in principle, unlimited in the sense that general international law does not contain norms by which its rules would be limited as to their temporal validity; treaty norms, on the other hand, often contain rules limiting their validity in time.

Unlimited also was the territorial sphere of validity of classic international law. It included, by 1914, not only the territories of nearly all the sovereign states, but, in addition, the high seas, the air space above the high seas, and the *terrae nullius*.

The material sphere of validity of international law is also unlimited. There are *no* matters which, by their nature, can *only* be regulated by municipal law. International law has the "compétence de la compétence"; it may, at any moment, regulate matters which hitherto have been regulated only by municipal law. In a federal state federal law is above the law of the states of the union, but this superiority says nothing about the actual division of competences, thus, the "compétence de la compétence" of international law says nothing as to the actual division of competences between international law and the sovereign states. This actual division of competences can always only be stated on the basis of the analysis of the positive law actually in force. Such analysis of classic international law shows that the majority of competences and the most important ones were actually given by international law to the sovereign states. This explains the relatively small range of the norms of general international law and is one of the reasons for the weakness of the international legal order.

Medieval Catholic western Europe had its constitution in the "Communitas Christiana" with its two highest powers, emperor and Pope. Beginning in the late Middle Ages, the gradual decentralization of this Christian community brought about the appearance of the national, territorial, sovereign states and the "international community" as the successor of the medieval Christian community as a loose union, now consisting of sovereign states, which disclaimed any allegiance to emperor and Pope. Their sovereignty was deprived, as Bodin stated for the king of France, "par Dieu et son épée." This would have brought about a situation of anarchy and constant threat of war. To prevent that, international law came into being to guarantee relative peace among the now sovereign states. It must also not be forgotten that these new states, insisting on their sovereignty, recognized the sovereignty of the other members of the western European Christian international community. The first and most urgent task of the new international law was, therefore, to secure the relatively *peaceful coexistence* of the sovereign states of Christian western Europe. This was done by delimiting the jurisdictions of the sovereign states and their legal orders *inter se* through rules of general international law created by custom. Every legal norm and order has a fourfold validity: as to time, as to matters, as to territory, and as to persons.

General international law delimited the validity of the legal orders of sovereign states in time.[11] It delimited their material validity, a problem of jurisdiction, by granting to the sovereign states in principle the highest and nearly exclusive jurisdiction within the territorial limits of the state; later general international norms came into being, limiting this jurisdiction in particular aspects.[12]

The sovereign states and the international community are, primarily, territorial communities; territory is, therefore, of the highest importance. The states looked for territorial expansion; jurisdiction was within the territorial limits of a state; territorial international conflicts have been and are today the most dangerous international conflicts and particularly likely to lead to war. It was, in consequence, of the highest importance for general international law to delimit the territorial validity of the legal orders of the sovereign states *inter se* by *norms of contents*. Thus, the norms concerning acquisition and loss of territorial sovereignty came into being. During the seventeenth century the fundamental norm of the freedom of the high seas and, simultaneously, the law of territorial waters came into being.

As the sovereign states and the international community were, primarily, territorial communities, the delimitation of the *personal* validity of the legal orders of the sovereign states was of lesser importance. This explains why the delimitation of the personal sphere of validity was not, as in the case of territory, done by general international *norms of contents*, but only by general international *norms of competence*. International law delegated to the sovereign states the competence to regulate, in principle, the acquisition and loss of their nationality by norms of their domestic law as they pleased. Thus, the granting of nationality has remained, up to the present day, in principle a "matter of domestic jurisdiction." But it is theoretically untenable to assert that this problem is *not* regulated by international law; it *is* only regulated by international norms of competence and the states are given this right by the international norm. But mere international rules of competence could not bring about a clear division of individuals between the different sovereign states. This state of things finds expression in the recognition by international law of multiple nationality as well as of statelessness.

In addition to delimiting the jurisdiction of sovereign states *inter se*, it was of primary importance to create norms for the official intercourse of sovereign states. The international law, concerning privileges and immunities of diplomatic agents, purely customary general international law, is among the oldest and best observed parts of general international law and even today in this highly divided world is least attacked.

As there was for every state a right to go to war, the regulations of the *laws of war* dominated the interest of early international law. It is no hazard that in Grotius' "De jure belli ac pacis" the laws of war come first.[13]

All that the basic development of general international law tried to solve was the first great problem, the problem of peaceful coexistence. But international law has a second great task—*international co-operation of sovereign states.* Here, general international law furnished an excellent instrument in the international treaty and the norm that sovereign states are free to conclude treaties, in principle, on any subject matter.

V

We have seen that classic general international law is primitive and unorganized, but the word "unorganized" has to be taken *cum grano salis*. Any community *must* have organs through which alone it can act. The international community is not "unorganized" in the sense of having *no* organs; it is only primitively organized. International law *has* its organs, it also has *its own* organs; but it has *no special* organs. Hence, the organs of the state have also to function as international organs. It is this phenomenon, to a great extent basic up to the present day, which Georges Scelle, with great insight, has called "le dédoublement fonctionel."

The primitiveness, the "unorganized" status of general international law could, even in the times of the classic law of nations, be tempered by norms of particular international law created by treaty. The treaty can create also special international organs; the treaty can serve for achieving the second great task of international law, international cooperation between sovereign states. With the advance of time, and particularly in the nineteenth century, it became obvious that the primitive unorganized international law was wholly inadequate for the needs of the times. The wish was to make international law a more advanced law. Taking the development of municipal legal orders from primitive to advanced ones as a model, it can be seen that this advancement had to be brought about by centralization. But here again a curious distinctiveness is shown. Were it possible to centralize international law in the same way as advanced municipal legal orders, then the international community would be a relatively centralized community, which we could call a sovereign state; hence, international law would come to an end and would be replaced by the municipal law of the world state. In consequence, it was tried to advance and centralize international law only so far as not to infringe upon the sovereignty of the members.

The idea of "organizing" the world—first the western European international community—is old in occidental thinking. Just as general international law had to solve, first, the problem of peaceful co-existence, these early thinkers thought first of "eternal peace" and only second of international co-operation. There is a long line of utopian proposals for "eternal peace" by international organizations from the beginning of the fourteenth to the end of the eighteenth century in occidental Europe.[14] But all of them show the typically European, occidental idea that peace can be guaranteed by a loose confederation of sovereign states and that, therefore, a world state is not only impossible but not even desirable.[15] This idea was adopted by Simon Bolivar and tried unsuccessfully in the First Pan-Americanism. On *this* idea the League of Nations, as well as the United Nations, was based. Not only general international law, but also international organization, even at the present time, is based on ancient western European ideas.

With this basic idea—no world state—in mind, the nineteenth century recognized that the advance of international law lies in international organization. The treaty, as stated, is an excellent instrument for international co-operation and can also create special international organs. The treaty holds, therefore, a very important place in international law and has seen a great development: from the bilateral to the multilateral and quasi-universal treaty; from the treaty, concerned with a single problem, lying in the past, and giving a settlement, creating only individual international norms to the so-called law-making treaty, creating general international norms *pro futuro*, or creating even a constitution of an international organization. It is certainly theoretically incorrect, even today, to speak of "international legislation," but it is true that in the absence of an international legislature the treaty is still the best substitute.

We see, further, under classic international law the great development of the international conference: peace congresses, "to remake the map of Europe";[16] *ad hoc* political conferences;[17] peace congresses, creating also some general rules of international law *pro futuro*;[18] international conferences, convoked in time of peace, exclusively for the purpose of creating general norms of international law [19] or for writing the constitution of a new particular international organization; international conferences as permanent organs of international organizations.[20]

There were attempts at regional organizations; Simon Bolivar, in this respect the forerunner of Woodrow Wilson and of the League of Nations, and then the second Pan-Americanism since 1889. There was an attempt at a political government for maintaining peace in Europe through the hegemony of the Great Powers, by the Holy Alliance and the Concert of Europe, although the attempt was wholly political rather than legal. Some ideas of this European experience reappear in the Security Council of the U.N. as it was planned by the makers of the U.N. Charter at San Francisco in 1945.

Since 1772 we see a revival of international arbitration, although it remained primitively organized and was, at the end of the nineteenth and the beginning of this century, strongly overestimated as the principal way of insuring international peace. The principle of compulsory jurisdiction of international tribunals was, just as today, rejected by sovereignty. There was even the first pre-established permanent international court, the Central American Court of Justice. The court, although restricted to Central America, of short duration and of no outstanding achievements, was the first of its kind in history.

There was, as the climax of classic international law, the system of the Hague Peace Conferences which partially codified the peaceful settlement of international conflicts, the law of war and neutrality; but no one dared even to question the right of unlimited resort to war by the sovereign states.

Multilateral treaties, sometimes quasi-universal, were concluded for international non-political co-operation in the fields of communications, economics, cultural co-operation, and the protection of men (against slave trade, for the suppression of traffic in women, beginnings of an international labor law). Even more important, some of these multilateral treaties created special international organs. There were the International River Commissions and particularly important, from the point of view of organization, the European Danube Commission which was empowered to make ordinances for the navigation of the lower Danube immediately binding on those who navigated this stream. The Commission which had its own courts, was independent and neutral from the country in which it sat, and had its own flag. Of the highest importance were the International Administrative Unions.[21] They survive and some of them have become U.N. specialized agencies. Here we have permanent, special international bureaucratic organs; here are the beginnings of an "internal law of international organization," the beginnings of an "international civil service." The typical, tripartite organization of these Unions has served as the model for all later international organizations, whether big or small, universal or regional, general or specialized. Here we see already the fact that these international organizations for non-political co-operation were much more successful than the attempts at international political organizations for maintaining the peace.

VI

The distinctiveness of classic international law by comparison and contrast lies in that it is, in general, a primitive legal order. But there is also another source of distinctiveness, particularities of a sociological nature, as writers like Max Huber, Dietrich Schindler, and the late Professor Brierly[22] have shown. Such sociological factors are, quite apart from primitiveness, also important reasons for the distinctiveness of the international legal order.

There is, first, the relatively small number of "persons" under classic international law—only the limited number of sovereign states—and each state is unique. It is, therefore, very difficult for general international law to create general, abstract norms contrary to municipal legal orders which can much more easily make norms for transactions, *e.g.*, contracts, which happen innumerable times between individuals whom the law has typified and schematized into "persons."

There are not only few persons in classic international law, but each is also "sovereign" and "equal" and disposes of power, whereas the international community has not only no monopoly of force, contrary to advanced municipal legal orders, but practically no power at all. This sociological fact, the individualistic distribution of power among the members, even small ones, and particularly the Great Powers, is fundamental for the distinctiveness of the international legal order, as Charles de Visscher has stressed.

In addition, the international community, even under classic international law, was, in the terms of German sociologists, as Brierly has underlined, not a community, but only a society; the French term for the League of Nations—"Société des Nations," society of states—was correct. There was, even prior to 1914, no real common axiological foundation, and, in general, no loyalty of individuals toward the international community. The lack of a common system of values makes a legal order weak. This weakness, Brierly has stated, goes deeper than the problem of sanctions; it is, he states, not the existence of a police which makes a legal order strong, but, to the contrary, it is the vigor of the law which makes a police force possible.

Finally, whereas advanced municipal law regulates the conduct of individuals who are powerless as compared with the monopoly of force at the disposal of the community, international law regulates the conduct of "sovereign

states," *i.e.*, of enormous groups of individuals, disposing
of power. This is the great difficulty of international sanctions, the importance of "vital interests."

This is a great source of distinctiveness of international
law by comparison and contrast. But in order not to lose
the right perspective for this distinctiveness, two things
must not be forgotten. First, even classic international law
functioned very well in the everyday problems of the conduct between sovereign states and in minor conflicts, and
it was only in the big problems of war and peace that it
often failed.[23] Second, this distinctiveness shows itself only
fully when comparison is with advanced municipal legal
orders and in normal times. This distinctiveness is much
less in comparison with states where there is no common
system of values, but internal strife. There is also, even
under advanced legal orders, the possibility of insurrection
and civil war. Here, like in international affairs, it is military victory which is also legally decisive; what, in the event
of failure, is treason,[24] becomes, in the event of success,
the starting-point of a new constitution of a new country.
The problem of a military execution by a federal state
against a state of the union is as delicate an operation as
an international military sanction. Where a great mass of
workers, disposing of power, strike, it is often preferred,
whether they are legally right or wrong, to negotiate rather
than to go into court.[25] The problems of international law,
whether in consequence of its primitiveness or because of
sociological particularities, are not unique with international law. The distinctiveness of classic international law
as compared with and contrasted against advanced municipal legal orders is very great but it is not absolute.

VII

After World War I the attempt was made to develop
international law much faster, to make a big leap forward
by way of centralization, *i.e.*, by international organization.

It was a turning point for, but not a break with, classic international law. This new international law has gone, and is going, up to now, through two periods: the period between the two World Wars, or the period of the League of Nations, and the present period since 1945, the period of the United Nations.

The League of Nations was the first successful attempt to set up in positive law a quasi-universal international organization which did not only successfully expand machinery for international, non-political co-operation [26] but dared also to regulate problems of "high politics": partial restriction of the right of sovereign states to go to war, declaration of certain matters as being of "international concern," the system of "collective security" through collective sanctions, and reduction of armaments. But the continuity with classic international law was, from the beginning, obvious. The League was based on the sovereignty of its members, on the occidental idea of keeping the peace through a mere loose confederation of sovereign states; it strongly rejected in its beginnings the idea of being a "super-state" and, most certainly, it was not. Its gradual decline and its final disappearance in the holocaust of World War II brought an illusion to an end. The individualistic distribution of power among the members remained untouched. Europe retained its hold on great parts of Asia and Africa and the exclusive values of the occidental culture as the basis of international law continued. The League became, more and more, a preponderantly European organization, run by Great Britain and France. The United States never was a member.

After the apocalyptic events of World War II, a period of much greater change of international law started in 1945. The new international law of the present period is one of flux, change, uncertainty, and crisis. But not only is the connection with the League of Nations period clear, but, up to now, no break with classic international law has occurred. There are many reasons for this far-reaching trans-

formation and crisis of international law, reasons which
can here only be briefly listed: [27] the complete change of
general conditions; the coming of totalitarian governments;
scientific and technological advances; the coming of the
atomic and space age; the appearance of new forms of
political warfare; the complete change of the strategy,
tactics, and goals of warfare; the relative decline of
Europe, creator of the occidental culture and of our international law; the "bipolarity" of the present world to which
China may soon have to be added besides the "uncommitted"
and "neutralist" states; the deep ideological split between
the democratic and the communistic world, each led by one
of the two Great Powers; the "cold war" and the continuous political crises on a world-wide scale; the "anti-colonial"
rebellion; the entry on the international stage of non-
occidental cultures; the "rebellion of rising expectations";
neo-Malthusian fears, often expressed in the pessimistic
slogan of the "population explosion"; growing nationalism;
an upsurge of sovereignty; signs of a weakening and decline of our occidental culture from within; a decline of the
respect for law. It is only natural that the combined influence of so many far-reaching causes in this terribly dynamic, rapidly changing world, in this revolutionary period
of transition, can hardly make the present status of international law a happy one. Let us briefly sketch the consequences of these causes, in order to arrive, by comparison
and contrast, at a judgment on the distinctiveness of
present-day international law.

1. There is, first, a very important change since 1945,
as to the composition and the value-system of the *international community*. Even prior to 1914, the international
community, as stated, was hardly a true community; the
expansion of international law in its territorial validity,
although it remained based exclusively on the values of the
occidental culture, was brought about at the cost of a
dilution of its contents. Since 1945 the existence of an

"international community" has become problematical and whatever unity of values may have existed before has been lost. This is, first, a consequence of the deep ideological split between the democratic and the communistic world, led by the Soviet Union, and of the "cold war." Some ideas, goals, and procedures of the Soviet Union are clearly incompatible with the values of the occidental culture. The real split is not between the different economic systems, but is a spiritual abyss between the occidental culture for which human dignity and liberty is basic, for which the state exists only for the individual, and collectivism, for which the individuals exist only for the state. To that extent the Soviet Union has openly admitted that its ultimate goal is a world dominated by communism and constantly expresses its deep conviction that this goal will be reached, although it expresses also its hope that this goal can be reached without a third world war. Hence, "a peaceful co-existence" —it has been clearly stated [28]—is only an instrument for the interim period, a more perfect form of the class struggle, the correct path to the "triumph of communism on a world-wide scale."

On the other hand, there is the appearance of many new states in former colonial or quasi-colonial areas of Asia and Africa, the appearance on the international stage of many non-occidental cultures.[29] Since 1945 the international community has become, for the first time, truly international and no longer primarily dominated by states of the occidental-Christian culture.

Both these developments have far-reaching consequences, not only as far as the unity of the international community is concerned, but also with regard to the universality, to the contents, and to the certainty of the norms of international law.

2. The international community has also been changed since 1945 by the *expansion of international law, as to its subjects*. The present-day international community, and its

law, is no longer exclusively restricted to sovereign states, although the latter remain, and probably will remain for any foreseeable time, not only the most numerous, but also by far the most important subjects of international law. But there are now many other subjects of international law, although, by no means, necessarily with the same legal status as sovereign states. There are "partial" subjects of international law, such as certain states of federal unions (Bielorussia, Ukraine); colonies, and territorial communities, created by treaty, such as the "Free Territory of Trieste" had it come into existence. There is the evergrowing number of international organizations, many of which have international personality. There is the attempt to make the individual a direct subject of international law; either a direct subject of international duties and responsibility— the attempted "international criminal law"—or the direct subject of international rights—the attempted law for the international protection of human rights. This development sometimes brings about doubts and uncertainty as to the contents of this "international community." There has not only been an expansion of the subjects but also of the *contents* of international law. It no longer deals exclusively with the rights and duties of sovereign states; its scope also includes today stateless persons and refugees; indigenous populations of trusteeship territories; international labor problems; the solution of international social, financial, economic, health, communication, educational problems; economic and technical aid to underdeveloped countries; and many more topics.

3. Even classic international law was to a great extent incomplete, inadequate, and uncertain. The present-day international law under the influence of all these causes of transformation and crisis is characterized by *rapid change* and a high degree of *inadequacy* and *uncertainty*. Even the present-day international law is, as to the making of norms

of international law, basically as "unorganized" and primitive as classic international law.

Great violations of the laws of war and neutrality in two world wars, the influence of the illusion that "war has been abolished," the coming of new and terrible arms of mass destruction, atomic and hydrogen bombs, intercontinental ballistic missiles, gas and bacteriological warfare, and the complete change of forms and goals of warfare have brought about since 1945 a chaotic state of the laws of war. Although in these last years some progress has been made, the laws of war remain to a high degree incomplete, inadequate, and uncertain. This is also true as far as the international law of neutrality is concerned. This uncertainty of present-day international law covers about one half of classic international law.

Not only the forms and techniques of actual warfare, but also those of political struggle in a deeply divided world have changed considerably. Political propaganda, psychological warfare against other states by means of powerful media of mass-communication, the system of "iron curtains," prevention of the free flow of men and ideas, political parties in many countries which are controlled, financed, and dominated by foreign, ideologically opposed states, highly developed techniques of subversion, veiled intervention, civil wars with foreign intervention, the use of "resistance movements" and so-called volunteers, "wars by proxy," delivery of technical, economic, and military aid to rebels in foreign countries for subversive purposes—all have made norms centering around the "prohibition of intervention" highly insecure.

The strong expansion of economic activities by states has made uncertain not only many norms of the laws of war and neutrality, but also many other norms, e.g., those concerning "sovereign immunity."

A great deal of inadequacy or uncertainty of rules of

international law is the consequence of new scientific and technological advancements such as the norms of aerial warfare, the use of weapons of mass destruction, the law of aviation, the atomic law, the law of outer space. Nearly all these problems have importance for peaceful as well as for military purposes.

Furthermore, we are faced with the ideological split between the democratic and the communistic world and the attitude of the new states of non-occidental cultures. That renders even old rules of international law, hitherto not questioned, uncertain and doubtful. The Soviet Union feels that certain rules are unacceptable, are an expression of "capitalism," or must be "re-interpreted"; hence, her reliance primarily on treaties concluded by herself. On the other hand, the new states, arising in former colonial or quasi-colonial territories, feel that most of general international law has been made by "colonial" powers exclusively in their own interest, not taking into consideration the interests of these new states. In addition, as they had no part in making these rules, they have never freely given their consent. It is interesting to note that some states of Latin America, although independent for one hundred and fifty years and belonging to the occidental Christian culture, have now, because of their economic backwardness and in consequence of the "revolution of rising expectations," sometimes joined communist or Afro-Asian states. This has led to a serious weakening of the Organization of American States. From all these reasons, it is easily understood that great departments of general international law of the highest importance—such as the norms concerning the sanctity of private property, the protection of citizens abroad, denial of justice, espousal, confiscation, nationalization, expropriation, and fulfillment of contracts concluded for the economic development of a country between a state and a foreign corporation — are in a status of high uncertainty.

4. All these developments have brought about a tremendous *growth of nationalism,* an *upsurge of the feeling and demands of sovereignty,* not only among communist and new states, but also among democratic states. This explains the uncertainty now surrounding the fundamental principle of the freedom of the high sea, and the new norms, concerning the continental shelf, the unilateral claims as to the width of territorial waters, contiguous zones, fishing rights, and so on. Also uncertain are the international norms concerning the use of great international streams for purposes other than navigation, such as irrigation or hydroelectric power.

This nationalism and upsurge of sovereignty has also intensified the wish of many states to be *judex in causa sua,* the rejection of third-party judgment. Communist states never submit a case to the International Court of Justice for they see in it a "loss of sovereignty." But the distrust in the present "capitalistic" international law, in the Court, the majority of the judges of which came from "capitalistic" countries, is also a prominent factor; only an angel, said Molotov, could be impartial in a case between "capitalism" and "socialism." For similar reasons, distrust of international law made by "colonial" powers, and distrust of the bench made up of a majority of judges coming from "colonial" powers, as well as the uncertainty of international law, keep the new states from going to the International Court of Justice. But the upsurge of sovereignty, even among democratic states, can be seen in the relatively small business of the Hague Court, the declining number of states accepting the "optional clause," the growing number of reservations, and the use of reservations as to contents and as to time limits which practically annul the effect of the

optional clause. Not only has it not been possible to accept
the principle of compulsory jurisdiction of the international
court, but the role of this Court has declined as compared
with League of Nations times. International law has not
only no sanctions, but an extreme scarcity of legal remedies.

5. Add to the above "Marxist dialectics" which makes
communication between the democratic and the communist
world even more difficult; the same words of basic norms,
as *e.g.*, "aggression," are interpreted in the opposite sense,
so that the two leading Great Powers, invoking the same
legal norm, can blame each other for "aggression."

The very weakening of the occidental culture from within
has led to a decline of law in general, and of the international rule of law in particular.

6. The rise of *international organizations* is a distinctive
feature of the present period. There is no doubt that the
growing number of specialized organizations, general and
regional, is not merely a fashion, but deeply corresponds,
even in the present-day divided world, to a true necessity.
While it has not yet changed the basic structure of the international community, there are possibilities of fruitful
development. It is recognized by states of all types of ideology that these international organizations are necessary.
It may well lead to an international community still based
on sovereign states but in which many functions, hitherto
in the hands of single sovereign states on a territorial basis,
may be delegated to international organizations on a functional basis, but transcending the territories of the member-
states either on a world-wide or a regional scale. There are
not only the "international" organizations in the traditional
sense; there are also the highly interesting "Public International Corporations"[30] and there are "supranational"
organs.[31] The expansion of international organizations has
brought many new and progressive norms of international

law: international organizations as subjects of the international community, norms in the field of international treaties, privileges and immunities, responsibility, capacity to claim indemnities. While international organizations are based on general international law, they have also influenced the latter.[32] The international organizations have led to new departments of international law such as "the internal law of international organizations," the "international law of the international civil service." In these cases as well as under the hypothesis of a trusteeship exercised directly by the U.N. itself, we have to deal with norms which, as to their origin, function, and sphere of validity, are strictly international norms, but which, as to their structure (directly binding on individuals, direct sanctions and so on), are not different from the norms of advanced municipal legal orders.

There has been progress concerning the U.N. Charter since 1945: the prohibition of the use or threat of force in international relations, collective security, the Security Council as an international organ which can decide and act with legally binding consequences for the members, the intended international protection of human rights. But basically the U.N., even as designed, is not more than a second League of Nations, based again on the occidental idea of international organization—a mere loose confederation of sovereign states with the remaining individualistic distribution of power among the sovereign states. The combined influences here discussed have, of course, made the U.N. in 1961 into a very different organization from what the makers of the Charter had intended. On the other hand, contrary to the League of Nations, the prestige of the U.N. has hitherto remained great. All new states immediately apply for membership. No state, up to now, has withdrawn from the U.N. Although collective security has proven again to be an illusion, although the U.N. is admittedly incapable of maintaining international peace, although not much has been achieved as regards the international protection of human rights, although the breakdown of collective and the prohibition of individual sanctions has rendered international law practically devoid of any sanctions of its norms, it retains great international usefulness. But even that is threatened in the present crisis: the uncertain operation in the Congo, the heavy attacks, particularly against the Secretary General by the Soviet Union and the communist bloc, the danger of financial bankruptcy, the strong indictment by the President of France who refused not only to make payments for the Congo operation, but spoke of the "global incoherence" of this "disorganization" and of the General Assembly as "tumultuous and scandalous meetings in which it is impossible to arrange an objective debate," make the future of the U.N. uncertain.

7. As every period of transition and crisis, the present period is full of contradictions and paradoxes. Although the U.N. Charter rests on peace, tolerance, and good-neighborliness, the present world is in one of the most bitter struggles for life and death. Although there is the wave of anti-colonialism, the Soviet Union in the words of General de Gaulle has set up "the greatest imperialism which the history of the world has seen." Although the U.N. Charter preaches the maintenance of human dignity, of human rights and fundamental freedoms, humanity has suffered in the last thirty years more cruel suppressions than at any time before. Although there is the tremendous longing for independence by small and unprepared communities, there is also a tendency of states to go closer together in regional or supranational unions. Whereas the U.N. Charter is based on respect for international law, there is a great deal of international lawlessness in the present-day world. Whereas the U.N. Charter wanted to bring collective sanctions, international law is today practically without any sanctions.

Whereas the U.N. Charter forbids the use or threat of force to render the world more lawful, this prohibition, coupled with the political possibilities of the "cold war," has had the effect of making even smaller states more lawless and has had the effect of creating an unwillingness in small states to submit to the jurisdiction of an international court. Whereas the U.N. Charter was designed to severely restrict the sovereignty of the members with the exception of the permanent members of the Security Council, there is everywhere an upsurge of sovereignty. Sovereignty, independence, equality, and non-intervention seem to be the only rule on which democratic, communist, and new states are in agreement. Whereas peace should rely on law and on collective security, such "peace," as we have today is based on the precarious "balance of terror"; the most uniting fact of the international community seems to be common fear of annihilation.

The general decline of law has made the rule of law, contrary to the League of Nations, of little importance in the U.N. Legal arguments are seldom used. In this period of uncertainty there is distrust and disrespect of law, and legal considerations are being treated under the contemptuous and pejorative term of "legalistic." The place of law has been taken by politics.

Many of the progressive rules of the new international law are uncertain, ineffective, experimental, and, in some cases, ephemeral.

The present situation of the world makes the most important issues of political tension unfit for a peaceful solution. In such a period not much real progress of international law can be expected; developments may be absolutely necessary, but they are impossible of achievement.[33] While a scientific analysis of the present situation of international law must by necessity be pessimistic, the same objectivity views more hopeful signs such as, in addition to those named earlier, the successes of codification by the International Law Commission, the Geneva Conventions of 1949, the Geneva Conference of 1958, the Second Vienna Congress, the International Geophysical Year, and the Treaty on Antarctica. There is also a strong hope that man, after having invented the weapons for his own self-destruction, will be unwilling to make use of them. It is difficult to say whether international law, seen as a whole and compared with former times has progressed or not. But as it stands today, there is no break yet, either with the League of Nations period or with classic international law.

Apart from the advances and retrogressions, the crises and dangers, the distinctiveness of international law is the same as before. It is based on (1) primitiveness (no superior, international legislature, highly decentralized, hardly any sanctions, no international courts with compulsory jurisdiction) and on (2) the sociological peculiarities (dealing with enormous groups of persons, sovereignty of states, vital interests, less a community than before, even a certain disintegration of the international community, a threat to the universality of the validity of international law, the same sociological foundation in the individualistic distribution of power among the sovereign states.)

This distinctiveness is great, but not absolute, by comparison with, and contrast against, other legal orders. The distinctiveness is greatest in comparison with the private law of advanced municipal legal orders, particularly in advanced and politically stable states; it is less in comparison with primitive municipal legal orders for here the primitiveness is a common factor. It is also less by comparison with certain fields of public law of advanced municipal legal orders, because they have some of the sociological particularities in common.

It is very possible that the present period of struggle, uncertainty, transition, and crisis will go for the rest of the present century. It is, therefore, impossible to predict the future of international law. The sentence which the President of the United States [34] applied to the present world situation applies also to the present status of international law, a "time of rising dangers and of persistent hope."

[1] Sanctions of religious norms are transcendent.

[2] See "Sanctions in International Law," pp. 621–60 in this volume.

[3] E.g., Inter-Hellenic law, ancient Hindu, ancient Chinese "international law."

[4] This "Communitas Christiana" was wider than the Holy Roman Empire of the Germanic nation, for England and Scandinavia never belonged to this Holy Roman Empire. There were, on the other hand, co-existent cultures, outside the "Communitas Christiana": the states of the Byzantine culture of eastern Europe and the Arabic-Islamic world.

[5] For example, acquisition of sovereignty by occupation of *terrae nullius*, *pacta sunt servanda*, rules concerning *alluvio* and *avulsio*, international servitudes, state succession, and so on. Roscoe Pound stated recently: "Grotius wrote to a picture of two second-century Romans owning adjoining land."—*A World Legal Order*, FLETCHER SCHOOL OF LAW AND DIPLOMACY 10 (1959).

[6] That the Holy See, contrary to all other churches, has been and is up to the present day, a permanent member of the international community, has an historical explanation. See "The Status of the Holy See in International Law," pp. 276–84 in this volume.

[7] "Existent international law is the creation of but one historical portion of one living culture."—Northrup, *Contemporaneous Jurisprudence and International Law*, 61 YALE L. J. 636 (1952).

[8] Exceptions: The Holy See, and insurgents, recognized as a belligerent party.

[9] Thus, the first sentence in I OPPENHEIM-LAUTERPACHT, INTERNATIONAL LAW 5 (8th ed. 1955).

[10] In connection with the problem dealt with in this section, see the full discussion in this writer's study in Spanish: TEORÍA DEL DERECHO INTERNACIONAL, Inter-American Academy of Comparative and International Law (Havana), 2 CURSOS MONOGRAFICOS 331–444 (1952).

[11] Coming into being and end of a sovereign state, problems of state succession, identity of states under international law.

[12] E.g., Immunity and privileges of foreign diplomatic agents; the right of "innocent passage" through territorial water; later the norms for the protection of citizens abroad.

[13] Prior to Grotius "seul le droit de la guerre se developpe sérieusement; il forme le noyeau du droit international."—E. NYS, LE DROIT DE LA GUERRE ET LES PRÉCURSEURS DE GROTIUS 7 (1882). "The most important as well as the first to spring into existence was that (part of international law) which occupied itself with the laws of war."—T. E. HOLLAND, STUDIES IN INTERNATIONAL LAW 45 (1898).

[14] Pierre Dubois (1305) to Abbé de St. Pierre (1716); KANT, ZUM EWIGEN FRIEDEN (1795).

[15] See WALTER SCHIFFER, THE LEGAL COMMUNITY OF MANKIND (1954).

[16] Westphalia, 1648; Utrecht, 1713.

[17] Berlin, 1878; Congo, 1885.

[18] Vienna, 1815; Paris, 1856.

[19] Hague Peace conferences, 1899 and 1907.

[20] International conferences of American states.

[21] See "Experience and Techniques in International Administration," pp. 467–91 in this volume.

[22] J. L. BRIERLY, THE LAW OF NATIONS (4th ed. 1944). See also CHARLES DE VISSCHER, THEORY AND REALITY IN PUBLIC INTERNATIONAL LAW (English transl. 1957).

[23] That is why the late Sir Hersh Lauterpacht applied to international law the contrary of the old Roman proverb: "In maximis non curat praetor."

[24] An old little English verse states ironically: "Treason cannot prosper; what's the reason? / For if it does, who would dare to call it treason?"

[25] Macchiavelli wrote in his Il Principe that "from superior to inferior one commands; but between equals one negotiates."

[26] Particularly the International Labor Organization, the only part of the League of Nations which survived in 1946; also the Institute of International Intellectual Co-operation at Paris, succeeded by UNESCO. For the international protection of persons or groups see the system of mandates, the Anti-Slavery Treaty of 1926, the Nansen Office of Refugees; the new, particular international law for the protection of national, linguistic, and religious minorities.

[27] For a full discussion see this writer's lectures in French at the Hague Academy of International Law, held in 1955: La Crise et les transformations du droit des gens (88 RECUEIL DES COURS, Pt. II, 1–104 [1955]); see also this writer's article "The Changing Law of Nations," pp. 3–12, above.

[28] Statement by leaders of eighty-one communist parties at the Moscow Meeting (N. Y. TIMES December 7, 1960, pp. 14, 15).

[29] See the writer's article "Pluralism of Legal and Value Systems and International Law," pp. 47–56 in this volume.

[30] See H. T. ADAM, LES ETABLISSEMENTS PUBLICS INTERNATIONAUX (1957).

[31] See this writer's article "Supranational Organs," pp. 600–612 in this volume.

[32] See "General International Law and the Law of International Organizations," pp. 492–501 in this volume.

[33] See JULIUS STONE, LAW AND POLICY IN THE QUEST FOR SURVIVAL (1960).

[34] President Kennedy's Special Message to Congress on Defense Spending, N. Y. Times, March 29, 1961, p. 16.

CHAPTER III: *Pluralism of Legal and Value Systems and International Law*

A LIFE DEDICATED to the study of international law, long studies on philosophy of law, and more recent studies in comparative law have convinced this writer that any legal order, and hence international law, in order to be fully understood, must be studied from three approaches: analytical, sociological-historical, and axiological. The analytical approach, the lawyer's approach par excellence, is indispensable; but it alone is not sufficient; it must first be supplemented—supplemented, not replaced—by the sociological-historical approach.[1] It must, second, be supplemented by an axiological approach, by the study of the different legal systems and of the different systems of values which underlie these legal systems and the cultures of which they are a part. For the purpose of this investigation it is not essential whether we speak of this system of values as "natural laws"[2] or as mere ideologies. For even if they were not more than ideologies—Verdross has recently stated —their knowlege would still be necessary in order to understand these legal orders. The faith shared in the system of values by those subject to a legal order is, further, of the highest importance to make this legal order effective. Just as the present sociological foundation of international law limits its effectiveness, so the effectiveness of international law is hampered by the lack of a system of truly international values. This approach, still ignored by the majority of international lawyers, is today particularly important.

Our international law is a creation of Christian Europe. It has its roots in the *Respublica Christiana* of medieval Europe. The present "international community" came into being through the decentralization of the medieval unity. It remained until toward the end of the eighteenth century restricted to Christian Europe [3] and its extension to the United States and Latin America did not change its legal and value basis. It was shaped by theologians and lawyers of the Roman law. Many of its norms are mere transplantations of norms of Roman private law into the international sphere. The great importance of natural law in the early development of international law merely corroborates the dominating influence of Roman law. For Roman law was regarded not only as a world law—"jus gentium"—but also as the "ratio scripta"; the contents of natural law were taken from Roman law and Catholic theology. Our international law is based on the value system of the occidental culture, on Christian,[4] and often Catholic, values. The Roman law–Catholic foundation has often been recognized by Protestant common-law lawyers.[5]

But even prior to 1856 the identity of legal and value systems was never complete. There were the states of Byzantine origin.[6] There was, at the very beginning, the antithesis between Catholicism and Protestantism. Protestant writers often claim that international law is a Protestant creation. On the other hand, modern Spanish writers [7] blame the present crisis of international law on the fact that Catholic ethics and universality,[8] on which the "Spanish Fathers" tried to build international law, have been abandoned. Also today there is *within* the occidental culture a difference between Catholic and Protestant cultures and "ways of life," between Ango-Saxon and Hispanic cultures, between England and the Continent, between the United States and Latin America, between Europe and America. There is further a duality of legal systems: civil law and common law. In view of the Roman-law basis of international law, common-law lawyers have sometimes voiced apprehension.[9] But these differences do not threaten international law and its development. For the bases are common: the values of occidental culture. It is a question of differences, but not of antagonisms; Catholic and Protestant, Anglo-Saxon and Hispanic, European and American values may be different, but they are also complementary.

Between 1856 and today the European Christian law of nations has, in an historical process, spread so as to constitute today the universal international law, binding also on nations of non-occidental legal and value systems. This development was generally welcomed and praised.[10] Although the reception of international law by non-occidental nations "made Oriental adjustments and interpretations necessary," [11] the problem of the binding value of European Christian international law on states of non-occidental legal and value systems was not seen in the West. For the occidental man was not only convinced of the eternity and absolute superiority of his culture, but believed also that it had been absorbed by the rest of the world to such a degree as to have become, in fact, the only one, world-wide culture.[12] Since 1920 positive international law has recognized the pluralism of the legal and value systems of the world, in the manner of elections to the Council of the League of Nations and the United Nations Security Council, to other organs of international organizations, in the equitable distribution, as to countries, of international civil servants and, particularly, in the Statute of the Permanent Court of International Justice and now in Article 9 of the Statute of the International Court of Justice, according to

which "in the body as a whole the representation of the
main forms of civilization and the *principal legal systems of
the world* should be assured."

The present situation is characterized by the decline of
Europe and the total crisis of our occidental culture. There
is, further, the deep split between the free and the communistic worlds, a split *within* the occidental cultures; if we
speak of the East-West split, the words "East" and "West"
are not used in the sense of Kipling. The Soviet law is of
Western origin; the Soviet ideology is based on Marx and
stems, therefore, in ultimate analysis, from Hegel. Yet
Soviet law is a new legal system, different from civil and
common law, as recognized in the free world and emphasized by Soviet scholars.[13] The Soviet ideology is not only
different from that of the free occidental world, but may
perhaps be found to be incompatible with it. The political
consequences of this split and of the "cold war" require no
enumeration. There are also deep-reaching influences on
international law and the law of international organization.
Just as Professor Jessup,[14] thinking of the "cold war," could
ask whether international law should not recognize a status
intermediate between war and peace, so others have asked
whether the same international law can rule both the capitalistic and the communistic worlds, whether this ideological
struggle will not lead to a disruption of the unity and universality of international law.[15] Although the early tendency
to regard international law merely as the "law of the transition period" [16] seems to have been abandoned in the Soviet
Union, there is no doubt that this split and the Soviet concept of international law [17] are posing and will pose many
difficult problems, *de lege lata* and *de lege ferenda,* for international law and the law of international organizations.

There is finally the fact that the international community
has today for the first time become, so to speak, *really* international through the definitive emergence and the great

activity on the international stage of states of non-occidental legal and value systems.[18] Nearly one third of the members of the United Nations are Asian and African states. They often form a bloc, supported in voting by the states of the Soviet bloc and a number of Latin-American states. They are primarily interested in bringing colonial issues before the Security Council or Assembly; they are very active within the framework of Chapter XI of the United Nations Charter.[19] There is also a definite policy of the states of Africa and Asia outside the United Nations.

While this "rebellion" of the present and former colonial and semi-colonial peoples is, in present-day world politics, strongly intermingled with the split between the free and the communistic world, it should not be overlooked that the issue is a separate one which would still exist if there were no East-West split. The independence idea pervades also the non-communistic states of Asia and Africa. Many of these peoples feel a deep resentment against centuries of Western conquest and domination. They no longer want to be regarded by the West merely as sources of raw materials, export markets, strategic bases, or tourist curiosities. Theirs is a new nationalism learned from Europe. But in addition to political and economic independence, they insist on their own culture, their own legal and value systems; they demand not only to be heard in international affairs, but to make their own legal and value contributions to international law. A new world is emerging, a world in which two out of every three human beings are non-white, a world in which white superiority is no longer conceded *a priori*, but must be earned.

Even the primitive legal and value systems of the Africa south of the Sahara begin to make themselves felt on the international stage. But most important is the active appearance of the states of the great non-occidental cultures. There is, first, the legal and value system of Islam, forming a vast

belt from Morocco to Indonesia. There is a renaissance of
Islam which wants to bring back the great days of Arabic
and Islamic culture; there is a movement in Syria and Pakistan to base the constitutions on the Koran, on Islamic law,[20]
and on the Islamic system of values. The emergence of an
Islamic ideology not only explains the Arab diffidence toward the West, but also the ideological abyss between the
Arab states and Israel, the conflict between Pakistan and
India.

There is the legal and value system of India. India's
influence under Prime Minister Jawaharlal Nehru is very
pronounced in international politics, law, the United Nations, and its leadership in the "Asia for the Asians" movement. There is finally the attitude of ancient China [21]
toward law, so entirely different and far removed from the
occidental approach, the value systems of Confucius, Lao-
Tse, and Buddha.

The question of an effective international law, in spite of
these wide differences in legal and value systems, is one
of the principal problems of Professor F. S. C. Northrop's [22]
research. His proposal of solution is to reduce the United
Nations Charter to two main articles. The first article would
declare the pluralism of ideologies as the basic principle.
Each member would be requested to state its specific
ideology. The Charter would guarantee to each member the
protection of its ideology within its geographical area. An
international judge would know that in every decision the
specific ideology of each member within its geographical
area must be protected, as long as this member has not
itself changed its ideology and so informed the United
Nations. Any speaker in the United Nations, attacking the
ideology of another member, would be automatically ruled
to be out of order. Thus, the author hopes, the "cold war"
could be ended. Each member, as stated, would inform the
United Nations of its ideology and of each change of it

made voluntarily by this member. But experts must investigate this ideology as far as its theory of international law is concerned. If this investigation shows that this ideology is also regarded as the only valid norm for the decision of international conflicts, the nation must, before being admitted, reject this part of its ideology in writing and take an oath to recognize instead the principle of the pluralism of ideologies. The second article would impose upon each member the duty to subject that part of its life which is international in character to the international organization. Every aggressive intervention or use of force against the ideology of another state is banned and each member obligates itself to participate in common action against the aggressor. Thus, the author hopes, the "veto" could be eliminated and at the same time an "international police force" of such strength might be created as to make resistance sheer insanity.

This writer has no space to refute this proposal in detail. He believes that it suffices to have given an exposé of it in order to make it clear that this proposal is wholly utopian. It is incapable of being realized; it cannot be translated into effective legal norms; and even if it could, it would be wholly illusory and insufficient. The pluralism of legal and value systems is, indeed, one of the problems for an effective international law, although not the only one. Hence, a comparative study of these legal and value systems on a grand scale and in a truly scientific manner would be of great importance. Such comparative analysis must not only study the non-occidental systems in their purity, but also take into consideration the far-reaching influences exercised on non-occidental systems by the civil and the common law. It must take into consideration that these non-occidental states are striving, out of poverty and misery, for prosperity, for industrial progress, for effective government and higher living standards. In these respects they must look to the West; technical assistance has a very great rôle to play, if it is given with no idea of domination. This writer believes that the non-occidental legal and value systems are different from, but not incompatible with, those of the occidental culture of the free world. They threaten neither the existence nor the development of universal international law. But they cannot be ignored; for they certainly will make their influence felt on the contents of international law: they will play a role in the formation of customary international law, in the contents of treaty-created norms, in the "general principles of law, recognized by civilized nations," and in the development of the law of international organizations.

[1] Max Huber, Dietrich Schindler, J. L. Brierly. The true sociological approach has, of course, nothing to do with current "neorealism." It is interesting to note that three very different writers put strong emphasis on this approach: JULIUS STONE, LEGAL CONTROLS OF INTERNATIONAL CONFLICT (1954); MARIANO AGUILAR NAVARRO, DERECHO INTERNACIONAL PÚBLICO (3 vols.; 1952–54); and CHARLES DE VISSCHER, THÉORIES ET RÉALITÉS EN DROIT INTERNATIONAL PUBLIC (1953). See also WALTER SCHIFFER, THE LEGAL COMMUNITY OF MANKIND (1954).

[2] It is, of course, necessary to recognize that "natural law," so called, is not law but ethics, a system of norms superior to law, by which to judge a legal order, not as law or non-law, but as good or bad law. In this sense, modern adherents of natural law: the German Coing, the Spaniard Legaz y Lacambra, the Mexican Rafael Preciado Hernández, and the Belgian Jean Dabin, an orthodox neo-Thomist, who now states unequivocally: "Au binôme: droit naturel-droit positif if faut substituer celui de: morale-droit."—THÉORIE GÉNÉRALE DU DROIT (1953).

[3] Up to the beginning of the nineteenth century, writers spoke of the "Droit des Gens de l'Europe." Still, in 1856, Turkey was admitted "to participate in the advantages of the Public Law and System of Europe."

[4] All other countries were referred to as "pays hors chrétienté."

[5] "Existent international law is the creation of *but one historical portion* of *one* living culture."—Northrop, *Contemporary Jurisprudence and International Law*, 61 YALE L.J. 636 (1952) (italics supplied).

[6] See the Russian scholar, Baron de Taube, *Etudes sur le développement historique du droit international dans l'Europe Orientale*, 11 RECUEIL DES COURS 345–535 (1926), and *L'apport de Byzance au*

développement du droit international occidental, 67 *ibid.* at 237–339 (1939). A modern Greek writer has seen the principal reason for the many Balkan crises of the nineteenth and twentieth centuries in the "total lack of understanding which the men of Occidental Europe have shown toward the states of Byzantine origin."—P. A. PAPALIGOURAS, THÉORIE DE LA SOCIÉTÉ INTERNATIONALE 489 (1941).

7 See Aguilar Navarro, *op. cit.,* and Antonio de Luna, *Fundamentación del Derecho Internacional,* 60 REVISTA DE DERECHO INTERNACIONAL 210–64 (1952).

8 "Humanum genus, quamvis in varios populos et regna divisum, semper habet aliquam unitatem non solum specificam, sed etiam quasi politicam et moralem."—FRANCISCO SUÁREZ, DE LEGIBUS AC DEO LEGISLATORE.

9 Thus Lauterpacht wrote some time ago that there is danger that states of the common law may be outvoted at international conferences, that international tribunals are mostly manned by Roman-law lawyers who have little (if any) knowledge of the common law, and that there is little justification today to make the development of international law exclusively dependent on Roman and civil law or to attribute to *one* system of law of a particular time and space the qualities of a *universal* law (PRIVATE LAW SOURCES AND ANALOGIES IN INTERNATIONAL LAW 178).

10 It remained for the leading National Socialist lawyer, Carl Schmitt, to attack what he called the "dissolution" of European order in a vague and universal, so-called international law (*Die Auflösung der europäischen Ordnung im International Law,* 5 DEUTSCHE RECHTSWISSENSCHAFT 267–78 (1940); against him, H. Wehberg, in 41 DIE FRIEDENS-WARTE 157–66 (1941)).

11 See the interesting account in *Japan's Reception of the Law of Nations,* by Professor Zengo Ohira, 4 ANNALS OF THE HITOTSUBASHI ACADEMY (Tokyo) 55–66 (1953).

12 Arnold Toynbee warned even in 1934 against the "misconception of the unity of culture."—1 A STUDY OF HISTORY 149 (1934).

13 "Soviet law is a completely unique type of law; it is not a further development of bourgeois law, but a new type of law."—A. Golumskii and M. S. Strogovitch, quoted in *Soviet Legal Philosophy,* 5 TWENTIETH-CENTURY LEGAL PHILOSOPHIES SERIES 385–86 (1951).

14 48 AM.J.INT'L L. 98–103 (1954).

15 Kurt Wilk in 45 *ibid.* at 648–70 (1951).

16 Thus, E. KOROVINE, DAS VÖLKERRECHT DER ÜBERGANGZEIT (1929) (German translation from Russian original of 1924).

17 See TARACOUZIO, THE SOVIET UNION AND INTERNATIONAL LAW (1935); S. Krylov, *La Doctrine soviétique du droit international,* 70 RECUEIL DES COURS 411–71 (1947).

18 For a broader treatment, see Josef L. Kunz, *Pluralismus de Naturrechte und Völkerrecht,* 6 ÖSTERREICHISCHE ZEITSCHRIFT FÜR ÖFFENTLICHES RECHT 185–220 (1954).

19 See this writer's editorial in 48 AM. J. INT'L L. 103–110 (1954).

[20] Moslem law has been studied, as far as the West is concerned, in England and France; see LOUIS MILLIOT, INTRODUCTION À L'ÉTUDE DU DROIT MUSULMAN (1953). Recently it has also attracted attention in the United States; see *Symposium on Moslem Law* in 22 GEO. WASH. L. REV. 1–39, and 127–86 (1953). In September, 1953, a Conference on Islamic Culture was held at Princeton University.

[21] F. A. SCHNITZER, VERGLEICHENDE RECHTSWISSENSCHAFT 260–67 (1945); RENÉ DAVID, TRAITÉ ÉLÉMENTAIRE DE DROIT COMPARÉ 377–93 (1950). See also JEAN ESCARRA, LE DROIT CHINOIS.

[22] See his books: THE MEETING OF EAST AND WEST (1947); (ed.), IDEOLOGICAL DIFFERENCES AND WORLD ORDER (1949); (ed.), THE TAMING OF THE NATIONS (1952), and his article, *loc. cit. supra*, note 5.

PART II

THE SCIENCE OF INTERNATIONAL LAW

THE "VIENNA SCHOOL"

THE SO-CALLED Vienna School of Jurisprudence was founded by Hans Kelsen and was developed by him and his disciples. The "Vienna School" stands for a "pure science of law" (*reine Rechtslehre*). The bond which unites all the adherents of the Vienna School is not a bond of interests, not a bond of common political convictions, but a bond of common theoretical thinking and of a common methodological approach.

Hans Kelsen's special field is constitutional and international law. He certainly is the greatest expert in Austrian constitutional law.[1] He is, indeed, the draftsman of the Austrian Federal Constitution of 1920, and has been for many years a member and a permanent *rapporteur* of the Austrian Constitutional Court (*Verfassungsgerichtshof*); but he is primarily interested in the *theory of law*.

I honestly believe—and I hope I am not prejudiced because he is my teacher as well as my friend—that the work of Hans Kelsen constitutes the greatest theoretical system [2] of law which has been produced in the last twenty years.

The doctrine of the pure science of law, so brilliantly expounded by Kelsen, has won many followers; his direct

disciples in Austria constitute the Vienna School. But the
influence of the Vienna School has by no means been restricted to Austria; it has been adopted, and sometimes
developed, by scholars in many countries: Germany, Czechoslovakia,[3] Yugoslavia,[4] Poland, Hungary, Italy, France,
Japan,[5] and many others. On the other hand—and this is
indicative also of its importance—it has met with violent
attacks,[6] attacks which are sometimes only the consequence
of misunderstandings, in other cases a determined enmity,
largely owing to *political* rather than scientific motives.

One of Kelsen's principal endeavors, as he stated himself,
was to bring back the science of law into the long neglected
province of philosophy, to show that no science is possible
without a philosophical foundation, to urge the necessity
of philosophical knowledge for a scholar of the law. Kelsen
is a great jurist—as distinguished from a mere lawyer—
because he is a great *thinker*.[7] But Kelsen's work is primarily a *theory* of law, not a philosophy of law.[8]

As a theory of *law,* Kelsen's work is not limited to any
special field of the law; it is a foundation for every field of
law; it will bear fruit, and has done so, in private, criminal,
administrative, constitutional, and international law.

THE PHILOSOPHICAL BASIS: KANT

To show how Kelsen's theory of law works in the particular field of international law is the task of this article.
But in order really to understand the conception of international law of the Vienna School, it is necessary to give a
short outline of the general theory of law of Kelsen.

Really to understand the Vienna theory of law, we must
in turn begin with a very short analysis of the relevant
points of the philosophy of Kant. For Kelsen's theory of
law is an attempt to apply Kant's transcendental method
to the science of law, in opposition to Kant himself, who,
although having established the critical method with regard

to natural sciences, remains in his *Rechtslehre* wholly within the traditional domain of the natural-law school. Kant's fundamental work for all times is his *Kritik der Reinen Vernunft* (Critique of Pure Reason), and it is on this philosophy, as interpreted by the Neo-Kantian school of philosophy, especially by Cohen, that Kelsen's pure science of law is based.[9]

It was Kant who, in his endeavor to found the independence of practical and pure reason, of morals and nature, of value and reality, discovered, so to speak, the fundamental contrast between 'to be" (*sein*) and 'to ought to be" (*sollen*). It was Kant who showed that every body of knowledge is called a science if it constitutes a *system, i.e.,* a totality of cognitions, arranged according to principles. It is his immense merit to have created a critique of cognition (*Erkenntniskritik*). His method is prior to experience, but related only to possible experience; it is *prior to,* but not *beyond,* experience. It is "transcendental" but not transcendent. Only things we can *know* can be treated scientifically. Kant has opposed the domain of *faith* to the domain of *science;* he has destroyed metaphysics in the old sense of the term. This is, of course, only a critical, theoretical clarification, not a judgment of value. Kant does not deny at all—he was a faithful Protestant—that there is metaphysics, that men can't do without it; all he says is that metaphysics cannot be a subject matter of science: We can *know* nothing about these things, although we may profoundly *believe* in them. To think scientifically means for Kant to avoid all mythological thinking which creates active beings behind the objects of our senses, which sees a dryad in every tree; a dryad is very legitimate as a poetical metaphor, but vicious scientifically from the moment we take it for a reality.

Every science, according to Kant, must have its own *subject matter,* clearly defined: For if not, the frontiers of sciences must run into one another. But a science, as stated above, is not a mere aggregate, but *a system;* and in order to arrive at a system, we must have a *method, i.e.,* a procedure according to principles of reason, by which alone a diversity of cognitions can become a system. This method must be one and the same for this science, and must not be confused with other methods which are not adequate to the very subject matter of the science in question. It is this *confusion of methods* which constitutes the deadly sin against scientific thinking. Clear frontiers, unity and purity of method, this is a fundamental postulate with Kant. Every science must have a basis, needs a hypothesis; no science is possible without logic; but Kant permanently warns against formulating *substantial* judgments by employing only logic, which is nothing else but the *formal* rules of thinking.

III

Pure Science of Law vs. Natural Sciences

Kelsen's theory of law [10] is Kantian as regards its starting point: Is jurisprudence a science? [11] Is jurisprudence *possible* as a science? In order to give an answer, Kelsen must first of all determine, what a science, what the *criterium* of a science is. But to give the answer to these necessary preliminary problems cannot be the task of jurisprudence, but only of philosophy as the theory of theories, the science of sciences. It is from this starting point that methodological questions are bound to play an important role in the work of Kelsen. He says, in accordance with Kant, that jurisprudence, in order to be a science, must have its own subject matter and must proceed by its own method. And Kelsen's fundamental proposition is that the subject matter of jurisprudence is the *law* and nothing but the law, that jurisprudence can work only and exclusively with *juridical* methods. This seems to be a truism; but the state of what commonly is taken as jurisprudence proves that it is urgently needed never to forget that the jurist has to deal with *law* only. To determine "the province of jurisprudence" [12] we must find the frontiers between this science and other sciences, we must uphold the unity and purity of the special method of this science, of the juridical method. That is what a "pure" science of law means, *i.e.,* a science purified from all metajuridical elements.

Kelsen started therefore with his classical research on the difference between a "law of nature" and a law in the juridical sense, and showed that, notwithstanding the use of the same *word* "law," these are two wholly different conceptions. The difference lies in the fact that they are to be found on two wholly different levels, in two different worlds: *Sein* and *Sollen.* The validity of a law of nature means that a certain effect *must* follow a certain cause. But this *must* in the realm of facts, of nature, is exclusively based on our experience, is the expression of a long experience. The validity of a law of nature holds good only so long as the facts correspond to it. If further experience shows that the facts do not correspond to it, it is not that the facts have violated our law of nature, but that further experience has shown that this law of nature is not valid. The law of nature is based on the relation of *causality.* Natural sciences are based on causality.

But the law in the juridical sense lies not in the domain of facts, but in the domain of the spirit. The law is a social phenomenon and therefore an object wholly outside of the realm of nature. The observation of facts can never lead to a juridical conclusion. Jurisprudence can never be run on the methods of the natural sciences. For the jurist it is not facts that matter, but the *significance* of facts. If *e.g.,* a man is shot and killed by other men, all that the man of natural sciences, for instance a doctor, can note is that a bullet has been fired, that this bullet has entered the heart of the victim and caused his death. A man shot through the heart *must* die; this is a law of nature. But how could the doctor as a doctor say that there has been a *murder?* The facts may be absolutely the same and yet they may constitute a manslaughter, an accident, an act of negligence, an execution, an act of war. Only the jurist can say so, because he is looking for the significance of these facts, and this significance cannot be observed with methods of natural sciences. A natural scientist may observe that in a room a few elderly gentlemen are sitting, that an individual is standing before them, and so on. But how could the physicist tell us that a court has given its decision? This cannot be concluded from the observation of facts; it is the *meaning* of these facts. And this meaning is produced by a norm. A law in the legal sense is on the level of "oughtness." The specific relation is here made by a rule, by a norm which connects facts with facts or facts with persons, not at all in terms of causality, but in terms of a *Sollen.* Jurisprudence is not and cannot be a natural science; it is a science of the spirit (*Geisteswissenschaft*). If a legal rule prescribes that he who commits a murder *shall* be executed, that does not mean that he *will* be executed necessarily. In the domain of facts, perhaps he will not be executed because he has escaped. But this circumstance takes nothing from the *validity* of the norm that he *shall* be executed. The *validity* (*Geltung*) of a norm, as its proper significance, wholly in the sphere of the *Sollen,* is by no means the same thing as the *efficiency* (*Wirksamkeit*) of a rule, a category in the domain of the *Sein,* of facts, of nature. The Eighteenth Amendment was no doubt a valid norm, although to a great extent inefficient.

Jurisprudence is not, and cannot be, anything else but a *normative* science. Kelsen's first great *actio finium regundorum* was to determine the province of jurisprudence *versus sociology.* The so-called sociological school is the very opposite of Kelsen's normative jurisprudence.[13]

That jurisprudence is a normative, not a natural, science means not only a delimitation *versus sociology* but also *versus biology* and *psychology.* The "man" of biology is by no means identical with the "person" in law. The person is a *creation* of the law. Kelsen has therefore done away with the dualism of "physical" and "legal" or "moral" persons by showing that *all* persons are legal persons.[14] To confuse the "man" with the "person" is another instance of confusing existential with normative sciences. The law may create a person which is not a human being, *e.g.,* a limited company. On the other hand, a human being in the sense of biology need not be a person in law, *e.g.,* the slave. Now, we demand that every human being *ought to be* a person in law; but that is *not a juridical* proposition but a *political,* an *ethical, postulate* as to the *contents* of a certain, or of every, law. Up to the Civil War, slavery certainly was a legal institution in the United States; that is all that the *jurist* can say. It is not within his competence *qua* jurist to state that it was an *immoral* institution; for the jurist looks at the world from the *juridical* point of view. To say that it was immoral is not possible taking the standard of *law* but only by taking the very different standard of *morals.* Whereas the proposition that slavery was a *legal* institution is a scientific statement, objectively valid, the question whether it was immoral depends on the speaker's subjective standard of morality; the South thought it was not.

The delimitation of jurisprudence *versus psychology* is also of the highest importance. The legal rule as a specific meaningfulness (*Sinngehalt*) is by no means the same thing as *my perception* of this legal rule. The validity of the rule remains intact, whether my perception is wrong or not, or whether I have no idea of its existence. How could one *psychologically* explain the positive rule of many juridical orders that *ignorantia juris nocet?* In the *existential* sphere, I certainly did not know of this rule, nevertheless I will be held responsible, because the *law* prescribes that I *should* have known it. Here again we see the difference between the objective validity (*Geltung*) of a legal norm and the wholly metajuridical question whether and how this rule exercises a motivating influence on the mind of human beings. Petrazycki's "theory of motivation" is therefore by no means a juridical, but a psychological theory.

This delimitation of law from psychology has been made by Kelsen's epoch-making research into the nature of the "will" in law.[15] Kelsen has shown that the "will" in law is something quite different from the "will" in psychology. To have operated in jurisprudence with the *psychological* conception of the will is another instance of confusing a natural with a normative science. It is only in consequence of this confusion that jurisprudence has been faced with many pseudo-problems; in private law, *e.g.*, the "real will" of the parties making a contract, the problem of the *reservatio mentalis*, of the "will" in spite of compulsion (*coactus tamen voluit*) ; in criminal law, the problem of crime and the "will," the juridical construction of delinquencies of omission, of delinquencies by negligence, the problem of the "freedom of the will"; these pseudo-problems are always the consequence of interpreting the "will" in law in terms of psychology, of interpreting a *normative* relation in terms of *causality*. He who makes a *reservatio mentalis* has not been willing to live up to the contract he has made; but this situation in the realm of facts is irrelevant in law, because the law holds him responsible, in spite of the non-existence of the psychological will. If a railwayman sleeps and a railway accident follows, has he had the "will" to produce this accident? No, but he ought to be punished because the law prescribes that he ought not to have slept, that it was his *duty*—a relation in law, not in the domain of nature—not to sleep. A man who is guilty of murder ought to be executed, not because he has *caused* the death of a man, but because the law connects a certain fact with a certain legal consequence. The *juridical fact (Tatbestand)* is not identical with the fact in natural science; the juridical fact always is a creation of the law; if we say that a juridical fact has been "established" in court, we speak of a juridical fact which can, but need not be, identical with the natural fact. If the court of last instance has established the fact that a man is guilty of murder, that need *not* necessarily mean that he has slain another man *in fact;* but it is the *legal* fact. On the other hand, if the court of last instance establishes the fact that this man has not slain another man, perhaps he *has* done so in fact. The English expression, "His Lordship was *satisfied,*" is very good, indeed; for this is the juridically relevant point, not how the facts *have been* in fact, but that the judge is satisfied that they have been so. Now, of course, we demand that the established legal fact *should* correspond to the fact in nature. But this is a postulate of an *ethical* nature as to the contents and procedure of a "good" law. A law prescribes, *e.g.,* that, if something happens, a *hostage* shall be executed. Is there any psychological, any connection in terms of causality, between this fact and the absolutely "innocent" hostage? Certainly not, but he shall be executed not because he has *done* something, but because he is held responsible for this act by the law in force. Here again, we certainly demand that the law should not make such a connection; but this again is only a metajuridical critique of the contents of a given positive law, which—from a *critical,* metajuridical point of view—still is a *primitive* law.

But the normative relation is not only quite different from the connection of *causality* (cause-effect) but also

from the *teleological* connection (means-end).[16] The specific
legal connection has to do neither with the causal nor with
the teleological nexus. It is a connection made by a norm in
terms of the *Sollen*. It is this specific normative connection
which Kelsen calls *juridical imputation* (*Zurechnung*).

But in order to avoid misunderstanding, a few further
observations are necessary. There are *facts*, of course, observable with our senses, facts which play in time and in
space, which are determined by causality. But these facts
obtain their juridical *significance* by a norm. The norm
functions as a scheme for attributing meanings (*Deutungsschema*). The norm as a specific meaningfulness (*Sinngehalt*) is very different from the factual act by which it is
produced. The judge must, of course, make an act of cognition, by interpreting, *e.g.*, facts as "larceny," and he must
further make an act of volition by which he creates the
individual norm of the decision. But the law is not identical
with the functions of the organ which creates or "applies"
the law.

It must further be borne in mind that the Vienna School
does not at all deny that the law can be made the subject
matter of other sciences, as well as of the science of law.
The *history of law* is, of course, a legitimate science; but
it is part of the science of history, working with *historical*
methods, giving an answer to the question how laws *have
been,* or how they have been brought about. Take, for example, the classical Roman law as a law which is no longer
in force; I can treat it historically, but I can treat it also
juridically, analyzing this law, presenting it as a system,
giving an answer not to the historical question how the
Roman law developed, but to the juristic question what the
classical Roman law *is*. It is legitimate to ask which psychological reactions are created by laws in the human mind,
how law operates as a motivating force; but this is not
science of law, but *Psychology* of law, a part of the natural

science of psychology, working not with juridical, but with psychological, methods. It is legitimate to ask *why* a parliament has made these statutes and not other ones, how these laws have worked socially, which economic, political, and other influences have made themselves felt on the activity of legislative bodies or tribunals; but the science of *law* can give no answer to these questions, they are the questions of *sociology,* a science in the domain of nature, connecting facts in terms of causality, whereas the problem of the pure science of law is and cannot be anything else but the *law* as the specific self-sufficiency of a sphere of meaning (*specifische Eigengesetzlichkeit einer Sinnsphäre*).

Pure Science of Law vs. Morals and Politics

But to have determined the science of law *versus* nature, means that we have found the *genus proximum*—the science of law is a *normative* science—but not yet the *differentia specifica.* For there are many normative sciences: ethics, the science of a positive religion, *et cetera.*

Whereas Kelsen in his first writings underlined mostly the contrast between the science of law and sociology, between normative and natural sciences, it has become more and more important in his work to delimit the science of law *within* the domain of normative sciences, *versus* ethics, morals; hence his struggle against natural law. The pure science of law is and cannot be anything else but the theory of positive law. The problem of the jurist is *Quid juris?* It is the problem of the moralist: *Quid est justum?* Justice expresses an absolute value, the contents of which cannot be determined by the pure science of law. Justice, according to Kelsen, as the history of human thought concerning justice has shown, is, in spite of its highest importance, in spite of the fact that it is indispensable for the actions

of men, not accessible to our cognition. Kelsen does not
deny natural law, he only recognizes that natural law is not
law in the sense of the jurist. Kelsen has shown that the
traditional jurisprudence, even after having repudiated
natural law in its most open forms, still abounds of natural
law, because it is not content to comprehend the essence
of the law and to understand it by an analysis of its structure—all the science of law can do—but wishes to *justify*
the law. The traditional jurisprudence confuses the law as
it is with the law as it *ought to be*. "Jurists" often are not
giving us the law but *their ideology* of the law. They either
endeavor to show that the law actually in force is not only
the law but also a "good" or the "best" law (*conservative*
natural law), or that the law actually in force is not only
the law but a "bad" law which should be replaced by a
"better" law (*revolutionary* natural law). In both cases
they not only do not state the law as it is but they falsify the
law. Now, *what* law ought to be depends, of course, on the
subjective political convictions of the writer and his epoch;
an aristocratic conservative has probably a very different
natural law from a socialist worker, a democrat from a
fascist. These struggles for a "good" law are naturally
of the highest importance and form a great part of human
history; but the jurist *qua* jurist can say nothing about it.

This *ideologic* treatment is to be found in every field of
the law, particularly so in constitutional and international
law. How often have we heard in Europe in "scientific"
works that "Soviet law" is no law at all; another could say
the same thing about "fascist" law. But the meaning can
only be that the writer does not like it; in a word, it is not a
juridical proposition, but a *political* judgment of value. To
delimit jurisprudence *versus politics*, this is the second
pillar of the pure science of law.

This delimitation, again, does not mean that it is not
legitimate to *study politics;* this does not mean that *politics*

of law is not very important. Political proposals for the further development of the law are, of course, legitimate and necessary.[17] But a man must make it clear whether he is speaking as a jurist or as a politician of the law.

The specific legal connection, as we have stated, is the juridical imputation: If there is *A*, there *shall* be *B*, whereas the scheme of a law in natural sciences is: If there is *A*, there *must* inevitably be *B*. The legal connection does not say anything about the normal or political value of this connection. Kelsen's "Rechtssatz" (norm) is a *hypothetical judgment*. It is the norm which connects a certain fact with a certain legal consequence, namely, penalty or execution. And this constitutes just the *specific difference* between a *juridical* and a *moral norm*; the juridical order is a *compulsory* order, regulating human conduct. This legal consequence (the "sanction") lies again, of course, in the normative sphere. Certainly, the contents of a norm are historically conditioned; but the law is not identical with these conditions.

Now, a last observation is necessary. If we distinguish law from natural law, as the law that *is* from the law that *ought to be,* and if, at the same time, we place the law that *is* in the domain of the "To Ought To Be," how is that possible? The answer is the following one: To say that law does not lie in the domain of nature does *not* mean that the law *has no existence;* it only means that the specific existence of the law in force is not an existence in the domain of nature. The creations of the human mind *do* have an existence, not in the corporeal world, but in the world of the spirit. The law that *is,* as opposed to the domain of nature, is a normative order in respect to the reality of facts in nature, it is the scheme of meanings (*Deutungsschema*) for the facts. There is a parallelism between the domain of *Sollen* and the domain of physical-psychological acts, which create and carry the mental contents of the law and

which, in a certain measure, must correspond to the law,
although they *do not* always correspond. There is a tension
between the factual and the normative. The normative juridical order has to hold good as a useful *Deutungsschema* for
the facts. It is only this normative order which gives to
these human acts a *sense*, a *meaning* as juridical acts, a
meaning which they do not possess in the system of nature.
The pure science of law points to the necessary relation between the juridical order and the realizing acts of *factual*
happenings, but it does not identify the spiritual existence
of the law with this relation between normative order and
factual reality. The pure science of law does not overlook
this relation, but determines the juridical order as a system
of norms, for which the acts of the realization of the norms
are, in terms of logic, the *conditio sine qua non,* but not the
conditio per quam.

The law that *is, exists* therefore, but in the domain of the
spirit. But the law that *ought to be,* is again a *Deutungsschema* which pretends that the *positive law* should correspond to something *outside* the law, to a natural law, to an
"ideal of justice." But a judgment of value lies in the domain of ethics or politics, not of pure cognition. The science
of law can only serve *cognition* if it is to be *science* and *not
politics.*

THE "PYRAMID OF LAW"

It is on these foundations that the pure science of law has
been built up. Kelsen has shown that the dualism dominating the traditional theory of law is nothing but the heir of
the theory of natural law, the consequence of an ideological,
political, but not a scientific, treatment of the problems.
These dualisms are not within the system of the law, but
are *transsystematic.* It is on these foundations that Kelsen
has done away with the dualism of law (*objektives Recht*)

and *right* (*subjektives Recht*). He has shown that the traditional position conceiving my right as something different and pre-existent to law, which only later is "guaranteed" by the law, is typically *jus naturae*. The right is only a subjective form of the law; a man has a right, juridically speaking, only insofar as it has been bestowed upon him by the juridical order in force. We have spoken already of Kelsen's doing away with the dualism of "natural" and "juridical" persons. Not only the dualism between right and law, but also the neglect of the conception of duty, as compared with the conception of the right, has purely ideological reasons. Duty is the very central problem, because the duty is the very essence of a compulsory normative order as the law is. And, of course, the legal duty is different from the moral duty. A conflict between law and morals is impossible within the system of the law; such a conflict may arise only in the heart of a man who is at the same time the bearer of a juridical as well as an ethical normative order.

Whereas Kelsen in his first principal work, the *Hauptprobleme*, while conceiving the law as a system of norms, has still identified the law with the *lex*, looking therefore at the law only from the *static* point of view of its *validity*, it is the great merit of Adolf Merkl to have introduced into the pure science of law the dynamic point of view of the creation of the law.[18]

If the law is a system of judicial norms, the first question which arises is: What does constitute the unity of a plurality of judicial norms? Why does a certain judicial norm belong to a given juridical order? And the answer is: A plurality of norms forms a system if their validity can be traced back to a single norm as the ultimate foundation of this validity. This ultimate norm is called the "basic norm" (*Grundnorm*). Every normative system must have a basic norm. But whereas the basic norm of an ethical order is a

substantive norm, from which the other norms can be
derived by a deduction from the general to the particular,
the juridical norms *are not valid on account of their contents: Every content can be law.* A juridical norm is valid
always and only if it has been created in a specifically determined way. Law is valid only as positive law. Therefore
the norms of a juridical order cannot be deduced logically
from the basic norm; they have to be brought into existence
by a *creative* act which is not an act of thinking, but of
volition. If, for example, the basic norm is, You shall obey
the Tsar, nothing is, as yet, said as to the *contents* of the
different norms of the juridical order of Imperial Russia.
But the basic norm is, according to Kelsen, only *hypothetical;* it means that if you take this basic norm as valid, then
and only then—Kelsen's relativism [19]—is the juridical order
valid. It is only under this hypothesis of the basic norm that
given materials can be determined as a system of juridical
norms. The theory of the basic norm shows the transcendental logical conditions of the positive method of juridical
cognition. The basic norm is, of course, not a positive, but
a hypothetical, norm; but the choice of the basic norm is
not an arbitrary matter, because it must be chosen in such
a way that it can function as a useful *Deutungsschema* for
the factual conduct of men.

The unity of a juridical order is a relationship of progressive delegation (*Erzeugungszusammenhang*). The different
norms of a juridical order do not stand on the same level;
the juridical order is a graduation of different strata of
juridical norms which stand to one another in the relation
of sub- and supra-ordination: The "pyramid of law"
(*Stufenbau des Rechts*). It is a gradual concretization and
individualization of the law. The scheme of a pyramid of
law would, for example, be: Basic norm, constitution—its
specific function is not to give certain contents, although
it can do so, of course, but to determine the organs and the

process of the creation of norms of a lower level; the *leges* —general abstract norms which connect juridically a certain fact *in abstracto* with a certain legal consequence *in abstracto*. These abstract rules, in order to have a meaning, need a further concretization; it is necessary to establish whether a fact which has been determined *in abstracto* by the general norm if the *lex* exists *in concreto*, and if a certain concrete compulsory act has to be set up for this concrete case; this is done by the administrative decision or by the decision of a court. The function of the judge is therefore by no means only declaratory, but constitutive, is *creation of the law:* The decision of the judge is a juridical individual norm, the individualization and concretization of the abstract and general norm.[20] On the other hand, the contract in private law is also a concrete, individual norm, set up by the parties who are authorized by a higher norm, the *lex*, to do so. The juridical validity of a contract has its legal foundation, not in the "coinciding will of the parties," but in the law which prescribes that the "coinciding will of the parties" *shall* be legally binding.

The basic norm has only the character of creation, the last compulsory act only the character of application of the law. But all intermediate stages of the pyramid of law partake at the same time of the character of creation as well as of application of norms. The constitution is an application of the basic norm and an act of creation of law; so are *leges*, and so forth. It is therefore clear that for a pure science of law there is no absolute, only a relative difference between "creation" and "application" of the law.

The conception of the gradual construction of the juridical order has important consequences as regards the problem of *interpretation*.[21] The interpretation is a mental proceeding accompanying the procedure of the creation and application of the law in its development from a higher to a lower stage. The interpretation is therefore by no means limited to the interpretation of a general rule (e.g., *lex*) or a concrete norm (of a contract) by the judge, but plays its role on all the stages of the pyramid of law. The legislator has to interpret the constitution. The "legality" of the creation of a norm is primarily dependent on the observance of the procedure of creation of this lower norm, a procedure regulated by the higher norm. A statute is a statute, in the first place, if it has been created in a procedure described by the constitution. But the higher norm *may* give also prescriptions as to the contents of norms of a lower stage. The difference between the legislator and the judge is therefore, in this respect, only a difference of degree, not a difference in kind. The legislator is juridically bound by the constitution; only such *leges* are valid as have been created by a procedure prescribed by the constitution *and* in conformity with the *contents* of the constitution, if the constitution contains also prescriptions as to the contents. But the constitution as the highest and therefore most abstract norm has only, generally speaking, a very general content and does therefore not limit the legislator so much with regard to the contents of the *leges*. As regards the judge, his decision is, of course, also bound by a procedure prescribed by the higher norm; but here determination of the higher norm, as regards the content, is usually more far reaching. But even here *the determination as regards the contents is never complete.* The higher norm always leaves to the organ which has to "apply" it a greater or lesser *liberum judicium.* The lower norm is therefore always, to a certain extent, undetermined by the higher norm.

This lack of complete determination can be *intentional.* The legislator needs not to determine everything, because the juridical order is not identical with the *lex;* because the juridical order is a dynamic process and it is the task of the organ which is *competent under the law* to continue the process of determination. If a statute prescribes that the judge shall condemn to a fine or imprisonment, or to imprisonment between five and ten years, the higher norm is only a *scheme* which has to be concretized in the individual case by the decision of the judge. *Ceteris paribus*, it is not possible to predict whether the judge will condemn in the concrete case, for example, to five or to eight years of imprisonment; *both* decisions are legal and legally valid. The general, abstract rules never can give a complete determination, and it is for this reason that the *lex* cannot determine all the cases and that the law prescribes that the concretization shall be done by the judge.

The undetermination of the individual, concrete norm can be the consequence of the *vagueness* of language in which the higher norm is expressed. Such a vagueness can again be intentional. If a fascist law prescribes that he who has done anything against the "prestige" of his country abroad shall, by the decision of the competent judge, be deprived of his citizenship and eventually of his fortune, it is the *intention* of the law to authorize the judge to fill out in a concrete case the intentionally vague expression "prestige." The higher norm, as a scheme, can also take the form of a mere blanket-norm, leaving it to the competent organ to fill it out in the concrete case according to its judgment.

The higher rule can choose the technique of referring to a rule that, *in itself*, is not a rule of law but, for example, of morals or usage; it can refer the competent organ to the "usages at the Stock Exchange of *X*" or to morals by prescribing, for example, that contracts *contra bonos mores* shall be void. In order to determine whether a concrete contract is immoral and therefore void, the judge must, of course, apply the standard of morals, but this moral rule is metajuridical only as regards its contents. The decision of the judge is, also in this case, based on the *law;* it is the *law* which so prescribes, the judge can act so only because

he is authorized by the law so to do, although the law does
not determine *in concreto* what an immoral contract is, but
leaves it to the judge.

The indetermination of the lower norm can also be *involuntary*, either because of "errors" of the legislator—law is
human work—or because of the ambiguity of the verbal
expression of the higher norm. Or it may happen that two
norms pretending to be valid at the same time are contradictory. In such cases, *every* one of the different possible
decisions that fills out the scheme of a higher norm is in
conformity with it. The "interpretation" by the judge must
therefore not lead only to one legal decision, but to different
decisions which are all equally legal, although only one of
them becomes the individual norm in the concrete case.
Many very different statutes can all be constitutional. It is
legally impossible to "predict" what concrete statutes will
be produced by parliament, all within the frame of the
constitution. Sometimes different judicial decisions are all
legal; it is, therefore, *juridically* impossible to *predict* the
decision of the judge. The judge is, for the "pure" science
of law, not an automaton, but a *creator of the law*. The
interpretation by the judge and the interpretation by a legal
scholar are, of course, very different things. The first is a
process *within* the law, an act of volition creating the individual, concrete, norm; the second is a mental process,
which lies outside of the law, within the science of law.
Therefore, when, in a case where various decisions are
legally possible, a "scientific" commentator tries to prove
that only one of them is the legal decision, he is not acting
as a scientist but as a politician of the law, trying to influence the court to give a decision in the sense *he* desires.

Here resides the fundamental difference between the pure
science of law and the "jurisprudence of conceptions"
(*Begriffsjurisprudenz*) [22] with which it is sometimes confused. The "mechanical" jurisprudence believes that the law

is a fixed order determining completely human conduct and especially the activity of the courts. The pure science of law, by its dynamic conception of the gradual concretization and individualization of the law, recognizes that the judge also is a creator of the law everywhere and not alone under the common-law systems.

The traditional jurisprudence attributes also to interpretation the role of filling out the *gaps* of the juridical order. Kelsen has shown that this is another remnant of natural-law thinking, a way by which, in a disguised manner, politics are introduced into the law. There are no gaps in the law. "Larceny" in old Austria, for example, could be committed only with regard to corporeal things, and *nulla poena sine lege*. As cases of larceny of electricity were brought before the courts, the Austrian judges, very correctly, acquitted the accused persons; for the judge has to apply the law as it *is*, even if he personally holds it to be a bad law. But many jurists, dissatisfied with this state of things, spoke of gaps in the Austrian law. Were there, juridically speaking, gaps? Not at all; the Austrian law provided a clear norm according to which larceny of electricity is not a punishable crime. But this law was, from a *metajuridical* point of view, held to be a bad law. The assertion of gaps, in a word, is nothing but a critique of the law in force; the word "gaps" points to a difference between the positive law—the only law in the legal sense—and a desired better law.

THE LAW AND THE STATE

This dynamic conception of the law leads Kelsen to do away also with the dualism between private and public law and between the law and the state. Already in his *Hauptprobleme* the identity of the state with the juridical order is foreshadowed; it becomes definite in his third principal book on the juridical and sociological conception of the state. In his *Allgemeine Staatslehre* (1925), Kelsen has given his whole theory of law, not only in a critical, but in a constructive, positive way.

Beginning once more to delimit the science of law from sociology, morals, and politics, Kelsen gives first the static theory of the validity of the law. He shows that the traditional doctrine of the state as composed of "three elements" (power, territory, people) is scientifically untenable. The "power" is the validity of the juridical order; the "territory" [23] is not a geographical conception but the sphere of validity of a juridical order in space; the people is the personal sphere of validity of this juridical order; the doctrine of local autonomy, self-government, colonies, union of states is developed as the doctrine of the centralization and decentralization of a juridical order.

The second part of his *Allgemeine Staatslehre* is dedicated to the dynamic problems of the creation of the law. The traditional doctrine of the different "powers" of the state (legislation, administration, judicial decision) is built up as the theory of the stages of creation of the law. This stage formation is brought about by the activity of the organs; Kelsen develops the theory of the organs of the state. The traditional theory of the different forms of the state is treated as the theory of the *methods of creation* of the law.

THE "PURE" SCIENCE OF LAW AS APPLIED TO THE SCIENCE OF INTERNATIONAL LAW

AFTER this survey of the basic theoretical ideas of the Vienna School, we have to show how this theory works in the particular field of international law. Within the Vienna School the study of international law has been the special field of work of Kelsen himself,[24] of Alfred Verdross,[25] of the writer of this article,[26] and of R. A. Métall.[27]

The influence of the Vienna School has asserted itself in other countries,[28] and many scholars belonging to different schools of thought share many ideas of the Vienna School in this field of international law.[29]

As the science of international law is a special branch of the science of law, it goes without saying that it only can be a *normative* science. The science of international law has therefore to deal exclusively with international *law* and can only work with juridical methods. The science of international law must therefore again be delimited from natural sciences,[30] from sociology, and, within the sphere of normative sciences, from morals, ethics, politics.[31]

Here again, this purification does not mean that international law cannot be made legitimately the subject matter of *other sciences* than the juridical one. We fully recognize the history of international law, its importance for a full understanding of the international law of today; but it is a part of history, working with historical methods. We fully recognize that it is legitimate to inquire into the sociological situations which condition the coming into existence and the development of international law. We recognize that there may be a science of international ethics, but it is different from the science of international law. We fully recognize the legitimacy of the politics of international law, which may perhaps be even more important than the science of international law. But we urge that the frontiers between the science and the politics of international law should be respected, the difference between the international law as *it is* and as it *ought to be*. Here again, the postulates as to the *future* development of international law depend on the speakers' subjective political and ethical convictions. The nationalist will have a very different politics of international law from that of the pacifist. But the international *jurist qua jurist* must not allow himself to be influenced by his nationalistic or pacifist convictions, for if he does so, he will falsify the law in force. It is from this confusion that most books on the international law of World War I are scientifically valueless, because the writer is a priori *politically prejudiced* in favor of the one or the other belligerent group; it is from this confusion that studies on such topics as the Covenant of the League of Nations, the Kellogg Pact, or neutrality so often today give us only the *political* convictions, nationalistic or pacifist, interventionist or isolationist, of the writer, but fail to give us a scientific, objective statement of what the Covenant, the Kellogg Pact, the law of neutrality really is in positive law.

Such a treatment cannot be an advancement, a scientifically valuable contribution to the science of international law. On the other hand, the Vienna School urges that no *politics* of international law are possible without, first, a *scientific* treatment. In order to make reasonable proposals for the development of international law, we must first start by knowing what the law actually in force *is*. This is only possible by a scientific, objective analysis, which, in its turn, presupposes a theory of international law. Many international lawyers therefore make a wrong beginning when they purposely neglect theoretical problems, either from a lack of philosophical education or because of the erroneous prejudice of practicality.[32] It is erroneous to believe that pure theory is nothing but a *jeu d'esprit* of scholars. The error is that anything, however practical, is possible without an underlying theory. The last decade, for example, has brought us, to borrow a word from Judge Moore, a real inflation in peace proposals; many of them are more than naïve because they lack completely the knowledge of the theoretical problems. They are wholly impractical because they have no theoretical basis. It is generally recognized that it is rather difficult to build a complicated railway bridge without the slightest knowledge of bridge building; it should at last be recognized also that it is rather difficult to make proposals for a new world organization without the slightest knowledge of the problems involved. If we, politically, wish to eliminate war, for instance, we must first theoretically understand what the place of war in positive international law is. A *politics* of international law—as regards contents and as regards technique [33]—is only possible on the basis of a *theory* of international law.

THE PRIMACY OF THE LAW OF NATIONS

THE fundamental problems [34] for a pure science of international law are the problems as to its nature, the systematic relations between the different parts of international law, and the relations between international and municipal law. It is by giving a *theory* that the Vienna School has endeavored to make out of international law a *science, i.e.,* a system, not a mere aggregate, whereas a look at even very well-known manuals often shows that, while they are giving us many very valuable materials, they do not even attempt to organize them.

In his first work, *Hauptprobleme,* Kelsen, while still identifying the juridical order with the *lex,* did not attack the problem of the law of nations; even in his study *Über Staats Unrecht* (1913) Kelsen still professes the typical dualistic doctrine, according to which municipal and international law constitute two different and independent spheres. Merkl, who introduced the dynamic conception of the pyramid of law, remained also within the orbit of the municipal law of one state.

It is the merit of Alfred Verdross to have been the first to adapt, as early as 1914, Kelsen's theory to the problems of international law. He has shown that, apart from the negation of international law as law, two constructions are possible: The *dualistic* [35] and the *monistic* constructions.

The dualistic construction, which endeavors to find the reason of validity of international law in the coinciding will of states, starts from the doctrine that municipal and international law are *toto genere* different. The writers of the Vienna School have shown—and we only can refer here to these writings for all details—that this theory cannot be maintained because it is in contradiction to positive international law, because it is unable to give a satisfactory construction of the universality of the law. Therefore, only a monistic construction is possible. But here again we have two possibilities: Either to base the validity of international law on the "will" of a single state (primacy of the law of the land)[36] or to base the validity of *all* law on international law (primacy of the law of nations).

It is self-evident that these problems are strongly connected with one of the principal problems of international law, namely, the "sovereignty" of states. In his second principal work,[37] Kelsen recognizes the conception of sovereignty as a necessary juridical conception, necessary as the expression of the unity and exclusiveness of the whole legal system. Sovereignty can therefore only be supreme and exclusive. It is for this reason that Kelsen, while recognizing the necessity of the conception of sovereignty, denies sovereignty to the single states; sovereignty can only be the attribute of the highest legal order, of international law.[38]

It is on this basis that Kelsen makes his research into the relations between municipal and international law. But here Kelsen takes a standpoint, different from and combated by Verdross and this writer, in asserting that there is a possibility of choice between the two monistic constructions, that both are, in theory, equally admissible, that there is no objective, theoretical criterium which would compel us to prefer the one to the other construction. This choice, Kelsen says, is not a theoretical question but a question of subjective conception of life.

Verdross, while accepting from the beginning only a
monistic construction, tried first in 1914 to build up the
universality of the law on the primacy of the law of the
land, anchoring international law in the constitutional rule
of municipal law, according to which the chief executive is
authorized to conclude international treaties. But he recognized soon that it is impossible to anchor the *whole* international law within this supposed constitutional rule, not
only because of the customary law of nations, but especially
because of the positive international norm according to
which the validity of international law is independent of
revolutionary change of the constitution; but in such a case,
the constitution in which international law was supposed
to be anchored disappears. It is for this reason that Verdross adopted the theory of the primacy of the law of
nations. He made, in his book on the unity of the juridical
world,[39] a further inquiry into the nature of the "sovereignty" of the states. He has shown that there are two
conceptions of sovereignty: Sovereignty as a presupposed
conception, and sovereignty as a conception deriving from
the contents of international law.[40] Verdross has shown
that Kelsen in his book on sovereignty was occupied only
with the first conception of sovereignty: This is indeed a
necessary conception and this *absolute* sovereignty can alone
belong to international law. But there is a second conception
of sovereignty, deriving from the contents of positive international law. This sovereignty is a *relative* conception and
means a relatively high level on the pyramid of law; it
means that the state is, of course, subordinated to international law, but that the state is *directly and immediately*
subordinated to international law alone; sovereignty means:
Völkerrechtsunmittelbarkeit. Sovereignty in this sense
means a *fullness of competences, given* to the single states
by international law. As under municipal law the "rights
of citizens" are not something preexistent and only later

"guaranteed" by the constitution (so the natural-law doctrine), but *granted* by the constitution and legally existing only insofar as the constitution positively grants them, the sovereignty of the single state is not something outside of and pre-existing to international law and only later "guaranteed" by it, but the competences are granted to the states by international law. This sovereignty is therefore by no means an absolute conception but an essentially *relative* conception which changes and is bound to change with the change of the supraordinated international law. What the competences of a sovereign state are can never be determined a priori but only through the analysis of the general and particular positive international law binding upon a given state at a given time. It is therefore self-evident that not only the sovereignty of the same state at different epochs but also the sovereignty of different states at the same moment do not have necessarily the same contents. Sovereign Great Britain was, in 1914, free to go to war, but not in 1933; sovereign Brazil, which is neither bound by the League of Nations Covenant nor by the Kellogg Pact, was free to do so even in 1933.

Hence *all* the activity of the single states is regulated by the supraordinated law of nations. The so-called domestic affairs of the single states are not the affairs which are *not* regulated by international law, but the affairs which a state *under international law,* has the exclusive competence to regulate as it pleases; they are, as paragraph 8 of Article XV of the Covenant states, "les affaires que le droit international laisse à la compétence exclusive des Etats." The domestic affairs are not such in virtue of their inherent nature and cannot be determined a priori—no affair is necessarily a "domestic" affair—but only by analyzing the positive international law. In 1933, the treatment of her minorities is a domestic affair for France, but not for Poland; but in *both* cases this is so in virtue of the supraordinated international law.

This basic cognition is rich in consequences for the theoretical treatment of *special* problems, *e.g.*, the "domestic" affairs, or the problem of nationality. That every state is free to confer its nationality upon whom it pleases and according to rules and principles of its own discretion means that the supraordinated law of nations confers such competence on the single states, but within the limits of international norms, stating namely that no state is allowed to confer its nationality upon individuals who are not reasonably connected with the state in question. If Austria, for example, were to make a statute according to which Austrian nationality is forcibly conferred on all Chinese resident at Peiping, this law, although fully valid according to the Austrian Constitution, would be clearly illegal under international law; Austria would be guilty of an *excès de compétence*. It is on this basis that this writer has built up a theoretical treatise of the problem of dual nationality [41] and of the international law concerning national minorities.[42]

It is the great merit of Verdross to have established the monistic construction of the primacy of the law of nations by proving through the *analysis of the positive law of nations* that this construction alone is theoretically possible because it alone is able to give a satisfactory explanation of the totality of legal experience. Verdross has shown, by an analysis of the positive law, that there is an uninterrupted relationship by delegation between international and municipal law. Verdross and this writer cannot therefore accept Kelsen's thesis of a possible choice between the two monistic constructions. But, after all, the difference between ours and Kelsen's standpoint is not so great. For it was exactly Kelsen who has shown that the construction of the primacy of the law of the land cannot lead to satisfactory results, that it cannot explain certain phenomena as being law, that it leads easily—and this writer would add, necessarily—to the negation of the legal character of internation-

al law. It is Kelsen who has shown that the primacy of the
law of the land which is based on the absolute sovereignty
of a single, of one's own, state inescapably must lead to
the consequence that one's own state *alone* is sovereign, that
this uniqueness and exclusiveness inherent *ex hypothesi* in
the conception of absolute sovereignty must lead to the
consequence that the other states cannot be regarded as
sovereign or can be regarded so only insofar as they are
regarded as being delegated by the juridical order of one's
own state. Kelsen has shown that the law of nations is by
no means, as the traditional doctrine asserts, a "law of co-
ordination." But if a single state has absolute sovereignty,
it cannot be subordinated to a higher law. Hegel, the spiritual father of the idea of absolute sovereignty of the single
state, was, as a philosopher, logical enough to take the consequence and to proclaim, not only that there is no international *law,* but to deny the very *possibility* of international *law.* But later writers on international law, while adopting Hegel's basis and being equally desirous to recognize
international law as real law, were under a necessity to
combine the two conceptions which do not go together, to
combine them at least apparently, by taking their refuge
in clear fictions, of which the theory of the "auto-limitation"
of the state has been most widely accepted; but if a state
is bound only by its own will, it can also cease to be bound
by its own will, which means that it is juridically not
bound at all.

It is Kelsen who has shown that the "equality" of states
is possible only under the supposition that international law
is supraordinated to the single states. The peers in England
were "equal" because they were all in the same way *subordinated* to the King; all men are equal before God or
before the law because they are all *subordinated* in the same
way to God or the law; all states are "equal" because they
are all *subordinated* in the same way to international law.

But this theoretically untenable conception of absolute sovereignty works still as a motivating force with statesmen and nations and is still defended by writers. It is therefore to be understood that the construction of the primacy of the law of nations has been attacked, especially by writers who are politically opposed to it. On the other hand, these attacks have in many cases been the consequence of misunderstandings, of reading into our construction many things which it does not mean at all. This writer has therefore endeavored [43] to clear up these misunderstandings by making it plain that the construction of the primacy of the law of nations as a theoretical, not a political, construction is the construction of the positive international law actually in force, neither a natural law nor a theoretical construction of an international law *de lege ferenda;* that the logical and legal supraordination of international to municipal law is not to be confused or identified with the quite different problem of historical priority; that the primacy of the law of nations is for us not a logical necessity a priori but built up on the analysis of the actual law of nations as it is; that our construction does not say, as such, anything with regard to the contents of international law. The *civitas maxima,* for example, as conceived by Wolff, is by no means implied in our construction; for this *civitas maxima* is today a political wish, not a statement of the positive law. The question whether individuals are or are not subjects of international law cannot be answered from the construction of the primacy of the law of nations but only from the analysis of the positive international law in force, the contents of which must appear in *every* theoretical construction as it actually is if this construction is to be a theoretical, not a political, one, if this construction is not going to falsify the law in force.

The primacy of the law of nations means the supraordination of the international juridical order to the munic-

ipal juridical orders of the single states, means that the
"sovereign states" are delegated partial juridical orders
(*delegierte Teilrechtsordnungen*) of the international juridical order, means that the pyramid of law does not end
with the basic norm of the juridical order of a given single
state but that at the top of the pyramid of law stands the
international juridical order, the norms of which must, in
their turn, be traced back again, in the ultimate analysis, to
the basic norm of international law.

As regards the basic norm of international law, Verdross
is of opinion that it must also be founded in an ultimate and
absolute value: *Justice*. This is, of course, in contradiction
to Kelsen's philosophy, not only in that it endangers the
independence, the self-sufficiency of the law, by giving a
strictly extralegal source as the ultimate reason of validity
of the law, but more so because Kelsen does not believe in
absolute values, such as justice, which are to him only
subjective, relative values as far as *science* is concerned.
Here play the different conceptions of life, Kelsen's essential philosophical relativism versus Verdross' Catholic philosophy and its faith in absolute values. This writer believes
that this problem, however important it may be for a philosophy of law, has no importance for a theory of law. We
can concede to Verdross that there are absolute values,
that it is philosophically legitimate to fit the whole universality of the law into the cosmic order, and yet say that this
task transcends the task of a pure theory of law, which
can be satisfied with the presupposed basic rule of international law and does not need to go further.

But the question, what the contents of this basic norm of
international law are, is, of course, of great importance for
the theory of law. The answer of Verdross is: *pacta sunt
servanda,* an answer accepted by Kelsen, and also by Anzilotti. But a deeper research must show that *pacta sunt
servanda* cannot be the *basic* norm of international law.

This critique has been made both from without and from within the Vienna School. It is not possible to trace back all international law to this basic norm. This writer has shown [44] that the binding validity of international law upon new states, of an international law in force prior to the coming into existence of this new state, cannot be founded in this basic norm. Métall [45] has shown that the *customary* law of nations cannot have its reason of validity in the norm *pacta sunt servanda,* except by understanding customary law as a *pactum taciturn,* which clearly amounts to a fiction. But *pacta sunt servanda* cannot be the basic norm of international law for two further and decisive reasons: first, it is a positive rule of customary international law, giving the reason of validity of international treaties. The whole treaty-law is therefore anchored in *customary* law. General international law is today still composed only of customary law and the "general principles recognized by civilized nations." [46] *Pacta sunt servanda* is therefore a positive, not a hypothetical, norm; now, we have seen that the basic norm is always and necessarily not a positive, but a presupposed, rule. Secondly, *pacta sunt servanda* cannot be the basic norm because of its structure; for it is a substantive norm, asking for the sanctity of treaties, whereas the basic norm must be purely formal; its unique function is to institute the method of creation of the law.

Verdross, taking into account these critiques, has now given a new formula of this basic rule: [47] The states shall behave in their relations with one another according to the general principles recognized by civilized nations, insofar as no special norms, derogating to these principles, have come into existence. This certainly is a presupposed and purely formal norm to which *all* the positive rules of international law can be traced back, although perhaps not yet a final solution of the problem of the contents of the basic norm of international law.

THE PROBLEMS OF THE STATIC THEORY OF INTERNATIONAL LAW: ITS VALIDITY

THE pure science of law distinguishes again in international law the static problems of the *validity* and the dynamic problems of the *creation* of the law of nations.

As regards the *static* problems,[48] the international juridical order has, as every juridical order, to be valid somewhere, at some time, for certain persons and with regard to certain matters. The domain of the temporal validity of international law is unlimited in principle.

The domain of the territorial validity of general international law is the international community. But this sphere of validity does not embrace a priori the whole world—this is a natural law conception—but changes with the contents of positive international law; restricted once to the Christian European states, it has been extended first to Christian non-European, and later to non-Christian European and non-European states, so as to comprise today nearly the whole globe.

As regards the material domain of the validity of international law, it is unlimited; there are no matters which are excluded from the *competence ratione materiae* of international law. All matters are regulated by international law, either directly by substantive international rules, or by international rules of competence, delegating to the single states certain matters which the states are authorized by international law to regulate as they please.

The problems of the personal domain of the validity of international law embraces the problems which are called by the traditional doctrine the problems of the "subjects of international law." Kelsen has made it clear that every law regulates and cannot regulate anything else but human conduct. International law, therefore, cannot regulate anything else but human conduct. If the traditional theory tells us, that the law of nations is *exclusively* binding upon *states,* it must not be taken literally. For a law which would not be binding, in ultimate analysis upon men, would be no law. But that does not mean a priori that individuals are subjects of international law. That international law is binding upon states means that it is individually binding on *certain* men, who, as competent organs under municipal law—and this municipal law is authorized by international law to create these organs according to municipal rules— have to execute the obligations imposed by international law; but all the other human beings, the subjects of the states, are collectively bound as possible objects of compulsory acts of international law (reprisals and war).

The pure theory of law has shown that the traditional theory, according to which states alone are—or even can be—subjects of international law, is theoretically wrong also, because it is in contradiction to the positive international law.

Every juridical order determines for itself the entities which are subjects of this order; so does international law. The question, which entities are 'subjects" of international law, cannot be answered by the traditional dogmatic statement, "States alone," but only by an analysis of the positive law. This analysis shows that sovereign states are full and permanent members of the international community; but not only states, but also certain unions of states,[49] such as confederations of states, or the League of Nations; and not only these communities on a *territorial* basis, but also communities on a *personal* basis, as the Roman Catholic church. But international law knows also subjects which are *not* states, e.g., insurgents recognized as a belligerent party,[50] or India.[51] International law knows permanent (the states, the Catholic church) and temporary subjects (recognized insurgents). It knows full and partial subjects. India is, for instance, a colony of Great Britain, theoreti-

cally, although in British constitutional law it is styled the
Empire of India; but it is neither a state nor a dominion.
From the point of view of general international law, India
is therefore not a subject of international law; but as a
separate member of the League of Nations, it is a partial
subject of international law, namely within the whole
sphere of the League, although remaining, in other respects,
a dependency of Great Britain.

The question whether individuals are or are not subjects
of international law is also exclusively a question of positive law. If the convention concerning the International
Prize Court had come into force, certain individuals would
have become subjects of international law within the sphere
of validity of this convention. Individuals have been subjects of international law during the validity of the convention creating a Central American Court. It is always
a question of the *contents* of positive international law.

The essential and necessary function of international law
is to determine the territorial, personal, and temporal
sphere of validity of the juridical orders of the different
sovereign states. The rules of international law are primarily rules of competence.[52]

The determination of the territorial validity [53] of the
juridical orders of the different sovereign states embraces
the problems with which the traditional doctrine deals with
under the heading "Territory." The "territory" of a sov-
erign state is, in law, not as most writers believe, "a certain
portion of the surface of the globe," *not a geographical,* but
a *legal* conception; it is the domain of validity of the juridical order of a given sovereign state. The unity of the
territory of a state, which may consist only of scattered
islands or of a mainland and far-flung colonies and possessions all over the world, is not a geographical, but a
legal, unity, constituted by the validity of one and the same
juridical order under international law. Verdross has shown

that there are three types of territorial competences under
positive international law: (1) A *competence ratione loci*
given by international law exclusively to a single state;
here we speak traditionally of the "territory" of a state.
It is from this point of view of a *competence ratione loci,*
granted by international law, that the pure theory of law
has to build up the theory of territorial sovereignty, of
frontiers, of the maritime belt, of the "modes of acquisition and loss of territory," of competences of a state on
the territory of a foreign state. (2) The second type is
the "territory of a community of states," where exclusive
territorial competence is given by international law, not
to a single state, but to a community of states (*condom-
inia*).[54] (3) Lastly, there are spheres where, according to
international law, no exclusive territorial competence of a
single state exists, but where *all* the states of the international community are territorially competent; these are
not *terrae nullius,* but territories of the international community; the high seas and unoccupied regions. But whereas
the high seas never can become the domain of exclusive
territorial competence of a single state, because the positive international law so prescribes, non-occupied regions
can become the domain of exclusive territorial competence
of a single state, as a legal consequence attached by international law to the fulfillment of conditions, also prescribed
by international law (occupatio). One of these conditions
is that the state in question must establish there an effective
authority. One of these conditions is therefore the existence
of facts; the state must exercise and continue to exercise
this authority in fact. This facticity is to be found often
as a legal condition in international law, e.g.,for the coming
into existence of a new state, or a so-called *de facto* government, or in the law of occupation, or in the law of blockade.
But by making them a legal condition, these facts become
normativized. If, for example, an international tribunal has

to decide which of two states is the sovereign over a formerly unoccupied region and if this decision depends on which of the states has there first exercised its authority *in fact,* here again we find that the legally decisive point is a *legal* fact; the decisive point is that the tribunal is satisfied that one or the other state has done so in fact.

It is from the point of view of the personal validity that the pure theory of law has to treat the problems of the "population" of a state, of nationality, and so on. It is from the point of view of temporal validity that the pure theory of law has to treat the problems of the coming into existence, of the extinction, of succession of states.

As every juridical order determines for itself who its members shall be and under which conditions membership shall be acquired, as every juridical order *creates* its subjects, it is international law which creates the states, which prescribes by its rules the conditions to which the legal consequence, coming into existence of a new state, is attached. The origin, the formation, of a new state is, therefore, by no means, as many writers believe, "a pure fact," something going on outside of the domain of law, in the realm of nature, but is a condition determined by a rule of international law. The same is true of the "extinction" of a state. The answer to the question, when has a state come into existence, cannot be given by the mere observation of facts but only by the analysis of positive international law. It is on this basis that this writer has built up his book on the recognition of states, showing that positive international law, determining by its rules the coming into existence of a new state, does not make this coming into existence dependent on the "recognition" by other states. This writer has therefore started with the analysis of the juridical position under international law of a new state which had not yet been recognized. The recognition of a new state is, by no means, a recognition of the legal existence of this new state, and even less the legal reason for its existence; recognition is not, as the dominating theory believes, constitutive but declaratory. From the recognition of a new state the recognition of a so-called *de facto* government [55] must be clearly distinguished; for in this case we have to deal with the problem of an unconstitutional change of government in a state already existing and recognized, a state which remains the same in international law. It is just this rule of international law (*regimine mutato non mutatur civitas ipsa*) which renders the "revolution" in a state juridically understandable; for whereas revolution, viewed from the point of view exclusively of the single state in question, means that the basic norm of this municipal juridical order has been overthrown by a procedure contrary to the law in force and therefore legally not understandable, whereas revolution, from this point of view, means a discontinuity of municipal juridical orders, it is this supraordinated norm of international law, prescribing the identity of a state in spite of revolution, which guarantees the continuity of the law.

As regards the determination of the competences *ratione materiae* by international law, international law delegates, in general, to the states the competence to regulate all matters. Insofar as international rules are only rules of competence, delegating to the states authority to regulate all and therefore the same matters, but within the territorial and personal competences delimited by international law, we have a concurring, as distinguished from an exclusive, competence of states. In the realm of concurring competences conflicts can naturally arise, where the same matters are regulated differently by different states, but everywhere within the competences conferred upon them by international law. Dual nationality or statelessness, for example, are necessary and permanent phenomena. Practical

proposals for the complete elimination of dual nationality
or statelessness must start with the theoretical insight that
to do so presupposes that international law, instead of
giving to the states merely the competence to regulate nationality according to their wishes, must regulate these
matters for all states by uniform and substantive rules, and,
as this writer has shown in his study on the problem of dual
nationality, not even that would be sufficient; it would
further be necessary to create an international tribunal
(International Court of Nationality) which would guarantee the uniform concretization and individualization (application) of this substantive uniform rule of international
law. It is the task of theory to make clear this necessary
condition for practical proposals; but the question whether
this condition can be achieved is no longer a theoretical
but a political question.

Among the competences conferred by international law
upon the single states, the competence to create their constitution according to their wishes merits particular attention. Sovereign states have, under international law, constitutional autonomy.

In his book on the *Unions of States* (1929), this writer
has tried to show that the word "state" includes two theoretically different conceptions. If we speak of a state, a
sovereign state, in international law, this state is a conception deriving from the *contents* of *international* law.
But a community which is *not* a state in international law
may be a "state" in terms of *municipal* law. This writer
has therefore distinguished between "states in the sense
of international law" and "states in the sense of municipal
law."

The first are communities which are exclusively, directly,
and immediately subordinated to international law; their
constitutional autonomy is directly granted by international
law. As sovereign states are competent, under international

law, to conclude treaties, and as every treaty creates a particular supraordinated juridical order supraordinated to the contracting parties, it is clear that every treaty creates a "union of states" in the broad sense of the term.[56] But, if we speak of unions of states in a technical sense, we speak of certain types, based either on inequality (international protectorate) or on *equality* (alliance, administrative union, real union, confederation of states, League of Nations, Pan-American Union). In all these cases the writer speaks here of genuine unions of states (we have a union of states in the sense of international law; created by an international treaty). But these unions of states are not conceptions of the law—there is no international rule determining a protectorate—but conceptions of the science of law; they are types created by the science of law on the basis of an abstraction, arrived at by the study of the contents of concrete international treaties of a certain, similar content.

But, if we come to the type of the *Suzerain-Vassal* or the federal state, it is clear that we have here unions of states in a very different sense; this writer calls them non-genuine unions of states. They may also have been created by an international treaty, but they may also have been created by constitutional law. These are not unions of states in the sense of international law; there is here *only one* state in the sense of international law, whereas the other states of which this one sovereign state is composed are states in the sense of municipal law. As every state in the sense of international law is competent, under international law, to adopt the constitution it likes, it can adopt as well a centralized as a highly decentralized form of government. The problem of the federal state is not a problem of international but of constitutional law, a problem of *decentralization*. A state in the sense of international law is competent to create states in the sense of municipal law, but it is not competent to create states in the sense of international law; only international law can do so. A centralized state can, therefore, by an act of its legislation become a federal state —as was historically the case with Brazil and the Republic of Austria—but not a confederation of states. This clear insight is of great importance, in regard to all problems of the federal state with respect to international law. This clear insight is often not to be found; and the reason is sometimes a lack of theoretical cognition, sometimes a purely political reason, because ideologically many communities believe that the name "State" confers upon them an extraordinary distinction compared with the *misera plebs* of simple "provinces" and so on. The forty-eight states of the United States are states in terms of the American constitution, but not states at all in terms of international law. There is only *one* state in the sense of international law: the United States. In international law, the American states are on the same level as the provinces of Austria or the former provinces of Germany or the provinces of Canada. International law has to deal neither with Ohio, nor Lübeck, nor Ontario, nor the Tyrol; it exclusively deals with the United States, Germany, Canada, Austria; and the sovereign states are *alone* internationally responsible for acts done by the organs of the states or province.

International law rules may be not only rules of competence but also *substantive* rules; here we have to speak of a *partition of competences* between international law and the municipal orders of the states. It is here, as Verdross was the first to point out, that an analogy, not identity, can be seen between this problem and the problem arising in the federal states. For one of the principal contents of a federal juridical order is the partition of competences between the federal union and its states. Now, in concrete federal laws, this partition can be very different; but, it is always the federal law which distributes the competences and which alone is competent to change this partition of competences; the "competence of competences" belongs to federal law. In an analogous way, the concrete partition of competences between international law and the municipal orders of the states is different at different epochs, changes with the change of contents of positive international law. But however wide the competences of a single state may be, this state has its competences only *in virtue* of international law; the "competence of competences" always belongs to international law. The "progress" of international law, from a political point of view, consists exactly in that international law is going to regulate more and more of the matters which are now delegated by international law to the states directly and by substantive international rules.

THE PROBLEMS OF THE DYNAMIC THEORY OF INTERNATIONAL LAW: ITS CREATION

THE dynamic theory of international law has to deal with the problems of the creation of international law: Problems of the stages of formation, of the organs, of the methods of creation of international law. As every juridical order, international law regulates the way in which it is to be created. International law is not identical with one single stage of its formation; here again the pyramid of law exists. The problems of the stage-formation of international law embrace the problems traditionally known as the problems of the "sources" of international law. It is characteristic for international law, as a primitive law, that the primary method of its creation still is custom. General international law is composed today only of customary law and the "general principles of law recognized by civilized nations." All treaty law is anchored in the customary rule: *Pacta sunt servanda.* For the binding force of international treaties—as well as the binding force of contracts in municipal law—has its reason of validity not, as the dominant doctrine teaches, in the "coinciding will of the parties," here the states, but in an objective norm of general international law which prescribes that this coinciding will of the contracting parties *shall* have this legally binding effect. The problems of the pyramid of international law have to deal with the juridical relation between customary and treaty law, with the relation of both with the general principles recognized by civilized nations, which, although belonging to general international law, have, in positive law, only a subsidiary character.

The rules standing on the highest level of the pyramid of international law may be called the *constitutional rules* [57] of international law. The problems of the pyramid of international law have to deal further with the problems of the relation between *general* and *particular* international law; with the problems of an international *jus cogens,* which cannot be derogated, and an international *jus dispositivum.* The distinction between general and particular international law—a distinction with regard to the domain of validity of international norms—must not be confused with the different distinction between general international law in the sense of abstract law and individual, concrete law—a distinction with regard to the level of an international norm on the pyramid of law, a distinction which is to be met with as well in the domain of general as of particular international law.

It is also to be borne in mind that the treaty has in the stage-formation of international law *two* different functions: The creation of *individual* norms—corresponding to the contracts in municipal law; and the creation of *abstract* norms— corresponding to municipal legislation.

Here again, the so-called gaps are only the expression of a difference between the law in force and a desired, "better" law. The conception of gaps means nothing but an ideological, political critique of the contents of positive law. If, for example, we are always told that the cases in which the League of Nations Covenant allows to its members recourse to war constitute the gaps of the Covenant; this means only that the critic is not satisfied with the positive Covenant as it is, that, according to *him,* the Covenant ought to admit recourse to war in *no* case; in a word, it is his political wish for a "better" Covenant; it is politics of law.

It is clear here again that under the conception of the dynamic creation of international law by a continuous concretization and individualization the difference between "creation" and "application" of international law is only a relative difference, that also the international judge is, to a certain extent, a *creator* of the law, that, on the other hand, even where an international judge decides *ex aequo et bono,* he is rendering nevertheless a legal decision; it is true that *aequitas* is materially not law, but the law, by referring to it, renders it legal, although leaving the determination of *aequitas* in the concrete case to the international judge. And he can give his decision *ex aequo et bono* only because he has been authorized by law, e.g., the *compromis.*

The so-called conflicts between international and municipal law are often quoted as an argument against the unity of all law, as conceived by the theory of the primacy of the law of nations. It is perfectly true that a single state may make a law contrary to international law, and yet it will be "valid" law in this state, binding upon its citizens, tribunals, and so on. Such a conflict can have two reasons: Either the municipal law is violating international law because the state in question has transcended its competence granted by international law, although perhaps the contents of this law are in harmony with international law (violation of an *international rule of competence*) ; or the municipal law, although remaining within the competence granted by international law, is violating international law

by its *contents* (violation of a *substantive* international
norm). But such "conflicts" arise also within municipal
law. A province ("Land") of Austria, for example, may
make a law which is, either by its contents or by its trans-
gression of competence, unconstitutional, and yet it is binding in this province. *But*—and here lies the decisive juridical factor—it is binding only so long as the Austrian Constitutional Court has not declared it unconstitutional, a
decision which has the annulment of this law as a legal
result. The juridically important factor for the unity of
every juridical order—as Verdross first has shown—is not
the impossibility of such conflicts but that this juridical
order provides itself a procedure for the solution of this
conflict. So does international law. A municipal law, contrary to international law, remains in force only so long
as it has not been annulled by an international procedure
(diplomatic negotiations, arbitration, war). Now, it is not
certain that international law will always lead to the desired
result. But it happens also in a federal state that the federal
law does not intervene, for instance for reasons of political
expediency, or that the province does not obey in fact. But
law, municipal as well as international, does not predict,
what always will, but prescribes, what shall follow.

International law also must designate the organs competent to create international law of the different stages. It is,
of course, theoretically untenable that, as the traditional
doctrine so often tells us, the international community is
"unorganized," an "anarchical" community, that international law has *no* organs. An "anarchical" juridical order
is a flat contradiction in terms; a juridical order without
organs would be no juridical order at all. But, on the contrary, international law does, *always* and necessarily, have
organs. The real sense of the quoted remarks is only a political critique of the contents of the actual international
law; it means that international law still is a primitive law.

In his *Allgemeine Staatslehre,* Kelsen has given us a masterly theory of the organs of the state; he has shown that an organ is the organ of the juridical order by which it is created. Verdross [58] has first attempted to give, within the Vienna School, a theory of international organs. This writer [59] has endeavored to complete the theory of international organs and to do away with the widely accepted doctrine of international organs as "common organs."

It is true that international law, up to the present time, has special organs only to a limited extent. This lack of special organs for the creation of international law of the different stages, according to the principle of division of labor, is a symptom of the primitiveness of international law, as it is symptomatic also for primitive municipal laws. But the lack of special organs does not mean the lack of its own organs.

It is theoretically wrong to pretend that international law has no legislative organs; to say that the creators of international law are at the same time the unities bound by the norms they have created themselves. If, for example, the United States concludes a treaty of commerce with Mexico, the international legislator [60] is neither the United States nor Mexico, but United States plus Mexico; whereas the United States and Mexico, taken individually, are bound by this treaty. Neither the one nor the other state alone is competent to create, to change, or to amend an international norm binding upon *both* of them. An international conference for the creation of international law is not, as is often said, a pure "assembly of the organs of the participating states" but it is an international organ; the representatives of the participating states—which are authorized by international law to choose these organs, according to their municipal law—are only partial organs of this international organ, the conference. It is a pure question of positive law whether the norms set up by this international conference shall be binding directly upon the states, members of this conference, or only subject to ratification by them, according to their municipal law; in this case we have a *legislation by two degrees*, characteristic also for most confederations of states. It is again only a question of positive law whether such international legislation shall be binding not only upon the "states," *i.e.*, upon their competent organs, but also immediately upon their subjects, or whether, in order to be binding upon these subjects, these international norms have to be "transformed" into municipal law.

Now, abstract international norms need, of course, "application," "execution," *i.e.*, further concretization and individualization. Here again, it is symptomatic of the primitiveness of actual international law that, generally speaking, it delegates this purpose to the states, that only indirect execution exists. We have here no special organs but the organs of international law itself. This again is no unique anomaly of international law. In the United States, it is true, the union has not only its own but also special organs for all the stages of the pyramid of federal law. But in Austria, as in most federal states, special federal organs exist only for the creation of abstract norms (the federal parliament) and for the highest stage of application of federal law (the federal ministries); but the application of the federal law in the lower stages is done by the governors of the provinces. But the governor, insofar as he executes *federal* law, is the organ of the federal state itself; whereas, insofar as he exercises the functions belonging under federal law to the province, he is the organ of the province. The governor combines in his person *two* organs, a federal and a provincial organ: As a federal organ he is directly subordinated to the federal ministries, but as a provincial organ he is only responsible to the *Dict* of the province.

As regards the solution of international conflicts, that general international law has not yet tribunals is a symptom of primitiveness shared by international law with all primitive municipal juridical orders. For the decision and execution of one's right is entrusted by all primitive laws to the party—here the state—whose right has been violated. This is, of course, very much open to criticism from a political point of view. But reprisals and war correspond exactly to blood feud and vendetta in primitive municipal laws. War is therefore not a mere "act of brute force," not something "outside of the law," not necessarily the outcome of "wicked" governments and nations, but a *necessary* and *legal* institution under a primitive international law, as every juridical order as an essentially compulsory order must be backed, in ultimate analysis, by the recourse to physical force. War, as has been pointed out, even prior to the Vienna School by the great Vienna scholar Leo Strisower [61] and within the Vienna School by Kelsen and Verdross, is a legal method for the assertion of a right of a state. This writer [62] has shown that war, apart from this function, namely to vindicate a right, has a second important function, namely as a method for *changing* the law in force, corresponding in this respect to revolution in municipal law. War has a static as well as a dynamic function. This writer's viewpoint has now been adopted by Verdross. Of course, war is a primitive means; the state entitled to a right is itself the judge and the sheriff in its own cause, which must easily lead to abuses; its ultimate success does not depend so much on its right but on its force; but exactly the same is true of blood feud or vendetta. But a state going to war—authorized by international law to do so—is nevertheless acting as an *organ* of international law, as well as men taking their recourse to blood feud under the law are acting as *organs* of this law. Just because

there is not yet an organization highly enough developed
to create special organs for the decision and execution of
conflicts, a primitive law is bound to leave all that to the
person or state injured. Here lies the difference between
blood feud, or vendetta, as a legal institution and mob
justice (lynching) as a crime; here would lie the difference
between war and international execution. This theoretical
insight is the *conditio sine qua non* for all political proposals for the elimination of war, if these proposals are to
be worth while and of a practical character. There can be
no elimination of war without, first, a higher organization
of the international community, without the creation of
special organs for the decision of all international conflicts,
static or dynamic, and for the execution of these decisions,
if necessary, against a recalcitrant member of the international community.

The primitiveness of war lies also in the institution of
collective responsibility. If the competent organ of a state
violates international law, the compulsory acts of international law (reprisals and war) are directed against all the
subjects of this state,[63] not because they are guilty, but
because the international law actually in force is built upon
responsibility, *not for fault*, but on *absolute liability* and on
collective responsibility.[64] But exactly the same is true of
primitive municipal laws. The progress of international law
lies in the above-mentioned creation of special organs. Elimination of war is theoretically and hence practically not a
problem of "outlawry of war," not a problem of "good will,"
but essentially a problem of international organization.

But international law has—prior to the League of Nations
and especially since—created also special organs for the
direct execution and application of international law.

There is, as Verdross has shown, a direct international
execution with regard to individuals where international
organs are competent to create juridical (legislative, ad-

ministrative, judicial) acts immediately binding upon certain individuals. Verdross has distinguished three types of such international organs: The lowest type, as regards extent of competences, is represented in positive international law by most international river commissions, international sanitary commissions, and so forth; a higher type is represented by the European Danube Commission; the highest type by the Government Commission of the Saar Basin, which exercises all the powers formerly belonging to Germany, Prussia, and Bavaria over this basin. International organs may directly govern a territory of the international community, as was proposed once with regard to the island of Spitzbergen.

Positive international law knows also a direct application of international law by special organs with regard to states. Here again Verdross has distinguished three types: International organs which are competent only to perform simply administrative acts—such as the bureaus of the international administrative unions or the Secretariat General of the League of Nations; and international organs competent only to elucidate facts—such as the international commissions of inquiry—or to try to conciliate, to make mediation proposals—such as the international commissions of conciliation, the Assembly and the Council of the League under Article XV of the Covenant. A second type is constituted by international organs competent to make political decisions directly binding upon states without ratification—the decisions of the Council of the League regarding the authority of mandatory powers, the exclusion of a member under Article XVI, paragraph 4, the election of non-permanent members of the Council, and so on.

There are, finally, special international organs competent to make judicial decisions directly binding upon states. Morelli [65] has shown that the authority to do so is always based on an international norm which he calls the instrumental norm (*la norma strumentale*), which may be special or general. In the case of isolated arbitration,[66] the instrumental norm is special with regard to the states in question and the matter to be decided. The instrumental norm has as its essential function to give *competence* to the arbitrator, but may, moreover, have a substantive content, as, for example, in the case of the "Alabama" *compromis*.

But even in the case of institutional arbitration (permanent arbitration treaties) the instrumental norm is special, insofar as a special *compromis* is required in every concrete case; the difference to the first hypothesis is that the states are here juridically bound to conclude the *compromis*. But a higher type is reached where the treaty provides for international arbitration independently of the co-operation of the parties, either by giving each party the right unilaterally to determine the formation of the arbitral tribunal or by giving each party the right to bring the case unilaterally before a preconstituted permanent tribunal (Permanent Court of International Justice).

But Morelli is profoundly wrong when he tells us that international arbitrators are bound by the *municipal* laws of the parties, that they are "common organs." This writer, who was the first to make clear the difference between *special* and *own* organs of international law, has combated this untenable theory of common organs (*organi communi, organi colletivi*) which holds a dominant place in the Italian science of international law.[67]

The case of common organs is to be found everywhere and only where *two* different juridical orders confer, independently of one another, the quality of being their organ upon the same individual. A typical, but by no means the unique, example is the so-called personal-union of states.[68] The king of Saxony and Poland was a common organ: king of Saxony only in virtue of the law of Saxony, king of Poland only in virtue of the law of Poland. Juridically speaking, it was a pure chance that both these juridical orders conferred the quality of a supreme organ upon the same physical person. The common organ means that the same individual combines the function of two different organs, that the same physical person is the bearer of the organ under two different juridical orders. But an international organ, whether a special organ or not, is the own and unitary organ of international law, created exclusively by international law, and not at all a common organ of different states. The Council of the League is, by no means, a common organ of the fourteen or fifteen states represented, but an international organ of the League; it is created exclusively by the Covenant; its creation, competence, function, exclusively derive from international law. The Council of the League is always the same organ although non-permanent members change.

The unitarian character of an international organ exists whether the organ consists only of one physical person, for example, the high Commissioner of the League for the Free City of Danzig, or whether it is composed of more than one physical person, for example, the Council of the League. All the persons constitute, as a whole in the latter case, the international organ, whereas every one of these persons alone is only a partial organ. H. M. Principal Secretary of State for Foreign Affairs is such in virtue of the British law and is a British organ; but the same secretary, sitting in the Council of the League at Geneva, is a partial organ of the international organ of the Council. His function in the Council is exclusively based on the Covenant, not at all on British law. The Council is not a common organ, but a unitarian international organ. The British secretary is a common organ, not in the sense of the Italian School, but in the above-mentioned sense, insofar as the same physical person is a British and a partial international organ.

The systems of creation of international organs, single or composite, can be very different in positive international law. The organ may be directly created by an international treaty (the permanent members of the Council, or Sir Eric Drummond, by the Covenant) ; or the organ may be directly created by an international organ (the non-permanent members of the Council, the Saar Government Commission, or, as example of a single organ, the high commissioner for Danzig). But international law can also delegate to the states the competence to choose for themselves the persons composing the international organ, and can further authorize the states to give to these persons binding instructions; but even in this case the states are free to do so only in virtue of the supraordinated international law.

The purpose of this article is to give a survey of the pure science of law of the Vienna School and its application to the domain of international law: First, to make this theory of the Vienna School more widely known in the United States; second, to show that we endeavor to give a scientific statement of international law as it is, a statement based on a theory; lastly, to make it clear that our work, however theoretical it may be, at the same time, is of a great practical importance; for the theoretical understanding of the problems involved is the *conditio sine qua non* for making worth-while and practical political proposals for a progressive development of international law, which no one desires more than the Vienna School. But let there be no mistake: At the very *basis* of every *practical* action always is *theory*.

---

[1] Cf. KELSEN, DIE VERFASSUNGSGESETZE DER REPUBLIK ÖSTERREICH, KOMMENTAR (1919–23) ; GRUNDRISS DES ÖSTERREICHEN STAATSRECHTS (1923). For a complete bibliography of Kelsen's writings up to 1931, see the bibliographical list prepared by Métall, in VERDROSS, GESELLSCHAFT, STAAT UND RECHT 417–41 (1931).

[2] For a French pure jurisprudence, independent of the Vienna School, but close to it as regards methods, see ROGUIN, LA SCIENCE JURIDIQUE PURE (1923) ; cf. Schreier, EINE FRANZÖSISCHE REINE RECHTSLEHRE, 2 REVUE INTERNATIONALE DE LA THÉORIE DU DROIT 57–66 (1927–28).

³ Cf. WEYR, *Zum Problem eines einheitlichen Rechtssystems*, 23 ARCHIV DES ÖFFENTLICHEN RECHTS, 529 (1908); *Über zwei Hauptpunkte der Kelsen'schen Staatsrechtslehre*, 40 GRÖNHUTS ZEITSCHRIFT, 175 (1913); *Zum Unterschied zwischen öffentlichem und privatem Recht*, 1 ÖSTERREICHISCHE ZEITSCHRIFT FÜR ÖFFENTLICHES RECHT 439 (1914); *Rechtsphilosophie und Rechtswissenschaft*, 2 ZEITSCHRIFT FÜR ÖFFENTLICHES RECHT 671 (1921); and his writings in Czech and French.

⁴ Cf. Pitamic, professor at the University of Lubljana, now minister plenipotentiary of Yugoslavia at Washington: *Denkökonomische Voraussetzungen der Rechtswissenschaft*, 3 ÖSTER. ZEITSCHRIFT FÜR ÖFFENTLICHES RECHT 339 (1918); *Eine juristische Grundlehre, ibid.* at 734; *Plato, Aristoteles und die reine Rechtslehre* 2 ZEITSCHRIFT FÜR ÖFFENTLICHES RECHT, 683 (1921); *Kritische Bemerkungen zum Gesellschafts—Staats und Gottesbegriff bei Kelsen*, 3 *ibid.*, (1923), A TREATISE ON THE STATE (1933).

⁵ Cf. the articles of Otaka and Yokota in VERDROSS, *op. cit.* at 106–35, 390–416.

⁶ Kelsen's genius is a fighting genius, not only in that his own theory has been built up by way of the critique of the theories of other writers, but also in that he has vigorously replied to attacks made upon his system. To this group of *polemical* writings belong *Rechtswissenschaft und Recht*, 3 ZEITSCHRIFT FÜR ÖFFENTLICHES RECHT, 103–235 (1922) (against Fritz Sander); DER STAAT ALS ÜBERMENSCH (1926) (against Hold-Ferneck, Vienna); RECHTSGESCHICHTE GEGEN RECHTSPHILOSOPHIE? (1928) (against Schwind, Vienna); DER STAATE ALS INTEGRATION (1930) (against Smend, Berlin); WER SOLL DER HÜTER DER VERFASSUNG SEIN (1932) (against C. Schmitt, Berlin).

⁷ Cf. HOLMES, COLLECTED LEGAL PAPERS 29 (1920). "The law is the calling of thinkers." The knowledge of documents, materials, and so on, is, of course, necessary for the legal scholar; but "the mark of a master is, that facts which before lay scattered in an inorganic mass, when he shoots through them the magnetic current of his *thought*, leap into an organic order, and live and bear fruit." *Ibid.* at 37.

⁸ It is for this reason that the new journal, edited since 1926 by Duguit, Kelsen, and Weyr is styled: REVUE INTERNATIONALE DE LA THÉORIE DU DROIT, and the preface to the first volume gives a clear account of what "theory of law" means— namely, the problems as to the nature of law, its relations to the state and society, as to the fundamental conceptions and the methods of cognition of law (*Rechtserkenntnis*), the relations in principle between the different juridical orders of the states and between municipal and international law. The theory of law is, therefore, to be distinguished, on the one hand, from a special field (private, criminal, and so on) and from the dogmatic analysis of a concrete positive law, and, on the other hand, from the *philosophy* of law, insofar as the problems of *justice*, of a natural, absolute, just, right law, are outside of its domain.

⁹ It is historically true, however, that Kelsen's first principal work, HAUPTPROBLEME DER STAATRECHTSLEHRE (1911) was an intuitive

creation written with no profound knowledge of Kant and with no knowledge at all of Cohen. It was a philosophical review on his first book which showed to Kelsen the far-reaching parallels between his thinking and the philosophy of Kant and Cohen.

[10] Kelsen's first book was DIE STAATSLEHRE DES DANTE ALIGHIERI (1905); his first standard work, HAUPTPROBLEME DER STAATSRECHTS-LEHRE (2d ed. 1923); his methodological study, ÜBER GRENZEN ZWISCHEN JURISTISCHER UND SOZIOLOGISCHER METHODE (1911). These works were followed by a group of further theoretical studies: *Über Staatsunrecht*, 40 ZEITSCHRIFT FÜR DAS PRIVAT-UND ÖFFENTLICHE RECHT DER GEGENWART, 1–114 (1913); *Zur Lehre vom öffentlichen Rechtsgeschäft*, 31 ARCHIV DES ÖFFENTLICHEN RECHTS, 53–249 (1913); *Die Rechtswissenschaft als Norm—oder als Kulturwissenschaft*, 40 SCHMOLLERS JAHRBUCH 1181 (1916); *Zur Theorie der juristischen Fiktionen*, 1 ANNALEN DER PHILOSOPHIE 630–58 (1919); *Das Verhältnis von Staat und Recht im Licht der Erkenntniskritik*, 2 ZEITSCHRIFT FÜR ÖFFENTLICHES RECHT, 453 (1921); his third standard work: DER SOZIOLOGISCHE UND DER JURISTISCHE STAATSBEGRIFF (2d ed. 1928); his fourth standard work: ALLGEMEINE STAATSLEHRE (1925). His articles: *Gott und Staat*, 11 LOGOS 261–84 (1922–23); *Die Bundesexekution*, FESTGABE FÜR FLEINER 127–87 (1927); *Naturrecht und positives Recht*, 2 REVUE INTERNATIONALE DE LA THÉORIE DU DROIT 71–94 (1927–28); *Die Idee des Naturrechts*, 7 ZEITSCHRIFT FÜR ÖFFENTLICHES RECHT, 221–50 (1928); DIE PHILOSOPHISCHEN GRUND-LAGEN DER NATURRECHTSLEHRE UND DES RECHTSPOSITIVISMUS (1928).

Many short writings by Kelsen have been published in various languages; books have been translated into Czech, Hungarian, Rumanian, Greek, Polish, Spanish, Italian, French, Japanese. Cf. also his French study, APERÇU D'UNE THÉORIE GÉNÉRALE DE L'ETAT (1927). The best short exposition of Kelsen's doctrine in English is to be found in H. Lauterpacht's lecture, *Kelsen's Pure Science of Law*, MODERN THEORIES OF LAW 105–38 (1933). The latest exposition of Kelsen's theory by himself is published in Italian, *La dottrina pura del diritto. Metodo e concetti fondamentali*, 26 ARCHIVIO GIURIDICO (1933).

For the development of Kelsen's theory by writers of the Vienna School (Merkl and Verdross will be quoted later; Weyr and Pitamic have already been quoted), see SEIDLER, DIE THEORIE DES RECHTS UND IHRE GRENZEN (1920–21); Henrich, *Das Sollen als Grundlage der Rechtswissenschaft*, 2 ZEITSCHRIFT FÜR ÖFFENTLICHES RECHT, 131–78 (1921); Löbl, *Zum Problem der reinen Rechtslehre*, 3 *ibid.* at 402–48 (1922–23); Voegelin, *Reine Rechtslehre und Staatslehre*, 4 *ibid.* at 80–131 (1925); Sander, *Das Faktum der Revolution und die Kontinuität der Rechtsordnung*, 1 *ibid.* at 132 (1919); *Die transendentale Methode der Rechtsphilosophie*, *ibid.* at 468; *Alte und neue Staatsrechtslehre*, 2 *ibid.* at 176 (1921); E. Winternitz, *Zum Gegenstandsproblem der Rechtstheorie*, 3 *ibid.* at 684 (1922–23). Two of Kelsen's disciples have developed his theory on phenomenological lines (under the joint influence of Kelsen and Husserl), namely, KAUFFMANN, LOGIK UND RECHTS-WISSENSCHAFT (1922); *Theorie der Rechtserfahrung und die reine Rechtslehre*, 3 ZEITSCHRIFT FÜR ÖFFENTLICHES RECHT 684 (1923);

Schreier, *Die Wiener rechtsphilosophische Schule,* 11 LOGOS 310 (1922–23); GRUNDBEGRIFFE UND GRUNDFORMEN DES RECHTS (1923). See also the articles in the above quoted volume, VERDROSS, *op. cit.*

[11] The word "science" is here always used in the broader sense, not restricted to natural sciences, but as an equivalent to the German word *Wissenschaft.*

[12] English authors stress the similarity of approach between Kelsen and Austin (cf. the lecture by Manning, in MODERN THEORIES OF LAW 180 (1933)); and there certainly is a similarity between Austin's "analytical" and Kelsen's "pure" jurisprudence. But this similarity must not be over-estimated by reading Austin too much in the light of Kelsen's theory.

[13] In the United States the sociological school seems to dominate now; but under this heading many different schools of thought are brought. We will deal here only with the "realistic school," the "behaviorist school," the "school of functional approach," or whatever its name be. The most extreme representative of this school is FRANK, LAW AND THE MODERN MIND (1930). It is symptomatic that such a book should have met with a great success; it shows the theoretical dissatisfaction amongst many American lawyers. But, from a *scientific* point of view, this book is the work of a dilettante: badly arranged, misleading in its quotations, full of contradictions, a good example of a confusion of methods, very naïve in its attempt to solve juridical problems with the one notion of the "father-substitute"—all-important for the author—a notion borrowed from Freud's psychoanalysis. The motto of the whole book is a famous quotation from Mr. Justice Holmes, but this quotation is completely misunderstood.

Other representatives of this school certainly do not go so far as to deny all general rules of law. But GRAY, THE NATURE AND SOURCES OF THE LAW (2d ed. 1921), tells us, at 99, "The judge is an investigator as was Sir Isaac Newton" (*sic!*). But, on the other hand, "A statute is a *general rule.*"—*Ibid.* at 161. Some twenty years ago, Bingham in *What is the Law?,* 11 MICH. L. REV. 1–25, 109–21 (1912–13), and *Legal Philosophy and the Law,* 9 ILL. L. REV. 98–119 (1914–15), said there are no rules or principles of law; he spoke of the "confusing error of conceiving the law as a system of rules and principles"; he told us that "the claims of causal facts and their actual legal effects are concrete phenomena in the external world analogous to the experimental phenomena of the scientist"; that "principles and rules cannot exist outside of the mind."

Llewellyn, in *A Realistic Jurisprudence,* 30 COLUM. L. REV. 431–65 (1930) lays the greatest emphasis on behavior, on the observable; "the real rules are predictions"; "they are descriptive, not prescriptive, they are on the level of isness, and not of oughtness", "a realistic understanding is possible only in terms of observable behavior."

But one of the most significant expressions this school has is found in the writings of Professor Cook. Now, I have the greatest admiration for the great talent of Professor Cook; but his methodological propositions, I respectfully submit, are fundamentally unsound. He abso-

lutely identifies the juridical method with the method of natural
sciences. Cook, *The Logical and Legal Basis of the Conflicts of Laws,*
33 YALE L. J. 457–88 (1923–24); *Scientific Method and the Law,*
29 A. B. A. J. 303–9, (1927) (that generalizations have no other purpose than "to *describe* in as simple a way as possible the concrete juridical phenomena observed." "We as lawyers like the physical scientists
are engaged in the study of objective physical phenomena" [*sic!*].
"The practising lawyer as much as an engineer or a doctor is engaged
to forecast future events"). Professor Cook tells us that he is only
interested in what "the judge will do." There are various reasons for
this attitude of the "realistic" school. One of them is that jurisprudence is here unduly narrowed to the decision of the judge. (Cf. the
critique by Goodhart, *Some American Interpretations of Law* in
MODERN THEORIES OF LAW 1–20, who characterizes this American
attitude with the words: "Le roi est mort, vive le juge!"). Another
reason is the effort of this American school to understand the process
by which the judge arrives at his decision; we shall deal with this
problem later in the text. A third reason, as Professor Cook's arguments make very clear, is the overestimation of natural sciences,
the belief, the superstitional belief, that the method of natural sciences
is the *only scientific method;* if therefore the science of law is to be a
science at all, it must—it is argued—be a natural science. The reason
why this superstition exists is given by the fact that natural sciences
have made enormous progress in the last hundred years. The superstitional belief in the method of natural sciences as the truly, *i.e.,*
only, scientific method is closely linked with the worship of progress,
which always means only mechanical progress—for men do not necessarily become better by progress in aviation—and the overestimation
of mechanical progress is responsible for an overestimation of a mere
civilization to the detriment of culture. Cf. the splendid pages in
MACIVER, THE MODERN STATE 325–30 (1926). Now, if Professor Cook
tells us that he is only interested in what the judge will *do*, it is easy
to show first that this is not quite true. He is really interested only
in what the *judge of the last instance* will do, and this probably will
be a *bench* of judges; and again only in what the *majority* of these
judges will do; lastly, not in what they will do, but in what that will
mean. But apart from all that, why is Professor Cook interested in
what the *judge* will do and not in what Mr. *X* will write about the
case? Because the judge is the *competent organ* to give the decision,
and he is the competent organ only on account of a *legal norm.* How
can Professor Cook, as a physicist, tell us that a man is a *judge?*
The doctor always will find only a biological, physiological unit belonging to the genus *homo sapiens*, but never a judge.

And if one would say, I conclude from the description of observable
facts—that this man is wearing a robe, and so on—that he is a judge,
that is clearly untrue. A man, an imposter, may play the role of a
judge. Is he a judge? No, he is a criminal, usurping the position of a
judge. In a word, if Professor Cook tells us that he is interested in
what the *judge* will do, he introduces, in a disguised manner, the
whole *normativity* of the law, because it is the *law* alone which makes

a man a judge. And if we are interested in what the *majority* of the Supreme Court will do, it is only because the *positive law* prescribes that the majority shall decide. If the positive law would prescribe that the decision must be taken unanimously, we would at once be interested, not in what the majority, but in what *all* the judges will do.

The superstitional belief in the methods of natural sciences plays also an important role in the valuation of the "case-method." This method *is* excellent for American law, because it goes back to the sources of the law, and common law *is* a "case-law." But a great deal of the estimation in which the case-method is held comes from the erroneous belief that it is an *inductive*, and therefore a "truly scientific," method. See REDLICH, THE CASE-METHOD IN AMERICAN LAW SCHOOLS 55 (1914).

There is opposition against the "realistic" school also in the United States. Dean Pound, himself a "sociological" jurist, is against this school. And *normative* American thinkers have made an excellent critique of this school, sometimes almost in terms of the Vienna School. Cf. COHEN, LAW AND THE SOCIAL ORDER (1933). This author speaks, at 189–90, of the "one-sidedness of Ehrlich who tends to confuse the sociologic with the juristic point of view." "Even if the behaviorists succeeded, they would have a descriptive sociology, *not a juristic science*" (*ibid.* at 205); "Penalties do *not* state what always *is* but what *ought to be*" (*ibid.* at 205); "categorical distinction between the existential or descriptive and the regulative or normative" (*ibid.* at 206); "The fact that legal norms are *conditioned* by historical situations and depend on certain social habits of obedience, does not make such norms identical with the uniformities of behaviour" (*ibid.* at 207); "To call a decision the behaviour of the judge is to confuse physically organic with social categories" (*ibid.* at 216); "Legal rules are normative in that they contain orders regulating what men *should* do" (*ibid.* at 240). Kocourek, in a review of Bingham 8 ILL. L. REV., 138 (1913–14), speaks of a "nihilistic theory" and hits to the very point by stating: "*The fundamental fallacy* of the propositions advanced lies in making legal phenomena analogous of natural phenomena." See especially KOCOUREK, AN INTRODUCTION TO THE SCIENCE OF LAW (1930): "The difficulty is in determining the pattern of liability and not in finding causation. The thing thought for is not in the physical facts, but can be found only in the rules of law."

The strongest case against this school has been made in this country by the writings of Dickinson: *The Law Behind the Law*, 29 COLUM. L. REV., 113–46, 285–319 (1929); *Social Order and Political Authority*, 23 AM. POL. SCI. REV. 293–328, 593–632 (1929) ("Lawyers are seldom philosophers enough . . ."); *Administrative Justice and the Supremacy of the Law* (1927); his articles in 79 U. of PA. L. REV. 833–68, 1052–96 (1931).

CARDOZO, THE NATURE OF THE JUDICIAL PROCESS (1921), takes his stand against the lawyers who believe "that there is no law except the decisions of the Courts." "A definition of law which in effect denies the possibility of law since it denies the possibility of rules of general operation must contain within itself the seeds of fallacy."—*Ibid.* at

127. "Nine-tenths, perhaps more, of the cases that come from a Court
are predetermined, their fate pre-established by inevitable laws;
the range of free activity is relatively small and even there is never
complete freedom."—CARDOZO, THE GROWTH OF THE LAW 60–61
(1924) ; and he warns against a "sceptical nihilism which is the negation of all law."—*Ibid.* at 31.

That a jurisprudence cannot be built upon sociology is clearly
shown by the work of Duguit, who says, "que le droit se trouve dans
la réalité sociale, que le moment est venu de tenter la construction
juridique de l'Etat, en utilisant uniquement les matériaux fournis par
la réalité sociale, et en écartant tous les concepts d'ordre méta-
physique," and who ends in natural law. Cf. Kunz, *Die Rechts und
Staatslehre L. Duguit's*, 1 REVUE INTERNATIONALE DE LA THÉORIE DU
DROIT, 140–52, 204–21 (1926-27) ; for a nearly identical critique see
Laski, *M. Duguit's Conception of the State*, MODERN THEORIES OF LAW
52–67.

14 Cf. Kocourek, AN INTRODUCTION TO THE SCIENCE OF LAW 177, 283
(1930). "A person in jurisprudence (*persona*) is not a material substance but only a concept; there are only juridical persons. A legal
person is a conceptual point of reference created by the law for the
attribution of rights and litigations."

15 KELSEN, HAUPTPROBLEME DER STAATSRECHTSLEHRE 97–188 (2d
ed. 1923).

16 This teleological conception has played an important role in the
German jurisprudence (*Ihering*) ; but it holds also a strong place
today in American thinking about the law. Cf. the writings of Mr.
Justice Cardozo and Mr. Justice Brandeis. Also Professor Cook, a
representative of the realistic school, tells us that "human laws are
tools. . . . If so, it follows that the worth or value of a given rule of
law can be determined only by finding out how it works." The philosophy of the leading American philosopher of law, Dean Roscoe Pound,
is also dominated by this teleological point of view: *Law as a means
toward Social Ends*, THE SPIRIT OF THE COMMON LAW, 205 (1921)
(Law in terms of social engineering. Legislation and judicial decisions must be governed by principles of social utility) ; *The Theory
of Judicial Decisions*, 36 HARV. L. REV. 641, 802, 940 (1922–23). Cf.
Pound, *Juristic Science and the Law*, 31 HARV. L. REV. 1047 (1917–
18) ; *The Need of a Sociological Jurisprudence*, 19 GREENBAG 607; *The
Philosophy of Law in America*, 7 ARCHIV FÜR RECHTS- UND WIRT-
SCHAFTSPHILOSOPHIE 213–23, 385–400 (1913) ; *The Scope and Purpose
of Sociological Jurisprudence*, 24 HARV. L. REV. 591–619 (1910–11),
25 HARV. L. REV. 140–68, 489–516 (1911–12). "The main problem to
which sociological jurists are addressing themselves today is to enable
and to *compel law-making* and interpretation and application of legal
rules to take more account and more intelligent account of the social
facts upon which law must proceed and to which it is to be applied."
—*Ibid.* at 512–13.

Now, the end of the law is clearly *outside* of the law. Everything on
earth can be used as a means to an end and misused. Mathematics can
be used as a means for physics. But the mathematician as such has

nothing to do with the *purpose* of mathematics. The chemist cannot advance his chemical studies by saying chemistry is a means for industrial production or for medicine or for poison gas warfare. The *end* of the law is *transcendent* to the law. Dean Pound does not so much give us a theoretical study about law as a means and the ends it can serve, as he stresses law as a means toward *social* ends, that is to say toward an end which *he* wishes. The law can be made a means to create democracy as well as dictatorship, equality as well as oppression; all depends on *which* end I choose and this again will depend on my ethical conception of life, on my political convictions. The jurist, as Dean Pound says, should *compel* law-making; but he never can do so *qua jurist*, but only as a *politician* of law. Dean Pound does not say what the law *is*, but he is giving us a "functional *critique* of the law," founded upon subjective ethico-political postulates. He will not make a research into what the American law *is*, but he will help and prepare that we may get a *better* American law. This is not judicial study, but, to quote the correct phrase of Mr. Justice Brandeis, "challenge of existing law."—*The Living Law*, 10 ILL. L. REV. 462 (1916). It is, in a word, *not science of law*, but *politics of law*.

[17] Kelsen himself has written many political writings: it would be a mistake to take all his writings as belonging to his pure science of law. Cf. his writings: VOM WESEN UND WERT DER DEMOKRATIE (2d ed. 1929); SOCIALISMUS UND STAAT (2d ed. 1923); MARX ODER LASSALLE? (1924); DAS PROBLEM DES PARLAMENTARISMUS (1925); STAATSFORM UND WELTANSCHAUUNG (1933).

[18] Cf. Merkl's writings: DAS DOPPELTE RECHTSANTLITZ, JURISTISCHE BLÄTTER (1917); DAS RECHT IM LICHTE SEINER ANWENDUNE (1917); *Hans Kelsen's System einer reinen Rechts theorie*, 41 ARCHIV DES ÖFFENTLICHEN RECHTS (1921); DIE LEHRE VON DER RECHTSKRAFT (1923); *Prolegomena einer Theorie des rechtlichen Stufenbaues in* VERDROSS, *op. cit.* See elso Verdross, *Zum Problem der Rechtsunterworfenheit des Gesetzgebers*, JURISTISCHE BLÄTTER 471 (1916).

[19] Kelsen's philosophy is essentially a *relativist* philosophy. It is for this reason, that in his *political* thinking, he stands for democracy as the expression of a *relativist* conception of life, which not only tolerates but needs an opposition, a minority, whereas autocracy ideologically pretends to be based on *absolute* values, the opposition to which is therefore a crime.

[20] It is this conception of the pyramid of law and of this function of the judge which gives the answer to the trouble of American lawyers about the character of a decision of a court, about law-making, not law-finding, about the famous argument of the "novel case." The theory that the judge is only an automation, rightly repudiated by modern American jurists, is fully repudiated too by the Vienna School. Cf. what is said in the text on the attitude of the Vienna School with regard to the problem of interpretation. Dickinson has clearly pointed out to the pyramid of law (he calls it "stage-formation") of the Vienna School as a solution of the legitimate trouble of the American sociological jurists, avoiding, at the same time, the theoretically

untenable, basically unsound position of the realistic school. Cf. Dickinson, *The Law Behind the Law*, 29 COLUM. L. REV. 319 (1929).

21 The problem of interpretation has for some time been neglected by the Vienna School and especially by Kelsen. But see the article of his disciple Ephrussi, *Interpretation and Analogie*, 4 ZEITSCHRIFT FÜR ÖFFENTLICHES RECHT, 132–59 (1925); and especially SCHREIER, DIE INTERPRETATION DER GESETZE UND RECHTSGESCHÄFTE (1927). In KELSEN, *op. cit.*, *supra* note 11, the author has given a complete theory of interpretation, which is followed in the text above.

22 The Vienna School stands, with Dean Pound, against "mechanical jurisprudence" 8 COLUM. L. REV. 605–23 (1908). The fear of mechanical jurisprudence is perhaps responsible in this country for not taking the *juridical* approach. Cf. GRAY, *op. cit.* at 2: "The analytic study . . . is not without dangers; it may easily result in a barren scholasticism."

23 As regards the conception of the territory of the state within the Vienna School, Cf. especially HENRICH, THEORIE DES STAATSGEBIETES (1922).

24 Cf. the following writings of Kelsen on International Law: DAS PROBLEM DER SOUVERÄNITÄT UND DIE THEORIE DES VÖLKERRECHTS (2d ed. 1928); *Les rapports de systéme entre le droit interne et le droit international public*, 4 RECUEIL DES COURS 231–331 (1926); *Théorie générale du Droit International Public*, 4 *ibid.* at 121–351 (1932); *Unrecht und Unrechtsfolge im Völkerrecht*, 17 ZEITSCHRIFT FÜR ÖFFENTLICHES RECHT 481–608 (1932);

25 Verdross, *Zur Konstruktion des Völkerrechts*, 8 ZEITSCHRIFT FÜR VÖLKERRECHT 329–59 (1914); DIE VÖLKERRECHTSWIDRIGE KRIEGSHANDLUNG UND DER STRAFANSPRUCH DER STAATEN (1920); *Grundlagen und Grundlegungen des Völkerrechts*, 29 NIEMEYER'S ZEITSCHRIFT, 65–91; *Völkerrecht und einheitliches Rechtssystem*, 12 ZEITSCHRIFT FÜR VÖLKERRECHT, 405–38 (1923); DIE EINHEIT DES RECHTLICHEN WELTBILDES AUF GRUNDLAGE DER VÖLKERRECHTSVERFASSUNG (1923); DIE VERFASSUNG DER VÖLKERRECHTSGEMEINSCHAFT (1926); *Völkerrechtsgemeinschaft und Bundesstaat*, REVUE INTERNATIONALE DE LA THÉORIE DU DROIT 15–22 (1927–28); *Zur neuesten Lehre von den Staatenverbindungen*, 35 NIEMEYER'S ZEITSCHRIFT 257–75 (1925–26); *Staatsgebiet, Staatengemeinschaftsgebiet und Staatengebiet*, 37 *ibid.* at 293–305 (1927); *Fondement du Droit International*, 1 RECUEIL DES COURS 251–321 (1927); *Règles générales du Droit International de la Paix*, 5 *ibid.* at 275–507 (1929); *Règles internationales concernant le traitement des étrangers*, 3 *ibid.* at 327–409 (1931); *Die Quellen des Völkerrechts*, Mitteilungen des Deutschen Gesellschaft für Völkerrecht, *Heft* 10; *Die allgemeinen Rechtsgrundsätze als Völkerrechtsquelle* in VERDOSS, *op. cit.*, *supra*, note 1 at 354–65; articles *in* the WÖRTERBUCH DES VÖLKERRECHTS (Strupp ed.); *L'excès de pouvoir du juge arbitral dans le droit international public*, REVUE DE DROIT INTERNATIONAL ET DE LÉGISLATION COMPARÉE (1928).

26 Cf. KUNZ: VÖLKERRECHTSWISSENSCHAFT UND REINE RECHTSLEHRE (1923); DIE VÖLKERRECHTLICHE OPTION (1925–28); GASKRIGG

UND VÖLKERRECHT (1927); DIE ANERKENNUNG VON STAATEN UND REGIERUNGEN IM VÖLKERRECHT (1928); DIE STAATENVERBINDUNGEN (1929); DIE INTRASYSTEMATISCHE STELLUNG DES ARTIKELS XI DER VÖLKERBUNDPAKTES (1931); DIE REVISION DES PARISER FRIEDENSVERTRÄGE (1932); *On the Theoretical Basis of the Law of Nations*, 10 TRANSACTIONS OF THE GROTIUS SOCIETY 115–41 (1925); *La Primauté du Droit des Gens*, 6 REVUE DE DROIT INTERNATIONAL ET DE LÉGISLATION COMPARÉE 556–98 (1925); *Zur Hypothesis vom Primat des Völkerrechts*, 5 REVUE DE DROIT INTERNATIONAL (GENÈVE) 1–15 (1927) (on the theory of Duguit); also article on dual nationality, 2 ZEITSCHRIFT FÜR OSTRECHT, 401–37 (1928); also articles in French on the theory of the federal state, REVUE DE DROIT INTERNATIONAL ET DE LÉGISLATION COMPARÉE (1930–31); an article in GESELLSCHAFT, STAAT UND RECHT 217–51 (1931); articles in WÖRTERBUCH DES VÖLKERRECHTS; a lecture on the Kellogg Pact in MITTEILUNGEN DER DEUTSCHEN GESELLSCHAFT FÜR VÖLKERRECHT (1929); French lectures at the Hague Academy of International Law, RECUEIL DES COURS 681–790 (1932); an article on the theory of the law concerning the international protection of national minorities, 12 ZEITSCHRIFT FÜR ÖFFENTLICHES RECHT (1932); critique of Morelli in 7 ANNUARIO DI DIRITTO COMPARATO E DI STUDI LEGISLATIVI; an article in 27 AM. J. INT'L L. 630–50 (1933).

Kelsen is primarily occupied with the *theory* of international law. In his Hague lectures 1932, *op. cit., supra*, note 29, at 121, he said that his general theory of international law is not intended to contribute an exposé of the positive international law, that it is *not* his intention to reproduce the *contents* of the norms of positive international law or to discuss the practical cases to which they are applied, but to give a *theory*, *i.e.*, an examination of the *nature* of international law, of the fundamental notions which alone allow us to know the positive phenomena in a scientific way. Such a theory of international law must, as must every real theory, he continued, necessarily be abstract and formal; for the task of theory is to simplify the complexity of concrete phenomena by reducing them to general aspects.

Verdross, who, as stated in the text, was the first to adapt Kelsen's pure science of law to the science of international law, is also very much interested in this purely theoretical aspect and has made important contributions to this theory. But he is also very much interested, more than Kelsen, in the *contents* of this positive international law; his theoretical studies are the foundation for a scientific and systematic exposé of the positive international law actually in force.

The writer of this article, too, is concerned with the purely theoretical aspect, but also with the positive contents of international law.

Whereas Verdross has primarily endeavored to give a scientific exposé of the *whole system* of peace, this writer has been occupied with clarifying special problems and has therefore chosen the way of rather extensive monographs. Professor Verdross is now preparing a new book on the whole international law of peace; this writer is preparing a new book on the law of war and neutrality. Both books

were published in German in the ENZYKLOPÄDIE DER RECHTS UND
STAATSWISSENSCHAFTEN at Berlin in 1934.

[27] Cf. Métall, *Skizzen zu einer Systematik der völkerrechtlichen
Quellenlehre*, 11 ZEITSCHRIFT FÜR ÖFFENTLICHES RECHT 416–28; *Das
allgemeine Völkerrecht und das innerstaatliche Verfassungsrecht*, 14
ZEITSCHRIFT FÜR VÖLKERRECHT 161–87 (1927).

[28] Cf. as one example among many: SUKIENNICKI LA SOUVERAINETÉ
DES ÉTATS (1927); Anzilotti has, changing his former ideas, accepted
the doctrine of the basic norm. The new book on international law by
P. Fedozzi defends in nearly all the decisive points the ideas of the
Vienna School.

[29] Cf. the many authors who are, with us, against the conception of
the absolute sovereignty of states. The work of Georges Scelle (Paris)
stands, as regards methods and results, very close to the Vienna
School. But, in spite of this great similarity and sometimes identity
of attitudes toward all important problems of international law, there
is a basic difference between this author and the Vienna School, insofar as *Scelle* proceeds from a *sociological* foundation which necessarily leads him, in some respects, to a pure natural-law reasoning.
In this respect he is a follower of L. Duguit. Cf. his book: PRÉCIS DE
DROIT DES GENS (1932), and my review in ZEITSCHRIFT FÜR ÖFFENT-
LICHES RECHT 448–53 (1933).

[30] Cf. the discussion on *methodological* problems, PROCEEDINGS OF
THE 5TH CONFERENCE OF TEACHERS OF INTERNATIONAL LAW AND RE-
LATED SUBJECTS 46–103 (1933). The brilliant paper of Professor W.
W. Cook (*ibid.* at 50–57) gives to jurists much highly interesting information about mathematics, physics, biology. We learn a great deal
about the *micrococcus Melitensis* and many other things; but it is
difficult to see what can be learned from this paper as to the science
of international law; and it is difficult to understand why this paper,
dealing exclusively with methods of *natural* sciences should have the
title: "The *Legal* Method."

[31] In his remarks on *The Part of Philosophy in International Law*,
PROCEEDINGS OF THE 6TH INTERNATIONAL CONFERENCE OF PHILOSOPHY
372 (1927), as well as in his splendid lectures on *Philosophical Theory
and International Law*, 1 BIBLIOTHECA VISSERIANA 73 (1923). See also
Hudson, *The Prospect for International Law for the Twentieth Century*, 10 CORNELL L. Q. 419 (1925). Dean Roscoe Pound makes a strong
case against repeating always "the received doctrine of the books,"
and for the "necessity of leadership"; he asks for a *functional critique
of international law in terms of social ends, not an analytical critique
in terms of itself;* he asks for a *"creative* work in law"; he would invite *"creative* juristic effort to shape existing legal institutions and
to make new ones in that image." Now, with all this the Vienna School
fully and heartily agrees; but it is self-evident that to do so can
neither be the task of the science, nor of the theory, but only of *politics*
of international law. It is difficult to see why Dean Pound, after urging all that, should say that the jurists of the nineteenth century had
no confidence in themselves *qua jurists;* exactly the reverse is true;

they had no confidence in themselves *qua politicians* of international law.

[32] Cf. WRIGHT, RESEARCH IN INTERNATIONAL LAW SINCE THE WAR (1930), who, at 3, notes the "predominantly *practical* turn of contemporary international law" and, at 34, the "practical character of recent international law."

[33] These are the two branches of politics of law (science of legislation).

[34] Cf. also B. Akzin, *L'école autrichienne et le fondement du droit des gens*, 1 REVUE DE DROIT INTERNATIONAL 342–72 (1927).

[35] Founded by TRIEPEL, VÖLKERRECHT UND LANDESRECHT (1899); cf. also his French lectures at the Hague Academy 1 RECUEIL DES COURS 77–118 (1923); and ANZILOTTI, TEORIA GENERALE DELLA RESPONSABILITA DELLO STATO NEL DIRITTO INTERNAZIONALE (1902); CORSO DI DIRITTO INTERNAZIONALE (1912). The dualistic conception is still dominant in the Italian science of international law.

[36] Cf. Phillip Zorn, A. Zorn, G. Jellinek, Bergbohm, Liszt, and many other writers of all nations.

[37] DAS PROBLEM DER SOUVERÄNITÄT UND DIE THEORIE DES VÖLKERRECHTS (2d ed. 1928).

[38] On the similarities and the differences between the theories on sovereignty of Kelsen and Professor John Dickinson, see E. Voegelin, *Die Souveränitätslehre Dickinson's und die reine Rechtslehre*, 8 ZEITSCHRIFT FÜR ÖFFENTLICHES RECHT 413–34 (1928–29).

[39] DIE EINHEIT DES RECHTLICHEN WELTBILDES (1923).

[40] This distinction between legal conceptions as supposed conceptions (*Rechtsvoraussetzungsbegriffe*) and as deriving from the contents of positive law (*Rechtsinhaltsbegriffe*) is of the highest importance; the merit first to have shown this difference belongs to the Hungarian philosopher of law Somló in his work JURISTISCHE GRUNDLEHRE (1917).

[41] 2 ZEITSCHRIFT FÜR OSTRECHT 401–37 (1928).

[42] 12 ZEITSCHRIFT FÜR ÖFFENTLICHES RECHT 221–72 (1932).

[43] 5 REVUE DE DROIT INTERNATIONAL 1–15 (1927).

[44] KUNZ, DIE ANERKENNUNG DER STAATEN UND REGIERUNGEN IM VÖLKERRECHT (1928).

[45] 11 ZEITSCHRIFT FÜR ÖFFENTLICHES RECHT 416–28 (1931).

[46] Which must not be confused with the "general principles of international law." It is just the merit of Verdross to have shown, by an analysis of the positive law, that these "general principles recognized by civilized nations" are a *source* of *positive* international law.

[47] In GESELLSCHAFT, STAAT UND RECHT 354–65 (1931).

[48] On this static theory of international law, cf. Kelsen 4 RECUEIL DES COURS 119-351 (1932).

[49] For details see KUNZ, UNIONS OF STATES (1929)

[50] For details see KUNZ, STATES AND GOVERNMENTS (1928).

[51] *Supra*, note 49.

52 Cf. Verdross 5 RECUEIL DES COURS 273–517 (1929).

53 *Ibid.*

54 *Supra,* note 49.

55 Cf. KUNZ, *Staatsgewalt de facto,* 2 WÖRTERBUCH DES VÖLKERRECHTS 605–15.

56 For all details, see KUNZ, DIE STAATENVERBINDUNGEN (1929).

57 Hence the title of Prof. Verdross' book: DIE VERFASSUNG DER VÖLKERRECHTSGEMEINSCHAFT (1926).

58 VERDROSS, *loc. cit., supra,* note 57, and in his Hague lectures of 1929.

59 KUNZ, DIE STAATENVERBINDUNGEN (1929); and an article in 8 ANNUARIO DI DIRITTO COMPARATO E DI STUDI LEGISLATIVI (1932).

60 It is the merit of Professor Manley O. Hudson to be a protagonist of this theoretically correct conception of international legislation.

61 STRISOWER, DER KRIEG UND DIE VÖLKERRECHTSORDNUNG (1919).

62 In GESELLSCHAFT STAAT UND RECHT 217, 251 (1931); Kunz, DIE REVISION DER PARISER FRIEDENSVERTRÄGE (1932), and the article in 27 AM. J. INT'L L. 630–50 (1933).

63 President Wilson's declaration therefore that "we are making war against the German government, but not against the German nation," was *not a juridical* proposition. War *was* made against the German nation, in law and in fact, and it could not have been otherwise under the international law in force, based upon the principle of collective responsibility.

64 This point has been especially made clear by Kelsen.

65 MORELLI, LA SENTENZA INTERNAZIONALE (1931).

66 The distinction between "isolated" and "institutional" arbitration was introduced by the great Vienna scholar of international law Heinrich Lammasch.

67 *Supra,* note 59.

68 For all details, see KUNZ, DIE STAATENVERBINDUNGEN (1929).

THE HISTORY of man's spiritual activities, of his attitude toward the world and life as a whole as well as toward particular problems, shows a continuous swing of the pendulum from one attitude to the opposite side. Philosophically we see a change between the different attitudes which can be taken—all outlined already by the thinkers of ancient Hellas. It may be that the first attitude has reached its fullness, that its possibilities seem, for the time being, exhausted. It may be that the first attitude has seemingly been disproved by historical events and no longer seems adequate to the needs of a changed situation. Then trends and tendencies appear which may ultimately climax in the establishment of the opposite attitude. And as, in order to establish the new attitude, very likely a distorted picture of the former one will be given, and as the new attitude, once established, itself often goes to extremes, the pendulum not only swings from one side to the other, but from one extreme to the other.

Thus classicism is followed by romanticism in the field of art, literature, and music. The pendulum of philosophy swings between idealism and realism, between idealism and materialism; only the spirit counts, says Hegel; there is only matter, says Marx. Centuries of faith in reason and natural law are followed by the utmost positivism of Comte. In the realm of law natural law with its extravagant claims is followed by strict legal positivism. The optimism of the nineteenth century is followed by the pessimism of the twentieth.

This swing of the pendulum is, of course, particularly great in periods of fundamental crisis like our present epoch, in which the very survival of our western Christian civilization is in question, in which the very ideals on which this civilization rests are questioned and attacked, in which, in consequence, everything is insecure. This insecurity and pessimism pervade the attitudes toward all problems. Doubts as to the fate of our culture can be found already in Pascal, they become pronounced in Kierkegaard, they are dogmatically laid down by Spengler, followed by Toynbee. Insecurity is the mark of our epoch, and it shows itself everywhere in musical atonalism just as much as in Heisenberg's uncertainty principle, in the insecurity of human relations within or between the states. Firm faith in science and progress is followed by doubt; natural sciences and reason are minimized in favor of intuitionism. The long appeal to reason is followed by an appeal to the irrational. The pessimism of an age of crisis makes men pessimistically doubt whether social relations are soluble at all.

As far as the attitude toward international law goes, a period of overestimation, so characteristic for the years between the two World Wars, is followed by a period of underestimation. It is, to a great extent, this change of attitude which spells the difference between the League of Nations and the United Nations.

At the end of World War I, fought under the leadership of Woodrow Wilson "to end war," boundless optimism prevailed. There was everywhere, in victors, neutrals, and vanquished, not only the will to achieve a better world through international law, but also the firm conviction that it could be done. Hence, the ambitious experiment of the League of Nations. Away with power politics! No more secret diplomacy, no more entangling alliances, no longer the forever discredited balance of power, no more war! Democracy and the rule of international law will change the world. The Covenant puts international law "in the actual conduct among Governments" and justice first, insists on disarmament as the way to peace, emphasizes the trust principle in the Mandates.

In all the dealings of the League, international law was at the heart of the discussion. Idealistic approach, optimism, emphasis on international law created the "Geneva atmosphere." This writer who was so often in Geneva between 1920 and 1932 knows it from experience. One must have been there in order to evaluate the impression, the genuine enthusiasm all around, when Aristide Briand made his famous speech: *"Plus de mitrailleuses!"* The legal department of the League played a great role; the Permanent Court of International Justice was frequently resorted to. The Mandates Commission was primarily moved by legal considerations. Legal arguments were the core of every debate; every delegate knew that he must justify his attitude legally. Hence, greatest importance was given to international law in the foreign offices. Many a delegate traveled to Geneva with a whole library of international law and always well accompanied by legal advisers. In the Hungarian-Rumanian Optants' Dispute both parties tried to produce the greatest number of opinions by leading international lawyers.

And, outside of Geneva, the very existence of the League, the foundation of the Permanent Court of International Justice, created enthusiasm and led to an overestimation of the efficacy of international law. An enormous number of legal studies on the League were published in all lan-

guages. The teaching of international relations centered on
international law and the League. The Rockefeller Foundation created the Geneva Institute, the Carnegie Endowment
the Hague Academy of International Law. The literature on
international law was greatly influenced by this general
trend of optimism.

The Covenant did not go to extremes; it recognized realistically that war can be successfully eliminated only insofar
as peaceful substitutes are created; it laid down only "obligations" (in the plural) not to resort to war. Article XVI
contains sanctions in a strictly juridical sense only against
a member which had violated its obligations under Articles
XII, XIII, or XV. The Covenant does not abolish war; is
by no means based on the doctrine of *bellum justum;* it does
not deal with the just cause of war, but contains merely
procedural obligations. Mr. Kellogg himself never made extravagant claims for the Kellogg Pact.

Even under this optimism the facts were, from the beginning, different. Old-fashioned alliances against Germany and
Hungary were concluded *"dans le cadre de la Société des
Nations,"* under the escape clause of Article XXI. The delegates to the League had mostly the interest of their own
states in view, so that Scelle could bitterly complain of
"merely multinational, not international gatherings."
Geneva oratory was contradicted by what the states did.
The Corfu incident in 1923 gave a foretaste of the unreality
of "collective security" in the face of a Great Power.

Then came the flagrant violations of the thirties, climaxing in World War II. They had, as a first effect, the going
to extremes especially by a literature of wishful thinking.
Fancy interpretations of the Kellogg Pact were put forward; the more "collective security" was shown to be non-
existent, the more the utopian writers emphasized it. The
more the facts were in contradiction to their writings, the
more lyrical they grew. The confusion between *lex lata* and

lex ferenda, the mistaking of often contradictory trends and tendencies for new rules of international law already established, the mistaking of Geneva—or Pan American—oratory for facts grew worse.

The events of the thirties also had the opposite effect: the time was ripe for the swing of the pendulum to the other extreme, from overestimation to underestimation of international law, from the emphasis on international law to the emphasis on power, from optimism to pessimism, to the new "realistic" approach. Already books published in the thirties show this new approach.[1]

During World War II, the new "realism" appeared in state action and literature. The three leading statesmen on our side were all realists. The bases-destroyer deal and Lend-Lease Act were moves of a realistic policy; legal considerations were less prominent. Not peace through law, but security through power, became the dominant idea and shaped the thinking as to a new world organization, built upon "more realistic bases" than the League. Power held by the Big Three, and, therefore, their predominance, became essential. In the literature, many war books not only condemned German geopolitics as aimed at imperialism, but tried also to brand it as a "pseudo-science." But at the same time attention was directed again to the writings of Sir Halford MacKinder—exactly from whom Karl Haushofer had started—and an American geopolitics was presented.[2] In the field of international law, important writers [3] came to the conclusion that it is for all practical purposes dead.

The Dumbarton Oaks Proposals do not even mention international law. Only the Chinese proposals and widespread criticism brought about the inclusion of international law in the Charter of the United Nations. The "realism" of the Charter can be seen in the Trusteeships, as distinguished from the League Mandates, in relative unimportance of the disarmament problem, in the powers of the Security Council as well as in the "veto" given to the permanent members, in the fact that the Security Council, deciding "upon the existence of any threat to the peace, breach of peace or act of aggression," is not bound by rules of international law, so that its "measures" must not necessarily be sanctions in the juridical sense, contrary to Article XVI of the Covenant. Also the practice of the United Nations is certainly very different from that of the League. Legal questions play a subordinate role at the United Nations and in diplomatic correspondence. The International Court of Justice is not overburdened; whether its advisory opinion on the admission of new members will be heeded remains to be seen. The oratory contrasts strikingly with that of Geneva. If the most undiplomatic language, bitterness, invectives, and political propaganda constitute realism, then there is plenty of realism at Lake Success (*lucus a non lucendo*).

The new realism makes itself felt everywhere. International law as a special subject has been dropped as an examination topic for entrance into the U.S. Foreign Service. It is significant that the Rockefeller Foundation and the Carnegie Endowment, although certainly many other motives were of influence, have withdrawn their subventions from the Geneva Institute and the Hague Academy. Although the Carnegie Endowment—traditionally a bulwark of international law—continues to do much for international law, for publications on and the teaching of international law, the new realistic tendencies can be seen in top decisions of recent years. The whole trend in teaching international relations shies away from international law and puts the focus on politics and power.[4] The Institutes at Yale and Princeton emhasize the realistic point of view. So does the new journal *World Politics*. Professor Harold Sprout states that earlier the study of international relations was carried on "in the sterile atmosphere of international law." [5] Excellent international lawyers like P. E. Corbett and Hans J. Morgenthau have, so to speak, "deserted" international law and gone with flying colors into the realistic camp. The latter has given us, one might say, the bible of realism.[6] The balance of power is being honored again and Macchiavelli quoted with approval.

Yet, even under the United Nations and in the literature, not everything is realism. The United Nations is based on the belief of the continued co-operation of the "Big Three," although a study of world history from oldest times could have shown that alliances of heterogeneous states are likely to disintegrate as soon as the common enemy is vanquished. It was not foreseen that the realistic veto may lead to paralysis. It was not seen that "collective security" and other tasks cannot be fulfilled by an association of "sovereign equal States," which has scrupulously to respect the *domaine réservé* of the members. The facts are as under the League. As there is no collective security, new alliances and counter-alliances are concluded, shamefully veiled as being "within the framework of the U.N."—only the language has changed since League times from French to English. And both camps again make use of the two escape clauses— the West of Article LI, the East of Article CVII.[7] Far-reaching utopian schemes appear also under the reign of the United Nations and a new utopian trend—"world government" and so on—can be seen in some parts of the literature.

Insofar as the new realism tends to correct mistakes of the earlier attitude, insofar as it is directed against the *overestimation* of international law, it is to be welcomed. International lawyers must not forget that international law does not operate in a vacuum, that even proposals *de lege ferenda* have sense only within the boundaries of political possibilities of being realized at a particular juncture of history. They must not confuse the law that is with

their wishful thinking. They must recognize that many of
their utopian proposals presuppose a world state under
world law, whereas the present international community is
only a loose society of sovereign states under international
law and is likely to remain such for the foreseeable future.
Good international lawyers, who, as lawyers, are trained
in looking to the law that is and to realities, rarely make
this mistake. Thus Edwin D. Dickinson [8] has given us a
severe—perhaps, too severe—critique of positive international law. Alf Ross [9] always urges a "sober, realistic attitude" toward international law. No one will say that J. L.
Brierly [10] neglects the realities.

But insofar as the new realism tells us that there is
nothing but power and that international law is "sterile,"
insofar as it tends toward an *underestimation* of international law, it must be opposed with all energy. In so doing,
it sins against its own realism. It is not true that problems
of international law "are largely irrelevant." International
law *is* a factor in international relations: Brierly [11] and
Jessup, in his *A Modern Law of Nations,* have recently
written pages proving convincingly that this is so. Municipal law, too, moves in a political atmosphere. Will this
country, therefore, accept Hitler's "Might is right" or
Lenin's "Law is politics"? *Ubi societas, ibi jus.* The law has
necessarily to play an important role, and so has international law. Extremes are always wrong: the truth lies in the
golden middle way. The correct attitude must be equidistant
from utopia, from superficial optimism and overestimation,
and from cynical minimizing; neither overestimation nor
underestimation: International law is "neither a panacea
nor a myth." [12]

[1] See, e.g., F. SCHUMAN, INTERNATIONAL POLITICS (1st ed. 1933);
SIMONDS and EMENY, THE GREAT POWERS IN WORLD POLITICS (1939);
and the writings of E. H. Carr in England.

[2] NICHOLAS J. SPYKMAN, AMERICAN STRATEGY IN WORLD POLITICS (1942).

[3] FRIEDMANN, WHAT'S WRONG WITH INTERNATIONAL LAW? (1941). See also papers and discussions during the war—Vols. XXVI to XXVIII (1940–42) of the TRANSACT. GROT. SOC'Y.

[4] See Wm. T. R. Fox, *Interwar International Relations Research,* 2 WORLD POLITICS No. 1 at 67–79 (1949); and Frederick S. Dunn, *The Present Course of International Relations Research, ibid.* at 80–95.

[5] 1 WORLD POLITICS No. 3 at 404 (1949).

[6] HANS J. MORGENTHAU, POLITICS AMONG NATIONS (1948).

[7] G. Schwarzenberger, *The North Atlantic Pact,* 2 WESTERN POLITICAL QUARTERLY No. 3 at 310–11 (1949).

[8] *International Law: An Inventory,* 33 CALIF. L. REV. No. 3 at 506–42 (1945).

[9] A TEXTBOOK OF INTERNATIONAL LAW (1947).

[10] THE OUTLOOK FOR INTERNATIONAL LAW (1947).

[11] *Op. cit.*

[12] J. L. BRIERLY, THE LAW OF NATIONS at v (4th ed.; 1949).

THE SYSTEMATIC PROBLEM OF THE SCIENCE OF INTERNATIONAL LAW [1]

THE FIRST AND PRINCIPAL TASK of the science of international law is to present the international law actually in force, to present it in its totality and in a systematic way. For a science is, in the words of Kant, not a mere aggregate, but a system; and in order to arrive at a system, we need a method, *i.e.*, a procedure according to principles of reason by which alone a diversity of cognitions can become a system. The science of international law has always been faced with the systematic problem. The system of public-private international law [2] is untenable, as it is not the system of one and the same science. Private international law, so called, is, apart from treaties on this subject, municipal law, although it ought to be cosmopolitan in its outlook. True, international law and conflict of laws are both a consequence of the present territorial organization of mankind, but in a very different way. International law results from the fact that the international community is composed of territorially organized sovereign states. Conflict of laws is necessary because of the coexistence at the same time of many different municipal legal orders, each with a territorial sphere of validity, which may, but need not, coincide with the territory of a sovereign state. Hence, international law would govern two or more sovereign states, even if they had absolutely identical municipal laws; on the other hand, conflict of laws may be necessary within one and the same sovereign state, whether federal or unitary. Equally, the coming into existence of a world state would bring international law in the actual sense to an end, but not necessarily conflict of laws. There is only one international law—often called "public" international law.

The oldest system of international law is that of peace, war, and neutrality. This system dominated from Grotius' *De jure belli ac pacis* until 1914. It corresponded to the continuity of the development of our international law from its beginning to World War I, to the classic international law of a primitively organized international community, a law limited in problems and content, dealing nearly exclusively with the rights and duties of sovereign states. The system of the first part ("Peace") corresponded to the concept of private law analogies: persons, things, contracts, torts, a system which goes back to Gaius—the system of Roman private law.

Since 1914 international law has been in flux, in a period of transition, of crises and transformations; it has seen, on the one hand, an ever-increasing expansion as to problems and content, and, on the other hand, a change in well-established norms and therefore uncertainty in many legal rules and whole departments. This development of international law since 1914 has challenged the science of international law in many ways: as to the general attitude toward international law—from the Utopians to the "neo-realists"; as to methodological problems—the attack against legal positivism, both from a revived natural law and strengthened sociological and realist schools; as to the

actual content of many international norms, theoretical
problems, and problems of construction and the outlook for
the future—from gloomy predictions of chaos to optimistic
prophecies of a "world law of humanity."

The development of international law since 1914 has also
put the systematic problem in a new light. Yet, although
the problem has been seen by some writers,[3] it has only
been lightly treated. As a consequence of the disastrous
neglect of the laws of war since 1920, treatises have sometimes been restricted to the law of peace,[4] or the laws of
war have been treated in a few pages in an "annex." But
in general the old and traditional system—peace, war, and
neutrality—has remained the dominating system since
1920.[5]

True, systematic changes have appeared since 1920. One
such change is related to the theory of the Vienna School.
As every legal norm must have a personal, territorial, material, and temporal sphere of validity, international law was
built up systematically in the following way: treating the
four spheres of validity of international law, then the
process of creating international norms; further—as a primary task of international law—the delimitation by international law of the four spheres of validity of the municipal
legal orders of the sovereign states; and finally the solution
of international conflicts.[6] Another systematic change stems
equally from theoretical considerations, namely, the growing attack against private-law analogies. The private-law
system, of persons, things, contracts, torts, has often been
replaced by a system of public law, taken from advanced
municipal legal orders: constitutional, administrative, procedural, and criminal law.[7] The concept of a 'constitutional
international law" has been made familiar by Verdross.[8]
Many works have been dedicated to international administrative law; in recent times many books on international
criminal law have been published. The concept of an "inter-

national law of procedure" has been created, including all
the norms for the pacific settlement of international conflicts as well as the laws of war and neutrality.[9]

Inspired by the continuous expansion of international
law, other attempts, having a merely pragmatic character,
have consisted in dividing international law systematically
into more and more divisions: international fiscal law,[10]
international law of communications, international air law,
international law of fisheries, international labor law, and
many others.[11] But these new systematic attempts are
hardly satisfactory; they are often only partially applied,[12]
they often overlap the traditional: peace, war and neutrality. To that end it must be added that it is necessary to
distinguish also between general and particular international law. Exactly for that reason a new system has been
tried: to divide a treatise on international law into two
great parts, "general international law" and "international
organization," a systematic division which often also overlaps other systems.[13] The clearest and most consequent application of this new system can be seen in the third edition
of Verdross' treatise.[14] The first part treats the whole general international law of peace, war, and neutrality; the
second part, "Constitution of the Organized Community of
States," deals with particular international law.

These new systematic attempts, inspired by theoretical reasons, by pragmatic considerations and by the
ever-increasing expansion of international law are clearly
reflected in the organization of "International Legal
Studies"[15] at the leading American law schools, which add
international administrative, aerial, labor, economic, investment, and taxation law, and so forth. International law and
international organization remain basic, although "International Legal Studies" go farther. But, as the Dean of
Harvard Law School stated, this newer group has nothing
to do with the teaching of "international relations," but

deals exclusively with international legal problems. But even the system of general-particular international law today is no longer adequate. On the one hand, "International Organization" cannot be presented without the general international law which is its very basis. On the other hand, the law of international organizations influences general international law; at a time when the United Nations has eighty-two members, it is no longer possible to present even general international law without taking the Charter of the United Nations into consideration.[16] Present international law is no longer restricted to sovereign states, their rights and duties, the traditional problems of recognition, nationality, territory, jurisdiction, treaties, international responsibility, and so forth. It deals also with universal and regional economic, financial, social, hygienic, and cultural problems, and with financial and technical aid to underdeveloped countries; it tries to deal with the international protection of human rights, stateless persons, refugees, aborigines of mandates and trusteeships. Non-states (units of federal states, colonies, the proposed "Free Territory of Trieste") may become partial subjects of international law. The new international law of atomic energy has come into existence; the new international law of outer space is beginning to develop. The ever-increasing number of international organizations, universal and regional, general and specialized, has created new problems: these international organizations are often persons in international law, have international privileges, and immunities, conclude treaties with member and non-member states as well as with other international organizations, have a right of diplomatic protection of their employees vis-à-vis states, have international responsibility. There is the whole "internal law" of international organizations, which is also international law, although on a hierarchically lower stage. There is the new "law of international functionaries."

Nor is this all. New developments have raised questions of the governing law in novel situations. What is the legal character of the contracts concluded by international organizations with their own functionaries? Which law has to be applied by the "International Administrative Tribunals"? What law governs contracts made by international organizations with foreign corporations for the supply of materials or services? What law governs the relations between international organizations and private international organizations admitted for purposes of consultation? [17]

New developments in the law of international organizations have appeared. The attempts at unification of free Europe often follow novel lines. There are now "supranational" organizations. Very new types of international organizations, referred to as *établissements publics internationaux*,[18] public international corporations, or, in appropriate cases, public international works, have come into existence, such as Eurofima in Europe, the *Entreprises Communes* of the Euratom Treaty, and the International Finance Corporation. They, too, are international organizations created by states through treaty; but they perform international services for the benefit of individuals. As operational units, independent of governments, they make contracts with an indefinite number of individuals. What law governs them? First of all, the law of the basic treaty. But as there is no international incorporation, they are constituted as banks or corporations under some municipal law, and the treaty, by international legislation, may change this municipal law and make it, through *renvoi*, applicable as the *lex fori* in the courts of the other participating states under principles of conflict of laws.

There are writers [19] who conceive the so-called international economic law as a new juridical department which extensively overlaps international law and conflict of laws. Jessup [20] has studied these frontier problems under the

heading of "transnational law." Of great importance today
are the problems of the repudiation of concessions granted
to a foreign corporation by a state. With regard to the
repudiation of *ultra vires* state contracts, Meron [21] has
shown that older international tribunals applied only the
relevant municipal law and, in case such law laid down
that such contract was void *ab initio,* decided in favor of
the state. But newer international decisions show the tendency to apply to such repudiation the international law of
state responsibility. They may, according to the case, apply
the principle of "unjust enrichment," or the argument that
the contract has been ratified by the conduct of the state,
or the general principles of law recognized by civilized
nations, or the rule of general international law concerning
the responsibility of the state for damage caused to aliens.
Even more important are the cases of expropriation, confiscation, or nationalization by a state vis-à-vis foreign
corporations, where a contract has been concluded between
a sovereign state and foreign corporations. Such contracts
often contain arbitration clauses. But the contracts may
not only regulate the problem of jurisdiction but also that
of the applicable law, e.g., the Iran Oil Consortium of 1954.
In the Serbian [22] and Brazilian [23] Loans cases, the Permanent Court of International Justice laid down that every
contract which is not a contract between sovereign states
in their capacity as persons in international law must be
based on the municipal law of some state. In consequence,
the international tribunal must apply municipal law, and
the decision as to which municipal law is applicable must
be determined according to the norms of conflict of laws.
Hence these agreements have been considered contracts, not
international treaties, and Lauterpacht has stated that the
tribunals instituted by these contracts are not genuine
international tribunals. But there is a strong tendency in
the free world to apply the norm *Pacta sunt servanda* to

these contracts. To this tendency Alfred Verdross, in an interesting article,[24] has recently given a theoretical foundation. Verdross distinguishes between property of aliens acquired under private law or concessions granted by the state on the basis of its administrative law (in both cases on the basis of the municipal law in question) and contracts between a sovereign state and foreign corporations for the economic development of the country, by which the concessions granted to the foreign corporation are put under this *lex contractus* and also contain arbitral clauses. Such contracts are neither international treaties nor municipal contracts. They belong to a third group of contracts. The dictum of the Permanent Court of International Justice that contracts can only be under international law or some municipal law is false. Such contracts were concluded under neither international nor municipal law; they have no positive legal order above them. The rights established by the contract are subordinated to a new legal order created by agreement of the parties, the *lex contractus*. These "quasi-international" contracts are legally characterized by the fact that the basis for their validity is directly in the suprapositive legal principle of *Pacta sunt servanda*, that they are contracts *inter pares* containing arbitral clauses, and that the *lex contractus* regulates exhaustively the relations between the parties. The investigations which Jessup made under the heading of "transnational law" have, therefore, counterparts in the writings of Adam, Erler, Verdross, and Zemanek.

All this shows the insufficiency of all the newer systematic attempts. This insufficiency has induced the eminent international lawyer C. Wilfred Jenks, to urge and propose a completely new system. Although he does not take the idea of a "transnational law" into consideration, he starts from his conviction that the development of international law in the first half of the twentieth century has transformed

the character and content of international law to such a
degree that it no longer can be presented within the framework of the classic law of nations. It is no longer possible,
he states, to take care of this new development by way of
mere additions to the pre-existing structure, by way of
casual and sometimes illogical modifications of the pre-
established system. It is no longer possible to understand
the actual development by starting from the classic presumptions. The systematic problem is today much more
fundamental; what is needed is an entirely new system.
Jenks sees the actual development of international law as
a tendency toward a common law of humanity, although
at this time only in an early, imperfect, insecure, and precarious stage. The actual trend, according to him, is toward
a law of the organized world community, still on the basis
of sovereign states, but fulfilling more and more common
functions through a complex of international organizations.
The law of sovereign states remains an important part, but
only a part, of the law of nations. The new status must be
reflected in a new system, and he tentatively proposes such
a new system. There is no doubt that such a new system
will only be gradually developed, but the task is undoubtedly
before us, for, to return to where we started, a science is
not a mere aggregate, but a system.

[1] See also this writer's study, *El Sistema del Derecho Internacional*,
in ESTUDIOS DE DERECHO INTERNACIONAL, HOMENAJE AL PROFESOR
CAMILO BARCIA TRELLES 87–102 (1958).

[2] Thus, the *Trattato di Diritto Internazionale* in twelve volumes,
edited by Prospero Fedozzi and Santi Romano, contains four volumes
on conflict of laws. In the newer *Trattato di Diritto Internazionale*,
edited by Balladore Pallieri, Gaetano Morelli, and Rolando Quadri,
one series of seven volumes treats international law, the other series
of seven volumes deals with conflict of laws. But the two series together constitute the "Treatise of International Law."

[3] Georges Scelle, *Essai de systématique du droit international public*, 30 REVUE GÉNÉRALE DE DROIT INTERNATIONAL PUBLIC 116–42 (1923).
See also MANLIO UDINA, IL DIRITTO INTERNAZIONALE TRIBUTARIO
1–15 (1949).

4 Thus still, the two-volume work by Marcel Sibert, TRAITÉ DE DROIT INTERNATIONAL PUBLIC (1951), is restricted to the "droit de la paix."

5 Thus the leading English treatise by Oppenheim, even in the newest edition by Sir Hersch Lauterpacht, is still based on this system. Also the treatise by Mariano Aguilar Navarro: whereas the first three parts (in seven volumes) will deal with the law of peace, the fourth part will treat the laws of war and neutrality.

6 This system is, for example, to be found in the treatises by Paul Guggenheim, 1 TRAITÉ DE DROIT INTERNATIONAL PUBLIC (1953), and by Alfred Verdross, VÖLKERRECHT (3rd ed.; 1955). See also JOSEF L. KUNZ, TEORÍA GENERAL DEL DERECHO INTERNACIONAL, Academia Interamericana de Derecho Comparado e Internacional, 2 CURSOS MONOGRAFICOS 327–444 (1955).

7 The only writer who has applied this system completely is Antonio Sánchez de Bustamante y Sirvén, DERECHO INTERNACIONAL PÚBLICO (5 vols. 1933–38).

8 ALFRED VERDROSS, DIE VERFASSUNG DER VÖLKERRECHTSGEMEINSCHAFT (1926). See also Georges Scelle, *Précis de Droit des Gens*, 2 DROIT CONSTITUTIONNEL (1934). The second part of the treatise by Mariano Aguilar Navarro (referred to in note 5 above) is entitled: "Constitución de la Comunidad Internacional."

9 Thus, for example, the second volume of P. Guggenheim's treatise (mentioned in note 6 above); thus also the planned fourth part of A. P. Sereni, *Diritto Internazionale*. See also JULIUS STONE, LEGAL CONTROLS OF INTERNATIONAL CONFLICT (1954).

10 See MANLIO UDINA, IL DIRITTO INTERNAZIONALE, TRIBUTARIO (1949).

11 Philip C. Jessup recently introduced the concept of an *International Parliamentary Law*, 51 AM. J. INT'L L. 396–402 (1957).

12 Thus the treatise, edited by Fedozzi and Santi Romano (referred to in note 2 above) contains, among twelve volumes, one on international administrative law, one on international tributary law, one on international labor law, and even one on international ecclesiastical law.

13 Thus the series dedicated to international law, in the treatise edited by Balladore Pallieri, Morelli, and Quadri (referred to in note 2 above), is based on the traditional system: peace, war and neutrality. But whereas the first four volumes will deal with classic international law, the fifth is dedicated to "International Organization." The treatise by Mariano Aguilar Navarro (referred to in note 5 above) is based on the same traditional system. But the second part (in four volumes) deals with general international law, whereas the third part will deal with "Cooperación Internacional y Servicios Internacionales," i.e., with international organization. This division appears in a different way in the *Diritto Internazionale*, by A. P. Sereni. The second part (in two volumes) is entitled: "Organizzazione Internazionale." But that means here the organization of the international community. The first volume, already published, treats "subjects of a territorial character" (states and insurgents recognized as belligerent parties),

i.e., general international law. The second volume will deal with "international persons of a functional character," i.e., primarily with international organization.

14 ALFRED VERDROSS, VÖLKERRECHT (3rd ed. 1955).

15 See Josef L. Kunz, *Der heutige Stand der Wissenschaft und des Unterrichts des Völkerrechts in den Vereinigten Staaten von Amerika*, 7 ÖSTERREICHISCHE ZEITSCHRIFT FÜR ÖFFENTLICHES RECHT 401–27 (1956).

16 This impossibility is confirmed by the newest edition of Oppenheim-Lauterpacht, (1 INTERNATIONAL LAW, A TREATISE, 8th ed. 1956). Sir Hersch Lauterpacht writes that this treatise is primarily dedicated to the presentation of the norms of general international law. But the norms of particular international law not only constantly appear as additions and notes in many places, but the editor has, characteristically, found it necessary to add a large chapter on "International Organization" (1 *ibid.* at 370–450), to treat the International Labor Organization, and to give us a large appendix on international specialized organizations (1 *ibid.* at 977–1029).

17 See, on these problems, KARL ZEMANEK, DAS VERTRAGSRECHT DER INTERNATIONALEN ORGANISATIONEN (1957), reviewed by the writer in 52 AM. J. INT'L L. 565–67 (1958).

18 See, on these problems, H. T. ADAM, LES ETABLISSEMENTS PUBLICS INTERNATIONAUX (1957), reviewed by the writer in 51 AM. J. INT'L L. 569–72 (1957).

19 See GEORG ERLER, GRUNDPROBLEME DES WIRTSCHAFTSRECHTES (1956).

20 PHILIP C. JESSUP, TRANSNATIONAL LAW (1956).

21 Theodore Meron, *Repudiation of Ultra Vires State Contracts and the International Responsibility of States*, 6 INT'L & COMP. L. Q. 273–89 (1957).

22 P.C.I.J., ser. A, No. 20 (1929).

23 *Ibid.* No. 21.

24 A. Vedross, *Die Sicherung von ausländischen Privatrechten aus Abkommen zur Wirtschaftlichen Entwicklung mit Schiedsklauseln*, 18 ZEITSCHRIFT FÜR AUSLÄNDISCHES ÖFFENTLICHES RECHT UND VÖLKERRECHT 635–51 (1958).

I

THERE IS NO DOUBT that in the modern science of international law currents of natural-law thinking, often coupled with severe criticism of positivism, do appear.[1] But there is no unity in this movement; quite to the contrary, there are very different approaches; there is much confusion as to what natural law can do for international law; even the very words "natural law" and "positivism" are used in very different meanings. This state of things invites some observations.

The problem of "natural law" was posed, two and a half thousand years ago, by the Greek sophists and, to the present day, has remained a permanent part of the occidental philosophy of law.[2] During antiquity and the Middle Ages there were many "schools" of natural law, yet a dominating school, the "traditional" natural law, was developed by a line of Greek and, later, Catholic thinkers:[3] a natural law on an ontological-teleological or metaphysical basis; it held that good law must be in harmony with the essential nature of man as a corporeal-spiritual individual and a social being. This traditional natural law during the Middle Ages not only dominated jurisprudence but also deeply influenced national legal systems, both the common law of England and the civil law of the Continent, where Roman law, itself considered as *ratio scripta,* had been received.

There is, therefore, small wonder that the new international law and its science should have been deeply influenced by Roman and natural law.[4] The masters of the first, the "Spanish" school of international law, were at the same time the leaders of Spanish neo-scholasticism, building upon Aristotelian-Thomistic lines. Suárez was a realistic thinker who fully recognized that the new "international community" of the sovereign states of western Christian Europe is here to stay; but he wanted to give the new international law a foundation in Catholic natural law, in the *"genus humanum, in varios populos et regna divisum."*

The Protestant Grotius, who wrote the first treatise on international law, was still strongly influenced by the traditional natural law, but he secularized it by stating that natural law would be valid even if there were no God. This secularization profoundly changed the character of natural law. True, the Catholic natural law is not based on divine revelation; it is to be discovered by man's *recta ratio*—a term stemming from the Stoics; yet the *jus naturae* is man's "participation in the *lex aeterna"*; it necessarily presupposes the Christian faith in the Creator who has written these norms into the hearts of all men. "Right reason" is only the tool to discover the natural law; with Grotius this right reason becomes the basis of natural law. Grotius distinguished the "natural" and the "voluntary" *jus gentium,* although modern international lawyers are sometimes of exactly opposite opinions as to what part he emphasized.[5]

International lawyers of the seventeenth and eighteenth centuries followed different paths: One school, eliminating the natural law of nations altogether, were strict positivists;[6] others, dominated by the "classic" law of nature, the *droit de la raison,* eliminated the voluntary law of nations;[7] even the later "Grotians" retained natural law only in appearance:

> Exaggerated emphasis on the independence of states had the effect in Vattel's system of reducing natural law . . . to little more than an aspiration after better relations between states.[8]

II

It is against the long predominance of the classic natural law and its extravagances that, at the beginning of the nineteenth century, positivism came as a reaction in Europe.[9] It took the form of a factual positivism, under the domination of the anti-metaphysical "positive philosophy" of Auguste Comte and of legal positivism. More and more, a rigid positivism swept the whole science of law [10] and the science of international law again followed the general trend. In the last decades of the nineteenth century, however, this trend began to change. There was the revival of the nearly-forgotten traditional Catholic natural law, due to the Encyclical *Aeterni Patris* of August 4, 1879, by Leo XIII. Neo-Thomistic philosophy of law developed, and this natural law was fostered in the Hispanic world, in the Catholic law schools of the United States, and in great law schools of Europe, such as those at Paris, Milan, Louvain, Freibourg. By 1870, there began in Germany a strong reaction against sociological positivism and the long predominance of Comte, with a return to Kant. Up to World War I the leadership in Germany was with the Marburg Neo-Kantian School. Within this school, we find Stammler's "natural law with a variable content," and Del Vecchio is not uninfluenced by the *Philosophia perennis* of St. Thomas. Since the beginning of this century, and particularly since the end of World War I new philosophical thinking, which

we may put under the general name of the "phenomenological movement," arises to challenge the Marburg Neo-
Kantianism. Hence, since the beginning of the twentieth
century and especially since World War II, a general revival
of natural law can be observed, as many writers state.[11]

Natural law flows from the Baden Neo-Kantian School.
The French "Institutionalists" know a "natural law with a
progressive content" (Renard). There is a strong connection
between natural law and all "intuitionist" philosophies:
Bergson, phenomenology, theories of values, existentialism.
Neo-Thomists often welcome certain types of these newer
philosophies. Phenomenology leads via Brentano to scholasticism. Strong influences lead from Bergson to Neo-
Thomism. Many Neo-Thomists are "jubilant followers of
Max Scheler." There is a "Catholic Phenomenology," a
"Catholic existentialism." Neo-Thomist philosophers, such
as Jacques Maritain and Heinrich Rommen, exercise wide
influence.[12] New treatises on Catholic natural law are being
written, such as that by Messner.[13] The Notre Dame Law
School has started its excellent Natural Law Forum.

The revival of natural law is by no means restricted to
Neo-Thomism. There is a revival of classic natural law.
Attempts at construing a modern natural law on the basis
of the "sentiment" or "conscience" of law are being made.[14]
There are proponents of natural law, not a part of Neo-
Thomism, in the United States. It is highly interesting to
see that sociological scholars of law, who strongly reject
natural law, build on a cryptic natural law, such as the
droit objectif of Léon Duguit or the *droit positif intuitif*
of Gurvitch. The leader of the American "sociological jurisprudence," Dean Roscoe Pound, has, in the spirit of Josef
Kohler, introduced a cryptic natural law.[15] There are all
kinds of natural law at the present time; as a professor of
the law school of the Catholic University of Louvain tells
us: "Natural law is now fashionable." [16]

This general trend toward natural law must also be understood historically in relation to the past and to the times in which we are living. The relatively peaceful nineteenth century had primarily to do with problems of interpretation, of codification of law. Western optimistic faith in "progress" sincerely held that law is and will be, generally speaking, in harmony with the postulates of natural law. In such times positivism can suffice. But the rapidly changing, violent twentieth century is faced by wars, revolutions, rebellions, by problems of reforming and of creating law. These are problems of law-making, of politics of law, for which rigid positivism has no answers. It is, therefore, understandable that positivism had to suffer a crisis, as a consequence of the fact and of the far-reaching consequences of World War I. To that must be added the deep inner crisis of our occidental culture; in such times cries, such as Scheler's, asking for a "knowledge of salvation" arise. Man was no longer satisfied with the formal, logical investigations of the Marburg Neo-Kantian School. A tendency toward the concrete, toward substantive richness, toward eternal values, toward metaphysics, toward natural law, made itself felt. Then there were the terrible experiences before, in, and after World War II, the unheard-of cruelties toward men by totalitarian regimes, the abuse of law for purposes of injustice, torture, and extermination, total war, the appearance of nuclear weapons, the bitter struggle in a world torn by an ideological abyss. Such periods of profound crisis foster a flight into natural law as ideas and values on which man can rely as a barrier against the misuse of law. These events of our time are part of the explanation why Gustav Radbruch, at the end of his life, returned from relativism, to natural law, why natural-law concepts appear in modern European constitutions and in the decisions of the highest courts of Western Germany, as well as in documents of the "new" international law.

III

In earlier centuries international lawyers followed the general trend, first of traditional, later of classic natural law. During the period of positivism they were mostly positivists; but even during the predominance of rigid positivism many an international lawyer still recognized natural law to a certain extent. Remnants of natural-law thinking can be found in the discussion of some problems, such as the fundamental rights of states. Now many international lawyers follow the general trend of the revival of natural law.

There is the great stream of the revived traditional Catholic natural law. We may mention in Germany Cathrein and Mausbach, in France Louis Le Fur.[17] J. T. Delos[18] has applied the teachings of the leaders of the French institutionalist school (Hauriou, Renard) to international law. Here belong the majority of Spanish international lawyers and others of the Hispanic world; to them the Catholic natural law, as developed by Spanish neo-scholasticism on the lines of St. Thomas, is a part of their national and historical civilization. Here must also be named prominently Professor Verdross who, according to his own words,[19] defends the natural-law doctrine of the Spanish school of international law, and, particularly, of Francisco Suárez.

Other international lawyers revive the classic natural law, especially with regard to the problem of the international protection of human rights and freedoms. The most prominent name is here that of the late Sir Hersch Lauterpacht, who openly returned to natural law in his plea for an international bill of the rights of man,[20] and who, in 1955,[21] spoke out against the triumph of positivism, which, notwithstanding its merits, "can no longer be regarded as being in accordance with existing International Law." With the misdeeds of totalitarian regimes in mind, he emphasized the importance and vitality of metapositive standards.

When it comes to the writers who are often indiscriminately named as "sociological" jurists, it is necessary to distinguish clearly. There are international lawyers who insist on the sociological factors, on the sociological foundation of the international law actually in force, and show their insistence upon the importance of a full understanding of that law as a prerequisite to reform, but who are normative jurists, sometimes favorable to, or adherents of, natural law. In this category, we may name Max Huber and Dietrich Schindler, who stood near to Nicolai Hartmann. Here belongs the professor at the University of Madrid, Mariano Aguilar Navarro.[22] Here belongs the late Professor Brierly, who wrote that

> if we are to explain why any kind of law is binding, we cannot avoid some such assumption as that which the Middle Ages made, and which Greece and Rome had made before them, when they spoke of natural law.[23].

Here we must also name Charles De Visscher,[24] who has emphasized sociological factors, but is a normative jurist and in favor of the traditional law of nature.

There are international lawyers who follow the cryptic natural law developed by anti-metaphysical scholars who reject natural law. The influence of Duguit's *droit objectif* on the science of international law was remarkable. Foremost is the late Professor Georges Scelle, whose *droit objectif*—pseudo-natural law, so to speak—is presented as a "biological necessity." Also Nicolas Politis [25] is to be mentioned here. Other international lawyers adhere to a natural law based on the "legal sentiment" or the "legal conscience" of men and nations (Krabbe,[26] Drost [27]) ; some, as Laun, in an unacceptable way simply confuse law with ethics.

Max Huber once remarked that ethical orders are, in the last analysis, anchored in metaphysics, whereas ethics anchored only in sociological observations are of a different

type. Indeed, a German sociological jurist has stated that
"sociology is the natural law of our times." [28] The realist
school considers "law as a fact," a prediction, not a prescription; in the same way natural law is not a system of ethical
norms, but a compilation of factual descriptions; statisti-
cally proven facts are spoken of as "values." Thus Professor
McDougal's "goal-values" are not values but, as he, when
pressed, must admit, simply "preferences." But the real
problem is not to state preferences or "interests" (Heck)
but to weigh them; and for that we need not a description
of factual behavior but a normative scale. The concept of
the "living law" of the Austrian scholar Eugen Ehrlich
has exercised a profound impression on the American realist
school.[29] It is also the basis for the earlier investigations of
western and eastern cultures by Professor Northrop. Yet in
his recent work [30] he felt the necessity of evaluating the
justice of the different "living laws." For that purpose he
needs, of course, a system of ethical norms, that is, of
natural law; but he believes he can solve this ethical problem by scientific means.

The far-reaching proposals for the progressive development of international law by the late Judge Alejandro
Alvarez [31] cannot be said to be based on natural law; he does
not start from supreme values, from highest ethical norms,
but from the *faits sociaux*, from the "new conditions of life."

IV

As in former times, many international lawyers follow
the trend of a return to natural law and toward severe criticism of positivism, a trend to be seen in the science of law in
general and understandable through the times in which we
are living, times of particular gravity for the future of international law. But we see also the split between many
forms of natural law, and sometimes only pseudo-natural

law. We find often the same lack of clarity as to the very terms of "natural law" and of "positivism."

As far as positivism is concerned, we must distinguish, first, the "naïve" positivism of the nineteenth, and the "critical" positivism of the twentieth century. The first has certainly been recognized as being untenable; we have to deal only with the second as represented by Hans Kelsen. Kelsen has, with his usual clarity, recognized that, in order to explain the legally binding validity of the law, at least one metapositive norm must be introduced, his "fundamental norm." The latter is only supposed; it has only hypothetical validity; it may be supposed, but must not be; but it must be supposed, if one wants to understand the given materials as law. The problem of the ultimate validity of law is not excluded by Kelsen. This is one of the fields of inquiry of natural law, a philosophical and ethical problem. But whereas true natural law stands on absolute values, Kelsen—and that is a general problem of our times [32]— feels that scientifically only a relativism of values can be maintained.

Secondly, there is legal (analytical) and factual (sociological) positivism. Thirdly, it is of the highest importance to distinguish between the philosophical and the juridical positivism. For the first, law is everything; as the neopositivism puts it: "Value judgments are nonsense." Yet law is a system of norms ordering human conduct; the exclusion of values is impossible. Juridical positivism correctly holds that there is only one law, the man-made law, whereas it is ready to recognize that there are other and higher ethical and religious values and norms. Critical and juridical positivism studies the law analytically; it excludes neither the study of the sociological factors nor the ethical evaluation of the law, which never can be eliminated. Law, as this writer has for a long time maintained,[33] has three components: norm, fact, and value. Analytical, sociological, and ethical studies are therefore justified. Their long-standing hostility should be replaced by co-operation, each working in its legitimate field and with legitimate methods.

Modern critical, juridical, analytical positivism is indispensable. That "positivism" is particularly attacked by the present science of international law also has a special reason. The rigid, naïve, philosophical positivism did not restrict itself to the study of the law in force, but served also its own political postulates, held under the conviction and defense of the omnipotence of, and the highest place on earth due to, the sovereign state. This positivism stood for the predominance of the state, for the dualistic construction, for the will of the state as the only basis of international law, for the unquestionable right of every sovereign state to go to war, against third-party judgment, against a progressive development of international organizations, and so on. The era of rigid positivism was therefore an unhappy one for international law. But all this has nothing to do with correct positivism. No one can deny that Kelsen, a critical positivist, is a protagonist of the most progressive development of international law.

Just as it is necessary to be clear about positivism, one must also be clear about natural law. It is, for instance, agreed that the classic natural law with its detailed natural-law codes on all problems is just as untenable as naïve positivism. Natural law, so called, is a system of highest ethical norms. Its adherents restrict it correctly to a few of the highest most general principles, whereas the application of these principles to concrete legal norms varies according to the contingent conditions of times and nations. There is no opposition to positive law; on the contrary, the latter is considered indispensable. But also in the traditional natural law, even today, the grave mistake is often made of asserting that natural law is *law*. This is untenable. The analytical, positivistic scholar studies from a legal point of view the law, that is, a system of norms according to which the real conduct of men can be evaluated as "legal" or "illegal." But the adherent of natural law is a philosopher, a moralist, evaluating the law in the light of higher, non-legal, but ethical norms, in order to decide, not whether it is or is not law, but whether the law is good or bad. When he speaks of the binding quality of the law, he does not mean its legally binding quality—for that is a question of law—but its ethically binding quality. It is fundamental to state that natural law is not law, but ethics. This is fully recognized by many modern Neo-Thomists.[34] It is particularly gratifying to see that a leading Neo-Thomist thinker, Professor Jean Dabin of the Catholic University of Louvain Law School, has strongly spoken against the long chain of mistakes being constantly made by the claim that natural law is law. He has said clearly that there cannot be a "juridical" natural law; he has stated unequivocally that the dichotomy of natural law—positive law must be replaced by the new one: ethics—law.[35]

A true natural law is not a system of legal norms, but a system of highest ethical principles. In this sense true natural law has a task to fulfil in these times; so difficult for international law. This task cannot be based on the pretense that natural law is law. It cannot be used to declare something to be law which is not law. Such uses can be seen often. There are three great problems for natural law as applied to international law: First, to study the ultimate foundation of the validity of international law; this is a problem of philosophy of law. Secondly, there is the problem of evaluating the international law actually in force from an ethical point of view; this is a problem of an ethical critique of international law. Thirdly, there is the problem of helping, from an ethical point of view, the progressive development of international law. These tasks are necessary for the international community which is today truly world-wide. Finally, in a period in which our occidental culture is fighting for its very survival, it seems necessary for its protagonists, and hence its international lawyers, to strongly reaffirm the supreme values and ethical norms of that civilization—flowing from the central idea of the *dignitas humana*—and show their faith in them by words and deeds.

[1] See, e.g., Luis García Arias, *Las concepciones jusnaturalistas sobre la fundamentación del derecho internacional*, TEMIS, No. 7 at 115–48 (1960) ; Ulrich Scheuner, *Naturrechtliche Strömungen in heutigen Völkerrecht*, 13 ZEITSCHRIFT FÜR AUSLÄNDISCHES ÖFFENTLICHES RECHT U. VÖLKERRECHT 556–614 (1950).

[2] See ALFRED VERDROSS, ABENDLÄNDISCHE RECHTSPHILOSOPHIE (1958).

[3] To name a few: Plato, Aristotle, the Stoics, Cicero, St. Augustine, St. Thomas of Aquinas, Vitoria, Suárez.

[4] International law was called for centuries *Jus Naturae et Gentium*. See E. REIBSTEIN, DIE ANFÄNGE DES NEUEREN NATUR UND VÖLKERRECHTS (1949) ; P. Guggenheim, *Jus naturae et Gentium*, FESTSCHRIFT SPIROPOULOS 213–25 (1957). This latter writer holds that natural law has been dissolved and that positivism is firmly and necessarily established; he foresees no success for present-day attempts at a revival of natural law.

[5] Thus, 1 OPPENHEIM-LAUTERPACHT, INTERNATIONAL LAW 93 (8th ed. 1955), holds that the bulk of Grotius' interest was in the natural law of nations; exactly to the contrary, Guggenheim, *op. cit.* at 233.

[6] Particularly Johann Jacob Moser.

[7] Particularly Samuel Pufendorf.

[8] J. L. BRIERLY, THE LAW OF NATIONS 39 (4th ed. 1949).

[9] Except Spain, where Krause's philosophy dominated—"el krausismo español."

[10] Bergbohm (JURISPRUDENZ UND RECHTSPHILOSOPHIE [1892] declared natural law dead.

[11] CHARMONT, LA RENAISSANCE DU DROIT NATUREL (1910) ; KELLER, DROIT NATUREL ET DROIT POSITIF EN DROIT INTERNATIONAL PUBLIC (1931) ; HAINES, THE REVIVAL OF NATURAL LAW CONCEPTS (1939).

[12] DIE EWIGE WIEDERKEHR DES NATURRECHTS (1949).

[13] NATURRECHT (1950).

[14] HELMUT COING, DIE OBERSTEN GRUNDSÄTZE DES RECHTS (1947).

[15] Cairns (LEGAL PHILOSOPHIES FROM PLATO TO HEGEL 113 [1949]) states that "Pound's 'postulates of civilized society in our time and place' are really natural law doctrines intentionally framed as the necessary presuppositions of a particular system or systems."

16 "The term natural law is fashionable, especially among Catholics who seek a rallying point against relativism. There are, therefore, many people using it, and they bring it up on any pretext, as other men use the term sociology."—J. Leclerq, in 2 NATURAL LAW FORUM 64 (1957).

17 On his "objective theory," see García Arias, *op. cit.* at 140–43.

18 LA SOCIÉTÉ INTERNATIONALE ET LES PRINCIPES DU DROIT INTERNATIONAL PUBLIC (1927).

19 A. VERDROSS, VÖLKERRECHT 55 (4th ed. 1959).

20 AN INTERNATIONAL BILL OF THE RIGHTS OF MAN (1945).

21 OPPENHEIM-LAUTERPACHT, *op. cit.* at 107.

22 DERECHO INTERNACIONAL PÚBLICO (1952–54).

23 *Op. cit.* at 57.

24 THEORY AND REALITY IN PUBLIC INTERNATIONAL LAW (1957). See this writer's book review in 70 HARV. L. REV. 1331–36 (1957).

25 LES NOUVELLES TENDANCES DU DROIT INTERNATIONAL (1926).

26 H. Krabbe, *L'idée moderne de l'Etat*, 13 RECEUIL DES COURS No. 3 (1926).

27 H. DROST, GRUNDLAGEN DES VÖLKERRECHTS (1936).

28 FRANZ W. JERUSALEM, KRITIK DER RECHTSWISSENSCHAFT 5 (1948).

29 The leading sociological jurist of Brazil, Pontes de Miranda, wants to determine justice positivistically and scientifically; he asks for "a justiça concreta, verificável e conferível com o fato."—I SISTEMA DE CIENCIA POSITIVA DO DIREITO 477 (1922).

30 F. S. C. NORTHROP, THE COMPLEXITY OF LEGAL AND ETHICAL EXPERIENCE (1959).

31 See his dissenting opinions as a judge of the International Court of Justice at The Hague, and his last two books: LE DROIT INTERNATIONAL NOUVEAU DANS SES RAPPORTS AVEC LA VIE ACTUELLE DES PEUPLES (1959), and LE DROIT INTERNATIONAL NOUVEAU. SON ACCEPTATION, SON ÉTUDE (1960).

32 See, on this problem, A. BRECHT, POLITICAL THEORY: THE FOUNDATION OF TWENTIETH CENTURY POLITICAL THOUGHT (1959), and the article by A. Means, Jr., *Legal Theory and Arnold Brecht*, 47 VA. L. REV. 264–76 (1961).

33 See his study in 8 ÖSTERREICHISCHE ZEITSCHRIFT FÜR ÖFFENTLICHES RECHT 1–26 (1957).

34 See, e.g., Joseph O'Meara, *Natural law fruitfully may be regarded as the contribution which ethics can make to law*, 5 NATURAL LAW FORUM 83 (1960); A. Utz, *Natural law is essentially normative ethics*, 3 *ibid.* at 170 (1958).

35 JEAN DABIN, THÉORIE GÉNÉRALE DU DROIT 324 (2nd ed. 1953).

CHAPTER VIII: The Changing Science of International Law

Πάνία ῥεῖ· — Heraklitos.

I

HALF A CENTURY AGO this writer began his life-long studies of international law at the Vienna University Law School under the great scholars Heinrich Lammasch and Leo Strisower. Looking back for a moment at these fifty years, it is amazing to compare international law and its science as they then were and as they are today.[1] Then, in 1911, international law was at the peak but also close to the end of its classic period. Now, in 1961, the new international law, which by 1920 had entered a turning-point of its history without undergoing a revolutionary break with its past, has seen a first era of change during the League of Nations period, followed by a period of much more far-reaching change since 1945. There can be no doubt that international law at present is not only in an era of full transformation, but is also in a profound crisis.

Corresponding to this changing law of nations, of course, is a changing science of international law. It reflects this crisis, all the progressions and retrogressions of international law, all its hopes and disillusion, all its contradictions, its uncertainty, inadequacy, its often experimental and sometimes ephemeral character. It is the science of an international law in a period of transition from the classic law of nations, which is definitively gone, to some new international law which has not yet arrived and the exact shape of which we do not yet know.

Hence the great changes and very different patterns of the science of international law everywhere. There are some particularities in this country because of the legal and political background, because of world-wide contacts, and because the leadership of the democratic world has fallen upon the United States. The present international law of transition has influenced the science of international law in every scientific and technical aspect. The question of what the scientific character of this science consists is again under full discussion. Is its first duty objectivity and the impartial search for truth? There are today, more than ever, the dangers of wishful thinking, of a confusion of methods, by presenting one's own wishes, mere proposals *de lege ferenda,* as the law actually in force. The whole question of the correct methods of this science is again under debate. The continuous expansion of international law as to its subjects and to the objects it governs has had its influence on the systematic problem of the science of international law.[2]

Yet, in one respect, we believe, there is scientific progress. The permanent and growing publication of all types of international law materials, sources, and documents has made it possible for scholars to know much more about the actual law than was the case fifty years ago. This development has also brought about a rapprochement, so long advocated by this writer, betwen the so-called Continental and Anglo-American methods. International lawyers of the common-law countries no longer rely exclusively on "cases," but take

other materials, particularly the literature, into consideration. International lawyers of the countries of the civil law
duly continue their theoretical investigations, continue to
use all the literature in the principal languages, but they
also use cases more and more; and thus modern continental
works on international law are very different from the
earlier literature.[3]

II

By 1945 we saw everywhere a disillusionment with international law. Outstanding writers and faithful adherents
of international law gave us perhaps too somber a critique.[4]
The whole occidental idea of international organization, an
idea according to which it is possible to maintain international peace by a mere loose union of sovereign states—an
idea developed since the fourteenth century in western European utopian writings, and on which the League of Nations
was based and the United Nations is still based—is being
critically analyzed and found ambiguous and unsatisfactory.[5] This disillusionment finds different reactions in different men. Some are simply in a state of despair, like the
late Professor Marcel Sibert; others begin to lose their
interest in the study of international law; a great scholar
like the late Professor Edwin Borchard tried to cling to the
classic law of nations and to stem with all his forces and
with all his learning the new international law—in vain;
for the wheel of history cannot be turned back.
There always had been deniers of international law, that is,
those who did not deny the existence of the "materials, commonly known as international law," but who denied their
legal character. Such deniers are again numerous at the
present time. The denial today is based primarily [6] on the
insufficient structure of international law as shown by an
analytical critique.[7]

The modern neo-realists go farther. They [8] cast international law aside as "sterile," as "largely irrelevant in international affairs"; they condemn the "moralistic-legalistic" approach in foreign policy and emphasize the "national interest." It is hardly necessary to state that this approach is untenable. As history has shown from the beginning, law is indispensable for the living together of men; and this is true, too, on the international level.

Theoretically it is easy to state the conditions for a strong and vigorous international law: centralization of the now primitive, highly decentralized legal order, an international legislature, international courts with compulsory jurisdiction, and so on. But an international community, thus relatively strongly centralized, would constitute what we call today a sovereign state. This is the ultimate goal of the adherents of the idea of the world state. It is not to be wondered that the number of adherents of the world state has recently relatively increased. They tend also toward the end of international law, although in a very different way from that of the neo-realists; they would replace international law by "world law," that is, by the municipal law of the world state. This tendency is now prominently represented by the book of Clark and Sohn.[9] The authors propose complete disarmament by stages and under strict inspection, the establishment of an international peace force and certain other world authorities. The guiding star is the maintenance of international peace; that is why the powers of this world federal state shall be "strictly limited" to make possible the carrying out of this one goal—peace. From a technical point of view the book is excellently done, even if some fallacies in basic presuppositions can be shown;[10] it has had many laudatory reviews and will be published in a number of translations. But has it any chance of being accepted by the whole world now, within the foreseeable future? We do not believe that there are

many who are convinced of that. It is exactly with regard
to a certain minimum chance of realization that the dividing
line between proposals *de lege ferenda* and utopias can be
drawn.[11]

III

The disillusionment in 1945 led to widespread dissatisfaction, not only with the international law then in force,
but with the whole traditional international law. The phrase
was coined that what was necessary was a "re-thinking
of international law," a "complete reconstrution of international law." This dissatisfaction with the traditional international law was often coupled with a dissatisfaction
with the whole traditional science of international law. This
science, wrote Professor Percy E. Corbett [12] from his present neo-realistic point of view, must have a new approach,
a sociological approach, better connected with the forces determining world political activities and must be less inclined "to imprint the elegant patterns of law upon the
unruly interactions of governments." The late Judge Alvarez even blamed the unsatisfactory status of international law on "faulty study" by the science of international law not connected with the *vie actuelle des peuples*.
On the other hand, the burden of reconstructing, of creating, new international law is put on the shoulders of the
science of international law. A radical change, not only of
international law, but also of the science, study, research,
and teaching of international law is postulated.

For some even a reconstruction is not enough; what is
necessary is the creation *ex novo* of a new international
legal order. The very name "international law" is attacked.
Some speak of the "World Rule of Law." Others demand
that the name "international law" be as rapidly as possible
replaced by the term "World Law," which allegedly is differ-

ent from the narrower international law and which, we are told, is "a new field of law." It seems clear to us that the quality of international law does not depend on its name. International law, like common law, is not a static, but a dynamic, legal order. There is no dogma that international law is "the law between sovereign states"; this was an adequate definition for the international law of an earlier period, but it is no longer true for present international law. On the other hand, the "law between the sovereign states" is still a very important part of international law. Sovereign states are no longer the only members, but they are still by far the most important members of the international community. The tendency to ignore the states is strictly unrealistic.

There is at the present time important literature on the concept of the rule of law.[13] The rule of law is the guiding star, the highest value, for the International Commission of Jurists [14] which is composed of individual lawyers of the democratic countries. Its ideal is the dignity of man and his protection in this dignity by law. It takes, therefore, a fighting attitude against the violation of human dignity, primarily by communist states but, as the fight against the "apartheid" of the Union of South Africa shows, if necessary, also by non-communist states. It has proclaimed its ideas in three Congresses of Jurists, held on three continents: "The Declaration of Athens" (1955); the "Declaration of New Delhi" (1959) and the "Law of Lagos" (1961).[15]

The movement World Peace through Law was initiated by Charles S. Rhyne, a former president of the American Bar Association and chairman of the Special Committee on World Peace through Law,[16] first appointed in 1958. The idea is to explore what lawyers can do of a practical, concrete character to advance the rule of law for achievement of world peace. Like the International Commission

of Jurists, it relies on private individual lawyers; it shows
the same respect for the rule of law. But there is an important difference: it tends toward an advancement of international law as such; its dominating goal, its supreme
value, as for the book by Clark and Sohn, is peace. Like
the International Commission of Jurists it works through
conferences of jurists. First a series of regional conferences were held in the United States, followed by four
continental conferences to culminate in a world conference.
The first continental conference, attended by lawyers of
the Western Hemisphere, took place at San José, Costa
Rica, in June, 1961. The resolution there adopted—the
"Consensus of San José"—asks for compulsory jurisdiction of the International Court of Justice and expansion
of its jurisdiction so as to embrace all legal questions
arising from commercial or private matters. A consensus
of universal principles was adopted, on which a structure
of world law can be built. There must be a struggle of
lawyers to obtain the collaboration of governments for
drafting treaties to create an international legal system.
It is fully recognized that the task will be hard and long.[17]
The second of these conferences was held at Tokyo in September, 1961, the third at Lagos, Nigeria, December 3-6,
1961. The last conference will be held in Rome in April,
1962.

The idea of world law—not in the sense used by this
writer as the municipal law of a world state—is often met.
It is interesting to note that Dean Roscoe Pound,[18] recognizing that a world state seems hardly attainable at this
time, has recently voiced his belief that a world law for
world relations *is* attainable. Based on his distinction between "law" and "laws," he denied that a universal legal
order presupposes a universal political order and sanctions. He considered that there exists a world regime of
due process of law, a generally recognized and received

body of principles to which men are expected to adhere in international relations, without any political super-organization behind them.

At the Duke Law School there is a World Rule of Law Center. Its director, Arthur Larson, has published a *Design for Research*.[19] His problem is nothing less than to *create* a world legal order; for him world law is a new topic, a "new and very important field of law." His principal object is peace, the avoidance of nuclear war. World law, he states, is wider than international law; it must be universal; is must be based on all legal systems. While the philosphy of world law is not to be neglected, we need first of all "activist," practical projects. The great responsibility of science and research for obtaining this world law is proclaimed. The *Design* contains in 233 pages the outline of 111 research projects on everything, from the "marshalling of existing materials on the body of world law" to "educational requisites to support world law." For the new world law we need a new casebook, a new treatise, a new full course on world law. Enthusiastic innovators must create not only new names—world law—but also speak in new phraseology; we need "pilot studies" for a successfull "break-through" toward "world law."

IV

The late Judge Alejandro Alvarez [20] proposed that the International Court of Justice directly apply the new international law, a proposal that would make the Court a legislator, a proposal in which his colleagues could not follow him. There are many "wishful thinkers" who try to persuade themselves and others that, for example, there is already a working system of collective security in the United Nations, that the United Nations *is* an adequate means for maintaining international peace. There are ex-

cellent international lawyers who do not want to create
an international legal system *ex novo,* because, in a mood
of generous overoptimism, they overestimate the present
law. Thus, García Amador,[21] a leading Latin-American international lawyer, is convinced that international law,
even if it has not yet reached the fullness of its development, has nevertheless already made enormous progress. He teaches that contemporary international law definitely guarantees the international protection of human
rights, that the individual is the subject par excellence of
international law. Hence his proposals for the responsibility of states in the International Law Commission; he
holds that both the "international minimum standard"
and the Latin American principle of "equality of for-
eigners with citizens" are obsolete under *present* international law; the individual is protected as such, not as
a national. The *Nottebohm* judgment has shown again that
this is certainly not the international law actually in force.

Dr. Jenks is a man of great knowledge, of vast experience in international organizations, of strong capacity
for work, of lovable enthusiasm, a brilliant writer. But
there is a certain overoptimism in his work, and for that,
as well as for certain methods, applied or proposed, he
has been criticized.[22] He already sees in *present* international law the "Common Law of Mankind," although admittedly only in an early stage of its development. He
hardly speaks of the great political crises of today, some
of which at this time seem to defy a solution by peaceful means; he skillfully uses the fine British art of under-
statement; his proposed "multicultural" method, so his
critics say, poses not only an endless task, but one which
is not appropriate. The overoptimism of others is already
expressed by their diagnosis of the present crisis of international law as a mere "crisis of growth."

"Re-thinking international law" puts the accent on the future. Hence the debate on the correct methods of our science. There is nowadays a general attack on analytical jurisprudence; it has come from two sides: natural-law and sociological, "realist" jurisprudence. Spanish international lawyers want to reconstruct international law by a "value-oriented" science, going back to the foundations of Suárez. There is a general revival of natural-law theories.[23] But the principal attack comes from the sociological side, from the postulate of the "functional" approach. This writer has often shown that this attack is not justified. On the other hand, the analytical approach will always be indispensable in order to know and present actual law systematically; that will always be the first task of the science of law. On the other hand, the analytical method by no means excludes sociological-historical investigations, nor the valuation from the point of view of ethics. To the contrary, they are very necessary to complete a full understanding of the law in force; but these are different investigations; they have to be made by different methods; they never can substitute for the analytical method. It is also clear that the international lawyer is entitled to make proposals *de lege ferenda* for new law. But that is a political task. Further, such proposals must start from the law actually in force; politics of law necessarily presupposes a theory and a science of law.

These methodological problems are very pertinent, if we consider the pattern of "re-thinking international law" as presented by Professor McDougal.[24] He stands and falls theoretically with "American legal realism." "Law is a decision-making process." What he has added is no longer to restrict himself exclusively to the decisions of the courts, but also to take into consideration the decisions of many other "decision-makers." He is glad

to state that "legal realism" has brought an end to a fright-
ful confusion in legal thinking. The "verbal propositions,
known as law" can only be meaningfully understood if
they are put into the continuous community process. With
the help of a new jargon, partly taken from the Lass-
wellian vocabulary, he asks for an end to the destructive
phase of legal learnedness and for a creative science of
international law. A science, he holds, which is nothing
but scientific does not suffice; it must apply not only the
normal but also other integrated and interrelated methods.
He feels that in this shrinking world more and more men
demand common values, transcending national frontiers.
Fortunately, we need today no longer torture ourselves
with circuitous deductions from metaphysics; we know
today how to verify values. We must study with precision the variable factors of environment which influence
human behavior all over the world—a task no less endless than Dr. Jenk's multicultural approach. We must
adopt methods for classification of goal values, for description of historical and contemporary trends in the
realization of values, critical perfection of trends into the
future, imaginative invention and evaluation of alterna-
tives of policies by which goal values can be most fully
attained. His is a contemporary and an American concept
as to contents. We must maintain a position of power
and make such use of our power as to achieve a compromise with rival ways of life that diminishes the anti-
democratic elements in them. We need a new understanding of law as an instrument for community values. For
all that we need a "policy-science" and, in the field of
teaching, law students must be stimulated to think of themselves as "policy-makers." He is a policy-maker, a strat-
egist, a protagonist of—again a new name—Public World
Order of Human Dignity.

Professor McDougal is a man of great gifts, of a great capacity for work, and of no small self-confidence. His writings are interesting and valuable from many points of view. But his theoretical basis has all the faults of American "legal realism." The latter was certainly by no means without merits, but as a movement it is already over: "Its premises were shaky and its promises over-stated."[25] First, sociological statements as to facts are not rules of law. Sociological statements connecting facts with facts on the basis of the principle of causality state what is. Norms of law prescribe what ought to be. It is significant to compare the attitude of Professor McDougal with that of Judge Charles De Visscher.[26] The latter attacks theory, stresses sociological conditions and their importance as the substratum of law or as necessary pre-conditions for making possible a reform of the law. But in spite of his attacks on Kelsen, in spite of the emphasis put on sociological considerations, he is far from confusing a sociological statement of facts with a legal rule; he always remains a normative jurist and, contrary to McDougal's antimetaphysical attitude, close to Catholic natural law. Second, just as sociological statements or predictions are not rules of law, thus Professor McDougal's "goal values" are not values but only factual preferences of behavior. Third, law is not fact, law is not identical with policy. Finally politics of law is as the name indicates, a part of politics; it is not identical with the science of law. The mistake is *to identify* his "policy science," that is, politics of law, with the science of law.

"Re-thinking international law" covers, as we have seen, innovations in international law and its science, in the study, research, and teaching of international law. Contrary to many earlier complaints about the relative neglect of international law in American law schools, inter-

national law is now being taught in an increasing number
of law schools and is being made obligatory. Introductory
courses and advanced courses on international law as well
as seminars are being offered. The reasons for this increase
lie not only in the general world situation and in the particular position of the United States, but also stem partly
from the particular, professional character of the American law school. It has been recognized and expressed in
many recent articles that international law is becoming
more and more *necessary* for the practicing lawyer, particularly in a metropolitan practice. The practicing lawyer is no longer seen exclusively as handling his client's
case in court, but also as a counselor, adviser, drafter,
and negotiator out of court.

The teaching of international law in American law
schools has not only increased but this teaching has also
been expanded into what is now known as "international
legal studies." This expansion is generously subventioned
by the Ford Foundation through grants to leading law
schools. At the same time the American Society of International Law has greatly expanded its activities and, in
its regular and many new regional meetings, also treats
apart from international law and international organization, a great number of topics belonging to international legal studies, such as organizing business abroad,
legal aspects of foreign investment, problems of international taxation, extraterritorial effects of antitrust laws,
legal problems of the American manufacturer in the European Common Market, and so on. As for the contents
and methods of this new branch of international legal
studies,[27] Dean Griswold stated a few years ago [28] that
they will continue to be based on international law and
international organization, but that they will go farther,
although exclusively devoted to legal problems. They will
include also comparative law and conflict of laws and the

leading aspects of international transactions of the American government, American corporations, and citizens. This corresponds to "transnational law." Judge Philip C. Jessup, a great scholar in the science of international law, devoted some of his talents to explorations on the periphery of this science and arrived at certain proposals *de lege ferenda.*[29] In a study dealing with particular cases, where no easy answer was at hand to solve the problems of jurisdiction and of what law governs, he suggested a possible use not only of international law but also of municipal law and conflict of laws, and spoke tentatively of "transnational law." But it is not a question of generally mixing up all types of law; the problem discussed by Judge Jessup arose in very particular and unusual cases. It is also restricted now to legal problems posed by international economics. This development concerning "transnational law" is by no means new or unique. On the Continent, Erler[30] had emphasized so-called international economic law. In problems of international economics, he pointed out, municipal laws are closely interwoven with international law; there is also a strong interconnection here between public and private law, both municipal and international private law.

For this "transnational" law we already have a new casebook by Katz and Brewster.[31] The sophisticated authors skeptically state that such phrases as "international legal order" or "international community" do not necessarily mean that these things do exist in fact. Being skeptical of the existence of an international community or of what it consists, they start their inquiry "with the practical everyday experience of individuals, business corporations and governments which engage in productive transactions spanning national boundaries."[32] The authors concentrate on "foreignness" and how that affects "a lawyer's job." Each problem is studied from the angle of opportunities and risks

under the foreigner's own municipal law, under the foreign
law, and under international law. It is an interesting book
and contains many useful cases and materials. The authors
are fully justified in stating that this book is a departure
from the familiar teaching materials in the international
field. On the other hand, it is certainly not a casebook on
international law; nor do the authors make any such claim,
to the contrary, they themselves declare that "they do not
reach the actual and potential role of international law
in providing a framework for international governmental
relations and settling international disputes which threaten
the peace.[33]

V

The preceding remarks are restricted to the science of
international law in different countries of the democratic
occidental world. But in order to see the change in full
depth it is necessary also to examine the science of international law outside of the democratic occidental world.
It is not possible here to go into any details. Only a few
words will be said in order not to leave the picture incomplete.

There are, first, the countries of the totalitarian communistic regime, whether or not they belong to the occident.
The Soviet science of international law is the leading one
in this group. It has been studied often by writers of, or
living in, countries of the democratic occidental world.
Although there are outstanding international lawyers in the
Soviet Union who, like Professor Tunkin, have a perfect
knowledge of the classic law of nations and are fully ac-
quainted with the science of international law in the different languages of the democratic occident, the ideological
basis, the political goals and concepts, the fact of being
bound by the "party line," the attack against rules of

international law as having been made by the "capitalists,"
all that is reflected even in questions of what looks to be
a problem of theoretical construction.[34]

There are, second, the countries of non-occidental civilization, even if they are democratic. Here belong particularly
the many new states of Asia and Africa which have become
independent since 1945. The Indian science of international
law may be named as representative. Even this development is not without precedent. The Latin-American republics, although now independent for one and a half centuries,
overwhelmingly Catholic, and emphasizing with pride their
belonging to the occidental culture, have, through their
statesmen and international lawyers, developed for a hundred years a series of "doctrines" all destined to weaken
norms and institutions of general international law as a
protest and defense of the weaker states against the powerful ones, first of Europe, later of the United States. And
they have done so with considerable success, as the development of Pan Americanism and now the Charter of Bogotá
prove. It is therefore not to be wondered if Indian international lawyers invoke, e.g., the Calvo clause.

These new states of non-occidental culture attack certain
norms and institutions of general international law as having been made by "colonialist" powers of Europe exclusively
in their own interest—rules to which these countries have
never consented, which belong only to the "general" customary western, but not to "universal," international law
and are, in consequence, not binding on them. An extremely
interesting example of this approach is the study by Judge
Guha Roy dealing specifically with the diplomatic protection
of citizens abroad.[35] It is also instructive to study the speech
made recently by the Indian representative on the Security
Council on the occasion of the incorporation of Goa by force
into India.[36] The defense and accusation, based on general
international law, by the Portuguese representative was for

the Indian representative only an "echo of the past." "Who gave Portugal," he asked, "sovereign rights for any part of India they occupied illegally and by force? Who gave them that right? Not the Indian people." And coming to the point of the science of international law, he remarked:

> There can be no question of aggression against your own frontier . . . and if any narrow-minded legalistic considerations, considerations arising from international law, were written by European international law writers, these writers are, after all, part of the atmosphere of colonialism.

The writer began this comment in the philosophical mood of "being amazed" at the change in international law and its science between 1911 and 1961. The change is indeed great. But it is probable that the change will be much greater and more radical fifty years from now.

---

[1] Compare, e.g., in German, the then celebrated treatise on international law by Franz von Liszt with the 1959 treatise by Alfred Verdross, or, in English, the first edition of Oppenheim's treatise with the latest edition by Lauterpacht.

[2] See "The Systematic Problem of the Science of International Law," above.

[3] See, as a recent example, the abundance of international and municipal "cases," quoted from the original sources, in 1 GEORG DAHM, VÖLKERRECHT (1958).

[4] See, e.g., Edwin D. Dickinson, *International Law: An Inventory*, 33 CALIF. L. REV. 506–49 (1945).

[5] WALTER SCHIFFER, THE LEGAL COMMUNITY OF MANKIND (1954).

[6] Hegel, for whose dialectic philosophy the sovereign state was "the reality of ethical idea," came to the conclusion that international law cannot even be thought, that it is *denkunmoeglich*. The influence of Hegel's glorification of the sovereign state finds expression in recent decades in the science of international law of the totalitarian states, whether fascist or communist. But there were always deniers whose denial was based merely on an analytical critique: e.g., Austin.

[7] Likewise, the doubts of the Neo-Thomist scholar Jean Dabin, as to whether international law is really law in the full sense, stem from an analytical critique.

[8] See HANS MORGENTHAU, POLITICS AMONG NATIONS (1948).

9 GRENVILLE CLARK and LOUIS SOHN, WORLD PEACE THROUGH WORLD LAW (2nd ed. 1960).

10 See Professor Lissitzyn's book review in 1959 CORNELL L. Q. 293–95.

11 That is why the occasional remark by W. Friedmann that the book is an exercise in drafting rather than a contribution to contemporary international law can be justified.

12 THE STUDY OF INTERNATIONAL LAW (1955).

13 See the special number: *Post-War Thinking on the Rule of Law*, 50 MICH. L. REV. 483–613 (1961). W. B. Harvey (*ibid.* at 487–500) distinguishes three concepts: the constitutional (A. V. Dicey), the American (due process of law), and traditional natural law. See also W. W. Bishop, *The International Rule of Law* (*Ibid.* at 553–74). See further, e.g., Judge Robert N. Williams, *World Rule of Law*, 63 W. VA. L. REV. 118–29 (1961); W. MCCLURE, WORLD LEGAL ORDER (1960).

14 See its pamphlet: BASIC FACTS (1961). It publishes the JOURNAL, THE BULLETIN, and newsletters, as well as special monographs.

15 It has also published reports on the rule of law in the United States, Italy, and the Federal Republic of Germany (1958), three reports on Hungary, two on Tibet, and one against apartheid in the Union of South Africa. See also Dudley B. Bonsal (American member of the International Commission of Jurists), *The Judiciary and the Bar*, 40 TEXAS L. REV. 2–17 (1961).

16 We may recall the old French Association: La Paix par le Droit.

17 On the rule of law and world law, see also the special number: *Next Steps in Extending the Rule of Law*, 30 NOTRE DAME LAW. (1961).

18 ROSCOE POUND, A WORLD LEGAL ORDER (1959).

19 ARTHUR LARSON, DESIGN FOR RESEARCH IN INTERNATIONAL RULE OF LAW 111 (1961).

20 See his dissenting opinions as a judge of the International Court of Justice; and his last book, LE DROIT INTERNATIONAL NOUVEAU (1960).

21 F. V. GARCÍA AMADOR, INTRODUCCIÓN AL ESTUDIO DEL DERECHO INTERNACIONAL CONTEMPORÁNEO (1959).

22 C. WILFRED JENKS, THE COMMON LAW OF MANKIND (1958). As to critical review articles, see R. A. Falk and S. M. Mendlowitz, *Some Criticisms of C. W. Jenks' Approach to International Law*, 1961 RUTGERS L. REV. 1–31; Julius Stone's review article in INTERNATIONAL STUDIES 414–41 (1960).

23 See this writer's editorial in 55 AM. J. INT'L L. 951–58 (1961). We read also in J. M. Hendry's *Canada and Modern International Law*, 39 CAN. B. REV. 59–77 (1961): "Our goal is the establishment of the international Rule of Law" (p. 63). It needs a value-oriented jurisprudence: "Aiding our quest for a new international legal order is the revival, in some form, of natural law doctrines" (p. 62).

24 Cf. Lasswell and McDougal, in 52 YALE L. J. 203 ff. (1943); McDougal, 50 *ibid.* 1345–55 (1947); *idem*, in 1 AM. J. COMP. L. 24–57

(1952); *idem, International Law, Power and Politics: A Contemporary Conception,* 82 RECUEIL DES COURS 137–258 (1961).

[25] Grant Gilmore, *Legal Realism: Its Cause and Cure,* 70 YALE L. J. 1037 (1961).

[26] CHARLES DE VISSCHER, THEORY AND REALITY IN PUBLIC INTERNATIONAL LAW (English trans. 1957). See this writer's book review in 70 HARV. L. REV. 1331–35 (1957).

[27] Milton Katz, *International Legal Studies: A New Vista for the Legal Profession,* 42 A.B.A.J. 53 (1956); David F. Cavers, *The Developing Field of International Legal Studies,* 47 POL. SCI. REV. 1056–75 (1957); John B. Howard, *International Legal Studies,* 26 U. Chi. L. REV. 577–96 (1959).

[28] REPORT ON HARVARD SCHOOL FOR 1954–55, at 1–11.

[29] PHILIP C. JESSUP, A MODERN LAW OF NATIONS (1948); TRANSNATIONAL LAW (1956), THE USE OF INTERNATIONAL LAW (1959).

[30] G. ERLER, GRUNDPROBLEME DES INTERNATIONALEN WIRTSCHAFTSRECHTS (1956).

[31] MILTON KATZ and KINGMAN BREWSTER, JR., THE LAW OF INTERNATIONAL TRANSACTIONS AND RELATIONS: CASES AND MATERIALS (1960).

[32] *Ibid.* at 3.

[33] *Ibid.* at 4–5.

[34] As a recent example, the defense of the obsolete and fictitious construction of international general customary law as *pactum tacitum,* a construction so dear to nationalistic writers, some time ago: G. I. Tunkin, *Remarks on the Juridical Nature of Customary Norms of International Law,* 49 CALIF. L. REV. 419–30 (1961).

[35] S. N. Guha Roy, *Is the Law of Responsibility of States for Injuries to Aliens a Part of Universal International Law?* 55 AM. J. INT'L L. (1961).

[36] N. Y. Times, December 19, 1961. We speak in the text only of the Indian arguments against Portugese rights under general international law. That the Indian representative defended also the taking of Goa by force, "Charter or no Charter, Council or no Council," is of course a very different matter; for the use of force, except in self-defense against an armed attack, is illegal even for enforcing a right. And here the Indian representative could not refer to a law made by the "colonialists." The U.N. Charter was drafted with the collaboration of India and was voluntarily ratified by India.

PART III

STATES, PERSONS, AND MINORITIES

CHAPTER IX: *The Italo-Austrian Agreement on the Austrian South Tyrol*

ALTHOUGH AUSTRIA is not a party to the Treaty of Peace with Italy of 1947, Part I of that document contains in Section III special clauses concerning Austria [1] and Annex IV [2] contains the text of the provisions agreed upon by the Austrian and Italian governments concerning the Austrian South Tyrol. This agreement must be viewed in the light of Austria's long fight for the Southern Tyrol, which goes back to the Paris Peace Conference of 1919 and even to 1914-15.

Two different problems are involved. The first problem is the territorial one.[3] Italian irredentism had, long before World War I, coveted those parts of the old Austria which were inhabited by an Italian-speaking population. That meant, in the case of Southern Tyrol, the province of Trento. In 1914-15, Italy, which had remained neutral at the outbreak of the war, carried on negotiations with Austria and, on the other hand, with Great Britain and France. Austria was unwilling to cede the Southern Tyrol, but Great Britain and France promised to Italy in the secret London Treaty of April, 1915, among many other things, the cession of the Southern Tyrol up to the strategic

frontier of the Brenner Pass as a prize for her entry into
the war on the side of the Entente Powers.

President Woodrow Wilson's Fourteen Points, the agreed
basis of the peace settlement, provided in Point 9: "A re-
adjustment of the frontiers of Italy should be effected along
clearly recognizable lines of nationality." Such clearly
recognizable lines of nationality had existed for a thousand
years. They passed through the Salurner Klause; south of
it was the Italian-inhabited province of Trento, north of it
the Austrian, German-speaking, Southern Tyrol including
Meran and Bozen. Italy should have obtained the province
of Trento. True, vis-à-vis Great Britain and France, she
could invoke the secret London Treaty, but the United
States was not bound by this treaty, and Wilson's point 9,
in conformity with the basic principle of national self-determination, was clearly in favor of Austria's retaining
the German-speaking part of the Southern Tyrol. The
Italian delegation at the Paris Peace Conference prepared
for a difficult battle with Wilson to obtain the frontier of
the Brenner Pass, and was agreeably surprised to get it
without difficulty, merely because President Wilson did not
know the facts: "Already, the President had, unfortunately,
promised the Brenner Pass boundary to Orlando, which gave
to Italy some 150,000 Tyrolese Germans—an action which
he subsequently regarded as a great mistake and deeply
regretted. It had been done before he had made a careful
study of the subject. . . ." [4]

The Austrian delegation at the Peace Conference had
fought desperately, but unsuccessfully, for the Austrian
Southern Tyrol.[5] The Austrian National Assembly resolved,
on September 6, 1919,[6] that "Austria expects that the
League of Nations will as soon as possible make good the
incomprehensible injustice inflicted upon the Southern
Tyrol."

This cession of the purely Austrian part of the Southern Tyrol, the German-speaking inhabitants of which had been Austrians for centuries, the land of Walther von der Vogelweide and of Andreas Hofer, a cession without a plebiscite, in open contradiction to Wilson's Point 9, remained during the whole inter-war period the main obstacle to good-neighborly relations between Austria and Italy. This cession led to the Austrian demand for territorial revision; to a real popular movement, especially in the Northern Tyrol; to demonstrations and symbolical acts; and to a rich literature on the subject.[7]

The second problem was that of the protection of the Austrian minority. The Paris Peace Conference did not impose special treaties for the protection of national minorities upon the Great Powers. Italy was, therefore, not bound by such treaty, and the League of Nations could not interfere. Democratic Italy had, however, not only given such promises unilaterally; these promises were also made internationally binding by their acceptance by the Peace Conference and by their insertion in Clemenceau's note to the Austrian Peace Delegation of September 2, 1919;[8] in addition the Austrian note of September 6, 1919,[9] emphasized that "the National Assembly expects that the promises given in the reply will be fulfilled by the Powers."

Democratic Italy kept these promises. But with Mussolini's fascism came one of Europe's worst examples of forcible denationalization.[10] Mussolini's thesis that fascist Italy was not bound by declarations made by pre-fascist governments involved, of course, a violation of international law. This policy of Italianizing the German-speaking mountain peasants in the *Alto Adige,* as the Austrian Southern Tyrol was now called, naturally impaired Italo-Austrian relations still further. In the great debate on the Southern Tyrol in the Austrian Parliament on February 23, 1928,

even a man so little nationalistic as the Austrian Chancellor
Dr. Seipel had, in cautious words, to recognize the difficulties arising out of the treatment of the Southern Tyrolese
by Italy.[11] Mussolini answered immediately by a speech in
Rome, in which he coined the sarcastic phrase: Austria is
what she is.

True, Mussolini's fear of an *Anschluss* made him, during
the 1930's, the quasi-protector of Austria; and, in 1934,
when Chancellor Dollfuss was murdered in the National
Socialist revolt in Vienna, Mussolini was ready to march
into Austria to prevent her annexation by Hitler. But
nothing was changed with regard to the Austrian minority
in the Southern Tyrol.

When Austria was annexed in 1938 by a powerful
Germany, Mussolini was unable to do anything against it.
But Hitler, the fanatical nationalist, was capable of political
expediency. In his Rome visit he solemnly promised Italy
the retention of the Brenner Pass frontier, abandoning a
mistreated German-speaking minority to its fate. By Hitler's treaties with Italy of 1939 and 1941, the Austrians in
the Southern Tyrol were free to opt for return to the Reich;
but if they did not so opt they were held to "deserve neither
protection nor the privilege of claiming collective rights as
a German minority."

It is understandable that Austria hoped that the present
peace settlement would correct Wilson's error. Austria
was, therefore, deeply disappointed, as the Paris Council
of Foreign Ministers in 1946, which took from Italy such
overwhelmingly Italian cities as Pola and Trieste, decided
against the return to Austria of the purely Austrian, German-speaking part of the Southern Tyrol. The disappointment and the resentment grew deeper when the Council
rejected the case for "minor frontier rectifications," presented by the Austrian Foreign Minister Dr. Karl Gruber,
who had been invited to submit this case.

Although the treaty for the re-establishment of an independent and democratic Austria is only in the making, the peace treaty with Italy of 1947 already lays down that Italy's frontier will remain at the Brenner Pass.[12] The only clause in favor of Austria is Part I, Section VIII, Article X, paragraph 1: "Italy shall enter into or confirm arrangements with Austria to guarantee free movement of passenger and freight traffic between the North and East Tyrol." This clause will remove a longstanding Austrian complaint.[13]

It was under these circumstances that Italy and Austria, at the Paris Peace Conference of 1946, both on the margins of the Conference, both representing countries in a terrible plight, began direct and independent negotiations, carried on by the Italian Prime Minister Alcide de Gasperi and the Austrian Foreign Minister Dr. Karl Gruber. These two men undoubtedly felt that the time had come to pave the way for good-neighborly relations between Italy and Austria. They must have felt that their two countries, although divided by historical events long antedating World War I, were bound by common ties as countries of a great and ancient culture, as countries definitely belonging to western Christian civilization.

These negotiations led to an agreement, the original English text of which was signed by the two parties at Paris on September 5, 1946, transmitted to the Paris Conference on the following day, and which now constitutes Annex IV of the Treaty of Peace with Italy. This brief agreement is basically a treaty for the protection of the German-speaking minority in the Southern Tyrol. From this point of view alone the agreement is highly interesting. For current peace settlements have abandoned the idea of international treaties for the protection of national minorities.[14] The Potsdam Agreement and the attitude taken by the United States and the United Kingdom at the Paris

Peace Conference of 1946, an attitude in favor of assimilation rather than of perpetuation of racial minorities, is certainly very different from the attitude taken by the Paris Peace Conference of 1919. The new idea of the international protection of "human rights" is a different idea which does not include specific minority rights, although the problem of the protection of minorities is bound to come up again within this new framework.[15]

The first paragraph of the agreement deals with the protection of the German-speaking minority in the Austrian Southern Tyrol, no longer called *Alto Adige*, but Bolzano Province. The German-speaking inhabitants of this province and of the neighboring bilingual townships of the Trento Province are assured of complete equality with Italian-speaking inhabitants within the framework of special provisions to safeguard the ethnic character and the cultural and economic development of the German-speaking element. In particular they are granted elementary and secondary teaching in the mother tongue, parity of the German and Italian languages in public offices and official documents and equality of rights in candidacy for public office, with a view to reaching a more appropriate proportion of employment between the two ethnical groups. In order to abolish fascist measures, they are granted bilingual topographic naming and the right to re-establish German family-names, which had been Italianized in recent years. There should be mentioned here also point (a) of paragraph 3, by which the Italian government pledges itself, in consultation with the Austrian government and within one year from the signing of the present treaty, to revise in a spirit of equity and broadmindedness the question of the options for citizenship resulting from the 1939 Hitler-Mussolini agreements.

The provisions of paragraph 1 are on the lines of the 1919 minorities treaties. The rights transcend "human rights"; they are specific minority rights. They reject the philosophy of assimilation; they are based not only on the preservation of the Austrian Tyrolese in their racial, linguistic, and cultural character but they also provide means for the cultural and economic development of the Tyrolese as a different ethnical group from the Italians. They are also on the lines of the 1919 minorities treaties in that they grant only individual, not collective, minority rights; they protect the individuals belonging to a national minority, but do not recognize the minority as such as a legal entity.

But paragraph 2 of the agreement goes considerably farther than the 1919 minority treaties. It grants to the Austrian Tyrolese regional autonomy, the exercise of autonomous legislative and executive regional powers. Two ways of granting collective minority rights exist: cultural autonomy and territorial autonomy.[16] Political or territorial autonomy, which is possible only in the case of a national minority compactly settled in a certain area, was granted after World War I, to the Podkarpatska Rus, the Aaland Islands, and the Territory of Memel. It has a territorial basis, embraces all individuals, including those not belonging to the minority, living in this area, and extends to all matters, not only to strictly cultural minority matters. It makes use, for the purpose of the protection of a national minority, of the device of decentralization by regional autonomy with a unitarian state.[17] Cultural autonomy,[18] on the other hand, is granted on a personal basis, to all individuals of the minority, wherever they live in the state. It recognizes the national minority as such, but as a personal group, with autonomous competence restricted to cultural matters. A cultural autonomy can also be locally determined, as long as it is on a personal basis and restricted to all or certain cultural matters.[19]

The true nature of the regional autonomy of paragraph 2 of the agreement will depend on the framework within

which the said provisions of autonomy apply, a framework
to be set up by Italy in consultation with local, representative, German-speaking elements. It looks like a new combination of cultural and territorial autonomy. It is territorial
in so far as it seems not to be restricted to strictly cultural
matters; but it is a locally determined cultural autonomy
in so far as it does not apply to all, but only to the German-
speaking, inhabitants of this area.

Paragraph 3 of the agreement, apart from the revision
of 1939 options and a pledge for free traffic between
northern and eastern Tyrol—in the latter respect Italy is
internationally bound by Article X, paragraph 1, of the
Peace Treaty—envisages the mutual recognition of the
validity of certain degrees and university diplomas, and, in
the economic field, facilitating of Austro-Italian border
traffic. But the agreement contains nothing about an Italo-
Austrian Customs Union, a project sometimes discussed
in England, though strongly resented by the Soviet Union
and the states under her influence.

The Italo-Austrian agreement was praised as a principal
achievement during, although outside of, the Paris Peace
Conference of 1946, and was hailed by the Western Powers
as a "very constructive step." But the equitable and beneficial purpose of the agreement and its success will depend
on legal problems, influenced by political considerations.
The minority rights of paragraph 1 depend on Italian
legislation "already enacted or awaiting enactment." The
regional autonomy of paragraph 2 depends equally on
Italian legislation. The carrying out of paragraph 3 depends
on Italian action and on the conclusion of further special
Austro-Italian agreements. The agreement is thus rather
a program awaiting implementation.

But the legal status of the agreement itself has to be
considered in the first line. This agreement is, no doubt,
an international treaty which has been signed, but needs,

it seems, ratification by Italy and Austria. The ratification by Austria will not prove to be easy politically. For, after all, the agreement implicitly renounces Austria's territorial claim, a question on which most Austrians and, particularly the North Tyrolese, feel very strongly. The agreement did not encounter a good reception by the political parties of Austria and caused resentment in North Tyrol. It is, finally, to be noted that the agreement is not put under the guarantee of the Allies, who, by Article X, paragraph 2, simply "take note" of this agreement.

And yet it is earnestly to be hoped that real, good-neighborly relations between Italy and Austria can be established. This will be to the benefit of the South Tyrolese and to the benefit of the two countries. It will promote not only the material but also the spiritual regeneration of Europe, of which Austria and Italy form so important a part. It will benefit the world and the United Nations. A basic precondition for the success of the United Nations, more vital than discussions about its Charter, is the conclusion of sound and just postwar settlements acceptable to all nations. A solid house must be built upon firm ground, not on shifting sand.

[1] Article X.

[2] September 5, 1946.

[3] See JOSEF L. KUNZ, DIE REVISION DER PARISER FRIEDENSVERTRÄGE VIENNA, 16–18, 209–10 (1932).

[4] 2 RAY STANNARD BAKER, WOODROW WILSON AND WORLD SETTLEMENT 146 (1922).

[5] 2 TÄTIGKEITSBERICHT DER ÖSTERREICHISCHEN FRIEDENSDELEGATION 210–12 (1919); see also the Austrian note on the Austrian Southern Tyrol: 1 *ibid.* at 140–41, 159–60.

[6] 2 TÄTIGKEITSBERICHT 629.

[7] F. KLEIN, DIE REVISION DES ST. GERMAINER VERTRAGES (1920); GRABMEYR, SÜDTIROL (1919); H. VOLTELINI, A. VERDROSS, W. WINKLER, DEUTSCH-SÜDTIROL (1925); A. VERDROSS, DIE RECHTLICHE LAGE DEUTSCH-SÜDTIROLS (1926); P. HERRE, DIE SÜDTIROLER FRAGE (1927); MAYREITER, DIE LITERATUR ÜBER SÜDTIROL (1926).

8 "Ainsi qu'il résulte des déclarations très nettes faites par le Président du Conseil des Ministres d'Italie au Parlement de Rome, le Gouvernment Italien se propose d'adopter une politique largement libérale envers les nouveaux sujets de race allemande, pour ce qui concerne leur langue, leur culture et leurs interêts éconcmiques."—2 TÄTIGKEITSBERICHT 323.

9 2 *ibid.* at 330.

10 See, apart from the literature quoted in note 7, S. M. BOUTON and C. H. HERFORD, ENGLISH AND AMERICAN VOICES ABOUT THE GERMAN SOUTH TYROL (1925); FINGELLER, DIE WAHRHEIT ÜBER SÜDTIROL (1918–26); C. H. HERFORD, THE CASE OF GERMAN SOUTH TYROL AGAINST ITALY (1926); F. K. HENNERSDORF, SÜDTIROL UNTER ITELIENISCHER HERRSCHAFT (1926); REUT-NICOLUSSI, TYROL UNDER THE AXE OF FASCISM (1930); see also for a brief report, Josef L. Kunz, *Italian Rule in German South Tyrol*, 5 FOREIGN AFFAIRS 500–505 (1927).

11 Fascist Italy pursued the same policy of Italianization toward her minority of four hundred thousand Yugoslavs.

12 Part I, § 1, art. I, lays down that "the frontiers of Italy shall, subject to the modifications set out in Articles II (France), III, XI (Yugoslavia), IV, XXII (Free Territory of Trieste), be those which existed on January 1, 1938."

13 The British Foreign Secretary Bevin had, on June 4, 1946, called the complication of Austrian rail transport caused by the amputation of South Tyrol "silly" (N.Y. Times, June 26, 1946, p. 10).

14 See "The Future of the International Law for the Protection of National Minorities," pp. 202–11, below.

15 The United Nations Human Rights Commission has appointed a subcommittee for the prevention of discrimination and protection of minorities.

16 See Josef L. Kunz, *Prolegomena zu einer allgemeinen Theorie des internationalen Rechtes nationaler Minderheiten*, 12 ZEITSCHRIFT FÜR ÖFFENTLICHES RECHT 221–72 (1932).

17 "La Tchécoslovaquie s'engage à organiser le territoire des Ruthènes au sud des Carpathes sous la forme d'une unité autonome á l'intérieur de l'état tchécoslovaque, munie de la plus grande autonomie compatible avec l'unité de l'état tchécoslovaque."—Czechoslovak Minority Treaty, Art. X.

18 Granted by the Esthonian Law of February 5, 1923.

19 Such as the "local autonomy concerning religious and school questions" granted to the "community of Szekler and Saxons in Transylvania" by Art. XI of the Rumanian Minority Treaty.

ALTHOUGH GENERAL INTERNATIONAL LAW, in order to delimit the spheres of validity of individual national legal systems, delegates in principle to the sovereign states the power to determine the rules for the acquisition and loss of their nationality by their own municipal law, so that the matter of nationality is, likewise in principle, within the exclusive jurisdiction of the states,[1] these states can, of course, conclude treaties on the subject and thus create norms of particular international law concerning nationality. This is being done especially in cases of transfer of territory by treaty and consequent change in the territorial jurisdiction of the states involved.

From feudal times onward the inhabitants of ceded territory shared its fate and owed allegiance to the new sovereign.[2] After the seventeenth century, however, we observe a tendency to protect the persons coming under the new allegiance. The means employed was the institution of option, first appearing in the Capitulation Treaty of the City of Arras of 1640. The option was orginally no more than a *beneficium emigrandi*, granted to all "inhabitants" of the ceded territory. After 1815, the newer form of option developed into a faculty granted to the nationals of the ceding state to retain their old nationality by an act of their own free will. From that time on, option, although still based only on treaty law, became more and more frequent[3] and played an enormous role after World War I, as millions of persons were involved in the new territorial settlements.[4]

As Italy suffers severe losses under the Peace Treaty of 1947, it is pertinent to inquire concerning the nationality and option clauses of this treaty. The purpose of this paper is to analyze these clauses as they stand, to study them in the light of the long history of the option clause and of the experience of the Paris Peace Treaties of 1920, and to investigate the extent to which they follow traditional lines or reveal modifications and innovations.

The territorial losses of Italy under the Treaty are of different kinds.

I. Of no importance in the Treaty are Italy's ephemeral annexations of the Province of Ljubljana[5] and of Dalmatia,[6] nor the setting-up of the "Independent State of Croatia," where Italy had "protective rights" and the nominal king of which was the Duke of Aosta.[7]

II. As to Ethiopia, Italy recognizes by Article XXXIII the sovereignty and independence of that state. Under Article XXXVI, Italian nationals in Ethiopia will enjoy the same juridical status as other foreign nationals but Italy recognizes the legality of all measures of the Ethiopian government annulling or modifying concessions or specific rights granted to Italian nationals, provided such measures are taken within a year from the coming into force of the present treaty.

III. Identical norms are laid down with regard to Albania.[8] Italy recognizes also that the Island of Saseno is part of the territory of Albania and renounces all claims thereto.[9]

IV. Italy renounces all right and title to the Italian colonies in Africa, namely Libya, Eritrea, and Italian Somaliland.[10] According to the Treaty the final disposal of these colonies shall be made jointly by Russia, the United States, Great Britain, and France within one year from the coming into force of the Treaty. Pending final disposal the colonies shall continue under their present (British) administration. Nothing is said as to nationality or a right of option of the inhabitants, natives or Italian citizens.

Under the Versailles Treaty, Germany ceded her colonies to the "Principal Allied and Associated Powers" and undertook the obligation to recognize the final measures taken by these powers. The natives, it was laid down, should be entitled to the diplomatic protection of the government which exercised authority over these territories. The colonies rested therefore, under the sovereignty of the principal powers, exercising this sovereignty in condominium until final disposition, which was made by granting these colonies as B and C mandates to certain mandatory powers under the League of Nations.

The regulation in the Treaty of 1947 is not so clear; Italy only "renounces all right and title" to her colonies but does not cede them to any particular power or powers. It is thus clear that Italy loses her sovereignty over her former colonies with the moment of the coming into force of the Treaty. Who is the sovereign of these colonies from this moment on, "pending final decision"? The Treaty is concluded between Italy and twenty-one "Allied and Associated Powers." Nevertheless it seems to follow from Article XXIII and Annex XI that the "Big Four" are sovereign over the ceded territories, Great Britain only "administering" them. As Italy loses her sovereignty with the coming into force of the Treaty she can no longer exercise any diplomatic protection over the natives. Is this protection to be granted by Great Britain, which administers these colonies as the agent of the four condominium sovereigns? Italian nationals in the former colonies will remain Italian nationals, subject perhaps to expulsion by the administering power.

The final determination can only be brought about by the final disposal of the colonies. Should they be given to one or more UN members in trusteeship [11] everything will depend on the trusteeship agreements; if the model of the League mandates is followed the natives will not become nationals of the trustee but merely "persons under the protection of the trustee." Should Libya, for example, be made into an independent state [12] the natives would become nationals of the new state. In both cases Italian nationals resident there will probably remain Italian nationals.

V. Although the Austrian South Tyrol remains Italian, Italy has pledged herself, under the Italo-Austrian Agreement, reproduced in Annex IV of the Treaty,[13] "to revise in a spirit of equity and broad-mindedness the question of the option for citizenship resulting from the 1939 Hitler-Mussolini agreements."

VI. As to territorial cessions, properly speaking Italy cedes certain small but strategic areas to France,[14] the Dodecanese Islands to Greece,[15] and vast areas—the greater part of the Istrian Peninsula, the island of Pelagosa, and the adjacent islands, as well as the community of Zara and all islands and adjacent islets—to Yugoslavia.[16] It is with regard to these ceded territories that the clauses concerning nationality and option are of particular significance. Whereas the Versailles Treaty gave these clauses separately in the case of each single cession, the Treaty of 1947 has adopted the technique of laying down these clauses in a special part of the Treaty [17] in a uniform way for all cases of cession.

Contrary to earlier treaties, but following the system of the Paris Peace Treaties of 1920, the Treaty of 1947 regulates first the legal consequence of the cession of territory as far as the nationality of the persons involved is concerned. This is theoretically correct and apt to avoid difficulties. For the right to opt is a means to escape a change of nationality; the circle of persons entitled to opt can only be clearly determined on the basis of the knowledge of the circle of persons changing their nationality in consequence of the cession. In this respect Article XIX, paragraph I, provides that Italian citizens who were domiciled in a ceded territory on June 10, 1940, and their children, born after that date, become citizens of the state to which the territory is transferred, with the exception of those who, under paragraph 2, are entitled to opt. This change of nationality is automatic *ipso jure* and takes effect at the date of the coming into force of the Treaty. As a measure to prevent dual nationality, the Treaty provides that these persons upon becoming citizens of the successor state lose their Italian nationality. The change of nationality hits, of course, only Italian nationals; beyond this the standard adopted is the pure principle of domicile, the classic principle which seems to be the most just. Birth in the ceded territory, without domicile there at the critical moment, is, therefore, irrelevant.

Whereas normally the critical moment is that of the coming into force of the treaty, the Treaty of 1947 follows the example of the Versailles Treaty [18] by asking domicile in a critical moment long before the date of the coming into force of the treaty, here June 10, 1940, the date of the Italian declaration of war on Great Britain and France. Thus Italian nationals domiciled in a ceded territory after that date remain Italian nationals; the reason for this innovation is, of course, political. The new institution of "reclamation of the nationality of the Successor" only by special authorization of the "Successor" has not been adopted by the Treaty of 1947.

It is interesting to note that the Treaty of 1947 rests on the traditional position according to which individuals are not subjects in international law and acquire no rights under a treaty which is binding only upon states. Article XIX, paragraph 1, prescribes that the acquisition of the nationality of the successor is brought about only "in accordance with legislation, to be introduced by that State within three months from the coming into force of the Treaty." In consequence it is municipal legislation which operates the change, but France, Greece, and Yugoslavia are internationally bound to enact corresponding laws.

The persons thus acquiring the new nationality have the guarantee that their property, rights, and interests in Italy must be respected by Italy in the same way as that of United Nations nationals and have a right to effect the transfer and liquidation of such property, in accordance with a special agreement to be concluded between Italy and the successor state.[19]

The determination of the conditions of the acquisition of the new nationality, namely "Italian nationality," and "domicile" at the critical moment is governed by Italian law.

Contrary to all precedents, not all the persons (Italian nationals domiciled in the ceded territory at the critical moment) acquire the new nationality but only those who are not entitled to opt.

The Treaty of 1947 recognizes two very different kinds of option:

1. There is, first, what this writer has called the "genuine option," under Article XIX, or option of the nationals of the ceding state in favor of the nationality of the ceding state, and only of such nationals, directly involved in the

cession of territory. Here again, it is provided that the successor state enacts appropriate municipal law concerning the option.

Traditionally all the persons determined, as here, by Italian nationality and domicile on June 10, 1940, who acquire the new nationality, are entitled to opt, so that the circle of persons changing their nationality and the circle of persons entitled to opt were identical. Exclusions from the right to opt were rare.[20] In this respect the Treaty of 1947 involves a profound innovation: of Italian nationals domiciled in a ceded territory on June 10, 1940, only those are entitled to opt "whose customary language is Italian." Whereas option was traditionally a means to enable the persons involved in a territorial cession to show their fidelity to the losing state, regardless of blood and language,[21] the option is here what this writer has called an "ethnical option." Such ethnical option,[22] introduced by the Paris Peace Treaties of 1920 only in cases of the "non-genuine option," has here been, for the first time, made the basis of the genuine option. This ethnical option is, of course, an expression of the principle of nationality, of an era in which nationalism precedes state allegiance. The Treaty of 1947 has dropped the criterium of "race" and has decided the problem of "language"—mother tongue or customary language—in the latter sense. On the other hand this criterium may in certain cases not express the "ethnic" character.[23] We see here, therefore, an emphasis on language alone and on the subjective side of the ethnic character, as the customary language depends on the will of the individual. The criterion of Italian as "customary language" must exist at the time of the coming into force of the Treaty.[24]

The Treaty recognizes, therefore, only a restricted or ethnical option which, in the case of the Dodecanese Islands, is a right of an ethnical minority, but in the case of cessions to Yugoslavia may be a right of the ethnical majority.

Because of this innovation the Treaty of 1947 also takes a new stand concerning the much discussed question of whether persons entitled to opt retain or reacquire their old nationality. Under the Versailles Treaty the change of nationality was automatic, so that option meant a reacquisition of the old nationality, although the problem of a possible retroactive effect of the option came up. Under the Treaty of 1947, only the persons not entitled to opt acquire the new nationality, whereas the persons entitled to opt and who have opted "shall retain Italian citizenship and shall not be considered to have acquired the citizenship of the Successor State." [25] Such persons will become citizens of the successor only with the expiration of the time-limit for option without having exercised the right to opt. In any case only one change of nationality is involved.

Many of the detailed norms concerning option follow traditional lines. The remarkable innovation of the Paris Peace Treaties of 1920 creating a special age for the capacity to opt, namely eighteen years, is here adopted, with the further innovation of an individual right to opt for all married persons—men or women—whether under or over that age. Option on the part of the father or, if the father is not alive, on the part of the mother is automatically to include all unmarried children under the age of 18 years.[26] As to the technique of option, the action must be exercised through a declaration.[27]

The norms concerning property rights of optants [28] follow traditional lines: freedom to take out movable property and transfer funds, provided —a new rule hitting fascist measures—they were lawfully acquired, in the case of emigration to Italy; freedom also to sell movable and immovable property; such sale is, therefore, in the traditional way, merely a right, not a duty.

The Treaty of 1947 contains also certain innovations: (a) Contrary to all previous treaties "the option of the husband shall not constitute an option on the part of the wife"; in consequence an individual right to opt on the part of married women arises, an expression of the movement for the emancipation of women; (b) contrary to the Paris Peace Treaties of 1920 which gave, generally, two years for the exercise of option, the time limit is here one year from the coming into force of the Treaty, and may in fact be only nine months, as the successor has to enact corresponding legislation within three months; (c) contrary to all previous treaties which prescribed emigration of the optants, the Treaty of 1947 leaves it to the discretion [29] of the successor whether it will require emigration. If so, the time limit for emigration is one year from the date when the option was exercised and does, therefore, not coincide with the time limit for option, an innovation, introduced by the Paris Peace Treaties of 1920. But, if prescribed, the emigration must be to Italy, and must be actual emigration, a giving up of the domicile in the ceded territory with an *animus non revertendi*. This is certainly the sense of the phrase: "move to Italy."

As to juridical persons, Annex XIV, paragraph 12, gives certain companies the right to remove their *siège social* to Italy with the benefits of paragraph 11 of this Annex, provided they fulfil the following conditions: having been incorporated under Italian law; having their *siège social* in a ceded territory; having more than 50 per cent of their capital owned by persons who opt for Italian nationality under the Treaty and move to Italy; finally, having the greater part of their activity carried on outside the ceded territory.

As in the Paris Peace Treaties so in the Treaty of 1947 there are important *lacunae:* no norms concerning the right to opt of illegitimate children, of unmarried persons under eighteen years of age who have no parents, of adopted children, of insane persons, and of persons in jail. Contrary to most of the Paris Peace Treaties, the Treaty of 1947 contains no norms guaranteeing the exercise of the right to opt. Many problems of option procedure are not dealt with, problems of examining and verifying the prerequisites for option, and so on. In these and other matters, differences and difficulties may arise. Much is left to the municipal law of the successor states. No doubt special agreements between Italy and each successor state for carrying-out these treaty norms will be necessary.

2. Article XX of the Treaty grants a "non-genuine" option. This writer speaks of a "non-genuine" option because it is not connected with the territorial cession; it is an option of persons, not connected with the ceded territory, and in favor of the successor state. This new type of option was introduced by the Versailles Treaty in favor of new states on an ethnical basis and developed in the case of the dismemberment of the Austro-Hungarian Monarchy.

Under Article XX, paragraph 1, all Italian citizens domiciled on Italian territory whose customary language is Serbian, Croatian or Slovene have a right to opt for Yugoslavia. All the other norms concerning this option are identical with those concerning the "genuine" option under Article XIX. But there are important differences: (a) the critical moment is here the date of the coming into force of the Treaty; (b) it is no real option, or a unilateral, constitutive act of the optant, but rather what the Versailles Treaty called a "reclamation of nationality," an innovation of that treaty. The persons in question have only a right to file a request with a Yugoslav diplomatic or consular representative in Italy. They acquire Yugoslav nationality only if the Yugoslav authorities accept their request, which is entirely discretionary with them. Yugoslavia will diplomatically communicate to Italy lists of persons who have thus acquired Yugoslav nationality; from the moment of this communication these persons automatically lose their Italian nationality.

Italy has no right to enact municipal law with regard to this option, but "may" require emigration from Italy.[30]

VII. A special case is that of the Free Territory of Trieste.[31] It is, under the Treaty, not a case of a ceded territory but of the creation of a new state. Under Article VI of the Permanent Statute, Italian citizens domiciled in the area of the Free Territory on June 10, 1940, and their children born after that date became *ipso jure* original citizens of the Free Territory and in the same moment lose their Italian nationality. Although the Permanent Statute will come into force only as determined by the U.N. Security Council, Italian sovereignty over that area comes to an end with the coming into force of the Treaty; at this date, therefore, the change of nationality of the persons involved will take place.

Article VI, paragraph 2, of the Permanent Statute grants a restricted right of "ethnical option" to those persons whose customary language is Italian. All the other rules are identical with those under Articles XIX and XX, but there are the following differences: (a) The conditions for the exercise of this right of option are to be laid down, in accordance with the forms of the Permanent Statute, by the constitution of the Free Territory. (b) The time limit for this option is only six months, running from the date of the coming into force of the constitution. (c) Contrary to Article XIX all persons, Italian nationals, and domiciled there on June 10, 1940, acquire the new citizenship whether they are entitled to opt or not. In consequence those entitled to opt for Italy who do so opt reacquire Italian nationality; hence a change of nationality twice. For this there are good reasons, as the overwhelming majority have Italian as a customary language. If the norm of Article XIX had been adopted here, the Free Territory might, at the moment of the coming into force of the Treaty, have no original citizens at all. (d) Again the option is limited and constitutes here a right of the ethnical majority. Italian nationals, domiciled there on June 10, 1940, whose customary language is, for example, Slovene are excluded from any right to option, not only for Italy, but also for Yugoslavia.

---

1 But not wholly; for the freedom of the states is limited by a superior norm of general international law, prescribing that individuals, on which the states confer their nationality, must have qualified points of contact with the state in question. *Nationality Draft of the Harvard Research in International Law*, 23 AM. J. INT'L L. (supp. 1929); Convention on the Conflict of Nationality Laws, 1930, Art. I (League of Nations, C. 351, M. 145 [1930] V); VERDROSS, VÖLKERRECHT 133 (1937); H. W. BRIGGS, THE LAW OF NATIONS 157, 165 (1938). That is why the language of the Permanent Court of International Justice in its Advisory Opinion No. 4 is not wholly unobjectionable.

2 This was common juridical doctrine; see the "règle de Pothier": "Lorsque une province est démembrée de la couronne, les habitants changent de domination." Even in England, notwithstanding the dogma of perpetual allegiance, "When the King cedes by treaty, the inhabitants of the ceded territory become aliens."

3 For a full historical and theoretical study of option see: 1 JOSEF L. KUNZ, DIE VÖLKERRECHTLICHE OPTION 1–170, 301–25 (1925).

4 For a full study of nationality and option in the Versailles and St. Germain Peace Treaties, see 1 KUNZ *op. cit.* at 171–300, 326–28, and 2 *ibid.* (1928).

5 Annexed by royal decree, law of May 3, 1941 (text in RAPHAEL LEMKIN, AXIS RULE IN OCCUPIED EUROPE 584–85 [1944]).

6 Annexed by royal decree of May 18, 1941 (LEMKIN, *op. cit.* at 587–88).

7 He never went there, and he resigned on July 31, 1943.

8 Articles XXVI, XXX.

9 Article XXVIII.

10 Article XXIII, Annex XI.

11 Although under Art. LXXVII, para. 1(b), of the U.N. Charter the trusteeship system is to apply to "territories which may be detached from enemy States as a result of the Second World War," para. 2 of this article leaves it entirely "for subsequent agreements as to which territories in the foregoing categories will be brought under the trusteeship system and upon what terms."

12 U.N. Charter, Art. LXXVIII.

13 See "The Italo-Austrian Agreement on the Austrian South Tyrol," above.

14 Treaty of 1947, Articles II and VI.

15 Article XIV.

16 Articles III and XI.

17 Articles XIX, XX, further Annex XIV, paras. 10–12.

[18] Versailles Treaty, Art. XXVI, para. 2; Art. XCI, para. 3; Art. CXII, para. 2.

[19] Annex XIV, para. 11.

[20] No option in the case of Alsace-Lorraine (Versailles Treaty, Annex to Art. LXXIX) and Neutral Moresnet (Versailles Treaty, Art. XXXII).

[21] It is well known that many Alsatians, German in blood and language, opted under the Treaty of 1871 for France.

[22] The ethnical option was newly introduced in the Versailles Treaty only in cases of "non-genuine" option, either for new states (Czechoslovakia, Versailles Treaty, Art. LXXXV, paras. 1, 3; Poland, Art. XCI, para. 4, para. 9) or, further developed as "option according to race and language" by the St. Germain Treaty, Art. LXXX, and the Trianon Treaty, Art. LXIV, finally only as an option for the "State of the race" in the Turkish Peace Treaty of Lausanne 1923, Articles XXXII, XXXIV.

[23] An Italian national, domiciled on June 10, 1940, in a territory ceded to Yugoslavia, who is, perhaps, a Slovene in blood and has Slovene as his mother tongue is entitled to opt for Italy if his "customary" language is Italian.

[24] Persons, "who were domiciled on June 10, 1940," but "whose customary language is Italian."

[25] Art. XIX, para. 2.

[26] This formula is clearer and better than the Versailles formula: option on the part of the "parents."

[27] The term "right to opt" can mean either the fulfillment of all the requirements for a valid option or merely the declaration. In the first case a declaration not followed by emigration would not be an "exercise" of the right to opt, or an *agere in fraudem legis*, so that the person in question would remain a national of the successor. Under the second hypothesis the successor could expell the person in question as an undesirable alien. The Treaty of 1947 calls the mere declaration the "exercise of option."

[28] Annex XIV, para. 10.

[29] Whereas they "shall" provide for other rules, they "may" require emigration.

[30] The question of interpretation comes up. The treaty uses the phrase "transfer their residence to Yugoslavia." Does that mean emigration? Is "residence" equivalent to domicile? Does the phrase of Art. XX ("transfer their residence to Yugoslavia") have the same legal meaning as the phrase of Art. XIX ("move to Italy")?

[31] Arts. IV, XXI, XXII, Annex VI.

CHAPTER XI: The Future of the International Law for the Protection of National Minorities

FOR TWELVE YEARS (1920-32), down to the time when he left Europe permanently for America, this writer studied intensively the theory of the League system of international protection of national minorities.[1] During the same period, in his capacity as director of the Austrian League of Nations Union and as a member of the Minorities Commission of the International Association of League of Nations Societies—so ably directed by its secretary-general, the French scholar Professor Theodore Ruyssen, an enthusiastic supporter of the League and a great friend of the minorities— he took part in innumerable international conferences all over Europe which dealt with this problem. He listened to minorities discussions at Geneva, knew the outstanding representatives of minorities and majorities, visited the regions of Europe where the minorities problem was most burning (the "Belt of Minorities States"); he attended many discussions between minorities and majorities, sometimes conducted on a high level and in a spirit of co-operation, sometimes leading to the most acrimonious debates, revealing deepest bitterness, dissatisfaction, and even hatred —at conferences, nevertheless, where everybody was supposed to be a full supporter of the League of Nations. From this long experience this writer has become firmly convinced that an adequate solution of the problem, which gave rise to an enormous literature,[2] is one of the conditions prerequisite for an enduring peace in Europe and, therefore, in the world.

In 1932, when this writer left Europe, the year after the collapse of the Vienna Credit-Anstalt and the beginning of the world-wide depression, the year after Japan's invasion of Manchuria—beginning of the end of the League—the year before Hitler's coming into power, the League's minorities system was already in a critical situation. The declaration of the Polish Foreign Minister Colonel Beck in the League Assembly on September 13, 1934, which amounted to an open repudiation of Poland's international minorities obligations, a breach of treaty against which the League did not react effectively, brought the League system to a virtual end and led finally to the complete disappearance of the Minorities Section of the League Secretariat. Important German minorities were Hitlerized and made a tool of the foreign policy of the Third Reich. Under these conditions little was heard about the whole League system of minorities protection several years before the outbreak of World War II.

But now, when the making of a European peace settlement is no longer a remote and theoretical but a practical and urgent problem, the perception that while the making of a "new map of Europe" may possibly prevent the creation of new artificial minorities it cannot, even under the hypothesis of the wisest and most just arrangements, eliminate the problem of national minorities entirely has led to a new discussion of this problem.[3] Just as the League of Nations is studied again in order to discover the extent to which and why it was a failure, so the system of the international protection of national minorities is re-examined and the question whether, and, if so, why, it was a failure is asked: the past experience and its critical analysis is used as a basis for future solutions.

It never will be possible to solve the European problem of national minorities merely by the application of the principle of the "self-determination of nations." The creators of the Paris Peace Treaties were fully aware of this impossibility and tried to supplement the principle of the self-determination of nations by an international law for the protection of national minorities under the guarantee of the League of Nations.

But it must be borne in mind that this experiment constitutes only one of the possible solutions of this problem. Another solution might be sought by purely municipal law. Such an attempt was made by the "law of Nationalities" of the Austrian Empire, based on Article XII of the Constitution of 1867, promising the "inviolable right of each nationality to preserve and develop its nationality and language," a law which became a model for the Paris Minorities Treaties. It tried to reconcile the permanent preservation and development of the national characteristics of each nationality with their living together in a multinational state. Such an attempt can be seen in the nationalities policy of the multinational U.S.S.R.—Stalin was in 1917 People's Commissar of Nationalities—although the Soviet leaders are not inspired by a romantic valuation of national language, folk-lore, and traditions.[4] Municipal legislation for this purpose was enacted in the postwar period by states not bound by minorities treaties, such as Germany and Denmark, or by states bound by such treaties but granting more than they were internationally bound to grant, such as the Estonian Law on Cultural Autonomy.

But the creators of the Paris Peace Treaties, distrusting an equitable solution by municipal law only, imposed international minorities obligations on certain states. Although there was some precedent for the protection of religious minorities, these treaties were an innovation insofar as the treatment by a sovereign state of its own citizens, belonging to national minorities, was subordinated to international law.

In recent literature, the work of Robinson and his colleagues is a scholarly and painstaking research into this experiment. The authors admit that there were many reasons for its failure: the ambiguity of many terms of the minorities treaties, or their vagueness and generality; their too schematic character—failing to distinguish between the very different types of different national minorities; the inadequacy of the substantive law; the failure to recognize the minorities as collective units; the lack of protection against economic discrimination—all this leading to the wish of the minorities for reform, particularly in the direction of an internationally guaranteed cultural autonomy. There further was the inadequacy of the procedural law and its inadequate handling by the organs of the League, with the striking exception of the Permanent Court of International Justice, and the attitude taken by the Great Powers. The minorities themselves are not free from blame, especially the "strong" German and Hungarian minorities after 1933. There was further the failure of the treaty-bound states to carry out their obligations in their municipal law and to co-operate properly with the League. But the authors attribute the failure of the system, in the first place, to the breakdown of the presuppositions of the whole Versailles system—democracy and economic liberalism—and to the continuously deteriorating general situation of Europe. They reach the conclusion that "despite all the faults and shortcomings the experience of twenty years does not justify the condemnation of a most remarkable experiment."

Professor Sulkowski's pamphlet, on the other hand, is a typical expression of the attitude of the majority peoples in the treaty-bound states. He gives a brief and absolutely correct survey of the origin and contents of the minorities treaties, but restates all the arguments *contra* which were already fully stated by Prime Minister Paderewski at the Paris Peace Conference: the merely particular character of this new international law, which involved a discrimination against the treaty-bound states, damage to their prestige, an unjustified restriction of their sovereignty, a violation of the principle of the equality of states, a humiliation, caused perpetual resentment. While, before World War II, the minorities wanted an extension of the contents of the treaty law, the treaty-bound states wanted an extension of this treaty law to all, or at least to all European, states. This proposal of generalization—politically hopeless because of the resistance of the unbound states and, particularly, of the Great Powers—was used as a means to undermine the whole treaty law, finding a climax in Colonel Beck's repudiation of 1934.

Sulkowski adds to the Paderewski arguments the powerful argument of the later 30's, the making of certain national minorities into fifth columns, undermining the very existence of the treaty-bound states, and reaches the conclusion that the experiment was a failure that should not be repeated. At the most, international law should guarantee to the national minorities only certain fundamental human rights and "leave the task of a more specific regulation of the legal situation of the various national minorities to the interested states."

The solutions, hitherto discussed, tend to preserve the ethnic characteristics of national minorities as minorities. But in a period where nationalism, often in its most fanatic and intolerant forms, is and will be the strongest emotional force in international politics, attempts have been made or are being considered of solving the problem of minorities through their elimination.

There were attempts of eliminating minorities by physical extermination, such as the massacres of Armenians in the Ottoman Empire, the outbreak in Iraq against the Assyrian minority, the horrible extermination of Jewish minorities by National Socialistic Germany in World War II. Certainly no one would dare to propose this method of solution.

There were attempts of a policy of denationalization by force, or the methods of "assimilation" or "absorption" of minorities. The Russification policy of the Czarist Empire towards its border-peoples, the Magyarization policy of the pre-1918 Hungary, the Italianization policy of fascist Italy with regard to its German and Slav minorities are examples. This type of "solution" is, quite apart from ethical considerations, highly questionable from the point of view of practical results: nothing inflames nationalism and irredentism more than oppression.

Other attempts were made at solving the problem through annexation of the territories inhabited by national minorities by the co-national state. The irredentisms of Italy, Serbia, and Rumania are examples. This solution was part of German and Hungarian revisionism, and led to the annexation of the area of the Sudeten Germans by the Munich Agreement of 1938.

Finally, a new type of solution has recently come into the foreground: transfer or exchange of populations, voluntary or compulsory.

The precedent for the voluntary exchange of population is the Greco-Bulgarian Treaty of November 27, 1919.[5] But the purpose of eliminating the national minorities cannot be reached by voluntary exchange. This type of solution was sponsored by Hitler in the German treaties of 1939 with Estonia and Latvia, the treaties of 1939 and 1941 with Italy, of 1930, 1940, and 1941 with the Soviet Union, of

1940 with Rumania, and of 1942 with Croatia.[6] Most of these treaties, which envisaged the transfer of German minorities in these countries into the Reich, were treaties for the unilateral transfer of a German minority: only the treaties with the Soviet Union provide for an exchange of populations. The transfer or exchange was voluntary; and yet the treaties aimed at the elimination of the problem of the minorities. The Austrians in the South Tyrol were free to opt for return into the Reich; if they did not so opt they were protected against forcible expulsion, but by not opting, they were left to the tender mercy of fascist Italy; they were held to "deserve neither protection nor the privilege of claiming collective rights as a German minority." In the case of Germany and the U.S.S.R., the treaties were based on the theory of the "protective right of the mother state."

The precedent for compulsory exchange of populations is the Greco-Turkish Convention of January 30, 1923.[7] This treaty was the outcome of the wish of victorious Turkey to rid herself definitively of her Greek minorities. It is well known that immense miseries were thereby caused to one and a half million Greeks who had been settled in Asia Minor for three thousand years; the problem of these Greek refugees could never have been solved by Greece without the magnificent aid given by the League of Nations. This certainly is a very pessimistic form of solution which brings misery to millions, which creates, in lieu of a minorities problem, an international problem of refugees. It has, therefore, been and is being condemned by the great majority of writers and by the minorities themselves. It has rightly been condemned with regard to the unilateral transfer, evacuation, or compulsory emigration imposed by National Socialist Germany before and during World War II on millions of Europe's population.

Nothing is yet known as to whether the "Big Three" intend to maintain—or even expand or generalize—or to drop the international law for the protection of national minorities. But there are signs that, at least in certain cases, a solution by transfer or exchange of populations—the most pessimistic solution—is favored.

The Soviet-sponsored Polish Committee of National Liberation in Lublin is reported to have concluded agreements with the governments of the Ukrainian,[8] White Russian,[8] and Lithuanian,[9] Soviet Socialist Republics for the voluntary transmigration of hundreds of thousands of Polish and Soviet citizens, affected by the Curzon line boundary or, generally, from each other's country. These agreements are said "to go far beyond the usual population exchange pacts to insure the protection of the best interests of those who desire to move from Poland to the Soviet Union or vice-versa."

On the other hand, proposals were made by writers for the compulsory transfer of the 3,600,000 Germans from Czechoslovakia, as well as for the removal of the millions of Germans [10] in East Prussia and Germany east of the Oder, territories promised to Poland by Stalin "by way of compensation" for taking Poland east of the Curzon line. Such a proposed solution can very well be understood psychologically,[11] but it certainly would have been no solution in effect:[12] apart from human considerations, it would have created an international problem of refugees; it would not have prevented an irredentism; it would have hardly been conducive to an enduring peace in Europe.

It shows the frailty of human nature that individuals and peoples proclaim general principles, but see no contradiction in asking those principles applied to themselves and denied to others. Often at the international minorities conferences in post-1920 Europe, this writer was struck by the double role of many peoples in Europe: accusers, where they constituted minorities; accused, where they formed the majority of the population of a state. This contradiction can now be seen even among American citizens of the same European stock. It is symptomatic that the demand for compulsory transfer of Germans from Poland was made by the Polish Labor Group at New York, whereas the memorandum presented to the President of the United States by the Polish-American Congress [13] asked for the President's assurance, not only "to defend Poland's territorial integrity," but also "to insist that not any part of Poland's population will ever be disposed of or transferred against the really freely expressed will of the Polish people."

[1] Josef L. Kunz, *La Question de la procédure en matière des minorités*, 3 REVUE SOTTILE 69–82 (1925) ; *Some Urgent and Practical Reforms Concerning the International Protection of Minorities*, International Law Association, 1926, PROCEEDINGS; *Der Schutz der nationalen Minderheiten als Rechtsproblem*, BULLETIN INTERNATIONAL DU DROIT DES MINORITÉS (1930) ; *Prolegomena zu einer allgemeinen Theorie des internationalen Rechts nationaler Minderheiten*, 12 ZEITSCHRIFT FÜR ÖFFENTLICHES RECHT 221–72 (1932).

[2] The standard bibliographical work is ROBINSON, DAS MINORITÄTENPROBLEM UND SEINE LITERATUR (1928).

[3] JACOB ROBINSON, *et al.*, WERE THE MINORITIES TREATIES A FAILURE? (1943) ; JOSEPH SULKOWSKI, THE PROBLEM OF INTERNATIONAL PROTECTION OF NATIONAL MINORITIES (1944) ; *The Minorities Problem*, 4 NEW EUROPE No. 6, 10–29 (July–August, 1944).

[4] Erich Hula, *The Nationalities Policy of the Soviet Union* in 11 SOCIAL RESEARCH No. 2 at 168–201 (1944).

[5] WURFBAIN, L'ECHANGE GRÉCO-BULGARE DES MINORITÉS ÉTHNIQUES (1930).

[6] J. B. Schechtmann, *The Option Clause in the Reich's Treaties on the Transfer of Populations*, 38 AM. J. INT'L L. 356–74 (1944). See also H. Wachenheim, *Hitler's Transfer of Populations in Eastern Europe*, 20 FOREIGN AFFAIRS No. 4 at 705–18 (July, 1942).

[7] G. STREIT, DER LAUSANNER VERTAG UND DER GRIECHISCHTÜRKISCHE BEVÖLKERUNGSAUSTAUSCH (1929) ; KIOSSEOGLOU, L'ECHANGE FORCÉ DES MINORITÉS D'APRÉS LE TRAITÉ DE LAUSANNE (1926) ; Ténékides, *Le Statut des minorités et l'échange obligatoire des populations grécoturques*, 31 REVUE GÉNÉRALE DE DROIT INTERNATIONAL PUBLIC 72–88 (1924).

[8] N. Y. Times, September 15, 1944, p. 5.

[9] *Ibid.*, September 25, 1944, p. 6.

[10] ROBERT MACHRAY, THE POLISH-GERMAN PROBLEM (1943).

[11] President Dr. Eduard Benes writes: "Czechoslovakia wishes to avoid any recurrence of the situation which led to Munich. She is

therefore considering the transfer of the greatest possible number of her German inhabitants. . . . "—23 FOREIGN AFFAIRS No. 1 at 36 (October, 1944).

[12] "The Nazi mentality is spreading outside of Germany. Nowadays we speak calmly of tossing millions of human beings from their homes to nowhere in order to get rid of troublesome 'racial minorities.' Hitler set the example in the countries that came under his control, and we seem ready to do the same. . . . "—Gaetano Salvemini, 23 FOREIGN AFFAIRS No. 1 at 58 (October, 1944). Fritz T. Epstein writes that "the transfer solution, in spite of its utter disregard for human rights, is regarded more and more as the only possible way out," but states that "the whole transfer mania is an illusion."—4 NEW EUROPE No. 6 at 29 (July-August, 1944).

[13] N. Y. Times, October 12, 1944, p. 8.

I

THE CREATION of the Free Territory of Trieste is a typical political compromise arrangement and the success of this creation is, to say the least, highly doubtful. But as a new experiment in international administration, it offers great interest. Within the framework of this study only a sketch can be given, although an effort will be made to outline, at least, some of the historical, political, and economic issues involved and the legal problems presented from the point of view of constitutional and international law.

Like Danzig, Trieste looks back on more than a thousand years of history. Incorporated in 791 into Charlemagne's empire, and conquered in 1202 by the Venetians, Trieste—apart from a few years under Napoleon's rule—had been united with the Austrian Empire from 1382 to 1918. Especially since the extension of the Austrian Southern Railway to Trieste in 1857, Trieste served as the principal commercial port of the Austrian Monarchy and enjoyed great prosperity until 1914. Being mainly inhabited by an Italian-speaking population, Trieste had long been coveted by Italian irredentism, had been promised to Italy by the secret London Treaty of April 26, 1915, and had come under Italian sovereignty through the Peace Treaties which brought World War I to an end.

After World War I the Italo-Yugoslav struggle centered around Fiume. In World War II fascist Italy annexed also the provinces of Ljubljana and Dalmatia [1] while Marshal Tito, backed by Moscow, claimed the province of Venezia Giulia and Trieste. On September 3, 1943, Italy, under Marshal Badoglio, surrendered unconditionally to Anglo-American forces and an armistice was signed. Later, Italy became a "co-belligerent." The Venezia Giulia crisis of May-June, 1945, was solved by the Trieste Area Agreement of June 9, 1945, by which the Morgan Line was established. In accordance with this agreement Yugoslav forces were to withdraw from the territory west of the Morgan Line, leaving the latter under Anglo-American occupation until final settlement of the dispute.[2]

Drafting the peace treaty with Italy was a long and delicate process.[3] Many reasons may be cited for the difficulties of the peace makers. In the first place the problem of Trieste is an Italo-Yugoslav problem. Ethnographically, the city is overwhelmingly Italian, yet it was strongly demanded by Yugoslavia. At the meeting of the Council of Foreign Ministers in London (September 11 to October 2, 1945), Yugoslavia presented her claims, including Trieste, through vice-premier Kardelj. The controversial Italo-Yugoslav boundary dispute was not settled. Though strongly pressed, the Yugoslav demands were opposed in Italy by a passionate Italian nationalism, shared even by the Communists under Togliatti. Finally it was agreed at the London meeting that "the boundary line should in the main be governed by ethnic considerations and that regardless of its sovereignty there should be a Free Port at Trieste under international control." The Italian Communists got an offer from Marshal Tito on November 7, 1947, proposing that Trieste might remain Italian territory if Yugoslavia, in exchange, could obtain Goriza. This offer was rejected by Italy.[4]

The question of Trieste is also a Central European problem; for as a commercial port Trieste is of greatest importance to the landlocked countries of Central Europe. This point was taken into consideration by the Council of Foreign Ministers. But the real controversy is directly connected with the East-West split. The "Iron Curtain" runs from Stettin to Trieste. A Slav Trieste would be likely to facilitate the bringing of the whole Danube Basin under Soviet political and economic control. For the Soviet Union, Trieste would be a starting point of further expansion, an important key point for the Slav "Drang nach dem Westen"; for Anglo-America, Trieste is significant in the strategy of "containing" Soviet and communist expansion. Here the two worlds "met and hold each other in equilibrium. In this contest, Italy and Yugoslavia had almost become secondary factors." [5]

The meeting of the Council of Foreign Ministers at Paris (April 25–May 16, 1946) did not advance the settlement of the problem. It was during the Paris Peace Conference that the French foreign minister Georges Bidault, in order to break the deadlock, made the suggestion, "liked by no one," to establish Trieste and its surroundings between Duino and Cittanova as the "Free Territory of Trieste." [6] Even after the creation of the Free Territory had been agreed upon, the Council was divided as to how the independence of Trieste should be assured by the Security Council of the United Nations. The struggle between East and West reappeared in a new form as the controversy over the statute of the Free Territory. The United States wanted a truly international, independent Trieste, protected only by the United Nations.[7] The Soviet Union proposed protection by joint agreement between Italy and Yugoslavia. France suggested protection by the principal Allied Powers. The

United States was anxious to guard against an internal coup and incorporation into Yugoslavia and wished, therefore, to vest the real power in a governor to be appointed by the United Nations, whereas the Soviet Union opposed this proposal as "undemocratic." [8]

Vital differences over the statute proposed for the Free Territory of Trieste existed still at the time when the Council of Foreign Ministers met at New York (November 4 to December 12, 1946). These differences concerned the designation and responsibilities of the governor, the allegiance of the police director, the settlement of disputes, and the problem of customs.[9] However, an arrangement on the basis of the American draft proposals was finally reached.[10] The Council of Foreign Ministers decided also that a Four Power commission be sent to Trieste to make an on the spot investigation of the financial requirements for operating the government of Trieste during the initial months of its existence and of problems in connection with the setting up of the territory's currency and customs regime. This commission made its report to the Council of Foreign Ministers at the meeting held in Moscow between March 10 and April 24, 1947.[11]

II

Although Yugoslavia and Italy had first threatened not to sign, still less to ratify, the Italian Peace Treaty primarily because of the articles concerning Trieste, they did sign it.[12] On December 12, 1946, Secretary Byrnes, as chairman of the Council of Foreign Ministers, wrote to the Security Council, asking it to approve these articles and to take the Free Territory under its guarantee.[13] On January 9, 1947, the Security Council approved the instruments concerning the provisional regime, the Permanent Statute, and the Free Port of Trieste.[14] On April 22, 1947, the Council

of Foreign Ministers, meeting in Moscow, agreed on a draft
providing for reciprocal free trade among Trieste, Italy,
and Yugoslavia, and recommended that the Security Council
put at the disposal of the governor of the Free Territory of
Trieste, if so requested, an amount up to five million dollars
to assist in meeting the pressing needs of the first period.[15]

After the adoption of the instruments concerning the Free
Territory of Trieste, the East-West split was transferred
to the problem of choosing a governor. Candidates proposed
by the western powers were not acceptable to the Soviet
Union; candidates proposed by the latter were not welcome
to the West.[16] In consequence the appointment of a governor
was referred back by the Big Four to the Security Council
and was put on its agenda on June 20, 1947. Naturally the
same deadlock prevailed in the Security Council. The Italian
and Yugoslav governments were asked to consult together
and to recommend a mutually satisfactory candidate by
January 5, 1948.[17] It is not surprising that the two governments could reach no agreement, and up to the time of this
writing the same deadlock has continued in the Security
Council.

III

In the meantime, the Italian peace treaty creating the
Free Territory of Trieste had come into force on September
5, 1947.[18] As the general political situation between West
and East has deteriorated and American policy to "contain
Soviet expansionism" has grown firmer, Italy, a short time
ago considered an enemy, has again gained greater importance in world politics. After the communist political coup
in Czechoslovakia, the Italian elections of April 18, 1948,
became a major contest in the struggle between East and
West. To help Premier Casperri against the Communists,
the three Western Powers recommended the return of the

Free Territory to Italy,[19] and this proposal was made public by Foreign Minister Bidault at the occasion of his visit in Turin. Italy naturally accepted the proposal.[20] As he had done earlier, Marshal Tito again offered Trieste in exchange for Gorizia, a proposal rejected by Italy. The Soviet Union kept silent. A United States note of April 9, 1948,[21] invited the Soviet Union, Great Britain, France, and Italy to begin drafting the changes in the Italian Peace Treaty. But the Soviet Union in a note to the three Western Powers of April 13, 1948,[22] rejected the invitation on the basis that the Peace Treaty had been concluded among twenty-one nations and that it could not be revised by means of correspondence or private conferences of four powers only. The proposal for the return of Trieste probably contributed to the Communists' defeat in the Italian elections; but the provisional, governorless situation in the Free Territory continued. The Italian Peace Treaty is, in Secretary Byrne's words, "unsatisfactory from many points of view"; but he added that no better solution was possible since the Soviet Union was determined not to leave Trieste as a part of Italy.

There was certainly less justification for the establishment of the Free Territory of Trieste than for the creation of the Free City of Danzig after World War I. In the Danzig case the solution was devised to reconcile the principles expressed in two of President Wilson's points, namely national self-determination and Poland's access to the sea. The Trieste solution had little to do with principles, but was a compromise of power politics. Ambassador Tarchiani, the spokesman for Italy at the meeting of the Council of Foreign Ministers, charged that the Italian Peace Treaty "was not in keeping with the principles of the Atlantic Charter and practically ignored Italy's co-belligerency during the war." The Trieste solution was seriously attacked by American writers [23] and ratification was opposed by many in the hearings of the United States Senate.[24] But, as stated by the

U. S. Secretary of State, Mr. Byrnes, without the acceptance of the Free Territory no common peace treaty with Italy would have been possible. Hence, the Western Powers had accepted this solution in the hope that the statute of the Free Territory would guarantee, with the co-operation of all parties concerned, the independence of the people of the area.

At the time of writing there exist four possible solutions of the Trieste situation: The return of the Free Territory to Italy, as proposed by the three Western Powers; the division of the Free Territory, with Zone A, including the city of Trieste, going to Italy, and Zone B to be incorporated into Yugoslavia; the appointment of a governor and the coming into force of the Permanent Statute of the Free Territory as foreseen by the Peace Treaty; and finally the continuation of the present, provisional, governorless situation. At this time the last possibility appears the most likely.

The whole arrangement is a consequence of the fact that Trieste is a focal point in the "international frontier," "the debatable no man's land into which the interests and policies of more than one Great Power penetrate, in which they compete for power and influence, but in which no one Power is supreme." [25] To avoid conflict in the international frontier, many types of compromise solutions have emerged: spheres of influence, protectorates, mandates, trusteeships, "strategic areas," buffer states, the special regime for the City of Tangiers, and others. Sometimes a special, small territory is set up. The Free Territory of Trieste has, therefore, its predecessors such as Sanjak of Alexandretta, the Republic of Cracow,[26] and, after the First World War, the "Free Territory of Memel," [27] the "State of Fiume" [28] and the "Free City of Danzig." [29] None of these creations lasted, but all of them led to experiments in international administration.

IV

Notwithstanding that the creation of the Free Territory of Trieste was the outcome of what has been termed the "international frontier," and in spite of the inherent difficulty of creating so small a territory as a separate entity, and warned, furthermore, by the fate of earlier similar experiments, the three Western Powers tried to provide for a viable and lasting creation. The provisions for the Free Territory of Trieste are carefully drawn and very elaborate, and make up one-fourth of the Italian Peace Treaty.

The Free Territory of Trieste,[30] as determined by the Italian Peace Treaty [31] includes the city of Trieste and a hinterland along the Adriatic Sea up to Duino in the north and Cittanova in the south. It comprises a total area of 305 square miles, with a population of about 325,000.[32] Under Article XXI the "Free Territory is hereby constituted and recognized by the Allies and Italy, which agree that its integrity and independence shall be assured by the Security Council of the United Nations." Under Article XXI, §5, Italy and Yugoslavia undertake to give to the Free Territory guarantees concerning water supply, electricity, and facilities for local frontier trade. Annex IX lays down in detail these "Technical Dispositions." Annex X contains elaborate economic and financial provisions relating to the Free Territory.

To protect the interests of Central Europe in the port of Trieste, Annex VIII, in 26 articles, contains the "Instrument for the Free Port of Trieste." [33] The port and transit facilities of Trieste will be available for use on general terms by all international trade and by Italy, Yugoslavia, and the states of Central Europe (Article I). A new development is introduced by giving the Free Port all the attributes of a juridical person. Thus, the Free Port shall be established and administered as a state corporation of the Free Territory (Article II). The administration of the Free Port shall be carried on by the director of the Free Port who shall not be a citizen of Yugoslavia or Italy, and who is to be appointed by the governor from a list submitted to him by the Council of Government of the Free Territory; in case of disagreement, the matter shall be referred to the Security Council (Article XVIII). The director of the Free Port shall issue such rules and by-laws as he considers necessary for the exercise of his functions and shall prepare the autonomous budget of the Free Port (Article XX). Highly interesting are the elaborate provisions for the creation of the International Commission of the Free Port [34] with a consultative function. This commission consists of a representative of the Free Territory as chairman and one representative each of the Big Four, Yugoslavia, Italy, Czechoslovakia, and Poland, and finally of the delegates of three states not parties to the Italian Peace Treaty, namely Austria, Hungary, and Switzerland (Article XXI). The offices and activities of the International Commission shall be exempt from local jurisdiction, and the members and officers of the Commission shall enjoy in the Free Territory such privileges and immunities as are necessary for the independent exercise of their functions (Article XXII). Proposals for amendment of this instrument may be submitted by the Council of Government or by three or more states represented in the International Commission (Article XXV).

V

The basic document is Annex VI of the Italian Peace Treaty. It contains the Permanent Statute of the Free Territory [35] the provisions of which shall govern the Free Territory from the date determined by the Security Council for its coming into force.[36] It is here that the effort for a lasting settlement can be seen. The Free Territory is not put under the protection of Great Powers as was the Republic of Cracow; it is not constituted as an autonomous unit within one sovereign state, as was the Territory of Memel; neither is it made into a sovereign state under the protection of the League of Nations with special rights given to Poland, as was the Free City of Danzig. The aim of the provisions contained in the Permanent Statute is direct government by the international organization.[37]

The organs of government of the Free Territory are the governor, the Council of Governmnet, the popular assembly and the judiciary (Article IX). It is stipulated that the constitution of the Free Territory shall be established in accordance with democratic principles and shall be adopted by a constituent assembly. Moreover, the constitution shall conform to the provisions of the Permanent Statute and shall not become effective prior to the coming into force of the latter (Article X).

Legislative authority is to be exercised by a one chamber popular assembly, elected on the basis of proportional representation by the citizens of both sexes through universal, equal, direct, and secret suffrage (Article XII). The assembly shall have the right to consider and discuss any matters affecting the interest of the Free Territory (Article XVIII). The Council of Government is the organ of executive authority and is formed by the popular assembly to which it is responsible. (Article XIII). It has to prepare the budget (Article XXI). The judicial authority is exercised by tribunals (Article XIV), and complete independence of the judiciary must be guaranteed by the constitution (Article XV).[38]

But the most important organ of government is the governor to whom the statute gives a powerful position. He is appointed by the Security Council after consultation with the governments of Yugoslavia and Italy (Article XI), he shall be neither a citizen of Yugoslavia nor of Italy nor of the Free Territory; the Security Council can suspend or dismiss the governor if he has failed to carry out his duties, and, in case of vacancy, the Security Council shall appoint another person as provisional governor, Article XI). The governor has the right to be present at all meetings of the Council of Government (Article XIII); he has a right of veto, subject to reference to the Security Council, against provisions of the constitution or any subsequent amendment if they are, in his opinion, in contradiction with the statute (Article X). The governor appoints the judiciary. He can initiate legislation in matters which affect the responsibilities of the Security Council; he has a veto right against legislation enacted by the assembly if he considers such legislation to be in contradiction with the statute. If the assembly refuses to withdraw such legislation, the governor shall immediately report the matter to the Security Council; such legislation shall be promulgated only upon the direction of the Security Council (Article XIX). The governor may require the Council of Government to suspend administrative measures which, in his view, conflict with his responsibilities (Article XX). Should the Council of Government object, the governor may suspend those measures, and he or the Council may refer the whole question to the Security Council for decision (Article XX). The power of pardon and reprieve shall be vested in the governor. (Article XXIII). In the performance of his duties the governor shall not seek or receive instructions from any government or authority except the Security Council (Article XXV). The governor, after consultation with the Council of Government, appoints and dismisses the director of public security. This director shall not be a citizen of Yugoslavia or of Italy. Normally, he shall be under the immediate authority of the Council of Government from which he receives his instructions. The director shall make regular reports to the governor (Article XXVII). Members of the police and security services shall be recruited by the director and shall be subject to dismissal by him.

The governor has further special emergency powers in order to carry out his responsibilities to the Security Council. In cases which in his opinion permit of no delay, threatening the independence and integrity of the Free Territory, public order, or respect of basic human rights, the governor can directly order and require the execution of appropriate measures, subject to an immediate report to the Security Council. In such circumstances the governor may himself assume, if he deems it necessary, control of the security services. The governor shall ensure that the foreign relations of the Free Territory are conducted in conformity with the statute, the constitution, and the laws of the Free Territory. He shall have authority to prevent the entry into force of treaties or agreements affecting foreign relations which, in his judgment, conflict with the statute, the constitution, or the laws of the Free Territory (Article XXIV).

The governor, as the representative of the Security Council, shall be responsible only to the Security Council to whom he shall present annual reports concerning the operation of the statute and the performance of his duties.

VI

Up to now, neither the Permanent Statute nor the constitution has become operative. Article XXI, §3, of the Italian Peace Treaty provides that from the termination of Italian sovereignty until the coming into force of the Permanent Statute, the territory shall be governed as laid down in Annex VII on the provisional regime of the Free Territory. This instrument deals primarily with the provisional regime after the assumption of office by the governor, who was to exercise authority at the earliest possible moment after the coming into force of the peace treaty (Article I). It is also stipulated that the provisions of the Permanent Statute shall be binding in this provisional period as and when they are applicable and in so far as they are not superseded by Annex VII (Article II). During this time the governor's position is further enhanced. From persons domiciled in the Free Territory, and after consultation with Yugoslav and Italian governments, he selects a provisional council. His actions shall be guided mainly by the needs of the population and its well-being (Article II). The seat of the government will be established in Trieste and the governor will address his reports directly to the chairman of the Security Council. (Article III). The governor's first concern is to be the maintenance of public order and security. Hence, he shall appoint provisionally the director of public security who is to organize and administer the police force and the security services (Article IV). There will be 5,000 Americans, 5,000 British, and 5,000 Yugoslav troops stationed in the Free Territory which shall be placed at the disposal of the governor for ninety days after his assumption of office in the Free Territory. They will then be withdrawn from the territory within a further period of forty-five days, unless the governor advises the Security Council that, in the interest of the territory, some or all of them shall not be withdrawn (Article V). The governor shall have the right at any time to call upon the commanders of such contingents for support which shall be given promptly (Article VI). The governor, in consultation with the provisional Council of Government, shall be responsible for organizing the elections of members of the constituent assembly (Article VIII). Existing laws and regulations shall remain valid unless and until revoked or suspended by the governor who can amend existing laws and introduce new laws and regulations in agreement with the majority of the provisional Council of Government (Article X). Pending the establishment of a separate currency regime the Italian lira shall continue to be the legal tender within the Free Territory.

VII

Until now, no governor has been appointed. But Italian sovereignty over the area was terminated on September 15, 1947, and on the same day the Free Territory of Trieste came into existence. Italian citizens who were domiciled within this area on June 10, 1940, as well as their children born after that date, lost their Italian nationality and became original citizens of the Free Territory on September 15, 1947. The right of option for Italy could not, as yet, be exercised, as this is permitted only within six months from the coming into force of the constitution of the Free Territory.[39]

Obviously, this provisional period was intended to be of shortest duration. Only one sentence of Annex VI, Article I, refers to it, stipulating that "pending assumption of office by the Governor, the Free Territory shall continue to be administered by the Allied military commanders within their respective zones." This is the period in which we still are. Naturally, this occupation is no longer an *occupatio bellica*, but constitutes an *occupatio pacifica*, the legal title of which stems from the Italian Peace Treaty.

At the present time the Free Territory is divided into Zones A and B. Zone A, the northern part of the Free Territory, including the city of Trieste, with an area of 101 square miles and a population of 282,000, is under British-American administration. Zone B, the southern part, with an area of 204 square miles and a population of 40,000, is under Yugoslav occupation. In a recent note the three Western Powers recommended the return of the Free Territory to Italy, asserting that they "have received abundant evidence to show that the Yugoslav zone has been completely transformed in character and has been virtually incorporated into Yugoslavia by procedures which do not respect the desire expressed by the Powers to give an independent and democratic status to the Territory." "Pending assumption of office by a governor," the note continues, "in the UK-US Zone the Anglo-American military authorities have acted as caretakers for the governor to be appointed," whereas "at the same time Yugoslavia has taken, in the zone under her charge, measures which definitely compromise the possibility of applying the Statute." [40]

The creation of the Free Territory must probably be considered a failure. The conditions for success in addition to full co-operation by Italy, Yugoslavia, and the Big Four would have been immediate appointment of a governor as well as a harmoniously working Security Council. None of these conditions have been fulfilled. How, one may ask, could the veto-crippled Security Council effectively administer the Free Territory? How is it possible to guarantee the independence and integrity of the Free Territory by the Security Council, while the latter, as a consequence of the non-implementation of Article XLIII of the Charter of the United Nations, has no armed forces at its disposal?

VIII

What would the international legal status of the Free Territory be as foreseen by the Permanent Statute? There can be no doubt that the new entity has been created by international law, although the coming into existence of the Free Territory depends on the fulfillment of the norm of effectivity of general international law. Under Article XXI, §4, of the Italian Peace Treaty, the Free Territory is not ceded by Italy. It comes into being with the termination of Italian sovereignty.

The Free Territory can hardly be considered a state in accordance with the rules of international law.[41] That the Territory is small, that it has been created by international law, and that the latter severely restricts its rights would not be decisive: a state under protectorate is a state in the sense of international law; the Treaty of Versailles which created the Free City of Danzig, although it limited Danzig's rights and her capacity to act by providing for the protection of the League of Nations and for very special relations with Poland, created, nevertheless, a state in the sense of international law; so is the Città del Vaticano. But Danzig was self-governing; the position of the League's high commissioner for Danzig was very different from that provided for the governor of the Free Territory of Trieste who is the representative of the Security Council and who is only responsible to the Security Council. True, the governor is a part of the government of the Free Territory; but he is primarily the representative of the Security Council, which itself is the highest organ of the Free Territory. Moreover, the Security Council has to exercise important functions under the Permanent Statute not only to assure the integrity and independence of the Free Territory but also its actual administration. No doubt exists that the Free Territory would be wholly and directly under the government of the United Nations as the Saar Basin was directly under the international administration of the League of Nations.

Duncan Hall says that, from a political point of view, the Free Territory belongs in the category of trusteeship, as a phenomenon of the "international frontier." [42] From a legal point of view, however, the Free Territory is certainly not a trusteeship in the sense of the Charter of the United Nations: it is subject to the Security Council, not to the Trusteeship Council.[43]

While the Free Territory is not a state in the sense of international law, it certainly is a particular territorial community, created by international law, with its own territory, population, and government, and with its own flag and coat of arms.[44] It is recognized by the Allies and Italy, which agree that its integrity and independence shall be assured by the Security Council. The Free Territory is demilitarized and declared permanently neutral;[45] no armed forces, except upon direction of the Security Council, shall be allowed in the territory.

Although not a state, the Free Territory, as an internationally created and guaranteed territorial community, is, no doubt, a person in international law.[46] For the sphere of international law is not, as often held, restricted to sovereign states. It is for international law itself to determine the entities which shall have international personality. In consequence, non-states can be persons in international law, as, for example, the Holy See, the League of Nations, and so on. Whether a certain entity is, in fact, a person in international law is a question to be determined by the analysis of positive international law. Such non-states which are persons in international law must, by no means, have an identical legal position with that given to sovereign states by international law. The determination of their position, again, is a problem of the analysis of international law. Such analysis shows that the Free Territory is a person in international law, but with internationally restricted rights. It can conclude treaties and agreements, as well as exequaturs and consular commissions, which shall be jointly signed by the governor and a representative of the Council of Government. The Free Territory may become a party to international conventions, or it may become a member of international organizations, provided the aim of such conventions or organizations is to settle economic, technical, cultural, social, or health questions. On the other hand, the

Free Territory cannot become a party to international conventions, or it cannot become a member of international organizations with other purposes. It cannot enter economic unions or associations of an exclusive character with any state. It has no right of legation. It cannot become a member of the United Nations. Being demilitarized and permanently neutral, the Free Territory is not allowed to make or to discuss any military arrangements or undertakings with any state.[47]

* The manuscript of this study was finished in the first days of May, 1948.

[1] Annexed by the royal decrees of May 3 and 18, 1941. For the text see RAPHAEL LEMKIN, AXIS RULE IN OCCUPIED EUROPE 584–85, 587–88 (1944).

[2] Mary E. Bradshaw, *Military Control of Zone A in Venezia Giulia*, 16 DEP'T STATE BULL. No. 417 at 1257–72 (June 29, 1947).

[3] See, in general, DEPARTMENT OF STATE, MAKING THE PEACE TREATIES 1941–1947, Publication 2774, European Series 24 (1947).

[4] N. Y. Times, November 8, 1947, pp. 1, 3.

[5] René Albrecht-Carrié, *Peace with Italy—An Appraisal*, 62 POL. SCI. Q. 492 (December, 1947).

[6] None of the foreign ministers considered ideal this agreement. But Secretary Byrnes said that it seemed the most reasonable decision which could be reached (MAKING THE PEACE TREATIES 1941–1947, at 27). See also the detailed remarks in Secretary Byrnes' report (*ibid.* at 103–5) and DOCUMENTI DELLA PACE ITALIANA (1947); see also GIUSEPPE VEDOVATO, IL TRATTATO DI PACE CON L'ITALIA (1947).

[7] See the remarks of Senator Connelly before the Italian Political and Territorial Commission of the Paris Peace Conference, in 15 DEP'T STATE BULL. No. 377 at 570–71 (September 29, 1946); see also MAKING THE PEACE TREATIES 1941–1947 at 114–17.

[8] The Soviet proposal "would make a figurehead of the United Nations Governor and would have given Yugoslavia virtual control of the customs, currency and foreign affairs of the Territory. It would make the Territory a protectorate of Yugoslavia and would have the United Nations powerless to prevent it from becoming a battleground between warring groups. There must be no seizure of power in Trieste after this war as there was in Fiume after the last war."—Secretary Byrnes' report of October 18, 1946, quoted in MAKING THE PEACE TREATIES 1941–1947, at 126.

[9] See the table of opposing views in N. Y. Times, November 18, 1946, p. 3.

[10] MAKING THE PEACE TREATIES 1941–1947, at 53–56. See also the statement of Secretary of State Byrnes before the Senate Committee

on Foreign Relations, March 4, 1947, in 16 DEP'T STATE BULL. No. 402 at 487–88 (March 16, 1947).

11 The report contains proposals as to budget, balance of payments, currency and banking, foreign exchange, and the customs system. See N. Y. Times, May 7, 1947, p. 9; 16 DEP'T STATE BULL. No. 405 at 609 (April 6, 1947). The report of the Commissioners is of February 27, 1947. For the decision of the Council of Foreign Ministers concerning the report of the Trieste Commission of Inquiry, see 17 DEP'T STATE BULL. No. 434 at 824–25 (October 26, 1947). See also U.N. Doc. No. S/577 (October 9, 1947).

12 MAKING THE PEACE TREATIES 1941–1947, at 39–41.

13 U.N. Doc. No. S/224, Rev. 1.

14 U.N. Doc. No. S/P.V./91. The representative of Australia expressed doubt as to the competence of the Security Council concerning the Free Territory of Trieste. However, a memorandum by the Secretary General of the United Nations stated that "the Security Council is not restricted to the specific powers set forth in Chapters VI, VII, and XII of the Charter of the United Nations." This was also the view taken by the Security Council. The affirmative vote was 10–0, with Australia abstaining, having already expressed the same doubt at the Paris Peace Conference of 1946.

15 For the text of the agreement, see N. Y. Times, April 23, 1947, p. 6; see also 12 CURRENT HISTORY 593 (1947). This agreement was forwarded to the Secretary General of the United Nations by Mr. Vishinsky on September 7, 1947. See 17 DEP'T STATE BULL. No. 434, 824 (October 26, 1947); see also U.N. Doc. No. S/577 (October 9, 1947).

16 As to the candidate proposed by different sides, see N. Y. Times, May 23, 1947, p. 7.

17 U.N. Doc. No. C/P.V./223.

18 For the text of the Italian Peace Treaty, see DEPARTMENT OF STATE, TREATIES OF PEACE WITH ITALY, BULGARIA, HUNGARY, ROUMANIA AND FINLAND, Pub. No. 2743, European Ser. 27 (1947). See also the text of the Italian Peace Treaty in 42 AM. J. INT'L L. 47–139 (1948).

19 18 DEP'T STATE BULL. No. 456 at 425 (March 28, 1948). The idea of a revision of the Italian Peace Treaty had already been voiced by Italy at the time of signing the treaty (N. Y. Times, February 10, 1947, p. 10). At the second Assembly meeting of the United Nations, Argentina submitted the topic of a revision of the Italian Peace Treaty, but withdrew the proposal later (U.N. Doc. No. A/500).

20 18 DEP'T STATE BULL. No. 457 at 453–54 (April 4, 1948).

21 18 ibid., No. 459 at 521–22 (April 18, 1948).

22 18 ibid., No. 460 at 549 (April 25, 1948).

23 See the sharp critique by Fred H. Cramer in 12 CURRENT HISTORY 101 (1947); see also René Albrecht-Carrié, op. cit. at 497.

24 N. Y. Times, April 15, 1947, p. 5. See also N. Y. Times, editorial, May 10, 1947, p. 12.

25 H. Duncan Hall, The International Frontier 42 AM. J. INT'L L. 42 (1948).

[26] Congress of Vienna, Act of June 9, 1815, Articles VI–X; Russian-Austrian-Prussian Treaty of May 3, 1815 (2 GEORGE F. MARTENS, NOUVEAU RECUEIL 251). The Republic of Cracow was recognized as a free, independent, and neutral state under the protection of these three powers. Each of the three powers delegated a "Commissar" to Cracow. But on the basis of the treaty, concluded between the same three powers on November 6, 1846 (9 MARTENS, NOUVEAU RECUEIL 375), the Republic came to an end and Cracow was incorporated into Austria (JOSEF L. KUNZ, DIE STAATENVERBINDUNGEN 289 [1929]).

[27] *Convention relative au Territoire de Memel, Paris, April 8, 1924*, 29 L.N.T.S., 1924, 87–115. The Memel Territory was an autonomous unit under Lithuanian sovereignty (JOSEF L. KUNZ, *op. cit.* at 232–36). See also A. ROGGE, DIE VERFASSUNG DES MEMELGEBIETES (1928).

[28] Fiume, a *corpus separatum* under the Hungarian Crown from 1779 to 1918, wanted after World War I by Italy and Yugoslavia, declared itself independent on October 29, 1918, and asked for its incorporation into Italy. After d'Annunzio's coup of September 12, 1919, it was made into the "Reggenzia del Carnaro." In the Italo-Yugoslav Treaty of Rapallo of November 12, 1920, the two states "recognize the full liberty and independence of the State of Fiume in perpetuity." But already under the Italo-Yugoslav Treaty of Rome concluded on January 27, 1924, Fiume was annexed by Italy. See LUIGI PETEANI, LA POSIZION INTERNAZIONALE DI FIUME (1940).

[29] JOSEF L. KUNZ, *op. cit.* at 289–91, 298–301. For a full treatment and an exhaustive bibliography, see JOHN BROWN MASON, THE DANZIG DILEMMA (1946).

[30] See, in general, Richard Schueller, *Trieste*, 13 SOCIAL RESEARCH 399–409 (1946); C. Grove Haines, *Trieste—A Storm Center of Europe*, FOREIGN POLICY REPORTS (April 1, 1946); MARTIN-CHAUFFIER, TRIESTE (1947); Bonetti, *Il territorio libero di Trieste*, BOLLETINO DELLA SOCIETA GEOGRAFICA ITALIANA 73–87 1947); J. F. KOVER, *Trieste et la paix*, 2 CAHIERS DU MONDE NOUVEAU 65–75 (1946); L. Unger, *The Economy of the Free Territory of Trieste*, 37 GEOGRAPHICAL REVIEW (1947).

[31] Articles IV, XXII.

[32] The city of Trieste has 240,000 inhabitants.

[33] Trieste was a free port under Austria, from 1779 to 1891. See LUZZATTO, IL PORTO DI TRIESTE (1945).

[34] See the regulations in the Treaty of Versailles concerning the harbor of Danzig and the institution of the "Danzig-Polish Harbor Board" (JOHN BROWN MASON, *op. cit.* at 115–29), indicating a "move toward international administration."

[35] For an investigation from the point of view of international law, see Manlio Udina, *La condizione giuridica internazionale del Territorio Libero di Trieste*, 2 RASSEGNA DI DIRITTO PUBBLICO (1947). See also A. Gervais, *Le Statut du Territoire Libre de Trieste*, 51 REVUE GÉNÉRALE DU DROIT INTERNATIONAL PUBLIC, PARIS 134–54.

[36] Italian Peace Treaty, Art. XXI, § 3; Permanent Statute, Art. XXXVIII.

[37] Thus the Saar Basin, from 1920 to 1935, was directly administered by the League of Nations; but the Saar Basin remained in law under the sovereignty of Germany which, in the Treaty of Versailles, only ceded for this period the "exercise of sovereignty."

[38] The statute contains also norms concerning local government (Art. XXIX), railways (Art. XXXI), commercial aviation (Art. XXXII), registration of vessels (Art. XXXIII), the Free Port (Art. XXXIV), and freedom of transit (Art. XXXV), as well as provisions concerning the interpretation (Art. XXXVI) and amendment (Art. XXXVII) of the Permanent Statute. The amendment has to be made by the Security Council, to which the popular assembly may present petitions. Italian and Slovene are the official languages of the Free Territory (Art. VII).

[39] Permanent Statute, art. VI. See "Nationality and Option Clauses in the Italian Peace Treaty of 1947," above.

[40] See 18 DEP'T STATE BULL. No. 456 (March 28, 1948); 18 *ibid.*, No. 457 (April 4, 1948); 18 *ibid.*, No. 459 at 521–22 (April 18, 1948); 18 *ibid.*, No. 460 at 549 (April 25, 1948).

[41] See Manlio Udina's detailed discussion, *op. cit.* at 6–11.

[42] Duncan Hall, *op. cit.* at n. 21.

[43] It is interesting to compare the Free Territory of Trieste with the "City of Jerusalem," created by Part III/A of the RECOMMENDATION OF THE UNITED NATIONS GENERAL ASSEMBLY (November 29, 1947), CONCERNING THE PARTITION OF PALESTINE (U.N. Doc. No. A/516). The City of Jerusalem is created under a special international regime as a *corpus separatum*. This designation is probably taken from the old Hungarian constitutional law concerning Fiume (see note 24, above). But the special international regime shall here be administered on behalf of the United Nations by the Trusteeship Council, which has to discharge the responsibilities of the administering authority and which will appoint the governor.

[44] Permanent Statute, art. VIII.

[45] Notwithstanding the trend against neutrality, the institution of permanent neutrality reappears here, as in the case of the Citta del Vaticano.

[46] In the same sense see Manlio Udina, *op. cit.* at 12–14.

[47] Permanent Statute, art. III, § 4.

CHAPTER XIII: *The Status of Occupied Germany under International Law: A Legal Dilemma*

I

GERMANY CERTAINLY PRESENTS the most important political problem in the present-day world. The ultimate outcome of the events of 1945, of subsequent developments, of the East-West struggle for Germany, will not only determine the fate of the Germans but may well decide also the fate of Europe and of the world, the question of peace or a third world war. In view of the political importance of the German problem, it stands to reason that the legal problem of the status of occupied Germany is also of paramount importance;[1] it is of more than academic interest, since it involves far-reaching political issues, and at the same time it is of the highest theoretical interest, since it touches upon fundamental problems of international law.

Yet in spite of the already large literature on this subject, hardly any theory that from a strictly legal point of view might be called really satisfactory and unobjectionable has been presented so far. It appears that the problem of the legal status of occupied Germany presents a legal dilemma which is hardly capable of such satisfactory and unobjectionable legal solution.

To show the reasons for the existence of this dilemma and to point to the lines of what seems to be the correct legal approach to the solution of this dilemma is the purpose of this study, which is limited by these objectives. The knowledge of the historical events and of the documentary evidence thereof is here taken for granted.[2] Neither is it the purpose of this study, nor is it necessary, to give a full survey and critique of all the theories hitherto presented. This task has been performed several times. This writer wants particularly to point to Rolf Stödter's book,[3] which presents a full and mostly excellent discussion of all the manifold problems involved and of all the theories elaborated, and which contains a very comprehensive bibliography of writings and an index of relevant court decisions up to the middle of 1948.

II

The first reason for this legal dilemma pertaining to the status of occupied Germany certainly consists in the fact that the defeat of Germany and the forms it took in 1945, as well as the subsequent situation, are without precedent in modern history. All the writers on the subject, however different their views may be, stress the point of the unique historical situation.

Precedents of military occupations abound. World War II was overrich in the most diverse types of occupations. But no one of these well-recognized types exactly fits the case. It certainly is not an *occupatio pacifica*.[4] It is not a belligerent occupation in the sense of the Fourth Hague Convention. It has nothing to do with the many belligerent occupations during World War II by Germany [5] or by the Allies, nor with the occupation of neutral countries. It is different from the many types of occupations by Great Britain in Africa,[6] which include particular and highly interesting cases. It is different from the legal status of German-occupied Denmark.[7] It certainly is not a so-called *occupatio mixta,* a military occupation on the basis of an armistice or a peace treaty, like the Rhineland occupation after World War I.[8] It is entirely different from the post-surrender occupations of Italy, Hungary, Romania, Bulgaria, which all had their legal basis in an armistice. It is, further, very different from the present occupation of Japan; for Japan accepted the Potsdam ultimatum and made, prior to her unconditional surrender, certain conditions concerning the position of the Emperor, conditions which the Allies accepted, so that Japan's occupation has its legal basis in an international agreement. Finally, the status of Germany cannot be compared with the equally unusual situation of the military occupation of "liberated" Austria.

Germany's unique situation, therefore, explains why the literature has produced many *ad hoc* solutions, such as an "occupation of intervention" [9] or a "fiduciary occupation." [10] But these *ad hoc* solutions are legally untenable, because they have no basis in general international law.[11] Intervention without a particular legal title is unlawful under general international law. The present situation of Germany in no way corresponds to the principles of the common-law "trust," [12] nor is the common-law trust an institution of general international law, although the trust idea has been applied by some institutions created by particular international law.[13] Historically, it is equally untenable to pretend that the Allies have occupied Germany solely for her own benefit.

Whereas some writers have thus constructed *ad hoc* theories, have invented new law to fit the facts, others have tried to put the situation on the Procrustes bed of well-known legal institutions, such as simple belligerent occupation, that do not fit the unique facts. Some—in despair, so to speak—have come to the conclusion that the present occu-

pation of Germany is an *occupatio sui generis,* which of
course is no legal solution at all, but merely an acknowledg-
ment that there is no solution. Finally, many writers hold,
in varying forms, that the occupation of Germany is an
occupatio imperii.

III

The previous discussion, dealing with the first reason for
this legal dilemma—the uniqueness of the historical facts—
leads to the question: Wherein does this uniqueness lie from
a legal point of view? The answer is that this uniqueness
lies in two facts, both of them unchallengeable but difficult
to reconcile legally: that Germany was undoubtedly conquered, but that equally undoubtedly Germany was not annexed. The problem of the legal status of occupied Germany,
and all further problems, such as the legal nature of the occupation authorities, or the character of the legal rules now
binding on individuals in the occupied territory, depend entirely on the solution of a preliminary question; namely,
whether Germany has or has not ceased to exist as a sovereign state, as a state in the sense of international law.

Only under the second hypothesis can the problem be
called the problem of the legal status of occupied Germany;
under the first hypothesis the problem would have to be
styled correctly as the problem of the status of the occupied
territory that once was Germany. All theories presented,
however different otherwise, can be clearly classified as
falling within two great categories, according to the attitude
taken toward the preliminary problem of the survival *vel
non* of Germany as a sovereign state.

The creator of the theory that Germany has ceased to exist
is Hans Kelsen. His first article, published in 1944,[14] is
written *de lege ferenda;* it shown the amazing foresight by

a man of genius of the problems that will arise after Germany's unconditional surrender. The article, being *de lege ferenda,* draws the legal consequences from the war slogan of unconditional surrender in a way which would have permitted the Allies to carry out their often-announced war aims in Germany in conformity with general international law. It was not Kelsen, but the announced policy of the Allies, which eliminated what Kelsen would have considered the best legal basis, namely an armistice, a peace treaty, or some type of agreement by which Germany in law would have given her consent. As the Allies had absolutely ruled out any form of agreement, Kelsen pointed out that a belligerent occupation could not permit the carrying-out of the Allied war aims in conformity with international law. Hence he emphasized that the only legal basis would be *debellatio.* Germany, Kelsen stated, will cease to exist on account of her conquest and subjugation; the victors will occupy ex-Germany in a condominium sovereignty; this will allow them to act as sovereigns; here a firm legal basis will also be given to the announced Allied intention to bring the principal war criminals to trial. The war will be terminated; no peace treaty will be possible. The Allies will later, when they think fit, create a new German state that legally has nothing to do with the Third Reich. This will also have the political advantage, from a German point of view, of freeing the government of a new democratic German state from liability, and from the politically unbearable burden of having been forced to sign a harsh peace treaty, which, although valid in law, would be assailed politically as a "diktat," like the Treaty of Versailles.

In his second article,[15] written after 1945, Kelsen interprets the events, particularly the Declaration of Berlin, as the carrying-out of his proposals of 1944. Kelsen has continued to maintain his *debellatio—condominium—*sover-

eignty thesis, and has voiced the opinion that contrary statements are untenable in law and must be regarded as mere
political fictions.[16]

It has been necessary to sketch, at least, the ideas of
Kelsen, because they constitute not only the first legal treatment of the German problem, but they have become—directly or in a modified form, positively or negatively—an
example to be followed or a target to be attacked, the very
center of the whole literature on this topic.

Kelsen's ideas have gained wide following, sometimes in
a modified form, in the United States, Great Britain, and
France, with writers such as Shears,[17] Green,[18], Finch,[19]
Quincy Wright,[20] Fahy,[21] Freeman,[22] Schwarzenberger,[23]
Lauterpacht,[24] Schick;[25], also, in a certain sense, Mann [26]
and Jennings;[27] further, Benoist,[28] Cuny,[29] and Virally.[30]
Recently, many Italian writers have sustained the theory
that Germany has ceased to exist by *debellatio;* but they
hold, contrary to Kelsen, that she has become *terra nullius;*
the activities of the occupying powers are not carried on
in a *condominium* of sovereigns, but simply on foreign soil
that constitutes a *terra nullius.* Representatives of this
theory are Ottolenghi, Bentivoglio,[31] Capotorti,[32] Guiliano,[33]
Quadri.[34]

Kelsen's thesis was the basis of the speech of the French
prosecutor de Menthon at the Nuremburg Trial. The Nuremberg Judgment itself, and the judgment of the American
Military Tribunal of December 3, 1947,[35] are likewise based
on Kelsen's ideas; these can also be found in some documents
of the Allies, and certainly have influenced the thinking
of Allied occupation authorities in Germany. Even there
Kelsen's thesis has found adherents, in a series of articles
published in a Berlin newspaper,[36] among which Professor
Becker's [37] deserves special mention. Moreover writings by
Richthofen,[38] Abendroth,[39] Pollak,[40] Jerusalem,[41] but particularly Kempski [42] and Dassel [43] have strongly maintained

Kelsen's thesis that Germany has ceased to exist as a sovereign state, in consequence of *debellatio*. Even in the Commission of Experts at Herrenchiemsee for the preparation of what later became the Bonn constitution, the majority defending the continued existence of Germany, was faced by a minority holding that Germany has ceased to exist as a sovereign state. This minority was led by so well known a German constitutional lawyer as Nawiasky.[44]

There exist also attacks and polemics against Kelsen's ideas from Allied,[45] neutral,[46] and German [47] sides. Generally speaking, Kelsen's ideas have been rejected by the great majority of German international lawyers; by the practice of foreign states, such as Switzerland, Sweden, Austria; by the attitude of authorities in the Allied countries; even by the occupation authorities in Germany; and by many court decisions,[48] some of them well known, rendered by British, Swiss, Austrian, German, and other courts.[49]

IV

As stated previously, the legal dilemma concerning the legal status of occupied Germany has its roots in the unique fact that Germany was fully conquered but not annexed, and it is intimately connected with the preliminary problem as to whether or not Germany has ceased to be a sovereign state. It appears necessary, therefore, to investigate the reasons why this preliminary problem presents such dilemma. The first reason may be seen in that this legal problem is of such political importance and involves often such a degree of emotion that most theories have a strong political flavor; political, not legal, considerations often dominate, consciously or unconsciously. On the Allied side theories have been favored that were born of the political wish to justify the Allied measures in Germany under international law. The connection with the Nuremberg Trial was particularly close, and the *debellatio*-sovereignty theory seemed to furnish a solid legal basis for the prosecution of German war criminals. There is no doubt that there sometimes entered latent feelings of revenge, of political or racial resentment of the unheard-of barbarities and atrocities of which National Socialist Germany had no doubt been guilty. On the other hand, with the change of the political situation between East and West, and therefore between the West and Germany, different theories were favored—seeing, for instance, in the Allied occupation merely a provisional regime pending the restoration of German sovereignty.

On the side of German scholars, there is an easily understandable, nearly overwhelming political wish inspiring most theories to prove legally that Germany, notwithstanding the events of 1945, has not ceased to exist as a sovereign state; that, in spite of total defeat, she is not entirely without rights as regards the victors; that she does not now form a territory in which no international law rules at all. It is these feelings which explain the bitter resentment and opposition against Kelsen's ideas. As German international lawyers cannot, contrary to their practice after World War I, base their case on agreements, such as Wilson's Fourteen Points, they must rely on the principles of general international law. Some try to bolster their case with recourse to common-law institutions, such as the trust, or the common-law principle of estoppel, and they attempt to transfer these doctrines into international law. Appeals may be found to the Atlantic Charter; to Anglo-American political convictions—such as the supremacy of democracy—to political fictions—e.g., that Hitler's regime was always illegal—exactly as the French reasoned after the defeat of Napoleon in 1815; to utopian reasonings; to "modern international law"; and finally one may discover a resort to ideas based on natural law. Indeed, it must be recognized as an unescapable fact that the great majority of German international lawyers had to prove to their own satisfaction that Germany survived the total defeat, and they had so resolved by a resolution passed at Hamburg in 1947; they could not have adopted a resolution to the contrary without giving themselves up politically.

V

If one reason for this German dilemma may be seen in the political prejudice of certain scholars, other reasons, equally political, lie in the political ambiguity of the declarations and actions of the occupying powers, which make it possible to quote such Allied behavior in support of the most divergent theories. This political ambiguity has many facets. First, there is the disunity among the occupying powers. Sometimes such disunity has existed, in a smaller degree, even between the United States and Great Britain. It has existed in a higher degree between these powers and France. France was not made to adhere to the Yalta and Potsdam agreements and did not consider herself bound as she had not participated in these conferences. French policy, born out of the eternal fear of Germany, even of a totally defeated and destroyed Germany, looked toward the dismemberment, the utmost decentralization, of Germany. At the same time France took unilateral and rather high-handed action with respect to the Saar.

But the principal disunity developed between the three western powers and the Soviet Union, a disunity that has grown continually worse under the impact of the "cold war." The Soviet Union had already strongly protested against the creation of "Bizonia" and the inclusion of the Western Zones in the Marshall Plan. The meetings of the Council of Foreign Ministers in Moscow (March–April, 1947) and in London (November–December, 1947) brought the final failure of agreement between West and East. On March 20, 1948, the Soviet Union walked out of the Allied Control Council, and by the end of June, 1948, she announced her intention to withdraw from the *Kommandatura* in Berlin. The "cold war" reached new heights with the Soviet-ordered "Berlin blockade." From now on, the "two Germanys" went different ways. The West went ahead with the consolidation of the three Western Zones,[50] which led to the so-called Bonn constitution.[51] There followed the establishment of an International Authority of the Ruhr and that of the Military Security Board; the promulgation of the Occupation Statute [52] and of the German Reparation Program;[53] the holding of free and democratic elections in Western Germany on August 7, 1949; the change from military to civilian control; the establishment of the Allied High Commission in Germany and, on September 7, 1949, the establishment of the "Federal Republic of Germany" (*Bundesrepublik Deutschland*), which includes neither the Saar nor the three western sectors of Berlin. On October 7, 1949, there was set up the "German Democratic Republic," comprising the Soviet Zone, with Berlin as its capital, and purporting to be the government of the whole Germany. In a note of October 2, 1949, the Soviet Union had made a strong protest against the setting-up of the Western Republic as "a violation of the Potsdam Agreement," charging the western powers with an illegal "splitting of Germany." The West rejected the Soviet protest and denounced the Eastern Republic as illegal, as lacking any democratic foundation, as a Soviet satellite and a Soviet puppet government. It is clear that the occupying powers are bound *inter se* by the treaties and agreements they have concluded. But the problem of the possible violation of these is merely a problem of particular international law. The solution of the problem pertaining to Germany's legal status must be sought in the rules of general international law. For the fundamental question is not How must the present situation be legally construed under the Potsdam Agreement?, but What is the legal title in general international law that empowered the Allies to establish *inter se* the norms contained in the Potsdam Agreement?

VI

Another political reason for the existing legal dilemma lies in the fact that the basic policies as to what should be done with Germany after her total defeat were not always clear or consistent but were often ambiguous, contradictory, or continuously shifting even in the formative pre-1945 period. This applies not only to policies within the same nation—e.g., the United States—but even more so to those among the Big Three.

There can be no doubt, historically, that prior to 1945 ideas were advocated, studies and preparations made, tending toward the destruction of Germany by way of dismemberment,[54] and not merely toward the disruption of the National Socialist regime in Germany. Sumner Welles, in a book published in 1944, advised the dismemberment of Germany and proposed a partition plan.[55] The United States Secretary of the Treasury proposed his Morgenthau Plan,[56] a plan that can be explained only as the outcome of a deep resentment, a plan that coupled the dismemberment of Germany with the proposal of her complete de-industrialization and "pasturalization," by making the Ruhr a pasture for goats. Dismemberment proposals and the Morgenthau Plan, to a certain extent, were favored by President Roosevelt who proposed at the Teheran Conference the partition of Germany into five "autonomous" states and two internationally controlled areas. Churchill advocated joining Bavaria with Austria. An intergovernmental Commission for the Dismemberment of Germany was set up.[57] But Americans in high position, such as Cordell Hull and Stimson, and many American governmental advisers, were opposed to the plan of dismemberment; also in time President Roosevelt lost his enthusiasm for the idea. The Soviet Union was strongly opposed; Stalin spoke his much-quoted words that "the Hitlers come and go, but the German people and the German state remain," and he declared on May 8, 1945, "the USSR does not intend to dismember or destroy Germany."

Thus the idea was discarded; but reminiscences of it remain even in the events and the documents of 1945. There is no doubt that one of the aims of the occupation was to punish the Germans,[58] to do nothing for the reconstruction of the German economy, to keep down the German living standard, to prohibit the fraternization of American occupation troops with German officials and the population.[59] All this shows the historical untenability of the theory of "fiduciary occupation." On the other hand, the Allies announced in unmistakable terms that Germany would not be annexed, they spoke of the unity of Germany within her frontiers as they existed on December 31, 1937, they declared that "so far as it is practicable, there shall be uniformity of treatment of the German population throughout Germany," and that "during the occupation Germany shall be treated as a single economic unit."

Western ideas as to Germany have changed with time. Many reasons explain this change: the ebbing of the original enmity, the enormous costs the occupation put on the shoulders of the American tax-payer; the insight that a nation like Germany—which notwithstanding the crimes of the Hitler period is by far the most advanced, the most populous and, even in total defeat and destruction, potentially the strongest nation of Europe proper, a nation that has made such enormous contributions of the highest magnitude in every field of western culture—simply cannot be held under the boots of the victors forever. With the

Marshall Plan, the conviction was emphasized that the reconstruction of German economy is the indispensable precondition of European economic recovery. It finally became evident to certain statesmen of the West that a Germany reconstructed and firmly integrated into Western Europe, and into the new community of the Atlantic Pact, is the only way to bring together the nations of the "free world" in their struggle against the "Communist menace." True, as Byrnes and Marshall stated, the new directive must at the same time avoid creating a new European menace in a reconstructed Germany.

The well-known address of Secretary of State Byrnes at Stuttgart, on September 6, 1946, constitutes the turning point of American policy toward Germany. The United States directive of July 11, 1947, to General Clay is, in spirit and contents, very different indeed from the directive of 1945, given to General Eisenhower. These new policies could be applied only to Western Germany. Eastern Germany went very different ways. The division of Germany has become a political reality, although East and West insist on the unity of Germany and each charges the other with the illegal splitting of Germany. It is fundamental to understand that this splitting of Germany is not only a consequence of events subsequent to 1945, and of the struggle between East and West; it had its roots in the agreed-upon measures of Yalta and Potsdam. These measures, whether it was so intended or not, whether the results were foreseen or not, made it congenitally impossible to carry out the equally agreed-upon territorial unity of Germany within her frontiers of 1937.

The economic unity of occupied Germany was made impossible from the moment it was decided at Potsdam to take reparations by zones. The dismemberment of the territorial unity started, in fact, when the Big Three agreed at the Crimean Conference to give half of Poland to the Soviet Union and recognized Poland's claim to ter-

ritorial compensation. At Potsdam, President Roosevelt and
Prime Minister Churchill agreed not only that Königsburg
and the adjacent area be put under Soviet administration,
but they agreed also in principle to their ultimate transfer
to the Soviet Union, promising to support this proposal at
the peace conference. At the same time they agreed that
Germany east of the rivers Neisse and Oder [60] be placed
under the administration of Poland, "and for such purposes
should not be considered as part of the Soviet Zone of occupation in Germany." Thus one-fourth of the Germany of
1937 was excluded from occupation.[61] In the West, apart
from certain small border rectifications, provisionally made,
France has virtually detached the Saar from Germany,[62] a
unilateral action of doubtful legal validity. The "autonomous" Saar Territory was set up and given a constitution.[63]

In addition to the territorial dismemberment of the Germany of 1937, the very ruling in the Statement on Machinery of Control in Germany provides that supreme authority
in Germany will be exercised by the four commanders-in-
chief, on instructions from their governments, *each in his
own zone* of occupation and also jointly in matters affecting
Germany as a whole, though the Control Council can make
decisions only by unanimity of vote. From the moment it
was decided to split Germany—rump Germany—even if
only for purposes of occupation, into four zones, each under
a different power following its own political aims, introducing and, in the East, imposing its own political ideology,
the maintenance of the agreed-upon unity of the Germany
of 1937 became impossible in fact.[64]

VII

A further reason for the dilemma analyzed in this paper
is the lack of legal clarity that surrounded from the beginning the political slogan of "unconditional surrender." This

postulate has been condemned politically as prolonging the war, as preventing a German revolt against the Hitler regime, as strengthening German resistance to the bitter end. The following, however, touches only upon the legal aspects of this once so popular slogan.

It is important to remember that the phrase "unconditional surrender" was coined during the American Civil War.[65] It stems, therefore, from a civil war, and in a civil war conquest alone is sufficient to terminate the war. President Roosevelt transferred this phrase to the vocabulary of World War II at the Casablanca Conference in January, 1943.

Military capitulations are, generally speaking, treaties concerning the capitulation of certain troops, or a certain fortress, or all the armed forces, upon agreed conditions.[66] The armed forces of different countries had to surrender to German commanders in the course of World War II. General international law directly delegates the commanders-in-chief to conclude these conventions, which need no ratification. These commanders, on the other hand, lack any jurisdiction to include political clauses, which therefore, if included, are invalid in law.

The German unconditional surrender—Berlin, May 8, 1945—differs from ordinary capitulations, even of all the armed forces, in two points: It was unconditional, and it did not take the form of a treaty but of a unilateral German declaration, made merely "in the presence" of representatives of the Allied High Commands. Yet it was nothing but a military surrender, signed by the competent German commanders, in accordance with general international law. They merely surrendered "all forces on land, at sea, and in the air who are at this date under German control." They expressly did so "acting by authority at the German High Command." The document is correctly styled "Act of Military Surrender."

There cannot therefore be the slightest doubt from a legal point of view that this document has only military—no political—significance. That is why the debate on the status of the so-called Dönitz government is entirely irrelevant here. Those who surrendered did not do so by authority of any government, nor did they make any political surrender.

Yet one source of the confusion is exactly the identification of the surrender of German military forces with the surrender of Germany. Writers who do so identify it can quote Allied documents. The preamble of the Declaration of June 10, 1945, regarding the defeat of Germany, after having started correctly with the unconditional surrender of the German armed forces, continues incorrectly: "The unconditional surrender of *Germany* has thereby been effected" (italics supplied). The Judgment of the Nuremberg Trial also speaks of the "unconditional surrender of Germany."

In close connection with this first, legally untenable, identification is another made by some writers; namely, the identification of the military surrender with the conquest and subjugation of Germany and the transfer of German sovereignty to the Allies. The legal untenability of this identification can be simply proved by the unchallengeable fact that all the allies of Germany had to surrender unconditionally and yet in no case— not even in the case of Japan —has anyone ever thought of arguing that these states have ceased to exist. Such identifications can be explained politically by the fact that the war slogan of unconditional surrender meant not only the total defeat of Germany and an imposed—not a negotiated—peace, but a complete remaking of Germany; also the thought of destroying Germany through dismemberment entered. Prior to the Act of Military Surrender, the idea was ventilated that the unconditional surrender should be coupled with a declaration of dismemberment. It was also remarked that if this were not done, only a normal belligerent occupation under the Hague rules would be legally possible. But, because of divergent opinions, unconditional surrender was finally accepted in the form that stands in history. Even at this late date the idea of another surrender, the surrender of *Germany,* was not wholly dismissed, as is shown by Point 4 of the Act of Military Surrender of May 8, 1945. Apart from the fact that it is doubtful whether general international law knows the legal concept of an unconditional surrender of a state, it is historically known that no such political surrender has ever been imposed.

VIII

It is legally untenable to identify the military surrender of the German armed forces with the political surrender of Germany. But such military surrender may have legal importance with regard to what on the Continent is known as *debellatio* and in Anglo-American countries as "conquest and subjugation." It is exactly the uncertainty of the practice of states, and the deeply divided opinions of the literature as to the real legal meaning of these terms, that furnish the principal juridical reason for the legal dilemma when considering the status of occupied Germany. In this connection even the problem whether "title by conquest" is still a valid legal title in present-day international law has been discussed. Title by conquest has been opposed by the adherents of natural law since the time of St. Augustine; it has also been criticized by modern writers, such as Geffcken and Stowell; but we have here only an ethical critique of positive international law. Grotius and Vattel, as well as the practice of states and courts, clearly affirmed the title by conquest. In recent times tendencies toward legal limitations of the title by conquest can be seen, which found expression, e.g., in the Drago doctrine, the Nine Power Treaty of 1922, in many Pan-American declarations, in the

Saavedra Lamas Treaty of 1933, in the so-called non-recognition doctrine. But all writers who have studied these developments agree that we have here only tendencies, and not yet a new rule of law.[67] "Conquest," as Sir John Fisher-Williams states, "is often a moral wrong. But it is not illegal and it produces legal results." [68]

Title by conquest is still the valid law. The Allies were entitled under general international law to annex Germany, but they did not. But what is *debellatio?* The practice of states is of little help. In this century there have been only two cases of *debellatio* (Boer Republics, 1902; Ethiopia, 1936), and in these, as in the more frequent cases of the nineteenth century, conquest was always followed immediately by the annexation of the conquered state.

The literature is not of great help either. First, the recent literature has no doubt given too little space to the problem of *debellatio* in its triple legal aspect as a means of terminating a war, as one of the forms of the extinction of a sovereign state, and as one of the methods of acquisition of territorial sovereignty—probably because it was held that the subject is no longer of great actuality. Second, there is a deep division in the literature as to the legal meaning of *debellatio.*

One school of thought, to which many more modern Continental writers belong,[69] sees in *debellatio* merely a factual situation, mostly defined as the complete annihilation of the enemy armed forces, total occupation of the enemy state, and lasting destruction of its government. If these facts are present, then, according to this school, the enemy state has ceased to exist as a sovereign state and its territory, according to many writers, has become *terra nullius.* According to this school, *debellatio* is identical with conquest; the annexation is merely a usual, not a legally necessary, presupposition for the extinction of the enemy state. Conquest alone extinguishes the enemy state; the victor may, or may not, annex what is now *terra nullius*. Especially the recent Italian doctrine has strongly upheld this point of view.[70] Some of the Italian writers think that the end of the enemy state through *debellatio* happens only when all the three quoted facts materialize; others see the decisive factor in the destruction of the enemy's governmental organization. Quadri goes so far as to identify the total occupation of the enemy state with *debellatio* in this sense. But this theory is certainly untenable. The practice of states and courts clearly shows that, under positive international law, total occupation of enemy territory has no such legal effects as long as allies continue fighting.[71] This rule operates also in favor of Germany. It was not on May 8, 1945, but only at the date of the surrender of Japan, that Germany was legally ripe for annexation.

Naturally, those writers on the German problem who belong to this school will conclude that Germany has ceased to exist as a sovereign state, as she was undoubtedly conquered. The Italian writers construe under this doctrine the present occupation of Germany not, like Kelsen, as a *condominium* sovereignty of the victors, but as activities by the Allies on a *terra nullius*. A *terra nullius*, however, can be acquired legally through effective occupation by any state; this is certainly not the legal situation of occupied Germany.

On the other hand, there is a very different school of thought, according to which *debellatio* consists of conquest plus subjugation, which must be exercised through annexation. Here the objective fact (conquest) must be coupled with the subjective animus of annexing the conquered enemy state. This school is also represented by Continental writers, particularly clearly by Strupp;[72] this point of view is, without exception, taken by Anglo-American writers.[73] It is sufficient to point to two recent statements by Hackworth [74] and Lauterpacht. "Subjugation," Lauterpacht writes, "may be correctly defined as extermination in war of one belligerent by another through annexation of the former's territory, after conquest, the enemy forces having been annihilated." [75]

If this second doctrine is adopted, Germany has not ceased to exist as a sovereign state, as she certainly has not been annexed. Thus the opposing doctrines on the status of occupied Germany can both claim to be correct, according to whether they are based on the one or the other school of a deeply divided doctrine. However, it seems that the second doctrine is not only advanced by a majority of experts, but that it is also the correct one; i.e., in conformity with positive international law. As two of the Big Three are Great Britain and the United States, and as the Anglo-American literature is unanimous in the sense of the second school, the documents of 1945, written under Anglo-American influence and clearly denying the intention to annex Germany, must be interpreted in the sense of the second school.

IX

The writers who correctly hold that an enemy state ceases to exist only through conquest plus subjugation often further hold that the victor who has conquered any enemy state has a legal right to annex it, but that there is only one alternative to annexation: a simple belligerent occupation under the Hague rules. *Tertium non datur.*

It is true that acts and declarations of the Allies as to the legal basis of occupation are often contradictory. That the status of Germany cannot be construed as a simple belligerent occupation has been strongly stated in documents, acts, and declarations. Thus point 2a of the directive of 1945 to General Eisenhower states: "The rights, power and status of the military government in Germany are based upon the unconditional surrender or total defeat of Germany." That this is by no means an *occupatio bellica* under the Hague rules is the legal opinion expressed in the Nuremberg Judgment. In a much-quoted statement the British commander-in-chief, General Sir Brian Robertson, declared: "The present occupation of Germany has no precedent . . . was never envisaged by the authors of the Hague convention. In view of the supreme authority vested in the four commanders-in-chief, there is no limit on their powers save those which they choose to adopt. Any allegation that measures taken by British Military Government constituted a violation of the said articles or of International Law are misconceived and beside the point."

On the other hand, the French and American military governments have, in their requisitions forms, often expressly referred to the corresponding Hague articles.[76] Such statements have also been made in the United States when e.g., funds were requested from Congress for relief in the area occupied by American forces, with reference to Article XLIII of the Hague rules.[77] To make the legal confusion even worse, General Clay once refuted the applicability of the Hague rules on belligerent occupation with the remark that "it cannot be claimed by a state which wages aggressive total war." But positive international law prescribes the application of the laws of war also against an illegal belligerent; nothing is more sure in law than that. On the other hand, in his proclamation in the autumn of 1944, when Allied troops first entered into Germany—i.e., at a time when there really was no more than a belligerent occupation under the Hague rules—General Eisenhower claimed powers far transcending those granted to a military occupant.

Writers such as Brabner-Smith,[78] Bagge,[79] and many Germans,[80] reasoning under the *tertium non datur* argument have come to the conclusion that as Germany has not

been annexed, her legal status is simply that of belligerent
occupation under the Hague rules. This theory has also
been strongly defended by Laun. From a German point of
view, this theory is politically valuable; it is a fighting
theory, to prove that much, perhaps most, of what the
Allies have been doing and are doing in Germany is in full
contradiction to the Hague rules, and therefore strictly
illegal under international law. Laun, at a time when it
might not yet have been advisable to say so openly, put
this accusation in the form that the Allies have created in
Germany a "special law" (*ein Sonderrecht*), that they are
manipulating with a "twofold international law" (*zweierlei
Völkerrecht*) ; but what he really meant was the assertion
of the strict illegality of Allied measures; and later writers
have made such statements openly.

However, this theory, too, is legally untenable. The law
of belligerent occupation is certainly still valid law, and
recognized as such by the Nuremberg Judgment; but it
applies, of course, only to belligerent occupation, and the
present occupation of Germany is not a belligerent occupation. It must be taken into consideration that in earlier
times any occupation of enemy territory constituted conquest. It was in order to distinguish a mere holding while
the war is going on from the firmly established occupation
after what already early writers called the "ultima victoria"
in a war that the new institution of belligerent occupation
had been created; and belligerent occupation became fully
recognized in the literature after Heffter, and was regulated
by the Hague rules. Belligerent occupation is therefore,
historically and legally, exactly the opposite of conquest. It
is characterized by being temporary, provisional, essentially
precarious, subject to all the vicissitudes of war. That is
the reason why in positive international law even the total
occupation of an enemy country whose armed forces have
been annihilated, and whose government has been driven

out, does not constitute conquest, as long as allies of the state whose armed forces have surrendered in defeat continue to fight. For here even such occupation is precarious, as the Allied liberation of German-occupied Europe has shown. It is this precarious situation which explains the limitations that international law puts on the powers of the belligerent occupant. Belligerent occupation presupposes that the war goes on, not only legally, but in fact, at least potentially. However, after the total defeat of Nazi Germany the situation was essentially different since the occupation had become firmly established; any resistance, any factual continuation of hostilities, any possibility that the occupant might be driven out by the military vicissitudes of war—all these were out of the question. Indeed, these are the very characteristics of conquest, which is historically and legally exactly the opposite of belligerent occupation.

Recently Stödter has presented a new theory which contends that Germany's status is that of mere belligerent occupation, and yet that the Allied measures are in general fully justified under the Hague rules.[81] This theory is legally untenable for two reasons: first, because Germany's status is not that of belligerent occupation; second, because if it were, the Allied measures certainly would be, to a great extent, illegal, as the aforementioned fighting theory holds. No amount of sophistication can prove legally that Article XLIII of the Hague rules authorizes a mere belligerent occupant to take, within certain limits, all such political measures as are necessary to realize his war aims. Exactly the contrary is the law. The whole development of the law from Lieber to 1907 was in the direction of limiting more and more the powers of the occupant. Russia's measures in Bulgaria during the Turco-Russian War were universally recognized as transcending by far the powers of a military occupant. When Germany in World War I divided Belgium into French and Flemish zones and encouraged Flemish nationalism—very mild measures, indeed, compared with Allied measures in Germany—this action was certainly in conformity with one of Germany's war aims, but it was held illegal in the professional literature and in the courts. Any attempt to construe the present status of occupied Germany as simple belligerent occupation must necessarily fail in view of the unsurmountable legal obstacle constituted by Article XLIII of the Hague rules.

X

The road of *tertium non datur* leads to no solution. That is why most theories try to show that there is a third way under international law. But these theories of the "third way" show again the two opposed solutions: extinction *vel non* of Germany as a sovereign state.

Leading among the writers of the first group is Kelsen who identifies "supreme authority" with sovereignty and holds that annexation is only one form, and not the only form, of taking over the sovereignty of the conquered state. All the adherents to Kelsen's theory adopt similar constructions; thus Pollack, Abendroth, Kempski, Benoist, Cuny, Schwarzenberger; thus also the Nuremberg Judgment [82] and the American Judgment in the Nuremberg Lawyers' Trial. Quincy Wright argues *a maiore ad minus*: [83] the victors had, no doubt, the right to annex the conquered state; they were thus entitled "to declare the lesser policy of exercising sovereignty temporarily for specific purposes with the intention of eventually transferring the sovereignty to someone else." For Wright, Germany has ceased to exist as a sovereign state; the victors are temporary sovereigns. This argument *a maiore ad minus* has found followers also among those who, like Verdross, affirm the continued existence of Germany as a state. German writers find comfort in Erich Kaufmann's phrase that what has been done is, in comparison with annexation, "not a *minus*, but an *aliud*." For Mario Giuliano, Germany is only a "geographical expression," but others see in her a separate entity, while her sovereignty is "absolutely suspended" (Virally).[84] For the latter, Germany's status is one of "international administration." For Abendroth, Germany, although extinct as a sovereign state, has remained a state in the sense of municipal law.[85] Lauterpacht holds that Germany has been conquered, but not subjugated;[86] he states that "the international personality of Germany must be deemed suspended until the setting up of an independent German government." But general international law knows no "suspension" of sovereignty. Mann holds too that Germany still exists as a state in the sense of municipal law.[87] Jennings construes the Potsdam Declaration as a "government in commission,"[88] as a special and temporary regime, as a separation of state and government, as a case of a succession, not of states, but of governments.

Other third-way constructions affirm the continued existence of Germany as a sovereign state. The theories of an "occupation of intervention" and of a "fiduciary occupation" have already been mentioned. Many writers hold, e.g., that the Allied Control Council is the German government. This is a wholly untenable theory which, if the continuance of war is asserted, would lead to the conclusion that the Allies are at war with themselves. Equally untenable is the theory of a "dual position" of the occupying authorities; thus Rheinstein,[89] although he is forced to recognize himself that this dual position—"qua victors" and "qua German government"—leads to "ambiguity and an intrinsic contradictoriness" of the situation.

Another theory, represented by Schätzel[90] and Verdross,[91] affirms that Germany continues to exist as a sovereign state, but that she has been "put under tutelage."[92] The writers upholding third-way theories and at the same time affirming the continued existence of Germany as a sovereign state can muster strong legal arguments. There are the official documents that expressly deny the annexation of Germany, which declare the intention to maintain the territorial unity of Germany as of 1937. The occupying powers—already this name is an argument—and the laws of the Allied Control Council always speak of Germany, of "Germany's frontiers," and so on. For example, the United States suggested at the Belgrade Danube Conference that Germany be made a member of the proposed Danube Commission. East and West continuously affirm that their policies aim at the unity of Germany. Many acts of the occupation authorities can be cited; the American Military Government, for example, censured Bavaria for separatist tendencies; German officials at Hamburg, in the British Zone, were sworn to keep allegiance to the Reich.

There are other strong legal arguments. The German nationality continues to exist; whereas when a state ceases to exist, its former nationals become stateless persons under general international law. The Allies have negotiated for years concerning the conclusion of a peace treaty; and certainly no peace treaty is legally possible with a state that has ceased to exist. Proclamation Number 2 of the Allied Control Council speaks of directions it will give concerning "the abrogation, bringing into force, revival or application of any treaty to which Germany *is* or has been a party" (italics supplied). A strong legal argument, upon which Verdross particularly insists, is the continuance of Germany as a unity of international responsibility for international delinquencies; reparations, the Allies state, have to be taken "from Germany." A good legal argument is, further, the attitude of neutral countries, such as Switzerland, Sweden, even Austria, which officially and through their courts voice their conviction of the continued existence of Germany as a sovereign state.

The thesis of Germany's continued existence as a state is, to a great extent, defended with arguments taken from the writings of Verdross; thus the distinction between *condominium* and *coimperium,* the distinction between sovereignty and mere exercise of sovereignty.[93] Here belongs also Verdross's distinction between territorial sovereignty and mere "territorial supremacy" (Bosnia 1878–1908). This distinction is certainly a correct one. He who, as in the case of "cession for administration," has only territorial supremacy is not the sovereign. He has only, to state it in the words of the Panama Treaty of 1903, all the rights "as if he were sovereign," but not *of* the sovereign; the right of sovereignty, although perhaps only a *nudum jus,* can be in another state. Only the sovereign has the *jus disponendi* over the territory, not he who has mere territorial supremacy. But is that the case here? In the declaration of June 5, 1945, the victors state that *"they* [not the peace treaty] will hereafter determine the boundaries of Germany or of any part thereof" (italics supplied). With regard to the factual dismemberments of Germany in the East and the West, it can be argued legally that these are only provisional measures and that it has always been expressly declared that all problems of Germany's frontiers must wait for their definitive solution at the peace conference. But East Germany has been ceded, at least for administration, to the Soviet Union and Poland, and that constitutes an exercise of the *jus disponendi* by the territorial sovereign. Verdross reasons that German state power has continued in the lower organs. But sovereignty cannot exist in the lower organs only. In addition, no such state power has continued even in the lower organs, as the victors assumed supreme authority, "including *all* the powers possessed by the German

Government, the High Command and *any state, municipal or local government or authority*" (italics added). The American military government, in the interest of decentralization, and democratization, began "to *transfer* authority to local German organs" (italics added).

All authority in occupied Germany has its legal reason in the "supreme authority" of the victors. Arndt states that laws by German bizonal authorities "are not German laws, but only laws for Germans." Stödter denies that for all German authorities to owe their origin and competence to measures of the occupation authorities destroys their German character. The competence of an organ depends either on considerations of jurisdiction; i.e., for whom the organ has to work; in this sense the German authorities are German organs. Or it depends on the legal source from which the authority of an organ is legally derived; this legal source is everywhere the "supreme authority" of the occupying powers.

There is further this legal difficulty: Can a sovereign state continue to exist if it has no central government? German writers take much comfort in the idea that a merely temporary lack of government does not have the extinction of the state as a legal consequence. Closely connected with this argument is the distinction between "capacity to have rights and duties in international law" and "capacity to act." Whereas for Lauterpacht the first capacity is "suspended," many argue that Germany has only lost her "capacity to act." Can this theory be legally maintained? The measures of the victors have abolished all Hitler laws, all state organs, have closed all courts, disarmed and demilitarized Germany, punished the war criminals; they have politically remade Germany; they tend toward "re-education," and complete control of German trade and finances; they have brought to an end all external relations of Germany; they have created the Länder and by Control Council Law Number 46, they have abolished the state of

Prussia; they have disposed of German territory and of the "orderly transfer of German populations"; they have dismantled factories and taken reparations. Now there is a norm of general international law according to which a state guilty of an international delinquency must make reparations. But as general international law contains no details, and as neither the guilty nor the injured state can unilaterally determine the amount and the modes of reparation, a previous agreement is necessary. German writers speak often of "performances in advance of reparations" (*Vorleistungen*); but where is the basis for that in general international law?

The case of occupied Germany is not one of a restriction of her capacity to act. It should be admitted that Germany had completely lost her capacity to act, in external as well as internal matters. Can a state under such conditions be sovereign? Even the proponents of continued existence of German sovereignty are forced to admit that Germany has become a "dependent state" (Rheinstein) or a "protectorate" (Verdross). Is a protected state that also has lost its whole capacity to act, even in internal matters, a sovereign state in law?

True, the German Federal Republic has made great progress. More and more sovereignty is "transferred" or "restored" to Germany. She may now, under certain conditions, conclude treaties. She will be admitted to international organizations; she will enter the Council of Europe; and she has taken part, on a basis of equality, at the Paris negotiations concerning the Schuman Plan. Germany will be more and more integrated into the so-called Western European and the Atlantic communities; the day may not be far when she will also participate in the defense of these groupings.

All that may be admirable and in the interest of Germany, of Europe, and of the whole "free world." But the problem of the legal status of occupied Germany remains.

The Western Republic is not a state, but only a "fragment of a state," as the experts at Herrenchiemsee expressed it. It is an artificial conglomeration of artificial Länder, often with absurd boundaries and an artificial capital. Western Germany has its legal *raison d'être* in the supreme authority of the three western powers. Even Grewe,[94] for whom the present status of Germany is one of "sequestration," sees in the Occupation Statute an act of sovereignty of the occupying powers. This Occupation Statute of April 17, 1949, has been unilaterally proclaimed by the western powers "in the exercise of supreme authority which is retained by their governments." Sovereignty means that a state is immediately and exclusively subordinated to international law, and not to any other legal order. The Occupation Statute does not give to Western Germany sovereignty, but "self-government to the maximum possible degree consistent with such occupation." Occupation rule, as Erich Kaufmann correctly states, is essentially foreign rule. The Occupation Statute contains not only reserved powers in wide and highly important fields but also the reserved power to resume, under certain conditions determined by the occupying powers, in whole or in part, the exercise of full authority.[95] That Western Germany will be admitted to the Council of Europe only as an associated member is explained by its lack of sovereignty.

In addition, Eastern Germany, too, is only a fragment, and certainly not a sovereign state. A sovereign state needs not only a government, but an independent government. The Germany of 1937 does not exist. There are two "Germanys," more and more divided not only in constitutional but also in private and criminal law, in organization and ideology. They symbolize the East-West split; so does Berlin, which legally belongs now neither to the Western nor to the Eastern fragment. How shall the Germany of 1937 be unified again as a sovereign state? The present situation is certainly a tragedy for Germany and for the world, a tragedy made gloomier by the recent events in equally split Korea.

XI

The occupying powers are bound by their treaties and agreements *inter se*; but these constitute merely particular international law. The legal source which justifies these agreements can be found only in general international law.

The occupying powers are, further, bound in any case by norms of general international law, not only toward aliens in the occupied territory, but also toward Germans. The latter are not without legal rights as regards the victors; they are protected by the norms established in the name of humanity that constitute positive international law. The Prisoners of War Convention remains binding also in case of conquest; as Fahy admits, not all the occupying powers have fully fulfilled their obligations in this respect.[96] He who takes over a territory, even if illegally, is under the legal obligation to care for the population. Rheinstein [97] is perfectly correct when he states that the importation of food into Germany is not simply an act of charity or generosity but the fulfillment of an international duty. To slaughter the population of a conquered territory, to sell them into slavery, or reduce them to forced labor— practices frequent in earlier times—are definitely prohibited by general international law actually in force. The power of the victors is not unlimited legally.

Giving one-fourth of Germany to the Soviet Union and Poland, always objectionable morally and politically, could have been done legally only by the sovereign of the conquered territory. The "orderly transfer" of millions of Germans, and the way it was carried out, Rheinstein writes, "cannot be called anything but a crime against humanity in the full sense and with all the implications of the term as determined in Nuremberg."

In certain ways the occupying powers have even done more than the sovereign can do under international law. This is the case of Law Number 5 of the Control Council of September 30, 1945, by which the control of all German property abroad was taken over and this property taken away from the German owners.[98] It is a well-settled rule of general international law that confiscatory measures of the sovereign have no extraterritorial effect. Hence also the necessity of special agreements with Switzerland and Sweden.

The status of occupied Germany is neither subjugation nor simple belligerent occupation. It is correct that, in general, the law cannot be deduced from the facts. But there is the principle of effectivity, which is a norm of positive general international law, and this norm applies to the status of states. As an ultimate construction of the status of occupied Germany it could be said that even if the present status of Germany had been brought about illegally, yet this illegality would have been healed by the norm of effectivity. And this norm is not valid, as is sometimes asserted, only against the aggressor. Italy's conquest of Ethiopia was certainly illegal, but it was effective, and Italy's sovereignty was recognized *de jure* by Great Britain and by many more states.

It is not necessary, however, to resort to the norm of effectivity, for general international law allows the conqueror not only to annex the conquered state, but also to determine its fate in a different way. He can restore the conquered state to its former sovereign and evacuate the territory; he can cede the conquered territory to a third state; he can partition it. He can take over the conquered territory temporarily with the intention of later restoring its sovereignty. Even if his intention is to continue the conquered territory as a sovereign state, the latter may cease to exist by subsequent events, such as dismemberment, even if this occurs against the intention of the conquerors. Should a unified, sovereign Germany emerge within foreseeable time, the question whether it is the old state continued or a new state will probably always remain controversial, not only because of strong political and emotional influences, but also because of the vagueness of the international norm concerning the so-called identity of a state in international law. Of course, there is no hope for the emergence of a unified, sovereign Germany within the frontiers of 1937.

General international law does not give to any victor, but to the conqueror, the right to take such measures with regard to the conquered territory as he thinks fit. This is the legal basis of the status of occupied Germany. The victors are not the German government, nor do they hold a dual position, nor are they the representatives of Germany. They act by virtue of a right given to them by general international law; all their acts, legislative, executive, or judicial, have the character of international law. Philip C. Jessup said in the United Nations Security Council debate on the Berlin blockade, "We are here by the right of victory." Sereni holds the same view.[99]

It is this right of the conqueror that is shown when writers state that the fate of the conquered territory depends on the will of the conqueror, when Lauterpacht notes that the conquered territory, even if not annexed, "remains in possession and under the sway" of the conqueror. That is why the same author can declare that the exercise of all rights and prerogatives is vested in the occupying powers "with full effect in International Law."

Especially within the Pan-American orbit, resolutions have been adopted to the effect that "victory gives no right." But that is not the general international law actually in

force. True, great progress has been made. The rights of
the conqueror are no longer legally unlimited, But within
these limits, the conqueror is entitled to determine the fate
of the conquered state by annexation or otherwise. It is
therefore not only a phrase of literature when the German
philosopher of a Christian existentialism, Karl Jaspers,
remarked that the only norm that applies to totally defeated
Germany is the ancient Roman rule: *Vae victis!*

What Kelsen tried to prevent by his article of 1944—
namely, the creation of a legally unclear and ambiguous
situation with regard to Germany—has in fact happened.
The situation of occupied Germany under international
law presents and will continue to present a legal dilemma.

On the one hand, the theories identifying either the unconditional surrender or the Potsdam Declaration with
subjugation are legally untenable. Germany was conquered,
but not subjugated. Conquest alone does not extinguish the
vanquished state, nor does it end the war automatically.
On the other hand, the theories construing the present situation as mere belligerent occupation under the Hague rules
are equally untenable in law; conquest is, historically and
legally, exactly the opposite of belligerent occupation. The
theories invented *ad hoc* are untenable, because they have
no basis in general international law. Neither does general
international law, to quote some "third-way constructions,"
know a "suspension" of sovereignty, or know a sovereign
state that has no government and is deprived of its total
capacity to act, in both external and internal matters.

While the situation, even if originally illegal, could be
construed as healed by the principle of effectivity that is a
norm of positive general international law, it is not necessary to resort to this construction. The legal basis of the
present occupation is conquest; the conqueror has a right
to annex the conquered state, but can also take other measures. He can, particularly, intend to preserve the sover-

eignty of the conquered state. That was the declared intention of the conquerors of Germany. But their very acts from the beginning, and also subsequent events, have made the carrying-out of this declared intention impossible. Where is the sovereign German state within the frontiers of 1937? From the beginning only rump Germany was made subject to occupation; and from this rump Germany, split into four occupation zones, the Saar, now a separate "associate" member in the Council of Europe, was virtually detached. At this time there are only two fragments, neither of them a sovereign state. And this situation is likely to last until either the victor in the next world war makes a completely new arrangement or, what would be too good to come true, a complete understanding between the United States of America and the Soviet Union can be reached.

Some writers voice the opinion that the present development of Western Germany may render the problem of the legal status of occupied Germany merely an academic question. This is not the case. This problem comes up continuously, diplomatically and internally. Recently, in the negotiations between the three western powers concerning the ending of the war, France took the position originated by Kelsen, but was persuaded to admit that Germany exists, although her sovereignty is *en sommeil.* Where is the legal basis in general international law for a "sleeping sovereignty"? Internally, the problem of the status of occupied Germany arises daily in Germany in legal business and leads to the greatest difficulties.

An analysis of the recent agreement of the three western powers of September 19, 1950, clearly shows that the basic dilemma continues.[100] True, this agreement "marks an important stage in the normalization of the relations," a "major advance toward the progressive return of Germany to partnership in Western Europe." It gives the Bonn government more powers; but Western Germany—and the agreement covers only this fragment—by no means becomes a sovereign state. True, all restrictions on commercial cargo ships are removed, steps for "German participation in an integrated force for the defense of European freedom" are envisaged. The Bonn government will be authorized to establish a Ministry of Foreign Affairs, far-reaching reductions in existing controls concerning internal economic matters will be made, a review of the agreement on prohibited and limited industries will be undertaken. The occupying powers are prepared to amend the Occupation Statute. They "will treat any attack against the Federal Republic or Berlin from any quarter as an attack upon themselves," and will increase their occupation forces. They will, finally, "take the necessary steps in their domestic legislation to terminate the state of war with Germany."

Again, it should be emphasized that all these blessings come from the authority of the occupying powers, and deal only with Western Germany. The Bonn government will be authorized by them to enter into diplomatic relations with foreign countries only "in suitable cases," and the occupying powers alone will determine what cases are "suitable." The supreme authority based on conquest is strongly reaffirmed. Thus the Occupying powers are prepared to amend the Occupation Statute "while maintaining the legal basis of occupation." The occupation troops will also be for the security of Western Germany, but "in addition to their occupation duties." Finally, the declaration to terminate the state of war with Germany "will not affect the rights and status of the three Powers in Germany, which rest upon other bases"—namely, upon conquest.

[1] See W. FRIEDMANN, THE ALLIED MILITARY GOVERNMENT OF GERMANY (1947); HAROLD ZINK, AMERICAN MILITARY GOVERNMENT IN GERMANY (1947), and, *Military Government*, THE ANNALS (January, 1950).

[2] See *A Decade of American Foreign Policy: Basic Documents 1941–1949*, S. Doc. No. 123, 81st Cong., 1st Sess. 1381; JAMES E. POL-

LOCK, JAMES H. MEISEL, HENRY L. BRETTON, GERMANY UNDER OCCUPA-TION: ILLUSTRATIVE MATERIALS AND DOCUMENTS (1949).

3 ROLF STÖDTER, DEUTSCHLAND'S RECHTSLAGE, Bibliography 275–86, Index of Court Decisions 287–90 (1948). Long after having finished this manuscript, this writer saw a report on non-German literature published by U. Meister in 13 ZEITSCHRIFT FÜR AUSLÄNDISCHES ÖFFENTLICHES RECHT UND VÖLKERRECHT 173–85 (1950).

4 See ROBIN, DES OCCUPATIONS MILITAIRES EN DEHORS DES OCCU-PATIONS DE GUERRE (1913).

5 See SERRA, L'OCCUPAZIONE BELLICA GERMANICA NEGLI ANNI 1939–1940 (1941); R. LEMKIN, AXIS RULE IN OCCUPIED EUROPE (1944); VAN NISPEN TOT SEVENAAR, L'OCCUPATION ALLEMANDE PENDANT LA DERNIÈRE GUERRE (1946).

6 See LORD RENNELL OF RODD, BRITISH MILITARY ADMINISTRATION OF OCCUPIED TERRITORIES IN AFRICA DURING THE YEARS 1941–1947 (1948).

7 See Alf Ross, *Denmark's Legal Status during the Occupation*, 1 JUS GENTIUM: NORDISK TIDSKRIFT FOR FOLKERET OG INTERNATIONAL PRIVATRET 3–21 (1949).

8 See HEYLAND, DIE RECHTSSTELLUNG DER BESETZTEN RHEINLANDE (1923); E. FRAENKEL, MILITARY OCCUPATION AND THE RULE OF LAW (1944).

9 The creator of this theory is Georg A. Zinn in 1 NEUE JURISTISCHE WOCHENSCHRIFT 8 (1947–48), and in 2 SÜDDEUTSCHE JURISTENZEITUNG 4 (1947). This theory has been adopted by A. Arndt in 2 DIE WANDLUNG 107–16 (1947); see also his article *Status and Development of Constitutional Law in Germany*, THE ANNALS 1–9 (1948); see also KARL GEILER, DIE GEGENWÄRTIGE VÖLKERRECHTLICHE LAGE DEUTSCHLANDS (1947). Karl Schmid and Alfons Steiniger, in 1 NEUE JUSTIZ 146, 205 (1947), give a juridical construction by holding that this type of occupation constitutes a third way open under international law, apart from the alternative of subjugation by annexation or mere belligerent occupation.

10 The creator of this theory is the Swiss G. Sauser-Hall, *L'Occupation de l'Allemagne par les Puissances Alliées*, 3 ANNUAIRE SUISSE DE DROIT INTERNATIONAL 9–63 (1946). This theory has found many followers, inside and outside of Germany, e.g., SAUER, GRUNDLEHRE DES VOLKERRECHTS 117 (2d ed. 1948); HERMANN V. MANGOLDT, GRUNDSÄTZLICHES ZUM NEUAUFBAU EINER DEUTSCHEN STAATSGEWALT (1947); Eberhard Menzel, Erich Kaufmann, Peters, Budde, and many others follow this theory; see also Max Rheinstein, *The Legal Status of Occupied Germany*, 47 MICH. L. REV. 23–40 (1948).

11 Both theories are adequately refuted by R. STÖDTER, *op. cit.* at 133–46.

12 For example, there must be three persons: settlor, trustee, *cestui que* trust. The trustee owes the beneficiary the duty of conducting the trust with the advantage of the *cestui que* trust solely in mind, must exclude his own advantage or profit and that of third parties from consideration in making decisions and taking action under the trust,

and has the duty of rendering account to the court (GEORGE G. BOGERT, HANDBOOK OF THE LAW OF TRUSTS 2, 331, 460 [2d ed. 1942]).

[13] League of Nations mandates (Covenant, Art. XXII). United Nations trusteeships. In both cases there is an international supervising organ. The phrase "United Nations" in the 1945 documents ("consultation with the United Nations") means here the wartime coalition of the victors. The "United Nations" in the sense of the international organization created by the Charter of the United Nations is expressly denied any jurisdiction with regard to enemy states (Art. CVII). The trust idea is in these cases always applied to "people not yet able to stand by themselves under the strenuous conditions of the modern world." By the United Nations resolution concerning the partition of Palestine the planned *corpus separatum* of Jerusalem was to be put under the Trusteeship Council, but the Free Territory of Trieste was placed under the Security Council.

[14] H. Kelsen, *The International Legal Status of Germany To Be Established Immediately upon Terminaton of the War*, 38 AM.J.INT'L L. 689–94 (1944).

[15] H. Kelsen, *The Legal Status of Germany According to the Declaration of Berlin*, 39 AM.J.INT'L L. 518–26 (1945).

[16] H. Kelsen, *German Peace Terms*, letter to the editor of the N. Y. Times, September 7, 1947; H. Kelsen, *Is a Peace Treaty with Germany Legally Possible and Politically Desirable?*, 41 AM. POL. SCI. REV. 1188–93 (1947).

[17] Curtis C. Shears, *Some Legal Implications of Unconditional Surrender*, PROCEEDINGS OF THE AMERICAN SOCIETY OF INTERNATIONAL LAW 44–52 (1945).

[18] L. C. Green, "Since Its Unconditional Surrender Germany Has By Debellatio Ceased To Exist," in *Berlin and the U.N.*, WORLD AFFAIRS 28 (January, 1949).

[19] G. A. Finch, *The Nuremberg Trial and International Law*, 41 AM.J.INT'L L. 22 (1947).

[20] Q. Wright, *The Law of the Nuremberg Trial*, 41 AM.J.INT'L L. 50 (1947).

[21] Charles Fahy, *Legal Problems of German Occupation*, 47 MICH. L. Rev. 11–22 (1948).

[22] Alwyn V. Freeman, *War Crimes by Enemy Nationals Administering Justice in Occupied Territory*, 41 AM.J.INT'L L. 584 (1947).

[23] G. SCHWARZENBERGER, A MANUAL OF INTERNATIONAL LAW 114 (1947).

[24] 1 OPPENHEIM-LAUTERPACHT, INTERNATIONAL LAW: A TREATISE 411, 520 (6th ed. 1947).

[25] F. B. Schick, *The Nuremberg Trial and the International Law of the Future*, 41 AM.J.INT'L L. 780 (1947).

[26] F. A. Mann, *The Present Legal Status of Germany*, 1 INT'L L. Q. 314–35 (Autumn, 1947).

[27] R. Y. Jennings, *Government in Commission*, 23 BRIT. YB. INT'L L. 112–41 (1946).

[28] Benoist, *Le Conseil de Contrôle et l'Occupation de l'Allemagne,* 11 POLITIQUE ETRANGÈRE 61 (1946).

[29] Cuny, La capitulation sans conditions de l'Allemagne (unpublished thesis, Paris, 1947).

[30] MIGUEL VIRALLY, L'ADMINISTRATION INTERNATIONALE DE L'ALLEMAGNE (1948).

[31] LUDOVICO M. BENTIVOGLIO, LA DEBELLATIO NEL DIRITTO INTERNAZIONALE (1948).

[32] FRANC CAPOTORTI, L'OCCUPAZIONE NEL DIRITTO DI GUERRA (1949).

[33] MARIO GIULIANO, LA SITUAZIONE ATTUALE DELLA GERMANIA SECONDO IL DIRITTO INTERNAZIONALE (1948).

[34] ROLANDO QUADRI, DIRITTO INTERNAZIONALE PUBBLICO (1949). He says, rather contemptuously, that, "taluni pedanti si ostinano a non considerare neppure la Germania como debellata" (p. 199).

[35] Case III, United States v. Josef Alstoetter.

[36] Tagesspiegel, January 21, February 11, 13, 1947.

[37] *Ibid.*, March 18, 1947.

[38] *Die völkerrechtliche Lage Deutschlands,* 1 EPOCHE, No. 11–12 (1947).

[39] 1 NEUE JUSTIZ 73 (1947).

[40] Gutachten, 1945.

[41] *Die völkerrechtliche Stellung Deutschlands,* 2 FRANKFURTER HEFTE 1254 (1947).

[42] Jürgen von Kempski, *Deutschland als Völkerrechtssubjekt,* 1 MERKUR, No. 2, 188–99 (1947).

[43] ULRICH VON DASSEL, DIE FRAGE NACH DEM DEUTSCHEN STAAT VON HEUTE (1948).

[44] BERICHT ÜBER DEN VERFASSUNGSKONVENT (1948).

[45] See, e.g., J. W. Brabner-Smith, *Has Germany Ceased To Exist?,* AMERICAN PERSPECTIVE 55–61 (May, 1948); Brabner-Smith, *Concluding the War—The Peace Settlement and Congressional Powers,* 34 VA. L. REV. 553–68 (1948).

[46] See, e.g., Algot Bagge, *The Legal Position of the Allied Powers in Germany,* 1 JUS GENTIUM: NORDISK TIDSKRIFT FOR FOLKERET OG INTERNATIONAL PRIVATRET 23–24 (1949). Modesto Suárez, *La existencia jurídica de Alemania: Esquema de una polémica originada por Kelsen,* 2 REVISTA ESPAÑOLA DE DERECHO INTERNACIONAL 129–43 (1949).

[47] See, e.g., Eberhard Menzel, *Deutschland ein Kondominium oder Koimperium?,* 1 JAHRBUCH FÜR INTERNATIONALES UND ANSLÄNDISCHES ÖFFENTLICHES RECHT 43–86 (1948).

[48] It must, of course, always be carefully investigated whether such court decisions—such as, e.g., the much quoted British decision Rex. v. Bottrill (1 All. E. R. 635; L. R. [1947], K. B. 41)—contain merely municipal law and are therefore not necessarily of legal value from the point of view of international law. Recently the judgment of the Oberlandesgericht Tübingen of May 4, 1949 (1 RECHTSPRECHUNG ZUM WIEDERGUTMACHUNGSRECHT 32 [1949]) has carefully reviewed the whole literature of state and court practice within Germany and

abroad and has reached the conclusion that neither the surrender nor other subsequent events have destroyed the international legal personality of Germany.

[49] For an excellent survey of this practice of states and courts, see STÖDTER, *op. cit.* at 91–104.

[50] Six Power Accord on Western Germany of June 1, 1948; currency reform of June, 1948; meeting of the minister presidents of the eleven western "Länder" at Frankfurt, July 21–26, 1948; meeting of German legal experts at Herrenschiemsee, Bavaria, August 10–23, 1948; session of the German Parliamentary Council at Bonn, starting on September 1, 1948, to write a constitution for Western Germany.

[51] *Basic Law* [Grundgesetz] *for the Federal Republic of Germany* (146 articles), DEPARTMENT OF STATE, Publication 3526 (1949).

[52] Text in 20 DEP'T STATE BULL., No. 511 at 500–501 (April 17, 1949).

[53] 20 *ibid.*, No. 512 at 524–31 (April 24, 1949).

[54] See P. E. Moseley, *Dismemberment of Germany: The Allied Negotiations from Yalta to Potsdam*, 28 FOREIGN AFFAIRS 487–98 (1950).

[55] SUMNER WELLES, THE TIME FOR DECISION (1944).

[56] To be found in the first pages of HENRY MORGENTHAU, JR., GERMANY IS OUR PROBLEM (1945).

[57] With Anthony Eden as chairman; see Point III of the Yalta Conference Protocol, 1945.

[58] The Potsdam Declaration states that "the German people has begun to atone for the terrible crimes committed under the leadership of those whom in the hour of their success they openly approved and blindly obeyed."

[59] See, for all details, the Joint Chiefs of Staff, directive to General Eisenhower (J.C.S. 1067, October, 1945).

[60] See for the Polish point of view: A. KLAPOWSKI, DIE RECHTS-GRUNDLAGE DER ODER-NEISSE LINIE (German trans. 1949); for the German point of view: P. H. SERAPHIM, R. MAURACH, and G. WOL-FRUM, OSTWÄRTS DER ODER-NEISSE LINIE (1949).

[61] Churchill was the first to state, as leader of the opposition, that the transfer of one-fourth of Germany to Poland does not augur well for the future peace of Europe. R. F. Maguire writes: "There is no difference in the effect on the German people from what would have arisen here, if Japan had been the victor in the war and had exacted a cession of the west coast of the United States. . . . It is not necessary to point out that even though we had been thus direly defeated, there would have been no real peace until by negotiations or by force those states were restored to us."—A.B.A.J. 907 (November, 1949).

[62] See Sidney B. Fay, *The Saar Problem*, 18 CURRENT HISTORY 251–62 (May, 1950).

[63] See G. Héraud, *Le statut politique de la Sarre dans le cadre du rattachement économique à la France*, 19 REVUE GÉNÉRALE DE

DROIT INTERNATIONAL PUBLIC (3e sér.) 186–209 (1948). The Constitution Sarroise of December 15, 1947 (*ibid.* at 210–22), lays down that the Saar Territory, economically integrated with France, has political independence vis-à-vis Germany. France controls the defense and the external relations of the territory, French laws concerning currency and tariff apply in the Saar. It is remarkable that the Saarlanders have lost their German nationality. A new law of July 15, 1948 (BULLETIN OFFICIAL DE LA SARRE, No. 61, August 14, 1948), concerning acquisition and loss of the *nationalité sarroise* has been adopted.

64 By 1949, Arnold Brecht could write: "Germany has been torn into four pieces, with absurd boundaries and governed by military governments that pursued highly divergent policies." He added: "The victors should not forget that it has remained their moral responsibility to terminate this compulsory state of undemocratic absurdity." —THE ANNALS 29 (January, 1950).

65 When Simon Bolivar Buckner at Fort Donelson sent word to General Grant on February 16, 1862, asking for the terms of capitulation, Grant answered: "No terms except an unconditional surrender can be accepted." This answer was approved by Lincoln (G.F. MILTON, CONFLICT: THE AMERICAN CIVIL WAR 167 [1941]; 3 CARL SANDBURG, ABRAHAM LINCOLN: THE WAR YEARS 462 [1940]; 4 *ibid.* at 358).

66 JOSEF L. KUNZ, KRIEGSRECHT UND NEUTRALITÄTSRECHT 157 (1935).

67 See Charles Cheney Hyde, *Conquest Today*, 30 AM.J.INT'L L. 471–76 (1936); MATTHEW M. MCMAHON, CONQUEST AND MODERN INTERNATIONAL LAW (1940).

68 *Sovereignty, Seisin and the League*, 7 BRIT.YB.INT'L L. 41 (1926).

69 Thus, e.g., Liszt, Meurer, Kirchenheim, Freytag-Loringhoven, Rivier, and others.

70 See the writers quoted *supra*, notes 31–34; for the conquest of Ethiopia see, M. Udina, *L'annessione dell'Etiopia*, 2 ARCHIVO DI DIRITTO PUBBLICO 247 (1937).

71 Belgium and Serbia in World War I, Poland and other states in World War II.

72 See his article, *Debellatio*, WÖRTERBUCH DES VÖLKERRECHTS 715, and 2 ELÉMENTS DU DROIT INTERNATIONAL PUBLIC 525 (1930). In the same sense, Schätzel and Waldkirch.

73 See, e.g., Westlake, Philipson, Lawrence, Hall, Halleck, Hershey, Wilson-Tucker, Pitt-Cobbett, Hyde, Fenwick.

74 "Conquest is the taking of possession of the territory of an enemy state by force; it becomes . . . transfer of sovereignty only if the conquered territory is effectively reduced to possession and annexed by the conquering state."—1 HACKWORTH, DIGEST OF INTERNATIONAL LAW 427 (1940).

75 "A belligerent, although he has annihilated the forces and conquered the whole of the territory of his adversary . . . may not choose to exterminate the enemy state by annexing it. Subjugation

takes place *only*, when a belligerent, after having annihilated the forces and conquered the territory of his adversary, *destroys* his existence by *annexing* the conquered territory.—2 OPPENHEIM-LAUTERPACHT, INTERNATIONAL LAW 467–68 (6th ed. 1946). See also 1 *ibid.* 518–20 (7th ed. 1948): "It is the very annexation which uno actu makes the vanquished state cease to exist, and bring the territory under the conqueror's sovereignty. Thus the subjugated territory *has not for one moment been no State's land,* but passes from the enemy to the conquerer . . . through annexation" (italics supplied).

[76] See references in STÖDTER, *op. cit.* at 178–79.

[77] House Select Comm. on Foreign Aid, *Report on Germany,* H.R. Doc. No. 1500, 80th Cong., 2d Sess. *Hearings before House Subcommittee on Appropriations for Government and Relief in Occupied Areas,* 80th Cong., 1st Sess. (1947).

[78] *Op. cit.*

[79] *Op. cit.*

[80] Thus the Bavarian minister, Dr. Baumgartner, in 1947; the resolution of German international lawyers at Hamburg in 1947: Peters, Budde, von der Decken, Scholz, Barandon, Wacke, Loening, Ipsen, Laun; also German court decisions.

[81] See his article in the 48 FRIEDENS-WARTE 111 (1948), and his book, *op. cit., supra,* note 3.

[82] "Making the (Nuremberg) Charter was the exercise of the sovereign legislative power by the countries to which the German Reich unconditionally surrendered."—41 AM. J. INT'L L. 216 (1947).

[83] *Op. cit., supra,* note 20.

[84] *Op. cit., supra,* note 30.

[85] *Op. cit., supra,* note 39.

[86] 1 OPPENHEIM-LAUTERPACHT, INTERNATIONAL LAW 519–20 (7th ed. 1948).

[87] *Op. cit., supra,* note 26.

[88] *Op. cit., supra,* note 27.

[89] *Op. cit., supra,* note 10.

[90] 2 DEUTSCHE RECHTS-ZEITSCHRIFT 69–72 (1947).

[91] Professor Verdross had the amiability to send to this writer a typed sketch of his legal construction of the status of occupied Germany.

[92] *Entmündigungstheorie.*

[93] Example, the Saar Territory, 1920–35.

[94] WILHELM GREWE, EIN BESETZUNGSSTATUT FÜR DEUTSCHLAND (1948).

[95] GUSTAV VON SCHMOLLER, DIE BEFUGNISSE DER BESATZUNGSMÄCHTE IN DER BUNDESREPUBLIK DEUTSCHLAND (1950).

[96] *Op. cit., supra,* note 21.

[97] *Op. cit., supra,* note 10.

[98] On this problem see F. A. Mann, *German Property in Switzerland,* BRIT. YB. INT'L L. 354–58 (1946). See also DIETRICH SCHINDLER,

ANNUAIRE SUISSE DE DROIT INTERNATIONAL 67 ff. (1946); F. X. PETERS, AUSLIEFERUNG DEUTSCHEN PRIVATEIGENTUMS? (1946); K. G. SEELIGER, DAS AUSLÄNDISCHE PRIVATVERMÖGEN IN DER SCHWEIZ (1949); Heinrich Drost, *Die Rechtslage des deutschen Auslandsvermögens*, 2 ARCHIV DES VÖLKERRECHTS 298–304 (1950); R. STÖDTER, DEUTSCHE VERMÖGENSWERTE IM NEUTRALEN AUSLAND (1950).

[99] ANGELO P. SERENI, LA REPRÉSENTATION EN DROIT INTERNATIONAL 30 (RECUEIL DES COURS, 1949): "C'est en leur qualité de vainqueurs qu'ils ont le droit absolu, reconnu par le droit international, d'établir le statut juridique actuel de l'Allemagne . . . qu'elles ont acquis par la victoire."

[100] N.Y. Times, September 20, 1950, p. 2.

CHAPTER XIV: *The Status of the Holy See in International Law*

THE PROTESTS in the United States against the nomination by the President of an American ambassador to the Vatican reveal an astonishing lack of knowledge and understanding of the legal problem of the status of the Holy See in international law. Even in the professional literature on international law in English, this problem is either neglected [1] or very briefly [2] and sometimes inaccurately handled; the same is true in some German treatises.[3] On the other hand, there are full and correct discussions in French, Italian, and German studies written before 1929 or after.[4]

Most of the erroneous treatments of this problem follow about this line: Until 1870 the Pope was the sovereign of the Papal State, a normal person in international law. Since the Lateran Treaty of February 11, 1929, the Pope is again the sovereign of the state of the City of the Vatican (*Stato della Città del Vaticano*). But between 1870 and 1929, there was no Papal State, hence no international personality. This line of reasoning, wholly untenable in the light of the practice of states, stems mostly from the pseudo-positivistic prejudice that only sovereign states *can* be persons in international law. But the Holy See was always a subject of general international law. Modern developments show, for instance, international organizations, which certainly are not states, as persons in international law.

To understand the problem correctly, we must start with a historical consideration. During the European Middle Ages the Holy See was the spiritual leader of the *communitas Christiana* of Europe. Our modern international community developed historically by way of decentralization of the medieval Christian community of Europe. Historically, the original members of our international community were only the Christian states of Europe and the Holy See. It is this historical development which explains the unique position in international law of the Holy See as the Supreme Head of the Catholic Church.[5]

The Holy See [6] is, therefore, a *permanent* [7] subject of *general* [8] customary international law vis-à-vis all states, Catholic or not. That does not mean that the Holy See has the same international status as a sovereign state.[9] But the Holy See has, under general international law, the capacity to conclude agreements with states (concordats). The Holy See can also conclude normal international treaties, formerly on behalf of the Papal State, now on behalf of the state of the City of the Vatican, but also in its own capacity.[10] Although the juridical nature of the concordats is a controversial question, they are not only expressly recognized as international treaties by a number of states, but they have all the characteristics of an international treaty: They are concluded on the basis of full equality. This sovereignty and independence of the Holy See is not only based on Canon Law [11] but on general customary international law, on the practice of states. The recognition of this sovereignty by the Italian municipal Law of Guarantee of May 13, 1871, and by the international Lateran Treaty of 1929 is purely declaratory in nature. Concordats are negotiated and signed like any international treaty. They need ratification. They can be modified only by common consent.

Their norms become binding on individuals only by their transformation into municipal law. As the Holy See is a person in *general* international law, its capacity to conclude concordats is by no means restricted to Catholic states.[12]

The Holy See has the active and passive right of legation under general international law, not restricted to Catholic states. The Protocol of Vienna of March 19, 1815, puts Papal nuncios into the rank of ambassadors under general international law. The Vienna Protocol also provides that "the present regulations shall not cause any innovation with regard to the representatives of the Pope," to whom Catholic states grant the privilege of being the Dean of the Diplomatic Corps. These norms are binding on all the states, Catholic or not.[13] Cardinals, on the other hand, are not diplomatic agents of the Holy See.[14]

Prior to 1870, there were two subjects of international law: the Papal State and the Holy See. The Pope constituted in his person a personal union of two different organs, the highest organs of two different subjects of international law. Even prior to 1870, the more important of these two subjects was the Holy See. It is clear that Catholic states granted the privilege of deanship to the Papal nuncios not because of the political importance of the Papal State, but because of the supreme spiritual sovereignty of the Holy See.

Of these two persons in international law the one, the Papal State, undoubtedly came to an end, under the rules of general international law, by Italian conquest and subjugation in 1870. But the Holy See remained, as always, a subject of general international law also in the period between 1870 and 1929. That this is so is fully proved by the practice of states.

The Holy See continued to conclude concordats and continued, with the consent of a majority of states, to exercise the active and passive right of legation. The legal position of its diplomatic agents—as the continuance of the Vienna Protocol also during this period proves—remained based on general international law, not on the Italian Law of Guarantee, a municipal law enacted under an international duty incumbent upon Italy. Hence, the confiscation by Italy in 1917 of the Palazzo Venezia, house of the Austro-Hungarian Ambassador to the Vatican, constituted a violation of international law.

It is interesting to note that after World War I more states established diplomatic relations with the Vatican than prior to 1914. The states did so because they recognized that the Vatican is a unique diplomatic observation point.[15] In 1930, about thirty states were diplomatically represented at the Vatican and the Vatican in about forty states. Among the states represented during this century at the Vatican were not only Catholic states, including states where the constitutional law of separation of state and church prevails, as e.g., in France, but Protestant states, such as Germany, Holland, Great Britain, and Switzerland, and Greek Orthodox states, such as Czarist Russia, Montenegro, Bulgaria, Rumania, Greece, and Yugoslavia. Heads of Protestant states paid visits to the Holy See: Edward VII, in 1903; Woodrow Wilson in 1919.

The Cardinal-Secretary of State of the Vatican exercises the functions of a foreign minister. In many other respects the status of the Holy See as a person in general international law was also clearly demonstrated in the period 1870–1929. Pope Leo XIII acted as a mediator in the Carolina Islands dispute between Germany and Spain.[16] The same Pope acted in 1895 as arbiter in a border conflict between Haiti and Santo Domingo. In 1898, Orthodox Russia sent her project for the Hague Peace Conference to the Holy See and solicited its support. The exclusion of the Holy See from the Hague Peace Conferences was due to the request by Italy, just as Italy in the London Treaty of 1915 made

it a condition of her joining Great Britain and France in
World War I that the Holy See would not be invited to the
Peace Conference. Italy also opposed the Holy See as a
member of the League of Nations; but the German project
for a League of Nations of 1919 provided expressly that
the Holy See could become a member. During World War I
its own flag was conceded to the Holy See and the vessel
flying this flag declared to be neutral and assimilated to a
state vessel. After World War I new states or governments
applied for recognition by the Holy See; such recognition
was, for instance, granted to Poland and Estonia.

The Lateran Treaty had the object of liquidating once
for all the "Roman Question" and bringing about a recon-
cilation between the Holy See and Italy,[17] but it in no way
created or changed the international position of the Holy
See.[18] The treaty concluded between the Holy See and Italy
presupposes the international personality of the Holy See.
Italian recognition, in Article II, of the sovereignty of the
Holy See and, in Article XII, of the active and passive right
of legation under the norms of general international law is
purely declaratory.

The Lateran Treaty created, furthermore, the state of
the City of the Vatican as a *new* state,[19] for which Italy
makes a cession of territory. The treaty, correctly speaking,
did not create this state, but laid down only the necessary
presuppositions. This state of the City of the Vatican is a
state, a subject of international law, different from the
Holy See.[20] It has become a member of the Universal Postal
Union. But it is not a sovereign state. As all writers correctly state, "Its activities are totally different from those
inherent in national States." [21] Its constitution is not autonomous, but derived from the Holy See.[22] It is a vassal state
of the Holy See.

During World War II, the Protestant occupying powers
of Italy—Great Britain and the United States—were bound

under international law to observe the neutrality of the state of the City of the Vatican and to grant free correspondence between the Holy See and all states, including those with which the occupying powers were at war.[23] In Article XXIV of the Lateran Treaty the Holy See makes a unilateral statement that it will remain aloof from the temporal competitions of states and from congresses convoked for such purposes, *except* that the contending parties by common consent may appeal to its mission of peace. The Holy See reserves in any event the right to exercise its moral spiritual influence. In this sense the Popes appealed to all belligerents during the two World Wars. In his Christmas address, 1951,[24] the Pope declared that the Holy See cannot remain neutral between right and wrong, but, on the other hand, can never consider political conflicts on purely political lines, but always "sub specie aeternitatis."

The Holy See, certainly, is not eligible to be a member of the United Nations because, under Article IV of the Charter, admission is only open to "States." The City of the Vatican would not be admitted because of its exiguity, just as the sovereign Principality of Liechtenstein was not admitted to the League of Nations. But the Holy See may participate in some activities of the United Nations, just as Papal delegates participated in the League of Nations meetings concerning calendar reform.[25] The Holy See can, of course, be chosen as a mediator or arbiter, and can be invited to international conferences. Recently the Holy See was invited to, and participated in, the diplomatic conference held at Geneva in 1949. It signed and ratified and is a contracting party to the four new Geneva Conventions of 1949. At this conference, nearly all the states, including the Soviet states, were represented; none objected to the invitation and participation of the Holy See.

Whether to send an American Ambassador to the Holy See [26] is, under international law, a political question. The political arguments to do so, given by the President, are, as this discussion shows, very strong; and the attempted refutation is in contradiction with the practice of states. But if this decision is made in an affirmative sense, this country merely enters into diplomatic relations with a subject of general international law. Such diplomatic relations —as the examples of Great Britain, Holland, other Protestant, Orthodox, and Islamic [27] states show—constitute, of course, no privilege for one or discrimination against other churches.

[1] Thus in two leading treatises: William Edward Hall (7th ed. 1917), and T. J. Lawrence (7th ed. 1925).

[2] Even CHARLES G. FENWICK, INTERNATIONAL LAW (3rd ed. 1948), discusses the problem briefly, only in relation to the City of the Vatican (pp. 124–25); and the full discussion in 1 OPPENHEIM-LAUTERPACHT, INTERNATIONAL LAW: A TREATISE 226–30 (7th ed. 1948), is not wholly free from ambiguous statements. Horace F. Cumbo's study, *The Holy See and International Law*, 2 INT'L L.Q. 603–20 (1948), although written with the express purpose of clarifying controversial issues, defends the untenable thesis that the Papal State did not come to an end in 1870 and that, therefore, the state of the City of the Vatican is not a new state. He follows in that respect D'AVACK, CHIESA, SANTA SEDE E CITTÀ DEL VATICANA (1937). The brief statements are correct in A. P. SERENI, THE ITALIAN CONCEPTION OF INTERNATIONAL LAW (1943), and ALF ROSS, A TEXTBOOK OF INTERNATIONAL LAW 103–4 (1947).

[3] See, e.g., F. v. LISZT, DAS VÖLKERRECHT 92–94 (12th ed. 1925); ERNST YANSELOW, VÖLKERRECHT (1931).

[4] See 1 P. FAUCHILLE, TRAITÉ DE DROIT INTERNATIONAL PUBLIC, Part 1 at 727–56 (1922); R. KNUBBEN, DIE SUBJEKTE DES VÖLKERRECHTS 427–38 (1928); G. DIENA, DIRITTO INTERNAZIONALE 195–216 (3rd ed. 1930); 1 A. HOLD-FERNECK, LEHRBUCH DES VÖLKERRECHTS 238–46 (1930); 1 K. STRUPP, ELÉMENTS DU DROIT INTERNATIONAL PUBLIC 44–49 (1930); P. FEDOZZI, CORSO DI DIRITTA INTERNAZIONALE 137–53 (1931). In all these works, as well as in OPPENHEIM-LAUTERPACHT, *op. cit.*, there are large bibliographies. The best, although a brief, discussion is now to be found in A. VERDROSS, VÖLKERRECHT 205–7, 211–13 (1950).

[5] That is why the recent attempt by an Austrian writer (Brandweiner) to treat relations between Protestant churches in different countries as falling under international law is legally untenable, because of being in contradiction with the practice of states. That is why the argument that American diplomatic relations could not be given to

all churches is not to the point. It is as if one would oppose American diplomatic relations with the new kingdom of Libya because they could not be given to the Arab communities of Algeria, Tunisia, and Morocco.

6 Not the Catholic Church as such; not the Pope. The relation between the concepts of the Holy See and of the Pope are analogous to the relation in British constitutional law between the concepts of the Crown and of the King.

7 Contrary, e.g., to insurgents, recognized as a belligerent party.

8 Contrary, e.g., to the Sovereign Maltese Order which is only a person in *particular* international law. The status of its representatives is not based on general international law but only on recognition by the receiving states.

9 See, as to the international personality of international organizations, the statement of the International Court of Justice in its advisory opinion of April 9, 1949 (Reports of Judgments, Advisory Opinions, and Orders, 1949, at 179).

10 The Lateran Treaty of 1929 is a normal international treaty. Recently the Holy See signed and ratified the four new Geneva Conventions of 1949.

11 "Romanus Pontifex . . . habet supremam et plenam potestatem jurisdictionis in universam Ecclesiam. Haec potestas est . . . a quavis humana auctoritate independens."—*Codex Juris Canonici*, Canon 218, at 1, 2.

12 Between 1920 and 1930, nine concordats were concluded with states, including Latvia and Prussia.

13 This is fully recognized by this country. See Secretary of State Fish to Mr. Cushing, Minister to Spain (1 MOORE, DIGEST OF INTERNATIONAL LAW 39), and Acting Secretary of State Adee to the American Minister of Costa Rica, April 29, 1908 (4 HACKWORTH, DIGEST OF INTERNATIONAL LAW 636).

14 A spokesman for the American Jewish Congress stated that "a Vatican Ambassador might become a disservice to the Roman Catholics in that the 'princes of the church' might be considered agents of another country and thus have to register as alien agents." This remark is rather strange since the leaders of American Zionism themselves warned that, after the independence of Israel, they must be careful not to become alien agents. The view is, furthermore, wholly untenable. "Cardinals," wrote Secretary of State Hughes to Mr. Cunliffe-Owen on April 21, 1924, "are not accredited to this Government, and have no official status before this Government. They are merely officers of a church."— 4 HACKWORTH, *op. cit.* at 637.

15 Le Vatican est en effet le point de l'univers d'où l'on peut le mieux observer l'ensemble des évènements politiques mondiaux."— Fauchille, *op cit.* at 742.)

16 See COELLA, LA CONFERENCIA DE BERLIN Y LA CUESTIÓN DE LAS CAROLINAS (1885); P. DE ANDRADE, HISTORIA DEL CONFLICTO DE LAS CAROLINAS (1886); SELOSSE, L'AFFAIRE DES CAROLINES (1886).

[17] DEL GIUDICE, LA QUESTIONE ROMANA E I RAPPORTI FRA STATO E CHIESA FINO ALLA CONCILIAZIONE (1948).

[18] It is, therefore, not correct, as OPPENHEIM-LAUTERPACHT, op. cit., at 228, states, that "the hitherto controversial international position of the Holy See was clarified as a result of the Treaty."

[19] The contrary position of D'Avack and Cumbo is legally untenable.

[20] The statement in OPPENHEIM-LAUTERPACHT, op. cit. at 229, is therefore incorrect: "The Lateran Treaty marks the resumption of the formal membership, interrupted in 1871, of the Holy See in the Society of States."

[21] OPPENHEIM-LAUTERPACHT, op. cit. at 230.

[22] VERDROSS, op. cit. at 87–88.

[23] See ROBERTO AGO, OCCUPAZIONE BELLICA DELL' ITALIA E TRATTATO LATERANENSE (1946).

[24] Text in the N.Y. Times, December 25, 1951, p. 4.

[25] G. P. CANSACCHI, IL PAPA E LA SOCIETÀ DELLE NAZIONI (1929).

[26] Not to the Pope; not to the state of the City of the Vatican. The phrase "American Ambassador to the Vatican" is merely a diplomatic one, just as we speak of the envoy to Great Britain as "the Ambassador to the Court of St. James," or as French or Austro-Hungarian foreign policy as diplomatically referred to as the foreign policy of the "Quai d'Orsay" or of the "Ballhausplatz."

[27] E.g., at this time Egypt and Indonesia. At the end of 1951, forty-three states—the majority of states—were diplomatically represented at the Vatican.

CHAPTER XV: Identity of States under International Law

THESE TROUBLED TIMES since 1914 have seen the coming into existence, transformation, extinction, and resurrection of many states. Whereas in many cases no difficulty has arisen in determining whether a certain state is a new state [1] or identical with a pre-existing state,[2] there are many doubtful cases. They all have significantly to do with cases of fusion [3] or dismemberment [4] of states or with so-called resurrected states [5] and, in one particularly important case,[6] with conquest not followed by annexation. These uncertainties in international law are by no means a new phenomenon. They arose in many cases during and after the long Napoleonic Wars, particularly with regard to "resurrected" states. Such uncertainties have also arisen in less troubled times.[7]

The identity *vel non* of a state is of the greatest practical importance. The international rule determining the identity of a state under certain conditions is not only in the interest of the state concerned, but guarantees a legally ordered development of international relations between states, gives security to third states by guaranteeing the continuity of treaties and international obligations, including concessions, contracts, debts, and so on; and furnishes the basis for the

continued international responsibility of the state. In view
of this importance, it seems strange that there is so much
uncertainty. What are the reasons for this state of things?

Apart from the fact that the whole problem of identity is
problematical from a philosophical point of view—some
writers speak rather of the "continuity" [8] of states—there
is, first of all confusion in the doctrine which has been unable to reach either a clear or a unanimous position with
regard to the problem of the identity of states under international law. The science of international law has given
to this problem relatively scant consideration and mostly
only incidentally, not as one problem. This is true of many
treatises, although those of Verdross [9] and Kelsen [10] are an
exception; the problem is also mostly only incidentally dealt
with in monographs on such topics as nationality, coming
into existence or extinction of states, and treaties. There is
a paucity of monographs [11] on this problem as such, although we have now the recent monographs of Verdross [12]
and Cansacchi.[13]

There is, moreover, the fact that political influences sway
many writers on this topic, so that they approach the problem with preconceived solutions corresponding to their
political wishes. But one of the principal reasons for the
confusion of the doctrine is the deep split among writers
as to fundamental problems. For many adherents of the
"dualistic" doctrine, Italians and Germans,[14] the coming
into existence and the extinction of states are purely historical, political facts, and international law has no competence to deal with these matters. The only logical consequence, in starting from this basis, is not only that international law does not, but that it *cannot*, contain norms concerning the identity of states. If, on the other hand, these
writers, in contradiction to their own basic theory, feel
compelled to admit that there *are* principles of international
law concerning the identity of states, they must take refuge

in wholly artificial explanations. Thus Quadri teaches that there is no problem of "identity" of states; in reality, this is only a particular case of state succession: a state which has undergone a revolutionary change of government thereby becomes extinct; a new state is formed immediately with universal succession to all the rights and duties of the old state. It is hardly necessary to point out that this construction is, in the light of the practice of states, wholly untenable. Cansacchi admits the international rule concerning the identity of states, but teaches that it constitutes a genuine "fiction" vis-à-vis "reality"; hence the title of his article. But Cansacchi means by "reality," not the reality of natural sciences, but of municipal law, a *legal* reality. Recently also Charles de Visscher [15] has taken the position that international law does not create the state but presupposes it. But, neither does municipal law "create" the individual: it attributes legal personality and it can make this personality extinct, even if "in reality" the human being remains identical.[16]

International law, like every legal order, must determine who its subjects are and what the conditions are for their coming into existence, extinction, and for their remaining identical in law. It is perfectly possible to speak historically, politically, of Poland of 1920 as being the same as the Poland which became extinct in 1795; but as a legal statement it would be untenable. The problem of the identity of states under international law is a *legal problem*.

Perhaps the most important reason for the lack of clarity and agreement in the doctrine concerning the problem of the identity of states is the uncertainty of the corresponding rules of international law itself. International law determines that a new sovereign state has come into existence if four conditions are fulfilled: an organized and effective legal order, valid for a certain territory and population; this legal order must, further, be exclusively and immediately subject to international law and not to any other national law. International law determines, further, that the disappearance of one of these four elements has as a legal consequence the extinction of the sovereign state. International law, finally, determines that *certain* changes as to the one or other or more elements will *not* have the legal consequence of the extinction of the state, but leaves its identity intact.

Let us first eliminate the hypotheses where the corresponding norm of international law is perfectly clear and precise. As changes are bound to occur, what may be called "normal" changes do not affect the identity of the state, such as changes in population through increase or decrease by births and deaths, through emigration and immigration, even if on a very high scale,[17] or changes in the ethnical composition of the population. Equally, normal changes in territory, as, e.g., by accretion or avulsion, while they have legal effects, do not affect the legal identity of the state or states concerned. The same is true of changes in government through death or election and of any change in the form of government or contents of the legal order brought about in conformity with the constitution of the state in question.

On the other hand, it is clear that the total loss of populaion would bring about the extinction of the state. Here it can already be seen—and that is true with regard to changes in any element—that the identity of the state continues, *except* where, by such change, it legally ceases to exist. The problem of the identity of states is not the antithesis of the problem of state succession but of the problem of the extinction of states.

Apart from "normal" territorial changes, there is also a principle of general international law which, insofar as it is clear, can be thus formulated: Territorial changes, whether by increase or reduction of territory, *in general* do not affect the identity of the state. Under this rule fall, for instance, the great territorial increase of the United States, the cession of a province by one state to another, the seccession of a part of the state or of a colony, constituting itself—often by revolution or war—a new independent state.[18] Thus far the law, the practice of states, and the doctrine [19] are unanimous. It is equally agreed that the *total change* of territory by a people which, under the same government and law, settles in a different territory, leaves the identity of the state intact.[20] But it is equally clear that total *loss* of territory, i.e, by total cession,[21] brings the identity of a state to an end.[22]

But, as stated, this norm of general international law is valid only *in general*. It constitutes only the general principle to which there are exceptions. Some writers [23] are of opinion that the exception is given by the circumstance that the territorial change is "quantitatively very considerable." But the practice of states shows that the Republic of Turkey, in spite of considerable territorial losses, was held identical with the Ottoman Empire; that Poland, although she lost in the east half of her territory and suffered a considerable decrease of population, is held to be identical today with the Poland of 1920. Other writers point rather to the real issue: the territorial change must leave "a part of the territory which can be recognized as an essential portion of the old state," [24] or the state concerned must retain its consistency.[25] While correct, these are rather tautological statements, telling us that territorial changes do not affect the identity of the state, except when they do. It really means that, under the rule of general international law, territorial changes do not affect the identity of the state, except if they legally lead to the extinction of the state. But international law does not contain universally valid and obligatory criteria as to what must be the extent or the nature of territorial changes in order to lead to the extinction of the state. The international norm does not specify

the exceptions to its general principle. It is this uncertainty
in the rule of general international law which leads, (particularly in cases of fusion, like Yugoslavia in 1918, or of
dismemberment, like the Republic of Austria in 1918) to
uncertainty both in the doctrine and in the practice of states.

There is also another old and fully recognized principle of
general international law under which the identity of a state
in international law is not affected by unconstitutional
changes in government, whether brought about by revolution or coup d'état. This rule is so unanimously recognized
by writers since Grotius and Bynkershoek, by the practice
of states, as illustrated by the well-known London Protocol
of February 19, 1831, and by national and international
court decisions that it is superfluous to give quotations. It is
irrelevant how far-reaching the revolutionary changes may
be; as is also the change of the name of the state. True, the
Soviet government insisted that the rule does not apply to
the case of the Bolshevik revolution; but all the other states
reaffirmed this rule of general international law, which
certainly is the international law actually in force. Occasional considerations that " there is room for reconsidera-
tion of the norm" [26] under exceptional circumstances are
proposals *de lege ferenda*. It is equally clear that the fact
that the revolutionary regime was a so-called intermediary
government or was not recognized in no way affects the
identity of the state.[27] For the non-recognition of a *de facto*
government leaves the recognition of the state intact.[28]

The theoretical construction is different with different
writers. Some adherents of the "dualistic" doctrine, following the reasoning of Aristotle, hold that the legal order is
the most important element of the state; hence, revolutionary change extinguishes the state.[29] But Kelsen does not
follow Aristotle; he says that this would be the case only if
there were no international law, but that revolutionary
change is now, by international law, a form of change that

does not affect the identity of the state. Kelsen holds that, with regard to the identity of the state, in spite of revolutionary changes, the most important element is territory: [30] revolutionary changes do not affect the identity of the state, "if the territory, by and large, remains the same." For many writers since Grotius and Bynkershoek,[31] population is the essential element, and this thesis has recently been vigorously defended by Verdross. But, apart from the fact that the Latin term *populus* and the English and French term "nation" means the *state* rather than the population, Verdross speaks of the population as "the people organized as a state." Where there is no organization at all the state becomes extinct in international law. Here again the problem of identity is the antithesis of the problem of the extinction of the state. The norm of general international law guarantees the identity of the state, in spite of revolutionary changes, as long as this state does not become extinct; for when a state becomes extinct under international law, there can, of course, be no identity,[32] even if territory and population remain the same.[33] Now general international law contains no special norms according to which, under certain conditions, a state which has lost *all* government and also its immediacy to international law nevertheless does not become extinct if it is "resurrected" within a reasonable time.

It is this uncertainty or lack of a norm of general international law regarding so-called resurrected states that is the reason for the uncertainty of the practice of states and of the doctrine, both of which use rather political arguments. Thus, in the case of Germany the argument is used that a state only becomes extinct if its territory and population are definitely imputed to other states, that in the case of Germany at least subordinate organs represented the state. But it is well known that the occupying powers took supremacy over all federal, state, and local organs, so that *all* organs depended on them. *All* law in occupied Germany

in 1945 after the unconditional surrender had its only
reason of validity in the supremacy of the occupying powers.
Even in 1954 there was still no sovereign Germany. Now
the Bonn Republic will finally become an almost sovereign
state, but a state which does not control the German Democratic Republic or the two Berlins, a state which contains
neither the prewar Germany east of the Oder and Weichsel,
nor the Saar, and where for nearly ten years there has been
no sovereign state at all. Under these conditions it seems
impossible not to recognize that it "is clearly not identical
with the former German Reich. It is a new state . . . a
successor state to the German Reich." [34]

In the cases of Ethiopia, Czechoslovakia, and Austria,
where it cannot be denied that population and territory
were imputed to other states, other arguments are used:
no sufficient duration, merely *de facto* recognition of the
annexation, unlawful character of the annexation making
it only an "occupation," and the "non-recognition-doctrine."
But none of the these arguments is very solid from a legal
point of view. Obviously, a certain duration is necessary; it
forms an element of the effectivity prescribed by international law; but four years in the case of Ethiopia, seven
years in the case of Austria, seem to fulfil this requirement,
especially as in 1936 and 1938 those annexations were taken
to be definitive; it was only the outbreak of war which
again put them in question.

These annexations *have* been recognized, however reluc-
tantly, by most states. No one can deny that the United
Kingdom recognized Italian sovereignty over Ethiopia *de
jure,* a recognition which is irrevocable in international law.
As far as the "non-recognition doctrine" goes, it is not pertinent in these cases. In addition, this doctrine is not, as is
sometimes believed, a sanction but merely a political statement which needs a sanction. If nothing is done to change
the situation, the illegal act will stand. But even if some-

thing is done successfully, it can, at the best, restore the *status quo ante;* it can act *as if* the illegal act had not occurred, but it cannot make the illegal act undone; just as municipal law can punish the murderer but cannot revive the dead man. The declarations that the annexation of Austria or the Munich Agreement are "null and void" are *ex post facto* political statements in time of war. As de Visscher [35] correctly states, the resurrection of Ethiopia was due to the outbreak of war, not to the "non-recognition doctrine." *A contrario,* we can point to the illegal annexation of the Baltic Republics by the Soviet Union, against which some states applied the "non-recognition doctrine." But even these states did not and do not now expect that this state of things will be changed. But in case of a new war, these problems might very well be revived and this annexation declared "null and void."

On the other hand, the doctrine *can* point to the practice of states which shows cases in which states acted in instances of "resurrected" states, recognizing the identity of such states, contrary to the norm of general international law under which they had become extinct. But the practice of states after the Napoleonic Wars and in our times not only differs among different states with regard to the same case and differs with the same state as to different cases, but it often changes in time with the same state toward the same case, and even in the same case diplomatic practice or even treaty norms are often ambiguous, lacking in consequence, or contradictory. Thus Ethiopia seems to represent an "automatic" revival since Italy in the Peace Treaty of 1947 only had to recognize Ethiopian sovereignty and not renounce Italian sovereignty, as should have been done in accordance with classic international law. On the other hand, the Allies promised only to *re*-establish a sovereign Austria; and Austria, whether a new state or identical with the 1938 Austria, is not yet a fully sovereign state even in

1954. On the one hand, Hitler's annexation was declared "null and void"; consequently what the Germans took in Austria should have been restored to Austria; but the Potsdam Declaration gave the "German assets in Austria" to the Soviet Union. It would be easy to show a long line of other ambiguities and contradictions in the practice of states.

In a word, a scrutiny of the practice of states after the Napoleonic Wars and since 1914 shows convincingly that no new general international rule concerning such cases has been developed; there is neither an established clear usage, nor the *opinio necessitatis*. States have acted, and do act, in such cases less according to legal considerations than according to what Lauterpacht once called "the amorphous principles of politics." It is the uncertainty of the law— the lack of the determination of exceptions to the general norm of identity in spite of territorial changes, and the lack of determination of the conditions under which the rule of identity works in spite of revolutionary changes, notwithstanding the extinction of the state under another norm of general international law—which is the ultimate reason for the lack of clarity and agreement in the doctrine.

---

[1] Thus Poland, Czechoslovakia, the Baltic republics, Finland, Iraq after World War I, and Syria, Lebanon, Libya, Israel, Burma, Ceylon, Indonesia, Pakistan after World War II.

[2] Thus the Turkish Republic and the Soviet Union, although the latter denied its identity with the Russian Empire.

[3] The Kingdom of the Serbs, Croats, and Slovenes. For identity with Serbia, see TOMITCH, LA FORMATION DE L'ÉTAT YOUGOSLAVE 1927; for a new state, with convincing arguments, see E. Kaufmann, in 31 ZEITSCHRIFT FÜR VÖLKERRECHT. 211–51 (1923–24).

[4] The Republic of Austria, 1918; Austria regarded herself as a new state; but for identity with the Empire of Austria, see the Peace Treaty of St. Germain; Hungary, 1918: for identity with pre-war Hungary, see the Peace Treaty of Trianon; this was also the attitude of postwar Hungary herself.

[5] Czechoslovakia, Albania, Ethiopia. See also the divergent opinions as to whether the Austria of 1945 is identical in law with the Austria of 1918. For identity, the Austrian government since 1945, and most Austrian writers (Adamovich, Verdross, Verosta, Klinghoffer, Seidl-

Hohenveldern). For a *new* state, the last Chancellor of the 1938 Austria, Schuschnigg (*The Austrian Peace*, ANNALS 106–18 [1948]), Kelsen, most German (e.g. W. Schätzel, H. Jellinek) and many foreign writers. The Moscow Declaration of 1943 is highly ambiguous in its wording; also doubtful is the Austrian Nationality Law of 1945. The practice of states at the time of the German annexation of Austria in 1938, in the period between 1938 and 1945, and in 1945 and after, varies not only with different states, but sometimes with one and the same state. There are national court decisions in favor of identity (e.g., Bruni *v.* Pizzorno, Corte d'Appello di Torino [1948]) and for the recognition of the German annexation (e.g., Matter of Mangold's Patent [1951], 68 R. Pat. cas. 1). See also the recent decision of the West German Federal Administrative Court in Berlin, ruling that 75,000 Austrians living in Germany must be regarded as German nationals. Judge Wichert ruled that the annexation of Austria by the Third Reich had been acknowledged in international law, and, therefore, the legality of German citizenship, acquired by the Austrians in 1938, could not be challenged. This, the judge said, was also the basis of the Austrian Citizenship Law of 1945. Only German law can determine, under international law, how German citizenship is acquired and lost. The Austrian state, the judge stated, had been restored as a result of a political decision of the Allies, without, however, regulating this problem. This problem, he stated, would have to be settled in the state treaty or by agreement between Austria and Germany (N. Y. Times, October 31, 1954, p. 2). Thus the present situation of Austria "is far from being free from dangerous ambiguities" (M. Rheinstein in 47 MICH. L. REV. 34 [1948]).

6 Germany, 1945. See "The Status of Occupied Germany under International Law: A Legal Dilemma," above.

7 The classical example is the formation of the Kingdom of Italy. For a new state, see D. Anzilotti, in RIVISTA DI DIRITTO INTERNAZIONALE 1–33 (1912); for identity with the Kingdom of Piedmont—and that has become the dominant opinion—Romano, *ibid*, at 345–67. The problem was still involved in a recent case, Gastaldi v. Lepage Hemery (Ann.Dig. 1929–30 No. 43).

8 But Cansacchi sees in "identity" and "continuity" two different problems, particularly with regard to "resurrected" states. "Identity," according to him, means only identity *after* the state has come into existence again, whereas "continuity" pretends that the state also continued during the period of its extinction.

9 A. VERDROSS, VÖLKERRECHT 161–63 (2nd ed. 1950).

10 H. KELSEN, PRINCIPLES OF INTERNATIONAL LAW 259–64, 416 (1953).

11 HERZ, DIE IDENTITÄT DER STAATEN (1931); ZEITSCHRIFT FÜR ÖFFENTLICHES RECHT 241–68 (1935); M. T. Badawi, La Continuité et l'extinction de la personnalité de l'état (thesis, 1940).

12 A. Verdross, *Die Völkerrechtliche Identität der Staaten*, in FESTSCHRIFT FÜR HEINRICH KLANG 18–21 (1950).

13 Giorgio Cansacchi, *Realtà e finzione nell'identità degli Stati*, in 4 COMUNICAZIONI E STUDI 23–97 (1952).

[14] E.g., Cavaglieri, Fedozzi, Strupp, but also de Louter. See recently, particularly, ARRANGIO RUIZ, GLI ENTI SOGGETTI DELL'ORDINAMENTO INTERNAZIONALE (1951); R. QUADRI, DIRITTO INTERNAZIONALE PUBBLICO (1951). This is also the basic presupposition of Cansacchi, whereby his whole, otherwise very interesting, investigation is vitiated a priori.

[15] THÉORIES ET RÉALITÉS EN DROIT INTERNATIONAL PUBLIC 204–5 (1953).

[16] E.g., under Roman law, loss of personality through becoming a prisoner of war. On the other hand, a slave, a thing in law, becomes a person through manumission; see also the *mort civile* of former French law.

[17] The young U.S. with five million and the present U.S. with one hundred and sixty million of inhabitants is, of course, the identical state in law.

[18] Thus, e.g., the identity of the British Empire in spite of the coming into existence of the United States; of Sweden in spite of the separation of Norway; of The Netherlands in spite of Belgium and Indonesia; of Russia in spite of the territorial loss brought about at the end of World War I through the coming into existence of Poland, Finland, and the Baltic republics.

[19] Hence the so-called principle of the variable limits of treaties.

[20] The Boer republics after the "trek."

[21] E.g., Korea, 1910.

[22] An exception, laid down by a norm of international law, is that even total occupation of the territory of a state and destitution of its government by a belligerent occupant does not constitute conquest and subjugation and leaves, therefore, the identity of the state in question intact as long as allies of the occupied state continue fighting (e.g., Poland, Yugoslavia in World War II).

[23] P. GUGGENHEIM, BEITRÄGE ZUR VÖLKERRECHTLICHEN LEHRE VOM STAATENWECHSEL 18, 19 (1925); 1 LEHRBUCH DES VÖLKERRECHTS 407 (1948).

[24] Thus, W. E. HALL, A TREATISE ON INTERNATIONAL LAW 22 (7th ed. 1917).

[25] Thus, F. v. LISZT, DAS VÖLKERRECHT 275 (12th ed. 1925).

[26] Thus, 1 OPPENHEIM-LAUTERPACHT, INTERNATIONAL LAW: A TREATISE 148 n. 2 (7th ed. 1948).

[27] *The Tinoco Arbitration*, 18 AM.J.INT'L L. 147 (1924).

[28] See acting-secretary of state to attorney-general of New Jersey, October 31, 1922, 2 U.S.For.Rel. 715 (1922), and many court decisions, e.g., *The Sapphire* U.S.Sup.Ct. (1871), 11 Wall. 164, Lehigh Valley R.R. *v.* State of Russia, U.S. (1927), 21 F.2nd 396, and many others.

[29] Cansacchi, following Kelsen on this point, holds that the state becomes extinguished only when the revolutionary change can no longer be based on the prerevolutionary "Grundnorm" of the constitution.

[30] Fricker and Preuss had, very differently, put the emphasis on territory as the most important element, by asserting that *any* territorial change, also without revolution, necessarily extinguishes the state, a statement fully in contradiction with positive international law.

[31] Thus, e.g., Anzilotti, Cavaglieri, Fedozzi, Ottolenghi. Cansacchi also insists on the element of population, but only as an element for what is for him basically a fiction.

[32] T. J. LAWRENCE, THE PRINCIPLES OF INTERNATIONAL LAW 89 (7th ed., 1925), writes that revolutionary changes, in spite of non-recognition of the *de facto* government, do not affect the identity of the state; but "a state loses its existence where it is obliterated as a subject of international law."

[33] As with the Boer republics in 1902 or Korea in 1910.

[34] E. Plischke, in 69 POLITICAL SCIENCE QUARTERLY 262 (1954).

[35] *Op. cit., supra,* note 15, at 208.

CHAPTER XVI: *The Present Status of the International Law for the Protection of Minorities*

HE WHO DEDICATES his life to the study of international law in these troubled times is sometimes struck by the appearance that there are fashions in international law just as in neckties. At the end of World War I "international protection of minorities" was the great fashion: treaties in abundance, conferences, League of Nations activities, an enormous literature. Recently this fashion has become nearly obsolete. Today, the well-dressed international lawyer wears "human rights." The decline of this whole department of international law is a fact often commented upon.[1] Why and how, did this decline happen and what is the present status of the international law for the protection of minorities?

The peace treaties concluded after the end of World War I were under the ideological impact of Woodrow Wilson's "principle of self-determination of nations"; under this inspiration new states were created, existing ones expanded, and the Austro-Hungarian Monarchy dismembered. But it was recognized that, no matter how frontiers would be drawn, there will always be groups in Europe who will have to live in a state the majority of whose inhabitants are ethnically, linguistically, or religiously different. Hence the international law for the protection of minorities as a substitute in cases where the application of the principle of self-determination of nations was, for one reason or another, not possible or not wanted. The international protection of minorities is, therefore, a strict and logical corollary of the principle of self-determination of nations. In accordance with the principle of protection of minorities, minorities have a right to be protected against physical extermination, "assimilation," or "absorption"; they have a right not only to preserve but to develop their specific characteristics and are entitled for that purpose to special rights, privileges, and services, transcending mere equality and non-discrimination, transcending the mere guarantee of human rights, due to all, majorities and minorities. Such special rights were official recognition and freedom of use of minority languages in public and private, in the courts, and before other authorities, and in the press, special minority schools, and allocation of state funds for the promotion and development of the educational, religious, and charitable institutions of minorities. The international law for the protection of minorities knew only "persons belonging to minorities." It did not make the persons belonging to minorities subjects of international law, but it created some supervisory machinery in the hands of the League of Nations. The greatest development, from the point of view of the evolution of international law, was that certain states were bound by international obligations vis-à-vis certain of their *own* citizens, namely, those belonging to minorities; whereas, under general international law, their treatment belongs to the "domestic jurisdiction" of those states.

The decline of this new international law has its reason in some congenital weaknesses of this law as well as in later political developments. First of all, the new law was not only restricted to Europe but not even general in Europe.

It was a strictly particular international law, binding only on certain states, not on all where there were minorities. The dividing line was not drawn, as in the case of "mandates," between victors and vanquished, but between big and small states. Hence such obligations were imposed on defeated Austria, Hungary, Bulgaria, but not on Germany; on the technically "victorious" new states Czechoslovakia, Poland, on the aggrandized states of Greece and Rumania, but not on Italy; likewise, on the new states of Albania, Finland, and the Baltic Republics. Some states gave by municipal law more than they were internationally bound to do; thus Estonia granted cultural autonomy. In some cases a treaty established even territorial autonomy for minorities, as in the case of the Podskarpatska Rus, the Aaland Islands, and the Memel Territory. Germany and Poland concluded the important treaty on Upper Silesia. Some states, internationally not bound, granted rights to their minorities by municipal law, e.g., Denmark. The impact of the whole law can also be seen in the division of Belgium into a purely Flemish zone in the north, a purely Walloon zone in the south, and a dual-language zone between. Protection of minorities also played a great role in the early Soviet Union; Stalin, the Georgian, began his political ascendancy as People's Commissar for Minorities. But the new international law was only binding on certain states. At the same time the world saw one of the worst cases of forcible denationalization of her Austrian and Yugoslav minorities by Fascist Italy, not bound by the new law. It is this particular character of the new law which exasperated many new states, all highly nationalistic, which saw in their numerous minorities, so to speak, stains on their "national" state. It is this protest, so strongly voiced by Paderewski at the Paris Peace Conference, which led in 1934 to the open repudiation of her corresponding international obligations by Poland.

Second, there was the procedural insufficiency of the League of Nations. Third, even at an early date, opinions unfavorable to this new law were voiced. Even in the twenties a Brazilian delegate, true to the policy of the "melting pot" in the Americas, spoke in favor of the most rapid assimilation of minorities. Fourth, even at an early time, we had attempts to get rid of the whole problem of minorities by way of population exchanges or transfers. Yet, the Greco-Turkish treaty of January 30, 1923, transferring compulsorily one and a half-million Greeks from Asia Minor, where they had lived since early Greek times, was overwhelmingly condemned as cruel and inhuman. To all that, later came the subversive activities of certain minorities, their being used for Hitler's political purposes, climaxing in the cession of the Sudetenland. On the other hand, Hitler sacrificed the Austrian minority in the South Tyrol to Mussolini and wanted to solve the problem of the German minorities in Europe through treaties destined "to bring them home into the Reich."

It is, therefore, not to be wondered that the new international law was already in decline some years prior to the outbreak of World War II and that there was no enthusiasm for its continuation.[2] Hence, the United Nations Charter contains exactly nothing about the protection of minorities, although it pays lip-service in Article II, paragraph 1, to "respect for the principle of self-determination of nations." Nor do later documents, such as the Peace Treaties of 1947, the disposal of Italian colonies, and so on, contain anything about the protection of minorities.

The first question is: What has happened to all these treaties, declarations, and so on, concerning the international protection of minorities, documents which have never been formally abrogated? To this question the Secretariat gave the answer in a study,[3] which comes to the conclusion that "between 1937 and 1947 circumstances as a whole

changed to such an extent that, generally speaking, the
League of Nations system of international protection of
minorities should be considered as having ceased to exist."
This study, in giving the conditions for the operation of the
clause *rebus sic stantibus,* follows closely the formulation
of the Harvard Law School Research in International Law,
Draft Convention on the Law of Treaties (1935), Article
XXVIII. But there is one startling deviation. This clause
does not bring a treaty automatically to an end; the treaty
becomes merely voidable and the clause must be invoked
by a state, which cannot terminate the treaty by its own
authority, but must get the consent of the other contracting
parties or the decision of a competent international organ.
In the case of the minorities treaties, it is supposed, they
lapsed automatically. Amongst the changes enumerated is
also "the recognition of human rights and non-discrimination" by the United Nations Charter. But it must be said
that "human rights and non-discrimination" are something
very different from, and no substitute for, the international
law for the protection of minorities. It is only natural that
Aristos Frydas,[4] representing a bound state, also comes to
the conclusion that the system of international protection
of minorities has been "definitively and irrevocably abrogated" without the necessity of any later abrogating act.
All that is a potent reminder that the "new" international
law is sometimes only an ephemeral episode. Frydas believes that not only the minorities treaties have lapsed but
that the whole idea of international protection of minorities
has been dropped, in consequence of "the evolution which
has taken place in international law." Guggenheim [5] also
writes that the difficulty in finding an adequate system of
protection for all minorities led to the postulate of its radical elimination by population exchange or transfer.

But, in spite of all that, the problem of minorities is still
with us. There is the Austro-Italian Agreement on the

South Tyrol of 1946.[6] The Italian Peace Treaty of 1947 introduced ethnical elements into the genuine option of nationality clause and continued the non-genuine ethnical option.[7] The recent clash between Italy and Yugoslavia over Trieste also involved minority rights; Yugoslavia thinks of Slovene minorities in Austria; there are minorities problems between the communist states of Czechoslovakia and Hungary. The Turkish president affirmed, while in this country, the rights of minorities in Turkey. At the same time minorities problems exist outside of Europe: Jewish and Arab, Moslems and Hindus in India and Pakistan, Indians in Ceylon, the Indian minority in the Union of South Africa; England wants to protect the pagan minority in the south of the Sudan, and so on.

The United Nations Genocide Convention certainly wants to protect minorities at least against "physical and biological" genocide, although it carefully avoids mentioning cultural genocide and fails to mention political minorities. Protection is certainly necessary today. What more than twelve million Germans, under the "orderly transfer" of the Potsdam dispensation, suffered, constitutes, as Max Rheinstein wrote a few years ago, a crime against humanity. Whole minorities peoples are now being shifted around in the Soviet Union. There is also today, therefore, a large field for the operation of the international law for the protection of minorities.

The latter has even a small bureaucratic niche in the huge apparatus of the United Nations in the form of the Subcommission for the Prevention of Discrimination and Protection of Minorities, a suborgan of the Commission on Human Rights. This subcommission has been closely studied by several writers;[8] it will, therefore, suffice to make a few general remarks and to speak of the most recent developments. The subcommission is an organ not composed of really independent experts nor of governmental delegates;

the members have often very different ideas, both as to
the nature of their task and as to the approach toward the
problem of minorities; the East-West split also finds here
its echo. The subcommission has met infrequently and for
short sessions;[9] its reports, it is complained, are being
neglected by the Commission on Human Rights; its proposals, it is equally complained, are rejected either by the
Social and Economic Council or by the General Assembly.
There is a feeling in the subcommission as if the United
Nations were reluctant to do something about the protection
of minorities. Last, not least, the subcommission has two
entirely different tasks: prevention of discrimination and
protection of minorities.[10] Prevention of discrimination is
constitutionally anchored in the United Nations Charter;
this is, of course, due to all minorities; but it is only a part
of "human rights," a problem of equality. Prevention of
discrimination is no part of the international law for the
protection of minorities; for the latter must give *more* than
mere equality and prevention of discrimination; it must
give specific minority rights, special privileges, and services.

A great deal of the subcommission's work has been, and
is being now, devoted to the task of prevention of discrimination. But it has also done something in the field of
protection of minorities. We quote here the proposals on
rights of minorities for inclusion in the Universal Declaration of Human Rights of December 11, 1948; but the
inclusion was definitively rejected by the General Assembly,
although it adopted a resolution to the effect that "the
United Nations cannot remain indifferent to the fate of the
minorities." The subcommission proposed "interim measures" for the minorities, facilities to be provided for them;
proposed, in the way of implementation, a right of petition
by individuals and groups; but no action was taken by the
superior bodies. The same is true of the subcommission's
proposed definition of minorities. The latter, preceded by a

very interesting memorandum by the Secretariat,[11] is extremely cautious:

> The term minority includes only those non-dominant groups in a population which possess and wish to preserve stable ethnic, religious or linguistic traditions or characteristics markedly different from those of the rest of the population; such minorities should properly include a number of persons sufficient by themselves to develop such characteristics and the members of such minorities must be loyal to the state of which they are nationals.

The depression of the subcommission is understandable when the Economic and Social Council decided to abolish the subcommission, at least until 1954. Hence, the subcommission tried to work out the tasks in this field which, in the future, will have to be carried out by other United Nations organs. It proposed also a particular study of definition and protection of political groups, and suggested that the Economic and Social Council prepare an international convention for the protection of minorities. The whole setup became somewhat more favorable when the Human Rights Commission at its ninth session (Geneva, April 7 —May 30, 1953) selected twelve persons as new members of the subcommission and proposed that the subcommission should meet annually. The latest session was held in January, 1954, in New York. While this session also dealt primarily with prevention of discrimination, particularly in education and employment, it recommended also a worldwide study by the United Nations of the present position of minorities. There is, therefore, some hope that the United Nations may in the future really do something theoretically and practically in the field, not only of prevention of discrimination, but also of the protection of minorities.

[1] See "The Future of the International Law for the Protection of National Minorities," above. See also the article by Joseph B. Schechtman in 4 WEST.POL.Q. 1–11 (1951).

² See, e.g., the special number, *The Minorities Problem*, 4 NEW EUROPE, No. 6 (July-August, 1944).

³ Study of the Legal Validity of the Undertakings concerning Minorities, U.N.Doc.No. E/CN. 4/367 (1950). The Secretariat had also published a memorandum on the International Protection of Minorities under the League of Nations, U.N.Doc.No. E/CN. 4/Sub. 2/6.

⁴ In 6 REVUE HELLÉNIQUE DE DROIT INTERNATIONAL, No. 1 at 60–63 (1953).

⁵ 1 LEHRBUCH DES VÖLKERRECHTS 270.

⁶ See "The Italo-Austrian Agreement on the Austrian South Tyrol," above.

⁷ See *ibid.* at 622–31.

⁸ See the article by Schechtman, *loc. cit.;* J. W. Bruegel, *Um einen wirksamen Schutz der Minderheiten*, 50 DIE FRIEDENS-WARTE, No. 1 at 40–50 (1950); Inis L. Claude, Jr., *The Nature and Status of the Subcommission on Prevention of Discrimination and Protection of Minorities*, 5 INTERNATIONAL ORGANIZATION, No. 2 at 300–312 (1951).

⁹ First session, Geneva, November 24—December 6, 1947; second session, Lake Success, June 13–27; third session, Lake Success, January 9–27, 1950; fourth session, New York, October 1–16, 1951; fifth session, New York, September 22—October 10, 1952; sixth session, New York, January, 1954.

¹⁰ This distinction is clearly laid down in the memorandum by the 4/Sub. 2/40 (1949).

¹¹ Definition and Classification of Minorities, U.N. Doc. No. E/CN. Secretariat on Prevention of Discrimination, U.N. Doc. No. E/CN. 4/Sub. 2/85 (1949).

BY THE SIGNATURE of the State Treaty with Austria in the Belvedere Palace at Vienna on May 15, 1955, the pledge given by the Big Three in the Moscow Declaration of November 1, 1943, has finally been redeemed. It was a long and hard road which led to this treaty. Nearly three hundred fruitless negotiation sessions had been held since 1946, although a draft treaty had been ready since 1949. The Berlin Conference, held at the beginning of 1954, led to a new deadlock, due to the insistence by the Soviet Union on continued occupation. The situation looked rather gloomy.[1] At the Berlin Conference, Mr. Molotov had asked for a new article, providing effective measures against *anschluss* and prohibiting Austria from entering any coalition or military alliance with any state which had fought Hitlerite Germany.

It was the Austrian government, bent as always on making use of any chance, which took the initiative. Chancellor Julius Raab visited Washington from November 22 to 26, 1954, where he was received in a friendly manner,[2] and also had talks with Great Britain and France. After a corresponding declaration by Mr. Molotov in Moscow and preliminary negotiations with the Austrian ambassador in

Moscow, the Soviet Union invited the Austrian chancellor
on March 24, 1955, to come to Moscow. Three Soviet-Austrian negotiations took place, and on April 15, 1955, a
Soviet-Austrian understanding [3] was signed in the Kremlin.
A Soviet note of April 19, 1955,[4] proposed to the West a
foreign ministers' meeting in Vienna for the purpose of
signing the treaty. The West wanted first a conference of
ambassadors and the Soviet Union agreed. This conference
took place in Vienna from May 1 to 13, 1955, and was
followed on May 15 by the signature of the treaty by the
five foreign ministers. The treaty went into force on July 27,
1955, upon completion of ratification by the five signatories.

The treaty [5] consists of a preamble and nine parts in
thirty-eight articles.[6] There can be no doubt that the terms
of this treaty are much more favorable to Austria than
those of the draft treaty, for it embodies the Soviet concessions contained in the Soviet-Austrian understanding of
April 15, 1955. At the Ambassador's Conference in Vienna
the Soviet Union wanted, first, the terms of the draft treaty
to stand, the Soviet concessions to be contained in a bilateral
Soviet-Austrian Protocol. But she accepted the American
compromise proposal to leave the old text of Article XXXV
of the draft treaty [7] and to include the Soviet concessions
in Annex II. At the same time, Article XXXVI of the treaty
declares the annexes to be integral parts of the treaty.
Two further concessions were made during the Ambassador's Conference in Vienna: dropping of Article XVI of
the draft treaty [8] and of other articles and eliminating from
Article XVII the limitation by which the size of the Austrian army was fixed at 53,000 men. Finally, the foreign
ministers themselves, at Austria's request, eliminated the
partial war-guilt [9] clause from the preamble.

The treaty is a bilateral treaty between Austria and the
four occupying powers. The latter are referred to as the

"Allied and Associated Powers." But whereas this formula, used in the peace treaties concluded after World War I, meant by "Associated Powers" the United States, it now means probably the Soviet Union. The treaty contains an accession clause.[10] It is in four equally authentic texts: Russian, English, French, and German, in that order.

From an Austrian point of view, the very heart of the treaty is Article XX, on evacuation. With the coming into force of the treaty, the Four-Power Agreement on Control of June 28, 1946, terminated and the Inter-Allied Command ceased to exercise any functions with regard to the administration of the City of Vienna. Upon completion of withdrawal of the occupation troops from Austria, the agreement on zones of occupation shall terminate. These forces shall be withdrawn from Austria within ninety days of the coming into force of the treaty and, "in so far as possible, not later than December 31, 1955."

Thus, after seven years of annexation by Hitlerite Germany and ten years of occupation by Hitler's conquerors, Austria is re-established as a sovereign, independent, and democratic state. This re-establishment is recognized by the Allied and Associated Powers, which declare that "they will respect the independence and territorial integrity of Austria." [11] The frontiers of Austria are the same as those existing on January 1, 1938.[12] By Article XI Austria undertakes to recognize the peace treaties with Italy, Rumania, Bulgaria, Hungary, Finland, and Japan, and a peace treaty which might be concluded with Germany.

Austria's sovereignty is limited by her obligations concerning the protection of human rights, by the guarantee of a democratic government, and her obligations concerning the protection of the rights of the Slovene and Croat minorities in Carinthia, Burgenland, and Styria.[13] It is highly interesting to see that, in spite of the disappearance of the minorities treaties concluded after World War I and in spite of the silence on this problem in the earlier peace treaties, the international protection of minorities again has its place here, as in the Understanding on Trieste.

Under Article IX of the treaty, Austria is bound to destroy all Nazi organizations. There are, further, two special clauses concerning Austrian legislation: Austria is bound to continue and maintain Austrian laws enacted since May 1, 1945, aimed at the liquidation of the remnants of the Nazi regime, and to maintain the Austrian law of April 3, 1919, concerning the House of Hapsburg-Lorraine.[14] Article IV contains the prohibition of *anschluss* with "Germany," which probably means the present Federal Republic of Germany as well as a possible reunited Germany. This prohibition is much more detailed than the corresponding Article LXXXVIII of the Versailles Treaty and Article LXXX of the St. Germain Treaty.

The treaty imposes no limitations on the size of the future Austrian army. But there are two types of restrictions: first, with respect to the prohibition of certain weapons, and duties as to the disposal of war matériel of Allied and German origin.[15] It is interesting to note that Austria shall not acquire or possess any war matériel of German manufacture, origin, or design, nor manufacture war matériel of German design;[16] and shall not acquire or manufacture civil aircraft of German or Japanese design.[17] Second, certain persons[18] are not permitted to serve in the Austrian armed forces. Austrian prisoners of war shall be repatriated as soon as possible.[19] Allied war graves in Austria will be respected, preserved, and maintained by Austria, as well as "the memorials to the military glory of the armies which fought on Austrian territory against Hitlerite Germany."[20] Each of the military clauses remains in force until modified in whole or in part by agreement between the Allied and Associated Powers and Austria, or, after Austria's membership in the United Nations, by agreement between the Security Council and Austria.[21]

The latter clause leads us to remark that the Allied and Associated Powers promise in the preamble "to support Austria's application for admission to the United Nations organization." Austria will, no doubt, apply very soon for admission and, under the treaty, there is little doubt that she will be admitted. Will Austria's admission break the deadlock as to the many other states which have been waiting in vain for years to be admitted?

It will also be interesting to see whether Austria as a permanently neutral state will be granted a special legal position as a member of the United Nations. For there is a further important limitation of Austria's sovereignty: her permanent neutrality. In Moscow the Austrian delegation gave assurances that

> the Austrian Republic intends not to join any military alliances or permit military bases on her territory, and will pursue a policy of independence in regard to all States.

The treaty contains nothing on Austria's permanent neutrality. In Vienna Mr. Molotov proposed that the four Powers "shall respect and observe a statement of Austria's permanent neutrality of the kind observed by Switzerland." The West had no objection in principle, but preferred to await the form and text of this Austrian declaration. Austria will soon enact a constitutional law declaring Austria's "perpetual neutrality" and will inform all states of this declaration and request its recognition. Austrian permanent neutrality will, therefore, be created by municipal law, although in consequence of the Soviet-Austrian understanding. But Austria will then ask for international recognition and guarantee of her permanent neutrality and of the inviolability of her territory.

As to the economic clauses of the treaty, Austria's status as a liberated country is shown by the fact that no reparations are asked,[22] and Austrian property in Germany is to be returned;[23] equally, all Austrian property in Allied territory is to be returned. Only Yugoslavia shall have the right to seize, retain, or liquidate Austrian property, rights, and interests within her territory.[24] But Austria is now negotiating with Yugoslavia for a return of Austrian assets. Whereas Article XXII (Article XXXV of the draft treaty) is as it was, Annex II contains the Soviet concessions; the details are not mentioned there but only in the Soviet-Austrian understanding. Austria will not only regain the other "German assets in Austria" but also her oilfields and the Danube Shipping Company. This means much to Austria not only economically, but also politically, in that there will be no "Soviet enclaves" in independent Austria. With respect to these returned assets Austria is only limited by Article XXII, paragraph 13: she is not allowed to pass foreign ownership rights and properties connected with the concessions regarding extraction and exploitation of oil; and, further, "none of the properties transferred as former German assets shall be returned to ownership of German juridical persons or where the value exceeds 260,000 shillings (ten thousand dollars) to the ownership of German natural persons."

Austria, on the other hand, waives all claims against Germany (except the return of Austrian property), and renounces all claims against the Allies; property of any of the United Nations in Austria must be restored.[25] The property of minority groups in Austria, who have suffered from racial or other persecution since March 13, 1938, is to be restored.[26] Pending the conclusion of commercial treaties, Austria, during a period of eighteen months from the coming into force of the treaty, must not discriminate against any of the United Nations and must grant them

national and most-favored-nations treatment, but only on
the condition of reciprocity. Austria shall grant to no
country exclusive or preferential rights with regard to the
operation of commercial aircraft in international traffic.[27]
Navigation on the Danube shall be free for national vessels and goods of all states.[28]

The clauses concerning the interpretation of the treaty
and the settlement of disputes contain no reference to the
International Court of Justice. There is, first, the organ
of the four "Heads of Mission" of the former occupying
powers. Under Article XXXIV, these Heads of Mission,
acting in concert, will, for a period not to exceed eighteen
months from the coming into force of the treaty, "represent the Allied and Associated Powers in dealing with the
Government of Austria in all matters concerning the execution and interpretation of the Treaty" and will "give guid-
ance, technical advice and clarification." The Heads of
Mission also have other functions, not limited to eighteen
months, under other articles. According to Article XXXV,
any dispute as to execution or interpretation of the treaty,
where not otherwise provided for, and which is not settled
by direct diplomatic negotiations, shall be referred to the
Heads of Mission. If the latter do not resolve the dispute
within two months, the dispute shall, unless another procedure is mutually agreed upon, be referred, at the request
of either party, to a Commission of Three, whose decision
is binding. The commission consists of one representative
of each party and a third member of a third country, selected by mutual agreement. In case of nonagreement within a month, either party may request the Secretary General
of the United Nations to make the appointment. In case
property, rights, or interests of minority groups are heir-
less or unclaimed, the Austrian government, under Article
XXVI, shall transfer these properties to agencies or organizations to be designated by the Heads of Mission by agree-

ment with the Austrian government. Any dispute concerning United Nations property in Austria (Article XXV) shall, under Article XXX, be referred to a conciliation commission of two members. If within three months no agreement has been reached, either government may ask for the addition of a third member selected by mutual agreement. If no such agreement can be reached within two months, the appointment will be made, at the request of either party, by the Heads of Mission. If the latter cannot agree within one month, the Secretary General of the United Nations may be requested by either party to make the appointment.

Whereas all agreements on West Germany, including the latest Paris Agreements, are (because of the remaining problems of a German peace treaty, Germany's frontiers and her reunification) provisional only, the State Treaty with Austria gives the impression of a treaty destined to form the basis of the international position of Austria for a long time to come. On the other hand, as the Austrian Treaty, although signed in 1955, dates back to the draft of 1949, in some ways it gives a curious impression in its clauses concerning Germany, signed at a time when West Germany had already become a sovereign state, an ally in NATO, and on the way to re-armament. Apart from the anti-anschluss clauses and from Article XXII, paragraph 13, already mentioned, we can point to Article XV which obliges Austria to co-operate in the prevention of German rearmament outside of German territory.

Although the State Treaty is much more favorable to Austria than the draft treaty, it still imposes heavy burdens on Austria. She must deliver each year for ten years one million tons of oil to the Soviet Union.[29] She has to pay in the next six years one hundred and fifty million dollars in goods [30] for the German assets in Austria held by the Soviet Union and to be returned to Austria under the treaty. This is no small burden. Austria has to pay two million dollars for the return of the Danube Shipping Company. But the Austrian chancellor declared that Austria will be able to carry these burdens without having to lower her standard of living. The returned German assets in Austria—about three hundred and forty enterprises, one hundred agrarian, two hundred and forty industrial—will create many problems. Perhaps one hundred enterprises, originally "aryanized" by Hitlerite Germany, have to be restored under the treaty. There are difficult problems concerning returned agrarian enterprises.[31] Many of the returned industrial enterprises are facing bankruptcy; all of them require much new capital for modernization. The evacuation of occupation troops, so highly welcomed, means on the other hand, a yearly loss of sixty million dollars in foreign currency. The creation of an Austrian army strong enough to protect her permanent neutrality, involves, of course, high costs. Negotiations are going on, as mentioned, with Yugoslavia. There will be negotiations with the holders of American oil concessions in Austria. Negotiations are pending with the Committee of Jewish Claims against Austria for the compensation of victims of naziism. There is the problem, arising out of Article XXII, paragraph 13, against which West Germany has protested both to the West and to Austria. But Chancellor Raab declared that the question of honestly acquired property of German citizens might lend itself to negotiations.

There will be, further, the many and often delicate problems of Austria's new permanent neutrality. There is the problem of the five-year commercial treaty to be concluded with the Soviet Union. There is need to remain in the best relations with the United States, which, up to now, has alone furnished Austria with capital. Notwithstanding the anti-German features of the treaty, Austria needs good relations with West Germany; these relations as to trade, capital, and tourist traffic are extremely important to Austria.

The treaty creates a sovereign, independent, democratic Austria which is treated as a liberated country. It is very interesting to inquire what the standpoint of the treaty is with regard to the problem of Austria's continuity and identity in law with pre-1938 Austria. We may say that the identity is upheld, without closing one's eyes to realities. First, the German annexation is recognized as a fact. The preamble states that Hitlerite Germany annexed Austria by force on March 13, 1938, and incorporated its territory into the German Reich. The Moscow Declaration is merely quoted as "regarding" the annexation null and void and as "affirming their wish to see Austria re-established as a free and independent State." The preamble expressly speaks of the annexation of Austria and of her "participation in the war as an *integral* part of Germany." Although in one case the phrase "during the German occupation of Austria" is used,[32] the treaty regularly uses the phrase "during the period of the German annexation of Austria," which is counted from March 13, 1938, to May 8, 1945. That is why the Austrian partial war-guilt clause was removed. That is why the treaty always speaks of the "war with Germany" or of "the war in Europe." That is why the treaty in Article XII, paragraph 2, discriminates against Austrian nationals "who were German nationals *before* March 13, 1938." It is also highly interesting to note that, in contrast to the clause concerning Ethiopia in the Peace Treaty of 1947 with Italy, the Allied and Associated Powers promise in Article III that they will incorporate into the German peace treaty a clause concerning "the renunciation by Germany of all territorial and political claims in respect of Austria and Austrian territory." This annexation is also the reason why, under Article XXVIII, "interest payments on Austrian Government securities, falling due after March

12, 1938 and before May 8, 1945 constitute a claim on Germany and not on Austria."

Second, an independent and sovereign Austria is, under Articles I and II, only re-established by this treaty. But Austria, even if not sovereign, has existed again since May, 1945. Third, this Austria since 1945, and the sovereign Austria re-established by the treaty, are identical in law with the Republic of Austria of 1918. That this is so, is clearly shown by Article X, paragraph 2, which obliges Austria to maintain the Austrian law of April 3, 1919. It is clearly shown by Article XXVIII, paragraphs 2 and 4, as to Austrian laws before March 13, 1938, and prewar contracts concluded by the government of Austria or persons who were nationals of Austria on March 12, 1938.

The treaty, therefore, recognizes Austria's extinction in fact between March 13, 1938, and May 8, 1945, and yet recognizes her identity and continuity. It is therefore a treaty proving Marek's [33] proposed "fourth rule" as to the identity of states: complete but illegal suppression of a state in time of peace, but continuance of a mere "ideal legal notion" of the state in question; identity and continuity, provided this state is re-established in fact within a reasonable time.

The treaty, of fundamental importance to Austria, also has world-wide political consequences. What will be the results of the Austrian Treaty in world politics remains to be seen. But there is no doubt that Austria will not only solve the economic problems arising from the treaty, but will manage her permanent neutrality successfully and in a manner advantageous for Austria and in the interest of world peace. Austria can in her new task be sure of the continued friendship of the United States, expressed in the message of the President of the United States to the President of Austria.[34] For, as the President said, the "conduct of the Austrian people during the ten long years they have labored under the heavy burden of foreign occupation has commanded the profound respect of all the American people."

¹ See this writer's editorial, *Infelix Austria,* 48 AM.J.INT'L L. 453–58 (1954).

² See text of U.S.–Austrian statement in N.Y. Times, November 27, 1954, p. 3. The United States recognize the "courage, resourcefulness and fortitude of the Austrian Government and its people."

³ Text in Sen.Exec. G, 84th Cong., 1st Sess. 40; supplement to 49 AM.J.INT'L L. 191 (1955).

⁴ Text in 32 DEP'T STATE BULL. 734 (1955); N.Y. Times, April 20, 1955, p. 4.

⁵ Official English text in Sen. Exec. G. 84th Cong., 1st Sess., reprinted in supplement to 49 AM.J.INT'L L. 162 (1955); see also N.Y. Times, May 16, 1955, pp. 6–8.

⁶ The draft treaty had fifty-nine articles.

⁷ Now Article XXII of the treaty.

⁸ Article XVI dealt with the "voluntary repatriation of displaced persons within Austrian territory," an article which might have endangered many refugees in Austria from behind the Iron Curtain. Text of this article in N.Y. Times, May 4, 1955, p. 12.

⁹ Original text in N.Y. Times, May 15, 1955, p. 13.

¹⁰ Art. XXXVII.

¹¹ Arts. I and II.

¹² Art. V.

¹³ Arts. VI, VII, VIII.

¹⁴ Art. X. The Austrian chancellor, it was reported, regretted this article as a "superfluous limitation of Austrian sovereignty."

¹⁵ Arts. XIII and XIV.

¹⁶ Art. XIV.

¹⁷ Art. XVI.

¹⁸ Art. XII; it is, in general, an anti-Nazi article.

¹⁹ Art. XVIII.

²⁰ Art. XIX.

²¹ Art. XVII.

²² Art. XXI.

²³ Art. XXIII.

²⁴ Art. XXVII.

²⁵ Arts. XXIII, XXIV, XXV.

²⁶ Art. XXVI.

²⁷ Art. XXIX.

²⁸ And not only for all of the United Nations (Art. XXXI).

²⁹ Austria's oil production was three million tons in 1954.

[30] This latter concession was already made by the Soviet Union at the Berlin Conference in 1954.

[31] E.g., those originally belonging to Jewish owners, but where for fifteen years small farmers have been compulsorily settled; or those still belonging to German nationals. A special case is that of the latifundia of Prince Esterházy in the Burgenland which certainly do not constitute "German assets," but were long ago confiscated by the Soviet Union. Later, Prince Esterházy, a Hungarian citizen, together with Cardinal Mindszenty, was condemned by communist Hungary and all his property declared confiscated.

[32] Art. XXV, par. 2–4a.

[33] KRYSTYNA MAREK, IDENTITY AND CONTINUITY OF STATES IN INTERNATIONAL LAW (1954).

[34] 32 DEPT. STATE BULL. 873 (1955); N.Y. Times, May 16, 1955, p. 6.

THE PERMANENTLY NEUTRAL STATE as a particular figure in international law is a creation of the nineteenth century: Switzerland and, for a certain period, Belgium and Luxembourg are the examples. Whereas the latter two states were made permanently neutral states through a treaty concluded between the great Powers, primarily in their political interest to create a "buffer state" (*état-tampon*), the treaty on Swiss neutrality corresponded to the wish and centuries-old policy of the Swiss people. This distinction is also shown in the manner of creating the status of permanent neutrality in international law: in the case of Belgium and Luxembourg by a treaty between the Great Powers; in the case of Switzerland by such treaty and the consent of the state concerned. On the other hand, a state cannot become permanently neutral in international law by its own unilateral declaration.[1] Permanent neutrality is the creation of a treaty; hence, it can only be modified or abolished with the consent of all the signatory powers and the consent of the permanently neutral state. The permanent neutrality can either be recognized by the third powers which have concluded the corresponding treaty and other states, or also be guaranteed. Recognition obliges the recognizing state to respect, guarantee to respect, and defend the permanent neutrality. The guarantee can be collective or single; in the first case the guarantors are only bound jointly, in the second case, jointly and severally. It is agreed that such permanent neutrality creates a legal situation valid *erga omnes*.

The permanently neutral state [2] foregoes the right to go to war except in self-defense. In any war between other states it is bound to observe strict, classic, integral neutrality and to remain neutral; neither can it participate in an international military execution. It is prohibited even in times of peace to follow any policy which might involve it in war. It can conclude no alliances, whether offensive or defensive, no treaties of military assistance, no treaties of protectorate or guarantee. It cannot guarantee the permanent neutrality of another state. It is not allowed to grant military bases on its territory to other states. It cannot allow the passage of troops of foreign belligerent states through, or the flying of foreign belligerent planes over, its territory, even if they are under the orders of a general international organization. The permanently neutral state has not only a right but a duty to go to war if attacked, to defend its permanent neutrality by arms. It has, therefore, not only a right but a duty to have an adequate army, to have fortifications,[3] and to make all necessary military preparations in order to be able to defend itself. Permanent neutrality is, like any treaty obligation, a restriction of sovereignty. But the permanently neutral state is a sovereign state. It has foregone the right to go to war except in self-defense, but it has not lost its legal capacity to make war; if it starts a war, such war is illegal, but it is, nevertheless, a war and the laws of war apply. In all nonmilitary aspects it has the right to conduct such internal and foreign policy as it thinks fit; it can participate in general and regional treaties and international organizations of a non-military nature; it has no duty of ideological neutrality, no duty to restrict the freedom of the press and of opinion.

Let us now apply these rules to the new case of Austria. First of all, it must be stated that the law of permanent neutrality, where it applies, as in the case of Switzerland, is positive international law also today.[4] The State Treaty with Austria of May 15, 1955,[5] which came into force on July 27, 1955, contains nothing about Austria's permanent neutrality. The latter idea is of Soviet origin. At the Berlin Conference of 1954, the Soviet foreign minister introduced proposals [6] with the object of a rapid resolution of the Austrian problem; among them was a clause preventing the establishment of foreign military bases on Austrian territory or the inclusion of Austria in any coalition or military alliance directed against any power which took part with its armed forces in the war against Germany and in the liberation of Austria. The Austrian delegation made a corresponding declaration at the Berlin Conference, but, for other reasons, the State Treaty could not be concluded. On February 9, 1955, the Soviet Union made new proposals on the Austrian question and, at Soviet initiative, a preliminary exchange of views took place in Moscow between the Soviet government and the Austrian ambassador during February and March, 1955; then followed the Soviet invitation to the Federal Chancellor of Austria to come to Moscow. There Soviet-Austrian negotiations were carried on from April 12 to April 15, 1955, and led to the so-called Moscow Memorandum of April 15, 1955.[7]

In Part I of the Moscow Memorandum, Austria obligates itself (1) to make a declaration in a form which will obligate Austria internationally to practice in perpetuity a neutrality of the type maintained [8] by Switzerland; (2) to submit this Austrian declaration, in accordance with the Federal Constitution, to the Austrian parliament for decision immediately after the ratification of the State Treaty with Austria; (3) to take all suitable steps to obtain international recognition of the declaration confirmed by the Austrian parliament; (4) to welcome a guarantee by the four Great Powers of the inviolability and integrity of the Austrian state territory; (5) to seek to obtain such guarantee. On the other hand, the Soviet Union obligates itself in Part II: (1) to recognize the declaration concerning the neutrality of Austria and (2) to participate in a guarantee by the four Great Powers of the inviolability and integrity of the Austrian state territory, according to the model of Switzerland.

The principal Committee of the Austrian Parliament recommended unanimously such declaration of permanent neutrality. On October 26, 1955, a constitutional federal statute on Austria's permanent neutrality [9] was enacted. This brief statute reads in its principal Article I:

> ARTICLE I. 1. For the purpose of the permanent maintenance of its external independence and for the purpose of the inviolability of its territory Austria, of its own free will, declares herewith its permanent neutrality. Austria will remain and defend it with all means at its disposal.
>
> 2. In order to secure these purposes Austria will never in the future accede to any military alliances nor permit the establishment of military bases of foreign states on its territory.

The purpose of the statute is Austria's permanent neutrality; but it is clear that, as such, it cannot have the legal effect of making Austria a permanently neutral state in international law. A self-declared neutrality, as was Switzerland's prior to 1815, is only a declaration of policy, or a part of municipal law. Permanent neutrality is by this statute a part of the Austrian federal constitution; but a municipal law, as such, can have no international legal effect. That Austria's permanent neutrality is self-declared seems enhanced by the emphasis on the fact that Austria

made this declaration "of its own free will." [10] If there were
nothing more to it, Austria could at any time, by the prescribed constitutional procedure, change or revoke its permanent neutrality. But there *is* more to it. For this statute
was enacted in fulfillment of an *international* obligation
arising out of the Moscow Memorandum. The statute binds
Austria, therefore, vis-à-vis the Soviet Union and could not
be changed or revoked, except with the consent of the
Soviet Union. It is the carrying out of the first two obligations undertaken in the Moscow Memorandum. That document binds Austria to make a declaration which will obligate it internationally to practice in perpetuity a neutrality
of the type maintained by Switzerland. The Memorandum
is, of course, from the point of view of legal technique,
badly drafted; for it is legally impossible for Austria to
make a unilateral declaration which will bind it *internationally*. But in spite of imperfect wording, the agreement
of the parties is clear: Austria has to take a *series* of steps
by which its permanent neutrality will by stages, come into
being. What is the sense of the phrase "of its own free will"
in the Austrian statute? It seems that these words mean
only that permanent neutrality has not been imposed upon
Austria, that is, its permanent neutrality is not a "neutrali-
zation" according to the model of Belgium and Luxembourg. For although the statute was enacted in fulfillment
of an obligation under the Moscow Memorandum, Austria
had already offered a declaration of this type at the Berlin
Conference of 1954. On the other hand, whereas the purposes given by the statute are external independence and
integrity of Austria's territory, the *reason* for the enactment of the statute was to fulfill a condition demanded by
the Soviet Union, and thus to finally get the State Treaty
and to see the withdrawal of the occupation troops.

Austria has also already fulfilled its duty under point 3
of the Moscow Memorandum: It has communicated this

statute to all states with which it has diplomatic relations and has asked for the international recognition of its permanent neutrality. Only the Soviet Union is, by the Moscow Memorandum, legally bound to grant this recognition. As far as the three Western Powers are concerned, Mr. Molotov proposed at the time of the signature of the State Treaty at Vienna that all four governments declare they would respect and observe Austria's permanent neutrality. The three Western Powers had no objection in principle, but preferred to await the form and text of Austria's declaration of neutrality. Their recognition was to be expected. Not only had they no "objection in principle" and full knowledge, but Annex II to the State Treaty refers to the Moscow Memorandum. True, the reference is to other matters, not to permanent neutrality; but this reference and the fact that Article XXXVI of the treaty makes the provisions of the annexes an integral part of the treaty seem to indicate that the Moscow Memorandum as a whole is recognized as an internationally binding agreement. In fulfillment of the next step prescribed by the Memorandum, Austria no doubt "will seek to obtain" from the four powers the guarantee [11] of the inviolability and integrity of its territory. Under the Moscow Memorandum the Soviet Union is only bound to "participate" in such guarantee which seems, therefore, to be a collective guarantee; whether the other three powers will be willing to give this guarantee remains to be seen.[12] It will be noticed that it is not a question of the guarantee of Austria's permanent neutrality, but only of the inviolability and integrity of its territory. Such guarantee is perhaps not fully identical with the guarantee of permanent neutrality, but it certainly covers a very substantial part of it.

The situation is therefore, at the beginning of 1956, the following one: As a starting point, Austria has declared its permanent neutrality by constitutional federal statute; it has asked all states to recognize its permanent neutrality. It is clear that only by this recognition can Austria's unilateral declaration have an international legal effect. As far as this writer knows, all the permanent members of the U.N. Security Council and many other states have already recognized Austria's permanent neutrality; [13] hence Austria has become a permanently neutral state in international law, regardless of whether the guarantee of its territorial integrity and inviolability is or is not given later by the four powers. Such guarantee will certainly be highly welcome to Austria; but the best guarantee of permanent neutrality is a strong army and the unshakable determination to defend this neutrality against any comer, as history has proved in the model case of Switzerland.

This brings us to another point. The Moscow Memorandum speaks of a permanent neutrality "of the type maintained by Switzerland" and "according to the model of Switzerland." This phrase is not found in the Austrian constitutional statute. In this writer's opinion the reference to Switzerland in the Moscow Memorandum serves only to determine the status of permanent neutrality, as Switzerland was at that time the only example, but does not mean that the Swiss model of practicing such permanent neutrality must be followed in every respect. This interpretation seems warranted by the Moscow Memorandum and the State Treaty. First, the historical background and the coming into existence of Swiss permanent neutrality [14] are totally different from the case of Austria. Second, there is a clear contradiction between Switzerland's policy, because of its permanent neutrality, not to apply for membership in the United Nations, and the preamble of the Austrian State Treaty, in which the four powers promise "to support Austria's application for admission to the United Nations." Article XVII of the State Treaty contains the phrase: "after Austria becomes a member of the United Nations."

Hence, the Soviet Union, as a contracting party to the Moscow Memorandum, considered Austria's membership in the United Nations fully compatible with its permanent neutrality "according to the model of Switzerland."

Indeed, the difference between Switzerland's and Austria's attitude is striking. Switzerland considered its entry into the League of Nations [15] possible because of the decentralization of the collective security system, but only on condition of being granted a special legal status exempting it from participation in the military *"action commune"* and later also from participation in economic sanctions. On the other hand, Switzerland holds its entry into the United Nations, because of the centralization of the collective security system in the Security Council, to be incompatable with its permanent neutrality, even with a special legal status granted to it.

Austria had already applied for admission into the United Nations in 1947, when it was not yet a fully sovereign, and of course not a permanently neutral state. Only the Soviet veto prevented its admission. Under the preamble to the State Treaty, its admission should have presented no difficulties. This preamble seemed to indicate that Austria's case would be handled specially, regardless of the deadlock with regard to many other applicants. But in fact Austria was simply included in the "package deal" and was first vetoed by the Soviet Union. The question arises whether the Soviet veto of the admission of Austria was legally compatible with the promise given in the preamble of the State Treaty with Austria. Anyway, under the compromise later offered by the Soviet Union, Austria was admitted into the United Nations like any other state and without being given a special legal status as a permanently neutral state. Austria was glad to be admitted. The Federal Chancellor of Austria has stated [16] that "for a country which had declared itself militarily neutral it is of special importance that it should belong to the United Nations, as this membership will give it security and support in its foreign policy." But it is also certain that unconditional membership in the United Nations is not compatible with permanent neutrality. Although the United Nations collective security system is, in contrast with the League of Nations, centralized, it is, on the other hand, different from that under the Covenant, not automatic; sanctions, as far as their legally binding character on members is concerned, depend on a decision of the Security Council under Article XXXIX of the U.N. Charter. That is why Verdross [17] has recently suggested that the Security Council, in conformity with the Charter, may by a basic resolution permanently relieve certain states from participation in economic and military sanctions. It is perfectly possible that the Security Council may adopt such a resolution and thus grant to Austria a special legal status in the United Nations. But even if no such resolution in principle is adopted, it seems that Austria's permanent neutrality is not endangered by its membership in the United Nations. For Austria's permanent neutrality has come into existence in international law by recognition on the part of the permanent members of the Security Council and many other states; recognition binds the recognizing states to respect permanent neutrality; this respect for permanent neutrality therefore obliges the members of the Security Council not to call on a permanently neutral state for participation in economic and military sanctions.

The Austrian constitutional federal statute expressly mentions only three duties: the negative duties not to accede to alliances, not to grant military bases on its territory to foreign states, and the positive duty to defend its neutrality with all means at its disposal. The first two duties meet the wishes of the Soviet Union; the last, the wish of the United States. The State Treaty gives Austria only the right to have an adequate army; but on the basis of its permanent neutrality this is not only a right, but at the same time a duty. The right of individual self-defense under Article LI of the U.N. Charter is at the same time a duty for a permanently neutral state. A statute on the Austrian army to be created is in preparation. The prominence given by the Austrian statute to these three duties also emphasizes the military character of Austria's permanent neutrality and its freedom of internal and foreign policy in all other respects, particularly in the ideological field.[18]

The carrying out of the Austrian constitutional statute by the federal government is not only a matter of international law and in this respect guided by legal considerations, but also a matter of neutrality policy, as distinguished from legal considerations. Such neutrality policy is, in the present world situation, a delicate task. But there can be no doubt that Austria, which has handled so well the problems arising out of a ten-year foreign occupation, will also handle its permanent neutrality in a manner advantageous to Austria and in the interest of world peace. For a permanently neutral state also has many occasions for an active international policy, as the example of Switzerland shows. And Austria will have the full support of the United States. In his message of friendship [19] the American deputy assistant secretary for European affairs said:

> The United States considers Austria now in a strong, stable political situation with a government well prepared and fully capable of carrying out its domestic and international responsibilities. Many new opportunities are opening up for Austria-United States relations. The United States salutes Austrian independence and looks forward with confidence to ever closer association between our two countries in the future.

American friendship was shown when the Secretary of State of the United States took part on November 5, 1955, in that event which more than anything else symbolizes

Austria's independence as well as its spiritual greatness—
the reopening of the Vienna Opera.

¹ The practice of states as well as the literature is nearly unanimous on this point. Iceland's unilateral declaration of permanent
neutrality, 1918, had only the value of a unilateral formulation of
policy; it had no international effect and did not render Iceland a
permanently neutral state in international law.

² See the treatises by FAUCHILLE, Vol 1, Part 1 at 693–714 (1922);
LISZT, op. cit. at 107–11 (12th ed. 1925); Cavaglieri, op. cit. at 164–74
(1925); DIENA, op. cit. at 105–13 (1930); 1 and 2 GUGGENHEIM,
TRAITÉ DE DROIT INTERNATIONAL PUBLIC 177–78, 547–61 (1953). Of the
many monographs, we mention K. STRUPP, NEUTRALISATION, BE-
FRIEDUNG, ENTMILITARISIERUNG (1933); Dollot, Essai sur la neutralité
permanente, 67 RECUEIL DES COURS 7 (1939).

³ Except if demilitarized by the basic treaty, as in the case of
Luxembourg.

⁴ It is, therefore, not correct that Professor Charles G. Fenwick, in
his INTERNATIONAL LAW 107 (3rd ed. 1948), puts the whole chapter
on permanent neutrality into the past tense.

⁵ See "The State Treaty with Austria," above.

⁶ See FOREIGN MINISTERS MEETING: BERLIN DISCUSSIONS (Department of State Pub. No. 5399) at 233.

⁷ It seems that the only authentic text of this Memorandum is in
Russian, as published by the Moscow Radio and TASS in May, 1955.
A German text was published by the Oesterreichische ZEITUNG (the
organ of the Soviet forces in Austria) of May 22, 1955, and by the
Oesterreichische Volksstimme (organ of the Austrian Communist
Party) of May 27, 1955. Up to now, the German text can only be
found in these newspapers. (This writer is indebted for this information as well as for the German text of the Moscow Memorandum and
the text of the Austrian Neutrality Statute to Minister Plenipotentiary Dr. Stephan Verosta of the Austrian Foreign Office.) English
text of the Moscow Memorandum in Supplement to NEW TIMES, No.
22 (1955); Sen. Exec. G, 84th Cong., 1st Sess. 40; 32 DEP'T STATE
BULL. 1011–13 (1955); and in Supplement to 49 AM.J.INT'L L. 191–94
(1955).

⁸ The German text is "gehandhabt," which rather corresponds to
handle, manage, administer, practice.

⁹ Bundesverfassungsgesetz vom. 26. Oktober 1955 über die Neutralität Österreichs (B. G. Bl. 1955 [November 4, 1955] No. 211).

¹⁰ In the German original: "aus freien Stücken."

¹¹ The four powers are already bound by Article II of the State
Treaty with Austria to "respect" the independence and territorial integrity of Austria.

¹² In his Report to the President, the American secretary of state
had this to say on this point: "The guarantee desire of the Austrian
Government is understandable, but the Government of the United
States has made no commitments with regard thereto."

13 The United States recognized Austria's perpetual neutrality by the U. S. note of December 6, 1955, in answer to the Austrian note of November 14, 1955 (33 DEP'T STATE BULL. 1011–12 [1955]).

14 See, e.g., SCHWEIZER, GESCHICHTE DER SCHWEIZERISCHEN NEU-TRALITÄT (1895); BONJOUR, GESCHICHTE DER SCHWEIZERISCHEN NEU-TRALITÄT (1946); C. GORGÉ, LA NEUTRALITÉ HELVÉTIQUE (1947); ROBERT, ETUDE SUR LA NEUTRALITÉ SUISSE (1950).

15 See, e.g., Borel, in 2 REVUE GÉNÉRALE DE DROIT INTERNATIONAL PUBLIC 2e sér. 153; W. RAPPARD, IN 1 MUNCH, L'ORIGINE ET L'OEUVRE DE LA SOCIÉTÉ DES NATIONS 379; METTETAL, LA NEUTRALITÉ ET LA SOCIÉTÉ DES NATIONS; SCHÜCKING-WEHBERG, DIE SATZUNG DES VÖL-KERBUNDES 207–10 (2nd ed.)

16 N.Y. Times, December 16, 1955, p. 4.

17 See his article in 50 AM.J.INT'L L. 61–68 (1956).

18 In the exercise of this freedom Austria has decided to join the Council of Europe. "We are a militarily neutral state, but there is no 'neutralism'," the Austrian foreign minister declared (N.Y. Times, February 22, 1956, p. 8). Switzerland has not joined. But as the Council of Europe is purely advisory and non-military in character, a permanently neutral state certainly has a right to join.

19 33 DEP'T STATE BULL. 788–90 (1955).

PART IV

SOURCES OF INTERNATIONAL LAW

THE ASCERTAINMENT of the existence or non-existence of a norm of customary international law and, in the affirmative case, the ascertainment of its contents—always a prominent task of international tribunals and courts—has played a strong role in the jurisprudence of the International Court of Justice. The court has had occasion to ascertain the existence,[1] or to deny the existence, of a rule of general[2] or particular[3] customary international law. The fact that sometimes the pronouncements of the court were rather to the surprise of the doctrine and of the practice of states has not only brought into being an extensive literature,[4] but has also directed attention once more to the problem of the nature of customary international law which justifies a brief survey of this problem.

There are two additional reasons. While many international lawyers have concentrated their studies since 1920 nearly exclusively on the particular international law of the League of Nations, and, now, of the United Nations, there is a transformation of customary general law going on, too. Finally, the problem of the nature of customary international law is still controversial within the science of international law. The nature of customary law is, of course, a general problem of law. But whereas customary law is today of lesser importance in the advanced municipal legal orders, it is fundamental in international law, since all general international law has been, up to now, customary law. Notwithstanding a vast literature on customary law in general [5] and on customary international law,[6] the words of Jules Basdevant,[7] that "les idées des juristes sur le caractère de la coutume n'ont atteint ni à l'unité ni à la clarté," are still true.

There are three principal reasons why the ideas of jurists as to the nature of customary law have reached neither unity nor clarity. The first reason is the use of the word "source," which, as Kelsen [8] often has pointed out, is "a figurative and highly ambiguous expression," which leads to confusion and should be dropped as a legal term.[9] Our problem must not be confused either with the "evidence" [10] or with the entirely different problem of the foundation of international law,[11] whether understood in a formal sense—as the "basic norm"—or in a material sense as the "ultimate" foundation. The latter problem is by its very essence a metajuridical problem, a problem not of the science but of the philosophy of law.

The second reason is the untenable construction of custom as *pactum tacitum*, a doctrine held by the early science of international law from Grotius to Vattel, and revived by the dualistic doctrine.[12] The purely fictitious character of this construction, its open contradiction to the practice of states, the untenable consequences to which it leads, its rejection by the overwhelming majority of writers, make it superfluous to refute this construction once more.

The third principal reason is the idea of seeing in custom, not a procedure for creating norms of international law, but merely the "proof," "evidence," "la constatation" of a preexisting rule of law. This is the typical approach of the natural-law doctrine.[13] It reappears in Savigny's Historical Jurisprudence (law as the product of the mystical *Volksgeist*, law to be found, not made) and, in recent times, in L. Duguit's sociological, and G. Scelle's [14] biological, jurisprudence. With Duguit, law is the product of "la solidarité sociale." For Scelle custom is the translation of a biological social necessity. The *droit objectif* is the sum total of *causal* laws which determine the appearance, permanence, and development of the social fact. Custom has a spontaneous and intuitive character. Similar ideas can be found in François,[15] and, at some stage of his development, in Lauterpacht.[16] This untenable theory is also responsible for the extremely bad drafting of Article XXXVIII (1) of the Statute of the International Court of Justice.[17] Close to this idea also is Roberto Ago,[18] for whom customary law is "spontaneous law, emerging in the conscience of members"; but its creation or approval by those members is irrelevant: the science of law is here occupied only with the ascertainment of the principle, not with its source.

To arrive at a legally correct understanding of the nature of customary international law, it is necessary to avoid these three errors. Customary law, like all law, is positive, man-made law. Law regulates its own creation. Treaty and custom are two different, independent procedures for creating international legal norms.[19] The treaty procedure leads only to norms of particular international law: custom can lead to norms of particular or general international law: but we speak of custom here only as a procedure for creating rules of general international law.

The custom procedure is, historically, a primitive procedure; hence its defects: slowness and uncertainty of ascertainment. Custom can create new norms, or change or abolish existing norms. Some writers [20] see in custom a secondary procedure. But it is, in fact, not only the older, but also the hierarchically higher form of creating norms of international law.[21] Custom-produced general international law is the basis; the customary principle of *pacta sunt servanda* is the reason for validity of all particular international law created by the treaty procedure.

International custom is, therefore, a procedure for the creation of norms of general international law. It is international law which lays down the conditions under which the procedure of custom creates valid norms of general international law. These conditions are two: usage and *opinio juris;* they have equal importance. This is admitted overwhelmingly by the writers, and proved by the practice of states and of international tribunals and courts.[22] Only Strupp, from his extreme *pactum tacitum* standpoint, denies the necessity of usage. As to the condition of *opinio juris,* Kopelmanas [23] took a position against its necessity, and recently Guggenheim has held that the condition of *opinio juris* is superfluous. But this theory is untenable; it would eliminate the distinction between customary rules of law, on the one hand, and rules of international morality and conventional international laws (*courtoisie internationale*), on the other hand; whereas the practice of states shows that the states and courts sharply distinguish between these international rules of different normative systems.

The elements of the first condition, "usage," are the following ones: There must be a "practice," whether of positive acts or omissions, whether in time of peace or war. This practice must refer to a type of situation falling within the domain of international relations. This practice must have been continued and repeated without interruption of continuity. But international law contains no rules as to how many times or for how long a time this practice must have been repeated. To require that the practice necessarily must be "ancient," [24] has no basis in positive international law.

Thus the new and undoubted rule of general customary international law concerning the sovereignty over the airspace [25] by the subjacent state was developed—contrary to the preceding proposals of the science of international law—during World War I. It is doubtful whether, as some writers [26] demand, the practice must be "just" and "humane" or must not be in violation of existing treaties or of valid international law. For custom may change a valid treaty norm—e.g., Article XVIII of the League of Nations Covenant—or a valid norm of general international law. As to the problem of how widely this usage must have been practiced, international law demands a "general" practice, not a unanimous one. That shows the untenability of the consent theory, of the *pactum tacitum* construction. For, if it is the case of a customary rule of general international law, created by general practice, such norm is valid for new states and for pre-existing states which hitherto had no opportunity of applying it.[27] The problem is, on the other hand, of importance as to the coming into existence of a new norm of customary general international law. Some writers say that such new norm cannot come into existence against the resistance of a leading state. That is why the so-called sector principle of the acquisition of sovereignty over polar regions has certainly not become a new norm of customary general international law, in consequence of the non-acceptance by the United States. On the other hand, even the concurrent attitude of the leading powers cannot create a norm of customary general international law against the resistance of other powers. That is why the three-mile limit of territorial waters, upheld by the leading maritime powers, the United States and Great Britain, has, in the light of non-acceptance by other states, not become a norm of customary general international law. The practice must be "general," not universal; but a mere majority of states is not enough.

The practice must have been applied by the overwhelming majority of states which hitherto had an opportunity of applying it.

The usage, thus determined, must be coupled with the *opinio juris*. The practice must have been applied in the conviction that it is legally binding. When the practice even for a long time and without interruption has been applied only in the conviction that it is morally binding or conventionally binding, a norm of international morality or a norm of *courtoisie internationale* may have come into being, but not a norm of customary general international law. Not only must the states which applied the practice have had this conviction, but this conviction must not have been challenged by other states. Protests by other states or declarations that they, even if submitting to this practice, do so only *ex gratia;* protests against the norm on which an international decision is based, even in carrying out this decision, prevent the coming into existence of a new norm of customary general international law.

There is a last problem as to the relations between those two conditions of "usage" and "*opinio juris,*" especially in time. We must distinguish two hypotheses. A norm of *courtoisie internationale* may become a norm of customary general international law: here the *opinio juris* is later added to the usage and no theoretical difficulty arises. But a difficult problem is presented when it is a case of the original foundation of a norm of customary general international law. On the one hand it is said that usage plus *opinio juris leads* to such norm; that, on the other hand, in order to lead to such norm, the states must already practice the first cases with the *opinio juris*. Hence, the very coming into existence of such norm would presuppose that the states acted in legal error. Kelsen [28] sees this dilemma, but it is hardly a solution to state "that it is sufficient that the states consider themselves bound by any norm whatever." For this would not explain why, then, in one case a legal rule, in another case a moral or conventional one, would come into existence, nor would it correspond to the condition which demands an *opinio juris,* not "of any norm whatever." Verdross resorts to the explanation that the first cases of this usage must be supported by the consciousness of helping a "principle of law which has not yet become positive law" to assert itself. But this solution comes close to the theory of custom as evidence of a pre-existing norm. There is here, certainly, a challenging theoretical problem which, as far as this writer can see, has not yet found a satisfactory solution.

The ascertainment whether the two conditions of the custom procedure have been fulfilled in a concrete case is a task of the competent international authority, and, preliminarily, of the science of international law. It is a difficult task. Evidence can be taken from diplomatic correspondence, instructions, and so on, municipal laws and court decisions, treaties, negotiations, international decisions, practice of international organizations. But the greatest caution is always necessary. Diplomatic correspondence and so on may carry the *opinio juris,* but may also constitute mere expressions of political convenience or expediency. A national court decision may be good evidence, but may also, in the words of the late Professor Borchard, only be evidence of what international law is *not.* Treaties may, under different circumstances, be evidence for the fulfillment of the two conditions, and, under other circumstances, evidence against it. Even similar clauses over a long time in corresponding treaties are not always evidence. Thus the option-of-nationality clause, although very frequently contained in corresponding treaties and in use a long time, has not lead to a rule of customary general international law which makes an option clause obligatory apart from treaty.[29] Repeated violations of international law may have occurred without changing the conviction that they constitute violations, but they may also have been committed with the *opinio juris* of creating new international law. That is, e.g., now the crucial and basic problem in the chaotic status of the laws of war.[30]

It is necessary to distinguish between internal laws as evidence of the coming into existence of a customary rule of general international law [31] and a mere parallelism of municipal statutes.[32] This research has not only to determine whether a norm of customary general international law, creating a new or changing or abolishing a pre-existing norm has come into existence but also when it has come into existence. Here is the difficult field of distinguishing between a new customary norm which has come into existence, and mere proposals for or tendencies toward creating such new norm. We give a few examples which will, at the same time, show how important this problem is in these times of transformation of general international law. Have recent international decisions [33] already created a principle of customary international law, lowering the degree of effectivity of occupation of certain *terrae nullius?* Have recent treaty clauses already lead to a new rule of customary general law concerning privileges and immunities of international organizations? Hardly. Is there a norm of general customary international law concerning so-called principle of contiguity? [34] Has a new norm of customary general international law come into existence abolishing the privilege of jurisdictional immunity for state-owned vessels engaged in normal commerce? The same question could be asked with regard to the acts *jure gestionis* of foreign states.[35] Has a norm of customary general international law come into existence granting to coastal states certain rights in the so-called contiguous zone beyond territorial waters? [36] It is certain that, contrary to the opinion of some writers, the so-called Nuremberg Principles have, up to now, not become principles of customary general international law. Has a new norm of general customary international law concerning the Continental Shelf come into existence? Lauterpacht [37] answered the question in the affirmative in 1950 insofar as the Truman Declaration is concerned. But not only are Mouton [38] and the Award of Lord Asquith of Bishopstone [39] of contrary opinion, but the proposals of the International Law Commission,[40] acting in its capacity for "progressive development of international law" and not "of its codification," would seem to show no more but a tendency, a trend toward the coming into existence of a new norm, and even that, perhaps, only by multilateral treaty. All the more so, certain recent extravagant unilateral declarations concerning the "epicontinental sea," the extension of territorial waters, the expansion of exclusive fishing rights have not led to the coming into existence of a new norm of customary general international law [41] in the light of the strong protests by the United States, Great Britain, and other states.

[1] Corfu Channel Case, [1949] I.C.J. Rep. 4; 43 AM.J.INT'L L. 558 (1949).

[2] Reservations to Genocide Convention, [1951] I.C.J.Rep. 15 (advisory opinion); 45 AM.J.INT'L L. 579 (1951); Anglo-Norwegian Fisheries Case, [1951] I.C.J. Rep. 116; 46 AM.J.INT'L L. 348 (1952).

[3] Asylum Case, [1950] I.C.J. Rep. 266; 45 AM.J.INT'L L. 179 (1951).

[4] See W. W. Cox, *Reservations to Multipartite Conventions*, PROCEEDINGS, AMERICAN SOCIETY OF INTERNATIONAL LAW 26–35 (1952); G. G. Fitzmaurice, *Reservations to Multilateral Conventions*, 2 INT'L & COMP.L.Q. 1–26 (1953); D. H. N. Johnson, *The Anglo-Norwegian Fisheries Case*, 1 INT'L & COMP.L.Q. 145–80 (1952); Jens Evensen, *The Anglo-Norwegian Fisheries Case and Its Legal Consequences*, 46 AM.J.INT'L L. 609–30 (1952); C. H. M. Waldock, *The Anglo-Norwegian Fisheries Case*, 28 BRIT.YB.INT'L L. 114–17 (1951); A. E. Evans, *The Colombian-Peruvian Asylum Case*, 46 AM.POL.SCI.REV. 142–57 (1952); C. Barcia Trelles, *El derecho de asilo diplomático*, 59 REVISTA DE DERECHO INTERNACIONAL 161–80 (1951), and 4 REVISTA ESPAÑOLA DE DERECHO INTERNACIONAL 59–66 (1951); P. F. Gonidec, *L'affaire du droit d'asile*, 22 REVUE GÉNÉRALE DE DROIT INTERNATIONAL PUBLIC, 3e sér. 547–92 (1951); J. L. F. Van Essen, 1 INT'L & COMP.L.Q. 533–39 (1952).

[5] See e.g., in German, PUCTA, DAS GEWOHNHEITSRECHT (1828–37); BRIE, DIE LEHRE VOM GEWOHNHEITSRECHT (1899); M. RÜMELIN, DIE BINDENDE KRAFT DES GEWOHNHEITSRECHTS (1919); W. Henrich, *Zur*

Problematik des Gewohnheitsrechts, 2 RECUEIL D'ETUDES SUR LES SOURCES DU DROIT EN L'HONNEUR DE FR. GÉNY 276 (1935).

6 See C. ROUSSEAU, PRINCIPES GÉNÉRAUX DU DROIT INTERNATIONAL PUBLIC 815–62, and the large bibliographies at 105–6, 815 (1949). Of later writings there must be added M. SORENSEN, LES SOURCES DU DROIT INTERNATIONAL (1946); MATEESCO, LA COUTUME DANS LES CYCLES JURIDIQUES INTERNATIONAUX (1947); 1 P. GUGGENHEIM, LEHRBUCH DES VÖLKERRECHTS 45–51 (1947); A. VERDROSS, VÖLKERRECHT 107–10 (2nd ed. 1950); H. KELSEN, PRINCIPLES OF INTERNATIONAL LAW 303–17 (1952).

7 RÈGLES GÉNÉRALES DE LA PAIX, 4 RECUEIL DES COURS 508 (1936).

8 E.g., *op. cit.* at 303.

9 See also H. W. BRIGGS, THE LAW OF NATIONS 44 (2nd ed. 1952).

10 This confusion is clearly to be seen in T. J. LAWRENCE, THE PRINCIPLES OF INTERNATIONAL LAW 95 (7th ed. 1915), and in ELLERY C. STOWELL, INTERNATIONAL LAW 26 (1931).

11 The books by ZICCARDI, LA COSTITUZIONE DELL' ORDINAMENTO INTERNAZIONALE (1943), and SPERDUTI, LA FONTE SUPREMA DELL' ORDINAMENTO INTERNAZIONALE (1946), wrestle with the problem of the "foundation," in connection with that of custom.

12 Most Italian writers; particularly strongly by 1 K. STRUPP, ELÉMENTS DU DROIT INTERNATIONAL PUBLIC 11 (1930), and *Règles générales de la paix*, 47 RECUEIL DES COURS 36 (1934): "Pas de normes là où il n'y a pas de traité explicite ou tacite." But there are, on the one hand, adherents of the dualistic doctrine who flatly reject this construction (e.g., BALLADORE PALLIERI, DIRITTO INTERNAZIONALE PUBBLICO 540 [5th ed. 1948]); on the other hand, this construction is accepted by some Anglo-American writers: LAWRENCE, *op. cit.* at 95; JOHN WESTLAKE, INTERNATIONAL LAW, Part 1, 14 (1904); A. S. HERSHEY, THE ESSENTIALS OF INTERNATIONAL PUBLIC LAW 19–20 (1921); P. E. Corbett, *The Consent of States and Sources of the Law of Nations*, 6 BRIT. YB.INT'L L. 25 (1925). See also S. Séfériades, 34 RECUEIL DES COURS 205, 209–10 (1930).

13 See in more recent times, 1 LORIMER, LAW OF NATIONS 27 (international custom as "unconscious interpreter of the law of nature in international relations"); and L. LE FUR: "L'usage présuppose l'existence d'une règle juridigue obligatoire: il la constate simplement."—*Règles générales de la paix*, 57 RECUEIL DES COURS 197 (1935).

14 G. Scelle, *Règles générales de la paix*, 4 RECUEIL DES COURS 348, 350, 358, 432–37 (1939); PRÉCIS DE DROIT DES GENS 5 (1932); DROIT INTERNATIONAL PUBLIC 13–14 (1949).

15 *Règles générales de la paix*, 66 RECUEIL DES COURS 173 (1938): "La coutume ne crée pas le droit, elle est un mode de constatation du droit: elle sanctionne des principes qui s'imposent d'eux-mêmes."

16 *Règles générales de la paix*, 62 RECUEIL DES COURS 158 (1937): "La coutume ne crée pas le droit: elle est la pratique actuelle qui se conforme à ce qui est déjà le droit"; and at 159: "La coutume est simplement la preuve de l'existence d'une règle indépendante de la volonté de ceux qui la suivent."

[17] "International custom, as evidence of a general practice accepted as law" ("La coutume internationale, comme preuve d'une pratique générale acceptée comme étant de droit.")

[18] ROBERTO AGO, SCIENZA GIURIDICA E DIRITTO INTERNAZIONALE (1950).

[19] That is why the norm *pacta sunt servanda* cannot serve as the basic norm of international law.

[20] E.g., G. SCHWARZENBERGER, A MANUAL OF INTERNATIONAL LAW 13 (1951).

[21] Thus 1 CHARLES CHENEY HYDE, INTERNATIONAL LAW 10 (2nd. ed. 1945); 1 OPPENHEIM-LAUTERPACHT, INTERNATIONAL LAW: A TREATISE 25 (7th ed. 1948); Verdross, 30 RECUEIL DES COURS 293 (1929); KELSEN, *op. cit.* at 314.

[22] The necessity of the condition of *opinio juris* plays a prominent role in international decisions; see the Lotus Case, P.C.I.J., ser. A, No. 10 at 28 (1928); and the Asylum Case, cited above.

[23] 18 BRIT.YB.INT'L L. 127–51 (1937).

[24] Thus 1 I. RUIZ MORENO, DERECHO INTERNACIONAL PÚBLICO 22–25 (2nd ed. 1940); and I D. ANTÓKOLETZ TRATADO DE DERECHO INTERNACIONAL PÚBLICO 46–47 (4th ed. 1949). Vattel speaks of a "long usage."

[25] See MARIO GIULIANO, LA NAVIGAZIONE AEREA NEL DIRITTO INTERNAZIONALE GENERALE (1941).

[26] Thus, Ruiz Moreno; ANTÓKOLETZ, *op. cit.;* previously Vattel.

[27] See The Paquete Habana, 175 U.S. 677 (1900).

[28] GENERAL THEORY OF LAW AND STATE 114 (1945).

[29] See 1 JOSEF L. KUNZ, DIE VÖLKERRECHTICHE OPTION (1925).

[30] "The Chaotic Status of the Laws of War and the Urgent Necessity for Their Revision," below.

[31] The Scotia, 14 Wall. 170 (1871).

[32] See Giesler v. Giesler's Heirs, Bundesgericht, July 11, 1935, ANN.DIG.REP.PUB.INT'L L.CAS. 1–2 (1935–37).

[33] *Island of Palmas Arbitration, 1928,* 22 AM.J.INT'L L. 867 (1928); Judgment in the Case of Eastern Greenland, P.C.I.J., ser. A/B, No. 53 (1933). On the other hand, the *Clipperton Island Arbitration, 1931,* 26 AM.J.INT'L L. 390 (1932), seems to this writer not in conformity with general international law.

[34] *Contra,* Judge Max Huber in the Island of Palmas Arbitration.

[35] See the very interesting decision and reasoning of the Austrian Supreme Court in the case Hans Hoffman v. Jiri Dralle, May 10, 1950, reprinted in 4 OSTERREICHISCHE ZEITSCHRIFT FÜR ÖFFENTLICHES RECHT 90–103 (1951).

[36] See OPPENHEIM-LAUTERPACHT, INTERNATIONAL LAW: A TREATISE 449 (7th ed. 1948), and *Report of the Third Session of the U.N. International Law Commission,* 45 AM.J.INT'L L. 146–47, Supplement (1951).

[37] *Sovereignty over Sub-Marine Areas,* 27 BRIT.YB.INT'L L. 376–433 (1950).

[38] THE CONTINENTAL SHELF (1952).

[39] Reprinted in 1 INT'L & COMP.L.Q. 247–61 (1952); digested in 47 AM.J.INT'L L. 156 (1953).

[40] *Op. cit.* at 139–44, *supra*, note 36.

[41] Hence, the statement by Professor Aramburu, in 47 AM.J.INT'L L. 120–23 (1953), is wholly untenable.

THE NORM [1] *pacta sunt servanda*,[2] which has constituted "since times immemorial the axiom, postulate and categorical imperative of the science of international law" [3] and has very rarely been denied on principle,[4] is undoubtedly a positive norm of general international law. But the meaning of this norm is controversial. Most writers lay the accent on the term *servanda*. One school of thought affirms that "treaties" are always binding, whereas a second tells us that the norm can only mean that valid treaties are binding.[5] Within this second school of thought some writers object that the norm appears as a *deus ex machina,* as international law does not lay down rules for the validity of international treaties,[6] whereas others maintain that not all, but only certain, treaties are binding, that the norm admits "exceptions," or speak of the *relativité de la règle pacta sunt servanda.*[7]

But if the meaning of the norm be that only valid treaties are binding then, we are told, the norm is only a special formulation of the general axiom that one must obey the law.[8] From there is it only one step to the further attitude that *pacta sunt servanda* says no more than that law is valid [9] and is, therefore, an empty tautology.[10]

The exponent of the principle is, in consequence, confronted with the following dilemma: Either everything which pretends to be a treaty is valid, or only valid treaties must be kept—indeed a tautology, as the characteristic attribute of every legal norm is its binding validity. But the conclusion, sometimes reached, that our norm is meaningless is by no means justified; it is only necessary to understand it correctly. Every legal order regulates for itself the creation of its norms. *Pacta sunt servanda* is a customary norm of general international law, a constitutional norm of a superior rank, which institutes a particular procedure for the creation of norms of international law, namely the treaty-procedure.[11] International law can be created by custom [12] or by treaties. These treaty-created norms, like the contents of a contract in municipal law,[13] have the legal reason of their obligatory force, not in the manifested concord of the will of the states, but in the superior norm *pacta sunt servanda,* which orders that the manifested concord of the will of the states shall produce, through the treaty procedure, valid norms of international law. Contrary to both the schools mentioned, which put the accent on *servanda,* the accent must be put on *pacta.*

II

To understand correctly the problem of the norm *pacta sunt servanda* it is necessary to avoid the confusion, often observable in the literature of the subject, which is produced by the fact that the term "treaty" is used in an equivocal way, sometimes meaning the procedure by which treaty law is created and at other times meaning the treaty norms created by this procedure.[14]

The meaning of our norm consists in the institution by general international law of a particular procedure—the treaty procedure—for the creation of norms of international law. The problem of the range of these norms is the problem of how far treaty-created norms are valid. In this respect it makes no difference whether the treaties are what is termed "contractual" or "legislative" in nature. For the real difference between these two types of treaties [15] is not that the first create no legal norms whereas the second do; the real difference is that the first create merely individual and concrete norms whereas the second create general and abstract norms.

Down to the present time all general international law is customary law. Treaties, whether "contractual" or "legislative," create only norms of particular international law. The present-day international law is highly decentralized, not only as to its creation, but also as to the spatial and personal sphere of its validity: relatively few norms are binding on all the members of the international community; the bulk of present-day international law is particular international law, treaty-created law. But this treaty law has its legal *raison d'être* in the norm of general international law *pacta sunt servanda*.

The validity of treaty-created norms, like that of all legal norms, is conditioned by the existence of a legal order, of which these norms form a part, by the presence of the norm-creating act and the absence of a norm-abolishing fact. Just as the Constitution of the United States lays down norms for the procedure by which federal law of a hierarchically lower grade—statutes—shall be created, and for the termination of statutory law, it is for general international law to lay down the legal conditions for the procedure by which treaty norms may be created and for the termination of treaty norms. It is intended to give a brief theoretical survey of these two problems and to discuss, at the end of this study, some general theoretical problems bearing on the validity and termination of treaties.

III

As far as the presence of the norm-creating act is concerned, the conditions for the validity of the treaty as a form of action [16] are primarily procedural in character, prescribing how the agreement of wills of the contracting parties has to be manifested; these conditions of validity deal with the capacity of the contracting parties, the competence of the concluding organs, real consent, form, conclusion of treaty. But general international law may contain also norms with regard to the contents of treaties.

The first condition for the validity of the treaty as a procedure is that it has been concluded between parties which, under international law, have the capacity to conclude treaties. Such capacity is by present-day international law vested primarily in sovereign states, i.e., in legal communities which are directly, immediately, and exclusively subject to international law, but also in the Holy See, certain confederations of states, the League of Nations, etc. Some communities may have a competence to conclude treaties limited in point of time or restricted to the conclusion of certain treaties.[17]

In consequence "treaties" concluded with parties which have no treaty-making power under international law do not create valid treaty norms;[18] on the other hand, treaties made by sovereign states contrary to restrictions imposed upon them by treaty law while illegal are nevertheless valid.[19]

From the problem of the capacity of the parties must be clearly distinguished the problem of the competence of the concluding organs. It is, of course, for international law alone to determine these organs. Sometimes international law determines these organs directly, as in the case of the competence of military commanders in the field to conclude treaties of armistice or capitulation. Similarly a fundamental treaty, such as the Universal Postal Convention, may authorize organs of the Union to conclude treaties of a specified character. In general the primitive international law of today has no special legislative organs of its own; it has nevertheless other organs, composite organs, composed of the organs of the states; and general international law delegates to the states the authority of determining these organs through their constitutions. The constitutional requirements, including such requirements as the necessity for parliamentary consent,[20] are internationally relevant for the validity of treaties,[21] because international law contains a *renvoi* to the constitutions of the states. Under the principle of effectivity, however, the *renvoi* is to the effective constitution.[22] That is why, e.g., so-called executive agreements [23] are internationally valid treaties.

In consequence treaties are invalid if the concluding organ was wholly incompetent or unauthorized under constitutional law or if it has acted in excess of authority.[24] Many further interesting problems arise which can only be mentioned here: can such invalidity be invoked only by the adverse party or by both the parties? Can such treaties be confirmed or is their invalidity waived by partial performance or by the fact that the treaty has, for a long time, been acted upon; in the latter case may a state be estopped from invoking the invalidity of the treaty? [25]

The law must further lay down rules with regard to the real consent [26] of the parties. Essential and excusable error, going to the fundamentals of the treaty, will be considered as a factor in the situation. It is equally universally recognized that a treaty may be invalidated by the fraud of one party. But error and fraud do not invalidate a treaty automatically: they must be invoked by the aggrieved party and can only be invoked by the aggrieved party; an international court will not consider these elements *ex officio*.

It is, similarly, unanimously agreed that duress [27] exercised against the person of the organ gives the aggrieved party the right to invoke the invalidity of the treaty thus concluded. But while the question of the effect of duress, exercised against the state, is the subject of great controversy in current literature on the subject, under positive international law treaties imposed by force are valid,[28] revealing again the primitive character of present-day international law.

Juristic doctrine and, to a certain extent, the practice of states [29] in the inter-war period have shown a tendency to hold treaties voidable on account of duress. The doctrine proceeded mostly along the lines of a revival of the distinction between justifiable and unjustifiable force. In a more restricted way, it was argued that peace treaties imposed by force are in general valid and are voidable only on account of illegal force; in a broader form the League resolution of March 11, 1932, the so-called Stimson Doctrine on non-recognition, and similar acts show a tendency to distinguish between legal and illegal force. But as a matter of positive international law, the norm of the validity of treaties imposed by force stands.

General international law prescribes no particular form for treaties;[30] treaties can, therefore, be concluded not only in writing, by telegram, by telephone, by wireless, but also orally and even by symbols.

As to the procedure of conclusion [31] of a treaty, there are, generally, three stages: negotiation, signature, ratification and exchange or deposit of ratifications. With regard to treaties subject to ratification this action (and exchange or deposit of ratifications) is a *conditio sine qua non* of the validity of treaties.[32] Ratification must be unconditional and embrace the entire treaty. There is no legal duty to ratify a treaty, signed by the plenipotentiaries of the state in question,[33] except, of course, if a state is bound by one treaty to ratify another treaty.[34] A treaty may provide that certain provisions shall come into force prior to ratification;[35] a multipartite treaty may provide that it shall come into force after the deposit of a certain number of ratifications or of ratifications by certain signatories.

A treaty is subject to ratification if the document itself so stipulates or if ratification was made a condition in the full-powers of the negotiators, but there exists further a general legal presumption for the necessity of ratification except where the treaty is clearly not subject to ratification. The latter is the case where negotiators are expressly authorized to conclude a treaty; with regard to military treaties concluded by commanders in time of war; with regard to treaties formerly concluded between absolute monarchs but recently between "leaders" of totalitarian states, except if they otherwise provide;[36] with regard to treaties which expressly stipulate that no ratification shall be necessary; with regard to executive agreements, except if they otherwise provide.

With regard to multipartite treaties, we may mention the special problems of accession [37] and reservations.[38]

General international law contains no rules as to registration or publication of a treaty as a condition for the validity of the treaty procedure; but particular international law may do so.[39]

As regards the contents of treaties, general international law authorizes the states to conclude treaties on any matter they like. This is the general rule but the problem arises whether general international law contains legal restrictions with regard to the contents of a valid treaty. Original impossibility invalidates a treaty. A treaty may be invalid on account of the illegality of its contents, namely if these contents are in violation of a hierarchically superior norm of general or particular international law which constitutes *jus cogens*. The problem of the invalidity of treaties because of the immorality of their contents (*pacta contra bonos mores*) has, like that of duress, become prominent again in the inter-war period.[40] Earlier writers asserted the principle of the invalidity of *pacta turpia* on the basis of natural law or on the equally *jus naturae* basis of the "inherent rights" of states.[41] Such a natural-law basis is again adopted by modern writers.[42] But, legally speaking, the problem is only a special case of the invalidity of treaties on account of the illegality of their contents; for the invalidity of treaties on account of their immoral contents can, of course, legally not be based on the norm of a metajuridical system such as ethics, but only on a norm of positive international law *juris cogentis*.[43]

IV

If the conditions laid down by international law for the treaty procedure have been fulfilled, the "treaty" in the second sense, i.e., the norms created by the treaty procedure, have come into force. The problem of the temporal sphere of validity deals with the moment of the beginning and of the ending of their legal validity. Treaty-created norms become valid in the moment of the conclusion of the treaty procedure; they remain valid in time, as long as no norm-abolishing fact,[44] as laid down by international law, has taken place.

General international law, first of all, provides that certain factors do not touch the binding validity of treaty norms: governmental or constitutional or territorial changes of the contracting parties, as long as they remain identical persons in the sense of international law.[45] Suspension of treaties, e.g., through the outbreak of war, nonrecognition by a foreign government only suspends the operation of treaties but leaves their binding validity intact.

As to the reasons for the termination of the validity of treaty-created norms, Chailley has insisted on the *principe de l'acte contraire*, but this theory is too narrow, for a treaty can legally come to an end, not only by mutual dissent, but also in a different way by operation of law. The only juridically correct formula would hold that treaty-created norms remain valid as long as no fact which, under international law, causes the termination of their validity has occurred.[46]

According to international law, treaty-created norms cease to be binding either according to the will of the parties or by operation of law. Among the first group we can distinguish norm-abolishing facts stipulated in the treaty itself or subsequent mutual agreement of all the parties. Treaty norms come to an end automatically through the expiration of any period of time for which the treaty has been concluded, subject to any provisions for its express or tacit renewal (it is also possible that the parties, before such expiration, will agree upon the continuance of the treaty); through the emergence of a resolutive condition in accordance with the treaty itself; through termination by the act of a third party, if the treaty so provides.[47] Treaty norms can also automatically come to an end, in accordance with the agreement, by the unilateral denunciation of one party, if this right to denounce the treaty is given by the treaty; normally this right will be given to both or all the parties but it is legally possible for the right to belong only to one party; multipartite treaties often provide that the denunciation by one party in no way touches the validity of the treaty norms for all the other parties.

Treaty norms come automatically to an end further through mutual consent of the parties. This, the *acte contraire*, can consist in the mere abrogation of a treaty without replacing it by a new treaty—so-called rescission—or in the conclusion of a new treaty which expressly abrogates the earlier treaty, or in the conclusion between the same parties of a new treaty, the contents of which are incompatible with the earlier treaty, even if the new treaty does not expressly abrogate the earlier one. The parties are entitled to abrogate a treaty by mutual consent even before the expiration of time for which it has been concluded, or to abrogate a treaty concluded *à perpetuité*.[48] The norm that mutual consent by all the parties is necessary in law applies also to multipartite treaties,[49] except if they otherwise provide. Renunciation by the beneficiary party to a bipartite, non-synallagmatic treaty is only a special case of termination by mutual consent, as acceptance of the renunciation is necessary.

But treaty norms can also come to an end automatically, independently of the will of the parties, by operation of law: extinction of one contracting party as a state in the sense of international law in a bilateral treaty; extinction of the object of the treaty; subsequent impossibility;[50] inconsistency of treaty norms with later general or particular international law, if the later law consists of hierarchically superior norms *juris cogentis;*[51] desuetude;[52] in some cases by outbreak of war,[53] or by way of reprisal.[54]

Treaty norms, finally, can come to an end by operation of law at the request of one party. To this group belong cancellation because of non-fulfillment by the other party[55] and operation of the rule of *clausula rebus sic stanibus*.[56] Breach of treaty by one party does not in itself affect the validity of the treaty norm, either for the guilty or for the innocent party; the latter is free to insist on the continued validity of the treaty and on its fulfillment, may apply sanctions or resort to reprisals, and may ask for the reparation in damages. But it is equally clearly a norm of positive international law that the innocent party has, at its option and discretion, the right to abrogate the treaty on account of previous breach by the other party. In this case the validity of the treaty norms does not come to an end automatically, however, but only if and when the innocent party makes use of its right to abrogate the treaty, a right which must be exercised within a reasonable time after the breach of the treaty has been committed.

The problem of the *clausula rebus sic stantibus*—it must be emphasized—is equally a problem of positive law, and, therefore, entirely different in nature from the purely political problem of revision of treaties. The *clausula*, insofar as it is positive law, is, further, by no means an exception to the norm *pacta sunt servanda*. The problem, finally, is not a specialty of international law, but exists also in municipal law.[57]

The problem of the clause is whether there exists in positive international law a norm according to which changed circumstances bring about the termination—not modification, not suspension—of treaty stipulations.[58] It is generally recognized that if at the conclusion of a treaty the existence of certain circumstances has been taken into consideration by the parties as a presupposition for the continuance of the obligations assumed, an essential change of these circumstances can produce the termination of the treaty. The further problem as to the effect of an essential change of circumstances which have not been taken into consideration by the parties on the legal validity of the treaty norms is controversial. While this question cannot be investigated here in detail, it is theoretically important to state that the legal basis for such termination of treaty

norms cannot be the "nature of things" or any other metajuridical argument, but solely a positive norm of international law which so prescribes.

V

The original validity of treaty norms depends on the
validity of the treaty procedure—the presence of the norm-
creating act—the continued validity of treaty norms depends on the absence of a norm-abolishing fact. The two
problems, although both of them problems *de lege lata*,
problems of positive law, are different. But they pose a few
common problems which it is proposed to investigate here
theoretically. As positive international law has to lay down
the norms for the original and for the continued validity of
treaty norms, the first problem that arises is that of the
legal sources of the validity of treaty norms in both respects. The first source, unquestionably, is general customary international law, to which the very norm *pacta sunt
servanda* belongs. The second source consists of treaties.
Often treaties contain themselves not only norms as to the
capacity of contracting parties, ratification, reservations,
but also as to duration, denunciation, compatibility *vel non*
of later treaties, and so on. It is also possible that a multipartite treaty creates general and abstract norms concerning the creation and termination of treaty norms. But no
such great codification exists at the present time. The only
collective treaty on this subject, the Havana Convention on
Treaties of 1928, is, as to its sphere of validity, continental
only; as to its contents it is extremely vague and by no
means complete, and it is, finally, in consequence of the
small number of ratifications, practically of little importance. It must also be borne in mind that conventional codification of the law on treaties would itself be a collective
treaty and, therefore, as to change or termination, be subject to the norms of general international law.

The "general principles of law, recognized by civilized nations" [59] as a third source of international law have in the inter-war period been particularly pressed into the service of determining the validity of treaty-created norms, especially with regard to the problems of duress and immoral subject matter.

In his report of 1930 to the *Institut de Droit International,* Verdross correctly took the position that the "general principles of law" as a third source of international law have to be clearly distinguished from the "general principles of international law"; that they are constituted by the general principles of law, recognized by the quasi-universality of civilized nations as positive law *in foro domestico;* that, even so, they must be applicable to international law; and, finally, that they are always merely subsidiary in character. But in his Hague lectures of 1935, Verdross adopted the hardly tenable thesis, developed in the meantime by his disciple Heydte, that these "general principles of law" are *juris cogentis,* hierarchically superior to customary and treaty law, with particular application to the doctrine of the validity of treaties. Under Verdross' influence this theory was adopted in 1935 by Härle. The "general principles of law" became thus a modern form of natural law and Le Fur called this new natural law the "ordre public international." In the meantime Alvarez and Raestad had launched the idea that the general principles of law include also the "general principles of international law." This idea was accepted by Verdross in his report to the Institut de Droit International of 1937. Here he returns to the subsidiary character of the "general principles of law" in the original sense, but proclaims that these principles in the second sense are *juris cogentis.*

Already this analysis of doctrinal developments shows that our theoretical problem of the sources of international law for the validity and termination of treaty-created norms is most intimately connected with the problem of the hierarchical position of these sources and with the problem of *jus cogens* and *jus dispositivum* ("pliable law").[60] For this problem determines the invalidity of treaties because of the illegality of contents *ab origine,* and also the termination of the validity of treaties because of subsequent illegality of their contents and the so-called conflict between treaties.[61]

The general principles of law are hierarchically strictly subsidiary in character, not *juris cogentis,* and cannot prevail against customary or treaty norms. As to the hierarchical order of customary international law, we must distinguish between general and particular customary law. General customary law is binding on all, particular law only on certain states. But this difference as to the sphere of validity does not yet solve the problem of their hierarchical position. All depends on whether the customary law is *juris cogentis* or not; contracting parties can by treaty derogate not only from "pliable" particular law, binding on the same states, but also from "pliable" general customary law if it constitutes *jus dispositivum.* They cannot legally derogate from general customary law *juris cogentis;* such derogation can invalidate treaties because of original, can terminate treaties because of subsequent, illegality of contents. Such norms are rare in present-day positive international law; examples are the norm of the freedom of the seas or the very norm *pacta sunt servanda.*

If a party concludes a second treaty, incompatible in contents with a first treaty, with the same party, the second treaty is valid and its conclusion constitutes a termination of the validity of the first treaty by mutual consent: *lex posterior derogat priori.* But if a state concludes a treaty with a third state, the contents of which is in violation of an earlier treaty with another state, the second treaty is, nevertheless, valid, although the party, having concluded both treaties, is guilty of an illegal act.[62]

As far as multipartite treaties are concerned, a later treaty, in conflict with an earlier treaty, is valid, if both treaties have been concluded between the same states. But more complicated problems arise if a later bilateral or multipartite treaty, concluded by two or more, but not by all, of the parties to the earlier multipartite treaty, is incompatible with this earlier treaty. We must here distinguish several hypotheses: If a bilateral or multipartite treaty has later been concluded between parties, all members of the original multipartite treaty, it depends again on whether the later treaty derogates from norms *juris cogentis* or merely norms *juris dispositivi* of the earlier treaty. The later treaty is valid if the earlier treaty expressly or impliedly permits treaties of this type,[63] or if the later treaty deals with norms expressly declared by the original treaty to be *juris dispositivi*.[64] It may be ordered by the earlier treaty that parties may by a new treaty replace the earlier treaty *inter se,* provided that the new treaty be open to the accession of the original parties; in such case the earlier treaty remains in force for the original parties which are not parties to the later treaty nor have adhered to it.[65] But the earlier treaty may contain norms *juris cogentis;*[66] in such case a later bilateral or multipartite treaty, not concluded between all the original parties, in derogation of these norms, is not only illegal but invalid. This problem applies not only to the original validity of the second but also to the termination of the validity of the first treaty; for in the case considered, less than all the contracting parties to the first multipartite treaty cannot legally change or abrogate the earlier treaty, not even *inter se.*[67]

But if the later treaty, bilateral or multilateral, has been concluded by a party or parties, members of the earlier treaty, with a third state, not a member of the earlier treaty, and if the later treaty derogates from norms *juris cogentis* of the earlier treaty, the later treaty is valid,[68] although the party or parties, members of the first treaty, are guilty of an illegal act, engaging their international responsibility.

This discussion shows the necessity of clearly distinguishing between the invalidity of treaty norms and the illegal creation of valid treaty norms.[69] Invalid treaties may be, it is said, either void or voidable. It is often said that a treaty is null (*nul et non avenu, void ab initio, nichtig*) if it is vitiated by such a great defect that the states attempting to conclude it do not succeed; that such a treaty is juridically *negotium nullum;* that the treaty is void automatically, needs no procedure of annulment; whereas voidable treaties are valid, as long as they are not declared void at the request of the aggrieved party. As a law does not deal with naked facts, however, but only with facts ascertained by the competent legal authority,[70] there is no absolute difference between the conceptions of "void" and "voidable." There may, on the other hand, well be a relative difference. Only research into positive international law can answer these questions: Is annulment of a treaty retroactive? Can a treaty be attacked as voidable by both or only by one party, or also by a third state? Can the defects of a treaty be healed by the action of the parties? Can such treaty be confirmed? Must the reasons of invalidity be pleaded by a party or can they be taken into consideration by an international court *ex officio*.

Generally speaking, cases of treaties void *ab initio* are rare under present-day international law. As to voidable treaties, only the aggrieved party has a right to attack them; the defect must be pleaded and will not be taken into consideration by an international court *ex officio*. The annulment of treaties has retroactive effect. The legal effect of termination is always *ex nunc*.

With regard to the validity and the termination of treaty-created norms the problem of the divisibility of treaties has arisen. Of course, a treaty may stipulate that it constitutes an indivisible whole.[71] But where treaties consist of different parts, dealing with completely different subject matters, it is now recognized by the majority of writers, by the treaties themselves, by international tribunals, and by the practice of states, that the problem of the validity or termination of treaty-created norms can arise not only with regard to the treaty as a whole, but also with regard to certain parts or articles of the treaty.

So far we have discussed the theoretical problems of the rules of international law as to the validity and termination of the validity of treaty-created norms. Now we come to the important distinction between these general, abstract norms and their application to a single concrete case. In such concrete cases a conflict may arise between the states in question either over the facts or over the law, or over both. It is one problem to determine the abstract, general norm according to which the occurrence of a resolutive condition, stipulated in the treaty, brings the treaty to an end. It is a different problem to ascertain whether in a concrete case this resolutive condition has arisen in fact.

The problem of the difference between the abstract, general norms as to the validity and termination of treaties and the conflicts between states as to their application to a concrete case is often not seen, or, if seen, is restricted to the cancellation of a treaty on account of breach by the other party and the *clausula rebus sic stantibus*. But it must be emphasized that such a conflict can and does arise with regard to any condition of the treaty's validity, and with regard to any condition of the termination of treaty-created norms.

In an advanced municipal legal order such conflicts are peacefully decided with authentic and final legal authority by centralized, special organs for the application of the law, organs different from the parties in conflict: impartial and independent courts, having compulsory jurisdiction.

The task of the court is to ascertain the facts with authority, to ascertain the law, to apply the law as ascertained, to the facts as ascertained, to order the application and execution of the sanction prescribed by the law.

If states are in conflict in a concrete case, as to the facts or the law, concerning the validity or termination of treaty norms, we are in the presence of an international conflict which, like any other international conflict, must be settled in accordance with the norms of general international law and of the particular international law binding upon the parties. The treaty may itself contain norms of procedure for the settlement of such conflicts, as in the case of the Locarno Treaty. The parties may be bound by the League Covenant or by a conciliation treaty. There may exist between them a treaty of obligatory arbitration or judicial settlement for these types of conflict. Then the parties are bound to follow this procedure, and a juridical solution is possible.

But where no such particular international law exists between the parties only general international law can be applied. And even where such particular law exists we may, in the last analysis, be thrown back on general international law; for a conflict may arise as to the meaning or interpretation of this particular treaty law or a party may become guilty of a breach of this particular treaty law.

As to the solutions of conflicts concerning the validity or termination of treaties under general international law, the juristic literature gives two opposite answers: the one, put forward, e.g., recently by Vitta,[72] says that withdrawal from a treaty, even if there is a conflict between the parties as to its validity or continued validity, is legally possible only with the consent of all the contracting parties; the other, put forward recently by Verdross[73] gives the aggrieved party under the general international law a right to decide the conflict itself.

In order to come to a correct understanding of this problem it must be borne in mind that present-day general international law, as a primitive legal order, lacks special organs for the application of general, abstract norms to concrete cases, and that, under general international law, the states themselves are the organs left to apply the law. It is for them, judges and parties in the same person, to ascertain the law and the facts, to apply the law as ascertained to the facts as ascertained, to order and execute the sanction, which, as in all primitive laws, takes the form of self-help: reprisals and war. As in all primitive laws, a peaceful juridical solution of the conflict is only possible by the agreement of the parties.[74] If no such agreement can be reached—and it will, of course, for political reasons often be impossible to reach such agreement—each party is entitled to ascertain the law and facts itself, to act accordingly, to apply reprisals and so on. But, on the other hand, neither the unilateral pretention of the one, nor the unilateral denial of the other party, can furnish an objective and impartial decision of the conflict.

The conclusion of this theoretical investigation is that, under present-day primitive and technically very imperfect general international law, conflicts between states as to the validity and termination of treaties cannot be settled juridically in a peaceful way [75] where no agreement between the parties can be reached, and it leads to the inescapable conclusion that the first and most important step on the road of progress toward international law and order must be the introduction into general international law of compulsory international courts. As long as this progress is not realized the whole problem of the validity and termination of treaties must remain, of necessity, in an entirely unsatisfactory condition and a condition which cannot be remedied by the science of international law. But, as the same is true with regard to general international law as a whole, the result

of this theoretical investigation of a limited problem leads
to a postulate of extreme importance today: If we are really
bent on bettering international relations, our task is to
transform present-day primitive general international law
into a more advanced legal order, and the first and most
important step is the establishment in general international
law of international courts, having compulsory jurisdiction
over all international conflicts in which states are in conflict as to the positive law.

VI

Pacta sunt servanda means the institution, by general international law, of a special procedure—the treaty procedure—for the creation of international norms. Norms, thus
created, are valid and must be kept as long as no norm-
abolishing fact, as laid down by norms of international law,
has occurred. *Pacta sunt servanda,* in consequence, and contrary to the opinion of many writers, admits no exceptions.
The problems of the norm *pacta sunt servanda* are exclusively problems of positive law. The revision of treaties,[76]
on the other hand, presupposes necessarily valid treaties
and brings up the purely political problem of a change or
termination of valid treaty norms, recognized as valid in
positive law by the conflicting parties, for metajuridical
reasons. Valid treaty norms must be kept, but they can, by
appropriate procedures, be revised. *Pacta sunt servanda*
means the inviolability, not the unchangeability, of treaties.
The revision of treaties is neither an exception to, nor in
contradiction with, the norm *pacta sunt servanda. Pacta
sunt servanda* belongs to the domain of positive law, the
lex lata; revision to politics of law, the *lex ferenda;* the
first deals with questions as to what the law is, the second
with questions as to what the law should be; the first is a
problem for the judge, the second for the legislator.

1 For literature see *Research in International Law under the Auspices of the Harvard Law School—Part III, Law of Treaties*, 29 AM.J.INT'L L. 671–85, Supplement and the literature there cited (1935). Further recent literature: *Traités*, 2 and 3 DICTIONNAIRE DE L'ACADÉMIE DIPLOMATIQUE INTERNATIONALE 954–70, (Vol. III not numbered); F. ARAGUEZ, EL TRATADO COMO NEGOCIO JURÍDICO (1933); H. Kraus, *Système et fonctions des traités internationaux*, 2 RECUEIL DES COURS 317–99 (1934); A. F. FRANGULIS, THÉORIE ET PRATIQUE DES TRAITÉS INTERNATIONAUX (1938); A. D. MCNAIR, THE LAW OF TREATIES: BRITISH PRACTICE AND OPINIONS (1938); H. Kelsen, *Contribution à la théorie des traités internationaux*, 10 REVUE INTERNATIONALE DE LA THÉORIE DU DROIT 253–92 (1936), and EL CONTRATO Y EL TRATADO ANALIZADOS DESDE EL PUNTO DE VISTA DE LA TEORÍA PURA DEL DERECHO (1943).

2 M. de Taube, *L'inviolabilité des traités*, 2 RECUEIL DES COURS 295–387 (1930); J. B. Whitton, *La règle pacta sunt servanda*, 2 *ibid.* at 151–276 (1934), in 18 REVUE DE DROIT INTERNATIONALE 440–80 (1936), and in INT'L. CONCIL. No. 317 at 395–430 (1935); H. BAUER, DER GRUNDSATZ PACTA SUNT SERVANDA IM HEUTIGEN VÖLKERRECHT (1934); H. Kaira in 7 ACTA SCANDINAVICA JURIS GENTIUM 39–67 (1936).

3 De Taube, *op. cit.* at 295.

4 Macchiavelli, Spinoza (on this thinker and international law, cf. Verdross in 7 ZEITSCHRIFT FÜR ÖFFENTLICHES RECHT 100 [1927]; H. Lauterpacht in 8 BRIT.YB.INT'L L. 89–107 [1927]). Cf. also R. SHAMASASTRY, KANTILIYA'S ARTHASÂSTRA (2nd ed. 1923).

5 Recently: E. VITTA, LA VALIDITÉ DES TRAITÉS INTERNATIONAUX 29–30 (1940). See also ULP. DE PACTIS: DIGEST 2, 14, 7; CODE CIVIL FRANÇAIS, Art. 1134. P.C.I.J., ser. B, No. 10 at 20: "A state which has contracted valid international obligations, is bound. . . . "

6 Thus J. L. BRIERLY, THE LAW OF NATIONS 208 (2nd ed. 1936). F. PFLUGER, DIE EINSEITIGEN RECHTSCHÄFTE IM VÖLKERRECHT 20–21 (1936).

7 Thus, 2 G. SCELLE, PRÉCIS DE DROIT DES GENS 336 (1934).

8 Thus Whitton, *op. cit.* at 218. Unequivocally Bourquin: "Pacta sunt servanda n'est qu'une forme particulière d'un principe plus vaste, d'un principe qui s'applique à toutes les normes: dans la mesure de sa compétence spatiale et temporelle, la loi doit être obéie universellement et continuellement."—*Règles générales du droit de la paix*, 1 RECUEIL DES COURS 5–229 at 80 (1931).

9 Thus BAUMGARTEN, GRUNDZÜGE DER JURISTISCHEN METHODENLEHRE 27 (1939). W. SCHIFFER, DIE LEHRE VOM PRIMAT DES VÖLKERRECHTS IN DER NEUEREN LITERATUR 183, 185, 188 (1937).

10 Thus H. HELLER, DIE SOUVERÄNITÄT 132.

11 This insight has been clearly formulated by P. Chailley: "Le traité est la procédure constitutionnelle suivant laquelle sont créés des normes juridiques communes à plusieurs Etats."—LA NATURE JURIDIQUE DES TRAITÉS INTERNATIONAUX SELON LE DROIT CONTEMPORAIN 331 (1932). In the same sense the two writings by Kelsen cited above, note 1.

[12] The fact that international law can also be created by custom renders the theory according to which the norm *pacta sunt servanda* constitutes the fundamental norm of international law untenable. This construction, originally defended by Kelsen and Verdross, has long been abandoned by these writers, while it is still retained by Anzilotti.

[13] Carnegie v. Morrison, Sup.Jud.C.Mass. (2 Met) (1841).

[14] This distinction is very clearly emphasized by CHAILLEY, *op. cit.* at 123, and in the two writings by Kelsen already cited.

[15] Fundamental the observations by Kelsen, *Contribution* at 260, and CONTRATO at 11–14, 25–36.

[16] See the literature quoted above, note 1. VITTA, *op. cit.*; G. CONMOUL, DES CONDITIONS DE VALIDITÉ DES TRAITÉS INTERNATIONAUX (1911); J. H. W. Verzijl, *La validité et la nullité des actes juridiques internationaux*, 15 REVUE DE DROIT INTERNATIONAL 284–339 (1935); M. HOULARD, LA NATURE JURIDIQUE DES TRAITÉS INTERNATIONAUX ET SON APPLICATION AUX THÉORIES DE LA NULLITÉ, DE LA CADUCITÉ ET DE LA RÉVISION DES TRAITÉS (1936); A. VERDROSS, VÖLKERRECHT 80–90 (1937).

[17] For example, India as a member of the League of Nations; insurgents recognized as a belligerent party.

[18] Such as "treaties" made with native chieftains.

[19] We may also mention the problem of treaties made with vassal or protected states; see Bulgarian-Serbian Peace Treaty of 1886; Anglo-Egyptian Sudan Treaty of January 19, 1899; in the case of the Anglo-Thibetan Treaty of September 7, 1904, China protested and Britain concluded, in consequence, the Convention of April 27, 1906, with China.

[20] With regard to this problem opinion is divided into at least four different schools of thought: the first distinguishes between the internal and the international validity of a treaty; the second pretends that municipal law alone controls; a third, or intermediary, doctrine holds treaties to be invalid only if constitutional restrictions have been "manifestly" violated. All these doctrines are untenable, as a treaty can only be either valid or not, and as the conditions for the validity of an international treaty can be determined only by international law. But the fourth doctrine, holding constitutional law to be internationally wholly irrelevant (Anzilotti, Verzijl, Vitta), is in contradiction with positive international law.

[21] That is why Article I of the Havana Convention on Treaties of 1928 is nothing but the restatement of the positive general international law.

[22] Problem of the validity of the Colombian-Peruvian Treaty of Frontiers of 1922–28 in the Leticia Conflict (see P. de Lapradelle in 11 REVUE DE DROIT INTERNATIONAL 185–209 [1933]).

[23] H. M. Catudal, *Executive Agreements: A Supplement to the Treaty-making Procedure*, 10 GEO. WASH. L. REV. 653–69 (1942).

[24] So a political agreement concluded by military commanders in time of war.

[25] McNAIR, *op. cit.* at 38–44.

²⁶ B. Shatsky, *La Validité des traités*, 13 REVUE DE DROIT INTER-
NATIONAL 545 (1933) ; Scialoja, *I vizi di volontà nelle leggi e nei
trattati internazionali*, RIVISTA DI DIRITTO PUBBLICO 4 (1929) ; H.
Weinschel, *Willensmängel bei völkerrechtlichen Verträgen*, 15 ZEIT-
SCHRIFT FÜR VÖLKERRECHT 446 (1930) ; ATASSY, LES VICES DE CON-
SENTEMENT DANS LES TRAITÉS INTERNATIONAUX À L'EXCLUSION DES
TRAITÉS DE PAIX (1930) ; J. TOMSITCH, LA RECONSTRUCTION DU DROIT
INTERNATIONAL EN MATIÈRE DES TRAITÉS (1931) ; W. Pasching, *Allge-
meine Rechtsgrundsätze über die Elemente der völkerrechtlichen Ver-
träge*, 14 ZEITSCHRIFT FÜR ÖFFENTLICHES RECHT 26–61 (1934).

²⁷ ROTH, ZWANG BEIM ABSCHLUSS VON VÖLKERRECHTLICHEN VER-
TRÄGEN (1923) ; SCIALOJA, VIOLENZA, ERRORE, E DOLO NEI TRATTATI
INTERNAZIONALI, SCRITTI . . . IN ONORE DI A. SALANDRA 25 (1928) ;
GOLBS-WILMS, ERZWUNGENE STAATSVERTRÄGE (1933) ; Zanten, *Over
verdragen totstandgekomen onder den invloed van dwang*, RECHTS-
GELEERT MAGAZIJN 97 (1934) ; A. Cavaglieri, *La violenza como motivo
di nullità dei trattati*, 27 RIVISTA DI DIRITTO INTERNAZIONALE 4–23
(1935) ; A. Verdross, *Anfechtbare und nichtige Staatsverträge*, 15
ZEITSCHRIFT FÜR ÖFFENTLICHES RECHT 289 (1935) ; F. Bleiber, *Auf-
gezwungene Verträge im Völkerrecht*, 19 ZEITSCHRIFT FÜR VÖLKER-
RECHT 385–402 (1935) ; P. Schön, *Erzwungene Friedensverträge*, 21
ibid. at 277–96 (1937) ; L. Buza, *Der Zwang im Völkerrecht*, 21 *ibid.*
at 420–40 (1937) ; H. WIDMER, DER ZWANG IM VÖLKERRECHT (1936) ;
MOIGLIANO, IN TEMA DI VIZI DI VOLONTÀ E DI TRATTATI IMPOSTI CON
VIOLENZA (1938).

²⁸ Scelle, while upholding the validity of peace treaties imposed by
force, wants to deprive them of their character of treaties. According
to him an imposed peace treaty is not a treaty but a unilateral legislative act of the victor; the signature of the vanquished is nothing
but the authentic recognition of the greater force of the victor; the
peace treaty as unilateral legislation by the victor comes into force
on the *hypothèse de la résignation du bien vaincu* (4 RECUEIL DES
COURS 675 [1933]; THÉORIE JURIDIQUE DE LA RÉVISION DES TRAITÉS 44,
56, 58 [1936]; 2 PRÉCIS DE DROIT DES GENS 339, 343 [1934]). This
construction has been adopted by Brierly (4 RECUEIL DES COURS 208
[1936]). But this construction is untenable. The truth is that treaties
imposed by force are valid in primitive international law, whereas
they are invalid in more advanced legal orders (cf. DIGEST 4.2 *quod
metus*). In municipal law also the vitiation of contracts by duress is
a later and gradual development (cf. for the common law, WILLISTON,
3 THE LAW OF CONTRACTS 2828 [1920]), a development which even
today is, by no means, at an end (cf. J. Gulzell, *Duress by Economic
Pressure*, 20 N. C. L. REV., No. 3 [1942]).

²⁹ Russian-Turkish Treaty of March 16, 1921, art. I: "Neither Contracting Party will recognize treaties which are imposed by force
on the other party."

³⁰ Particular international law may prescribe the written form:
Havana Convention on Treaties, 1928, Art. II.

³¹ MAKOWSKI, THÉORIE ET TECHNIQUE DE LA CONFECTION DES ACTES
INTERNATIONAUX (1921) ; B HERZOG, DER BEGRIFF DER RATIFIKATION

UND DIE BEDEUTUNG SEINER TECHNIK FÜR DAS VÖLKERRECHT (1929);
F. DEHOUSSE, LA RATIFICATION DES TRAITÉS (1935); F. O. WILCOX, THE
RATIFICATION OF INTERNATIONAL CONVENTIONS (1935).

[32] Havana Convention on Treaties, 1928, art. V.

[33] Ibid. art. VII.

[34] Peace Treaty of Versailles, arts. XCIII, DXXXIV.

[35] Morocco Convention, Madrid, July 3, 1880; Martens N. R. G.,
art. XI, para. 1; German–U. S. S. R. Treaty, Rapallo, April 16, 1922,
20 L.N.T.S. 247–49 (1923); Convention Regarding the Regime of the
Straits, 173 *ibid.* at 215–41.

[36] Some such recent treaties, as the German-U.S.S.R. Treaty on
the Soviet-German Frontier, of January 10, 1941, provide that the
treaty comes into force at the moment of signature (art. IV), but
that it is subject to ratification (N. Y. Times, January 11, 1941, p. 8).
The legal significance of ratification in such cases seems to be doubtful.

[37] SCHABER, DER BEITRITT ZU VÖLKERRECHTLICHEN VERTRÄGEN
(1937).

[38] K. SCHEIDTMANN, DER VORBEHALT BEIM ABSCHLUSS VÖLKER-
RECHTLICHER VERTRÄGE (1939); W. Sanders, *Reservations to Multilateral Treaties*, 33 AM. J. INT'L L. 488–99 (1939).

[39] Thus Article XVIII of the Covenant. See, apart from commen-
taries on the Covenant, Adatci–de Visscher in 30 ANNUAIRE DE
L'INSTITUT DE DROIT INTERNATIONAL 47 (1923); C. SEVENS, LE
RÉGIME NOUVEAU DES TRAITÉS INTERNATIONAUX (1925); KÖNIG, VOLKS-
BEFRAGUNG UND REGISTRIERUNG BEIM VÖLKERBUND (1927); Stieger
in 7 ZEITSCHRIFT FÜR ÖFFENTLICHES RECHT 227 (1928); F. DEHOUSSE,
L'ENREGISTREMENT DES TRAITÉS (1929); Keydel in 9 REVUE DE DROIT
INTERNATIONAL 141–60 (1931); SCHWAB, DIE REGISTRIERUNG DER
INTERNATIONALEN VERTRÄGE BEIM VÖLKERBUND (1932); L. Reitzer in
11 REVUE GÉNÉRALE DE DROIT INTERNATIONAL PUBLIC 76–89 (1937).

[40] M. FRÖHLICH, DIE SITTLICHKEIT IN VÖLKERRECHTLICHEN VER-
TRÄGEN (1924); Bradner, *Pacta contra bonos mores im Völkerrecht*,
JAHRBUCH DER KONSULARAKADEMIE ZU WIEN 33 (1937); A. Verdross
in 15 ZEITSCHRIFT FÜR ÖFFENTLICHES RECHT 289–99 (1935); and in
16 *ibid.* at 79–86 (1936); also *Trattati contra bonos mores* in RIVISTA
DI DIRITTO INTERNAZIONALE 3–11 (1937) and *Forbidden Treaties in
International Law*, 31 AM. J. INT'L L. 571 (1937).

[41] M. OHMANN, DISSERTATIO DE PACTIS SUB CONDITIONE TURPI
(1770); E. VATTEL, LE DROIT DES GENS, Book LII, chap. XII, para.
160, and Book LIV, chap. IV, para. 36.

[42] G. Scelle in 4 RECUEIL DES COURS 448 (1933); Salvioli, *id.* at 75.

[43] Thus Oppenheim, who asserts a customary general norm of international law to this effect (1 INTERNATIONAL LAW 713–14 [4th ed.
McNair]).

[44] See recent writings, apart from literature already quoted: J. L.
Brierly in 11 TRANSACT. GROT. SOC'Y 11 (1926); A. D. McNair, *La
terminaison et la dissolution des traités* 2 RECUEIL DES COURS 463
(1928); M. PERLOWSKI, LES CAUSES D'EXTINCTION DES OBLIGATIONS

INTERNATIONALES CONTRACTUELLES (1928); H. J. TOBIN, THE TERMINATION OF MULTIPARTITE TREATIES (1933).

45 KIATIBIAN, CONSÉQUENCES JURIDIQUES DES TRANSFORMATIONS TERRITORIALES DES ETATS SUR LES TRAITÉS (1892); L. LARIVIÈRE, DES CONSÉQUENCES DES MODIFICATIONS TERRITORIALES DES ETATS SUR LES TRAITÉS ANTÉRIEURS (1892).

46 Thus G. BALLADORE PALLIERI, DIRITTO INTERNAZIONALE PUBBLICO 137 (2nd ed. 1938).

47 Article VIII of the Locarno Treaty, 1925.

48 *Contra*, KELSEN, CONTRATO at 74.

49 M. SORENSEN, THE MODIFICATION OF COLLECTIVE TREATIES WITHOUT THE CONSENT OF ALL CONTRACTING PARTIES (ACTA SCANDINAVICA JURIS GENTIUM, Vol. IX [1938]) at 150–73. On the question of the abrogation of the permanent neutrality of Belgium by the Versailles Treaty, to which Russia and Holland were not parties, cf. LE ROY, L'ABROGATION DE LA NEUTRALITÉ DE LA BELGIQUE (1923); H. Tobin in 26 AM. J. INT'L L. 514 (1932); Moscato, *Le sorti della neutralizzazione belga dopo la guerra*, 22 RIVISTA DI DIRITTO INTERNAZIONALE 379–95, 526–41 (1930), and 23 *ibid*. 54–66, 199–215 (1931).

50 Subsequent physical and permanent impossibility as a reason for the termination of treaties is to be distinguished from original impossibility as a reason for the invalidity of treaties.

51 Article XX of the Covenant; H. Lauterpacht, *The Covenant as "Higher Law,"* BRIT.YB.INT'L L. 54–65 (1936).

52 Yuille Shortridge & Co. (Great Britain v. Portugal) in 2 DE LAPRADELLE–POLITIS, RECUEIL DES ARBITRAGES INTERNATIONAUX 105 (1932); J. L. Kunz, *Observations on the De Facto Revision of the Covenant*, 4 N.COMMW.Q 131–43 (1938).

53 Recently: J. L. KUNZ, KRIEGSRECHT UND NEUTRALITÄTSRECHT 41–44 (1935); L. ERADES, DE INVLOED VAN OORLOG OP DE GELDIGHEIT VAN VERDRAGEN (1938).

54 On the other hand, complete execution of a treaty is not a legal reason for the termination of its legal validity, notwithstanding the contrary opinion of many writers. See K. Hofbauer, *L'éxécution, cause d'extinction du traité international*, 20 REVUE DE DROIT INTERNATIONAL 92–103 (1937).

55 Woolsey in 20 AM. J. INT'L L. 346–53 (1926); G. WACKERNAGEL, ZUR LEHRE VON DER EINSEITIGEN AUFHEBUNG VÖLKERRECHTLICHER VERTRÄGE (1926).

56 Of recent writings, see T. YOUNG HUANG, THE DOCTRINE OF REBUS SIC STANTIBUS IN INTERNATIONAL LAW (1935). C. Fairman, *Implied Resolutive Conditions in Treaties*, 29 AM.J.INT'L L. 219–36 (1935); FUSCO, LA CLAUSULA REBUS SIC STANTIBUS NEL DIRITTO INTERNAZIONALE (1936); C. LIPARTITI, LA CLAUSOLA REBUS SIC STANTIBUS (1938).

57 L. PFAFF, DIE CLAUSEL REBUS SIC STANTIBUS IN DER DOKTRIN UND DER ÖSTERREICHISCHEN GESETZGEBUNG (1898); M. HERZFELD, DIE STELLUNG DER CLAUSULA REBUS SIC STANTIBUS IM BURGERLICHEN GE-

SETZBUCH (1917). On the common-law doctrine of "frustration," see
Fairman, *op. cit.* On the French theory of "imprévision," see A.
BRUZIN, ESSAI SUR LA NOTION D'IMPRÉVISION ET SUR SON RÔLE EN
MATIÈRE CONTRACTUELLE (1922); J. MAGNAN DE BORNIER, ESSAI SUR
LA THÉORIE D'IMPRÉVISION (1924); LOUVEAU, THÉORIE D'IMPRÉVISION
EN DROIT CIVIL ET EN DROIT ADMINISTRATIF (1920); JACQUEMARD, LA
THÉORIE DE L'IMPRÉVISION (1928).

[58] On this point see H. W. Briggs in 36 AM.J.INT'L L. 89–96 (1942).

[59] An enormous literature on this subject has sprung up in the
inter-war period. The principal writer on the subject is Verdross: 37
ANNUAIRE DE L'INSTITUT DE DROIT INTERNATIONAL 283–98 (Oslo
1932); *ibid.* at 490–507 (Paris 1934); *ibid.* at 183–89 (Luxemburg
1937); 8 REVUE DE DROIT INTERNATIONAL 484–98 (1934); 2 RECUEIL
DES COURS 195–251 (1935); VÖLKERRECHT 75–79 (1937); 12 REVUE
GÉNÉRALE DE DROIT INTERNATIONAL PUBLIC 44–52 (1938). See further,
Heilborn in 1 RECUEIL DES COURS 5–63 (1926); SPIROPOULOS, DIE
ALLGEMEINEN RECHTSGRUNDSÄTZE IM VÖLKERRECHT (1928); BALLA-
DORE PALLIERI, I PRINCIPI GENERALI DEL DIRITTO RICONOSCIUTI DALLE
NAZIONI CIVILI (1931); Heydte in 16 ZEITSCHRIFT FÜR VÖLKERRECHT
461–78 (1932) and in 33 DIE FRIEDENSWARTE 289 (1933); Wolff in 2
RECUEIL DES COURS 483–551 (1932); SCERNI, I PRINCIPI GENERALI DI
DIRITTO RICONOSCUTI DALLE NAZIONI CIVILI (1932); Harle in REVUE
DE DROIT INTERNATIONAL LÉGISLATION COMPARÉE 663–87 (1935); C. de
Visscher in *ibid.* at 395–420 (1933); Ripert in 2 RECUEIL DES COURS
569–664 (1933); RAESTAD, DROIT CONTUMIER ET PRINCIPES GÉNÉRAUX
EN DROIT INTERNATIONAL (1933); Pasching in 14 ZEITSCHRIFT FÜR
ÖFFENTLICHES RECHT 26–61 (1934); Kopelmanas in 15 REVUE GÉN-
ÉRALE DE DROIT INTERNATIONAL PUBLIC 285–308 (1936); W. KÜNZEL,
UNGESCHRIEBENES VÖLKERRECHT (1935); P. GRAPIN, VALEUR INTER-
NATIONALE DES PRINCIPES GÉNÉRAUX DU DROIT (1934); CEGLER, DIE
BEDEUTUNG DER ALLGEMEINEN RECHTSGRUNDSÄTZE FÜR DIE QUELLEN-
LEHRE DES VÖLKERRECHTS (1936).

[60] Radnitzky, *Dispositives Völkerrecht*, 1 ÖSTERREICHISCHE ZEIT-
SCHRIFT FÜR ÖFFENTLICHES RECHT 656 (1914); C. Rousseau, *De la
compatibilité des normes juridiques contradictoires dans l'ordre international*, REVUE GÉNÉRALE DE DROIT INTERNATIONAL PUBLIC 133–92
(1932); MORELLI, NORME DISPOSITIVE DI DIRITTO INTERNAZIONALE
(1931); J. JURT, ZWINGENDES VÖLKERRECHT (1933); C. de Visscher
in REVUE DE DROIT INTERNATIONAL LÉGISLATION COMPARÉE 395–420
(1933); J. Ray, *Des Conflits entre principes abstraits et stipulations
conventionnelles*, 2 RECUEIL DES COURS 635–707 (1934); R. L. Buell,
The Suez Canal and League Sanctions, 6 GENEVA SPECIAL STUDIES,
No. 3 (1935); H. Lauterpacht, *op. cit.;* M. SORENSEN, *op. cit.;* VITTA,
op. cit., supra, note 5, at 172–208.

[61] On the last problem see KELSEN, CONTRATO at 83–111.

[62] See the Bryan-Chamorro Treaty (U.S.–Nicaragua) of 1914. In
the case of Costa Rica *v.* Nicaragua, the plaintiff state petitioned the
Central American Court of Justice to decide that the treaty in question

violated the rights of the plaintiff, acquired by the Canas-Jerez Treaty, and that this violation rendered the Bryan-Chamorro Treaty void ("que la violación de los derechos de Costa Rica vicia de nulidad el dicho Pacto Bryan-Chamorro."—5 ANALES DE LA CORTE DE JUSTICIA CENTROAMERICANA, Nos. 14–16 at 149, 150). But the Court decided that the Bryan-Chamorro Treaty was illegal, but not void (at 176). Similar decision in the case of El Salvador *v.* Nicaragua (6 *ibid.*, Nos. 16–18 at 168, 169–70 [1917]).

63 Covenant, art. XXI. Convention to co-ordinate, extend, and assure the fulfilment of certain treaties between the American states, Buenos Aires, 1936, art. VII.

64 Fifth Hague Convention of 1907, art. XII.

65 First Hague Convention I of 1907 arts. 91, 93, 94; fourth convention, arts. 4, 6.

66 General act of the Brussels Conference relative to the African slave trade of July 2, 1890, art. XCVI (Martens N.R.G. [2e ser.] 345), Covenant, art. XX. See also the article of the Universal Postal Conventions which forbids members to conclude more restricted unions in derogation of the norms of the Convention.

67 Examples of such modification or abrogation of norms of multipartite treaties without the consent of all the original parties: Treaty of Versailles (abrogation of the permanent neutrality of Belgium); Agreement for the Evacuation of the Rhineland, 1929; agreements of the Little Entente with Bulgaria and Hungary, concerning their equality in armaments, 1938; Montreux Convention of July 20, 1936, concerning the regime of the Straits, without the participation of Italy, party to the Lausanne Convention, 1923 (but Italy acceded to the 1936 Convention in 1938). See also the dissenting opinion of Judge Negolescu in P.C.I.J., ser. B, No. 14 at 73, 129, and the separate opinions of Judges van Eysinga and Schücking in the Chinn Case (P.C.I.J., ser. A/B, No. 63 at 131, 148–50).

68 Covenant, art. XX.

69 See the language of President Hurst in the Chinn Case, as cited, at 122–23.

70 This idea has now become pivotal in the system of Kelsen, but see also Scelle: "Il existe un instant entre le moment où la nullité est alleguée et celui où elle est constatée par l'autorité compétente."—2 PRÉCIS DE DROIT DES GENS 419 (1934).

71 Thus Article LXV of the unratified London Declaration of 1909.

72 *Op. cit., supra,* note 5, at 29–30.

73 VÖLKERRECHT at 89, 95.

74 D. ANZILOTTI, III CORSO DI DIRITTO INTERNAZIONALE, Part 1, 8 (1915): "Poichè non esiste un potere superiore agli Stati, le loro controversie non hanno che un modo di resoluzione, consistente nell'accordo degli Stati medesimi."

75 Thus clearly Oppenheim, although limited to the *clausula rebus sic stantibus:* "If such abrogation be refused, a conflict arises between

the treaty obligations and the right to be released from them, which, in absence of an international Court that could give judgment in the matter, cannot be settle juridically."—1 INTERNATIONAL LAW at 751. See also G. del Vecchio: "The old illusion that the maxim *pacta sunt servanda*, independently of any jurisdiction which ascertains the subjective and objective requisites of the validity of a contract, is sufficient to regulate the relations between states, is vanishing from the field of international law."—50 POL.SCI.Q. 529 (1935). In the same sense Kelsen and Verzijl, as cited. For an excellent treatment of the whole problem, see G. BALLADORE PALLIERI, DIRITTO INTERNAZIONALE PUBBLICO 312–13 (2nd ed. 1938).

[76] Kunz, *The Problem of Revision in International Law.* 33 AM.J. INT'L L. 40–43 (1939).

LAW IS A DYNAMIC SYSTEM of norms which, in continuous concretization and individualization, develops from the basic norm above to the last act of mere execution below. Law is a normative system which itself regulates the creation of its own norms. The legal order must, therefore, establish norms which give determined organs the power to create, change, abolish, apply, and execute the norms of a particular legal order. Such power we call competence or jurisdiction. The order of competences of a particular legal community we call its constitution. The constitution must define what persons shall act as organs, what their competence is, and by what procedure it is to be exercised. It may, in addition, prescribe, positively or negatively, certain contents. A legal norm is, therefore, valid if it has been created by the constitutionally prescribed procedure and (or) is in conformity, as to contents, with the constitution or the immediately higher norm. It remains valid as long as it has not been changed or abolished by a procedure also provided for by the constitution. The constitution may also contain norms for its own change, perhaps prescribing particular procedures for such action.

But law can also be changed or created otherwise than by the constitutionally prescribed procedures, this also "illegally": *ex injuria jus oritur*. "The principle of legitimacy is qualified by the principle of effectiveness." [1] In a broader sense, any "illegal" creation of a norm, whether general (a statute) or individual (a judicial decision), which, in spite of its "illegality," asserts itself as law, may be called a "revolutionary" creation of law. But we must distinguish between a truly revolutionary and a merely "unconstitutional" creation of law.

Let us look, first, at municipal law. The "unconstitutional statute," the "illegal" decision of a court of last instance [2] is, nevertheless, valid law, if the constitution provides no particular procedure for abolishing it, or, if such procedure is provided, as long as the decision has not been abolished by this procedure. "Illegality of a norm means possibility of abrogating the norm (otherwise than in the normal way) or punishing the norm-creating organ." [3] Such "illegal" creation of law must, therefore, be regarded as authorized by the constitution, although the constitution may provide a special procedure for abolishing it. The "unconstitutional statute" is a legal feature which, paradoxically, may, but must not, appear in a legal order. But the revolutionary creation of law is a universal phenomenon under any municipal legal order.

Revolution in the legal sense occurs if a constitution, particularly its basic norm, is changed contrary to the constitutionally prescribed procedure. It is legally irrelevant whether such change is peaceful or violent, whether the revolution starts from below or above—the *coup d'état*—whether the triumphant new regime entirely changes the legal order or accepts most of the legal order of the previous regime, whether the new legal order which the revolution brings about is better or worse than the old, whether the revolution is of far-reaching historical importance or only a game of politicians. Even the most drastic change in the contents of a constitution is legally not revolutionary if it is brought about by constitutionally prescribed procedure.[4] Even a slight and peaceful change is legally revolutionary if brought about by a procedure not provided by, or in violation of, the constitution in force.[5] Revolution means the discontinuity of the legal order. It cannot be understood from the point of view of the legal order which has been violated. According to that legal order it constitutes an illegality. A "right to revolution" cannot exist as a right in the sense of positive law. In such a case everything depends on effectiveness. If the revolution succeeds, it abolishes the old and creates a new legal order; if it fails, the revolutionaries are, under the old legal order, traitors.[6]

But, while revolutionary creation of law cannot be legally understood from the point of view of the old municipal law, it is the positive norm of effectiveness of the supra-ordinated international law which guarantees the continuity of the municipal legal order and the identity of the international personality of the state. Revolution, therefore, must be understood as a procedure of creating municipal law provided for by international law. There is also a procedure of international law itself, *debellatio*, which constitutes a revolutionary form of creation of municipal law. The revolutionary creation of municipal law, which leads us to international law, has been the subject of many studies. But little attention has been given to the possibility of a revolutionary creation of law on the level of international law itself.

International law also has its constitutional norms; there is the constitution of general international law, there are the constitutions of particular international communities, like the United Nations, based on particular, treaty-created, international law. International law also regulates the creation of its own norms, by custom or by the treaty procedure.[7] Here, too, norms of international law may be created in contradiction to the constitutionally prescribed procedure, or in violation of certain contents of hierarchically superior norms of international law. Here again there is no revolutionary creation of law, however drastic the change in contents may be, if the new law has been created in conformity with the procedure prescribed by the international law in force.[8]

We need first to consider a possible revolutionary creation of general international law by overthrowing the whole present international legal order and its basic norm, so that apparently the new international law could not be legally understood from the point of view of the international law actually (or previously) in force. It is true that general international law, although a primitive legal order, has shown since the Renaissance a high degree of stability, far superior to that of the more advanced municipal legal orders. But such revolutionary change is thinkable. Such an idea was held widely in early bolshevik Russia. The idea, as expressed by the leading Soviet international lawyer, Eugene Korovin,[9] was to look at the present international law as something intrinsically bad from a Marxist point of view and theoretically superfluous. The aim was to overthrow by a world revolution the present system of a plurality of sovereign, capitalistic states, and to replace it by a worldwide Soviet state, of which the Union of Soviet Socialist Republics, an open state under the Constitution of 1923, was to be the nucleus. In such case the present international law would be overthrown and replaced by a Marxist world law, a wholly intra-Soviet municipal law. Only for the period prior to the victory of the world revolution was Korovin willing to recognize an "international law of the transition period": general international law, he held, had lost its validity between a Soviet state and the capitalistic world; the Soviets would be bound only by treaties. This construction is already theoretically untenable; for the norm *pacta sunt servanda* of general international law is the reason for the validity of all treaty-made law. And as the Soviet world revolution has, up to now, not succeeded, the present international law has remained in force and is binding on the Soviet Union.

Undoubtedly such "revolutionary" change of the present international legal order would again depend on effectiveness for validity. But the question arises whether such creation of new law, even if effective, would legally have the character of revolutionary creation of law. Revolutionary creation of municipal law is revolutionary because it is illegal under municipal law; it is only the positive norm of effectiveness of international law which validates the revolutionary creation of municipal law. The latter is, therefore, a legal form of creation of municipal law provided for by international law. But general international law has no superior positive law above it and contains the positive norm of effectiveness. There is no rule of general international law which makes such "revolutionary" change illegal. In consequence the so-called revolutionary change of general international law must be understood as a legal procedure for the change of its constitution provided for by the constitution itself, on condition of effectiveness. It follows that the legal figure of "revolution" has no place in general international law, which is the only legal order in which there can be no revolution in the legal sense.

But there is the possibility of the creation of particular treaty-made international law made not in conformity with the supra-ordinated general international law. Examples are not rare today.

We may refer to the creation of the norms—both as to procedure and contents—which form the basis of the War Crime Trials in Germany and Japan. A jurist can hardly admit that he is dealing here with normal, or long-estab-

lished, international law, with a mere routine application
of international law already previously valid. But this problem would demand a whole volume for its investigation.

There are other recent examples, such as Article II, paragraph 6 of the Charter of the United Nations, according to
which the organization shall ensure that non-members act
in accordance with the principles of Article II; so far as
may be necessary for the maintenance of international peace
and security. This paragraph has a predecessor in Article
XVII of the Covenant of the League of Nations.[10] Article
XVII left it entirely to the discretion of non-member states
whether they should accept or not accept the invitation of
the Council. In the Eastern Carelian case, Tchitcherin
sharply rejected the invitation and Soviet Russia declared
that any attempt to apply Article XVII against her would
be considered as a hostile act. Article XVII does not attempt
legally to bind non-member states. True, it provides that,
if the third state rejects the invitation and resorts to war
against a member state, the provisions of Article XVI shall
be applicable against it. But such measures would not have
the legal character of sanctions, for sanctions in the legal
sense presuppose the violation of a legal duty and non-
members are not bound by the Covenant. Article XVII was,
therefore, not in violation of the general international law
then in force. Article II, paragraph 6, of the Charter takes
a different approach. Two completely different interpretations of it have already been given. Goodrich and Hambro [11]
state emphatically that "the Charter does not of course
create any legal obligations for non-member States. They
are, therefore, not obligated in a legal sense to act according
to the principles of the Charter for any purpose whatever."
True, there is, under Article XXXV, the possibility of the
acceptance of the Charter *pro hac vice* by non-members,
as under Article XVII of the Covenant. But it is also true
that the U.N. is bound to ensure that non-members act in

accordance with the principles of the Charter whether they have accepted or not. In this case the organization, according to Goodrich and Hambro, "assumes authority not based on the consent of the States affected" and the Charter "provides for the imposition by force, if necessary, of the prescribed conduct without any legal basis in contractual agreement." But that is no solution and no juridical explanation. For the authors can only mean that such action constitutes either old-fashioned intervention and war, not sanctions, or that the Charter imposes upon the organization the duty to act with no basis in law at all, or a duty to act illegally.

Kelsen,[12] on the other hand, interprets Article II, paragraph 6, as claiming that the Charter is legally binding upon non-member states. Under Article II, paragraph 6, only Article II would be binding, but Article II, paragraph 2, covers all the obligations under the Charter. Kelsen considers[13] that non-members are even legally bound to register their treaties (Article CII). He even goes so far[14] as to say that the Charter claims to constitute general international law and that, if this interpretation is accepted, all the states of the world would be "members" of the U.N.

This interpretation seems to go too far in any case. Article II, paragraph 2, covers all the obligations under the Charter, it is true, but imposes this duty "in order to ensure to all of them the rights and benefits resulting from membership," a purpose which naturally makes no sense in the case of non-members. Such wide interpretation would, under Article XVII, bind non-members even to bear the expenses of the organization. The fact that the Charter distinguishes between members and non-members, the exclusion of Franco's Spain from membership, and the unsuccessful application for membership by a number of states, show that the Charter only constitutes particular international law, although it may have, like the League, a tendency toward universality. It seems to follow that Article II, paragraph 6, cannot intend to bind non-members by all the norms of the Charter. But by what norms? Would a non-member state be legally bound to make available armed forces to the Security Council under Article XLIII? Is Switzerland legally bound to grant rights of passage to U.N. troops? Finally the restricting phrase "so far as may be necessary for the maintenance of peace and security" must not be forgotten.

We need, first, the "jurisprudence" of the U.N. to determine the meaning and range of Article II, paragraph 6. The wording of this clause does not compel the adoption of the construction that non-members are thereby legally bound. But if this interpretation is adopted then Article II, paragraph 6, as Kelsen fully recognizes, "is not in conformity with general international law as prevailing at the moment the Charter came into force." For under general international law a treaty creates only legal rights and duties among the contracting parties.[15]

While Article II, paragraph 6, of the Charter is not so worded as clearly to claim that non-members are legally bound, this issue is unequivocally raised in the draft treaty for the outlawing of atomic bombs, proposed by the Soviet Union, and read by Mr. Gromyko [16] in the session of the Atomic Energy Commission of the U.N. The proposed treaty, it is true, is open to accession by all states, whether members of the U.N. or not. But under Article VI the treaty is to come into effect after the approval of the Security Council and after ratification by half of the signatory states, including all states members of the U.N., and Article VII reads: "After the entry into force of the present agreement, it shall be an obligation upon all States, members or not of the UN." This clause is clearly not in conformity with general international law. For treaties do not legally bind non-contracting parties and "save in exceptional cases are binding only in virtue of their ratification." [17]

The draft treaties of peace with the minor European Axis states purport to be legally binding after ratification by one party only. A peace treaty is valid even if imposed by force but it is, nevertheless a treaty and needs, therefore, in order to be a treaty at all, signature and ratification by the vanquished as well as by the victor. But in Article LXXVIII of the Draft Peace Treaty with Italy[18] we read that the treaty "shall be ratified by the Allied Powers. It shall be ratified also by Italy. It will come into force upon the deposit of ratification by France, the United Kingdom, the United States, and the Union of Soviet Socialist Republics." What is in this case, by the way, the legal significance of ratification by Italy?

As we have seen, "revolution" has no place in general international law, for the reason that such so-called revolutionary change is not illegal under the international law, at any moment in force, in view of the norm of effectiveness. But the examples of the creation of treaty norms already discussed, not in conformity with general international law, are in a very different category. For here this creation is illegal under general international law. And it cannot be said that here everything depends on effectiveness. As Verdross [19] correctly states, "the principle of effectiveness can create new law only within the framework of international law; for a *boundless* recognition of the principle of effectiveness would legalize *any* illegality and thus abolish international law itself."

Such illegal creation of treaty law will need a healing of the illegality in order to become valid international law, as by general recognition. Or it may be rejected as illegal in a procedure and by an organ of international law. Indeed Article II, paragraph 6, is, as Kelsen [20] asserts, "problematical." Kelsen says that an arbitration tribunal *ad hoc*, established between a member and a non-member state, may possibly not consider the non-member state as bound by the Charter. But there is more to the problem than this. Even the International Court of Justice at The Hague, although, under Article III of the Charter, it is a "princpal organ" of the U.N., may not only possibly, but will be bound to, decide that a non-member is not legally bound by the Charter, or that Italy is not legally bound by an Italian Peace Treaty not ratified by her. For this Court, under Article XXXVIII of its statute, is bound to apply general customary international law, under which these treaty norms are not legally binding, and can apply international conventions only if they "establish rules expressly recognized by the contesting parties."

The problems of "revolutionary" and illegal creation of norms of international law have hardly been considered as yet by the writers on that subject. These problems call for further investigation. They are highly interesting theoretically and, therefore, highly important practically. For there is no practice without theory, and in the relation between them it is theory which holds the commanding position; as the great Leonardo Da Vinci has put it: "La teoria è il capitano, e la prattica sono i soldadi."

---

[1] H. KELSEN, GENERAL THEORY OF LAW AND STATE 119 (1945).

[2] Erie R.R. v. Tompkins, 304 U.S. 64, 58 S.Ct 817 (1938), not only overruled Swift v. Tyson, but held repeating the words of Justice Holmes that "Swift v. Tyson was an unconstitutional assumption of power, by courts of the United States." Nevertheless, under the principle of res judicata, Swift v. Tyson, 16 Pet. 1, 10 L.Ed. 865 (1842), was valid law for ninety-six years.

[3] KELSEN, op. cit. at 371.

[4] Whether Italy's change from monarchy to republic was legally a revolutionary creation of law depends on whether such change was or was not brought about in conformity with a procedure provided by the constitution of the Kingdom of Italy in force at that time.

[5] The American republics held the change from the Vargas regime in Brazil to be constitutional for diplomatic reasons, so as to avoid the problem of the recognition of a de facto government. But the overthrow of President Vargas by a palace revolution was, from a legal point of view, certainly revolutionary, as contrary to the Vargas constitution of 1937, then in force.

6 Hence the paradoxical situation of the crime of treason. In positive common law, it is the highest crime, standing in a category apart. But a successful revolution leads to an original creation of law. "Those who lose are the traitors," says the King in Calderon's *La Vida es Sueño*. An old English verse reads: "Treason cannot prosper, What's the reason? / For if it does, who would dare to call it treason?"

7 See "The Meaning and the Range of the Norm *Pacta Sunt Servanda*," above.

8 At the World Health Conference, held in the summer of 1946 in New York, it was proposed that the World Health Assembly of the new World Health Organization should have jurisdiction of enacting regulations immediately binding upon member states without ratification, except if specifically rejected by a member state. The Belgian representative, rejecting this proposal, spoke of a "revolutionary change of international law." But legally such a norm, created by the treaty procedure, with the consent and ratification of the contracting parties, and binding only upon member states, would not be revolutionary at all.

9 E. A. KOROVIN, DAS VÖLKERRECHT DER UBERGANGSZEIT (German trans. 1929). See also T. A. TARACOUZIO, THE SOVIET UNION AND INTERNATIONAL LAW (1935).

10 Article XVII: "1. In the event of a dispute between a Member of the League and a State which is not a Member of the League, or between States not Members of the League, the State or States not Members of the League shall be invited to accept the obligations of Membership in the League for the purposes of such dispute, upon such conditions as the Council may deem just. If such invitation is accepted, the provisions of Articles 12 to 16 inclusive shall be applied with such modifications as may be deemed necessary by the Council.

"2. Upon such invitation being given the Council shall immediately institute an inquiry into the circumstances of the dispute and recommend such actions as may seem best and most effectual in the circumstances.

"3. If a State so invited shall refuse to accept the obligation of membership in the League for the purposes of such dispute, and shall resort to war against a Member of the League, the provisions of Article XVI shall be applicable as against the State taking such action.

"4. If both parties to the dispute when so invited refuse to accept the obligations of membership in the League for the purposes of such dispute, the Council may take such measures and make such recommendation as will prevent hostilities and will result in the settlement of the dispute."

See the well-known commentaries on the Covenant by Schücking and Wehberg, Ray and Goppert, as well as the following monographs: E. Morpurgo, *L'articolo 17 del Patto della Società delle Nazioni ed il diritto internazionale consuetudinario*, in REVUE DE DROIT INTERNATIONAL 177–85 (1925); A. BAVAJ, L'INTERPRETAZIONE DELL' ARTICOLO 17 DEL PATTO DELLA SOCIETA DELLA NAZIONI (1931); R. WEINBERG, VÖLKERBUND UND NICHTMITGLIEDSTAATEN (1932).

[11] LELAND M. GOODRICH and EDWARD HAMBRO, CHARTER OF THE UNITED NATIONS: COMMENTARY AND DOCUMENTS 70–71 (1946).

[12] H. Kelsen, *Sanctions in International Law under the Charter of the UN*, 31 IOWA L.REV. 499–543, at 502 (1946).

[13] *Ibid.* at 512.

[14] H. Kelsen, *Membership in the United Nations*, 46 COLUM.L.REV. 391–411, at 394, 411 (1946).

[15] P.C.I.J., No. A/22 at 17, No. A/B/46 at 141, 143.

[16] N.Y. Times, June 20, 1946, p. 4.

[17] P.C.I.J., No. A/23 at 20.

[18] N.Y. Times, July 27, 1946, p. 9. Analogously Article XXXVII of the Hungarian, XXXVIII of the Rumanian, XXXVI of the Bulgarian, and XXXIV of the Finnish draft peace treaties (*ibid.*, July 31, 1946, pp. 15, 18, 19, and 21), only with the difference that the first three treaties come into force immediately upon deposit of ratification by the U.K., the U.S., and the U.S.S.R., the last upon deposit of ratification by the U.K. and the U.S.S.R.

[19] A. VERDROSS, VÖLKERRECHT 126 (1937).

[20] Kelsen, *op. cit.* at 512–13.

SOME YEARS AGO at an annual meeting of the American Society of International Law, as this writer recalls, there was a discussion from the floor as to cases decided by the United States Supreme Court concerning river boundaries between states of this union. The opinion was voiced tentatively that this Court perhaps no longer applies international law in such cases and that perhaps the maxim "International law is a part of the law of the land" is in decline. Such and similar opinions, it is submitted, are based on two theoretical errors, and it is the purpose of this paper to clarify them.

The first error has to do with the legal significance of the quoted maxim which, it is said, is typical of the common law.[1] That international law, to its *full extent,* is a part of the law of England and of the United States, has been stated frequently by English and American judges.[2] There are, further, Article VI, clause 2, of the Constitution of the United States and articles in recent European constitutions.[3]

Where such municipal rules are in force, international law can thus far be directly and immediately applied by national courts. But even under such an hypothesis, the international and municipal validity need not necessarily coincide. For instance, treaties may need, in addition to their coming into force in international law, internal promulgation. There is, further, in this country the important distinction between self-executing treaties and treaties requiring legislation.[4] Finally, a treaty does not prevail over a later federal statute.[5]

Naturally, even under such rules of municipal law, it must be the question of a true norm of international law, not, for instance, of recommendations by international organizations, a declaration which is not legally binding, a statement by the International Law Commission, or even clauses in treaties where these clauses do not constitute legally binding norms but merely ethical considerations or political programs for the future.[6] The often voiced opinion that British Prize Courts are "courts of international law" is, of course, theoretically untenable. These courts are courts of His Britannic Majesty and are, as was fully recognized in the case of "The Zamora," bound by a British act of Parliament, even if it is not in conformity with international law. Municipal law can naturally go further, as the norms of the American and some European constitutions do. Under Swiss law the rules of international treaties to which Switzerland is a party prevail not only over cantonal law but even over *later* Swiss federal laws which are in contradiction to international law.[7]

"The doctrine that international law is a part of the law of the land." writes Lauterpacht,[8] "is a rule of law." That is correct insofar as this rule is a norm of *municipal* law; but it is not a norm of international law. The latter binds the states legally to execute and enforce rules of general and particular international law binding upon them. But it delegates to the sovereign states the competence to do so according to their discretion. They can enact such municipal law, but it is equally in conformity with international law if they choose to "transform" [9] the norms of international law into municipal law in each single case.

Lauterpacht further states correctly that the maxim that international law is a part of the law of the land must not be confused with the issue of the supremacy of international law. But if he continues that one may assert the first, but deny the second proposition, we would rather emphasize exactly the contrary. International law does not bind the states to have a municipal law of the "part of the law of the land" type. But whether a state has such municipal law or not, the norms of international law are always and, by their very nature, intrinsically superior to municipal law. Whatever the municipal law of a state may be, violation of the superior norms of international law, whether by its legislative, administrative, or judicial organs—even if the latter are under a legal duty to apply municipal law which is in contradiction to international law—always makes the state internationally responsible. It is of the greatest importance to distinguish clearly between a municipal norm of the "part of the law of the land" type and the clear supra-statal validity of international law regardless of the contents of municipal law.[10]

The second theoretical error in the discussion, quoted at the beginning, is of an entirely different nature. In most discussions and treatments of "international law in national courts," certain decisions by the United States Supreme Court in conflicts between states of this union are quoted simply as applications of international law.[11] The Supreme Court has, indeed, often applied rules of international law in controversies between states of this union; the same has been done by the German *Staatsgerichtshof* in controversies between member states and by the Swiss Federal Tribunal in conflicts between the cantons,[12] as, e.g., in determining the mountain borderline between the cantons of St. Gallen and

Appenzell. Rules of international law have been applied here, in Germany and Switzerland, in controversies between member states, concerning bays,[13] diversion of water and utilization of rivers and lakes,[14] nuisances,[15] river boundaries,[16] problems of accretion and avulsion,[17] jurisdiction,[18] boundaries (prescription),[19] navigation, state succession.[20] American cases abound.

But in order to gain a theoretically correct insight into this type of application of international law it is necessary first to consider that the sovereign states, although they are no longer the only persons in international law, are still the most important, permanent, and full persons in international law and, at the same time, its creators. In this sense, the Permanent Court of International Justice [21] could say, although not absolutely correctly, that "international law governs relations between *independent* States." One must distinguish, in the terminology of this writer,[22] between "States in the sense of international law" and "States in the sense of municipal law." Member states of a federal state are, generally speaking, not states in the sense of international law,[23] although they may have a partial personality in international law, which is, naturally, derived from international, not from municipal, constitutional law.[24] But the member states of this union, as well as the cantons of Switzerland, are merely "States in the sense of municipal law," and not sovereign states.[25] This correct insight is often expressed in decisions of the United States Supreme Court.[26] The legal relations between the states of this union or the cantons of Switzerland do not belong to international, but to 'interstate" or "intercantonal," i.e., national law.

The norms of international law concerning international rivers apply, by the supremacy of international law, only to *international* rivers which flow through or form the boundary between two or more *independent* states. But the rivers involved in these interstate cases, like the Arkansas,

Colorado, Laramie Rivers, are, unlike the Rio Grande, not international, but "interstate" rivers.[27] International law, of course, raises no objection to the application of international rules to interstate conflicts or to interstate rivers. In Wisconsin v. Michigan (1935) Justice Butler stated that "principles of international law apply also to boundaries between States constituting the United States." But it must be understood that, if they do, they apply by force of municipal, not international, law. This legal situation fully justifies the fact that the United States Supreme Court in these cases sometimes applies rules which, as to their contents, are identical with the corresponding norms of international law and sometimes does not, but instead applies common law, statutory law, local customary law, interstate agreements, long usage, or acquiescence.[28] In Iowa v. Illinois (1893) Justice Field stated that the rules of international law "will be held to obtain, unless changed by statute or usage."

We must distinguish between what this writer, for purposes of theoretical clarification, would call *genuine* international law and international law *by analogy*. The application of international norms in these interstate cases is neither a duty imposed by international law, nor has it anything to do with the municipal "part of the law of the land" rule which envisages only *genuine* international law. It is purely a matter of municipal law to apply in such cases international law *by analogy*.[29]

Such international law by analogy appears also in other fields. Genuine international law binds the states to grant to diplomatic agents the immunities prescribed by international rules. But the states are free to grant the same privileges *by analogy* to inter-imperial delegates who are *not* diplomatic agents in the sense of international law.[30]

The two theoretical clarifications here given—distinction between the municipal character of the "part of the law of the land" rule and the always existing supremacy of inter-

national law, on the one hand, and the distinction between
genuine international law and international law by analogy,
on the other—are by no means, as some would believe, a
consequence of the theoretical construction known as the
"dualistic doctrine." The latter is certainly untenable, because it is unable to construe positive international law as
superior to national law. Only the monistic doctrine of the
supremacy of international law is correct, for the sole
reason that it alone is able to furnish a construction in conformity with the positive international law actually in
force. But it is a theoretical construction of positive international law, not an a priori natural law hypothesis, out
of which rules of positive international law could be gained
by mere logical deduction. What the rules of positive international law at a given time are can only be found by its
analysis.

Such analysis clearly shows that present-day positive
international law does not prescribe that the states must
have a "part of the law of the land" norm—although such
municipal norm is welcome, convenient, and beneficial; on
the other hand, international law is always, and regardless
of the contents of municipal law, superior to the national
legal orders. Such analysis further shows that, like every
legal rule, the rules of international law have a certain
temporal, personal, territorial, and material sphere of
validity; they are binding upon the sovereign states and
superior to national law. The sovereign states may also
apply international law rules beyond their spheres of
validity. But this is a matter of municipal law. If the states
do so, they do not apply genuine international law but
apply international law merely by analogy.

1 See on this problem: BLACKSTONE, COMMENTARIES UPON THE LAWS
OF ENGLAND, Book IV, chap. 5; 1 J. B. MOORE, A DIGEST OF INTER-
NATIONAL LAW 9–11 (1906); PICCIOTTO, THE RELATION OF INTER-
NATIONAL LAW TO THE LAWS OF ENGLAND AND OF THE UNITED STATES

(1915); H. Lauterpacht, *Is International Law a Part of the Law of England?*, 25 TRANSACT.GROT.SOC'Y. 51–88; E. D. Dickinson in 26 AM.J.INT'L L. 239–60 (1932); WALZ, VÖLKERRECHT UND STAATLICHES RECHT (1933); 1 OPPENHEIM-LAUTERPACHT, INTERNATIONAL LAW 37–44 (7th ed. 1948).

2 See the Earl of Mansfield in Triquet v. Bath, 3 Barrows 1478 (1764); Respublica v. DeLongchamps, 1 Dallas 111 (1784); Marshall, C.J., in *The Nereid*, 9 Cranch 388 (1815); Lord Campbell, C.J., in Magdalena Steam Navigation Co. v. Martin, 2 Ellis and Ellis 94 (1859); Turner. L. J., in Emperor of Austria v. Day and Kossuth, (1861), 2 Gilfard 621 (Ch.); Lord Alverstone, C.J., in West Rand Central Gold Mining Co. v. The King, 2 K.B. 391 (1905).

3 Weimar Constitution, 1919, art. IV; Austrian Constitutions, 1920, art. IX; 1934, art. IX; Spanish Constitution, 1931, art. IX. See also the present so-called Bonn Constitution (*Grundgesetz*).

4 See Marshall, C.J., in Foster and Elam v. Neilson, 2 Peters 253 (1829); Robertson v. General Electric Co., 32 F. (2d) 495 (1929).

5 See Hooper v. U. S., 22 Ct.Cl. 408 (1887).

6 That is why the decision in Sei Fujii v. State of California, Calif. Dist.Ct.App., 2d Dist. (1950), is doubly attackable: The corresponding clauses of the United Nations Charter are not self-executory, nor do they constitute legally binding norms. See Manley O. Hudson in 44 AM.J.INT'L L. 542–48 (1950).

7 GUGGENHEIM, LEHRBUCH DES VÖLKERRECHTS 34, 35 (1948).

8 In 1 OPPENHEIM-LAUTERPACHT, *op. cit.* at 44.

9 H. Kelsen, *La Transformation du droit international en droit interne*, REVUE GÉNÉRALE DE DROIT INTERNATIONAL PUBLIC 5 (1936).

10 This distinction is now brought out with the utmost clarity by A. VERDROSS, VÖLKERRECHT 65–66 (1950).

11 See Charls K. Burdick's paper *Decisions of National Tribunals* and discussion in PROCEEDINGS OF THE FIFTH CONFERENCE OF TEACHERS OF INTERNATIONAL LAW AND RELATED SUBJECTS 162–66, 172 (1933). See also the digests of international law by Moore and Hackworth and the treatise by Oppenheim-Lauterpacht. On the subject of international law in national courts, see in general: D. ANZILOTTI, IL DIRITTO INTERNAZIONALE NEI GIUDIZI INTERNI (1905); JAMES BROWN SCOTT, JUDICIAL SETTLEMENT OF CONTROVERSIES BETWEEN STATES OF THE AMERICAN UNION (1918); H. A. SMITH, THE AMERICAN SUPREME COURT AS AN INTERNATIONAL TRIBUNAL (1921); RUTH D. MASTERS, INTERNATIONAL LAW IN NATIONAL COURTS (1932). It seems also that Professor Willard B. Cowles, in his 1950 lectures on the application of international law within federal states at the Hague Academy of International Law, taught that international law as such is applicable in the relations between non-sovereign parts of federal states, and even to provinces and municipalities.

12 On Swiss cases see 1 Guggenheim, *op. cit.* at 34, note 33.

13 See Louisiana v. Mississippi, 202 U.S. 1; Michigan v. Wisconsin, 270 U.S. 295 (1926); Wisconsin v. Michigan, 295 U.S. 455 (1935); decision of the German *Staatsgerichtshof* of July, 1928, in the con-

troversy between Lübeck and Mecklenburg-Schwerin (Ann.Dig., case no. 88 [1927-28]).

14 See Kansas v. Colorado, 206 U.S. 46 (1907); Wyoming v. Colorado, 259 U.S. 419 (1922), and 298 U.S. 573 (1936); Connecticut v. Massachusetts, 282 U.S. 660 (1931); New Jersey v. New York, 283 U.S. 336 (1931); Washington v. Oregon, 297 U.S. 517 (1936); Wisconsin v. Illinois, 278 U.S. 367 (1929), 281 U.S. 179 (1930), and 289 U.S. 395 (1933); decision of the German *Staatsgerichtshof* between Baden and Württemberg of June 19, 1927.

15 Missouri v. Illinois, 200 U.S. 496 (1906); New Jersey v. City of New York, 283 U.S. 473 (1931).

16 Iowa v. Illinois, 147 U.S. 1 (1893); Louisiana v. Mississippi, 202 U.S. 1 (1906); Indiana v. Kentucky, 136 U.S. 479 (1890); Nebraska v. Iowa, 143 U.S. 359 (1892); Washington v. Oregon, 211 U.S. 127 (1908), and 214 U.S. 205 (1909); Arkansas v. Tennessee, 246 U.S. 158 (1918); Arkansas v. Mississippi, 250 U.S. 39 (1919); Oklahoma v. Texas, 252 U.S. 372 (1920); and 260 U.S. 606 (1923); Minnesota v. Wisconsin, 252 U.S. 273 (1920); Georgia v. South Carolina, 257 U.S. 516 (1922); New Mexico v. Texas, 275 U.S. 279 (1927); Vermont v. New Hampshire, 289 U.S. 593 (1933); New Jersey v. Delaware, 291 U.S. 361 (1934).

17 See Nebraska v. Iowa, 143 U.S. 359 (1892); Louisiana v. Mississippi, 282 U.S. 458 (1931); Jraolo v. Province of Buenos Aires, Supreme Court of Argentina (Ann. Dig., case no. 62 [1919-22]).

18 See Central R.R. Co. v. Jersey City, 209 U.S. 473 (1908).

19 See Rhode Island v. Massachusetts, 12 Peters 657 (1838); Virginia v. Tennessee, 148 U.S. 503 (1893); Louisiana v. Mississippi, 202 U.S. 1 (1906), and 282 U.S. 458 (1931); Maryland v. West Virginia, 217 U.S. 1 (1910); Arkansas v. Tennessee, 246 U.S. 158 (1918); Arkansas v. Mississippi, 250 U.S. 39 (1919); Michigan v. Wisconsin, 270 U.S. 295 (1926).

20 Virginia v. West Virginia, 220 U.S. 1 (1911), and 246 U.S. 568 (1918).

21 In the *S.S. Lotus Case*, P.C.I.J., Ser. A, No. 10 at 16, 18 (1927).

22 JOSEF L. KUNZ, DIE STAATENVERBINDUNGEN (1929).

23 They are not members of the international community; that is why the federal state alone is internationally responsible for them; that is why they enjoy no immunity in foreign courts (State of Ceara, a member state of Brazil, v. Dorr, France, Cour de Cassation 1932, RECUEIL DALLOZ at 196 [1936]), The U.S. Supreme Court decision in Monaco v. Mississippi, 292 U.S. 573 (1934), is based on American constitutional, not on international, law.

24 See now Byelorussia and the Ukraine. Treaties can, of course, confer a limited international personality even on a territorial entity which is not a state and is not independent and self-governing, such as the proposed Free Territory of Trieste (see Josef L. Kunz in 1 WEST.POL.Q., No. 2 at 99-112 [1948]).

25 That they are often called "sovereign" means sovereignty in the sense of the Constitution of the United States, not sovereignty in the sense of international law.

26 Thus, Justice Holmes, in Missouri v. Illinois (1905), distinguished between "international" and "interstate" law. Justice Cardozo, in New Jersey v. Delaware (1934), said of the rule of the "thalweg" that "such considerations have less importance for states united under a general government than for States wholly independent." Justice Field, in Iowa v. Illinois (1893), spoke of the application in this interstate controversy "of the same rule when a navigable river constitutes the boundary between two *independent* States," and added that "the reasons and necessity of the rule of international law may not be as urgent in this country where neighboring States are under the same general government." In New Jersey v. New York (1931), the Court held: *"Different* considerations come in when we are dealing with *independent* sovereigns. . . . In a lesser degree, perhaps, the same is true of the *quasi-sovereignties* bound together in the Union" (italics supplied).

27 Thus, Justice Van Devanter, in Wyoming v. Colorado (1922), spoke of the Laramie River correctly as an "interstate stream."

28 It depends on the case. In Wyoming v. Colorado (1922), not international law, but the local "doctrine of appropriation," shared by both states, was applied. But see Kansas v. Colorado (1907), in which Colorado had the appropriation, but Kansas the common-law system; or Connecticut v. Massachusetts (1937), in which both states had the common-law system. See also the "Colorado River Compact" of 1922. In Central R.R. Co. v. Jersey City (1908), Justice Holmes applied, not international law, but an agreement and statutory law.

29 Guggenheim (1 *op. cit.* at 344 n. 38) correctly states that the Swiss Federal Tribunal applies to intercantonal cases international law "in analoger Weise."

30 "Representatives which Great Britain and the Dominions send to one another as High Commissioners do not enjoy diplomatic status."—1 OPPENHEIM-LAUTERPACHT, *op. cit.* at 692. But "the Finance Acts of 1923 and 1928 confer upon High Commissioners of the Dominions and India . . . the same immunity from income tax, super tax and land tax as is enjoyed by the accredited ministers of a foreign State."—*idem* at 692–93 n. 5.

CHAPTER XXIII: Roberto Ago's Theory of "Spontaneous" International Law

PROFESSOR ROBERTO AGO, a leading Italian scholar of international law, the excellent editor of *Comunicazioni e Studi,* a member of the United Nations International Law Commission, has elaborated a critique of legal postivism which has led him to his theory of "spontaneous" law. He wants to impress upon us the necessity of distinguishing, within the law actually in force, between "positive" law—law owing its origin to a certain "source," created historically by certain authorities in a prescribed procedure—and "spontaneous" law, which is also law actually in force, but not so created. This spontaneous law must be discovered by an inductive method, and to formulate it is the task of the science of law. Naturally, this is a problem of the general theory of all law. But as Ago takes customary law as his main type of spontaneous law, this distinction would be of particular importance in the law of nations, as all general international law is customary and therefore, for the author, spontaneous law.

Ago's theory was first developed in a small book.[1] The importance which the author gives to his theory can be seen from the fact that he has presented it in a more elaborate form in the principal Western languages.[2] Ago obviously presents this theory as a new and original one; but it was first developed by Mario Giuliano and then taken over with a few minor changes by Ago.[3] Now, *is duo faciunt idem, non est idem*. The same theory has a completely different standing in Giuliano and in Ago. Mario Giuliano is not only an adherent of the "realist school," but also a theoretical Marxist and politically pro-communist, whereas Ago is not. Giuliano stands on the Marxist philosophy of historical materialism; for him *all* law and not only the spontaneous law of Ago, is merely an ideological superstructure of the economic conditions of a certain society at a given time.

Prima facie, Ago's theory gives the impression of an attack on legal positivism, so fashionable since the end of World War II, be it by the adherents of a naked sociologism (law as a fact) or by the adherents of natural law. But Ago tells us that he does not want to attack positivism as such. He fully recognizes the great merits of legal positivism, namely, to have the law separated from mere aspirations and subjective expressions of ideal exigencies of justice. He starts his investigations from a semantic angle. He believes that the trouble with "positive" law is the ambiguity of language which prevents clarity of thinking.

He gives an elaborate historical study of the meanings of the term "positive law" since the creation of this term in the Middle Ages. This term means etymologically "jus positum" and, according to Ago, has been so understood from the beginning, namely, as the law established by a special authority and created by a procedure prescribed by legal norms; stemming therefore, from a formal "source," from what Italian doctrine calls "normative facts." [4] In this sense, he states, the term was used by international law doctrine of the seventeenth and eighteenth centuries. The legal positivism of the nineteenth century, he continues, rejected natural law, restricted law to positive law, but did not change the meaning of the term. At the same time it was asserted that only the sovereign state can create law. In the further development, positive law was identified with the "law in force." Hence, it is argued, for positivism law is not a phenomenon distinguished by certain characteristics of its own, but simply everything posited by a certain authority in a certain prescribed procedure. Thus only the "posited," enacted, law remained. But spontaneous law, which is of spontaneous creation, neither posited nor willed, is also an integral part of the law. The untenability of positivism, the author asserts, was brought into the open by Perassi's "first norm" and Kelsen's "basic norm": here it is admitted that the most basic norms are not "posited," and hence not positive law. The present confusion as to positive law, the author holds, stems from overlooking the fact that in all legal orders there is a whole category of legal norms which do not owe their origin to a certain "source," which are not posited, but spontaneous, law. To the latter belongs customary law, of particular importance in international law.

The author proposes, therefore, either to use the term "positive law" in the sense of all "law actually in force"— then, another name must be found to designate the enacted law—or to restrict the term "positive" to its etymological sense of "posited"—in the latter case positive law is not identical with the law in force. While Ago's writings are always interesting and full of learning, it is clearly impossible to accept the author's theory.

First of all, from a purely practical point of view, this writer cannot see the slightest difference, as far as customary international law is concerned, between Ago's spontaneous law and the manner in which the courts and doctrine handle this problem.[5] But Ago's theory is also theoretically wholly unacceptable. First we must question Ago's historical investigation as to the term "positive law." Certainly mistakes have been made, but we seriously question Ago's identification of "positive" with "enacted" law in his sense. If we also do a bit of semantics, it is clear that the term "positive" has many meanings, e.g., as the antithesis of negative or of relative. But in the realm of law, the term, from the earliest times of occidental culture, has been understood as the antithesis of "natural." Thus in classical Greece the distinction was between the law by nature (φύσει δίκαιον) and by enactment (νομῷ δίκαιον). Only the alleged existence of a "natural" law has brought forward the term "positive law." That was so in the classic Catholic natural law of the scholastic and the Spanish neo-scholastic [6] period as well as in the naïve positivism of the nineteeth century. Thus, St. Thomas of Aquinas contrasts the "natural law" which for him is "participatio creaturae humanae in lege aeterna," and which can, contrary to the revealed *jus divinum*, be found by the "recta ratio," with the *jus humanum*. At all times the term "positive law" was not restricted to enacted law, but to man-made law. It is exactly in this sense that the term was used by earliest writers.[7] Thus positive law means from the earliest times, not just enacted, but man-made law in contrast to natural law; and that is the meaning today.[8] Law is positive law, not because it has been posited by a certain authority, but because it is man-made. Legal positivism, as Ago fully recognizes, is by no means necessarily tied up with philosophical positivism. Legal positivism can very well recognize religious and ethical values as being hierarchically superior to legal norms; what legal positivism states is only that these higher norms are *not law;* and that is conceded now by so orthodox a neo-Thomist as the Belgian, Jean Dabin.

Exactly because "positive" law has always meant manmade, in contrast to natural, law, the problem is not of the "sources" of law. Speaking semantically, we have the impression that Ago is a victim of the term "source."

Kelsen has often warned that the term "sources of the law" is a figurative and highly ambiguous expression [9] which should be dropped as a legal technical term. Law is a normative order which regulates its own creation. The metaphorical term "sources of the law" means theoretically the procedures regulated by the legal norms which prescribe the methods of creating legal norms.[10] One of these procedures regulated by these norms is the creation of customary law. We can hardly understand Ago's dictum that legal positivism has restricted positive law to enacted law and has excluded customary (his "spontaneous") law. Who are the international lawyers who have excluded customary from positive international law? There is no real basis for Ago's dictum and his critique seems to be mere shadow-boxing.

Positive law does not merely consist of enacted law, created by certain special law-making authorities in a certain prescribed procedure. Custom, too, is a well-recognized procedure for creating positive law. Positive law can be created consciously by special law-making organs, but it can also be created by custom; and where, as in primitive international law, no special law-creating organs exist, it can only be created in this way. The same is true of any primitive municipal legal order. Were the *coutumes de France* not positive law? True, the procedure of custom is a decentralized procedure; but so is the procedure of treaty-created particular international law, for the simple reason that primitive international law is characterized by a high degree of decentralization. The creators of customary international law are, partly at least, at the same time those who are subject to these norms; but the same is not true with regard to treaty-created norms. It is true that enacted and treaty-created law is created consciously, and customary law may be created unconsciously. But it is positive international law which prescribes the procedure by which customary international law can be created (usage plus *opinio juris*) ; the latter is the product of a legally prescribed procedure and must be sharply distinguished from norms of international morality or from conventional norms of *courtoisie internationale*.

From the point of view of a general theory of law, Ago's attitude of distinguishing merely between enacted and customary ("spontaneous") law erroneously restricts the law to general abstract norms. But the "whole law in force" consists also of individual concrete norms, created by judicial and administrative decisions, by contract ("la loi entre les parties" of the Code Napoléon), by international treaties. Enactment, custom, judicial and administrative decisions, contracts, treaties, are all for the creation of law, regulated by corresponding legal norms. If it were true, as Ago asserts, that customary (his "spontaneous") law is excluded from positive law, then the United Kingdom would have no positive constitutional law and even the positive, i.e., enacted, law would have its *raison d'être* in non-positive, i.e., spontaneous, law. Have the countries of the common law no positive law? Now, the common law is unwritten, customary law,[11] but the law-making function of the courts is a procedure for creating law prescribed by corresponding norms. If Ago were right, the United Kingdom, with no written constitution and the "case law" of the common law, based on precedents and the rule of *stare decisis*, would have no positive law at all, except the acts of Parliament, standing like a lonely flower of positive law in a desert of spontaneous law. It seems clear that the author is not familiar with the common-law system.

Customary law, like enacted law, is positive law, the creation of which is regulated by legal norms. This is fully recognized today, and has always been recognized. The distinction between *jus scriptum* and *jus non scriptum*, is a distinction *within* positive law.[12] Ago is entirely right that

the problem of the "sources" of the law—that is, correctly
stated, of the law-regulated procedures for the creation
of legal norms, including custom—has nothing to do with
the philosophical problem of the "foundation of law." That
is why it is inadmissible to quote Kelsen's "basic norm"
in favor of Ago's spontaneous law. The basic norm is *not*
a rule of positive law, but only the presupposition for the
validity of the whole legal order. The basic norm is the
recognition by critical positivism that positivism has its
limits. Such presupposition is just as necessary in a system
of natural law. If rules can be deduced from nature, be it
physical or human, it is further necessary, in order to
explain *why* they are binding, to presuppose here also a
norm according to which men ought to obey the dictates
to nature.[13]

Ago's dictum that for legal positivism the law is nothing
but the product of a certain authority which has no characteristics of its own, is equally untenable. On the one
hand, there is the revolutionary creation of positive law;
on the other hand, not everything created by a certain
competent authority in a certain prescribed procedure constitutes legal norms; that depends on the essence of law: "a
rule is a legal norm, because it provides for a sanction." [14]
Statutes, like treaties, often contain expressions such as diplomatic phrases, political theories, mere exhortations, and
so on, which do not constitute legal norms. On the other
hand, even a rule intended as a rule of law is not a legal
norm if no sanction is provided, for instance, with regard
to the duties of a supreme organ. Such duties are moral,
not legal, duties. Now, from all that, one may deduce with
Verdross that positive law is not a closed autonomous body,
but anchored in ethics; but one can hardly deduce with
Ago that such non-legal norms are spontaneous law. Finally,
even a legal rule, created by the competent authority in a
prescribed procedure and providing for a sanction, is not

a legal norm if it is not "by and large effective." Mere paper rules are not legal norms.

A further point, unacceptable in Ago's theory, is the author's statement that customary law is not created at all, has no "source." Customary norms, the author holds, arise in the conscience of the members of a community; but this conscience is not their "source," but only their "seat." This is a typical pseudo-natural-law construction of customary law as it has often been presented under varying names: customary law is not "made," but pre-existing; there is no procedure of creation, but only "proof," "evidence," "la constatation" of a pre-existing, not man-made, rule of law. To this type of construction belongs the "Volksgeist" of German historical jurisprudence, the "solidarité sociale" of L. Duguit, the "biological necessity" of G. Scelle, the realist-Marxist version in Mario Giuliano, Barile's "rilevazione" of customary international law.

In close connection with this pseudo-natural-law construction is Ago's unacceptable teaching that the formulation of customary international law is the task of the science of law, exactly as Leon Duguit stated of his "droit objectif" that "the man feels it and the scholar formulates it." [15] Now, it is well settled that the science of law is *not* an organ of the creation of law. It can and should help the judge and the legislator by its scientific work; it can historically and theorically be of great importance to the development and interpretation of the law, but it is most certainly not a law-creating organ; its authority is not legally binding, although, by the intrinsic reasonableness of its findings, its authority may, to use the common-law term, be persuasive. That the science of law, to speak in this metaphorical term, is not a source of positive international law, whereas customary law, of course, is such source, is also clearly expressed in Article XXXVIII of the Statute of the International Court of Justice.

Apart from the historical and theoretical errors, Ago's theory of an ill-defined spontaneous law, to be formulated by the science of law, leads also to the danger—and that is Sereni's basic criticism [16]—of blurring the dividing line between law and non-law, to identify law with the *fait accompli;* for, in order to end this critique with a bit of semantics, what is "spontaneous"? [17]

[1] ROBERTO AGO, SCIENZA GIURIDICA E IL DIRITTO INTERNAZIONALE (1950).

[2] Ago, *Diritto Positivo e Diritto Internazionale*, originally published in 3 COMUNICAZIONI E STUDI 33–86 (1955). He lectured on this subject in French at the Hague Academy of International Law in 1955, and his lectures have been published in the RECUEIL DES COURS. For a version in German, cf., 6 ARCHIV DES VÖLKERRECHTS 257–307 (1957). For a version in English, see his article, *Positive Law and International Law*, 51 AM.J.INT'L L. 691 (1957).

[3] See Angelo Piero Sereni's critique, *Dottrine Italiane di Diritto Internazionale*, in 2 SCRITTI DI DIRITTO INTERNAZIONALE IN ONORE DI T. PERASSI 281–300, particularly at 285–89.

[4] *Fatti normativi.*

[5] See "The Nature of Customary International Law," above.

[6] Francisco a Vitoria, who uses the term "jus gentium' in the Roman sense and in the sense of later international law, says that the *jus gentium* is different from natural law. Francisco Suárez, who, first, uses the term "jus gentium" in the modern sense of international law, wrote unambiguously: "jus gentium simpliciter esse *humanum ac positivum.*"—De legibus, lib. II, cap. XIX.

[7] Ago himself quotes the definition of Damaso (1215): "jus positivum, expositum ab homine," and of Abelard: positive law is "quod ab hominibus institutum est." In both cases the term is used in contrast to natural law. In his discussion "De Indis," Vitoria writes that "paganism takes away neither natural, nor positive human law."

[8] "Law is always positive law, and its positivity lies in the fact that it is created and annulled by acts of human beings."—H. KELSEN, GENERAL THEORY OF LAW AND STATE 114 (1945).

[9] *Op. cit.* at 131.

[10] See, e.g., A. VERDROSS, VÖLKERRECHT 118 (3rd ed. 1955).

[11] "The rules of case law are the by-product of the continuous process of judicial settlement of particular controversies. The latter rules are not contained in official text form."—John Hanna, *The Role of Precedent in Judicial Decision*, VILL.L.R. 367–84 at 380 (1957).

[12] Abelard, defining positive as man-made law, distinguishes within positive law written and unwritten positive law. Suarez, defining *jus gentium* as positive, man-made law, states at the same time that it

is a law "quae magis traditione et consuetudine quam constitutione aliqua introductum est"; it is positive law, although primarily "non scriptum," but "ab usu."—De legibus, lib. III. cap. 2, no. 6.

13 H. KELSEN, WHAT IS JUSTICE? 258 (1957), reviewed in 51 AM. J.INT'L L. 830 (1957).

14 KELSEN, *op. cit.* at 45.

15 DUGUIT, L'ETAT, LE DROIT OBJECTIF ET LA LOI 16 (1901).

16 *Op. cit., supra,* note 3.

17 According to Funk and Wagnalls' *New Standard Dictionary of the English Language* (1956) p. 2349, "spontaneous" may mean many, even contrary, things: "Automatic, instinctive, involuntary, voluntary, willing. Voluntary and involuntary are both partial synonyms of spontaneous."

INTRODUCTION

FRIEDRICH NOTTEBOHM was born at Hamburg, Germany, a German national by birth and remained a German national until 1939. Since 1905, he had resided in Guatemala, where he carried on prosperous activities in the fields of commerce, banking, and plantation. At the end of March or the beginning of April, 1939, he left for Germany and applied in October, 1939, after the outbreak of World War II, for naturalization in the Principality of Liechtenstein and was naturalized on October 13, 1939. From this moment on he conducted himself exclusively as a national of Liechtenstein, particularly with regard to Guatemala, where he returned in 1940. On October 19, 1943, he was arrested by Guatemalan authorities and turned over to the armed forces of the United States in Guatemala. He was deported to the United States and interned there for two years and three months. During his internment in this country, in 1944, fifty-seven legal proceedings were commenced against him in Guatemala, designed to confiscate all his movable and immovable properties. When he was released from internment in the United States in 1946 and wanted to return to Guatamala to take up the defense against all the litigations pending against him there, he was refused readmission to Guatemala. In 1946 he went to Liechtenstein, where he has resided ever since. In 1949, three years after he had made Liechtenstein his effective and permanent domicile, his properties in Guatemala were confiscated under Guatemalan law.

By application, filed on December 11, 1951, at a time when Nottebohm had been domiciled in Liechtenstein for five years, the Principality, espousing his case, instituted proceedings in the International Court of Justice against Guatemala. By the judgment of November 18, 1953, the Court rejected the preliminary objection raised by Guatemala against the jurisdiction of the Court. In the second phase public hearings were held in February and March, 1955. In its memorial, Liechtenstein asked the Court, as far as the merits were concerned, to adjudge and declare that the government of Guatemala, by arresting, detaining, expelling, and refusing to readmit Nottebohm, and by seizing and retaining his property without compensation, acted in breach of its obligations under international law and, consequently, in a manner requiring the payment of reparation, and asked for payment by Guatemala, under various headings, of a sum perhaps running into ten million Swiss francs.

Guatemala had raised three pleas in bar, which, in the final submission, stated in substance:

> May it please the Court, as to admissibility, to declare that the claim of Liechtenstein is inadmissible.
>
> (1) on the ground of the absence of any prior diplomatic negotiations;
>
> (2) (a) on the ground that Nottebohm has not properly acquired Liechtenstein nationality in accordance with the law of Liechtenstein.
>
> (2) (b) on the ground that naturalization was not granted to Nottebohm in accordance with the generally recognized principles in regard to nationality;

(2) (c) in any case, on the ground that Nottebohm appears to have solicited Liechtenstein nationality fraudulently, that is to say, with the sole object of acquiring the status of a neutral national before returning to Guatemala and without any genuine intention to establish a durable link, excluding German nationality, between the Principality and himself.

(3) on the ground of the non-exhaustion by Nottebohm of the local remedies.

As to the merits, Guatemala asked the Court to hold that no violation of international law had been shown to have been committed in regard to Nottebohm, either in respect of his property or his person; more especially, in regard to the liquidation of his property, to declare that Guatemala was not obliged to regard the naturalization by Liechtenstein as binding upon her or as a bar to his treatment as an enemy national in the circumstances of the case.

Liechtenstein, in its reply and final submission, asked the Court to reject Guatemala's pleas in bar and to declare that the naturalization of Nottebohm was granted in accordance with the municipal law of Liechtenstein and was not contrary to international law. As to the merits, Liechtenstein, in its final submission, asked the Court to adjourn the oral proceedings for not less than three months.

The Court, considering only the admissibility of the claims before it, decided, by a majority of eleven to three, that Liechtenstein was not entitled to extend its protection vis-à-vis Guatemala, and declared, therefore, the claim to be inadmissible *a limine*.

The *Nottebohm Judgment* (Second Phase) of April 6, 1955,[1] has already provoked a vast literature.[2] Much of this literature is highly critical of the judgment, particularly the studies by Glazer, Jones, Löwenfeld, Makarov, Seidl-Hohenveldern, and Verzijl. These critical attacks follow the sharp critique of the judgment by the three dissenting judges.[3] Criticism of this judgment can also be found in recent treatises on international law,[4] and has inspired a whole book.[5] On the other hand, the study by Mme. Bastid, daughter of Judge Basdevant, is extremely favorable to the judgment. Favorable voices, particularly American and Italian, have also been heard in recent years. Some of these statements are made without going into any analysis,[6] others on the basis of doubtful reasoning.[7] A very favorable opinion on the judgment has recently been voiced by Professor Jessup.[8] It is highly to be regretted that Judge Lauterpacht, in his recent brilliant book on the Court,[9] could not treat the *Nottebohm Judgment* (Second Phase), since it was rendered after he himself had been elected one of the judges of the Court.

The judgment remains, therefore, highly controversial. On the other hand, all writers, whether they approve or attack the judgment, agree that it is of particular interest, of the highest importance, and possibly, of the most far-reaching effects. Under these circumstances, it seems justified to analyze the judgment once more. Naturally, this writer is absolutely in favor of judicial settlement of international conflicts and has the greatest respect for the two Courts and for their mission, not only to decide concrete cases, but also to develop international law. The *Nottebohm Judgment* is entitled to the highest respect. The majority with which it has been rendered is impressive; there is also a legal presumption in favor of the legal superiority of the majority opinion. But dissenting opinions may later become the law,[10] and "the degree of precariousness of the line dividing the content of a decision from the opposite is not invariably indicated by the size of the majority by which it was rendered." [11]

It is not intended here to go once more into all the relevant details of the practice of states, precedents, and literature, insofar as they have already been covered in previous writings on this judgment; the statement of the issue and references can here suffice; only newer developments, not

yet covered in the literature, will be treated in more detail.
What is intended here is to give a complete and comprehensive analysis, considering the arguments *pro* and *con*; to
study the judgment from all its aspects: from the point of
view of theoretical and methodological problems, to study it
de lege lata—from the points of view of matters of procedure and matters of substance—and to study it *de lege
ferenda*.

Such analysis is in the sole interest of international
justice; for scientific criticism takes away nothing from the
legally binding force of the judgment for the parties in this
case, and "the pronouncements of the Court, even if unanimous or approaching unanimity, are a legitimate object
of scientific scrutiny." [12]

THE JUDGMENT (SECOND PHASE)—DE LEGE LATA

A. Matters of Procedure

1. *The Issue of Exhaustiveness of Judicial Reasoning*

Judge Klaestad starts his dissenting opinion [13] with the
statement that the judgment deals with only one of the
three pleas in bar, and some writers criticize this procedure.
Common-law courts, it is true, have often given many
reasons, where one reason would have been sufficient, but
in other cases have also restricted themselves to a narrow
ground.[14] We fully recognize, with Judge Lauterpacht, the
great difference between a municipal court with compulsory
jurisdiction and private parties and an international court
with, in the last analysis, its voluntary and therefore precarious jurisdiction and sovereign states as parties. That
is why Judge Lauterpacht [15] devotes many pages to showing the necessity of exhaustive judicial reasoning and cu-
mulation of *rationes decidendi*, and gives many reasons and
examples; but he admits that "not every argument put for-

ward by a party requires an answer." Although, therefore, Judge Klaestad's statement is correct,[16] this is, in our opinion, no ground for criticism. The ground chosen by the Court is sufficient for its decision, and the decision is fully reasoned.

2. *The Narrow Ground and Narrow Range of the Judgment*

Notwithstanding what has been stated in the first paragraph, it is essential to keep the narrow ground and range of the judgment fully in mind in order to understand it correctly and to evaluate it, both *de lege lata* and *de lege ferenda.* It was the Court itself which underlined the narrow basis and range of the decision.[17] The judgment is, therefore, very much cut to this particular case. This fact has made some commentators raise the question whether the Court was not, however, unconsciously, too much under the impact of the fact that Nottebohm *had* been a German national and of the facts of Hitlerite aggression. But even the voicing of such doubt must be firmly rejected; for "judges, like Caesar's wife, should be above suspicion." [18]

Nevertheless, the narrow basis and range of the judgment have several consequences: (1) There is the possibility of a dangerously wide interpretation of the judgment.[19] (2) On the other hand, taking the narrowness seriously, coupled with the Court's "functional approach," may lead to paradoxical consequences. (3) The narrow basis and range of the judgment make the whole reasoning of the Court rather hybrid, as this reasoning goes, and is bound to go much beyond the task of giving adequate reasons for this narrow judgment.[20]

3. *The Basic Decision Was Neither Invoked Nor Discussed by the Parties*

When the Court limited its task to adjudication upon the admissibility of Liechtenstein's claim vis-à-vis Guatemala, it added that it would adjudicate this issue "on the basis of such reasons as it may itself consider relevant and proper." And that it did, on a basis, as Mervyn Jones states, "not even contended for by Guatemala nor discussed by Liechtenstein." [21] Judge Klaestad severely criticizes the solution upon these lines: on the ground that it does not conform with the argument and evidence submitted by the parties; and he adds that some facts "show how necessary it would have been, in the interest of a proper administration of justice, to afford to the Parties an opportunity to argue this point before it is decided." [22] Judge Read [23] goes even farther, and states that the matter is governed by the principle which the Court applied in the *Ambatielos Case* (Jurisdiction) of July 1, 1952: "The point raised here has not yet been fully argued by the parties and cannot, therefore, be decided at this stage." [24]

4. *The Issue of Adjournment*

Guatemala contended that Nottebohm had applied for and obtained Liechtenstein nationality fraudulently. As no documentary evidence had been given by Guatemala with regard to this allegation in the course of the written proceedings, the agent of Guatemala, after the close of the written proceedings and a few days before the oral hearings, submitted to the Court a considerable number of new documents. The agent of Liechtenstein objected to the production of these documents. The Court decided on February 14, 1955, to permit the production of all these new documents, but

> reserved to the Agent of the Government of Liechtenstein the right . . . to avail himself of the opportunity provided for in the second paragraph of Article 48 of the Rules of the Court, after having heard the contentions of the Agent of the Government of Guatemala based on these documents, and after such lapse of time as the Court might, on his request, deem just.[25]

On the basis of these new documents, Guatemala submitted in the oral proceedings the new allegations of
fraudulent concealment of enemy property. Liechtenstein,
in its final submission as to the merits, requested the Court
"to adjourn the oral pleadings for not less than three
months in order that Liechtenstein may obtain and as-
semble documents in support of comments on the new
documents produced by Guatemala."

But the judgment considered it "unnecessary to have
regard to the documents," and rejected Liechtenstein's demand for adjournment, also on the technical ground that
Liechtenstein, in asking for an adjournment, "did so only
for the eventuality of the Application being held to be admissible and not for the purpose of throwing further light
upon the question of the admissibility of the Application." [26]

This procedure was — we believe rightly — severely
attacked by Judge Klaestad [27] and *ad hoc* Judge Guggenheim,[28] who strongly felt, in view of Article XLVIII, paragraph 2, of the Rules of the Court and the Court's decision
of February 14, 1955, as well as of Liechtenstein's demand,
that adjournment should have been granted by the Court;
all the more so, as, in Judge Klaestad's opinion, "these
allegations of fraud now appear to constitute the main
aspect of the case." In fact, *ad hoc* Judge Guggenheim
opens, and Judge Klaestad begins and ends his dissenting
opinion, with the statement that the case should have been
adjourned.

5. *The Issue of Joining the Pleas in Bar with the Merits*

The problem of adjournment is closely connected with
the issue of joining the pleas in bar with the merits. A
plea in bar may be so closely connected with the merits that
it is impossible to adjudicate the former without prejudging
the latter. Judge Lauterpacht [29] fully discusses the problem
of joinder of jurisdictional objections to the merits and
cites many cases in which the Court has ordered such

joinder.[30] All the considerations given by the Court for such joinder in earlier cases apply eminently to Guatemala's pleas in bar. Such joinder to the merits was, therefore, strongly insisted upon by Judges Klaestad[31] and Read,[32] and *ad hoc* Judge Guggenheim.[33]

6. *Granting the Plea in Bar Cuts off the Decision on the Merits*

Just as the issue of adjournment is closely connected with the issue of joining the pleas in bar with the merits, thus both these issues are closely related to the obvious consequence of granting the plea in bar, namely, of preventing the Court from adjudicating upon the merits of the case. Judge Read forcefully states:

> The allowance of a plea in bar prevents an examination by the Court of the issues of law and fact which constitute the merits of the case. It would be unjust to refuse to examine a claim on the merits on the basis of findings of law or fact which might be reversed if the merits were considered and dealt with.[34]

And he equally forcefully brings out a second consequence:

> . . . The allowance of the plea in bar would ensure that justice would not be done on any plane, national or international. I do not think that a plea in bar, which would have such an effect, should be granted, unless the grounds on which it is based are beyond doubt.[35]

Ad hoc Judge Guggenheim emphasizes that a preliminary objection must be strictly interpreted and must not prevent justice from being done.[36]

The consequences of the granting of the pleas in bar and thereby cutting off adjudication as to the merits are, indeed, far reaching in two aspects:

(A) The real issue in the *Nottebohm* case—apart from the complaints of arresting, deporting, and not re-admitting him—is that of the legality under international law of the confiscation of his property, even if he had been, which he was not, a German national, i.e., an alien enemy, at the critical time. Many writers hold this confiscation of private property as a war measure to be illegal [37] and, particularly, confiscation by states which have made only paper declarations of war. Here was a rare opportunity for the Court to adjudicate authoritatively upon the legality under international law of these war confiscations. It deprived itself of this opportunity.

(B) The judgment prevented justice from being done to Nottebohm,[38] making him, for all practical purposes, a stateless person and depriving him of the only legal remedy he had.[39]

There are other issues in this case which have procedural aspects, such as whether it is allowed to consider the motives, the problem of burden of proof, the issues of estoppel and of denial of justice; but they will be more conveniently dealt with in considering matters of substance.

B. Matters of Substance

1. *Competence of an International Tribunal to Investigate and Decide upon the Nationality of Claims*

It is universally recognized that an international court or tribunal is competent to investigate and decide the true nationality of a claim; this is not only its right, but also its duty, as its own jurisdiction depends on the true nationality of the claim. Hence also an official document concerning nationality has, it is true, particular value, constituting prima facie evidence, but is rebuttable. That this is the law is shown by the unanimity of the literature and by many international decisions, such as the *Flutie Cases*.[40] Invoking the *Flutie Cases* and the precedents there quoted, the United States–Italian Conciliation Commission, established

under the Peace Treaty with Italy of 1947, in a recent case
has taken a particularly strong stand. The Commission
stated:

> Abundant doctrine in international law confirms the power of
> an international court to investigate the existence of the nation-
> ality of the claimant, even when this is established *prima facie*
> by the documents issued by the State to which he owes allegiance
> and in conformity with the legislation of said State. . . .
>   The Commission, in conformity with the case law of interna-
> tional tribunals . . . is not bound by the provisions of the na-
> tional law in question, either as regards the manner or as regards
> the form in which proof of nationality must be submitted.[41]

That this is so, is fully granted by *ad hoc* Judge Guggenheim, but he also states the limitations:

> The plaintiff must therefore *prove* that nationality has been
> conferred by means of a valid act in accordance with the mu-
> nicipal law of the claimant State; and the defendant, if he dis-
> putes this, must establish the contrary.[42]

The burden of proof was, therefore, here on Guatemala.
Further, an international court can only "up to a certain
extent" ascertain whether the nationality exists; the court
"*cannot freely* examine the application and interpretation
of municipal law"; particularly the court cannot decide
with regard to the discretionary power of administrative
authorities; "it cannot exercise the power of a Court of
Appeal with regard to municipal law"; in the same sense
Judge Klaestad [43] and Judge Read.[44]

Here the issue of an international court's powers to investigate and decide the nationality of claims must be discussed, because of the reasoning of the parties and because
of Guatemala's pleas in bar (2a and 2b). The judgment, it
is true, is not based on the exercise of such competence;

for, without deciding the validity of Nottebohm's nationality, it takes it for granted.

2. *Nationality in International Law* [45]

To create a theoretical framework for the evaluation of the judgment, it seems necessary to give a brief exposé on nationality in international law.[46] Our international law came historically into being by the decentralization of the medieval European *communitas Christiana* into a plurality of sovereign states. International law and sovereignty developed, therefore, *uno actu*. Sovereignty, a basic concept of present international law, as a legal concept, is a bundle of competences conferred by international law. Any a priori or unlimited political concept of sovereignty must, with inescapable logic, lead to the non-existence of international law as law. Sovereignty is, therefore, essentially a relative notion; its content depends on the stage of development of international law. In order to guarantee a somewhat peaceful living together of a plurality of sovereign states, international law, as its first task, had to delimit the competences of the legal order of the sovereign states as to space, as to persons, as to matters, and as to time.

As the sovereign states and the international community are primarily territorial communities today, international law delimited the competences between sovereign states as to space by direct rules of international law, rules of content. But international law delimited the personal competence of sovereign states only indirectly, by rules of competence, giving to the sovereign states, and only to them,[47] the competence to regulate the acquisition and loss of their nationality in principle through their municipal legislation, as they think fit. This is positive international law, recognized by the Hague Codification Conference of 1930, by the Harvard Research in International Law,[48] by

international courts and tribunals, by the literature. "In
the present state of international law,"—this phrase is
revealing—stated the Permanent Court of International
Justice, "Questions of nationality are, in principle, within
the reserved domain"; [49] Article I of the Hague Convention
on the Conflict of Nationality Laws of April 12, 1930,
states: "It is for each State to determine under its own law
who are its nationals." [50]

Furthermore, it is necessary to distinguish clearly between "nationality" and "citizenship." Nationality is a
concept of international law, citizenship a concept of municipal law. International law is only concerned with nationality, the "belonging of a person to a state." As the quoted
Article I correctly states, sovereign states are given the
competence to determine who are their "nationals," not
merely their citizens. The *Nottebohm* case turns on his
nationality, not his Liechtenstein citizenship.

This determination of nationality belongs to the *domaine
réservé* of the sovereign states; but what belongs to this
exclusive jurisdiction is, as the Permanent Court of International Justice in 1923 correctly stated, "an essentially
relative question; it depends upon the development of international relations." There are *no* matters at all which "by
nature" belong to this reserved domain, which "can" only
be regulated by municipal law. And this right of the sovereign states is, as the Court in 1923 also correctly stated,
a competence given to them *by* international law. But it is
incorrect, as the Court in 1923 did, to speak of matters of
reserved domain as "matters not regulated by international
law." They *are* regulated by international law through this
attribution of competence to the sovereign states; if a
federal constitution attributes to the states of the union the
exclusive competence to legislate upon matters of the law
of domestic relations, it cannot be said that this matter is
not regulated by federal law. Because of the *compétence de*

la compétence in favor of international law, the latter may regulate problems of nationality directly by rules of international law, rules of content, as is often done by peace treaties, treaties of cession, the minorities treaties concluded at the end of World War I. States may conclude treaties on problems of nationality bilaterally or multilaterally.

International law gives to sovereign states the competence to determine by municipal law who are their nationals only *in principle.* They have a wide discretionary competence, but their competence is *not* unlimited; it is indeed, in a wide and somewhat vague way, *limited* by general international law. The states may choose between many and different connections for granting their nationality; all these often conflicting principles, such as *jus soli* and *jus sanguinis*, may be legally applied by different states. It is evident that no clear repartition of human beings between the different states can result; hence, international law recognizes multiple nationality as well as statelessness.

But all these various principles, however different, have one thing in common: there is between the state granting its nationality and the person to which it is granted *some* connection which present-day international law considers sufficient. In *this* sense, we may speak of a wide "link" necessity, as pertaining to the international law actually in force.

Hence, if a state confers its nationality on a person in consequence of the competence given to it by international law and *within* this widest limitation established by general international law, it executes not only an act of municipal law, but it executes an international competence given to it. That is why "this law shall be recognized by other states"; that is why "any question as to whether a person possesses the nationality of a particular state shall be determined in accordance with the law of that state." [51] If, on the other hand, a state confers its nationality in disregard of this broad limitation, it acts in violation of international law by conferring it, e.g., on a person who has no connection at all with this state or a connection which, under present-day international law, is not recognized as sufficient, such as mere acquisition of real estate in a country or compulsory naturalization. In such a case, foreign states not only need not recognize the nationality thus conferred, but may protest against the statute, demand its abolition regardless of damage suffered, and not merely refuse to recognize it in connection with diplomatic protection.

General international law may contain other rules limiting the validity of the grant of nationality; but such norms seem to have developed only with regard to fraud and with regard to the still controversial concept of abuse of rights (*abus de droit*).

3. *The Issue of Estoppel and the "Functional Approach"*

Was not Guatemala estopped by her own acts from denying that she had recognized Nottebohm's Liechtenstein nationality? The judgment itself enumerates all these acts: granting a visa of Guatemala to Nottebohm's Liechtenstein passport; registering him in Guatemala in the Register of Aliens as a Liechtenstein national, changing his identity document in the same sense; issuance of a certificate to the same effect by the Civil Registry of Guatemala.[52] But the Court reasoned that "no proof has been adduced that Guatemala had recognized the title to the exercise of protection relied upon by Liechtenstein as being derived from the naturalization it granted to Nottebohm." A number of writers state that a case of estoppel could have been made, but that the judgment rejected the estoppel. That analysis is incorrect. Van Panhuys is right when he says that "even the principle of estoppel was applied in a functional way," [53] for the Court held that these acts of recognition by Guatemala refer only to "control of aliens," and not to diplomatic protection.

This "functional approach"—so dear to the American "Realist School"—applied throughout the judgment, has far-reaching consequences. The first is the tearing apart of the "recognition by other states," [54] for all purposes of which Article I of the 1930 Hague Convention speaks. Second, this "functional approach" has the paradoxical consequence that Guatemala *is*, perhaps, estopped from denying Nottebohm's Liechtenstein nationality for all other purposes except diplomatic protection. Here Judge Read's argumentation comes in.[55] Nottebohm's admission as a Liechtenstein national brought into play the obligations which general international law prescribes as to the treatment of resident aliens. Guatemala contended that Nottebohm, who had been admitted to Guatemala as a Liechtenstein national, had, with regard to his person and with regard to the confiscation of his property, not been treated in violation of international law. But the treatment by Guatemala made Judge Read declare: "I am bound, in such circumstances, to proceed on the assumption that Liechtenstein might be entitled to a finding of denial of justice, if the case should be considered on the merits." Hence Guatemala will be estopped from denying Nottebohm's Liechtenstein nationality for all purposes, yet, as she is not estopped so far as diplomatic protection is concerned, Nottebohm is deprived of the *only* legal remedy he had.

4. *Was Liechtenstein Nationality Granted to Nottebohm in Accordance with Liechtenstein Law?*

That it was not was Guatemala's plea in bar (2a) as a ground for the inadmissibility of the application. The judgment merely briefly states that Liechtenstein produced a certificate of naturalization, and gives the circumstances under which naturalization was granted to Nottebohm under the Liechtenstein Nationality Law of January 4, 1934.[56] Guatemala had attacked the validity of the naturalization, particularly with regard to two points.

One point made was that Nottebohm had not lost his German nationality. The answer to this allegation is: (A) Nottebohm *did* lose his German nationality automatically under the German Nationality Law of July 22, 1913, Article XXV. A certificate of the Senate of Hamburg of June 15, 1954, was produced attesting the loss of German nationality by Nottebohm in consequence of his naturalization by Liechtenstein. Under Article II of the Hague Convention of 1930, the question whether a person possesses German nationality must be determined in accordance with German law. (B) Guatemala was unable to prove its allegation, and the burden of proof was on the defendant.[57] (C) Under international law, the validity of a naturalization does not depend on the loss of earlier nationality.

Guatemala's other point was that the Liechtenstein law demands that the "applicant must have ordinarily resided in the territory of Liechtenstein for at least three years"; but, under the same law, "the applicant can be exempted from this requirement by way of exception." The grant of this exception is, under Liechtenstein law, by discretionary decision of the reigning prince, a decision which cannot be reviewed by the State Court of Liechtenstein The reigning prince *had* granted the exemption. There cannot be the slightest doubt that, as far as Liechtenstein law is concerned, Nottebohm had been a Liechtenstein national since 1939, and Guatemala's contention to the contrary "fails through lack of evidence to support it."[58]

5. *Was Liechtenstein Nationality Granted to Nottebohm in Accordance with International Law?*

That it was not was Guatemala's plea in bar (2b) as a ground for the inadmissibility of the application. Both parties agreed that, under Articles I and II of the Hague Convention of 1930, it is for each state to determine under its own law who are its nationals, and that this law shall be recognized by other states "in so far as it is consistent with international conventions, international custom, and the principles of law generally recognized with regard to nationality." This agreement on Article II resolves nothing; neither does its invocation by the Court, as this article is in abstract terms and contains no criteria; it had been controversial in the literature. There were, of course, no treaties between Liechtenstein and Guatemala. Guatemala conceded that "there is no system of customary rules nor any rigid principles by which States are bound"; only rules concerning fraud and abuse of rights exist.[59]

(A) The issue of abuse of right (*abus de droit*).—This issue is still controversial.[60] It is not necessary to investigate it further because it is recognized that

> the doctrine . . . cannot be invoked by one State against another unless the State which is admittedly exercising its rights under international law causes damage to the State invoking the doctrine.
> . . . It is sufficient to point out that Liechtenstein caused no damage to Guatemala. . . . "

(B) The issue of fraud.—The issue of fraud was brought up by Guatemala in different ways. It was said that Liechtenstein had acted fraudulently in granting its nationality to Nottebohm. But, as Judge Klaestad stated, the burden of proof was on Guatemala, and "no evidence has been given in support of such contention." No damage was caused to Liechtenstein; finally, Guatemala was not at war with Germany.

It was further contended that Nottebohm did not act in good faith, but fraudulently, in applying for and in obtaining the certificate of naturalization. Here again no

proof was given by Guatemala. It was said that his motive
was not to dissociate himself from Germany but solely "to
escape from the consequences of his German nationality
under the shield of a neutral nationality." But, as the dissenting opinions and many writers state, this contention is
untenable for many reasons. First, the burden of proof was
on Guatemala and no such proof was given. Second, it is
hardly admissible for the Court to consider the motives of
Nottebohm and it is extremely difficult to prove them. Third,
he *did* lose his German nationality. Fourth, it is of the greatest importance to insist upon the fact that Guatemala in
October, 1939, was not at war with Germany. This was the
time of the First Consultative Meeting of the Foreign Ministers of the American Republics at Panama, where a declaration of Pan-American neutrality was adopted, a "Pan
American Neutrality Zone" was established, and the Inter-
American Neutrality Committee was set up. Fifth, even
if Nottebohm had changed his nationality for the purpose
of becoming the national of a neutral state, there existed
no rule of municipal or international law rendering his
naturalization invalid for that reason only.

Finally, Guatemala charged later that Nottebohm's case
was a "cloaking case," to use such naturalization as a
cloak for the property of enemy nationals in Guatemala.
But, as has been stated before, these allegations were not
proved and could be considered only by granting an adjournment and joining the pleas in bar to the merits.[62]

6. *The Judgment's Dualistic Conception of International Law*

As the case stood, it must be said that Nottebohm certainly did acquire Liechtenstein nationality, and did so validly, both under Liechtenstein and international law. Nor
did the judgment adopt the allegations of Guatemala's
pleas in bar (2a and 2b), although it is unfortunate that

the Court twice,[63] rather one-sidedly, refers to allegations concerning fraud, which had not been proved by Guatemala. The judgment does not adjudicate upon the validity of the acquisition of Liechtenstein nationality by Nottebohm.[64]

The judgment approaches the issue of nationality in an orthodox way:

> It is for Liechtenstein, as it is for every sovereign State, to settle by its own legislation the rules relating to acquisition of its nationality. . . . It is not necessary to determine whether international law imposes any limitations on its freedom of decision in this domain. Furthermore, nationality has its most immediate, its most far-reaching and, for most people, its only effects within the legal system of the State conferring it. Nationality serves above all to determine that the person upon whom it is conferred enjoys the rights and is bound by the obligations which the law of the State in question grants to or imposes on its nationals. This is implied in the wider concept that nationality is within the domestic jurisdiction of the State.
>
> To exercise protection, to apply to the Court, is to place oneself on the plane of international law. . . .
>
> The naturalization of Nottebohm was an act performed by Liechtenstein in the exercise of its domestic jurisdiction. The question to be decided is whether that act has the international effect here under consideration.[65]

These dicta cannot be accepted. First, there is an obvious confusion between nationality, a concept relevant in international law, and citizenship. The question here turns on Nottebohm's nationality, not on his Liechtenstein citizenship.

Second, it is highly to be regretted that this judgment of the highest international court reveals an extreme dualistic conception of international law, a conception which is theoretically untenable and apt to lead to the denial of international law as law. The judgment, in typically extreme dualistic fashion, makes a complete separation between municipal and international law. It creates the impression that a sovereign state, in granting its nationality and in making its nationality law, acts on a purely domestic level and by its own authority,[66] and that a state's "reserved domain" has nothing to do with international law. This exclusive jurisdiction is, as the Permanent Court of International Justice correctly stated, given to the state *by* international law. The states, having the attribution of competence given to them by international law, a competence authorizing them to confer their nationality, not only their citizenship, perform an international act. That is why third states have to recognize this nationality; that is why third states have to determine the nationality of a person under the law of the state in question. But this competence granted to the states is not unlimited but limited by what we have called the link theory in the widest sense. If, on the other hand, states enact a nationality law or confer nationality of this widest limitation set by international law, they commit an international delinquency.

7. *The Specific Link Theory*

While recognizing indirectly the validity of Nottebohm's Liechtenstein nationality, the judgment creates the specific link theory *ex novo*. This theory can be stated in the judgment's own words:

> . . . Nationality is a legal bond having as its basis a social fact of attachment, a genuine connection of existence, interests and sentiments, together with the existence of reciprocal rights and duties. It may be said to constitute the juridical expression of the fact that the individual upon whom it is conferred, either directly by the law or as the result of an act of the authorities, is in fact more closely connected with the population of the State conferring nationality than with that of any other State . . . it constitutes a translation into juridical terms of the individual's connection with the State which has made him its national.[67]

And the Court states apodictically: "This is the character which nationality must present." [68]

8. *Critique of the Specific Link Theory*

It is, of course, true, that the judgment does not create the specific link theory as a precondition for the validity of a nationality, but, always using the "functional approach," only as a sufficient title for Liechtenstein's right to exercise diplomatic protection with regard to Nottebohm, and even so only with regard to diplomatic protection exercised by an application to the International Court of Justice, and only vis-à-vis Guatemala. The Court had to consider the case of the acquisition of nationality by way of naturalization. But, in spite of the narrow basis and the narrow range of the judgment, it referred to all kinds of acquisition of nationality. That can be seen by the Court's mentioning the different principles, basic for the grant of nationality and necessary by the diversity of ethnographic conditions. The judgment declared that

> a State cannot claim that the rules it has thus laid down are entitled to recognition by another State unless it has acted in conformity with this general aim of making the legal bond of nationality accord with the individual's genuine connection with the State.[69]

That the genuine link is thus a functional precondition for all types of grants of nationality is further affirmed by the Court's dictum speaking of nationality "conferred, either directly by the law or as the result of an act of the authorities."

(A) We have noted before that this basic decision was neither claimed nor discussed by the parties. The "genuine link" theory was only indirectly discussed on behalf of Guatemala in connection with the argument of abuse of right. Here Professor Henri Rolin (Belgium), counsel for Guatemala, the brilliant international advocate who may be said to have won by his pleadings the *Anglo-Iranian Case* for Iran, developed this theory with his usual skill and subtlety. But it is not in this sense that the Court adopted it.

(B) Whether the genuine link theory would be desirable *de lege ferenda,* has, of course, no importance in evaluating the judgment *de lege lata.* The Court stated correctly, as it was bound to do, that "it must decide this question on the basis of international law," [70] Did it do so? With regard to this problem, the statement of Judge Read is pertinent:

> . . . I do not question the desirability of establishing some lim-
> itation on the wide discretionary power possessed by sovereign
> States: the right, under international law, to determine . . .
> who are their own nationals and to protect such nationals.
> Nevertheless, I am bound, by Article 38 of the Statute, to
> apply international law as it is—positive law—and not inter-
> national law as it might be if a Codification Conference suc-
> ceeded in establishing new rules limiting the conferring of
> nationality by sovereign States. . . .[71]

Under Article XXXVIII of the Statute, the Court is under a duty "to decide in accordance with international law," i.e., in accordance with international conventions, international customary law, or, as a source, if there are no conventions and customary law, the general principles of law recognized by civilized nations; and, finally, as a mere subsidiary means for the determination of rules of international law, judicial decisions and the teachings of the most highly qualified publicists of the various nations. This wording constitutes a compromise between civil-law and common-law jurists.

(C) True, the "genuine link" theory was not invented by the Court. But the Court was unable to quote treaties or to show any general principles of law. There are writers (like Redslob) who have defended this theory; but the sharp attack to which the *Nottebohm Judgment* has been sub-jected by many writers of different nations proves con-vincingly that this theory by no means constitutes the *communis doctorum opinio.* The Court, like Guatemala, was unable to quote a single judicial precedent in favor of the genuine link theory as constituting positive international law. It is certainly true that the genuine link theory finds expression in the practice of a number of states, such as the United States and many others.[72] It is perfectly true that many nationality laws demand previous domicile for granting nationality by way of naturalization. But it is one-sided if the Court states that "the Liechtenstein Law of January 4th, 1934, is a good example" of the genuine link theory.[73] Liechtenstein and Guatemala had agreed that dispensations from the requirements of previous domicile are frequent. As Mervyn Jones states,[74] Guatemala's own nationality law exempts from the condition of five-years' residence "Spaniards and Ibero-Americans without defining them." The Court could, therefore, have stated equally well that Guatemala's own nationality law is a good example of the dispensation from the requirement of previous domicile. There are states which allow naturalization, "as an exceptional measure" without any connection.[75] There are, finally, states granting naturalization without any condition;[76] none of these laws has been attacked as being in violation of international law. Certainly, compulsory naturalization is internationally illegal; there must be, as Sereni states, a minimum link; but "even the most tenuous links are sufficient to justify the grant of nationality to one who voluntarily applies for it";[77] or, as Van Panhuys formulates it, "the voluntary application by the applicant and the willingness of the state to grant its nationality constitute the minimum link which general international law demands." [78] The practice of states proves the statement by Judge Klaestad that "international law does not, however, require previous residence in the country as a condition for naturalization, nor does it presuppose a subsequent residence in the country as a condition for naturalization, nor does it presuppose a subsequent residence there." [79]

The Court has not been able to prove a rule of customary general international law establishing the condition of a genuine link for other forms of acquisition of nationality. It is clear that the acquisition of nationality *jure soli* may be wholly fortuitous, and a child may have no specific link at all with the country in which it has been born. On the other hand, a person may be a national of a state *jure sanguinis* without having the slightest genuine link with that country. Both types of situations are very frequent and never have been regarded illegal by the practice of states. In this sense Judge Read remarks:

> In the case of many countries such as China, France, the United Kingdom and the Netherlands, the non-resident citizens form an important part of the body politic and are numbered in their hundreds of thousands or millions. Many of these non-resident citizens have never been within the confines of the home State.[80]

Ad hoc Judge Guggenheim states:

> International law does not, for example, in any way prohibit a State from claiming as its nationals, at the moment of their birth, the descendants of its nationals who have been resident abroad for centuries and whose only link with the State which grants its nationality is to be found in descent, without the requirement of any other element connecting them with that State. . . .[81]

The Court has, therefore, been unable to quote precedents or to show a rule of customary general international law in favor of the requirement of a genuine link, particularly if we take into consideration the very stringent conditions which the Court laid down in the *Asylum Case* for the coming into existence of a rule of customary international law.[82]

(D) It is highly interesting to note—a circumstance not mentioned in the judgment—that five years prior to the *Nottebohm Judgment,* when Nottebohm brought an action against the United States for reparation as the result of the seizure of his property as that of an alien enemy, the action was settled out of court in favor of Nottebohm; it was recognized by the United States that "the evidence showed the party . . . as non-enemy."[83]

(E) There is another critique, valid also *de lege ferenda*. The Court itself states that previous or subsequent domicile in the country of naturalization is, by no means, the only proof of a genuine link:

> Different factors are taken into consideration, and their importance will vary from one case to the next: the habitual residence of the individual concerned is an important factor, but there are other factors such as the centre of his interests, his family ties, his participation in public life, attachment shown by him for a given country and inculcated in his children, etc.[84]

Thus, the *new* rule created by the Court replaces the objective criteria of nationality with vague and subjective criteria, a replacement that is bound to lead to uncertainty. Judge Read makes a strong attack.

> . . . When one considers the occasions for invoking [nationality] . . . it becomes evident that certainty is essential. There must be objective tests, readily established, for the existence and recognition of the status. That is why the practice of States has steadfastly rejected vague and subjective tests . . . sincerity, fidelity, durability, lack of substantial connection. . . .[85]

In the same sense *ad hoc* Judge Guggenheim attacks the replacement of objective by subjective considerations, points to the fact that the new rule is in no way in accordance with present practice, and warns of the danger that such vague principles would open the door to arbitrary decisions.[86]

(F) As the Court, by its own authority, established the *new* rule of the "genuine link," it measured the facts of the case as against this new rule and tried to show that the

conditions of this new rule are not fulfilled. The Court
asked "whether the factual connection between Nottebohm
and Liechtenstein in the period preceding, contemporaneous
with and following his naturalization appears to be sufficiently close, so preponderant in relation to any connection
which may have existed between him and any other State,
that it is possible to regard the nationality conferred upon
him as real and effective, as the exact juridical expression
of a social fact." Let us repeat that nothing in positive
international law authorized this question. The Court then
goes on to say that Nottebohm had no settled abode in
Liechtenstein, no interests exercised or to be exercised
there, no intention to transfer all or some of his interests
and business activities there; that the naturalization was
lacking in the genuineness requisite to an act of such importance.[87] All these statements are legally irrelevant, because they do not refer to conditions established by positive
international law.

But there are also one-sided statements in the judgment,
based on motives or referring to allegations by Guatemala
which she has failed to prove. Thus the Court states that he
had always retained his connections with members of his
family who had remained in Germany, and always had business connections with that country. Quite correct; but is
there here anything illegal under municipal or international
law? And when the Court continues that "there is nothing
to indicate that the application for naturalization . . . was
motivated by any desire to dissociate himself from the
Government of his country," we are amazed; not only is this
a statement of motives, but there is no proof that Nottebohm, while having business and family connections with
Germany, was politically an adherent of the Hitler government. The Court, in rather strange statements, says that in
1946 he attempted to return to Guatemala, "and he now
complains of Guatemala's refusal to admit him"; that

"there, too, were several members of his family who sought to safeguard his interests"; that he went to Liechtenstein only because of the refusal of Guatemala to admit him; that he did not in any way alter his manner of life.[88]

This extremely one-sided recital is vigorously attacked by Judge Klaestad, who correctly states that Guatemala had taken measures to confiscate his property during his internment in the United States and that it was only natural that he wanted to return to Guatemala to defend his interests. The dissenting judge recalls that Nottebohm's property was confiscated in 1949, at a time when he had been domiciled for more than three years in Liechtenstein.[89] At the time of the judgment, we may add, Nottebohm had been a Liechtenstein national for sixteen years and had fulfilled even the "genuine link" condition by a domicile in Liechtenstein for nine years. Much more detailed is the criticism by Judge Read [90] and by *ad hoc* Judge Guggenheim.[91]

9. *The Special Problem of Dual and Multiple Nationality*

As the Court was unable to prove that its new genuine link theory is positive international law with regard to the case at bar, namely, with regard to an individual who, at all times of his life, had only one nationality, it took refuge in its reasonings as to the very particular and entirely different problem of dual and multiple nationality. It is, therefore, necessary to investigate this problem. The judgment [92] bases its reasoning on the problem of dual nationality, which in no way fits this case. The Court, considering the narrow basis and the narrow range of the judgment, had to deal with the acquisition of nationality by naturalization and the validity of the naturalization as a sufficient title for Liechtenstein's right to exercise diplo-

matic protection by way of an application to the International Court of Justice vis-à-vis Guatemala. But, in spite of this narrow range, in spite of its functional approach, the reasoning of the judgment necessarily goes farther. It speaks of all types of double nationality, e.g., through a conflict of the *jus soli* and *jus sanguinis*. It speaks of a conflict of nationality not only from the point of view of the exercise of diplomatic protection through an application to the International Court of Justice vis-à-vis a particular state. The judgment is forced to admit that "in most cases arbitrators have not strictly speaking had to decide a conflict of nationality as between States"; that "courts of third States . . . have done so not in connection with the exercise of protection, which did not arise before them." [93]
    The judgment states that

> International arbitrators [in cases of dual nationality] . . . have given their preference to the real and effective nationality, that which accorded with the facts, that based on stronger factual ties between the person concerned and one of the States whose nationality is involved.[94]

The judgment cites the Bancroft Treaties, and concludes wrongly that the "genuine link" theory is proved by the practice of states, arbitral and judical decisions, and the opinion of the writers. The judgment itself does not invoke any established rule of international law, but speaks only of "tendencies." [95] The judgment invokes the studies under the auspices of the League of Nations and the United Nations and Articles I and V of the 1930 Hague Convention.
    Has the judgment, at least with regard to the entirely different problem of dual or multiple nationality, proved the genuine link theory as a condition established by general international law? We think not. First, such problems arose in third states, not with regard to diplomatic protection, but with regard to conflicts concerning military

service, with regard to treaty rights enjoyed by the nationals of a particular state, with regard to problems of conflict of laws, where nationality may play a subordinate role, as e.g., in common-law countries the connecting factor is not nationality, but domicile; there are, therefore, no precedents for the case at bar. The quotation of the Bancroft Treaties is not pertinent, as Judge Read [96] and *ad hoc* Judge Guggenheim,[97] as well as many writers, point out; they do not constitute a precedent for the *Nottebohm* case. These treaties were bilateral treaties, binding only on the contracting parties, to which neither Liechtenstein nor Guatemala belonged; they were abrogated on November 6, 1917, and cannot be regarded as reflecting the rules of general international law. The present case, as *ad hoc* Judge Guggenheim points out, is entirely different: Nottebohm was not a Liechtenstein national who went to Guatemala, was naturalized there, and returned to Liechtenstein. Also the Judgment's invocation of Articles I and V of the 1930 Hague Convention means little; the judgment does not invoke the first sentence of Article I, nor the very different, but basic, Articles III and IV. In order to show a customary rule of general international law, it is necessary, as the Court did in the *Asylum Case*,[98] to point out to repeated and recurrent acts; no evidence of such custom has been given.[99]

As to precedents concerning double nationality in municipal courts and international tribunals, the pattern is, by no means, so simple, but rather involved. In *Re Chamberlain's Settlement* [100] the court decided to take over Chamberlain's assets in England under the Treaty of Versailles, holding him to be a German, i.e., an ex-enemy national, under German law, although he was also a native-born British subject and his German naturalization at a time when the King was at war with Germany would, under English law, normally not be recognized. At the same time, the court made it crystal clear that, should he ever return to England, he would be hanged for high treason, the court regarding him for purposes of *that* action exclusively as a British subject.

As to the international tribunals occupied with the problem of dual or multiple nationality, we must distinguish:

(A) If a person has two or more nationalities, he may be regarded as its national by each of the states whose nationality he possesses. This is the basic rule of Article III of the Hague Convention of 1930. Each state may regard him *exclusively* as its own national, regardless of any "genuine link" requirement. Hence, *each* state may exercise diplomatic protection vis-à vis *third* states. Thus, in *William MacKenzie v. Germany*,[101] the United States espoused the case of a British subject, born in Canada of a British father, who *jure soli* was also an American national, who had returned to England while still a minor. No "genuine link" with the United States prior to settling in Massachusetts in 1894 could have been claimed.

(B) An exception is when the problem of dual nationality arises within a third state, and only for this hypothesis the exceptional rule of Article V of the Hague Convention of 1930 is made. But the same problem may arise in an international tribunal, if a state espouses the case of a dual national against a state of which he is *not* a national. The same problem may also arise, apart from diplomatic protection, if a dual national himself can bring an action against a state of which he does not possess the nationality, as was possible under the Mixed Arbitral Tribunals established by the Peace Treaties concluded after World War I.[102] Here the relatively closer link prevailed.

(C) Further exception from the first general hypothesis is the diplomatic protection exercised by a state through the espousal of a case of a double national against a state whose nationality he equally possesses. The great majority of cases are those in which the action is brought against the state of the other nationality, with which state the individual has closer relations and which is, at the same time, the state responsible for the wrong. In such a situation the international tribunal may, as in the *Flutie Cases* and the *Flegenheimer Case,* decide that the person in question does not possess one of the two nationalities, and specifically not the nationality of the espousing state. But also in the normal case, when both nationalities are recognized as valid, the many decisions of international tribunals, as Briggs states, "have not led to a uniform rule." [103] Van Panhuys [104] has now made a careful study on this subject and has convincingly proved that there is much confusion and a great lack of clarity, but that the principle of equality will be considered as the primary rule of general international law. In this sense the basic Article IV of the Hague Convention of 1930—an article quoted by the judgment—provides:

> A State may not afford diplomatic protection to one of its nationals against a State whose nationality such person also possesses.

The mere fact that a person has the nationality of two states, regardless of the question with which state he has relatively closer factual ties, prevents either of these two states from exercising diplomatic protection against the other state. This principle, reaffirmed by Article IV of the Hague Convention of 1930, has also prevailed in the practice of international tribunals. It is true that sometimes, as in the *Canevaro Case,*[105] the principle of relatively closer ties with the defendant state has also been invoked. But it can be said, with Van Panhuys, that both principles were used, that the second served only to reinforce the first, and that, under the circumstances of the case, both principles would have led to exactly the same result. To that must be added that it by no means follows from the *Canevaro* decision that

Peru could exercise diplomatic protection of this double national against Italy.

It is, therefore, doubtful whether there is, even under the special hypothesis of double or multiple nationality, a general rule of international law requiring a "genuine link" as a prerequisite for the exercise of diplomatic protection. But even where the "closer link" test was applied by international tribunals, they prove nothing as to the case at bar, and this for two different reasons.

The judgment, speaking of cases of double nationality, says:

> In order to decide this question arbitrators have evolved certain principles for determining whether full international effect was to be attributed to the nationality invoked. The same issue is now before the Court.[106]

But this is obviously not the case. Nottebohm was at no time a double national. He never was a national of Guatemala. Judge Read is right in stating that "the problems presented by conflicting claims to nationality and by double nationality do not arise in this case." He is equally right in stating: "I do not think that it is permissible to transfer criteria designed for cases of double nationality to an essentially different type of relationship." [107] *Ad hoc* Judge Guggenheim also emphasizes that

> The test of *effective connection* with respect to nationality has only been laid down for the purpose of resolving conflicts arising out of dual nationality. . . .[108]

The much-invoked Hague Convention of 1930 is *not* a convention concerning problems relating to nationality laws in general, but only a convention concerning questions relating to the *conflict* of nationality laws. Judge Basdevant long ago, in scientific writing,[109] defended the "genuine link" theory, but he dealt there with problems of *double* nationality. Van Panhuys maintains that the Court in the *Reparation Case* referred "to the ordinary practice whereby a state does not exercise protection on behalf of one of its nationals against a state which regards him as its own national," [110] hence to the equality doctrine. But in the *Nottebohm* case, Van Panhuys continues, 'the Court openly declared itself in favor of the principle of effective nationality, but it did so in a *completely different context.*"

The second reason is, that even where courts of third states or international tribunals, in cases of double nationality, did apply the effective nationality test, they did so because they had to choose between two nationalities; and they did not create a precedent for the "genuine link" theory of the judgment; they did not ask for a link, "so preponderant in relation to any connection which may have existed between him and *any other state,*" but only for stronger links with one or the other state, of which he possessed nationality. It is arguable that a dual national has equally strong links with both the states of which he is a national, or that he has the closest links with a third state of which he is not a national but in which he is domiciled; but all that is irrelevant. The test, as applied by courts of third states or international tribunals, does not evaluate an *absolute* genuine link but only *relatively* stronger links as between those states of which he possesses the nationality.

The judgment has hardly proved the existence of an "absolute link" rule even in cases of double nationality, having nothing to do with the case at bar. Nor has the judgment proved the genuine link as a requirement of positive international law in cases where the person involved has had at all times only one nationality. The genuine link theory, as Mervyn Jones states,[111] is a novel one, based only on the authority of the Court; the conclusion is, therefore, inescapable that the genuine link theory is not required by international law and, as applied in the *Nottebohm* case, constitutes a clear-cut instance of judicial legislation.

General international law actually in force contains norms for the treatment of aliens, including the rule of the international minimum standard; a violation of these rules by the state of the residence of the alien constitutes an international delinquency. Under general international law, the state of nationality has the right of diplomatic protection on behalf of its nationals abroad. This is merely a right, not an international duty; how and whether the state of nationality in a concrete case will or will not exercise diplomatic protection is, as far as international law is concerned, discretionary with that state. Diplomatic protection can be exercised through the state of nationality's embassies, legations, consulates, by diplomatic protests and demands; it may be exercised by coercive measures; it may also be exercised by espousing the case of its injured national before international tribunals or an international court. The state exercises *its* right and does not act as an agent or attorney of the injured private individual. Under general international law, individuals are not subjects of international law and cannot bring *their* case into an international court against another state. Statements to the contrary by defenders of human rights [112] are not correct statements of the international law in force but merely critiques of this law or proposals *de lege ferenda*. The Permanent Court of International Justice stated in the *Mavrommatis Case,* 1924,[113] and in the *Panevezys-Saldutiskis Railway Case,* 1939,[114] that

the rule of international law is that in taking up the case of one of its nationals, by resorting to diplomatic protection or international judicial proceedings on his behalf, a state is in reality asserting its own right, the right to ensure in the person of its nationals respect for the rules of international law.

That is why international tribunals have held that the case, which in the prior exhaustion of local remedies was between the private individual and a local court, entirely changes its character by the espousal of the state of nationality. It becomes, then, an international procedure between states; the espousing state has a right to dispose of the claim, can compromise it, can accept less than the damage suffered by its national. The payment of indemnities is from state to state and the espousing state is not bound by international law to give the full indemnity to its national. Diplomatic protection is the right of the state; that is why a private individual cannot, through a Calvo clause, contract away the right of his state. While there are cases in which diplomatic protection can be exercised for non-nationals, the general rule is that diplomatic protection can be exercised only by a state and only on behalf of a person who was its national, both at the time of the alleged injury and at the time when diplomatic protection was being exercised.[115] The *Panevezys Case* states:

> The right [of diplomatic protection] is necessarily limited to intervention on behalf of its own national, because, in the absence of a special agreement, *it is the bond of nationality* between the state and the individual which *alone* confers upon the state the right of diplomatic protection.[116].

The *Nottebohm Judgment* approaches, first, the problem of diplomatic protection, as well as that of nationality, in an orthodox fashion, invoking cases of the Permanent Court of International Justice.[117] But, although granting the Leichtenstein nationality of Nottebohm, it decides that the exercise of diplomatic protection on his behalf is inadmissible vis-à-vis Guatemala. The international law actually in force restricts the right of diplomatic protection only where nationality does not have to be recognized, and in cases of dual nationality, where the action is brought against a state whose nationality the individual also possesses. No such condition arises in the *Nottebohm* case. That is why Judge Klaestad attacks the "severance of diplomatic protection from the question of nationality." [118] And Judge Read states: "Nationality and diplomatic protection are closely inter-related. The general rule of international law is that nationality gives rise to a right of diplomatic protection."[119] *Ad hoc* Judge Guggenheim treats this problem clearly: There are examples of situations in which the grant of nationality is invalid with the direct consequence that it cannot form the basis of diplomatic protection; none of these situations applies here.[120] As to other situations, a rule of law would have to be proved and it has not been proved. There is no precedent vis-à-vis a state of mere domicile.

The judgment adds, therefore, a new restriction on a state's right to exercise diplomatic protection and this new restriction has no basis in international law. It is, as Mervyn Jones says, "a *novel* principle," an "entirely *new* theory of international claims." [121] And the *Lotus Judgment* stated: "Restrictions upon the independence of states cannot be presumed."

The extreme dualistic conception, upon which the *Nottebohm Judgment* is based, has separated municipal and international law. The functional approach which the judgment uses has severed the conferring of nationality from its recognition by foreign states, has severed nationality from diplomatic protection, has severed the different forms of diplomatic protection, and has questioned the recognition of nationality as a sufficient title for diplomatic protection vis-à-vis different states. By severing nationality from the closely interrelated diplomatic protection, "diplomatic protection has been diluted," "the decision represents a departure from international tradition, and facts of the case do not warrant such a departure." [122]

The judgment severs not only nationality as the link for the exercise of diplomatic protection by the state. It also severs nationality as the link between the individual and the law of nations. It deprives Nottebohm of the *only* legal remedy he had, sixteen years after his acquisition of Liechtenstein nationality, with the result that no justice is being done to him either on the national or international level.

THE JUDGMENT (SECOND PHASE)—DE LEGE FERENDA

It must be stated *de lege lata* that the *Nottebohm Judgment* is not based on international law actually in force. Judge Lauterpacht has stated that the Court must apply the law in force; it is not its function deliberately to change the law so as to make it conform with its own views of justice and expediency; and he speaks of the "hazardous course of judicial legislation." [123] Even common law courts, as Mr. Justice Holmes stated, can change the law only "interstitially." On the other hand, it is recognized that the International Court of Justice has an important task to fulfil in developing international law. Where is the borderline between development of international law and judicial legislation? Judge Lauterpacht gives four examples of judicial legislation: relying on general principles of law, relying on parallel developments, absence of a generally accepted rule of international law, and a certain flexibility of international law.[124] None of these examples applies here.

Most writers speak of the *Nottebohm Judgment* as of a "novel" or "entirely new" doctrine; even those who approve the judgment call it "revolutionary." Professor Oliver Lissitzyn and Mr. Loftus Becker agreed that "the Nottebohm decision could be called fairly unpredictable." [125] This is dangerous for the Court's own activity, since it does not have very much to do. Communist states and new Asian and African states do not go to the Court. It is usually the

European states which resort to the Court. But Judge
Lauterpacht has asserted that

> an International Court which yields conspicuously to the urge
> to modify the existing law may bring about a drastic curtail-
> ment of its activity. Governments may refuse to submit disputes
> to it.[126]

And so devoted an adherent of international judicial procedure as Mr. C. Wilfred Jenks states that

> one of the main qualities in a Court likely to make it attractive
> to governments is not . . . the extent to which they are attempt-
> ing to develop the law imaginatively on constructive lines, but
> the predictability of the Court as a whole. . . . There must exist
> a reasonable degree of confidence that the Court will follow those
> rules of law, right or wrong, which have hitherto been regarded
> as usually accepted. . . . When an international court suffers
> from a certain lack of predictability, compulsory jurisdiction is
> likely to suffer.[127].

In evaluating the *Nottebohm Judgment de lege lata,* the
eventual desirability of the new norm created by the judgment does not enter. But in evaluating the judgment *de lege
ferenda,* it is exactly this desirability, together with the
willingness of states, which has to be considered. Although
the judgment is binding only for the specific case on the
parties, and *stare decisis* is no part of international law
actually in force, naturally the prestige of the Court will
give to its judgment a high degree of persuasive authority.
States have followed in their practice the line laid down in
a judgment of the Court. But, from a legal point of view,
the judgments do not constitute international law. As Judge
Lauterpacht has stated, "they are not binding upon *states,*
nor are they *binding* upon the Court." [128] Whether the new
doctrines, on which the *Nottebohm Judgment* is based, will
become international law depends entirely on the practice
of states.

There is no doubt that it might be desirable to achieve a clean distribution of the world's population among the existing sovereign states and thus avoid all conflicts of dual or multiple nationality as well as of statelessness. But in order to achieve that, it would be necessary for international law to regulate the problems of nationality, not by a mere attribution of competence to the sovereign states, but directly by substantive rules establishing uniform principles for the grant of nationality. Even that, as this writer stated thirty-two years ago, would not be sufficient. For even if a universal treaty to this effect were concluded and ratified, the difference of languages and the difference of interpretation by municipal courts would soon again introduce causes of conflict. It would, therefore, be necessary also to create a Supreme International Court of Nationality to keep the application of the universal treaty uniform. But the achievement of such a universal treaty is not politically possible. Much that would be desirable *de lege ferenda* cannot be done. It would, for instance, be highly desirable to end the chaotic status of American divorce laws by a uniform federal statute on divorce; but it cannot be done. The *Nottebohm Judgment* itself recognizes the political impossibility because of "the diversity of demographic conditions." [129] But it lays down the new rule that every principle for the grant of nationality, however diverse, must embody the genuine link doctrine as laid down by the Court.

Such a development of international law seems to us entirely undesirable. First, it is not always possible, under the conditions of modern life, to determine with what state a person has a factual connection, absolutely preponderant in relation to any connection which may have existed between him and any other state. Second, the important link of nationality which, under present international law, is a legal link, imperiously demands objective and secure criteria, whereas the "genuine link doctrine" introduces purely subjective criteria, shifting from case to case, and would therefore necessarily lead to a situation of uncertainty as to nationality which would be undesirable from all points of view.

It is, of course, technically true that the judicial legislation concerning the genuine link theory, introduced by the *Nottebohm Judgment,* does not touch nationality as such, but only nationality as a sufficient title for Liechtenstein to exercise diplomatic protection, and that only by an application to the International Court of Justice, and even so only vis-à-vis Guatemala. But as the inadmissibility of Liechtenstein's application is not based on any special reason which Guatemala may have had for refusing to recognize the effects of the nationality in the field of diplomatic protection, but exclusively on the allegedly missing "genuine link" in granting nationality by naturalization, the result is practically the same. In spite of the Court's dualistic conception and functional approach, the judgment is exposed to a wide interpretation as to the other effects of nationality, "for example, treaty rights enjoyed by the nationals of a particular State in regard to monetary exchange, establishment and access to municipal courts of a third State, etc." [130] The Nottebohm legislation would not only introduce the highest degree of insecurity and uncertainty into the problem of nationality, but also tear apart the unity of the institution of nationality.

The International Court of Justice has, by its judgments, made two additions to the law of diplomatic protection. The case on *Reparations for Injuries Suffered in the Service of the United Nations* [131] brought an extension of the right of diplomatic protection from states to international organizations. While this approached international legislation, it can be fully justified as falling under the legitimate task of the Court to develop international law. For the Court reasoned not only by analogy, but on the basis of the positive international law of the U.N. Charter, bringing out the implied powers of the United Nations. There is little doubt that this decision is on the way to becoming international law. But the *Nottebohm Judgment* diluted the long-established right of diplomatic protection by states. Not only this is judicial legislation *de lege lata* in complete contradiction to the rule of international law that nationality should not be dissociated from diplomatic protection in cases where the protected person has only *one* nationality, but it is also undesirable *de lege ferenda*.

True, it could be said that it would be desirable in the interest of peaceful relations to prevent states from exercising diplomatic protection on behalf of persons who are not really their nationals. It is also true that the exercise of diplomatic protection can and has been abused by powerful states vis-à-vis weaker states. Yet the necessity of retaining the institution of diplomatic protection is universally recognized and is today, perhaps, more important than ever. The growing international connections, the mass migrations from state to state, the activity of investment and establishment abroad, often furthered by the state also in states where there is, as in communist states or the new African and Asian states, less legal security for foreign persons and assets, have led writers even to consider the question whether municipal law should not create a legal duty for the state to exercise diplomatic protection on behalf of its nationals.[132]

The judicial legislation laid down by the *Nottebohm Judgment* restricts the right of diplomatic protection by states without any basis in positive international law and severs nationality as the principal link from diplomatic protection. Nor can it be said that the *Nottebohm* doctrine is "progressive" in the sense of enhancing the individual's right to protect himself independently of his state. For the judgment stands not only on the orthodox viewpoint that a state exercises its own right through diplomatic protec-

tion, but enhances this exclusive right of the state by its
doctrine. On the other hand, it is true that, under general
international law, the individual has no standing in an
international court; that, in spite of the emphasis by the
United Nations on "human rights," international law, as
it is today, and international organizations are still inadequate to give direct international protection to individuals.
Private persons must rely on diplomatic protection by their
states. Hence, the severance of nationality from diplomatic
protection, as nationality is the link between an individual
and the law of nations, is of far-reaching consequence. Under its novel doctrine the *Nottebohm Judgment* declared the
application of Liechtenstein inadmissible at a time when
Nottebohm had been a Liechtenstein national for sixteen
years and had had his permanent domicile in Liechtenstein
for nine years. As there is no other state in the world that
could exercise diplomatic protection on behalf of Nottebohm, the latter, for all practical purposes, has been rendered stateless. Is that progressive? Is it in accordance with
Article XV of the Universal Declaration of Human Rights,
which, although containing no legal norms, lays down moral
principles that "everyone has the right to a nationality"?
Is that in accordance with the efforts of the United Nations? [133] The *Nottebohm Judgment* has not only precluded
the Court from the possibility of adjudicating the important issue of war confiscation measures, but it has also
deprived Nottebohm of the only legal remedy he had, has
made him practically stateless, and has prevented justice
from being done to him, either on the municipal or international level. That cannot be a proper administration of
international justice.

It must also be taken into consideration that the *Notte-
bohn Judgment* declared Liechtenstein's application inadmissible vis-à-vis a mere state of domicile. This brings up

serious problems *de lege ferenda*. Latin American states, disappointed with the *Asylum Case* [134] and the *Haya de la Torre Case*,[135] should approve the *Nottebohm Judgment*. Does this judicial legislation not look like abolishing diplomatic protection in behalf of aliens domiciled in the country, a goal for which, by way of the Calvo clause, they have aimed, at least, to make the individual renounce the invocation of diplomatic protection by his state. Shall there be no more diplomatic protection on behalf of nationals domiciled abroad for business purposes? Today, when the states of nationality are no longer allowed to exercise diplomatic protection on behalf of nationals abroad through coercive measures involving the use or threat of force, or under the Charter of the Organization of American States, not even through non-military reprisals, such a rule would be in contradiction with the maintenance of international order and involve the danger of anarchy. Such a rule would be undesirable not only from the point of view of the state of nationality and of the national involved, but also from a world point of view and from the point of view of the underdeveloped countries themselves. For all these reasons, Seidl-Hohenveldern hopes that the practice of states will not follow the *Nottebohm Judgment*.

Not only is the new norm, on which the judgment is based, undesirable *de lege ferenda*, but it is also irreconcilably in conflict with the policies of a number of states which, up to now, have not been changed, either as far as the granting of nationality or the claim to exercise diplomatic protection on behalf of their nationals is concerned. There are many states which do not demand a "genuine link" as a precondition for granting nationality by naturalization. There are many states which consider as their nationals individuals born by mere chance as their nationals *jure soli,* and who for a long time have had no connection

with the country of their birth. There are many states
which consider as their nationals persons whose parents
have lived for centuries abroad and are nationals only *jure
sanguinis*. There are, as Mervyn Jones states, "hundreds
of thousands of British subjects in foreign countries who
have never seen their native land and who, from generation
to generation have acquired British nationality by de-
scent." [136] There are millions of "overseas Chinese," and so
on. Practically all states regard as their nationals even
those nationals who have been domiciled abroad for a long
time for carrying on business activities, like Nottebohm in
Guatemala, and claim to exercise diplomatic protection on
their behalf.

Judgments of the International Court of Justice are
binding in the specific case on the parties concerned but do
not constitute international law. But they may become
international law by the practice of states through custom
or treaty. On the other hand, the practice of states may
act in such a way as to preclude the norm laid down in a
judgment from becoming international law. Thus the rule
laid down in accordance with international law actually
in force by the *Lotus Case*,[137] which was not liked by a
number of maritime states and by a part of legal opinion,
was changed by the Brussels Convention of 1952,[138] and
this change has now also entered the 1958 Geneva Convention on the High Seas.[139] The same may happen to the
Nottebohm Judgment. Mervyn Jones suggests that "in
future Claims Conventions the prudent draftsman will endeavor to limit, to define or even perhaps to exclude the
link theory." [140] It should be added here *de lege ferenda*
that the genuine link theory would not only bring about
uncertainty, but would make proof by the complainant state
much more intricate and difficult, whereas the application
may be held inadmissible, as in the *Nottebohm* case, under

the mere attack by the defendant state, even if it did not ask for it, and even without having furnished proof.

The continuing criticism of the *Nottebohm Judgment* by writers furnishes ample proof that the genuine link doctrine is far from corresponding to the *communis doctorum opinio*. Nor has the genuine link doctrine been applied by later international decisions. It is particularly necessary to say a few words with regard to the decision in the case of *Florence Strunsky-Mergé v. Italy*,[141] rendered on June 10, 1955, by the United States-Italian Conciliation Commission, established under the Peace Treaty with Italy of 1947; for this decision, rendered after the *Nottebohm Judgment,* is often quoted as confirming the "genuine link" doctrine established by this judgment. But Professor de Yanguas Messía (Madrid), the "Third Member," i.e., the deciding judge in this case, himself told this writer at the 1959 Neuchâtel Session of the Institut de Droit International that this decision had nothing to do with the *Nottebohm Judgment,* that the situation before the Commission was entirely different, namely, a situation of dual nationality. A later decision, rendered by the same Italian–United States Conciliation Commission on September 20, 1958, in the case of *United States ex rel. Flegenheimer v. Italy*,[142] limited the link theory of the *Nottebohm Judgment* to cases of dual nationality and beyond these limits repudiated it *expressis verbis,* stating:

There does not in fact exist any criterion of proven effectiveness for disclosing the effectiveness of a bond with a political collectivity, and the persons by the thousands who, because of the facility of travel in the modern world, possess the positive legal nationality of a State, but live in foreign States where they are domiciled and where their family and business center is located, would be exposed to non-recognition, at the international level, of the nationality with which they are undeniably vested by

virtue of the laws of their national State, if this doctrine were
to be generalized.[143]

The "genuine link" legislation of the *Nottebohm Judg-*
ment may, by analogy, be extended to problems of the
nationality of corporations and of the nationality of ships.
The rule concerning the nationality of ships is that international law gives to each state the competence to attribute
national character to a ship through registration and documentation; international law traditionally has left each
state free to determine under what conditions it will register and thereby confer its nationality upon a ship.[144] There
are, therefore, a great variety of criteria. While the legislation of some maritime states has required as conditions, for
example, that the ship must have been built in the state;
that all or a prescribed part of the crew must be nationals;
that the ship must be wholly, or as to a prescribed part,
owned by nationals; and so on; there are states which
make it extremely easy and inexpensive to get ships registered, to become national ships of the state in question,
and to acquire the right to fly the flag of that state. These
are the so-called flags of convenience. Among these states
Liberia and Panama are outstanding. It is certainly amazing that at the end of 1957 these two states had more than
fifteen per cent of world tonnage under their flag, that the
United States flag-of-convenience fleet now has over six
million gross tons, which correspond to thirty-six per cent
of all American privately-owned, or five per cent of world
merchant tonnage. But, in a similar way, a great many
American corporations are incorporated in Delaware and
are, therefore, Delaware corporations, although otherwise
they have nothing to do with that state.

American high-cost, producing shipping owners make use
of flags of convenience primarily to cut their costs to about
half, and thus to meet European competition. European

shipowners attack flags of convenience because this system deprives them to a great extent of the economic advantage which they otherwise would have over their Amreican competitors. This explains why the United States government supports flag-of-convenience shipping, whereas European maritime nations file diplomatic protests against this practice; why American international lawyers are, generally speaking, in favor of, and European international lawyers against, this practice. The states of the flag of convenience have, of course, a fiscal interest in the preservation of this practice; labor, on the other hand, combats it for its own reasons.[145]

International law gives to each state the competence to confer its nationality on a ship as it pleases. This nationality has to be recognized by other states. The state of the flag alone has competence to extend its protection to the ships of its flag, regardless of the nationality of its owners, and to control its movements and activities. Just as the enemies of flags of convenience charge that such states have no adequate laws and machinery to prescribe and control efficient building safety, internal conditions, guarantees for employed personnel,[146] thus they say that these states, because of the extreme smallness of their consular corps, are unable to protect their ships, adequately.

In this long-standing economic battle for and against the flags of convenience, the International Law Commission of the United Nations took a stand against the flag-of-convenience fleet by introducing into the corresponding article of its Report on the High Seas in 1956—after the *Nottebohm Judgment* had been rendered—the "genuine link" doctrine as to nationality of ships in exactly the same fashion as the *Nottebohm Judgment* created it. After having stated that "ships have the nationality of the state whose flag they are entitled to fly," the draft article continued: "Nevertheless, for purposes of recognition of the national character of the ship by other states, there must exist a genuine link between the state and the ship." [147] We have here the same dualistic conception of international law, the same distinction between municipal validity and recognition by other states, the same complete lack of definition of "genuine link," the same severance of nationality and protection.

As this draft was the principal basis of discussion at the 1958 Geneva Conference on the Law of the Sea, it was exactly this requirement of the genuine link which led to lengthy debates at Geneva. Finally, Article V of the 1958 Convention on the High Seas states, according to traditional international law, that

> Each state shall fix the conditions for the grant of its nationality to ships, for the registration of ships in its territory, and for the right to fly its flag. Ships have the nationality of the state whose flag they are entitled to fly. There must exist a genuine link between the state and the ship; in particular, the state must effectively exercise its jurisdiction and control in administrative, technical and social matters over ships flying its flag.[148]

As in the debates of the International Labor Organization, and at the Geneva Conference, Europeans spoke mostly in favor of, Americans against, this genuine link requirement. In this respect it is particularly interesting that Mr. Van Panhuys, so sharp a critic of the *Nottebohm Judgment*, at Geneva was emphatically in favor of the genuine link theory as applied to the problem of the nationality of ships. In the scientific evaluation of the 1958 Geneva Convention we see Europeans [149] defending the genuine link theory, whereas we now have the massive attack by Professor Myres McDougal and his associates,[150] who see in the genuine link requirement an "ill-conceived innovation," creating "dangers for the free and ordered use of a great common resource on the basis of equality and certainty of expectations, which [dangers] can hardly be exaggerated." [151] and who ask for the deletion of the last sentence of Article V of the 1958 Geneva Convention on the Law of the Sea.

The same issue, as Professor Jessup states,[152] "nearly disrupted the inaugural meeting of the U.N. Inter-Governmental Maritime Consultative Organization in London, January, 1959," because Liberia and Panama were not elected to the Maritime Safety Committee, where certain places were reserved for "the largest ship-owning nations." The Assembly has asked the International Court of Justice for an advisory opinion on the question whether the committee was constituted in accordance with the Convention for the Establishment of the Organization.[153]

The international law of nationality and the international law concerning the nationality of ships could certainly bear improvements. But the adoption of the genuine link requirement is undesirable and does not constitute progress. For, as far as individuals are concerned, this requirement separates nationality from its recognition by other states, replaces a clear and objective criterion by vague and subjective criteria, severs nationality from diplomatic protection, dilutes diplomatic protection, contains no definition, makes it possible to deprive an individual of the only legal remedy he has, threatens millions of persons with statelessness, makes the diplomatic protection of nationals domiciled abroad for business activities questionable, and thus endangers business and investment activity abroad, tears apart the unity of the institution of nationality, and separates the different aspects of diplomatic protection. Its over-all effect would, therefore, be international uncertainty and insecurity. The *Nottebohm Judgment's* judicial legislation *stricto sensu* has, up to now, no chance of becoming international law; the municipal legislation and practice of many states are opposed to it, writers continue to attack it, and a recent international decision has expressly rejected it.

The problem of nationality of ships is, at the best, analogous to, but by no means identical with, that of the nationality of individuals from many points of view. They differ legally also in this important aspect: whereas international law knows dual or multiple nationality of individuals, every ship must have one nationality. Positive international law knows no genuine link theory; but it has evolved the test of the relatively stronger ties between two states exclusively in the situation of dual nationality in which a choice between two nationalities has to be made. Such a problem cannot arise with regard to the nationality of ships. The genuine link requirement here is also undesirable: it replaces a clear and objective criterion by vague and subjective criteria, severs nationality of a ship from recognition by other states, severs granting of nationality to a ship from protection, contains no definition, gives third states a seeming right to determine subjectively and unilaterally whether the genuine link requirement is fulfilled, threatens thereby to make ships stateless and unprotected, and endangers international certainty in the use of the high seas. But, contrary to the *Nottebohm Judgment's* judicial legislation *stricto sensu,* the genuine link theory with regard to the nationality of ships has found entrance into the practice of states (International Law Commission, 1958 Geneva Convention on the Law of the Sea, the U.N. Inter-Governmental Consultative Maritime Organization, acceptance by a number of governments and writers). But here it also remains controversial: contrary views of governments, the advisory opinion of the International Court, adverse comments by writers. Professor McDougal's frontal attack is, of course, at the same time, a strong attack on the *Nottebohm Judgment.*

[1] I.C.J. Rep. 4 (1955); digested in 49 AM.J.INT'L L. 396 (1955).

[2] See I. Seidl-Hohenveldern, *Der Fall Nottebohm*, RECHT DER INTERNATIONALEN WIRTSCHAFT 147-49 (1955); A. Migliazza, in 7 COMUNICAZIONI E STUDI 582-94 (1955); Erwin H. Loewenfeld, *Der Fall Nottebohm*, 5 ARCHIV DES VÖLKERRECHTS 387-410 (1956); Jack H. Glazer, *Affaire Nottebohm—A Critique*, 44 GEO.L.J. 313-23 (1955-56); J. Mervyn Jones, *The Nottebohm Case*, 5 INT'L & COMP.L.Q. 230-46 (1956); unsigned note in 31 N.Y.U.L.REV. 1135-39 (1956); A.N. Makarov, *Das Urteil des Internationalen Gerichtshofes im Fall Nottebohm*, 16 ZEITSCHRIFT FÜR AUSLÄNDISCHES ÖFFENTLICHES RECHT UND VÖLKERRECHT 407-26 (1956); *idem, Consideraciones sobre el derecho de la protección diplomatica*, 8 REVISTA ESPAÑOLA DE DERECHO INTERNACIONAL 519-24 (1955); Paul de Visscher, *L'Affaire Nottebohm*, 60 REVUE GÉNÉRALE DE DROIT INTERNATIONAL PUBLIC 238-66 (1956); Suzanne Bastid, *L'Affaire Nottebohm devant la Cour Internationale de Justice*, 45 REVUE CRITIQUE DE DROIT INTERNATIONAL PRIVÉ 607-33 (1956); J. H. W. Verzijl in 3 NEDERLANDS TIJDSKRIFT VOOR INTERNATIONAL RECHT 33 (1956); Maury, *L'Arrêt Nottebohm et la Condition de la Nationalité Effective*, 23 ZEITSCHRIFT FÜR AUSLANDISCHES UND INTERNATIONALES PRIVATRECHT 515 (1958); Mariano Aguilar Navarro, *Reglementacion internacional del Derecho de Nacionalidad*, 10 REVISTA ESPAÑOLA DE DERECHO INTERNACIONAL 333-72 (1957). These writings will further be quoted only by the names of their authors. See also Hans Goldschmidt in FORDHAM L. REV. 689 (1960).

[3] Judges Klaestad and Read, and *ad hoc* Judge Guggenheim. The majority of the Court was composed of: Judge Hackworth, president; Judge Badawi, vice president; Judges Basdevant, Zoričić, Hsu Mo, Armand-Ugon, Kojevnikov, Sir Muhammad Zafrulla Khan, Moreno Quintana, Córdova; *ad hoc* Judge M. García Bauer.

[4] See the critical remarks in 1 GEORG DAHM, VÖLKERRECHT 446, note 1, 447, note 6, 458 459, note 13 (1958); VERDROSS-ZEMANEK, VÖLKERRECHT 237, note 3 (4th ed. 1959); 2 A. P. SERENI, DIRITTO INTERNAZIONALE 691 (1958), states correctly that there must be "some link," but it cannot be said in general terms what the criteria of this link must be which justify the grant of nationality for international purposes; he adds that "even the most tenuous links are sufficient to justify the grant of nationality to one who voluntarily applies for it."

[5] H. F. VAN PANHUYS, THE ROLE OF NATIONALITY IN INTERNATIONAL LAW (1959).

[6] G. BATTAGLINI, LA PROTEZIONE DIPLOMATICA DELLE SOCIETÀ 216-17 (1957). Professor McDougal, in 4 S. D. L. REV. 45-46 (1959), quotes the *Nottebohm Judgment* as "sufficiently dramatic" and seemingly with approval, but does not go into any analysis. But now, apropos his violent attack on the link theory with regard to the nationality of ships, he also has his doubts about the *Nottebohm Judgment*; see 54 AM.J.INT'L L. 36-40 (1960). Z. R. Rode, *Dual Nationality and the Doctrine of Dominant Nationality*, 53 AM.J.INT'L L. 139-49 (1959), takes no stand with regard to the *Nottebohm Judgment*, but only

quotes, for the purposes of his study, the dicta of the Court concerning dual nationality.

7 Mario Giuliano, *La sudditanza degli individui e il suo rilievo nell'ordinamento internazionale*, 8 COMUNICAZIONI E STUDI 50–54 (1956), accepts the link theory as "autorevole." It is surprising that this sharply critical mind does not see that the Nottebohm case has nothing whatsoever to do with the special problem of dual nationality, and that there is no basis at all in positive international law for the link theory in the case of an individual who, at all times, had only one nationality.

8 See Philip C. Jessup, in PROCEEDINGS, SECOND SUMMER CONFERENCE ON INTERNATIONAL LAW, Cornell Law School, 43, 49 (1958).

9 SIR HERSCH LAUTERPACHT, THE DEVELOPMENT OF INTERNATIONAL LAW BY THE INTERNATIONAL COURT (1958). The discussions on pp. 13, 15, 349 all refer to the *Nottebohm Judgment* of 1953, with which we are not concerned here.

10 "A dissent in a court of last resort is an appeal to the broadening spirit of the law, to the intelligence of a future day where a later decision may possibly correct the error into which the dissenting judge believes the court to have been betrayed."—CHARLES EVANS HUGHES, THE SUPREME COURT OF THE UNITED STATES 68 (1928).

11 LAUTERPACHT, *op. cit.* at 398.

12 *Ibid.* at 62.

13 I.C.J. Rep. 28 (1955).

14 See, e.g., People of State of New York *ex rel*. Halvey v. Halvey, 330 U. S. 616, where the U. S. Supreme Court stated: "The narrow ground on which we rest the decision makes it unnecessary to consider several other questions argued." At the 1959 Neuchâtel Session of the *Institut de Droit International*, during discussion of Article XV No. 15, of the Draft Resolution on Arbitration in Private International Law, an article which states that foreign arbitral awards shall not be recognized, "lorsque la sentence n'a pas prononcé sur toutes les conclusions des parties," Lord McNair stated that this point could not be accepted by a lawyer of a common-law country.

15 LAUTERPACHT, *op. cit.* at 37–49.

16 "The Court is not therefore called upon to deal with the other pleas in bar put forward by Guatemala or the Conclusions of the Parties other than those on which it is adjudicating in accordance with the reasons indicated above."—I.C.J. Rep. 26 (1955).

17 "The present task of the Court is limited to adjudicating upon the admissibility of the claim of Liechtenstein in respect of Nottebohm on the basis of such reasons as it may itself consider relevant and proper."—*Ibid.* at 16; see also at 17.

18 Bowen, L. J., in Leeson v. General Council of Medical Education, 43 Ch. D. 366, 385 (1889).

19 *Ad hoc* Judge Guggenheim, I.C.J. Rep. 60–61 (1955).

20 The points 2 and 3 made in the text have been fully considered by Van Panhuys.

21 *Loc. cit.* at 238.

22 I.C.J. Rep. 30–31 (1955).

23 *Ibid.* at 38.

24 I.C.J. Rep. 45 (1952).

25 I.C.J. Rep. 6 (1955).

26 *Ibid,* at 24–25.

27 *Ibid.* at 32.

28 *Ibid.* at 65.

29 LAUTERPACHT, *op. cit.* at 113–15.

30 It is interesting to see the reasons given by the Court for such joinder: "When the interests of the good administration of justice require it."—P.C.I.J., ser. A/B, No. 75 at 56 (1939). "Where the preliminary question at issue appears to be entirely bound up with the facts, adduced by the Application, and can only be decided on the basis of a full knowledge of these facts, such as can only be obtained from the proceedings of the merits."—P.C.I.J., ser A/B, No. 52 at 14 (1933).

31 "This question of fraud is so closely connected with the merits of the case that it cannot be decided apart from them and without any appraisal of the various relevant facts which may be disclosed by a consideration of the merits. . . . "—I.C.J. Rep. 33 (1955).

32 *Ibid.* at 38

33 *Ibid.* at 65.

34 *Ibid.* at 34.

35 *Ibid.* at 35. Mervyn Jones, *op. cit.* at 234, asks, "Is it the case that under international law a claim may be rejected *a limine* by an international tribunal without reference to the merits, although the procedural rules concerning the nationality of the claim have been complied with?" See also VAN PANHUYS, *op. cit.* at 98.

36 I.C.J. Rep. 64 (1955).

37 See, e.g., Philip C. Jessup, 49 AM.J.INT'L L. 57 (1955); Glazer, *op. cit.* at 321; Seidl-Hohenveldern, *op. cit.* at 149.

38 See dissenting opinions; unsigned note (cited note 2, above) at 1139. Glazer states that the retroactive effect of the judgment, sixteen years afer Nottebohm's naturalization, six years after he had established his permanent domicile in Liechtenstein, is "extremely harsh" and calls the judgment "but a hollow triumph of form."—*Op. cit.* at 325.

39 Common-law courts are careful not to deprive a plaintiff of his only legal remedy. Thus, the application of the doctrine of *forum non conveniens* "presupposes *at least two forums* in which the defendant is amenable to process."—Gulf Oil Corp. v. Gilbert, 330 U.S. 501 (1947); see also Slater v. Mexican Nat.R.Co., 194 U.S. 120: "The defendant can always be found in Mexico"; and, e.g., B. Bramwell: "So that in all cases there will be a remedy."—Crawley v. Isaacs, 16 L.T. (N.S.) 529, 531 (1867).

40 U.S.—Venezuelan Arbitrations, 1903, in RALSTON, VENEZUELAN ARBITRATIONS OF 1903 at 34.

41 U.S. *ex rel.* Flegenheimer v. Italy, September 20, 1958, excerpted in 53 AM.J.INT'L L. 944–58 (1959).

[42] I.C.J. Rep. 50 (1955).

[43] *Ibid.* at 28–29.

[44] *Ibid.* at 35–37.

[45] See H. W. BRIGGS, THE LAW OF NATIONS 452–524 (2nd ed. 1952); A. VERDROSS and K. ZEMANEK, VÖLKERRECHT 234–47 (4th ed. 1959); 1 DAHM, VÖLKERRECHT 444–95 (1958); Rundstein, 16 ZEITSCHRIFT FÜR VÖLKERRECHT 14; Naujoks, 6 TEMP. L. Q. 451 (1932), 7 *ibid.* 176 (1953); MAKAROV, ALLGEMEINE LEHREN DER STAATSANGEHÖRIGKEIT (1947).

[46] This writer developed these ideas thirty-two years ago in his study, *Zum Problem der doppelten Staatsangehörigkeit*, 2 ZEIT-SCHRIFT FÜR ÖSTRECHT 401–37 (1928). These ideas are today to a wide extent recognized by the literature; they are strongly emphasized by VAN PANHUYS, *op. cit.* at 149. See also Josef L. Kunz, *La Teoría General del Derecho Internacional*, 2 ACADEMÍA INTERAMERICANA DE DERECHO COMPARADO E INTERNACIONAL, Cursos Monográficos, 327–444 (1952).

[47] Not necessarily to the protecting state as regards the protected state, P.C.I.J., ser. B, No. 4 (1923); nor to the mandatory power with regard to the inhabitants of a territory under mandate, LEAGUE OF NATIONS OFF. J. 604 (1923).

[48] Draft on the Law of Nationality, 23 AM.J.INT'L L. Spec. Supp. (1929).

[49] P.C.I.J., ser. B, No. 4 (1923).

[50] 179 L. N. T. S. 89; 24 AM.J.INT'L L., Supp. 192 (1930).

[51] Hague Convention, 1930, arts. I, II; Stoeck v. Public Trustee, 2 Ch. 67 (1921).

[52] I.C.J. Rep. 17–20 (1955).

[53] *Op. cit.* at 66.

[54] Clive Parry, *The Duty to Recognize Foreign Nationality Laws*, 1 MAKAROV FESTGABE 337–68 (1958), deals with a different problem, namely, the recognition of foreign nationality laws by a state in shaping its own law of nationality.

[55] I.C.J. Rep. 46–48 (1955).

[56] *Ibid.* at 15–16.

[57] Mavrommatis Case, P.C.I.J., ser. A, No. 5 at 30.

[58] Judge Read, I.C.J. Rep. 36 (1955).

[59] *Ibid.* at 40.

[60] See Mervyn Jones, *op. cit.* at 237; LAUTERPACHT, *op. cit.* at 162; VAN PANHUYS, *op. cit.* at 164.

[61] Judge Read, I.C.J. Rep. 37–38 (1955).

[62] Judge Klaestad, *ibid.* at 32–33; *ad hoc* Judge Guggenheim, *ibid.* at 58, 64–65.

[63] *Ibid.* at 25, 26.

[64] *Ibid.* at 20. "The present Judgment does not decide the question, in dispute between the Parties, whether the naturalization granted to Mr. Nottebohm was valid or invalid either under the national law of Liechtenstein or under international law."—Judge Klaestad, *ibid.* at 30.

[65] *Ibid.* at 20–21.

[66] Mario Giuliano, a dualist, speaks, therefore, of a "mera libertà di fatto."

[67] I.C.J. Rep. 23 (1955).

[68] *Ibid.* at 24.

[69] *Ibid.* at 23.

[70] *Ibid.* at 17.

[71] *Ibid.* at 39.

[72] See *Laws Concerning Nationality*, U.N. St./Leg./Ser., No. IV, B 4, and Add. 1 and 2 (1954), as well as Supplement, St./Leg./Ser. No. 59,3, B 9. We find, e.g., the following Cambodian Statute of 1954, art. XXI: "La nationalité combodgienne est la lien à la fois spirituel et politique qui unit une personne physique ou morale à l'Etat cambodgien."

[73] I.C.J. Rep. 22 (1955).

[74] *Op. cit.* at 236.

[75] *Ibid.* at note 12.

[76] "A special nationality law exists in the Soviet Union in enabling aliens, whatever their nationality or race, to acquire Soviet Union citizenship. No special conditions have to be fulfilled for that purpose." —Kojevnikov, in 1952 YEARBOOK OF THE INTERNATIONAL LAW COMMISSION 7 (1958).

[77] See footnote 4, above.

[78] *Op. cit.* at 156.

[79] I.C.J. Rep. 29 (1955).

[80] *Ibid.* at 44.

[81] *Ibid.* at 56. See also Mervyn Jones, *op. cit.* at 239–40.

[82] This point is made by Judge Klaestad, I.C.J. Rep. 30 (1955).

[83] See the detailed statement in Glazer, *op. cit.* at 323.

[84] I.C.J. Rep. 22 (1955).

[85] *Ibid.* at 46.

[86] *Ibid.* at 55–56.

[87] *Ibid.* at 24–26.

[88] *Ibid.* at 25–26.

[89] *Ibid.* at 31.

[90] *Ibid.* at 44–46.

[91] *Ibid.* at 56, 61–62.

[92] *Ibid.* at 21–23.

[93] *Ibid.* at 21–22.

[94] *Ibid* at 22.

[95] *Ibid.*

[96] *Ibid.* at 41.

[97] *Ibid.* at 59–60.

[98] I.C.J. Rep. 276 (1950).

[99] The U.S.–Italian Peace Commission considered the Bancroft Treaties carefully and took them for the basis of its decision, but under completely different circumstances; for there the two nation-

alities claimed were those of two states bound by a Bancroft Treaty, and the time involved was a time when this treaty was fully in force.

[100] Great Britain, 2 Ch. 533 (1927).

[101] U.S.–Germany, Mixed Claims Commission, 1925. Decisions and Opinions of the Commission 628; 20 AM.J.INT'L L. 595 (1926).

[102] See, e.g., Baron Frederic de Born v. Yugoslavia, Hungary-Yugoslavia, Mixed Arbitral Tribunal, 1926, 3 RECUEIL DES DÉCISIONS DES TRIBUNAUX ARBITRAUX MIXTES 501.

[103] Op. cit., supra, note 45, at 516.

[104] Op. cit. at 73–81.

[105] Tribunal of the Permanent Court of Arbitration, 1912, in JAMES BROWN SCOTT, HAGUE COURT REPORTS 284 (1916).

[106] I.C.J. Rep. 22 (1955).

[107] Ibid at 42.

[108] Ibid. at 59.

[109] JULES BASDEVANT, CONFLITS DE NATIONALITÉ DANS LES ARBITRAGES VÉNÉZUELIENS DE 1903–1905 (1909).

[110] Op. cit. at 78.

[111] Op. cit. at 242.

[112] INSTITUT DE DROIT INTERNATIONAL (1931 and 1932); H. LAUTERPACHT, INTERNATIONAL LAW AND HUMAN RIGHTS 27 (1950).

[113] P.C.I.J., ser. A, No. 2 at 12.

[114] P.C.I.J., ser. A/B, No. 76 at 16.

[115] LAUTERPACHT, op. cit. at 183.

[116] P.C.I.J., ser. A/B, No. 76 at 16 (1939).

[117] I.C.J. Rep. 24 (1955).

[118] Ibid. at 30.

[119] Ibid. at 46.

[120] Ibid. at 53–54.

[121] Op. cit. at 231, 243.

[122] Glazer, op. cit. at 314.

[123] Op. cit. at 75, 19.

[124] Ibid. at 155–220.

[125] PROCEEDINGS, SECOND SUMMER CONFERENCE ON INTERNATIONAL LAW, Cornell Law School 146–47 (1958).

[126] Op. cit. at 76.

[127] 1 INSTITUT DE DROIT INTERNATIONAL, ANNUAIRE 169–71 (1957). also E. Giraud, in ibid. at 272–73.

[128] Op. cit. at 22.

[129] I.C.J. Rep. 23 (1955).

[130] Ad hoc Judge Guggenheim, ibid. at 63.

[131] I.C.J. Rep. 174 (1949), 43 AM.J.INT'L L. 589 (1949).

[132] See KARL DOEHRING, DIE PFLICHT DES STAATES ZUR GEWÄHRUNG DIPLOMATISCHEN SCHUTZES (1959).

[133] Convention on Refugees, 1951; Convention on Stateless Persons, 1954.

[134] I.C.J. Rep. 266 (1950); 45 AM.J.INT'L L. 179 (1951).

[135] I.C.J. Rep. 71 (1951); 45 AM.J.INT'L L. 781 (1951).

[136] *Op. cit.* at 239.

[137] P.C.I.J., ser. A, No. 10 (1927).

[138] International Convention for the Unification of Certain Rules Relating to General Jurisdiction in Matters of Collision or Other Incidents of Navigation, Brussels, May 10, 1952, 53 AM.J.INT'L L. 532 (1959).

[139] Geneva Convention on the General Regime of the High Seas, 1958, 52 AM.J.INT'L L. 842 (1958).

[140] *Op. cit.* at 243.

[141] RIVISTA DI DIRITTO INTERNAZIONALE 70–90 (1956); digested in 50 AM.J.INT'L L. 154 (1956).

[142] It is interesting to note that the "Third Member," i.e., the deciding judge, in this case was Professor Georges Sauser-Hall (Switzerland), who had also been Counsel to the agent of Liechtenstein in the Nottebohm case.

[143] 53 AM.J.INT'L L. 944 at 957 (1959).

[144] U.N. Laws Concerning the Nationality of Ships, St./Leg./Ser./B/5 and Add. 1, (1956); Supp. St./Leg./Ser./B/8 at 113–34 (1959).

[145] See *The Effect of U.S. Labor Legislation on the Flag of Convenience Fleet*, 69 YALE L.J. 498–530 (1960).

[146] It is from this angle that the International Labor Organization was occupied with this problem.

[147] U.N.GEN.ASS.OFF.REC., 11th Sess., Supp. No. 9 (A/3159); 51 AM.J.INT'L L. 154 at 168 (1957).

[148] U.N. Doc. No. A/CONF. 13/L. at 53; 53 AM.J.INT'L L. 842 at 843 (1958).

[149] Max Sorensen, *The Law of the Sea*, INT'L CONC. No. 520 (1958); see also Philip C. Jessup, *The United Nations Conference on the Law of the Sea*, 59 COLUM.L.REV. 234–68 at 255–57 (1959).

[150] Myres S. McDougal, William T. Burke, and Ivan A. Vlasic, *The Maintenance of Public Order at Sea and the Nationality of Ships*, 54 AM.J.INT'L L. 25–116 (1960).

[151] *Ibid.* at 41.

[152] *Loc. cit.*, note 149, above.

[153] On June 8, 1960, the Court handed down its advisory opinion, in which it held that the Maritime Safety Committee was not constituted in accordance with the convention establishing the Intergovernmental Maritime Consultative Organization, and that, under Article XXVIII(a) of that convention relating to the constitution of the Committee, the largest ship-owning nations were those having the largest registered ship tonnage.

PART V

INTERNATIONAL ORGANIZATIONS IN GENERAL AND THE UNITED NATIONS

I

SINCE THE BEGINNING of the second half of the nineteenth century, developments have taken place tending toward the creation of an administrative law on an international level. And since that very time, the character and nature of "international administration" and of "international administrative law" have been the object of far-flung scientific debates.

We can distinguish two completely different conceptions. The first conception, defended by Italian scholars,[1] but primarily made into a whole system, a new juridical discipline, by Professor Neumeyer,[2] conceives administrative international law as the ensemble of norms fixing the spatial sphere of competence of administrative institutions, delimiting the administrative competence of a state vis-à-vis the competence of the other states. Administrative international law, a part of private international law, is, therefore, wholly a part of municipal law.

This conception, entirely tenable and justified, has nothing to do with the second conception of administrative international law as a part of the law of nations. Neumeyer, it is true, denies the very possibility of this second conception, as the international community is an unorganized community and cannot exercise administrative functions, so that even in the case of treaties of an administrative content, these activities must be carried out by organs of the states, under municipal administrative law. But his arguments, as will be shown later, are not only in contradiction with reality, but also theoretically unsound.

The second conception has again many different shades of meaning: identifying practically the whole law of nations with international administrative law (Martens),[3] or thinking primarily at the activities of one state in the international field, or finally characterizing the international administrative law as the collaboration of states, based exclusively on international treaties, in certain fields of administrative character (von Stein).[4] It is this last conception which prevails in the increasingly rich literature on this topic.[5] International administrative law is a part of the law of nations, not a field distinct from international law, as Negulesco asserts.

But in order to arrive at a workable definition, we must consider that international administration must not be narrowed down to institutions with special organs (thus Burns), not limited to multilateral treaties setting up special organs [6] and less so restricted to international administrative unions. On the other hand, it must not be enlarged so as to identify administration with executive power, with government (thus Sayre). Within these limits international administration will have to include merely preparatory and mediate as well as supervisory and immediate administration, and even merely informational and ministerial functions.

II

International treaties of an administrative content may be bilateral, multilateral, and quasi-universal. They may create special organs or not. In the latter case [7] the contracting states carry out the obligations of the treaty through their municipal organs. The field of international administration is larger than that of international administrative agencies.

With regard to the development of international administrative agencies, we may distinguish the period prior to World War I, the League of Nations period between the two wars, and the present war and post-war period.

Naturally, international treaties on administrative matters and leading to the creation of special organs have always been frequent. They may be on a strictly bilateral basis or concluded between a group of states, permanent or temporary, the outcome of war or inspired by peace activities. As examples, we mention the boundary commissions, the International Joint Commission U. S.–Canada, and many others. Equally monetary unions and customs unions may create special international administrative agencies.

Such agencies were, further, created in the interest of a certain power or powers, e.g., the international control commissions for the Turkish, Egyptian, and Greek public debts.[8] But the new development, starting at the beginning of the second half of the nineteenth century, lies in the creation of international administrative agencies to take care of certain social interests, common to many or all states, interests which are vital to all states and yet cannot be adequately taken care of by any single state alone, interests which make international collaboration necessary; these agencies were, therefore, not the outcome of international rivalries but of the need for international co-operation.

Organizationally two types developed: the "international commission" and the "international bureau." The international commission was used for the protection of the world against epidemics [9] and for the administration of international rivers.[10] The international river commissions owed their origin often to "high politics"; the Great Powers sometimes held a preponderant role; they did take care of international interests, but limited to a certain area and to a smaller number of states; on the other hand, some of these commissions are given much more far-reaching authority than the organs of the international administrative unions.

It is the creation of these unions that has brought about the most important progress in international administration. It is fully understandable that early writers on this topic, such as Moynier or Descamps, speak with enthusiasm of them, see in them the beginning of an era of organization of the international community, of true and genuine international co-operation. The importance of these unions, prior to and subsequent to World War I, explains the rich literature on this subject.[11]

They have continuously grown in number; while some disappeared [12] and others have been replaced,[13] most of them have survived World War I and new ones have been created since 1920. These unions, existing at the present time, are: (1) the Universal Postal Union (1874);[14] (2) the Union of Measures and Weights (1875);[15] (3) the Union for the Protection of Industrial Property (1883);[16] (4) the Union for the Protection of Works of Literature and Art (1886);[17] (5) the International Union for the Publication of Tariffs (1890);[18] (6) the Union of International Transport by Rail (1890);[19] (7) the Union for the Establishment of the International Institute of Agriculture at Rome (1905);[20] (8) the Union for the Establishment of the International Hygiene Office (1907);[21] (9) the Union for the Creation of the International Hydrographic Bureau (1919);[22] (10) the Union for the Establishment of an International Institute for Research of Cold (1920);[23] (11) the Union for the Establishment of the International Bureau for Combating Contagious Animal Diseases (1924);[24]

(12) the Union for the Creation of the International Wine Office (1924);[25] (13) the Union Internationale de Secours (1927); [26] (14) the Union for the Establishment of the International Bureau for Chemistry (1927);[27] and (15) the International Telecommunications Union (1932).[28]

The international administrative unions are unions of sovereign states,[29] based on treaty. As in every treaty, we must here too carefully distinguish between the "treaty" as an act, a procedure, and the treaty as the ensemble of norms, created by the treaty as a procedure. The norms created by the fundamental treaty constitute the constitution of these unions. This fundamental treaty creates a particular international community, although positive international law has not made them subjects of international law.[30] The territory of the members constitutes for the purpose of the union a single territory.[31]

It is characteristic and typical, although not absolutely essential, for the international administrative unions that they are intended as permanent unions,[32] that the treaties creating them are not only concluded between many states but contain also an adhesion clause, are open conventions, that they aspire at universality, which in the case of the Universal Postal Union is practically achieved.

But while these features are typical, it is essential that the international administrative unions regulate administrative, non-political matters, which may embrace any field of international social activity, and that they are organized unions, creating special, international organs, maintained by the contributions of the member states. A tripartite scheme of organization—general congress, permanent committee, international bureau—is highly characteristic.

The fact that the international administrative unions deal with non-political matters has made their success possible. They are expressions of interests which do not divide, but unite the sovereign states. These unions have rendered and are rendering great service; they not only mark the start of international organization, but they have, as will be shown later, quietly and without much advertisement, introduced far-reaching new developments in international law. They have by their objects and activities, by their methods and techniques, and by their tripartite scheme of organization served as a model for Pan-American developments and for the League of Nations.

III

The Pan-American Union, founded in 1890 and slowly extended and built up into a very important international agency, is of the type of the international bureau. It shares with this type the administrative, non-political character, the nature of its organization, and of its activities. It is distinguished from this type by its non-universal, strictly regional, continental, inter-American character and by the fact that its activities are not restricted to one particular field. But it does not constitute the only inter-American agency. Other inter-American agencies have been set up in increasing numbers. The regional, continental character of the Pan-American Union expresses itself in its independence, both vis-à-vis the international administrative unions and the League of Nations.

IV

The peace treaties at the end of World War I have not only created an enormous number of bilaterial or multilateral international administrative agencies of a temporary character but also the League of Nations. The League's agencies profited from the experience of inter-Allied organs, set up during the war, particularly the new type of the consultative commission, the Commission of Experts, which goes back to the Royal Commission in British practice; but these agencies profited equally from the experience of the international administrative unions.

The League was, of course, primarily a political, not an administrative, organization; its principal task was the maintenance of peace. But its relations with experiences of earlier international administrative agencies are manifold:

1. The League adopted in assembly, council, and secretariat the tripartite scheme of organization of the international administrative unions. Assembly and council were naturally primarily political organs, but they had also administrative functions. The secretariat is clearly modeled after the type of the international bureau.

2. The second task of the League was international cooperation in non-political matters. For such international administrative functions the League created many auxiliary organs of international administrative character: the many consultative commissions; commissions for the internal administration of the League, such as the Budget Control Commission and others; administrative agencies such as the High Commissioner for Dantzig, the different commissioners for refugees, the Saar Government Commission, and many others; the three technical organizations of the League (Economics and Finance, Public Hygiene, and Communications and Transit) ; the autonomous International Labor Organization with its tripartite scheme of organization; finally, the special institutes of the League,[33] offered to the League by a single state; they did not technically form part of the League, but they were strictly international administrative agencies, closely co-operating with the League and placed under the League's "high authority."

3. The international administrative unions were universal in space, but each was restricted to a particular field. They had grown and were working completely independent

of each other; the prewar international administration was highly decentralized. The League in its administrative aspects was conceived as universal in space and functions, a "Union of Unions," centralizing international administration.[34] This idea found expression in Article XXIV of the Covenant. The League secretariat could function as the bureau in all administrative matters, regulated by collective treaties, not creating special international administrative agencies; all international bureaus or commissions created after 1920 were to have been automatically placed under the authority of the League, whereas those created prior to 1920 were equally to have been placed under the authority of the League if the member states of these unions consented. But although the Hanotaux Report of June 26, 1921, adopted by the Council, defined the League's "authority" very mildly, Article XXIV remained on paper; [35] the prewar and postwar international administrative unions as well as the Pan-American agencies remained independent from the League.

V

World War II again saw the creation of many inter-Allied administrative agencies,[36] some strictly bilateral, some multilateral. There are further congresses of agencies of all the United Nations: the conference on Food and Agriculture (Hot Springs, Va., May 18–June 2, 1943), the Monetary Conference (Bretton Woods, N. H., July, 1944), and particularly the Agreement for United Nations Relief and Rehabilitation Administration, signed on November 6, 1943, which set up an inter-United Nations administrative agency, the UNRRA.

It is probable that international administration will again constitute the second task of whatever postwar international organization may be set up.

VI

The development of international administration has brought about legal problems of great theoretical interest and practical importance.

If we speak of international administrative organs, the first problem which arises is: Whose organs are they? [37] For a long time the international character of these organs has been denied by French, German, and Italian authors. Anzilotti saw, e.g., in Universal Postal Congresses merely "reunions of organs of the single states"; for international commission or bureaus, the theory of the "common organs" was developed. And while the theory of the common organs has now been abandoned even by its former defenders, a residuum has remained in the theory of "collective organs." It was said, first, that the international community as an unorganized community can have no organs of its own; second, that an international administrative union can have no organs, as it is not a subject of international law.

All these theories are in contradiction with reality and theoretically untenable, based on a misunderstanding.[38] A juridical community can only act through organs; the general international community is "unorganized," not in the sense that it has no organs of its own, but in the particular sense, that it has, as a primitive legal order, not yet developed special organs. But the treaties creating the international administrative union or the League of Nations constitute particular international communities and are "organized" in the particular sense that they no longer merely delegate the member states to carry out these treaties but create *special* organs for this purpose.

An organ is the organ either of the legal order which has created it or of the legal order for which it is authorized to function. The international administrative agencies are, both according to their creation and their function, truly international organs. But they are not subjects of international law.[39]

International administrative organs may be temporary or permanent; they may be created by the fundamental treaty or by another organ. They may be simple or composite. Simple organs are organs composed of a single individual, such as the High Commissioner for Dantzig and so on.

Composite organs are constituted by more than one individual; but the composite organ as such is always a unitarian organ. Composite organs may be organized according to the collegiate or the bureaucratic principle.

An excellent example of the first type is the International River Commissions composed of persons appointed by the contracting states, representing them and having to act in conformity with the instructions of their states. But the International River Commissions are unitarian, international organs. Recently, especially in the League, the International Commission of Experts has gained importance. These are composite organs, the members of which are not appointed by the states, but by another organ, e.g., the Assembly or Council of the League. The members are not representatives of the states of their nationality, are not instructed by them, but are independent experts. Pan-American developments have equally brought forward similar tendencies: the Inter-American Neutrality Committee (now Inter-American Juridical Committee) at Rio de Janeiro, and particularly, the Emergency Advisory Committee for Political Defense at Montevideo,[40] the members of which were elected by the governing board of the Pan-American Union; they do not represent their states, but all the twenty-one American republics.

To the first type of composite organs belong also the general congresses or conferences of the international administrative unions; they are constituted by the diplomatic representatives of the member states; as these congresses are provided for by the fundamental treaties, which also give them a periodic character, they are not simple, isolated, international conferences, but true international organs of these unions. Their functions are mostly of a legislative character, but they may also be charged with administrative activities. Increasingly—an interesting development— only a qualified or simple majority is necessary for their resolutions.

Examples of composite international administrative agencies of the bureaucratic type are the international bureaus,[41] Central offices or institutes of the international administrative unions, the Pan-American Union, the League secretariat, the International Labor Office. Here the individuals composing the organ are not co-ordinated but hierarchically subordinated to the head of the organ. This leading official—director, secretary general—may be named in the fundamental treaty or elected or appointed by international organs. The rest of the personnel are appointed by the leading official; with regard to certain high officials, sometimes the appointment by a superior international organ or its approval is provided for.

Between congress and international bureau there is generally an intermediate organ. In the so-called dependent type, used by the older international administrative unions, the bureau is placed under the authority of the state in which it has its seat (Switzerland, Belgium). This "directing state" has certain important functions with regard to the creation, supervision, and control of the bureau. It creates the bureau, appoints and dismisses its officials, regulates their salaries, advances the funds, controls the financial administration, exercises disciplinary authority over the officials. But the bureau is an international bureau, its officers are international, not Swiss or Belgian officials. The control of the directing state is of a purely formal character. It in no way intervenes with the activity of the bureau. The director has an independent position, full freedom of action, and full responsibility. The directing state exercises its functions on the basis of the fundamental treaty, as a mandatory, as an international organ of the union.

The later international administrative unions, Pan-America, and the League of Nations have chosen the "independent type," in which the bureau is entirely disconnected from the local authorities of the state of its seat. Here the general congress, apart from its legislative functions, exercises the functions which under the dependent type belong to the directing state; and beyond that it is also charged with the direction of the bureau and the control of its administration. In addition, these unions have created a special administrative organ intermediate between congress and bureau—permanent commission, permanent committee, governing board of the Pan-American Union, the governing body of the International Labor Organization. This commission supervises, directs, and controls the activities of the bureau, appoints its director, makes the report to the general congress. It is composed either, like the general congress, of representatives of each of the member states—thus the permanent committee of the International Institute of Agriculture, or the governing board of the Pan-American Union—or the members are elected by the general conference—thus the permanent committee of the Union of Weights and Measures. Resolutions are mostly taken by the majority of votes.

VII

The juridically most important classification of international organs is according to their functions — legislative, judicial, administrative — and to the range of their competence.

International administrative agencies may, sometimes, also have *judicial*,[42] sometimes also *legislative*, functions. In the latter respect, extremely interesting developments have taken place. The diplomatic conference creating the fundamental treaty may be considered as the constituent assembly. The general congresses or conferences of the international administrative unions are the legislative organ for revising the fundamental treaty. They do not differ in their nature from the normal, diplomatic international conference.

The international bureaus have no legislative competence. But a new development has been brought about through the delegation, by the fundamental treaty, to international organs of the authority of creating general, abstract norms, binding, without need of ratification, either upon states or upon individuals. Contrary to what is commonly loosely called "international legislation," in these cases a genuine international legislation has come into existence.[43] Just as within a state, administrative authorities may be authorized by statute to make general, abstract norms immediately binding upon individuals (administrative ordinances), thus the fundamental treaty may delegate to international administrative agencies competence to make general, abstract, immediately binding norms. But while these norms are norms of international law, they constitute international law of a hierarchical lower type. The norms of the fundamental treaty have their legal ground of validity in the norm *pacta sunt servanda* of general international law; but these norms have their legal basis in the superior fundamental treaty. This type of general norms of international law has been called "droit interne des communautés d' Etats" (Gascón y Marin) or "inneres Staatengemeinschaftsrecht" (Verdross) ; we may call them *International Administrative Ordinances*. They are of different types:

(1) Those immediately binding upon the states of the union; this is the case of the *Règlement* ("Regulations of Execution"), as distinguished from the convention, if they are made not by the general congress but by another delegated organ, e.g., the permanent committee of the union.

(2) Those immediately binding upon individuals. The European Danube Commission has jurisdiction to make regulations for the navigation on the Danube which are immediately binding upon the individuals navigating on this river.[44]

(3) The internal regulations of procedure of international commissions, or of assembly and council of the League, as often the fundamental treaty delegates to these organs competence of regulating their own procedure.

(4) The fundamental treaty may delegate to international administrative agencies the competence of regulating the status, obligations, and rights of the personnel. Here we have again a genuine, delegated international legislation, immediately binding upon individuals.

The *administrative* competence of international administrative agencies may range from modest to far-reaching competences. We may distinguish between general and auxiliary, between general and technical, between administrating, certifying, controlling, and consultative functions, between organs without and with real power of control, between organs with only preparatory administrative functions and organs which set binding administrative acts, between organs with functions of merely mediate or of immediate administration.

We may distinguish international administrative agencies which merely *co-ordinate* the administrative activities of the member states—thus the international administra-

tive bureaus—or those which *replace* national administra-
ton as in the case of the European Danube Commission
or the former Commission of the Straits. In the first case,
e.g., in the Universal Postal Union, the immediate administrative activities are carried out by the member states
through their municipal administrations. The fundamental
treaty lays down certain norms superior to the domestic
laws of the members; the members are bound not to derogate to the norms of the convention. They are free to conclude, within the general union, more restricted unions,[45]
insofar as they are not in contradiction with the norms of
the fundamental treaty.

As to the range of competences, international bureaus
have generally less far-reaching competences than the international commissions.

1. The international bureaus, the Pan-American Union,
the Secretariat of the League, the International Labor Office have mostly only preparatory administrative functions,
functions primarily of a secretarial, informational, and
ministerial character. They have no authority of their own,
no power of compulsion; they do not set acts of immediate
administration. The modesty of their competence is not in
contradiction with their importance, their great prestige,
and sometimes powerful influence. To quote from the
Universal Postal Convention, as this bureau has served
as a model for many others, this bureau is charged with
collecting, co-ordinating, publishing, and distributing information, including documents and municipal laws, concerning the international postal service, with publishing the
journal of the union and an annual general statistics; it
has to hold itself at the service of the member states and
give them all information they want; the bureaus mostly
give also information to private persons. The director
participates ex officio at the Universal Postal congresses

with right to take part in the discussions, but no right to vote; he has to make an annual report to the members of the union.[46]

2. The international bureaus mostly serve also as an intermediary between the member states. They have further to administer the private property of the union, to take care of the archives and library.

3. Many international bureaus and institutes are charged with scientific functions, studies, and research.[47]

4. The international bureaus and the Pan-American Union have further to stimulate and prepare the activities of the union. They register the demand for modification of the acts of congresses, notify the adopted changes, prepare the meetings of the congresses, make the studies with which they may be entrusted in the interest of the union; they may prepare revisions of the convention or make proposals to this effect. They have to publish the acts and proceedings of the conferences.

5. Sometimes the international bureaus have to give advisory opinions on the interpretation of the convention or on controversial questions.

6. In all these respects the bureaus are organs of liaison, information, and consultation. But some international bereaus are also charged with acting as a clearing house and providing for the settlement of unsatisfied balances; they function, in the words of Reinsch, as a fiscal center for the collection of arrears and the settlement of balances.[48]

7. The international river commissions have not only informational and ministerial functions but, nevertheless, with the exception of the European Danube Commission, also preparatory and supervisory, mediate, not immediate, administrative functions.

8. International administrative agencies may be empowered to set acts of immediate international administrative

character: e.g., the registration of trade marks within the framework of the restricted Union of the Madrid Treaty of 1891, by the Bureau for the Protection of Industrial Property, or the registration of trade marks by the corresponding Pan-American Bureau at Havana.

9. International administrative agencies may be empowered to set acts of immediate international administration binding upon individuals; thus the European Danube Commission administers directly in complete independence from local authorities, has legislative and judicial competence, has taxing power, has its own flags, and enjoys the privileges of neutrality and exterritoriality.

10. International administrative agencies may even be empowered to set acts of immediate international administration directly binding upon states; thus boundary commissions, the former Commission of the Straits, and especially the former International Sugar Commission, which had authority to collect surtaxes and to adjust the sugar tariffs of the member states even without their consent.

But where international organs are created for the *government* of a certain territory,[49] we have international governing, not international administrative, agencies.

VIII

The organ has to be distinguished from the person or persons which compose the organ. If the organ is simple, the difference is analogous to the distinction between the Crown and the King in British constitutional law. If the organ is composite, the physical persons composing the organ may realize in their person a personal union as the bearers of two different organs. The delegates, e.g., to the Universal Postal Congress may be at the same time organs of their states and partial organs of this unitarian, although composite, international organ known as the Universal Postal Congress.

But among the individuals composing an international organ, we must again distinguish between international agents and international public officials ("fonctionnaires internationaux").[50] The delegates to the Universal Postal Congress, e.g., are as such international agents, but not international public officials. International public officials are persons who, on the basis of an international treaty constituting a particular international community, are charged by this international community or by an organ of this community and under its control to exercise, in a continuous way, functions in the interest of this particular international community, and who are subject to a particular personal status.

The problem arose already with regard to the personnel of the international river commissions [51] and with regard to the officials of the international administrative unions. The personnel of these unions is mostly small, below ten in number. But the International Institute of Agriculture, the Pan-American Union, with a personnel of nearly a hundred persons each, and particularly the League of Nations and the International Labor Organizations with their vast bodies of officials, have rendered the problem a very important one.

The legal position of these international public officials, who, of course, are neither private officials nor public officials of any particular state, is not based on municipal law but on international law, on the "internal law" of a particular community of states, on these international administrative ordinances,[52] mentioned above, brought about by true and genuine international legislation, which the organs of this particular international community are delegated by the fundamental treaty to make and which have juridical validity immediately binding upon the individuals of the personnel.

The international law of public international officials ("internationales Beamtenrecht") has become a vast and important field of law. We can here only indicate the principal problems with which it has to deal. First of all, the legal position of these officials is not based on a contract of private law but on a normative situation, laid down in international administrative ordinances. These ordinances contain the legal rules as to the nomination or appointment of these officials, the conditions of appointment (physical status, intellectual capacity, education, nationality, languages, and many other problems of vital importance for a capable, reliable, independent "international civil service"). They regulate their duties (fulfillment of their functions, incompatibilities, hierarchial subordination to their superiors, professional secrecy, independence from the state of their nationality, international loyalty) and their rights (salary, tenure, advancement, vacations, pension, and so on; sometimes diplomatic privileges and immunities). They regulate the problem of disciplinary measures and the ending of their position (expiration of time, necessity of reorganization, age limit, resignation, dismissal).

Finally there is the problem of their remedies in case of conflicts with their international administrative agency. As public international officials they cannot bring a conflict with their organization before the municipal courts of the state of the seat of this organization. They have only a purely hierarchial appeal to their superiors, and, in the last instance, to the leading officer; they further have an administrative appeal to the supervising organ, such as the

permanent committee of an international administrative
union, the governing body of the Pan-American Union and
so on.

But it has been felt more and more that a mere appeal
to the same instance which, e.g., has ordered their dismissal is not sufficient to protect their rights, that they need
a judicial appeal to courts. Thus—an extremely interesting
development—real international administrative courts have
been created: the administrative tribunals, established by
the League of Nations in 1927 and by the International
Institute of Agriculture in 1933.

---

[1] Cf. G. FUSINATO, DI UNA PARTE ALQUANTO TRASCURATA DEL DIRITTO
INTERNAZIONALE (1892); P. FEDOZZI, IL DIROTTO AMMINISTRATIVO IN-
TERNAZIONALE (1901); D. DONATI, I TRATTATI INTERNAZIONALI 385
(1906); U. Borsi, *Carattere ed oggetto del diritto amministrativo
internazionale*, 6 RIVISTA DI DIRITTO INTERNAZIONALE 368 (1912).

[2] Karl Neumeyer, *Le droit administratif international*, 18 REVUE
GÉNÉRALE DE DROIT INTERNATIONAL PUBLIC 492–99 (1911), and INTER-
NATIONALES VERWALTUNGSRECHT (4 vols.; 1910–36), particularly
Volume IV at 1–25, 378–401 (1936); further in 1 STRUPP, WÖRTER-
BUCH DES VÖLKERRECHTS 577–81.

[3] TRAITÉ DE DROIT INTERNATIONAL PUBLIC 3–19.

[4] *Einige Bemerkungen uber das internationale Verwaltungsrecht*,
SCHMOLLER'S JAHRBUCH 395 (1882).

[5] P. Kazansky, *Théorie de l'administration internationale*, 9 REVUE
GÉNÉRALE DE DROIT INTERNATIONAL PUBLIC 353–67 (1902); GEMMA,
PRIME LINEE D'UN DIRITTO INTERNAZIONALE AMMINISTRATIVO (1902);
Alessio, *Il diritto amministrativo e le sue fonti*, 5 REVISTA DI DIRITTO
PUBLICO 276 (1913); L. S. WOOLF, INTERNATIONAL GOVERNMENT
(1916); F. B. SAYRE, EXPERIMENTS IN INTERNATIONAL ADMINISTRA-
TION (1919); C. Delisle Burns, *International Administration*, BRIT.
YB.INT'L L. 54–72 (1926); M. O. HUDSON, CURRENT INTERNATIONAL
COOPERATION (1927); I RUIZ MORENO, LA TEORÍA DE LA ADMINISTRA-
CIÓN INTERNACIONAL (1929); A. S. DE BUSTAMANTE, DERECHO INTER-
NACIONAL PÚBLICO (1934); A. RAPISARDI-MIRABELLI, IL DIRITTO IN-
TERNAZIONALE AMMINISTRATIVO (1939). Further the following lec-
tures at the Hague Academy of International Law: M. Pilotti, *Les
Unions d'Etats*, 4 RECUEIL DES COURS 455–545 (1928); J. Gascón y
Marin, *Les transformations du droit administratif international*, 4
RECUEIL DES COURS 5–75 (1930); P. Negulesco, *Principes du droit in-
ternational administratif*, 1 RECUEIL DES COURS 583–691 (1935); M.
Dendias, *Les principaux services internationaux administratifs*, 1
RECUEIL DES COURS 247–366 (1938).

6 Thus the definition given by P. S. REINSCH, PUBLIC INTERNATIONAL UNIONS 130 (1911).

7 As examples we name the Phylloxera Convention, Berne, 1878 (Additional Convention, 1889), the Hague Treaties of 1882 and 1887 concerning fishing in the Baltic Sea, the Convention on Automobile Traffic, Paris, October 11, 1909, replaced by the Convention of April 24, 1926 (3 M. O. HUDSON, INTERNATIONAL LEGISLATION [1859]), the Rome Convention for the Protection of Plants of April 16, 1929 (4 HUDSON, *op. cit.* at 2680).

8 Cf. A. Andréades, *Les Contrôles financiers*, 4 RECUEIL DES COURS 5–108 (1924).

9 Conseil supérieur de santé at Constantinople, abolished by Article CXIV of the Turkish Peace Treaty of Lausanne of 1923. Conseil international de santé at Bucharest (1881). Conseil sanitaire maritime et quarantenaire at Alexandria, confirmed by the Sanitary Convention of June 21, 1926.

10 European Danube Commission (created by the Peace Treaty of Paris, 1856; continued by the Versailles Treaty; cf. also the Statut définitif du Danube of July 23, 1921). Central Commission of the Rhine, equally continued by the Versailles Treaty. This treaty further created the International Commission of the Danube (art. CCCXLVII), the International Commissions of the Elbe (art. CCCXL), and of the Oder (art. CCCXLI). Cf. also the Commission of the Straits (Commission des Detroits), created by the Turkish Peace Treaty of Lausanne of 1923, abolished by the Convention of Montreux of July 20, 1936.

11 Cf. JOSEF L. KUNZ, DIE STAATENVERBINDUNGEN 373–404 (1929); F. MEILI, DIE INTERNATIONALEN UNIONEN (1889); G. MOYNIER, LES BUREAUX INTERNATIONAUX DES UNIONS UNIVERSELLES (1892); E. DESCAMPS, LES OFFICES INTERNATIONAUX ET LEUR AVENIR (1894); L. Renault, *Les Unions Internationales, leurs avantages et leurs inconvénients*, REVUE GÉNÉRALE DE DROIT INTERNATIONAL PUBLIC 14–26 (1896); L. POINSARD, LES UNIONS ET ENTENTES (2nd ed. 1901); V. GUASTELLA, LE UNIONI INTERNAZIONALI AMMINISTRATIVE (1903); A. RAPISARDI-MIRABELLI, IL DIRITTO INTERNAZIONALE AMMINISTRATIVO E LE GRANDI UNIONI FRA GLI STATI (1907); VON TOLL, DIE INTERNATIONALEN BUREAUX DER ALLEGEMEINEN VÖLKERRECHTLICHEN VERWALTUNGSVEREINE (1910); P. S. REINSCH, PUBLIC INTERNATIONAL UNIONS (1911); K. Strupp in 1 WÖRTERBUCH DES VÖLKERRECHTS 573–77; F. Roussel-Despierres, *Les Unions internationales*, REVUE INTERNATIONAL DE SOCIOLOGIE (1916); K. Neumeyer, *Les Unions Internationales*, 2 REVUE DE DROIT INTERNATIONAL, DES SCIENCES DIPLOMATIQUES, POLITIQUES ET SOCIALES 16–40, 139–44, 343–62 (1924); W. Kaufman, *Les Unions Internationales de nature économique*, 2 RECUEIL DES COURS 181–290 (1924); A. Rapisardi-Mirabelli, *Théorie Générale des Unions Internationales*, 7 *ibid* at 345–90 (1925); the same in 7 ZEITSCHRIFT FÜR ÖFFENTLICHES RECHT 11–21 (1927); F. Ruffini, *La natura giuridica della Unioni Internationali Amministrative*, RIVISTA DI DIRITTO PUBBLICO (1928); M. Udina, *Unioni Internazionali*, NUOVO DIGESTO ITALIANO (1939).

[12] Namely the International Geodetic Union of 1862; the International Seismological Union, based on the Conventions of 1903 and 1905; the International Sugar Union, created by the Brussels Convention of March 5, 1902 (31 Martens N.R.G. [2e sér.] 272), with an international bureau at Brussels; this union came to an end on September 1, 1920.

[13] The International Telecommunications Union (1932) has replaced the former International Telegraphic Union (1865) and the former International Radio-Telegraphic Union (1906). The Anti-Slave Trade Union (1890) was replaced by the St. Germain Treaty of 1919.

[14]. Based on the Treaty of Berne of October 9, 1874 (1 Martens N.R.G. [2e sér.] 651), revised by the International Postal Congresses of Paris, 1878, Lisbon, 1885, Vienna, 1891, Washington, 1897, Rome, 1906, Madrid, 1920, Stockholm, 1924, London, 1929, Cairo, 1934, and Buenos Aires, 1939. International bureau in Berne. Monographs: L. RENAULT, ETUDES SUR LES RAPPORTS INTERNATIONAUX, LA POSTE ET LE TÉLÉGRAPHE (1877); G. LACROIS, EXPOSÉ DU SYSTÈME GÉNÉRAL DE L'UNION POSTALE UNIVERSELLE; Kirchenheim on the International Postal Congresses in 12 REVUE DE DROIT INTERNATIONAL LEGISLATION COMPARÉE 467; H. WEITHASE, GESCHICHTE DES WELTPOSTVEREINS (1895); C. SCHRÖTER DER WELTPOSTVEREIN (1900); L. ROLAND, DE LA CORRESPONDANCE POSTALE ET TÉLÉGRAPHIQUE DANS LES RELATIONS INTERNATIONALES (1901); J. JUNG, DER WELTPOSTVEREIN (1903); H. KRAINS, L'UNION POSTALE UNIVERSELLE (1910); L. CAPPELLI, STORIA DELLE CONVENZIONI POSTALI INTERNAZIONALI (1917); L'UNION POSTALE UNIVERSELLE, SA FONDATION ET SON DÉVELOPPEMENT (1924), and Supplement (1929); John F. Sly, *The Genesis of the Universal Postal Union*, INT'L CONC., No. 233, 393–443 (1927); H. R. Turkel, *International Postal Congresses*, BRIT. YB. INT'L L. 171–80 (1929); BUHLER, DER WELTPOSTVEREIN (1930); and Universal Postal Union, Convention of Buenos Aires, May 23, 1939, and Washington, 1940.

[15] Union des Poids et Mesures, based on the Paris Treaty of May 20, 1875 (1 Martens N.R.G. [2e sér.] 663). International bureau at St. Cloud near Paris. Cf. C. E. GUILLAUME, LA CRÉATION DU BUREAU INTERNATIONAL DES POIDS ET MESURES (1927).

[16] Based on the Paris Treaty of March 20, 1883 (10 Martens N.R.G. [2e sér] 133; 30 *ibid.* at 449). Act of Washington of January 2, 1911, (8 *ibid.* [3e sér.] 760). International bureau at Berne.

[17] Based on the Berne Convention of September 9, 1886 (12 Martens N.R.G. [2e sér.] 173). International bureau at Berne. Cf. F. Ruffini, *La protection internationale des droits sur les œuvres littéraires et Artistiques*, 2 RECUEIL DES COURS 391–571 (1926).

[18] Based on the Brussels Convention of July 5, 1890 (16 Martens N.R.G. [2e sér.] 532; 18 *ibid.* at 558). International bureau at Brussels. We may mention here also the Brussels Treaty of December 31, 1913, for the creation of an International Bureau of Commercial Statistics (11 Martens N.R.G. [3e sér.] 304). Bureau at Brussels.

[19] Created by the Berne Convention of October 14, 1890 (19 Martens N.R.G. [2e sér.] 289). Revised by the two Berne Conventions of

October 23, 1924 (2 HUDSON, INTERNATIONAL LEGISLATION 1393. International bureau at Berne. Monographs: van der Leyen in 1 WÖRTERBUCH DES VÖLKERRECHTS 266, 3 *ibid.* at 817; SCHNEIDER, ENTWICKLUNG DES INTERNATIONALEN EISENBAHNRECHTS SEIT DEM BERNER UBEREINKOMMEN VOM JAHRE 1890 (1926); STIELER, DER INTERNATIONALE EISEN BAHNVERBAND (1926); JOSSERAND, TRANSPORTS EN SERVICE INTÉRIEUR ET EN SERVICE INTERNATIONAL (1926); BRUNET, DURAND, and FOURCOULD, LES TRANSPORTS INTERNATIONAUX PAR VOIES FERRÉES (1927).

[20] Created by the Rome Convention of June 7, 1905 (3 Martens N.R.G. [3e sér.] 139). Monographs: VON STOCKHAMERN, DAS INTERNATIONALE LANDWIRTSCHAFLICHE INSTITUT IN ROM (1928); A. HOBSON, THE INTERNATIONAL INSTITUTE OF AGRICULTURE (1931).

[21] Based on the Paris Treaty of November 3, 1903; the Office International d'Hygiène Publique at Paris was created by the agreement of December 9, 1907.

[22] Treaty of June 30, 1919; the Bureau International Hydrographique at Monaco was created in 1922.

[23] Paris Treaty of June 21, 1920 (1 HUDSON, *op. cit.* at 464). Bureau International du Froid in Paris.

[24] Paris Treaty of January 25, 1924 (2 HUDSON, *op. cit.* at 1239). Office International des Epizooties in Paris.

[25] Paris Treaty of November 29, 1924 (2 HUDSON, *op. cit.* at 1533). Office International du Vin at Paris.

[26] Created by the Geneva Treaty of July 12, 1927 (3 HUDSON, *op. cit.* at 2090).

[27] Treaty of October 29, 1927. Bureau in Paris.

[28] Convention of December 9, 1932. Bureau in Paris.

[29] Not of particular administrations of the states. The International Telegraphic Bureau, originally known as the Bureau International des Administrations télégraphiques, was rebaptized in 1908 as the Bureau International de l'Union télégraphique. Sometimes colonies or other non-sovereign territories are admitted in varying degrees to membership. The Universal Postal Convention designates the members with the non-technical term of "countries." For a painstaking study of this problem, cf. B. Akzin, *Membership in the Universal Postal Union,* 27 AM.J.INT'L L. 651–74 (1933). Cf. also the special position of certain private corporations in the International Telegraphic Union. Although international administrative unions have sometimes historically developed from private international organizations (such as the Geodetic Union or the Institut International du Froid) or owe their creation to private initiative (as in the case of the International Institute of Agriculture), they must be clearly distinguished from international private organizations. On these latter, cf. W. Kaufmann in 2 ZEITSCHRIFT FÜR VÖLKERRECHT 419–40 (1908); VAN OVERBERGH, L'ASSOCIATION INTERNATIONALE (1907); A. Guillois, *Les Associations internationales,* REVUE GÉNÉRALE DE DROIT INTERNATIONAL PUBLIC 5–127 (1915); *Rapport et project politis in* 30 ANNUAIRE DE L'INSTITUT DE DROIT INTERNATIONAL 97–173, 348–81 (1923); P. SCHRAG, INTERNATIONALE IDEALVEREINE (1936).

30 On this problem cf. G. Ottolenghi, *Sulla personalità internazionale delle Unioni di Stati*, 17 RIVISTA DI DIRITTO INTERNAZIONALE 313–57, 461–99 (1925).

31 Cf. Universal Postal Conventions, art. I.

32 The fundamental treaty contains, nevertheless, a denunciation clause. But the denunciation has as a juridical consequence only the exit of that particular member, whereas the union as such continues. The union is, further, not dissolved by war; the norms are only suspended as between the belligerents. Practically, a resignation, e.g., from the Universal Postal Union, is out of the question.

33 Institute of Intellectual Co-operation, Paris (1925); International Institute for the Unification of Private Law, Rome (1926); International Institute of Educational Films, Rome (1928).

34 Cf. C. GRASSI, LE UNIONI INTERNAZIONALI AMMINISTRATIVE E LA SOCIETÀ DELLA NAZIONI (1919); A. RAPISARDI-MIRABELLI, GLI STADI DELL'ORGANIZZAZIONE INTERNAZIONALE DALLE UNIONI INTERNAZIONALI ALLA SOCIETÀ DELLA NAZIONI (1926); H. BOISSON, LA SOCIÉTÉ DES NATIONS ET LES BUREAUX INTERNATIONAUX DES UNIONS UNIVERSELLES POSTALE ET TÉLÉGRAPHIQUE (1932).

35 Only the Commission Internationale de Navigation Aérienne (CINA), created by the Paris Convention of 1919, the Bureau Hydrographique International at Monaco, and the Office Central pour le Contrôle du Commerce des Spiritueux en Afrique, created by the St. Germain Treaty of September 10, 1919 (1 HUDSON, *op. cit.* at 323), were placed under the authority of the League. Interesting are the negotiations of the League with th Office International d'Hygiène Publique in Paris leading to the creation of the Hygiene Organization of the League.

36 For a list see 10 DEP'T STATE BULL. No. 241 at 152–61 (February 5, 1944).

37 Cf. the literature quoted in notes 5 and 11, above, and D. Anzilotti, *Gli organi comuni nella Società di Stati*, 8 RIVISTA DI DIRITTO INTERNAZIONALE 156–64 (1914); and C. Baldoni, *Gli organi e gli Instituti nelle Unioni Internazionali*, 23 *ibid.* at 352–85, 464–89 (1931).

38 For a fuller treatment of this problem cf. KUNZ, DIE STAATEN-VERBINDUNGEN 393–404 (1929).

39 This latter problem was particularly discussed with reference to the International Institute of Agriculture. Cf. G. Fusinato in 8 RIVISTA DI DIRITTO INTERNAZIONALE 149–55 (1914); and to the judgment of the Corte di Cassazione in Rome of February 26, 1931 (23 RIVISTA DI DIRITTO INTERNAZIONALE 385 [1921]); also in 4 ZEITSCHRIFT FÜR AUSLÄNDISCHES ÖFFENTLICHES RECHT UND VÖLKERRECHT 165 (1934); English translation of the judgment in M. O. HUDSON, CASES AND MATERIALS ON INTERNATIONAL LAW 39–40 (2nd ed. 1936).

40 Cf., on this committee, the study of Carl B. Spaeth and William Sanders in 38 AM.J.INT'L L. 218–41 (1944).

41 Only the special bureau at Zanzibar, created by the Brussels Anti-Slavery Convention of 1890, was composed of the representatives

of the member states. But the type of its functions was exactly the same as those of any international bureau.

[42] E.g., the Central Office of International Transport by Rail at Berne, according to Article LVII, point 3, of the Berne Convention of 1890. Cf. M. O. Hudson and L. B. Sohn, *Fifty Years of Arbitration in the Union of International Transport by Rail*, 37 AM.J.INT'L L. 597–610 (1943). Further the Rhine Central Commission (Article XLVc of the Rhine Navigation Act of Mannheim of October 17, 1868); similarly the jurisdiction of the Elbe Commission (art. II) of the Elbe Navigation Act of February 22, 1922. Additional agreement of January 27, 1923. Particularly the European Danube Commission exercises judicial functions in civil and criminal cases, in first and in second instance.

[43] Cf. SCERNI, SULLA NATURA GIURIDICA DELLE NORME EMANATE DAGLI ORGANI CREATI CON ATTI INTERNAZIONALI (1931); A. Verdross, VÖLKERRECHT 42, 44, 69, 78–79, 105 (1937).

[44] Such "pouvior règlementaire" belonged also to the former Commission of the Straits.

[45] Cf. the more restricted union, within the Union for the Protection of Industrial Property, on the registration of trade marks, according to the Madrid Treaty of April 14, 1891, and the additional act of Brussels of December 14, 1900. Cf. also the Postal Union of the Americas and Spain, with the bureau at Montevideo.

[46] Sometimes the union intends also the unification of the law concerning the particular field of the union; great success has been achieved in this respect by the Union of International Transport by Rail.

[47] Thus the Union of Weights and Measures or the International Hydrographic Bureau at Monaco. The International Institute of Agriculture in Rome, on the other hand, has no scientific functions.

[48] Thus the Universal Postal Bureau and the Central Office of International Transport by Rail.

[49] Thus the contemplated Albanian International Commission of Control, created by the London Ambassadors Conference, 1913; thus the Leticia Governing Commission of the League of Nations (June, 1933, to June, 1934) and, particularly, the Saar Governing Commission, 1920–35.

[50] Cf. SUZANNE BASDEVANT, LES FONCTIONNAIRES INTERNATIONAUX (1931); José Gascón y Marin, *Les fonctionnaires internationaux*, 3 RECUEIL DES COURS 725–91 (1932).

[51] The European Danube Commission has not only officials—as distinguished from the members of the Commission—but also subordinate organs: the Captain of the Port of Sulina and the Inspector of Navigation at Toulcea.

[52] Cf. the Statutes of the International Institute of Agriculture, and the Statutes of the Personnel of the League of Nations, made by the Secretary General.

WITHIN THE REALM of international law, general and particular [1] international law have to be distinguished, the first consisting of norms binding all members of the international community, whereas the norms of the latter are binding on less than all members. The range of spatial validity, not the procedure of the creation of norms, is the distinctive criterion. For while general international law is created only by custom,[2] particular international law may also be created by custom, although the bulk of it consists of treaty-created norms. Treaty-created norms always constitute particular international law only, whether the treaties are bilateral, regional, or "quasi-universal," and whether the treaties create only concrete, individual or general abstract norms.

General international law is, up to now, a primitive law lacking special organs. Particular international law may—although it need not—create special international organs. It constitutes, therefore, a way to develop primitive international law into a more advanced "organized" international legal order. Hence, the great emphasis on "international organization." [3]

Yet, even the law created by "quasi-universal" treaties must clearly be distinguished from general international law. This was always recognized as a matter of course. Only recently Article II, paragraph 6, of the Chapter of the United Nations has led some writers to assert that this Charter constitutes, or pretends to constitute, general international law. Article XVII of the League of Nations Covenant, in some way a predecessor, never purported to bind non-members. There was never any doubt, theoretically or practically, that the United States was never bound by the League Covenant. The Permanent Court of International Justice stated in an advisory opinion [4] that "international organizations cannot impose legal obligations on third States against their own will." And in the Eastern Karelian case (1923) [5] the Court laid down that "States not members of the League are not bound by the Covenant." and refused to give even an advisory opinion, in the absence of consent by the Soviet Union.

Kelsen [6] interprets Article II, paragraph 6, as "showing the tendency to be general, not only particular international law." [7] He admits, however, that this interpretation makes that provision, being in contradiction to general international law, a revolutionary norm the very validity of which in consequence, depends on effectivity. But this interpretation is by no means necessary and has not been accepted by the majority of writers. [8]

In any case, the law of the United Nations has to be carefully distinguished from general international law. The latter continues to exist independently of the Charter. The rule of general international law, *pacta sunt servanda,* is the basis of validity of the Charter. The Charter is not only based on general international law, but also presupposes it in its very principles. The Preamble pledges respect for the obligations arising from treaties (including

the Charter) and "international law." Article I speaks of
the "principles of international law." These are references
to general international law. Equally, Article XIII (a)
speaks of the "progressive development of international
law and its codification."

The Charter, like any treaty, is itself under the impact
of general international law. Its coming into force, its
change, its end, are governed by rules of general international law in addition to the rules provided in the Charter. It may be changed by custom, as in the case of
Article XVIII of the League Covenant, without an amendment; the norm of *desuetudo* applies. The interpretation
of the Charter is governed by general international law.
The so-called political interpretation of the Charter, now
often advocated, "is nothing but an attempt to justify
the non-application of the existing law in case its application is in conflict with some interest, or rather, with
what the respective writer considers to be the interest
of his State." [9] The Permanent Court of International Justice always interpreted the League of Nations Covenant
according to the principles of general international law.
The International Court of Justice, interpreting the Charter in the advisory opinion on admission to the United
Nations,[10] has clearly stated that "to determine the meaning
of a treaty provision [here the Charter] . . . is a problem
of interpretation and consequently a legal question," "an
essentially judicial task." If a norm of the particular law
of an international organization does not function, the
corresponding norm of general international law reappears.
The United Nations has no legislative authority to abolish
rules of general international law. The particular law even
of a quasi-universal international organization may be
ephemeral; the law of the League Covenant is no longer
valid, but general international law continues.

But while the law of international organizations is based upon, presupposes, and stands under the impact of, general international law, it exercises, on the other hand, an influence on general international law. The laws of war and neutrality have been very much influenced by the particular law of the League and of the United Nations so that they stand today in a chaotic condition. Treaty law may, under the rules of general international law, become general international law by custom.

The hopes concerning the maintenance of peace raised by the League of Nations amidst a wave of enthusiasm have been disappointed. It is often said that "the true measure of the League" was "to be essentially a universal communal organization of nations committed to the maintenance of peace, the assertion of the rule of law over national power interests, and the solidarity of all against any law-breaking aggressor," [11] and that, in consequence, all the League's achievements in the field of non-political international co-operation "have only marginal significance." Equally, over-optimism in the United Nations has quickly been followed by disappointment. "Realistic," sociological international lawyers like Georg Schwarzenberger speak of these two experiments as mere "superstructures" above the primitive general international law, as mere "power politics in disguise."

It is true that these experiments have not had a full success so far. Sir Gladwyn Jebb, the British permanent delegate to the United Nations, recently warned strongly against over-optimism in this field.[12] He stated that no enforcement action can be taken against a Great Power without a major war; that it would be unrealistic to expect too much from the work of the Collective Measures Committee; that we must frankly recognize the comparative weakness of the United Nations—a weakness deep-rooted in the facts of the world situation—as an instrument for providing the physical force to resist aggression; that, perhaps, the United Nations has a greater role before it as an organ of conciliation. Naturally, a real end of the "Cold War" could enhance the role of the United Nations also in this field. But even if unsuccessful so far, these new ideas have opened new vistas. The League of Nations, although dead, will stand in history as the first experiment in this direction. The United Nations is the second experiment; and even if it should fail, too, certainly a third experiment will have to be, and will be, made.

In the meantime, the law of international organizations, dealing with non-political international co-operation, has made, and is making its influence felt also in the realm of general international law. International organizations have become subjects of international law and have thus widened the international community, hitherto composed nearly exclusively of sovereign states. A new type of international treaties concluded by international organizations with member and non-member states or *inter se* has appeared. We see an embryonic law of succession of international organizations developing.[13] New problems of privileges and immunities of international organizations have been created and these problems have their repercussions also in general international law.

This inter-action between the law of international organizations and general international law began with the coming of the international administrative unions.[14] The enthusiasm of early writers on this development, such as Moynier or Descamps, is fully understandable and justified. With their tripartite scheme of organization they established the model for most of the later international organizations, regional or quasi-universal. Such unions contain the germ of what has now become a vast international civil service. A true international legislation, based on the basic treaty, was created—legislation *pro foro interno,* binding upon member states or upon individuals. Non-sovereign territories were admitted as full or restricted members. The basic treaty rules were clearly superior to the domestic laws of the members. The basic treaty of the Universal Postal Union made the territories of all the members one territory for purposes of postal communications. In the same Union a development took place to treat resolutions as being in force without waiting for all ratifications. Attempts were made to depart from the unanimity rule. A modern uniform law in many important fields was created. The fields covered by international administrative unions were more and more enlarged. Limitations of sovereignty became an accepted thing. The necessity of solving certain problems internationally, the inevitable interdependence of the modern world, were recognized. Even in this beginning period we can see, step by step, and done in a non-sensational way, the developments which might lead to changing patterns in the international community.

The League of Nations excellently carried on and expanded this work. International co-operation in financial matters had great success. The Geneva Conventions of 1930 and 1931 concerning Bills of Exchange and Checks constitute great progress in the field of unification of private law. The problem of refugees and stateless persons entered the field of international organizations. The mandates system, even if created from political considerations and applied only to ex-enemy territories, marks an important change in the development of thought concerning the adminstration of not fully self-governing peoples. The International Labor Organization set a new pattern of organization, admitting representatives of private labor and employers' organizations, and created the International Labor Code.

Since 1945 we have seen an unheard-of development of international organizations, principal and specialized, quasi-universal and regional. A new problem of their co-ordination [15] has been created in international law. International non-governmental organizations, by having been brought into relationship with intergovernmental organizations, have reached a place in international law. "Higher standards of living, full employment, conditions of economic and social progress and development, solution of international economic, social, health, cultural and educational cooperation" hold a prominent place in the United Nations Charter.[16] The number and importance of international economic and financial organizations has strongly increased.[17]

At the latest annual meeting of the Academy of Political Science [18] the question on the agenda was: "United Nations —Success or Failure?" It is characteristic that many speakers,[19] to prove success, dealt with non-political international co-operation. David Mitrany [20] stressed the enormous importance of the International Technical Assistance Program; he held it to be "the most vital and promising line of action in our varied efforts toward a peaceful and contented world community." He went so far as to state that this Technical Assistance Program, by which all, for the first time in history, accept the principle of common international responsibility for general conditions everywhere "may prove infinitely more important than the prohibition of war in the Charter of the U. N."

Similar ideas were voiced recently in a long and excellent article by Roberto Ago,[21] who rightly says that just as was earlier over-optimism, present-day pessimism is superficial and unjustified. Certainly, even in the field of non-political international co-operation, the present East-West split is hampering progress. Certainly, notwithstanding all international organizations in this field the leadership of the United States is indispensable. But there are signs that technological progress and a worldwide ideology for higher living standards and economic and social development are leading us to a unifying world. These international organizations have, therefore, a firm basis in the real necessities and in the wishes of nations. Contrary to the "neo-realists" of today who would like to persuade us that there is nothing but power, force, and national self-interest and that the role of international law in international relations is negligible, it is clear that there can be no coexistence of men, under whatever system of government, whether within one state or internationally, without law. And faith in the rule of law, in liberty under law, is a basic element of our Western culture. While most international organizations have not so far changed the character of the international community, and while the impact exercised by these international organizations is step by step and nonsensational, unknown by the great masses, this impact may pave the way even for a structural change in the law of nations.

---

[1] OPPENHEIM-LAUTERPACHT, INTERNATIONAL LAW: A TREATISE 4–5 (7th ed. 1948), call what this writer calls "general" international law "universal," and restrict "particular" international law to treaty norms binding only on two or a few states. The third category of "general" international law is claimed "for the body of rules binding upon a great many States, including the leading Powers." This new category can hardly be admitted from a theoretical point of view; there is no juridical criterion between general and particular international law, thus defined. This writer's use of "quasi-universal" international law covers more than Oppenheim-Lauterpacht's "general" international law without introducing a new category. Quasi-universal international law is not a new category; it is particular international law, too; the term denotes only a greater extension of validity, not a legal difference. For this writer the League of Nations Covenant constituted quasi-universal international law. But it would not be general international law in the sense of Oppenheim-Lauterpacht, as the Soviet Union and Germany were at one time not yet bound, and

later both, as well as Japan, no longer bound, and as the United States never was bound, by the Covenant. A. Verdross (VÖLKERRECHT 73 [2nd ed. 1950]) correctly speaks of "universal" and "general" international law as synonymous terms. The recent term "world law"—to designate quasi-universal particular international law—is technically unjustified, not only because even quasi-universal treaties constitute only particular international law, but also because the term "world law" suggests the end of international law; it refers to the municipal law of a world state.

2 P. Guggenheim (1 LEHRBUCH DES VÖLKERRECHTS at 48) calls, following Max Huber, "droit international commun" the norms valid in the whole spatial sphere of international law, but is of the opinion that to them also belong norms not created by custom.

3 It is, therefore, easy to agree with Percy E. Corbett's sentence (LAW AND SOCIETY IN THE RELATIONS OF STATES 12 [1951]) "that the future of international law is one with the future of international organization," because it means only that the future of international law lies in the progress to a more advanced international law.

4 P.C.I.J., ser. B, Nos. 2 and 3 (Competence of International Labor Organization).

5 P.C.I.J., ser. B, No. 5 at 27–28.

6 THE LAW OF THE UNITED NATIONS 106–10 (1950).

7 That is why Kelsen in his new work, PRINCIPLES OF INTERNATIONAL LAW (1952), which deals with general international law, includes a detailed analysis of fundamental principles of the U.N. Charter (p. vii). This interpretation is also accepted by ALF ROSS, CONSTITUTION OF THE UNITED NATIONS 32–33 (1950).

8 See "Revolutionary Creation of Norms of International Law," above. GOODRICH and HAMBRO, CHARTER OF THE UNITED NATIONS 108–10 (2nd ed. 1949); OPPENHEIM-LAUTERPACHT, op cit. at 371: "Without imposing legal obligations upon non-member States"; N. BENTWICH and A. MARTIN, A COMMENTARY ON THE CHARTER OF THE UNITED NATIONS 14 (1950): "The Charter does not purport to impose legal obligations on non-members. . . . [They] will have to obey not as a matter of law, but as the result of the realities of power"; 1 P. GUGGENHEIM, op. cit. at 92.

9 KELSON, op. cit. at viii.

10 I.C.J. Reports 61 (1948).

11 G. Niemeyer, The Balance Sheet of the League Experiment, 6 INTERNATIONAL ORGANIZATION, No. 4, 537–58 at 542 (November, 1952).

12 Sir Gladwyn Jebb, The Role of the United Nations, ibid. at 509–20.

13 League of Nations—U.N.; International Institute of Agriculture —FAO; International Institute of Intellectual Cooperation—UNESCO.

14 See "Experience and Techniques in International Administration," above.

15 See Wilfred Jenks, Co-ordination: A New Problem of International Organization, 2 RECUEIL DES COURS 157–302 (1950), and in 28 BRIT.YB.INT'L L. 28–29 (1952).

16 Article LV.

17 See CHARLES H. ALEXANDROWICZ, INTERNATIONAL ECONOMIC OR-GANIZATIONS (1952).

18 25 PROCEEDINGS, No. 2 (1953).

19 Boudreau on WHO and FAO (*ibid.* at 134–43) ; Basch on financing economic developments (*ibid.* at 157–70) ; Klineberg on UNESCO (*ibid.* at 187–97).

20 *Ibid.* at 145–55.

21 *Considerazioni su alcuni sviluppi dell'organizzaione internazionale,* 7 LA COMUNITÀ INTERNAZIONALE, No. 4 at 527–67.

CHAPTER XXVII: Privileges and Immunities of International Organizations

THE PROBLEM of the privileges and immunities of international organizations has become very prominent in recent times and has raised not a few difficult questions. While many aspects of this problem cannot yet be regarded as definitively settled, there is, on the other hand, a trend toward the development of a new uniform and general international law concerning this topic. It seems, therefore, timely to investigate briefly this problem in its different ramifications historical and theoretical.

HISTORICAL SURVEY

The problem is not quite as new as it is sometimes supposed to be. It dates from the beginning of the nineteenth century.

1. *From the beginning of the nineteenth century to 1920.* One of the earliest examples of the grant of diplomatic immunities to non-diplomatic functionaries international is to be found in the Convention of Contingents of the Panama Congress of 1826.[1] Mexico invested its commissioners on the Mixed Claims Commission under the United States–Mexico Convention of April 11, 1839 [2] with diplomatic

character. Diplomatic privileges were later granted to the members of the International Finance Control Commission of Greece by the Hellenic Statute of February 26 (March 10) 1898.[3] The privileges of "independence and neutrality" were originally given to the Central Commission for the Navigation of the Rhine [4] and permanently to the European Danube Commission; [5] "inviolability" was granted to the International Congo Commission provided by the Berlin Congo Act of 1885.[6]

Diplomatic privileges were granted to the judges of the Permanent Court of Arbitration.[7] The same privileges were envisaged for the proposed Court of Arbitral Justice [8] and the International Prize Court.[9] Of the judges of the Central American Court of Justice, it was provided that

> whilst they remain in the Country of their appointment, shall enjoy the personal immunity which the respective laws grant to the magistrates of the Supreme Court, and in the four other contracting Republics they shall have the privileges and immunities of diplomatic agents.[10]

The Central American Treaty of 1907 created a Central American Bureau composed of representatives of the five republics, having its seat in Guatemala City, and provided that the delegates should have in their own country the immunities of members of the legislative body and in the other four republics diplomatic immunities. After a long struggle between the different conceptions of the bureau and of the governments of San Salvador and Costa Rica,[11] the Central American Conference of 1910 adopted the interpretative Convention of February 3, 1910, Article IV which provided for diplomatic immunities of the delegates in the Republic of Guatemala.

2. *1920–39.* Prior to 1920 granting of diplomatic privileges and immunities to international organizations was clearly an exception based on particular treaties or statutes.

No such privileges existed in the case of other finance control commissions, of other river commissions, of the international sanitary councils, of all the administrative unions, or in the case of the Pan-American Union. This remained in principle the law also during the period from 1920 to 1939, but the granting of such privileges by treaty or statute was greatly extended. Only the United States took, prior to 1941, a negative attitude, on the basis that under international law diplomatic privileges were due only to members of diplomatic missions.[12] The great increase in grants of diplomatic privileges to international organizations has brought into being a rich literature on this topic,[13] which has already begun to be studied by learned societies and international organs.[14]

Such privileges and immunities were in this period confirmed and continued for the European Danube Commission,[15] were granted by French decree of 1922 to representatives and agents of the Central Commission for the Navigation of the Rhine, by the Italian law of June, 1930, to the members of the General Assembly and of the Permanent Committee as well as to the officials of the first and second categories of the International Institute of Agriculture at Rome, by treaty to the newly created international river commissions, the International Danube Commission,[16] the Elbe Commission,[17] the Oder Commission, and the Commission Technique Permanente du Régime des Eaux du Danube;[18] they were granted further to many organs created by the Paris Peace Treaties or by later treaties: to the Interallied Rhineland High Commission,[19] to the Reparations Commission,[20] the Ambassador's Conference, boundary commissions, international plebiscite commissions, to the organs and agents created to execute the Dawes Plan; by a Polish-Danzig treaty to the Polish-Danzig Harbor Board,[21] and the Polish Commissioner General in Danzig. Diplomatic status of the Uruguayan delegate on the Commission of Inquiry and Conciliation in the conflict between Paraguay and Bolivia (1929) [22] was recognized. Diplomatic privileges were granted to the members of the mixed arbitral tribunals created by the Paris Peace Treaties.[23] The German-Polish Convention of 1922 granted diplomatic privileges and immunities to the members and the chief of the bureau and to the agents of the member states, but not to a state's own nationals, in the Arbitral Tribunal of Upper Silesia.

Article XIX of the Statute of the Permanent Court of International Justice granted to the judges diplomatic privileges and immunities in the exercise of their functions and outside of their own country. A detailed regulation concerning diplomatic privileges and immunities of the judges and officials of the Registry in the Netherlands was brought about by the letter to President Anzilotti of the Court to the Dutch Foreign Minister Beelaerts van Blokland of May 22, 1928.[24]

Diplomatic privileges were also envisaged for the Bank of International Settlements.[25] Finally Article VII, paragraph 4, of the Covenant of the League of Nations gives to the representatives of the members and the agents of the League diplomatic privileges and immunities.[26] As far as their enjoyment in Switzerland was concerned first a provisional agreement of July 17, 1921, and later a *modus vivendi* [27] were agreed upon between Switzerland and the Secretary General of the League on September 18, 1926.

3. *Since 1939.*[28] The Charter of the United Nations contains several articles [29] on privileges and immunities. These articles were carefully studied by the preparatory commission of the United Nations in London,[30] which annexed to its report a draft convention on privileges and immunities [31] and a draft convention between the United Nations and the United States.[32] The first convention was studied by the fifth [33] and sixth [34] Committee of the First Part of the General Assembly of the United Nations, held in London; on

February 13, 1946, the General Assembly adopted the
General Convention on the Privileges and Immunities of
the United Nations.[35] This convention had been ratified so
far only by the United Kingdom.

A negotiating committee of the United Nations reached
an interim agreement with Switzerland, which provided
privileges and immunities for the United Nations and its
personnel, more extensive than those offered by this country. The League building and other buildings have been
acquired by the United Nations in the former League of
Nations area at Geneva. The first report of the Secretary
General and the negotiating committee on the interim arrangement on privileges and immunities of the United Nations concluded with the Swiss Federal Council and on
arrangements concerning the Ariana site came before the
sixth (Legal) Committee of the Second Part of the General
Assembly of the United Nations, held in New York in November and December, 1946. The same committee had before it also a joint report of the Secretary General and the
Committee of Negotiations with the competent authorities
of the United States regarding the arrangements required
as a result of the establishment of the seat of the United
Nations in the United States. The fact that the United
Nations Headquarters Committee adopted a midtown site
in New York City as the permanent headquarters of the
United Nations has somewhat changed the legal problem,
as the original draft convention was made with a rural area
in mind. On June 26, 1947, the second anniversary of the
signing of the Charter, Secretary of State Marshall and
Secretary General of the U.N. Trygve Lie signed at Lake
Success the agreement between the U.N. and the United
States. The agreement will be brought into force by an exchange of notes between the Secretary General and the
President of the United States after they have been authorized to approve it by the General Assembly and by both
Houses of Congress by a majority vote.

The Statute of the International Court of Justice contains a clause,[36] identical with Article XIX of the statute of the former court, giving diplomatic privileges to the judges, "when engaged on the business of the Court"; Article XXXII, paragraph 8, of the statute stipulates that salaries, allowances, and compensations shall be free from taxation. New is Article XLII, paragraph 3: "The agents, counsel, and advocates of parties before the Court shall enjoy the privileges and immunities necessary to the independent exercise of their duties." Part II of the General Convention on the Privileges and Immunities of the United Nations of February 13, 1946, invites the members of the Court at their first session to consider the question of ensuring that the Court shall enjoy the privileges, immunities, and facilities necessary for the exercise of its functions and the fulfilment of its purposes, in the country of its seat and elsewhere, and to inform the Secretary General of their recommendations. The problem of immunities and privileges for the judges and staff officials of the Court came before the sixth (Legal) Committee of the Second Part of the General Assembly of the United Nations, held in New York. Negotiations between the Court and the government of the Netherlands led to an agreement, confirmed by an exchange of notes between the president of the Court and the Dutch minister of foreign affairs, on June 26, 1946.[37] This agreement was approved by a resolution of the General Assembly of December 11, 1946, which also approved the proposals of the Court as to privileges and immunities of the Court in countries other than Holland.[38]

Clauses concerning privileges and immunities are frequently to be found in the constitutions of the specialized agencies. The United Nations Relief and Rehabilitation Administration (UNRRA), at the first session of its council,[39] adopted Resolutions 32, 34, and 36, concerning this problem. The International Labor Organization (ILO), which had enjoyed diplomatic privileges under Article VII, paragraph

4, of the League Covenant, has included corresponding clauses in its "Philadelphia Charter" (1944).[40]

Article VIII, paragraph 4, and Article XV of the constitution of the Food and Agriculture Organization (FAO),[41] Article IX of the International Monetary Fund agreement, Article VII of the agreement creating the International Bank for Reconstruction and Development,[42] Articles IV and VIII; points 14–17, of the European Central Inland Transportation Organization (ECITO),[43] Article I, section 4, of the Provisional International Civil Aviation Organization (PICAO),[44] Article XII of the constitution of the United Nations Educational, Scientific, and Cultural Organization (UNESCO),[45] the constitution of the International Refugee Organization (IRO), the constitution of the World Health Organization (WHO),[46] Articles LXXIII and LXIV of the suggested charter of an International Trade Organization [47] deal with privileges and immunities. Other specialized agencies may follow.

The same trend is also visible outside of the United Nations, particularly in the Inter-American system. We can point here to the project of an Inter-American Court of Justice, to the convention concerning the creation of an Inter-American Bank, to the granting of diplomatic privileges and immunities to the members of the newly organized governing board of the Pan-American Union,[48] and to the project of an organic pact of the Inter-American system.[49]

We see the same trend even in respect to bilateral organs: The recent U.S.–Mexican Water Treaty,[50] which came into force on November 28, 1945, creates an International Boundary and Water Commission. Under Article III, paragraph 4, of the treaty,

> each government shall accord diplomatic status to the Commissioner designated by the other government. The Commissioner, two principal engineers, a legal adviser, and a secretary, designated by each government as members of its Section of the Com-

mission, shall be entitled in the territory of the other country
to the privileges and immunities appertaining to diplomatic
officers.

Municipal statutes and ordinances have recently appeared
in many states to the same effect; thus in China,[51] Canada,[52]
Great Britain,[53] and, reversing a longstanding attitude to
the contrary, in the United States.[54]

THEORETICAL SURVEY

It is not intended here to describe in detail the privileges
and immunities of the League of Nations, of the United
Nations, of any particular, or even of all international organizations. The purpose of this study is not to furnish a
commentary on any particular treaty stipulations, but rather
to study the whole problem on a comparative basis and,
theoretically, to give a theory of this problem. Systematically we will deal, first, with the general problems involved,
and then with the problems of privileges and immunities
first of the representatives of the members, then of the international organizations themselves, and, lastly, of their
agents and officials.

1. *General Problems*

The granting of privileges and immunities to international organizations always had and has today basically the
same reason and purpose: to secure for them both legal and
pratical independence, so that these international organizations should be able to fulfil their task. The standard has,
however, changed for calculating the action to be taken in
recent times. The older principle, as applied in the case
of the European Danube Commission, was formulated by
reference to "complete independence from the territorial
authority" and "the benefits of neutrality." From the begin-

ning of the nineteenth century onward the favorite standard
was that of diplomatic privileges and immunities. The whole
problem then developed historically as one of extending
diplomatic privileges and immunities to non-diplomatic
functionaries. This standard also dominated, through Article VII, paragraph 4, of the League Covenant, the inter-war
period. This seemed not only logical in view of the historical
development of the problem but also highly advantageous,
because of the relative clarity of international law concerning diplomatic privileges and immunities. The phrase of
"diplomatic privileges and immunities," found in Article
VII, paragraph 4, was, thus, technically an abbreviated
form of international legislation, bringing about a reception
of the whole general international law of this subject.[55]

It seems, therefore, necessary to outline briefly the status
of the law concerning diplomatic privileges and immunities.
These go back to the Roman law; *Sancti habeantur legati*
and *ne impediatur legatio*. In Roman law are also to be
found the roots of the different doctrines on which these
immunities have been justified. The three most important
doctrines, which have all played a role in the development
of the law, are the doctrines of the representative character
of diplomatic agents, the fiction of exterritoriality, and the
functional theory. Exterritoriality as a basis to explain
these immunities can already be found in Grotius.[56] It is
today universally recognized that we encounter here with
an untenable fiction. But the idea that Roman ambassadors
represent the *majestas populi Romani,* that modern diplomatic agents "represent their sovereign" [57] has undoubtedly
exercised a powerful influence; hence the pomp and cere-
mony, the importance of "diplomatic rank" and of the
"problem of precedence." If the functional theory is most
widely adopted today in this pragmatistic age, it is, on the
other hand, true that it always has played a great role, and
is stressed already by Grotius and Vattel.[58]

The diplomatic privileges and immunities universally recognized today under positive general international law may be distinguished, according to Strisower and Verdross,[59] into two great categories: inviolability and so-called exterritoriality, which word has nothing to do with the out-dated fiction of the same name, but is only used to designate a bundle of immunities.

Inviolability means that the receiving state is under an international obligation to grant a special and extraordinary protection to diplomatic agents against illegal attacks.

Exterritoriality means the exemption of diplomatic agents from the criminal, administrative, and civil jurisdictions of the receiving state, with a few recognized exceptions (voluntary submission, real estate, counterclaims). It must be emphasized that the exemption from local jurisdiction of diplomatic agents pertains exclusively to the private acts of diplomatic agents. Their exemption from local jurisdiction for their official acts has nothing to do with diplomatic privileges and immunities; their official acts are "acts of state" and are legally imputed not to them but to the sending state. That this is so can be seen from the fact that the same immunity from local jurisdiction pertains also to the official acts of consuls who enjoy no diplomatic privileges.

Equally the premises (offices and residences) of diplomatic agents enjoy these immunities, together with goods therein, carriages, records, and archives of missions. They cannot, without the consent of the sending state, be entered, searched, or detained by local authorities, even under process of law. Diplomatic officers have the right of free communication with their states, inviolability of diplomatic correspondence, pouches, and couriers.

But these immunities constitute only an immunity from local jurisdiction, not from local law.[60] That is why diplomatic agents can be held liable after the termination of the diplomatic mission. There is further the possibility of bringing civil action against them in their own countries. A means of conciliating the exemptions from local jurisdiction with the necessities of local life is the institution of the waiver of diplomatic privileges. But as they are functional, not personal, privileges, such waiver must, in the case of subordinate diplomatic officers, be made by the chief of their mission, and, in the case of a chief of mission, by his government. Finally, the receiving state may ask for the recall of diplomatic agents.

The inviolability and immunities extend not only to the chiefs of mission and all diplomatic personnel, but also to the administrative personnel and clerks, and, in a derivative way, to the suite, members of family, and servants.

Exemption from taxation (income taxes, excise taxes) and freedom from custom duties is not a matter of strict law, but rather of international courtesy. When granted, however, it consists legally of an exemption from the laws themselves, so that no claim can be made after the termination of the diplomatic mission.

It was generally held that a state will not grant diplomatic privileges and immunities to an envoy who is a citizen of the receiving state. The legal situation of diplomatic agents in third states was hardly strictly regulated by general international law. As to the immunity of servants, nationals of the receiving state, there was no uniformity of state practice.

Contrary to the period 1919–39, the standard has now been changed again, although privileges and immunities have been given increasingly to international organizations. Instead of the formula of "diplomatic privileges and immunities," Article CV of the Charter of the U.N. grants "such privileges and immunities as are necessary for the fulfillment of its purposes." [61]

Prima facie it might have seemed that the intention would be that of lowering the standard to be applied. Anxiety concerning possible abuse, or the ever increasing number of persons enjoying these privileges, and the influence of nationalistic considerations certainly played a role. "Any excess or abuse of immunity or privilege is as detrimental to the interests of the International Organization itself as it is to the countries who are asked to grant such immunities," states the Report of the Preparatory Commission of the U.N.[62] Even resistance to the grant of diplomatic privileges *stricto sensu* was not unkown in the inter-war period. The Italian School endeavoured to restrict the circle of persons entitled to diplomatic immunities. It excluded the non-official suite or held that only certain privileges should be granted. Some governments distinguished between diplomatic personnel and simple employees. The draft convention of the Harvard Research in International Law does not accord diplomatic immunity to the administrative personnel which is, therefore, subject to local jurisdiction for acts not within the scope of their official functions.

Yet the impression that the new formula means a lowering of the standard cannot be maintained if the problem is studied more closely.

First, it must be remembered that general international law knew no uniformity as to the status of servants who were nationals of the receiving state. The legal situation of diplomatic agents in third states and the exemption of diplomatic agents from taxation and custom duties were rather matters of international courtesy than of international law. There did not exist, therefore, that certainty in the general international law on the subject which was considered to be one of the principal advantages of the formula of Article VII, paragraph 4, of the Covenant. The diplomatic privileges and immunities of general international law themselves are in need of revision and codification.

The diplomatic privileges and immunities also varied from country to country, in consequence of courtesy, special customs, different national attitudes, or special treaties, and under the influence of reciprocity. Under Article VII, paragraph 4, of the Covenant, functionaries of the League were assimilated to the status of diplomatic envoys accredited to Switzerland or to Holland. Thus the second advantage of the formula of Article VII, paragraph 4, the uniformity of the law, was more apparent than real.

On the other hand, this formula proved not to be applicable to all officials of the League. The *modus vivendi* with Switzerland of 1926 distinguished between members of the staff of the first category, or extraterritorial staff, and members of the staff of the second category.

Most writers argued that diplomatic privileges and immunities constitute a maximum, but Schücking and Wehberg emphatically stated that they constitute a minimum; the position of officials of the League is superior to that of diplomatic agents who represent only a single state.

Percy E. Corbett [63] recently wrote that "diplomatic privilege for the officials of international organizations is of doubtful utility" and declared that even "the case for maintaining diplomatic immunities in the modern world is not above controversy." But this opinion is not only erroneous, because the author thinks only in terms of the "mystical dignity of the sovereign state," not in terms of functional necessity, but is also completely isolated. All the officials of international organizations, all the writers on this subject, such as Ray, Schücking and Wehberg, Göppert, van Vollenhaven, Rey, Jacques Secrétan, Roger Secrétan, S. Kaufmann, A. Hamarskjöld, and Ranshofen-Wertheimer, agree that privileges and immunities are indispenable for the efficient working of international organizations. This absolute necessity has recently been sharply underlined by the legal adviser to the International Labor Organization.[64]

But these privileges pose a new problem—and this is the main reason why the new formula cannot be considered as a lowering of the standard but rather as a recognition that the problem is new. While most writers of the inter-war period, under the impact of Article VII, paragraph 4, of the Covenant, dealt with the problem as one of the extension of diplomatic privileges to non-diplomatists, the insight into the fact that we have here to do with a new development, different from that of the privileges of diplomatic agents, is to be found, here and there, already in this period. The Adatci–de Visscher report of 1924 emphasizes the difference between our problem and that of diplomatic agents. Van Vollenhoven underlines the fact that we are dealing here with a new development, and similar hints can be found in the writings of Suzanne Basdevant. Sir Cecil Hurst wrote in 1929 that the formula of diplomatic privileges is "unfortunate," as international functionaries exercise no diplomatic function.

It is the confusion between the two problems which explains the negative attitude taken in the report of David Jayne Hill in the Institute de Droit International, [65] where it is considered an exaggeration to ask for diplomatic privileges for international functionaries as the League is not a state, there is no reciprocity, and no state responsibility. It is the same confusion which has hampered and even still hampers the building up of an adequate law of privileges and immunities for international organizations. From this confusion stems the attitude of discrimination against nationals, the restriction to the state in which the organization has its seat, the quarrel about the immunity from income tax, and other aspects of the problem. Diplomatic privileges cannot serve either as a maximum or as a minimum standard. In some respects less, in others more, is necessary. New privileges and immunities, not necessary to diplomatic agents, have to be created. The problems posed by the privileges and immunities of the international organizations themselves and, in particular, of public international corporations are completely new.

Just as the first railroad coaches and motorcars looked like horsedrawn vehicles without horses, and it was some time before these new means of transport found a form adequate to their functions, so the problem of privileges and immunities of international organizations started historically, by analogy, as an extension of diplomatic privileges to non-diplomatists. Now the development has reached a point, however, at which the different nature of the new problem is realized and where a new law, independent and emancipated from that of the privileges of diplomatic agents, has to be created. Such a creation of a new law has also become necessary through the dropping of the formula of Article VII, paragraph 4, of the Covenant which brought about a reception of the corresponding general international law.

This new law tends, first, to a codification of the privileges and immunities of the U.N., and, second, to the unification of these privileges with those of the specialized agencies. Such codification and unification will have to lay down the basis, ways, and methods of granting these privileges and immunities and regulate in detail the privileges of the representatives of members, of the international organizations themselves, of international judges, and of all international agents and officials.

Finally, the ultimate end is the creation of a new, general international law on this topic. Here the already existing privileges of other international organizations will have to be taken into consideration. It will have to be considered whether and how far such privileges shall be granted the other international tribunals, international administrative unions, and so on, already existing or to be created in the future.[66] The problem will, therefore, also enter into the problem of the codification of international law, with which the U.N. is charged by Article XIII, paragraph 1a, of the Charter.

2. *Privileges and Immunities of the Representatives of the Members*

In building up a new international law, concerning privileges and immunities of international organizations, a new law independent from that of the privileges of diplomatic agents, it is logical to start with the problem of the privileges of representatives of the members. Jacques Secrétan wrote in 1928 that Article VII, paragraph 4, of the Covenant does not constitute an innovation in this respect. This is true to a certain extent, but, as we shall see, only to a certain extent. For these representatives represent a single, sovereign state which appoints, instructs, and recalls them and to which they are responsible. The Vienna Protocol of March 9, 1815, already gave full diplomatic privileges to "diplomatic agents on an extra-ordinary mission." True, the representatives of a member are, contrary even to extraordinary diplomatic envoys, not accredited to a sovereign state. But long ago extraordinary envoys, representatives of their states at general international conferences and accredited to these conferences, were held to be extraordinary envoys in the sense of the Vienna Protocol.

Yet the position of the representatives of members is somewhat different. They are not accredited to conferences held within the framework of general international law but to meetings of international organs which function on the basis of a particular, treaty-created, constitution. They are, at one and the same time, national organs and a part of an international organ; they constitute in their person a personal union of two organs. Even so, they can be taken as extraordinary diplomatic envoys, as expressly stated in Article II of the Havana Convention of 1928 on diplomatic officers.

If the representatives of members are diplomatic agents or invested with "diplomatic rank," they enjoy full diplomatic privileges and immunities on the basis of general international law. That is why these privileges were given in the League also to representatives of non-members, who could not invoke Article VII, paragraph 4, of the Covenant.

Such representatives of members appear at international conferences and congresses, at the congresses of international administrative unions, on river commissions, and so on, on many temporary commissions and boards created by the Paris Peace Treaties or which will be created by the new peace treaties, at the Assembly and Council of the League of Nations, in the conferences convoked by and held under the auspices of the League and the League's consultative organisms, permanent or temporary commissions, at the General Conference and the governing board of the International Labor Organization, at the general conferences, commissions, and boards of the special organizations of the League and of the institutes put at the disposal of the League by single states.[67]

Diplomatic privileges and immunities pertain to the representatives of the American Republics at the Conferences of American States, special Inter-American Conferences, the Meetings of Foreign Ministers, and other official Pan-American or Central American conferences. The members of the governing board of the Pan-American Union are now, on the basis of Resolution IX of the Mexico City Conference of 1945, special envoys, but they have each the rank of ambassador and naturally enjoy full diplomatic privileges. Thus in Washington a second, "Pan-American," diplomatic corps has come into existence, and a third one in this country in New York, made up of representatives in the U.N. Security Council.

Yet Article VII, paragraph 4, of the Covenant did contain some innovations in this respect. There are to be mentioned, first, representatives of members who are not diplomatic agents nor invested with "diplomatic rank," such as foreign ministers, prime ministers, or other non-diplomatic official personalities. Full diplomatic privileges granted to them can hardly be based on general international law. The representatives of members in the International Labor Organization were given full diplomatic privileges and immunities, even if they represented states not members of the League. Further the problem of representatives who were private persons arose. Full diplomatic privileges and immunities were granted at the General Conference of the ILO to the delegates of workers and employers. Finally a completely new issue arose with regard to the permanent delegates of member states accredited to the League at Geneva.[68] They represented their state but were accredited to the League in the person of the Secretary General and differed from other representatives in that they were not members of international organs. The League had, contrary to the opinion of Schücking and Wehberg, no active and passive right of legation. Switzerland granted to these delegates diplomatic privileges.[69]

Article VII, paragraph 4, of the Covenant granted to the representatives of the members diplomatic privileges and immunities.[70] Article CV, paragraph 2, of the U.N. Charter grants only "such privileges and immunities as are necessary for the independent exercise of their functions in connection with the Organization," [71] and Article CV paragraph 3, enables the General Assembly of the U.N. to make recommendations or propose conventions to the member states for determining the details of the application of paragraph 2.[72] But Article IV of the U.N. Convention, section 1, paragraphs f and g, gives to the representatives of the members diplomatic privileges and immunities. It is made clear by section 11 that these privileges pertain to all representatives of members in all the principal and subsidiary organs of the U.N.—the General Assembly, the Security Council, the Economic and Social Council, the Trusteeship Council, the Military Staff Committee, the Atomic Energy

Commission, the Balkan Commission, and so on—and to conferences convoked by the U.N.

The granting of "diplomatic" privileges again results in a reception of general international law. All diplomatic privileges and immunities are granted to the representatives of members, for instance, that of "inviolability." [73] Because of this reception of general international law, which does not concede diplomatic privileges to the *agent diplomatique régnicole,* diplomatic privileges are not accorded to representatives of the members in relation to the states of which they are nationals or—an innovation—of which they are or have been the representatives.[74] These privileges are naturally enjoyed by the representatives also with regard to their private acts, and during the whole time of their being representatives of the members.[75]

These privileges are not only enjoyed by the representatives themselves, but also by the "deputy delegates, advisers, technical experts, and secretaries of delegations." [76]

But the representatives need more privileges than those granted by general international law. Article IV, section 11, paragraphs a–e, enumerates immunity from personal arrest or detention from seizure of personal baggage, inviolability of all papers and documents, the right to use codes and to receive papers or correspondence by courier or in sealed bags; all these privileges are already given by general international law. Further exemptions in respect of themselves and their spouses from immigration restrictions, aliens' registration or national service obligations, and from currency or exchange restrictions are granted to them. The exemption from taxation is made by section 13 a matter of law. That section 11a grants them immunity from legal process of any kind in respect to words spoken or written and all acts done by them in their capacity as representatives, and that under section 12 this immunity is continued even if they are no longer the representatives of members, has, as in the case of ordinary diplomatic agents, nothing to do with their diplomatic privileges and does not constitute an innovation. These acts are "acts of state" and are imputed by law not to them but to the state they represent. But the insistence by section 12 on complete freedom of speech and independence in the discharge of their duties is important. Another new development, not contained in general international law, but made necessary by the functions of the representatives of members, is that all these privileges are granted them, under Article IV, section 11, also "during their journey to and from the place of the meeting" of the international organs. The privileges are, further, not only enjoyed in a single state, but in any state member of the international organization.

A special problem arises from the fact that, contrary to ordinary diplomatic agents, the state of the place of the meeting does not have at its disposal the extraordinary procedure of asking the sending state for the recall of the representatives. To conciliate and counterbalance their privileges with the territorial needs of the state of the meeting, Article IV, section 14, gives the members not only a right but imposes upon them a duty "to waive the immunity of its representative in any case where in the opinion of the member the immunity would impede the course of justice, and it can be waived without prejudice to the purpose for which the immunity is accorded." [77] True, this is more a moral than a legal duty, as its fulfilment is left to the non-revisable judgment of the member itself.

All the representatives of the members enjoy these privileges. But they must be representatives of the members. International judges are not representatives of the members. And there are representatives of the members or non-members of the parties before the Court who are not extraordinary diplomatic envoys and were up to now not given special privileges. Article XLII, paragraph 3, of the Statute of the Court of International Justice now gives—an innovation—"to the agents, counsel, and advocates of parties [that is members or not] before the Court the privileges and immunities necessary to the independent exercise of their duties."

Finally members of the commissions of international organizations, who are directly appointed by the organization to be partial organs of international organs, are not representatives of the members. They represent the international organization. Their privileges, therefore, constitute a different problem.

3. *Privileges and Immunities of the International Organizations*

The problem of privileges and immunities of the international organizations themselves is obviously a new problem, different from that of the immunities of diplomatic agents. While there are precedents, even dating back prior to 1920, the writers of the inter-war period, mostly concerned with the immunities of international functionaries, paid little attention to this specific problem. The problem does not constitute a small, secondary matter, however, but is, just as is the problem of financing international organizations,[78] a vital one, and one which constitutes an indispensable condition for the efficient work of international organizations. It is from the immunities of the organizations themselves that the immunities of their different institutions, organs, and officials are derived. The building-up of a new and complete international law concerning this topic will have to take into consideration the following problems.

(A) *Basis*. The functional principle as the basis seems now almost universally recognized. Complete independence from the local authority, as granted to the European Danube Commission, in order to enable it to fulfill its international functions, constitutes the *raison d'etre*. The functional principle furnishes not only the basis but also the standard of the extent of the privileges and immunities required. The "necessary" privileges and immunities must be granted. The accent obviously will have to be on the "immunities" necessary for independent functioning, rather than on "privileges," which deal more with questions of honor, courtesy, and protocol. Nevertheless the dignity and prestige of an international organization may very well be an important point. The principle of the equality of states also constitutes a basis in some respects.

(B) *Methods of granting privileges and immunities.* Jenks [79] envisages three different ways in which immunities may be granted. One way would be to grant an international organization statehood over an internationalized area, as over an internationalized Austria. But this writer would not be in favor of making a state out of an international organization. Jenks would prefer the second way, "internationalized headquarters, governed by international authority and not subject to the jurisdiction of any one state" and cites Vatican City and the District of Columbia as examples. But Vatican City is a sovereign state and the District of Columbia is certainly a part of the United States. While there was some talk to establish an "internationalized area" around Geneva, by the cession of territory by Switzerland and France, the practical possibilities of this method are slight. The U.N. certainly will have its headquarters in New York City, that is, in the United States.

As international organizations will, in all likelihood, continue to be located on the territory of one or more sovereign states, the functional principle demands that they be made independent from the local territorial authorities. The granting of immunities merely by municipal statute, whether to a particular organization, or by an act of a more

general nature, a voluntary granting, is certainly no adequate method, as such law may at any time be changed or
repealed by the state in question. It would also make impossible the uniformity of the law of immunities.

An "agreement" between the organization and the state
of its seat, as the Swiss *modus vivendi* of 1926, is equally
not an adequate method. The legal nature of such agreement is doubtful; it is not an international treaty; both
parties can at any time renounce it in part or as a whole.
It leads only to an agreement with a single member state
and "fails to afford a solid legal foundation for the permanent independence of the international organization." [80]

The only adequate method is to grant these immunities
in the basic international treaty, creating identical and
binding international obligations upon all member states.
The constitution, like the Charter of the U.N., may contain
only the standard and leave the details to further action.
The U.N. correctly decided, for the laying down of these
details, against mere recommendations to the members,
but in favor of a treaty. This U.N. General Convention is
contrary to the *modus vivendi* of 1926, a genuine international treaty, which has to be ratified by each member; the
vote of approval by the General Assembly was equivalent
to ratification by the U.N. The contracting parties are, on
the other hand, each member state and, on the other, the
U.N. as such. Thus, identical norms are created for all
member states, the coming into force of which as well as
amendments are controlled by the U.N. Under section 36
of the General Convention, the Secretary General may conclude with any member states supplementary agreements;
but he acts on behalf of the U.N. and this agreement is
subject to the approval, *i.e.*, ratification, of the General
Assembly. As the law is laid down by the supra-ordinated
treaty, it is inadmissible to put in phrases, such as "insofar
as it may be possible under the constitutional procedure of
a Member." [81]

(C) *International Personality of International Organizations.* Prior to the problem of immunities arises the problem of the legal status of international organizations. Here the first problem is that of its international personality. This problem has been obscured by the traditional theory according to which only sovereign states can be persons in international law. For that reason the possibility of the international personality of international organizations has either been denied or untenable attempts to construe it as a sovereign state have been made.[82] But it is clear that, while sovereign states are the normal and full persons in international law, non-states may be such persons [83] if international personality is granted to them, expressly or impliedly. It follows that an international organization is not *ipso facto* a person in international law, and, if it is, its legal status is not necessarily identical with that of a sovereign state. It is always a question of the analysis of positive international law. Such analysis shows that most international organizations do not have international personality.[84] But the League of Nations, no doubt, had international personality.[85] The same is true of the U.N. as shown by its capacity of concluding international treaties under Articles XLIII and CV, paragraph 3.[86]

(D) *Legal capacity of international organizations under private municipal law.* From the problem of the international personality of international organizations must be clearly distinguished the very different second problem of their legal status, namely the problem of their legal capacity under private municipal law. This latter capacity is indispensable, as these organizations have to "enter into innumerable transactions governed by the municipal law of different countries which are incidental to their daily operations." [87] Such legal capacity has indeed always been granted by the state of the seat and it can be said that this state was under an international obligation to grant it, so far as it is necessary for the fulfillment of its functions and not beyond the powers granted to it by its Constitution.[88] Such legal capacity is now expressly granted—capacity to contract, to acquire and dispose of movable and immovable property, and to institute legal proceedings—by the Charter of the U.N. and the constitutions of the specialized agencies. The new development consists only in that that the basic treaty imposes such obligation for each member state.

(E) *The single privileges and immunities.* From legal capacity, which is enjoyed by any private corporation, must be distinguished special privileges and immunities. There are earlier precedents; Article VII, paragraph 5, of the League Covenant granted inviolability to the buildings and other property occupied by the League. The *modus vivendi* of 1926 specified the details. Article CV, paragraph 1, of the Charter gives the U.N. the "necessary" privileges and immunities on a functional basis. The new development is here again that these immunities are granted in the territory of each member state; for the U.N. can have offices and assets elsewhere than at its seat. The study of the U.N. General Convention, sections 2-10, exhibits the following privileges and immunities: immunity for U.N. property and assets, wherever located and by whomsoever held, from every form of legal process,[89] inviolability of premises, immunity from search, requisition, confiscation, expropriation, and any other form of interference (whether by executive, administrative, judicial, or legislative action), inviolability of archives and premises, freedom from financial controls, regulations, or *moratoria* of any kind, right to hold funds and gold or currency of any kind and to operate accounts in any currency, freedom to transfer funds, exemption of assets, income, and other property from all direct taxes, exemption from custom duties and prohibition of and restrictions on imports and exports needed for its official use, most favored diplomatic treatment as to priorities, rates, and taxes on mails, cables, telegrams, radiograms, telephoto, telephone, and other communications, freedom from censorship, and right to use codes, dispatches, and receive its correspondence by courier or in bags under diplomatic privileges and immunities.[90] Nevertheless the U.N. Zone in New York, for example, is in the United States; there is no fiction of "exterritoriality." The normal United States civil and criminal law applies also in the U.N. Zone. Under the U.N.–U.S. agreement of June 26, 1947, the site of the New York City headquarters of the U.N. is declared "under the control and authority of the U.N." and is granted "inviolability" but no exterritorial rights. The area remains United States territory and the laws of the United States, federal, state, and local, will apply in all cases, except where specifically laid down otherwise. Federal, state, or local officials can enter only with the consent of the Secretary General of the U.N. Service of legal process, including seizure of private property, can take place within the area only by consent of the Secretary General. The U.N. has the right to establish its own radio station, airport, and postal service. Disputes between the United States and the U.N. on interpretation and application of the agreement are to be settled by a tribunal of three arbitrators.

(F) *The special problems of international public corporations.* Special problems arise with regard to the so-called international public corporations.[91] as they existed in the Bank of International Settlements,[92] to which special privileges and immunities had been granted. They exist today in the Inter-American Bank, in the International Monetary Fund, the International Bank for Reconstruction and Development, and they may be created on a great scale in the Atomic Energy Development Authority. They are, in Friedmann's definition, "international corporate bodies established for purposes of international government, but constituted as commercial enterprises." Such an institution must be really international in character with managerial and financial autonomy. It should have, according to this author, its constitution in a basic international treaty, independent financial existence, legal ownership of funds, constitute an international public service, but be subject to the control of an appropriate international organ. Friedmann asked for them the status of an "international legal person." But it is clear that he is not thinking of personality in international law but only of full corporate status in every member state, although they remain in their private transactions subject to municipal law, to be determined according to the rules of conflict of laws. But he asked for corporate status in all member states and on the basis of an international charter of incorporation.[93]

(G) *Methods of counterbalancing the privileges and immunities.* As international organizations are nationals of no sovereign state the counterbalance in the case of diplomatic immunities—recall, civil and criminal jurisdiction of the sending state—is here lacking. Shall international organizations be immune from any jurisdiction? Here again the new character of our problem, which calls for a solution, is demonstrated. There is another difference: The immunity of diplomatic agents from the jurisdiction of the receiving state lasts only as long as they are diplomatic agents; later action can be brought against them and a statute of limitations cannot be set up as a defense.[94] But international organizations are supposed to have a permanent existence.

The oldest way of effecting a counterbalance, taken from the law of diplomatic agents, is the waiver of immunity. Such waiver can be made in a special case, but must be made expressly. There is no duty to waive the immunity, and section 2 of the U.N. General Convention adds: "It is understood that no waiver of immunity shall extend to any measure of execution."

Section 6 of the General Convention states that in respect of freedom from financial controls the "U.N. shall pay due regard to any representation made by the Government of any member, in so far as it is considered that effect can be given to such representations without detriment to the interests of the U.N." Here again there is no legal duty, as the decision is left within the discretion of the U.N.

It must be remembered that international organizations are immune in most cases only from local jurisdiction, but not from local laws which they are, therefore, in duty bound strictly to observe. In torts cases this counterbalancing can be done by obligatory insurance against third-party risks, as now provided by Part IV of the U.N. General Convention.

Already writers of the interwar period have proposed the creation of special *fora* for the settlement of conflicts in which international organizations are involved. While these suggestions have not as yet been followed, section 20a of the U.N. General Convention prescribes that the U.N. shall make provisions for appropriate modes of settlement of disputes arising out of contracts or other disputes of a private-law character to which the U.N. is a party. The problem is of particular importance in the case of public international corporations. It is, in this respect, interesting to compare Article IX, section 3, of the Monetary Fund Constitution, which grants immunity from judicial process, except if expressly waived for any proceedings or in the terms of any contract, with Article VII, section 3, of the International Bank Constitution, which provides the conditions under which action against the Bank may be brought.

4. *Privileges and Immunities of International Functionaries*

A. *International Judges.* International judges stand in a category by themselves. They are neither representatives of members, nor "officials" of an international organization.

Since 1899, international conventions have granted diplomatic privileges and immunities to certain international judges. Agents, counsel, and advocates of parties before the court are representatives of members; the registrar and officials of the registry are international officials.

In the agreement of 1928 wth Holland the judges of the Permanent Court of International Justice were granted the diplomatic privileges and immunities granted to heads of diplomatic missions, accredited to the Netherlands, and had a position analogous with the diplomatic corps, enjoying precedence immediately after that body. This gave rise to interesting questions of precedence.[95] It shows that not only the functional principle but also honor and prestige can be involved in these problems. Manley O. Hudson [96] calls the Dutch agreement of 1928 "hardly altogether satisfactory" and finds that the Court was not sufficiently exigent in this respect, that the proper respect for the Court as an international institution seems to demand that international judges be given precedence over the representatives of any single state. It shows also that the analogy with the diplomatic corps does not fit the situation, that a new law has to be created. Already van Vollenhoven had stated that the conditions and necessities of an international judge are different from those of diplomats. Hudson says that "new standards are needed for determining the status of high international officials and that they should be developed without a slavish regard for the past."

Indeed, an international judge does not need free communication with his own government. On the other hand, he needs the necessary privileges and immunities in each member state; he needs the right of free transit on his way to and from his duties, a right which is of vital interest. Also the national discrimination, as found in the conventions of 1899 and 1907,[97] as practiced in the Dutch agreement of 1928 [98] is to be explained from the law of diplomatic privileges and immunities.

(B) *International Experts.* A special position is that of international experts, technical counsel, members of a consultative commission, appointed by an international organization, but not working under its control. They were, under Article VII, paragraph 4, of the Covenant, mostly excluded from diplomatic privileges and immunities.[99] Roger Secrétan called this regulation in 1925 a *solution bâtarde.* Sections 22 and 23 of the U.N. General Convention grant now to "experts on missions for the U.N.," such privileges and immunities "as are necessary for the independent exercise of their functions during the period of their missions."

(C) *International Officials.* That function is the true basis of the immunities of international officials is now widely recognized; not representation, not state responsibility, not reciprocity. The problem derives from that of the immunities of international organizations themselves. Sometimes the principle of the equality of states has been declared to form the real basis; thus Hammarskjöld and, especially, Suzanne Basdevant: no state must be allowed to have a privileged position vis-à-vis the international organization, not even the state of the seat. The principle of the equality of states has particularly been insisted upon as the true basis for the immunity of international officials from direct taxation. The problem is a new one,[100] different from that of diplomatic privileges and immunities.

(1) *Definition.* In building up this new law it is first necessary to define the concept of "international officials," to recognize that this concept is not identical with the wider concept of "persons invested with functions of international interest," that the concept must be delimited as against international judges, international experts, and representatives of members who can very well be parts of an international organ. We can accept Suzanne Basdevant's definition: "International public officials are persons, who, on the basis of an international treaty constituting a par-

ticular international community, are appointed by this
international community or by an organ of it [here lies the
difference from the representatives of members] and under
its control [here lies the difference from international ex-
perts] to exercise, in a continuous way, functions in the
interest of this particular international community, and
who are subject to a particular personal status." [101] A uniform and general law of privileges and immunities for
international officials is a task; but at the present time it
seems that no such general customary international law
has yet come into existence.

(2) *Extension.* Shall privileges and immunities be
granted to all international organizations and their officials,
or only to "important" international organizations? The
present tendency seems to be in the latter sense. International administrative unions are still for the most part
excluded. It seems also that the standard for "importance"
is found in the consideration that the international organization must be charged with more than mere technical
functions. But recently the Universal Postal Union and the
International Telecommunication Union were brought into
relation with the U.N.

The functional principle must also protect the states
against too high demands and too great an extension of
international immunities. Shall they be granted to all officials of the "important" international organizations? Article
VII, paragraph 4, of the Covenant made no distinction
whatsoever between the "officials" of the League. Rougier
wanted the immunities restricted to the Secretary General
and the Assistant Secretaries General. But Borsi stated in
1923 that such interpretation is in flagrant contradiction
with the text. Yet in practice some discrimination had to
be made. The *modus vivendi* of 1926 distinguished between
members of the first category and the staff of the second
category, who enjoy immunity only with regard to official

acts and fiscal immunity from direct taxation, but remained, with regard to acts of their private life, subject to the laws and jurisdiction of Switzerland. The same distinction between the higher and the other international officials was made by the Dutch agreement of 1928 and the Italian law of 1930, concerning privileges and immunities of the International Institute of Agriculture. The Adatci–de Visscher report distinguished between higher and "purely technical or manual personnel"; Politis proposed at the Institut de Droit International to distinguish between *agents de fonction* and *agents de gestion;* Jenks speaks of "senior officers."

(3) *Duration.* International officials enjoy the privileges and immunities not only at the occasion of exercising their functions, but during the whole time they are exercising their functions.

(4) *Immunity from jurisdiction for official acts.* This immunity must be granted to all international officials of whatever category. Such immunity is not part of special "international privileges and immunities," just as such immunity of diplomats does not stem from their diplomatic immunities. Immunity for official acts is, as the Adatci–de Visscher report has put it, *ratione materiae, par le caractère intrinsèque de ces actes.* Such immunity of all members of an international staff, irrespective of nation or rank, is, in the words of Jenks, "a *sine qua non* of the effectiveness of the immunities of the organizations themselves." Official acts are by the law not imputed to the officials, but to the international organizations.

(5) *Acts of private life.* In order to speak truly of an international immunity from jurisdiction, such immunity must cover the acts of the private life of the international officials. Such immunities, contrary to the immunity for official acts, are *ratione personae,* although their basis and reason lies also in the functional principle. Complete im-

munity must be granted, at least, for the higher officers of an international organization and such guarantee against national control, as Jenks emphasizes, must be unqualified; for "if the local State can exercise jurisdiction without waiver, then the determination of the official or private character of a particular act passes from international to national control." [102]

(6) *Place of immunity.* International officials must be granted the necessary privileges and immunities not only in the state of the seat of the organization, but in each and all member states.

(7) *The single privileges and immunities.* Diplomatic privileges granted to international officials include inviolability for his person, effects, papers, and correspondence. Article VII, paragraph 5, of the Covenant granted inviolability also to the residence of officials of the League. The privileges will include immunity from local administrative, police, criminal, and civil jurisdiction,[103] and immunity from direct taxation. To these privileges belong immunity from immigration restrictions, alien registration requirements, national service obligations, exchange restriction, facilities for travel. As to the problem of an international passport, the Secretary General of the League had already submitted to the International Conference on Passports a memorandum on the granting of a diplomatic passport to the members of the Secretariat General. But serious arguments were made against this proposal. The granting of a passport, it was said, is an act of sovereignty; the League is not a state with sovereign rights; the Secretary General has no subjects. The proposed diplomatic passport should be valid in the territory of all members without visa. Probably mindful of this precedent,[104] section 24 of the U.N. General Convention now creates a U.N. *laissez-passer,* issued by the U.N. to its officials and which shall be recognized and accepted as a

valid travel document by the authorities of members; but it needs visa. This U.N. *laissez-passer* extends, under section 17, only to specified categories of U.N. officials.

(8) *Wives, children, immediate family.* Diplomatic privileges include, in a derivative way, the extension to families living under the same roof. The *modus vivendi* of 1926 granted this extension to officials of the first category.[105] F. Rey, S. Kaufman, and other writers of the interwar period opposed this extension and asked only that wives and children be freed from police restrictions of residence and certain conditions of admission.

(9) *Private suite, servants.* As to the extension of the privileges and immunities of international officials to their private suite and servants, with the exclusion of the nationals of the territorial state, opinions of the writers of the inter-war period were divided; Hammarskjöld was in favor, Roger Secrétan and F. Rey opposed. The first test cases [106] concerning servants of the U.N. do not allow yet to speak of a settled law in this respect, as the immunity has been either waived or the immunity appeal withdrawn.

(10) *The problem of national discrimination.* A particular consequence of treating international immunities as diplomatic immunities has been to deny these immunities to international officials who are nationals of the state of the seat of the international organization or to deny them these immunities in their own country. The figure of the *agent diplomatique régnicole* has been duplicated by that of the *agent international régnicole*. Already the treaties of 1899 and 1907 gave international judges diplomatic privileges only "when outside of their country." This principle of "national discrimination" dominated also the interwar period. The *modus vivendi* of 1926 gave officials of the League of Swiss nationality only immunity from Swiss jurisdiction for official acts, exemptions of League salaries from

cantonal and municipal direct taxes, and exemption from
or postponement of military service only if the necessity of
training and the interests of the country permit and if their
convocation for military service would be likely to interfere
with the normal working of the League. A similar solution
was reached in the Dutch agreement of 1928. This principle
was confirmed by decisions of courts.[107]

The same idea is to be found today in municipal legislation [108] as well as in the constitutions of specialized agencies.[109] The report of the Preparatory Commission [110] states:
"It is also a principle that no official can have in the
country of which he is a national immunity from being
sued in respect of his non-official acts and from criminal
prosecution."

But this principle of "national discrimination" has been
strongly attacked already by the literature of the interwar
period. The Adatci–de Visscher report asked that no member shall deny diplomatic privileges to its own nationals
who exercise a mission in the name of the League in their
own territory. Schücking and Wehberg termed the national
discrimination "not unobjectionable." S. Kaufmann, F. Rey,
Jacques Secrétan, Suzanne Basdevant, and Hammarskjöld
took a stand against national discrimination. The necessity
of independence from the control of national authorities, the
principle of the equality of states were the principal reasons.
Jenks recently demanded immunity for all members of international staffs, irrespective of nation and rank, at least
for official acts.

"National discrimination" plays, apart from the problem
of exemption from military service, a principal role in two
respects: immunity from jurisdiction and immunity from
direct taxation. The problem is different as to each of these
two aspects.

(11) *The regulation in the U.N. General Convention.*
Article V, sections 17–21, deal with the privileges and im-

munities of officials. These norms are based on the granting of privileges and immunities in all member states, without "national discrimination," and on the basis of a differentiation of U.N. officials into different categories. As to the contents, in some cases full diplomatic privileges are granted, in accordance with general international law, in other cases specified "necessary" privileges and immunities.

There are three classes of officials. The Secretary General and all Assistant Secretaries General have full diplomatic privileges "in respect of themselves, their spouses, and minor children." [111] On the other hand, here and everywhere, privileges and immunities, flowing from general international law, in respect of their private suite and servants, are excluded. This section, therefore, adopts the suggestion, presented in 1921 by Rougier, and presented at that time as a hardly tenable interpretation of Article VII, paragraph 4 of the Covenant.

As to the U.N. officials below these ranks, section 17 leaves it to the Secretary General to specify the categories of officials to which the provisions of this article shall apply; these categories shall be submitted to the General Assembly and communicated thereafter to the governments of all members as well as the names of the officials included in these categories. Only the categories thus specified will enjoy the privileges of section 18. But in carrying out his function under section 17 of the General Convention, the Secretary General proposed that "the categories of officials to which the provisions of Art. V and VI shall apply should include all members of the staff of the UN, with the exception of those who are recruited locally and are assigned to hourly rates," and this proposal was adopted unanimously by resolution of the General Assembly, 1st session, 2nd part, on December 7, 1946.[112]

Section 18a grants immunity from legal process in respects of words spoken or written and all acts performed in their official capacity. It is obvious that this immunity should not be restricted to officials of certain specified categories but granted to all officials irrespective of rank and nationality.

Diplomatic privileges are granted in respect of exchange facilities and repatriation facilities in time of international crisis, further immunity from immigration restrictions and alien restrictions. While all other privileges are strictly personal, the last two privileges mentioned are given to the officials, "together with their spouses and relatives." It is interesting to note that whereas the full diplomatic spouses and "minor children," here the word "relatives" is used which goes much farther than minor children. Here again the private suite and servants of the officials are excluded.

The officials of the specified categories are further granted, in the territories of all member states and without national discrimination, immunity from national service obligations and exemption from taxation on the salaries and emoluments paid to them by the U.N. It remains to be seen whether the member states, or all of them, will accept this proviso.

The problem of exemption from taxation, even restricted to international salaries and emoluments, is the problem where the principle of "national discrimination" has established its strongest bastions. While Switzerland and Holland granted to officials of the League and the Court also of Swiss and Dutch nationality exemption from taxation for their salaries, and the Italian law of 1930 took the same attitude as to Italian officials of the International Institute of Agriculture, the French Ministry of Finance refused tax exemption for French officials of the Institute of International Intellectual Cooperation at Paris.

Suzanne Basdevant has strongly defended the tax exemption of nationals exclusively on the principle of the equality of states, according to which the state of the seat should not have a privileged position vis-à-vis the international organization. It is not a question of a favor for international officials. Jenks [113] has insisted that "fiscal immunity is both an element in the independence of international institutions and a device to prevent the imposition in the fiscal interest of a particular state of inequitable burden on funds held for common international purposes." National discrimination also leads to inequality of payment of international officials for equal work; hence the Paris Institute of International Intellectual Cooperation paid the taxes on salaries for French officials.

The fight against national discrimination in tax exemption of international officials played a large role in the fifth and sixth Committee of the First Part of the General Assembly of the U.N. held in London. The principal stand in favor of national discrimination was taken by Senator Vandenberg, who, primarily, invoked the necessity of congressional action and the "evils of a tax-free class." But in his report as chairman of a subcommittee, he had to recognize that the subcommittee "believes that there is no alternative to the proposition that tax exemption for U.N. salaries is indispensable to equity between members and equality between personnel."

All kinds of proposals were made: that in order to avoid creating a "tax-free" class, a tax should be imposed by the U.N. (Holland); but the United Kingdom objected; such tax would have no real purpose, and the U.N. is not a sovereign state [114] but an employer; no precedent exists anywhere of an employer taxing an employee. In order to have equal pay for equal work, Norway proposed to increase the salaries of officials who have to pay taxes. Finally it was agreed that tax exemption should be granted to nationals but that in the meantime allowances be paid by U.N. for tax payments, following the precedents of the Paris

Institute. But Australia objected that taxing members should have to pay increased contributions. In the New York meeting of the U.N. General Assembly, the Soviet Union, while exempting their own nationals from taxation and opposing U.N. taxation of its own employees, attempted to terminate U.N. compensation to the employees for income taxes; the attempt was defeated, but the Soviet Union saw in it a "subsidizing" of the United States.[115]

(12) *Counterbalancing the privileges and immunities of international officials.* Already the writers of the interwar period had recognized that immunity from jurisdiction for international officials also in their own state leads, contrary to the situation with regard to diplomatists, to difficult problems; in such case there would be "no jurisdiction at all" for League officials (Adatci–de Visscher report), there would be a "gap" which creates the necessity of special regulation (Schücking and Wehberg), a "denial of justice" (Jacques Secrétan), a "juridical vacuum" (Schwelb).[116]

The remedy most favored, taken from the law of diplomatic immunities, is the waiver of immunity by the leading international official.[117] Section 20 of the U.N. General Convention makes it the right and duty of the Secretary General of the U.N. to waive the immunity of any official in any case where, in his opinion, the immunity would impede the course of justice and can be waived without prejudice to the interests of the U.N. Waiver of immunity for the Secretary General is the right of the Security Council.

The U.N. General Convention further provides, to prevent the occurrence of any abuse, that the Secretary General be instructed that the drivers of all official motor cars of the U.N. and all members of the staff who own or drive motor cars shall be properly insured against third-party risks. Section 29b provides that the U.N. make provisions for appropriate modes of settlement of disputes involving any official of the U.N. who by reason of his official position enjoys immunity if immunity has not been waived by the

Secretary General. Decision by arbitration, perhaps inserted into a contract, or recognition of a particular tribunal or court may be such means. The idea of creating special *fora*, perhaps an international tribunal to be utilized exclusively for these purposes, has been advocated by Grunebaum-Ballin, by S. Kaufman, and by Hammarskjöld.

It must also be remembered that the international, like the diplomatic, immunity is only an immunity from local jurisdiction, not from local law. Section 21 of the U.N. General Convention provides that the U.N. shall co-operate at all times with the appropriate authorities of members to facilitate the proper administration of justice, secure the observance of police regulations, and prevent the occurrence of any abuse in connection with the privileges and immunities. The strict observance of all local laws and ordinances by the officials of the U.N. can be made their duty by the regulations for the members of the staff of the U.N. and be put under appropriate sanctions, going up to the dismissal from the U.N. staff.

On the other hand the drastic restriction of immunity from local jurisdiction sems not to be an adequate means. Under the U.N. General Convention apart from the Secretary General and the Assistant Secretaries General, not even the U.N. officials of the specified categories enjoy immunity from criminal, civil, administrative, and police jurisdiction, in connection with acts of their private life. But jurisdiction of local courts without waiver for acts of private life empowers the local courts to determine whether a certain act is an official act or an act of private life. The determination of the character of an act passes, therefore, as Jenks has warned, from international to national control and endangers the independence of the international organizations themselves.

Special problems will arise with regard to the personnel of international public corporations. Such personnel, as Friedmann states, is not an international civil service, but a service fulfilling public functions in the employment of an enterprise constituted as a commercial corporation. Friedmann [118] stands for immunity from national jurisdiction also in the home state, but demands an international administrative tribunal which shall have not only adequate jurisdiction, but also adequate authority and power of enforcement. The coming into being of large international public corporations, especially an International Atomic Energy Development Authority, which should run mines and take on the administration and performance of actual engineering projects, will make it necessary, as Jessup [119] recently remarked, to develop new rules of international law, defining the legal status of such personnel and the rights and duties as well as the international responsibility of such international agencies.

[1] Article XIII and XIV of this convention created a special organ, the Comisión Directiva, for the Atlantic confederate navy. The commission was to consist of three members, each appointed by its own government (Colombia, Central America, Mexico). To give this commission full independence and liberty, each member of the commission was to enjoy all the immunities and exemptions of a diplomatic agent, wherever he reside (Article XV).

[2] 1 MALLOY, TREATIES at 110.

[3] Article II: "Les délégués des Puissances jouiront des mêmes droits que le personnel des Légations en Grèce."

[4] German-French Treaty of August 15, 1804, 3 Martens N.R.G. 201, art. 231; Congress of Vienna, 1815, Articles on the Navigation of the Rhine, 2 Martens N.R.G. 431. Convention and *règlement* concerning the navigation of the Rhine, Mainz, March 31, 1831, 9 Martens N.R.G. 252, art. 108. But the revised Mannheim Rhine Navigation Act of October 11, 1868, 20 Martens N.R.G. 355, contains no clause on diplomatic immunities.

[5] Treaty of the Congress of Paris of March 30, 1856, Article XVI, 15 Martens N.R.G. 766–77 (1856); Acte public relatif à la navigation des embouchûres du Danube, Galatz, November 2, 1865, Article XXI, 18 Martens N.R.G. 144: "benefits of neutrality." London Treaty of March 13, 1877, Article VII, 18 Martens N.R.G. 303; Berlin Congress Act of July 13, 1878, Articles LII–LVII, 3 Martens N.R.G. (2e sér.) 449, "Dans une complète indépendance de l'autorité territoriale" (Article LIII).

[6] Congo Navigation Act. 1885, Article XVIII. To the commission and the agents appointed by it was granted the "privilège de l'inviola-

bilité dans l'exercise de ses fonctions" and the same *garantie* was extended to the offices and archives of the commission.

7 Hague Convention of July 29, 1899, Article XXIV. Hague Convention of October 18, 1907, Article XLVI: "The members of the Tribunal in the exercise of their duties, and out of their own country enjoy diplomatic privileges and immunities."

8 Article V of the draft convention, annexed to the voeu, adopted on October 18, 1907.

9 Hague Convention of October 18, 1907, Article XIII.

10 Convention of December 20, 1907, establishing the Central American Court of Justice, U. S. FOREIGN RELATIONS 692–741 (1907), and in 2 AM.J.IN'TL L., Supplement 219–65 (1908). M. O. Hudson in his study on this court (in 26 AM.J.INT'L L. 759–86 at 765 [1932]) surveys the attitudes taken by the Central American governments and concludes: "At no time were the privileges and immunities of the judges made very definite."

11 Francis Rey, *L'Union Centro-Américaine*, 18 REVUE GÉNÉRALE DE DROIT INTERNATIONAL PUBLIC 69–89 (1911).

12 G. H. HACKWORTH, 4 DIGEST OF INTERNATIONAL LAW 419–23 (1942).

13 See the commentaries upon the Covenant of the League of Nations by Ray (at 289–99 [1930]), Schücking and Wehberg (Vol. 1 at 588–604 [3rd ed. 1931]), Göppert (at 147–50 [1938]). F. RANSHOFEN-WERTHEIMER, THE INTERNATIONAL SECRETARIAT 268–73 (1945); SUZANNE BASDEVANT, LES FONCTIONNAIRES INTERNATIONAUX 292 (1931). See also Grunebaum-Ballin in 2 REVUE DE DROIT INTERNATIONAL ET DE LÉGISLATION COMPARÉE (3e sér.) 67–82 (1921); A. Rougier in 28 REVUE GÉNÉRALE DE DROIT INTERNATIONAL PUBLIC 275–79 1921); Ramón de Orúe, *Extensión de los privilegios diplomáticos en el Pacto de la Liga de las Naciones*, REVISTA DE CIENCIAS JURIDICAS Y SOCIALES 167 (1922); U. Borsi, *Il rapporto d'impiego nella Società delle Nazioni*, 15 RIVISTA DI DIRITTO INTERNAZIONALE 437–40 (1923); C. van Vollenhoven, *Diplomatic Prerogatives of Non-Diplomats*, 19 AM.J.INT'L L. 469–74 (1925); R. Secrétan, *Les privilèges et immunités diplomatiques des agents de la Société des Nations*, 20 REVUE DE DROIT INTERNATIONAL PRIVÉ 1–25 (1925); CHARLES MORTON, LES PRIVILÈGES ET IMMUNITÉS DIPLOMATIQUES (1927); Francis Rey, *Les immunités des fonctionnaires internationaux*, REVUE DE DROIT INTERNATIONAL PRIVÉ 253–78, 432–63 (1928); J. SECRÉTAN, LES IMMUNITÉS DIPLO-MATIQUES DES REPRÉSENTANTS DES ETATS MEMBRES ET DES AGENTS DE LA SOCIÉTÉ DES NATIONS (1928); K. G. HIRSCH, DIE RECHTLICHE STEL-LUNG DER INTERNATIONALEN BEAMTEN UNTER BESONDERER BERÜCKS-ICHTIGUNG DER FUNKTIONÄRE DES VÖLKERBUNDSEKRETARIATS IN GENF. (1928); P. FREI, DE LA SITUATION JURIDIQUE DES REPRÉSENTANTS DES ETATS MEMBRES DE LA S.D.N. ET DE SES AGENTS (1929); Sir Cecil Hurst, *Diplomatic Immunities—Modern Development*, BRIT.YB.INT'L L. 1 (1929); KURT POSEGA, DIE VORRECHTE UND REFREIUNGEN DER INTER-NATIONALEN FUNKTIONÄRE (1929); F. SCHMIDT, DIE VÖLKERRECHT-LICHE STELLUNG DER MITGLIEDER DES STÄNDIGEN SEKRETARIATS DES VÖLKERBUNDES (1930); N. Hill, *Diplomatic Privileges and Immuni-*

ties in International Organizations, 20 GEO.L.J. 44–56 (1931); L.
Preuss, *Diplomatic Privileges and Immunities of Agents Invested with
Functions of an International Interest,* 25 AM.J.INT'LL. 694–710
(1931); H. R. BALZ, DIE BESONDEREN STAATENVERTRETER UND IHRE
VÖLKERRECHTLICHE STELLUNG (1931); H. P. Benet, *Recent Developments Affecting Diplomatic Privileges,* J.COMP.LEG. & INT'L L. 84
(1931); S. KAUFMANN, DIE IMMUNITÄT DER NICHT-DIPLOMATEN
(1932); J. Secrétan, *The Independence Granted to Agents of the International Community in Their Relations with National Public Authorities,* BRIT.YB.INT'L L. 56–78 (1935); A. Hammarskjöld, *Les
immunités des personnes investies de fonctions d'intérêt international,*
16 REVUE DE DROIT INTERNATIONAL ET DE LÉGISLATION COMPARÉE (3ᵉ
sér.) 6–31 (1935); the same, *Rapport,* in ANNUAIRE DE L'INSTITUT DE
DROIT INTERNATIONAL, SESSION DE PARIS (1934); the same, *Les immunités des personnes investies de fonctions internationales,* 2 RE-
CUEIL DES COURS 110–209 (1936). A monograph by Martin Hill, DIPLO-
MATIC PRIVILEGES AND IMMUNITIES OF LEAGUE OF NATIONS OFFICIALS,
is also pertinent to the subject.

[14] Adatci–de Visscher, *Rapport,* 31 ANNUAIRE DE L'INSTITUT DE
DROIT INTERNATIONAL, SESSION DE VIENNE 1–19 (1924); David Jayne
Hill, *Rapport,* 33 ANNUAIRE DE L'INSTITUT DE DROIT INTERNATIONAL,
SESSION DE LAUSANNE 420–30 (1924); observation by Francis Rey,
ibid. at 442–47; A. Hammarskjöld, *Rapport,* ANNUAIRE DE L'INSTITUT
DE DROIT INTERNATIONAL, SESSION DE PARIS 358–413 (1934); Commis-
sion of Experts for the Progressive Codification of International Law
in 20 AM.J.INT'L L., Supplement 148–75 (1926); J. Blociszewski,
L'Institut de Droit International, Session de Vienne, 32 REVUE GÉN-
ÉRALE DE DROIT INTERNATIONAL PUBLIC 261–67 (1925).

[15] Paris Peace Treaties, Statut définitif du Danube (1921).

[16] Versailles Treaty, art. CCCXLVII, Statut définitif du Danube,
Paris, July 23, 1921, 26 L.N.T.S. 173, art. XXXVII (1924): "The
property of the International Commission and the persons of Commissioners are entitled to privileges and immunities which are accorded in peace and war to accredited diplomatic agents."

[17] Convention, Dresden, February 22, 1922, 26 L.N.T.S. 219, art.
VIII (1924): "The delegates to the International Commission, the
Secretary General and his assistant, will enjoy the usual diplomatic
privileges."

[18] Convention, October 27, 1923, art. XIX, grants diplomatic privileges for the president, the delegate, and their assistants, the members
and personnel of the secretariat and of the delegations *dans l'exercice
de leurs fonctions.*

[19] Versailles Treaty, art. CDXXXII. Treaty of June 24, 1919,
L.N.T.S. No. 7, art. III (1919).

[20] Treaties of Versailles, art. CCXL. St. Germain, art. CLXXXVI,
Triannon, art. CCLXX, Neuilly, art. CXXX (obligations for the ex-
enemies). French decree of April 30, 1920.

[21] Polish-Danzig Convention, Paris, November 9, 1920, art. XIV.
The Danzig Commissioners of the Board enjoyed diplomatic privileges

and immunities in the territory of Poland, and the Polish members in the territory of Danzig, the president of the Board in both states. The president, even if appointed by the Council of the League of Nations, was not an official of the League, as the Council expressly stated (LEAGUE OF NATIONS OFF.J. 158 [1921]).

22 4 HACKWORTH, *op. cit.* at 420.

23 German law of August 10, 1920. French decrees of May 29, December 13, December 15, 1925.

24 P.C.I.J., ser. D, No. 1, at 69–79 (3rd. ed. 1936).

25 Hague Convention, January 20, 1930, 5 M. O. HUDSON, INTERNATIONAL LEGISLATION 309–13 (1936).

26 Art. VII, para. 4: "Representatives of the Members of the League and officials of the League, when engaged on the business of the League, shall enjoy diplomatic privileges and immunities." Slightly different, the equally authentic French text: "Les représentants des Membres de la Societé et ses agents jouissent dans l'exercise de leurs fonctions des privilèges et immunités diplomatiques."

27 L. N. Doc. No. C. 555. (1926); LEAGUE OF NATIONS OFF. J. 1422 (1926); 1 M. O. HUDSON, *op. cit.* at 224–28.

28 P. C. Jessup in 38 AM.J.INT'L L. 658–62 (1944); LELAND M. GOODRICH and EDVARD HAMBRO, CHARTER OF THE U.N.: COMMENTARY AND DOCUMENTS 281–85 (1946).

29 Arts. CIV–CV.

30 PC/20, 60–80, December 23, 1945. See also Henry Reiff in 15 DEP'T STATE BULL. No. 372, 305–6, 311–12 (August 18, 1946).

31 15 DEP'T STATE BULL. Appendix B, 72–74 (August 18, 1946).

32 *Ibid.* Appendix C. 75–80.

33 Faris al-Khoury (Syria), chairman; Aghnides (Greece), *rapporteur* (U.N.GEN.ASS.J. Nos. 11 and 23, Supplement 5). See also Henry Reiff in 15 DEP'T STATE BULL. No. 30, 345, 349–51 (August 25, 1946).

34 R. Jimenez (Panama), chairman; Read (Canada), rapporteur (U.N.GEN.ASS.J. Nos. 14, 18, 26, Supplement 6). Meetings of the subcommittee (Vandenberg [U.S.], chairman). See Doc. Nos. A.C/6.14, A.C/6.20, A.C/6.21, A.C/6.23, A.C/6.28, and the report of W. E. Beckett (U.K.), reporter, of the sixth committee of the General Assembly (U.N. Doc. No. A/43 [Feburary 9, 1946]).

35 Annex to U.N. Doc. No. A/43—Comd. 6753 (1946) (Miscellaneous Docs. No. 6 [1946]). U.N.GEN.ASS.J. No. 34 at 687–93 (March 7, 1946).

36 Art. XIX.

37 I.C.J. ser. D, No. 1 at 84.

38 M. O. Hudson in 41 AM.J.INT'L L. 16–17 (1947).

39 First session of the Council of the UNRRA, Atlantic City, N.J., November 10–December 1, 1943, Selected Documents. Dep't State Pub. No. 2040, Conf. Ser. 53 at 215.

40 International Labor Conference, 26th Sess., Philadelphia, 1944. REPORT OF PROCEEDINGS 647 (1944).

41 U.N. Conference, Hot Springs, Va., May 18–June 3, 1943, Final Act and Section Reports. Dep't State Conf. Ser. 52 at 67 (1948). Constitution of FAO in 40 AM.J.INT'L L. SUPPLEMENT, 76–85 (1946).

42 U.N. Monetary and Financial Conference, Bretton Woods, N.H., July 1–22, 1944, Final Act and Related Documents. Dep't State Pub. No. 2187, Conf. Ser. 55 at 122; Articles of Agreement, U.S. Treasury, p. 88.

43 40 AM.J.INT'L L. Supplement 31–45 (1946).

44 International Civil Aviation Conference, Chicago, Ill., November 1–December 7, 1944, Final Act and Related Documents. Dep't State Pub. No. 2282, Conf. Ser. 64 at 284. Interim Agreement in 40 AM.J. INT'L L. 63–76 (1946).

45 London Conference, November 1–16, 1945, Final Act. DEP'T STATE, THE DEFENSE OF PEACE: DOCUMENTS RELATING TO UNESCO Part 1, 13–22 (1946); "The privileges of Art. 104 and 105 of the Charter of the UN concerning the legal status of that organization, its privileges and immunities shall apply in the same way to this organization."

46 Proposal for the constitution of WHO, U.N. ECON. & SOC. COUNCIL J. No. 13 (May 22, 1946). Article XVI of the constitution (15 DEP'T STATE BULL. No. 370 at 211–19 (August 4, 1946), arts LXVI–LXVIII.

47 15 DEP'T STATE BULL. 44–45 (September, 1946).

48 Inter-American Conference on Problems of War and Peace, Mexico City, Final Act, resolution IX at 44–48 (1945).

49 Pan-American Union 33, arts. XIX, XLV (1946) (mimeo.).

50 13 DEP'T STATE BULL. No. 336 at 901 (December 2, 1945).

51 For the ILO (1943).

52 Status of the ILO Order, August 14, 1941.

53 The Diplomatic Privileges (Extension) Act, 1944 (8 Geo. 6 [Ch. 44]). Text also in 39 AM.J.INT'L L. Supplement at 163–67 (1945). See Egon Schwelb in 8 MODERN L. REV. 50–63, 163–67 (1945). Diplomatic Privileges (UNRRA) Order in Council, January 24, 1945 (S.R.O. No. 79 [1945]). Order in Council, January 24, 1945 (S.R.O. No. 84 [1945]), aplied to U.N. Information Organization, Intergovernmental Committee for Refugees, and European Advisory Commission.

54 International Organizations Immunities Act, Public Law 299, 79th Cong. (1945). Text also in 40 AM.J.INT'L L. Supplement at 85–91 (1946). See Lawrence Preuss in 40 AM.J.INT'L L. 332–45 (1946). By Executive Order 9698 of February 19, 1946 (11 FEDERAL REGISTER [1809]; 14 DEP'T STATE BULL. 348–49 [March 3, 1946]) were designated the U.N., the UNRRA, ILO, FAO, and the Pan-American Union, Further extension by the later Executive Orders 9751 of July 11, 1946 (2 DEP'T STATE BULL. No. 131 at 7713) and 9823 of January 24, 1947 (12 ibid. No. 19 at 551).

55 Of the imense literature on this subject we cite here only a few writings: 4 HACKWORTH, op. cit. at 513–623; FRANÇOIS PIÉTRI, ETUDE CRITIQUE SUR LA FICTION D'EXTERRITORIALITÉ (1895); E. BELING, DIE

STRAFRECHTLICHE BEBEUTUNG DER EXTERRITORIALITÄT (1898); FRISCH, DER VÖLKERRECHTLICHE BEGRIFF DER EXTERRITORIALITÄT (1917); L. Strisower; *L'exterritorialité et ses principales applications*, 1 RECUEIL DES COURS 233–86 (1923); HEYKING, L'EXTERRITORIALITÉ (1926); Sir Cecil Hurst, *Les immunités diplomatiques*, 2 RECUEIL DES COURS 119–240 (1926) J. L. F. VAN ESSEN, ONTWICKKELING EN CODIFICATIE VAN DE DIPLOMATIKE VOORECHTEN (1928); F. Deák, *Classification, immunités et privilèges des agents diplomatiques*, 9 REVUE DE DROIT INTERNATIONAL ET DE LÉGISLATION COMPARÉE (3e sér.) 173–206, 522–67 (1928); 1 PAUL GENET, TRAITÉ DE DIPLOMATIE ET DE DROIT DIPLOMATIQUE 417–598 (1931); SIR ERNEST SATOW, A GUIDE TO DIPLOMATIC PRACTICE 161–80 (3rd ed. 1932); L. Preuss, *Capacity for Legation and the Theoretical Basis of Diplomatic Immunities*, 10 REVUE DE DROIT INTERNATIONAL 1–18 (1932); JAIME EYZAGUIRRE, PRIVILEGIOS DIPLOMÁTICOS: SÍNTESIS TEÓRICA Y DE LEGISLACIÓN COMPARADA (1932); VAN PRAAG, JURIDICTION ET DROIT INTERNATIONAL PUBLIC (1935); MONTELL OGDON, BASES OF DIPLOMATIC IMMUNITY (1936); M. M. SAVELBERG, LE PROBLÈME DU DROIT INTERNATIONAL AMERICAIN (1946). Treaties: Vienna, 1815; Havana Convention, 1928. INSTITUT DE DROIT INTERNATIONAL, RÈGLEMENT SUR LES IMMUNITÉS DIPLOMATIQUES 240 (ANNUAIRE No. 14, 1895); Epitacio Pessôa, *Projecto de Codigo de direito Internacional Publico*, 22 AM.J.INT'L L. Supplement at 249–524 (1928); Giulio Dienn, *Rapport au Sous-Comité pour les privilèges et immunités diplomatiques*, League of Nations Doc. No. 196, M. 70, IV at 78–85 (1927); also in 20 AM.J.INT'L L. Suplement at 148–65 (1926); Harvard Research in International Law, *Draft Convention on Diplomatic Privileges and Immunities*, 26 AM.J.INT'L L. Supplement at 15–18 (1932).

[56] DE JURE BELLI AC PACIS 2.184.5.

[57] MONTESQUIEU, *Ils sont la parole du prince qui les envoie*, ESPRIT DES LOIS, Bk. XXVI, chap. 21.

[58] VATTEL, *Tous les privilèges qui assurent l'exercice de leurs fonctions*, LE DROIT DES GENS, Bk. IV, chaps. 7, 92.

[59] VÖLKERRECHT 207–14 (1937).

[60] Dickinson v. Del Solar, [1930], 1 K.B. 376: "Diplomatic agents are not in virtue of their privileges, as such, immune from legal liability for any wrongful acts. The accurate statement is that they are not liable to be sued in English Courts unless they submit to the jurisdiction. Diplomatic privilege does not import immunity from legal liability but only exemption from local jurisdiction." In the Iranian minister's case, 1935 (4 HACKWORTH, *op. cit.* at 515–16), Secretary Hull wrote: "This Government has at all times impressed upon its own diplomatic officers in foreign countries that the enjoyment of diplomatic immunities imposes upon them the obligation and responsibility of according scrupulous regard to the laws and regulations, both national and local, of the countries to which they are accredited."

[61] Similar formulas are to be found in Article LXXIV of the ITO constitution and Article LXVII of the constitution of WHO. The same formula is used in Articles XIX and XLV of the Project of Organic

Pact of the Inter-American System (Pan-American Union, Washington, D. C., 1946). On the other hand, the formula of "diplomatic privileges and immunities" is to be found in FAO, art. XV, para 2, art. VII, para. 4, ECITO, art. VIII, Statute of the International Court of Justice, art. XIX, and in U.N. General Convention on the Privileges and Immunities of the U.N., art. IV, sec. 11, paras. f and g, art. V, sec. 18, paras. e and f, and sec 19.

62 See also U.N. General Convention, art. IV, § 14; art V, §§ 20, 21; art. VI, § 23. The functional basis and the principle is stressed that these privileges are given to the officials of the U.N. in the interest of the organization, and in no way for the benefit of the individual concerned.

63 POST-WAR WORLDS 173 (1942).

64 C. WILFRED JENKS, THE HEADQUARTERS OF INTERNATIONAL INSTITUTIONS, A STUDY OF THEIR LOCATION AND STATUS (1945).

65 33 ANNUAIRE. 1 SESSION DE LAUSANNE 420–38 (1927).

66 A. Hammarskjöld proposed extension even to *fonctionnaires internationaux à statut national*, such as the judges at the Mixed Courts of Egypt or the administrative officials of the International Zone at Tangiers, and even to members of private organizations, acting in the international interest, such as the members of the International Red Cross Committee.

67 Institute of Intellectual Co-operation, Paris, Institute for the Unification of Private Law, Institute for Educational Films, both at Rome; International University of Hygiene, Paris, 1930; International Institute for the Study of Leprosy, Rio de Janeiro, 1931.

68 William Martin, *Représentation permanente des Etats membres auprès de la Société des Nations à Genève, in* REVUE DE DROIT INTERNATIONAL 150–52 (1925).

69 Answer of Switzerland to Questionnaire 3B of the Committee of Experts for the Codification of International Law, in League of Nations Doc. No. C. 196, M. 70, I at 249 (1927).

70 The same formula in ECITO, art VIII, para. 18, equally § 3 of the British Act of 1944. The constitutions of some specialized agencies do not mention the legal status of representatives of the members.

71 Similarly Resolution 32 of the UNRRA Council, art. LXXIV, para. 2, of the suggested charter of the ITO, art. LXVII of the constitution of WHO.

72 Equally art. LXIV, para. 3, of ITO, art. LXVIII of WHO.

73 See Swiss Confederation v. Justh. Switzerland, [1927] Fed.Ass. 1st Dist. (40 REVUE PÉNALE SUISSE 179 [1927]) (English transl. in M. O. HUDSON, CASES AND OTHER MATERIALS ON INTERNATIONAL LAW 795–97 [2nd ed. 1936]). See now also the letter of Ukrainian Foreign Minister Dmitri Z. Manuilsky to Secretary of State Byrnes at the occasion of the criminal attack upon two members of the Ukrainian delegation to the General Assembly of the U.N. (N.Y. Times, November 24, 1946, p. 58).

74 U.N. General Convention, art. IV, § 15. Thus also British act of 1944, American act of 1945, § 7a.

75 "While exercising their functions" (U.N. General Convention, art. IV, § 11.

76 U.N. General Convention, art. IV, §16.

77 Thus the Argentinian delegate Dr. José Arce waived his immunity and paid a $15.00 fine for contravention of the New York laws (N.Y. Times, November 14, 1946, p. 11). Equally Dr. Max Steemberger, financial adviser to the Netherlands government (*ibid.*, November 23, 1946).

78 C. W. Jenks, *Some Legal Aspects of the Financing of International Institutions*, 28 TRANSACT.GROT.SOC'Y 87–132 (1943).

79 *Op. cit.*

80 JENKS, *op. cit.* at 46.

81 This phrase stands in FAO, art. XV, para. 2.

82 See Holtzendorff's construction of the European Danube Commission as a "fluvial state."

83 R. KNUBBEN, DIE SUBJEKTE DES VÖLKERRECHTS, (1928). M. Siotto Pintor, *Les sujets du droit international autres que les Etats*, 3 RECUEIL DES COURS, 251–361 (1932).

84 See "Experience and Techniques in International Administration," above.

85 Recognized by Switzerland in the *modus vivendi* of 1926. There is a rich monographic literature on this subject. See also the literature on the international personality of the International Institute of Agriculture. JOSEF L. KUNZ, DIE STAATENVERBINDUNGEN 50 (1929); and, in general, VAN DER LÜBE, DIE INTERNATIONALE JURISTISCHE PERSON (1931).

86 That is why, under section 30 of the U.N. General Convention, differences between the U.N. and a member are to be decided by an advisory, but binding, opinion of the International Court of Justice. Different is Article LXVIII of WHO which provides for the establishment of details concerning immunities by a separate agreement which is to be prepared by the organization but is to be concluded between the members. Jenks, *op. cit.* at 39, asks for the recognition of the international personality of international institutions as the basis of their capacity to conclude with states and other international institutions agreements governed by international law.

87 JENKS, *op. cit.* at 39.

88 See for the Pan-American Union, Josef L. Kunz, *The Pan-American Union in the Field of International Administration*, 31 IOWA L. REV. 58–89 at 79–80 (1945).

89 See for the Pan-American Union, Penfield, 20 AM.J.INT'L L. 257–62 (1926); for the International Institute of Agriculture, Italian Court of Cassation, 1931 (ANNUAL DIGEST OF PUBLIC INTERNATIONAL LAW CASES, 1929–1930, No. 254).

90 Similarly the constitutions of the specialized agencies. For details as regards the U.N. in the state of the seat, see Draft Convention, P/C, Rep. 75–80.

91 W. Friedmann, *International Public Corporations*, 6 MODERN L. REV. 185–207 (1942-43).

92 Created by the Hague Convention of January 20, 1930, see 5 M. O. HUDSON, INTERNATIONAL LEGISLATION 307–13; 104 L.N.T.S. 441. See J. F. Williams in 24 AM.J.INT'L L. 665–73 (1930); C. Cereti, *La personalità giuridica della Banca dei Regolamenti Internazionali*, 23 RIVISTA DI DIRITTO PUBBLICO 169–93 (1931); G. BEITZKE, DIE RECHTSSTELLUNG DER BANK FÜR INTERNATIONALEN-ZAHLUNGSAUS-GLEICH IM VÖLKERRECHT (1932); Reynolds, *The Legal Structure of the Bank of International Settlements*, 19 A.B.A.J. 289–93 (1933).

93 The Bank of International Settlements at Basel was, notwithstanding its creation by international treaty and its far-reaching immunities, legally a Swiss corporation that received its charter from Switzerland. In the same way the Inter-American Bank gets its charter from the United States. A recent Inter-American Institute of Agriculture, which has its seat in Turrialba, Costa Rica, is incorporated under the laws of the District of Columbia.

94 Musurus Bey v. Gadban, [1894] 2 Q. B. 352.

95 R. Genet, *Un problème de préséance*, 14 REVUE DE DROIT INTER-NATIONAL ET DE LÉGISLATION COMPARÉE 254 (1933); A. Hammarskjöld, *Un problème de préséance*, 4 ACTA SCANDINAVICA JURIS GENTIUM 158–65 (1933); L. Aubain, *Un nouveau Protocole de Vienne?*, 15 REVUE DE DROIT INTERNATIONAL ET DE LÉGISLATION COMPARÉE 129–43 (1934).

96 THE PERMANENT COURT OF INTERNATIONAL JUSTICE 325–31 (1943).

97 "In the exercise of their duties and out of their own country" (art. XLVI [1907]).

98 At the time of preparing Article XIX of the Statute of the Permanent Court of International Justice, Sir Cecil Hurst proposed to drop the phrase "en dehors de leurs pays," but this proposal was opposed by Huber and Loder. It has now been dropped in Article XIX of the Statute of the International Court of Justice.

99 In X v. Y and the Greek State (ANNUAL DIGEST OF PUBLIC IN-TERNATIONAL LAW CASES, 1933–34 at 387–88 [1940]), the Court of Appeals of Athens (1934) held that the members of the Greco-Bulgarian Mixed Emigration Commission enjoyed no jurisdictional immunity, as the Neuilly Convention of November 27, 1919, did not confer immunity upon them and as they performed independent duties and exercised their functions not for and under the League of Nations; they were not "officials" in the sense of Article VII, para, 4, of the Covenant.

100 Already the Adatci-de Visscher report stated that the agreement with the state of the seat and the assimilation of the League officials with diplomatic agents is "theoretically inexact and would practically lead to an inadmissible inequality."

101 "International officials" in the sense of Article VII, para. 4, of the Covenant were the officials of the Secretariat General, of the ILO, of the Saar Governing Commission, of the Registry of the Permanent Court, the High Commissioner at Danzig, the High Commissioner for Refugees, officials of the Paris and Rome Institutes, members of the

Mandate Commission and of the many commissions of the League, insofar as they had not the status of "international experts" or were representatives of the members, the high commissioners of the League at Vienna and Budapest, personnel of Nansen office, and so on.

102 *Op. cit.* at 40.

103 In Assurance Générale des Eaux et Accidents v. F.B., Cour de Justice Civile (Geneva), May 6, 1929 (Annual Digest, 1929–30 at 315–16 [1935]), the Swiss court decided that an official of the first category of the ILO is immune from civil jurisdiction and cannot validly renounce his privilege; proceedings cannot be continued as long as his immunity is not waived by the director of the ILO.

104 The report of the Preparatory Commission (p. 62) proposed the creation of an international passport which "would not, of course, impair the sovereign rights of members in respect of granting visas." The word "passport" has now been lowered to "laissez-passer."

105 Parents of officials do not enjoy benefits of immunity. The mother of an official of the ILO of the second category was held not to be entitled to claim any privilege (W. K. v. Office des Poursuites, Cours de Justice Civile [Geneva] February 16, 1929; ANNUAL DIGEST, 1929–30 at 314–15 [1935]).

106 Case of David Sission (N.Y. Queens Traffic Court), the U.N. waived immunity. Case of Andrew Jackson before the City Judge at Yonkers; no plea of immunity was made in this case (N.Y. Times, November 5, 1946, p. 5). The most interesting case is that of William Ranallo, chauffeur of Secretary General Trygve Lie, who was before a court of New Rochell, N.Y., for speeding. Counsel for the U.N. stated that "immunity is not the same as the broad, unrestricted immunity of diplomats. It is only when the U.N. official is carrying out his duties that the immunity is involved." Judge Rubin took exception to the contention that all U.N. personnel, from the highest to lowest, should have immunity if engaged on U.N. "functions." He said: "To establish such a principle would in effect create a large preferred class. Under diplomatic immunity the law violator is subject to return to his own country for punishment of violations of U.S. law. Immunity to U.N. personnel could result in offenses receiving no punishment."—N.Y. Times, November 9, 1946, pp. 1, 7. The immunity appeal was later withdrawn by Trygve Lie. The judge regretted this withdrawal, "as it left the question of right to immunity unsettled for future cases." For a detailed examination of the Ranallo Case, see L. Preuss, *Immunity of Officers and Employees of the UN for Official Acts: The Ranallo Case,* 41 AM.J.INT'L L. 555–78 (1947).

107 C. M. v. A. C., Cour de Justice Civile (Geneva) March 2, 1929 (ANNUAL DIGEST, 1929–30 at 313–14 [1935]): Creditors of a League official of Swiss nationality applied for an attachment of salary for debt. The Court held that A. C., a Swiss national, was not entitled to immunity. But as the League premises were inviolable, an attachment of his salary in the hands of the employer could not be made. See Avenol v. Avenol, Juge de Paix, XVIe arrondissement de Paris, March 8, 1935 (ANNUAL DIGEST, 1935–37 at 395–97 [1941]): sentence in absentia to pay 12,500 francs per month to his wife from whom he

was separated as maintenance. Avenol appealed: as secretary-general of the League he was exempt, under Article VII, para. 4, from the jurisdiction of the courts of any member state, including that of French courts. The court dismissed the appeal, holding that (1) his privileges were strictly limited to Geneva and Switzerland, and (2) League officials enjoy no exemption in their own country.

[108] British act, 1944, American act, 1945, § 7a ("other than Nationals of the U.S.").

[109] Monetary Fund, art. IX, sec. 8b: "Not being nationals"; and sec. 9b: tax exemption on salaries and emoluments "for those, who are not local citizens, local subjects, or other local nationals." ECITO, art. VII, § 17c: exemption from taxation "except in the case of their own nationals." UNRRA, resolution 32: "Each Member shall determine to what extent the privileges shall apply to its own nationals, and to non-nationals in permanent residence in its territories."

[110] P. 62.

[111] Sec. 19.

[112] U.N. JOURNAL, No. 54, A/P.v/50, Supplement A (December 9, 1946).

[113] *Op cit.* at 42–43.

[114] Same argument as against an international passport in the League of Nations.

[115] The U.N. budget for 1947 provided $350,000 for income-tax refunds; of this sum, $330,000 was needed for U.S. income-tax refunds (N.Y. Times, November 13, 1946, p. 11).

[116] See the reasoning of the French court in Avenol v. Avenol and of Judge Rubin, above, note 107.

[117] See Parlett v. Parlett, Tribunal de première instance (Geneva), July 21, 1927. Divorce proceedings against an official of the first catagory of the ILO, waiver of immunity from civil jurisdiction by director of ILO: Johnstone v. Ruttle, Superior Court of the Province of Quebec, August 4, 1942 (ANNUAL DIGEST, 1941–1942 at 376–77 [1945]). Suit for annulment of marriage, waiver from civil jurisdiction, signed by director of ILO.

[118] *Op. cit.* at 199.

[119] P. C. Jessup, *Responsibility of States for Injuries to Individuals*, 16 COLUM.L.REV. 903–28 at 927, 928 (1946).

CHAPTER XXVIII: The Legal Position of the Secretary General of the United Nations

THE INTERVENTION by Secretary General Trygve Lie of the United Nations in the Iranian case, pending in the Security Council, has brought up again the problem of the range of his competence under the Charter. The problem is not only important as far as the U.N. is concerned but also is interesting from the point of view of the development of international organization. As the makers of the Charter carefully took into consideration the law and the experience of the League of Nations, it may be helpful to start with a brief sketch of the legal position of the Secretary General of that organization.

The Secretary General of the League of Nations was primarily the chief administrative officer of the League. He had, first, to organize the Secretariat and to act as its chief. In this capacity he had broad powers. He was the superior of all the staff members. He made all appointments to the staff; the approval of the Council, under Article IV, para. 3, of the Covenant, was, to a large extent, a formality and was given once for all, as far as all the lower posts were concerned, at an early date. He alone was responsible to Assembly and Council for the work of the Secretariat. He had important functions concerning the budget of the League.

He acted as Secretary General at all meetings of the Assembly and the Council. He had specific duties under Article I, para. 1, Article XVIII, and Article XXIV, para. 2, as well as under Article XI, para. 1 and Article XV, para. 1 of the Covenant. He had to prepare the work and to execute the resolutions of the various organs of the League. He had administrative and technical functions specified in the rules of procedure of the organs of the League, under the Statute of the Permanent Court of International Justice, with regard to the International Labor Organization, and under special treaties. He represented the League to a certain extent. His emoluments were adequate and he enjoyed full diplomatic privileges and immunities.

Developments in the League caused certain difficulties however. The pressure brought by members for the appointment to higher staff posts of their nationals handicapped his freedom of choice and the dangerous trend to regard these officials rather as the representatives of their countries than as true international civil servants threatened to compromise the international character of the Secretariat. The Secretary General also had to struggle for the adoption of his budget and the Supervisory Commission of the League rose from its original modest task of assisting the Secretary General to a role of supervising and controlling him.

The political functions of the Secretary General were severely restricted by the Covenant. This had already been suggested by the history of the drafting of the Covenant. The title originally proposed for this office, that of "Chancellor," was lowered to "Secretary General." The original "and" in Article II, putting the Secretariat on the same level as the Assembly and Council, was changed into "with." [1] The fact that the Secretary General was "appointed" (*nomine*) pointed in the same direction. At the very beginning of the League the Noblemaire report [2] insisted urgently that the

Secretariat should not extend the sphere of its activities beyond preparing and executing the decisions of the various organs of the League, without suggesting what these decisions should be. It was the time when orators in Geneva frequently found it necessary to emphasize that the League was not a "super-state." But as late as 1930, the Report of the Committee of Thirteen [3] stated emphatically that the Secretariat had no political initiative and formed only an administrative organism.

Most students of the League have, nevertheless, concluded that the Secretariat was more: Ray wrote in 1930 that the position of the Secretary General was considerable, although badly defined juridically.[4] Schücking-Wehberg pointed in 1931 to the permanency of the Secretariat, to the fact that it was the central point of all incoming information, the guardian of the tradition of the League, and the adviser of all the delegations, and concluded that it was not merely a technical but also a political organ.[5] And this view was shared in 1938 by Göppert.[6] Ranshofen-Wertheimer in 1945 recognized the limitations and restrictions put by the Covenant upon the external powers of the Secretary General but pointed also to the personality of the two Secretaries-General of the League: "the two Secretaries-General kept scrupulously, even over-scrupulously, within the constitutional limits and did not even avail themselves as fully as they could have done of the marginal possibilities for action and influence open to them," [7] e.g. to address the Assembly and the Council; "they fell short of international leadership." [8] He suggested that a future international organization should give political powers to the Secretary General, who should be chosen rather from statesmen than civil servants.

It is against this background and experience that the legal position of the Secretary General of the U.N. has to be studied. The Dumbarton Oaks Proposals [9] contained already *in nuce* the relevant provisos of the Charter of the United Nations.[10] The Secretary General of the U.N. has also functions under the Statute of the International Court of Justice.[11] The preparatory commission of the U.N., set up by the interim arrangements adopted at San Francisco,[12] sat in London from November 23 to December 23, 1945, and its report [13] deals in Chapter VIII with the Secretariat. The first part of the First General Assembly of the U.N. met in London from January 10 to February 14, 1946; and it was its fifth committee [14] which dealt with the problems of the Secretariat. The excellent work done by the preparatory commission made it possible for the fifth committee to adopt, to a great extent, the proposals of the preparatory commission, without substantial change.[15]

The title of "Secretary General" was retained as in the Covenant. The word "elected" in the Dumbarton Oaks Proposals had been changed to "appointed" in the Charter. Under Article XCVII the appointment has to be made by the General Assembly, by a simple majority of votes, upon the recommendation of the Security Council. This recommendation needs seven votes, including the concurrent vote of the five permanent members, who, therefore, have the right of veto. The General Assembly is not bound to appoint the person recommended, but, if it does not, it must wait for a further recommendation by the Security Council. As determined by the General Assembly, nomination and appointment are to be made in private meetings and the vote taken by secret ballot. It further determined that the appointment of the first Secretary General should run for five years, renewable for a further five-year term.

The recommendation by the Security Council was a matter of compromise between an eastern European, sponsored by the Soviet Union, and the Canadian ambassador in Washington, sponsored by this country and Great Britain, but whose nomination the Soviet representative threatened to veto. On January 29, 1946, the Security Council unanimously agreed on Trygve Lie for Secretary General.[16] The appointment was made by the General Assembly by secret ballot, with 46 votes in favor and three against. The installation of the Secretary General took place in the twenty-second Plenary Meeting on February 2, 1946,[17] and he took an oath of loyalty absolutely identical with the oath taken by the Secretary General of the League of Nations. Contrary to the practice under the League, the appointment of the foreign minister of Norway as Secretary General brought a statesman of a small power, not a civil servant of a Great Power, into this office.

The Secretary General of the U.N. is, in first place, the "chief administrative officer of the United Nations" (Article XCVII); he is the Secretary General of the General Assembly, the Security Council, the Social and Economic Council and the Trusteeship Council (Article XCVIII). He has to present an annual report on the work of the organization to the General Assembly (Article XCVIII). Specific administrative and executive functions are given to him under the provisional rules of procedure of the General Assembly.[18] He has to prepare the agenda, convoke the sessions, provide the necessary staff, prepare the minutes and other documents of the various organs of the U.N. He is the channel of communication with the U.N. and all of its organs. He is responsible for the preparation of the work of the various organs and for the execution of their decisions. He has wide responsibilities concerning the financial administration of the U.N. He is the head of the Secretariat and appoints all staff members (Article CI). He alone is responsible to the other principal organs of the U.N. for the work of the Secretariat. His emoluments are adequate; he enjoys full diplomatic privileges and immunities. He is strictly an international officer; he may not seek or receive instructions from any authority external of the

U.N.; each member undertakes fully to respect the exclusively international character of his responsibilities
(Article C).

The report of the preparatory commission emphasized the
"key position of the Secretariat in the U.N." The report of
the fifth committee states that it was guided by the consideration "to enable a man of eminence and high attain-
ment to accept and maintain the position." It is fully recognized that "his choice of staff and his leadership will
largely determine the character and efficiency of the Secretariat as a whole," [19] that "the manner in which the Secretariat performs its tasks will largely determine the degree
in which the objectives of the Charter will be realized." [20]

With regard to these administrative and technical functions, his position is analogous to that of the Secretary
General of the League. But the preparatory commission
and the General Assembly in London took measures to enhance the prestige of his position and to guard against the
handicaps of which the Secretary General of the League
became the victim. The fifth committee proposed that, as
the Secretary General is the confidant of many governments, members will not offer him positions, at least immediately after his retirement, nor will he accept those in
which his confidential knowledge might be a source of
embarassment to other members. This proposal, no doubt,
was inspired by the fact that the first Secretary General
of the League had become British ambassador to fascist
Italy. To prevent such happenings, the financial position
of the Secretary General after retirement must be secured.

The General Assembly insisted that the Secretary General should have a completely free hand to set up and organize the Secretariat, choose his collaborators, appoint the
members of the staff, prepare the rules for the staff, set up
classification schedules and salary scales. The preparatory

commission and the General Assembly have also seen to it that the Secretary General should formulate and present the annual budget of the U.N. to the General Assembly and that the proposed Advisory Committee for Administrative and Budgetary Questions be an assisting body and may not develop into an organ of control like the Supervisory Commission of the League.

Contrary to the Covenant, Article XCIX of the Charter, under which "the Secretary General may bring to the attention of the Security Council any matter which in his opinion may threaten the maintenance of international peace and security," certainly gives the Secretary General an important and far-reaching right of political initiative, the exercise of which is left entirely to his discretion. The report of the preparatory commission [21] stated that "the responsibility which Article XCIX confers upon the Secretary General will require the exercise of the highest qualities of political judgment, tact, and integrity" and points out that Article XCIX "confers a special right which goes beyond any power previously accorded to the head of an international organization"; it states at the same time that "it is impossible to foresee how this article will be applied."

Already Rule 48 of the provisional rules of procedure of the General Assembly gives the Secretary General the right, at any time, upon invitation by the president, to make to the General Assembly either oral or written statements— whereas the Secretary General of the League could only "address" the Assembly—concerning any question which is being considered by the General Assembly. But the problem of the range of Article XCIX came really up in the Iranian case. This article certainly does not give the Secretary General a right to make the policy of the U.N. In his first speech as Secretary General Trygve Lie had said: "Your Secretary General is not called upon to formulate the policy of the

U.N." [22] In his letter to the Security Council [23] the Secretary General suggested that the Council may have no authority to retain the Iranian case on its agenda. We are here not concerned with the contents of this letter; but merely that it was presented involved the problem of the Secretary General's competence under the Charter.

The motives of this intervention were differently interpreted; the press hinted even at the possibility of a desire on the part of the Secretary to be agreeable to the Soviet delegation, which had supported Trygve Lie first for president of the General Assembly, then for Secretary General. But such a motive is surely out of the question; perhaps the Secretary General wanted to make use of the first opportunity to test the range of Article XCIX. Gromyko (Soviet Union) and Lange (Poland) [24] took a strong stand in favor of this competence of the Secretary General under Article XCIX. On the other hand, it was reported in the press that the American representative (Stettinius) had questioned Lie's authority to intervene and that perhaps one or two more members of the Security Council were of opinion that the Secretary General had overstepped his powers in the Council. Trygve Lie defended his right to intervene under Article XCIX and urged a clear and definite decision.

The report of the Council's Committee of Experts [25] was unanimously adopted in the meeting of June 6, 1946 and under it "the Council recognizes that the Secretary General may make oral or written statements to the Council regarding any matter submitted to it for consideration." The Council, further, granted authority to the Secretary General to participate in the discussions of the Atomic Energy Committee, the Military Staff Committee and any other subsidiary organ of the Council. It was, moreover, decided that the Council "could, if it and Mr. Lie chose, appoint the Secretary General as a rapporteur or mediator in any controversy in the Council." Finally, the same powers were granted to the Secretary General's deputy (Arkady Sobolev), when acting on behalf of the Secretary General.

It was reported that the Secretary General would reorganize his "cabinet" so that it should consist of persons of highest rank, with the intention of delegating more authority to them as far as administrative and technical functions were concerned, so that the Secretary General might devote the greater part of his time and energy to his political functions. The legal position of the Secretary General of the U.N., therefore, transcends by far that of the Secretary General of the League.

[1] Still more indicative, the equally authentic French text: "Assistés d'un Secrétariat permanent." JEAN RAY, COMMENTAIRE DU PACTE DE LA SOCIÉTÉ DES NATIONS 237 (1930): Le Secrétariat apparait ainsi, dès le début, comme un organisme subordonné."

[2] League of Nations Doc. No. C.424, M.305, X (1921).

[3] Doc. No. A.16 (1930).

[4] *Op. cit.* at 231, 248–49, 250.

[5] 1 DIE SATZUNG DES VÖLKERBUNDES 542 (3rd ed. 1931).

[6] DER VÖLKERBUND 140 (1938).

[7] EGON F. RANSHOFEN-WERTHEIMER, THE INTERNATIONAL SECRETARIAT 38 (1945).

[8] *Ibid.* at 429.

[9] 11 DEP'T STATE BULL. No. 276 at 368–74 (October 8, 1944), chaps. IV, 1, d, and X, paras. 1–3. See also the amendments proposed by the four sponsoring powers at the San Francisco Conference on May 5, 1945 (11 *ibid.* No. 306 at 851–55 [May 6, 1945]).

[10] 12 *ibid.* No. 313 at 1119–34 (June 24, 1945), art. VII, para. 1; art. XII, para. 2; and arts. XX, XCVII-CI, CIV-CV. See LELAND M. GOODRICH and EDVARD HAMBRO, CHARTER OF THE UNITED NATIONS: COMMENTARY AND DOCUMENTS 32–33, 90, 100–101, 114–16, 268–76 (1946).

[11] 12 *ibid.* No. 313 at 1134–42 (June 24, 1945), art. V. para. 1; art. VII; art. XIII, paras. 2, 4; art. XVIII, para. 2; art. XL, para. 3; and arts. LXVII and LXX.

[12] 12 *ibid.* No. 313 at 1142–43 (June 24, 1945).

[13] Report of the Preparatory Commission of the United Nations. U.N. Doc. No. P/C20 (December 23, 1945), chap. VIII at 81–103.

14 Administrative and Budgetary Committee: Faris al-Khoury (Syria), chairman; Aghnides (Greece), rapporteur.

15 Reports of the fifth committee, U.N. Doc. No. A/11 (January 23, 1946); Doc. No. A/41 (February 8, 1946); Doc. No. A/44 (February 11, 1946).

16 U.N.Gen.Ass.J. No. 18 at 355; No. 20 at 369.

17 *Ibid.* No. 22 at 402 (February 4, 1946).

18 U.N. Doc. No. A/4 (January 10, 1946).

19 U.N. Doc. No. P/C20 at 86 (December 23, 1945).

20 U.N. Doc. No. P/C20 at 85 (December 23, 1945).

21 U.N. Doc. No. P/C20 at 87 (December 23, 1945).

22 U.N.GEN.ASS.J. No. 22 at 404 (February 4, 1946).

23 J. SECURITY COUNCIL No. 27 at 522–25 (May 18, 1946).

24 *Ibid.* at 530.

25 J. SECURITY COUNCIL No. 37 at 721–22 (June 12, 1946).

ARTICLE LI of the Charter of the United Nations [1] poses the problem of the meaning of the concept of "individual and collective self-defense," of its connection with other parts of the Charter, and of the range of its application.[2]

This article, not contained in the Dumbarton Oaks Proposals, was added at San Francisco. It was the notion of "collective self-defense" which was needed, and it was needed as a diplomatic step to solve the so-called Latin–American crisis at San Francisco. It was the means to save the relative independence of the Inter–American System and the continued validity of the Act of Chapultepec and of the proposed permanent Inter–American Defense Treaty without endangering the universality of the jurisdiction of the Security Council. It was for purposes of fitting regional arrangements, and particularly the Inter–American system, into the general international organization. That this was so is clearly shown by the history of the San Francisco Conference, where what is now Article LI was worked out by Committee III/4, dealing with regional arrangements. Latin Americans had originally feared that the Security Council might override the Act of Chapultepec but soon became anxious rather for fear of action under this act might be blocked through the inactivity of the Security Council, paralyzed by the exercise of the veto. A great number of Latin–American proposals were introduced between May 4 and 23, 1945, in Committee III/4, the chairman of which was Alberto Lleras Camargo, then foreign minister of Colombia, now director general of the Pan–American Union. But only the United States proposal of what is now Article LI solved the dilemma. Lleras Camargo, speaking for Colombia, declared [3] in the fourth meeting of Committee III/4 on May 23, 1945:

> The Latin American countries understood, as Senator Vandenberg has said, that the origin of the term "self-defense" is identified with the necessity of preserving regional systems like the Inter-American one. . . . It may be deduced that the approval of this article implies that Chapultepec is not in contravention of the Charter.

and again: [4]

> In the case of the American states, an aggression against one American state constitutes an aggression against all the other American states and all of them exercise their right of legitimate defense by giving support to the state attacked, in order to repel such aggression. *This is what is meant by the right of collective self defense.*

All the Latin–American representatives associated themselves with these declarations. When the report of Committee III/4 was adopted [5] on June 13, 1945, at the second meeting of Commission III, the Mexican Castillo Nájera spoke in the same sense. [6]

The proposals of the Latin–American governments for the Inter–American Defense Treaty to be considered at the Rio de Janiero conference and the report and draft treaty of the committee of the governing board, presented [7] at the session of May 22, 1946, distinguish between acts and threats of aggression having the form of "armed attack," where full advantage is taken of Article LI, and other acts and threats of aggression.

Historically, therefore, the connection of Article LI with the Inter–American system is clear. But this historical background is not necessarily decisive for the juridical interpretation of Article LI as it stands. The Permanent Court of International Justice held that, where a text is clear and unambiguous, no resort should be had to *travaux prépara- toires* for its interpretation. There are to be noted further that Article LI is not included in the chapter on regional arrangements, that the Inter–American system—this question was debated at San Francisco and decided negatively— is not specifically mentioned, and that the negotiations themselves did not discuss the issue. The representative of Egypt stated that Article LI also extended to the Pan- Arab League, but he declared himself against the inclusion of alliances and mutual-assistance pacts. But Paul-Boncour (France) emphatically stated that the formula of Article LI "extends in general to cases of mutual assistance against aggression." Thus the "collective self-defense" of Article LI may play the same role for a new system of alliances as the *ententes régionales* of Article XXI of the Covenant.

This development, apart from the original wish of saving the relative autonomy of Pan–America, reflects the lack of complete faith in the ability of the United Nations to maintain international peace and security, a lack of faith brought about by the fact that Article XLIII, calling for the placing of armed forces at the disposal of the Security Council, had not yet been implemented and by the possible paralysis of the Council through the exercise of the veto. Yet the developments discussed give the right of "collective defense" only to members bound by regional, or, at least, by particular treaty ties. But may Article LI not be invoked by any and all members, even those which have no special treaties with the state attacked? Such use was intimated by the British representative on the occasion of the discussion of the report of the military staff committee [8] as a substitute for non-existing "collective security." For the report had, realistically, proposed to build up only a relatively small armed force to be used against small and medium-sized states, not against Great Powers.

The obligation of Article II, paragraph 4, that the members "refrain in their international relations from the use of force" is subject, therefore, apart from Articles CVI and CVII, to the following exceptions: (1) the right of individual self-defense, (2) the right of collective self-defense: (a) by the Inter-American system, (b) by the Pan-Arab League, (c) by possible new continental or regional organizations, (d) by states having alliances or mutual assistance pacts against aggression, and (f) eventually by any and all states members.

Whether such development will, in fact, substitute the independent use of force for the enforcement action by the United Nations is, first of all, a political problem; but it is also a juridical problem, depending on the legal meaning of the concept "individual and collective self-defense."

Let us analyze, first, the legal meaning of the concept of "collective self-defense." The term is new, but the thing was known previously. Military assistance to another state is the heart of any treaty of alliance. Prior to the League of Nations this problem was primarily political, as a state could at all times go to war, and as states could also conclude alliances for offensive purposes. Yet the idea of helping another state only to defend itself had often also a legal significance; the *casus foederis* was often restricted to an *attaque non-provoquée*.[9] The alliances and mutual-assistance pacts of the inter-war period, concluded "within the framework of the League of Nations," all take this attitude. The idea of Pan-American solidarity, often proclaimed, was raised to the idea of Pan-American continental defense. It culminates in Declaration XV signed at Havana in 1940, and the Act of Chapultepec, of 1945, which, for the first time, envisaged "the use of armed force to repel aggression."

A special problem is raised by the wording of Article LI, which gives the right of collective self-defense only "if an armed attack occurs against a member of the United Nations." In the hypothetical case of an illegal armed attack by a member of the United Nations against Portugal, with which Great Britain has a centuries-old alliance, has Great Britain a right of collective self-defense under Article LI?

The term "collective self-defense" is not a happy one. It is not self-defense, but defense of another state; [10] it corresponds, in municipal law, not to self-defense, but to the defense of others.[11] Neither is "collective self-defense" an action in the name and by authority of the United Nations. It is not a means to realize collective security. It does not correspond to the military *action commune* under Article XVI of the Covenant. It is an autonomous exercise of force, legalized by the Charter only under the conditions and within the limits of Article LI.

Is the exercise of collective defense merely a right, or is it also a legal duty? [12] If a state or states are bound by regional or mutual-assistance treaties they are under a duty to act, imposed by particular international law. But for any state or states not having such particular obligations the exercise of collective defense is for it under Article LI merely a right and not a legal duty.

The right to defend others in municipal law is often restricted to persons having a special family relation with the person defended and always made dependent on whether the person defended has himself a legal right of self-defense.[13] Here, too, the legality of the exercise of the right of collective self-defense depends on whether the state in whose favor it is being exercised has a right of individual self-defense. In consequence all further legal problems concerning collective self-defense depend on the problem of individual self-defense.

Self-defense must be distinguished from self-help. Self-help is a procedure of realizing and enforcing the law in a primitive legal order. In an advanced legal order self-help is excluded. As international law is, or at least was, a primitive legal order, it had to admit self-help (reprisals, war). In consequence the notion of self-defense had a political rather than a legal character. Self-defense as a truly juridical institution presupposes an advanced legal order and international self-defense is, therefore, closely bound up with a more advanced international organization. Only where self-help is forbidden does self-defense become legally meaningful. Only the attempts to restrict or eliminate the right of resort to war make international self-defense legally meaningful. The notion of international self-defense depends on the illegality of war, or, as the Charter puts it more sharply, on the illegality of the use of force by individual states.

Self-defense is, further, in municipal and international law, clearly to be distinguished from the so-called state of necessity.[14] Self-defense is a full justification; it is a right, not only an excuse. But it is a right established by positive law, a right in the lawyer's sense, not merely a political or ethical principle. That is why it is unfortunate that Article LI puts it as a "right" of natural law,[15] although this phrase is also found in municipal law.[16] While the right of self-defense is granted by practically all legal orders, it may be denied, or it may constitute only an excuse, or it may be made dependent on particular conditions.[17] The phrase "inherent right" can only serve to obscure the legal meaning. As a legal right, granted by positive international law, it has to be defined by this positive law. Only thus can its legal meaning be discovered; only thus can we see whether Article LI constitutes a progressive development and measure it against the institution of "self-defense" in advanced municipal legal orders.

As in municipal law, self-defense under Article LI is not a procedure to enforce the law, is not designed to punish the aggressor or to obtain indemnities, is not an enforcement action by the United Nations, but serves primarily to repel an illegal armed attack. But, contrary to municipal law, it may not stop here: it seems to give the state or states exercising the right of individual or collective self-defense the right to resort to a justified war, to carry this war to victory, to impose a peace treaty upon the vanquished aggressor, always presupposing that the Security Council has failed and continues to fail of taking the measures necessary to maintain international peace and security. The right of self-defense is, in such cases, a right to resort to war. But as the action is war, even if illegal on the side of the aggressor, the state or states acting in self-defense are bound by the laws of war.

It seems also that the conditions of necessity, reasonableness, and a certain proportionality, which the municipal law prescribes for the exercise of the right of self-defense, are lacking in Article LI.

Self-defense in municipal law presupposes an illegal attack; this is certainly true also in international law.[18] In consequence the right of Article LI cannot be exercised legally against the legal use of force, as against an enforcement action by the United Nations, or against a state or states legally exercising the right of self-defense under Article LI.

As self-defense is legal only against an illegal attack, the problem of when self-defense is legitimate is of the utmost importance; the problem of the limits of self-defense is coordinate with the problem of the "definition of aggression." The recognition of a vague "right of self-defense," to be determined by the state which claims to act in self-defense, is apt to make the prohibition of "wars of aggression" illusory. That is why it could logically be asked whether the Pact of Paris could be violated at all. It is a commonplace that all states, determined to go to war, plead self-defense. The term "self-defense" has been diplomatically used in a very extended fashion, including the Monroe Doctrine,[19] the so-called British Monroe Doctrine, and, in general, the doctrine of the so-called vital interests,[20] the justification of the lend-lease bill,[21] and so on. "Self-defense" has been recognized as an exception in the abortive Geneva Protocol of 1924, in Article II of the Locarno Treaty of 1925, and under the Kellogg Pact.[22] In addition it was often insisted, as Hughes said in 1923 with regard to the Monroe Doctrine, "that the U. S. in the exercise of this right of self-defense must have an unhampered discretion," or, as the Kellogg Note puts it, that "each nation is the sole judge of what constitutes the right of self-defense and the necessity and extent of the same."

In this respect Article LI constitutes an important progress by limiting the right of individual and collective self-defense to the one case of armed attack against a member of the U.N. Various problems arise with regard to the interpretation of the term "armed attack." The word "attack" is a strategic, not a legal, word. It is clear that "armed attack" can only mean an illegal armed attack,[23] an "aggression." But the problem of the definition of aggression has not only not yet been solved: the very desirability of the definition of aggression has been rejected by Pan-America[24] and at San Francisco.[25] Under Article XXXIX of the Charter it is for the Security Council to determine the existence of any act of aggression at its discretion.

If "armed attack" means illegal armed attack, it means, on the other hand, any illegal armed attack, even a small border incident; necessity or proportionality are no conditions for the exercise of self-defense under Article LI. It is clear that there is no self-defense against a legal enforcement action by the United Nations or against a legal exercise of self-defense. An armed attack may also be unlawful, and thus give the right of self-defense if it constitutes an unlawful intervention, individual or collective; Article LI must be interpreted with regard to the doctrine of non-intervention and Article II, para. 7, of the Charter.[26] Armed attack gives the right of self-defense if directed against a member of the U.N.; how it is done, on land, by sea, in the air, by invasion of territory by armed forces, or by long-range guided missiles, and so on, is legally irrelevant. It is also irrelevant whether such armed attack is made ultimately against the sovereignty, territorial integrity, and independence of the U.N. member or whether any such purpose is expressly denied. Such interpretation would make illegal an armed intervention under the Monroe Doctrine or for the purpose of protecting citizens abroad. Is, in the latter case, an armed intervention the dispatching of, men-of-war without attack, legal or does it already give rise to self-defense under Article LI? But the armed attack must not only be directed against a state, it must also be made by a state or with the approval of a state. One may think of the Pancho Villa affair, or now of the situation of Greece and Yugoslavia.

Armed attack as the only condition of the right of self-defense under Article LI may, in conceivable circumstances, mean too little. For this right does not exist against any form of aggression which does not constitute armed attack. Secondly, this term means something that has taken place. Article LI prohibits "preventive war." The "threat of aggression" does not justify self-defense under Article LI. Now in municipal law self-defense is justified only against an actual danger, but it is sufficient that the danger is *imminent*. The "imminent" armed attack does not suffice under Article LI.

Apart from the problem of the definition of aggression, there is the problem of determining the aggressor. The aggressor, or he who has "provoked" an aggression, has no right of self-defense under municipal law; also in municipal law there are situations where neither of two fighting persons can invoke the right of self-defense. To determine the aggressor must, in cases of self-defense, be left, in the first instance, to the person in question. But self-defense becomes a truly juridical institution in municipal law only through the control of self-defense by independent courts with compulsory jurisdiction. No such judicial control is provided in Article LI. But here, too, some progress has been achieved, through giving a certain control over the exercise of the right of self-defense to the Security Council. The latter remains, notwithstanding Article LI, all authority and responsibility to take at any time the necessary measures, and thus to determine an act of aggression and, consequently, the legality of self-defense. The state or states acting in the exercise of self-defense, are, moreover, legally bound to report immediately to the Security Council the measures taken in the exercise of the right of self-defense, and they can take such measures only until the Security Council has taken the measures necessary to maintain international peace and security.

The concept of self-defense in Article LI, to sum up, reveals a progressive development, although it is, of course, still far away from the juridical precision which the legal institution of self-defense has in advanced municipal law.

---

[1] "Nothing in the present Charter shall impair the inherent right of individual or collective self-defense if an armed attack occurs against a member of the United Nations, until the Security Council has taken the measures necessary to maintain international peace and security. Measures taken by members in the exercise of the right of self-defense shall be immediately reported to the Security Council and shall not in any way affect the authority and responsibility of the Security Council under the present Charter to take at any time such action

as it deems necessary in order to maintain or restore international peace and security."

² For a preliminary discussion of Article LI, see LELAND M. GOOD-RICH and EDVARD HAMBRO, CHARTER OF THE UNITED NATIONS: COMMENTARY AND DOCUMENTS 174–81 (1946). For a more thorough discussion, but one written when the San Francisco documents were not yet available, see E. ALBANELL MACCALL, LA LEGÍTIMA DEFENSA EN EL ARTICULO 51 DE LA CARTA DE LAS NACIÓNES UNIDAS (1945). A synthesis of this Uruguayan study is given by A. Schwerest Ferrer in 51 RIVISTA DE DERECHO INTERNACIONAL No. 101 at 14–23 (1947). The Uruguayan study is primarily based on the excellent Hague lectures of Emile Giraud, *La théorie de la légitime défense*, 3 RECUEIL DES COURS 691-865 (1934).

³ 3 UNITED NATIONS CONFERENCE ON INTERNATIONAL ORGANIZATION: DOCUMENTS, 1945 at 680–81.

⁴ *Ibid.* at 687.

⁶ 11 *ibid.* at 54–55.

⁶ In the same sense, also, REPORT ON THE ACTION OF THE SAN FRANCISCO CONFERENCE ON REGIONAL ARRANGEMENTS, SUBMITTED TO THE GOVERNING BOARD BY THE DIRECTOR GENERAL (Congress and Conference Series No. 48, 1945).

⁷ INTER-AMERICAN CONFERENCE FOR THE MAINTENANCE OF CONTINENTAL PEACE AND SECURITY, RIO DE JANEIRO 145 (1946) (mimeo.).

⁸ Security Council, U.N. Doc. No. S/336 (April 30, 1947).

⁹ See W. STEINLEIN, DER BEGRIFF DES NICHT HERAUSGEFORDERTEN ANGRIFFS IN BÜNDNISVERTRÄGEN (1927).

¹⁰ Descamps (1 RECUEIL DES COURS 469–85 [1930]) speaks of the *concours à la légitime défense d'autrui*.

¹¹ In German, *Nothilfe* as distinguished from *Notwehr*.

¹² In Roman law a slave had not only the right, but also the legal duty, to defend his master if the master found himself in a situation of self-defense.

¹³ Such person "has only the same right to defend another as he would have to defend himself under the same circumstances," although "even a stranger may take life, if necessary, in order to prevent the commission of a felony by violence or surprise."—CLARK and MARSHALL, A TREATISE ON THE LAW OF CRIMES, 359 (4th ed. 1940).

¹⁴ It was, therefore, not correct, when Secretary of State Webster spoke, with regard to the Caroline Case of 1837, of the "great law of self-defense" (2 J. B. MOORE, DIGEST OF INTERNATIONAL LAW, 412). Necessity may be an excuse, but never a justification; in the common law of crimes, necessity even as an excuse for homicide is doubtful. See Regina v. Dudley and Stephens, [1884] Q.B. 273. See also JEROME HALL, GENERAL PRINCIPLES OF CRIMINAL LAW (1949).

¹⁵ "Inherent right"; in the French text, "droit naturel"; in the Spanish text, "derecho inmanente."

¹⁶ Already in Roman law: "vim vi repellere licere Cassius scribit idque ius natura comparatur."—DIG. 43. 16. 1. 27.

[17] See the development in the common law of crimes: orginally no excuse at all; then, under the Statute of Gloucester (1278, 6 Edw. 1, c. 9), the life of one who had killed *se defendendo* was released but his chattels forfeited; later a full justification under the Statute of 1532, 24 Henry VIII, c. 5. Yet the exercise of the right of self-defense presupposes the "retreat to the wall," a condition wholly unknown to the countries of the Roman law.

[18] 1 C. C. HYDE, INTERNATIONAL LAW, 106 (1922).

[19] C. H. Hughes, in 4 HACKWORTH, DIGEST OF INTERNATIONAL LAW 451.

[20] J. L. BRIERLY, THE OUTLOOK FOR INTERNATIONAL LAW 33–45 (1944).

[21] H. R. 18, 77th Cong., 1st Sess. at 5 (7 HACKWORTH, *op. cit.* at 692–93).

[22] Circular note of Secretary of State Kellogg of June 23, 1928.

[23] Whereas the English and the Spanish texts use "armed attack" and *ataque armado*, the French text has the clearer term *agréssion militaire*.

[24]Resolution XXIV, Lima Conference, 1938.

[25] 12 UNITED NATIONS CONFERENCE ON INTERNATIONAL ORGANIZATIONS: DOCUMENTS, 1945, at 341–49.

[26] Luis E. Nieto Arteta, *Intervención y dominio reservado del Estado*, REVISTA COLOMBIANA DE DERECHO INTERNACIONAL (1947).

CHAPTER XXX: *Bellum Justum and Bellum Legale*

BELLUM JUSTUM AND BELLUM LEGALE

IN 1914 AND LONG BEFORE the right of every sovereign state to go to war was recognized by the practice of states and by the overwhelming majority of writers, war, the *ultima ratio regum,* served in the primitive international community a double purpose: a method of self-help to enforce a right in the absence of international courts with compulsory jurisdiction, and a method of self-help to change the law, analagous to internal revolution, in the absence of an organ of international legislation in the true sense of this term.

In this century the old *bellum justum* doctrine, which played so great a role in the literature from the times of St. Augustine to Vattel, was, first, historically re-studied in great detail.[1] After World War I, attempts at the revival of this doctrine were even made: it was asserted that this doctrine is a norm of positive international law, often coupled with the further assertion that recent developments in international organization constitute a return to this doctrine. These assertions, however, are not tenable in law, but are only political ideologies or the consequence of a theoretically incorrect analysis.

While Catholic international lawyers, such as Mausbach and Cathrein, retained the traditional concept of *bellum justum*, the revival was inspired by very different motives in other writers. Louis Le Fur,[2] an adherent of Catholic natural law, used the doctrine as a political instrument to prove the Treaty of Versailles to be a *justa pax* in the beginning struggle over the revision of this treaty. Leo Strisower [3] could, in his book, state with the utmost sincerity that he was not inspired by political motives. His approach was wholly ethical, a consequence of his basic philosophical conviction that law is a part of ethics. But exactly for this reason his argumentation is moral rather than legal. Hans Kelsen, the bitter antagonist of natural law, became the principal champion of the doctrine of *bellum justum*, which he felt compelled to defend for wholly logical reasons: If war cannot be interpreted either as a delict or as a sanction against a delict, then it is no longer possible to consider international law as such at all. But in his most recent treatment [4] he does not decide whether this doctrine is a norm of positive international law, and states forcefully the grave objections against the workability of this doctrine.

That this doctrine was not positive law in 1914, and long before, seems settled;[5] even in earlier times it was hardly ever a norm of positive international law.[6] It is of Catholic origin, anchored in natural law, a theological, not a legal, concept. That is proved by its content as well as by its historical origin. The early Church under the pagan Roman Empire took a strictly pacifist attitude, an attitude preserved even today by some Protestant sects. It was the anti-state attitude of the early Christians which led to their persecution. The Romans of the Empire had long ceased to believe in Roman mythology; many foreign cults were not only tolerated in imperial Rome, but some of them were extremely fashionable among the élite. The Romans further failed entirely to understand the transcendental importance and future of Christianity; for them the Christians were no more than an insignificant Jewish sect. The persecutions were not directed against a religion, but against what would be called today a "subversive movement."

But when, with Constantine, Christianity became the official religion of the *orbis terrarum,* when Christian persecutions were followed by those of the pagans, the Church had naturally to revise its attitude toward the Empire. In this connection the purely theological problem arose: How can a Catholic participate in a war without committing a sin? It was a theological, not a legal, problem. To this theological problem St. Augustine gave the answer: He can do so, provided the war is just. Transforming the formal criterion of the ancient Roman *jus fetiale* into the substantive criterion of objective, intrinsic justice of the cause of war, he created this doctrine, which was later elaborated by other theologians, consolidated by St. Thomas of Aquinas, Victoria, Suárez and others, and secularized, divorced from its Catholic soil, by Gentili, Grotius, and their successors.

In its purity the doctrine is wholly an ethical one. There must be an objectively just cause of war waged by the authority of the prince, and he must be inspired by the *recta intentio.* Even the prince who has a just cause of war can make an unjust war if he acts from wrong motives, such as territorial aggrandizement or elimination of the enemy as a competitor in the future. And, if all these are fulfilled, the war can still cease to be just if the prince imposes an *injusta pax.* Thus Victoria lays down that the victor in a just war can impose upon the vanquished only conditions proportionate to the wrong committed, must always act with moderation and Christian modesty, and never has the right to ruin the vanquished enemy as a nation.

Just war is, therefore, a reaction against a wrong,[7] a
procedure either in tort (restitution, reparations, guarantees) or in criminal law (punishment, sanctions).[8]

The *bellum justum* doctrine presupposes, therefore, the
continuance of war and distinguishes between objectively
just and unjust wars. If all the conditions of a just war are
fulfilled, just war can be either a war of self-defense against
the *injustus aggressor* or a war of execution to enforce one's
right. In both cases it makes no difference whether the
just war is, from a military point of view, waged defensively or offensively, nor is the factor of who resorts to
war first decisive.

This doctrine in its purity, even if it might have been
or were a norm of positive international law, would be
practically valueless because of the grave objections against
its workability. This very circumstance forced later writers
to develop the doctrine in such a way as to deform it.

(A) There are no objective criteria between "just" and
"unjust" wars. If the just war is one of self-defense, it is
just if directed against a present or imminent unjust attack. When is an attack in a concrete case unjust? Gentili
went so far as to call just wars even preventive wars, wars
"which anticipate dangers, not premeditated, but probable
or possible." In a war of execution to enforce a right, the
right and its violation need definition.

(B) Who is to decide in an objective way which belligerent has a just cause and who is the *injustus aggressor?*
This decision must be left to each state itself, a consequence
which, as Verdross states, deforms the *bellum justum* doctrine. Hence, even the classic doctrine distinguished between
"absolute" and "relative," [9] between "objective" and "subjective" justice. Therefore, war can be subjectively just on
both sides, Gentili's "bellum justum ex utraque parte"; the
same is proclaimed by Guggenheim today. Hence, practic-

ally every war is just, a doctrine identical with the traditional freedom of a state to resort to war. Sociological jurists, therefore, go so far as to see in this doctrine, which "invites subjectivism and abuse by State practice," nothing but a "degeneration into a mere ideology of power politics." [10]

Many other problems arise:[11] What of a belligerent who joins a war only in the last moment to participate in the advantages of victory? Or who changes sides during the course of the same war? Or who, with regard to partial wars constituting the same world war, has a just cause in one partial war, but is an *injustus aggressor* in others? The two world wars have given examples for all these hypotheses.

(C) There is, further, the gravest objection that war is not an adequate means of enforcing the law: the *injustus aggressor* may be the victor. That is why Cayetano advises the prince not to go to war, even if he has a just cause, if he has not also the moral certainty of victory. Suárez' probabilism asks, at least, for the probability of victory. These statements show the radical deficiency, the "tragic confession of the negligible practical range of the classic bellum justum doctrine." [12]

Recent developments through the League of Nations, Kellogg Pact, and United Nations, here mentioned as representative of the newer trend, do not constitute a return to the classic *bellum justum* doctrine.[13]

First, it must be emphasized that these treaties, as well as writers such as Strisower and Kelsen, are in a fundamental point different from the classic doctrine. They understand by the term "wrong" exclusively a violation of *positive* international law, whereas the classic doctrine means by "wrong" a violation both of positive and of *natural* law.[14] A just war can be waged to enforce not only a positive, but also a *natural,* right, e.g., the natural right of commerce. It is exactly by the enforcement of this *natural* right that Victoria ultimately justifies the conquest of America. Thus, just war is given a *double* function: enforcement of *law* and enforcement of *justice;* law and justice need not be identical.

The League of Nations Covenant did not abolish war but discriminated between different wars. The basis of distinction was *not,* as in the classic doctrine, between just and unjust wars but between legal and illegal wars. The concept of *bellum legale* replaced the concept of *bellum justum.* The illegality of resort to war was not a function of the intrinsic injustice of the cause of war but of the breach of a formal, procedural requirement. Hence, a legal war could have been waged even between members of the League by a state which had no just cause of war, whereas a state which fully had a just cause of war could have been guilty of resorting to an illegal war. This is a very different thing from the *bellum justum* doctrine. The military *action commune* under Article XVI was a sanction in a truly legal sense, not against the *injustus aggressor,* but against an *illegal* belligerent who had "resorted to war in disregard of his covenants under Articles XII, XIII or XV."

The Kellogg Pact, if taken at its surface value, could not constitute a return to the classic doctrine, as it did not distinguish between wars but renounced war completely as an instrument of national policy. But the admitted legality of self-defense and the delegation to each state of the right to be the only judge to determine whether the conditions of self-defense exist make this pact practically only a restatement of general international law. Compared with the classic doctrine, war is also renounced as a war of execution to enforce a right.

Experience had shown that the Covenant and the Kellogg Pact, because of the aura of uncertainty hovering around the legal concept of "war," made it possible to wage "wars in disguise." Hence, the United Nations Charter, in making great progress from the point of view of legal technique, replaced the concept of "war" by that of the "threat or use of force." The Charter, therefore, distinguishes between legal and illegal use of force; the distinction is again based on the legality, not on the intrinsic justice of the cause. Use of force is, generally speaking, forbidden; but under Article LI force can legally be used against an "armed attack" "until the Security Council has taken the necessary measures." If the Security Council is paralyzed by the veto, we are back to general international law. On the other hand, the military measures which can be decided by the Security Council are, contrary to Article XVI of the Covenant, not necessarily sanctions in a juridical sense.[15]

Furthermore, these new developments have hardly been able to avoid the grave objections which have been stated above against the *bellum justum* doctrine.[16]

Roscoe Pound has stated that a primitive and weak law wants, first of all, to establish peace, i.e., absence of violence, and to guarantee the status quo. It puts peace above justice, whereas the intrinsic justice of the cause was the heart of the classic doctrine. This emphasis on security, more than justice, can be seen in recent developments. The Kellogg Pact renounces war, the Charter forbids the use of force—except in self-defense—without giving the states as a substitute the compulsory peaceful settlement of international conflicts, without guaranteeing the enforcement of their rights, without creating a workable procedure of peaceful change, without a guarantee that United Nations force will be brought to bear, not only against an illegal aggressor, but also against a state which, without using force, does not fulfil an international obligation, without guarantee that, if such force is exercised by the United Nations, its use will be reasonably assured of success.

Two world wars and the fear of more catastrophic wars have made the avoidance of war more important than the achievement of justice. The first aim in the preamble of the United Nations Charter is "to save succeeding generations from the scourge of war." The first purpose in Article I is not to achieve and maintain justice but to "maintain international peace and security." Again, we are faced with the antinomy between the two juridical values of security and justice. Security is the lower but most basic value. "La sécurité d'abord," as the French thesis ran after World War I; only then the intrinsic settlement of conflicts; here lies the difference between Chapters VI and VII of the Charter, between, within the Pan-American orbit, the Rio Treaty and the Pact of Bogotá. First to establish security is the philosophy of recent developments, in the conviction that security is the indispensable pre-condition of later achieving justice. This philosophy may be wholly justified, but it is not the philosophy underlying the bellum justum doctrine.

[1] See, apart from monographs on St. Augustine, St. Thomas, Victoria, Suárez, Gentili, Grotius and others, the following works: A. VANDERPOL, LE DROIT DE LA GUERRE JUSTE D'APRÈS LES THÉOLOGIENS ET LES CANONISTES DU MOYEN-AGE (1911); idem, LA DOCTRINE SCHOLASTIQUE DU DROIT DE LA GUERRE (1919); G. SALVIOLI, IL CONCETTO DELLA GUERRA GIUSTA NEGLI SCRITTORI ANTERIORI A GROTIUS (1915); P. Yves de la Brière, Les droits de la juste victoire selon la tradition des théologiens catholiques, 32 REVUE GÉNÉRALE DE DROIT INTERNATIONAL PUBLIC, (1925); idem, Les étapes de la tradition théologique concernant le droit de la guerre juste, ibid. 129 (1937); idem, LE DROIT DE JUSTE GUERRE (1938); V. BEAUFORT, LA GUERRE COMME INSTRUMENT DE SECOURS OU DE PUNITION (1933); REGOUT, LA DOCTRINE DE LA GUERRE JUSTE DE ST. AUGUSTIN À NOS JOURS D'APRÈS LES THÉOLOGIENS ET CANONISTES CATHOLIQUES (1935); KIPP, MODERNE PROBLEME DES KRIEGSBRECHTS IN DER SPÄTSCHOLASTIK (1935); J. von Elbe, The Evolution of the Concept of Just War in International Law, 33 AM.J. INT'L L. 665–88 (1939).

[2] Guerre juste et juste paix, 26 REVUE GÉNÉRALE DE DROIT INTERNATIONAL PUBLIC 9–75, 268–309, 349–405 (1919).

[3] DER KRIEG UND DIE VÖLKERRECHTSORDNUNG (1919).

4 H. KELSEN, GENERAL THEORY OF LAW AND STATE pp. 331–38 (1945). He is followed by 1 P. GUGGENHEIM, LEHRBUCH DES VÖLKER-RECHTS 590–93.

5 Naturally, an ethical and political critique of a concrete war has always existed; the ethical critique of the postve law, whether municipal or international, is socially indispensable. For, as the Romans said, "Non omne quod licet, honestum."

6 See also A. Nussbaum, *Just War—A Legal Concept*, 42 MICH. L. REV. 453–79 (1943–44).

7 Thus Victoria: "Unica est et sola causa justa inferendi bellum injuria accepta"; Grotius: "Causa justi belli suscipiendi nulla alia esse potest nisi injuria."

8 Thus e.g., Cayetano: "Habens justum bellum gerit personam judicis criminaliter procedentis."

9 One belligerent can have a just cause, whereas the other has a "still more just" cause.

10 Thus G. Schwarzenberger, *Jus Pacis ac Belli*, 37 AM.J.INT'L L. 460–77 at 465 (1943).

11 See Antonio Truyol y Serra, *Crímenes de guerra y derecho natural*, 1 REVISTA ESPAÑOLA DE DERECHO INTERNACIONAL No. 1 at 45–73 (1948).

12 *Ibid.* at 60.

13 See VERDROSS, *op. cit.*; ALF ROSS, CONSTITUTION OF THE UNITED NATIONS 140–41 (1950); W. Schatzel, *Friede und Gerechtigkeit*, 50 DIE FRIEDENS-WARTE No. 2 at 97–107 (1950).

14 This essential distinction is pointed out in JOSEF L. KUNZ, KRIEGSRECHT UND NEUTRALITÄTSRECHT 2 n. 3 (1935), and in A. VERDROSS, VÖLKERRECHT 339 (1950).

15 H KELSEN, THE LAW OF THE UNITED NATIONS 732–39 (1950); ALF ROSS, *op. cit.* at 141.

16 See Robert W. Tucker, *The Interpretation of War*, 4 INT'L L.Q. No. 1 at 11–38 (1951).

CHAPTER XXXI: Compulsory International Adjudication and Maintenance of Peace

WHILE IT IS STILL TOO EARLY to draw up a detailed blueprint of postwar international organization, there seems to be substantial agreement among statesmen and writers on the necessity for the creation of a general international organization of which an international court of justice shall form an important part. Many writers and proposals insist on compulsory jurisdiction for this court.[1] But no writer has pressed this view with more vigor than Hans Kelsen.[2] Coming from a leading protagonist of democracy and peace, a person who, as a scholar, is one of the greatest jurists of the century, these ideas deserve careful study.

Generally speaking, Kelsen's reasoning and arguments in favor of compulsory international adjudication are theoretically faultless and carry great weight: (1) Conditions at the present juncture in world history make any attempt at the creation of a world state or world federal state wholly utopian; the only politically possible solution must be sought within the framework of international law and must be compatible with the principle of the "sovereign equality" of states as laid down by the Moscow Declaration. The only non-utopian goal is, therefore, the establishment of an international court with compulsory jurisdiction. (2) This achievement would constitute, not only the first step in time, but the most important step toward making the present primitive international law a more advanced legal order. As long as states—and here Kelsen points to the very crux of the problem—are legally free to determine the question of right and wrong by themselves, as long as each state is *judex in causa sua*, as long as there is no impartial and objective judicial decision, the basic question of right and wrong cannot be answered with juridical authenticity. (3) The decision of right and wrong by impartial and objective judicial judgment would constitute the greatest advance in world history even if the court could not execute its judgment by force. The cry for an international police force rather than judical action is not only politically utopian [3] but also theoretically untenable: there can be no execution before there is a judgment. "One cannot bring to perfection the process of implementing the sanction of the law through its centralization, while leaving the first phase, i.e., determination of the fact of wrong in a condition of utter primitiveness." [4] (4) In municipal law, also, courts preceded legislatures. By analogy compulsory international adjudication corresponds to the law of historical evolution.[5] (5) The pragmatic argument points in the same direction: arbitration has been widely accepted already by sovereign states, here majority decisions have proven possible, arbitration has actually been effective, judicial decisions have overwhelmingly been carried out bona fide by the states; the creation of compulsory international adjudication is, therefore, "the line of least resistance."

It is with regard to this last point that Kelsen seems to this writer to be overoptimistic. What he says concerning the effectiveness of arbitration is true, but under *optional* arbitration. *Compulsory* adjudication, even if restricted to "legal" disputes, might be a very different matter. For the cause of compulsory adjudication, even of only "legal" disputes, has unfortunately not made great advances, either prior or subsequent to World War I,[6] either at The Hague or in the League of Nations or in Pan-American developments. Even under compulsory arbitration treaties, far-reaching reservations are accepted; even Argentina, the protagonist of "arbitraje amplio" has a favorite very broad reservation: constitutional questions. It is unfortunately a fact that the great majority of international judicial decisions, prior and subsequent to World War I, were given on conflicts of relatively minor importance.[7] The Inter-American Treaty of Washington of 1929 has not yet been applied a single time. When the United States proposed in 1940 to submit the strictly legal question of the conformity with international law *vel non* of the Mexican oil expropriations to an international court, Mexico refused.

As for the acceptance by the states of compulsory international adjudication, there is no logical, legal, or theoretical difficulty; the difficulty is wholly political. And this political difficulty of persuading the sovereign states is, we believe, underestimated by Kelsen. For the same reason it seems to this writer that Kelsen's proposal, contrary to the Covenant of the League, to place the court in the center of a new international organization (which would not be based on the principle of universality, which would have no duties of international co-operation in non-political fields, but merely be a Permanent League for the Maintenance of Peace), so that its council would only be a subsidiary organ of the court, a sheriff which, at the court's order, would execute the court's judgments, has not the slightest chance of being realized.[8]

These remarks touch only political estimates as to practical possibilities. But Kelsen goes farther than any other writer by demanding compulsory international adjudication of all international conflicts of whatever nature and without any reservation or exception. Here again Kelsen seems to be overoptimistic as to the chance that this postulate may be accepted by the states. There are no multilateral treaties, down to the present time, which go this far. Even proposals to this effect are very rare.[9] Bilateral treaties of this type are equally rare; a number of such treaties exist but contain very important reservations. The objection to the proposal of compulsory international adjudication over *all* conflicts is, moreover, not only a political but also a theoretical one.

Kelsen is, of course, entirely right that all the objections based on the existence of "gaps" in international law, the possibility of a *non liquet*, the deficiency or inadequacy of present-day international law, are theoretically entirely untenable, insofar as they lead to the conclusion that it would not be logically possible to give a judicial decision on any conceivable international conflict of whatever nature. He is entirely right that no objective criterion as to the nature of international conflicts can be found, with regard to the question of their justiciability *vel non*.[10] It is necessarily true that every conflict can be decided according to positive international law, at least by giving judgment in favor of the defendant and dismissing a state's claim when the latter cannot be founded on a norm of positive international law. It is also true that a court will adapt the positive law to its idea of justice and equity.

But our problem is not whether any conflict can be decided, but whether it can be settled. In this respect we must distinguish between international conflicts as to what the law is and conflicts as to what the law should be.[11] But this distinction, based, as it is, on a subjective criterion, is violently attacked by Kelsen. States, he says, must be obligated to treat all their conflicts as legal conflicts, like citizens. And he adds that compulsory international adjudication is perhaps the most efficient means of maintaining positive international law.

But the possibility that states, contrary to citizens, may advance metajuridical arguments in a conflict—"such as justice and the like," as Kelsen says—is first a consequence of the fact that states are not only the executors of positive international law, but also the makers of new international law; in consequence conflicts may arise between them in both their capacities. Furthermore, citizens are not obligated to treat all their conflicts as legal conflicts; in some of the bitterest conflicts courts could do nothing; positive law as a guarantee of peace must not be overestimated. Citizens are only obligated not to resort to force; but they may settle their conflicts out of court, and they are free to leave them unsettled. The basic obligation of states must be not to resort to force; they are free to leave their conflicts unsettled; but if they want to settle them they must settle them by peaceful means, whether the conflicts involve the law that is or the law that should be.

But the peaceful means of settling these two types of conflicts are different in municipal law, too. Within a state bitter political conflicts arise; they can be decided, but not settled, by the courts. The means of settling them consists in changing the law by legislation, or, if necessary, by constitutional amendments. Where such means of peaceful change do not exist or do not work, political conflicts may lead to revolution or civil war. Could any one imagine the courts of the United States to have abolished the eighteenth amendment? Courts are wholly unfit and unequipped for changing the law, just as political agencies are unfit for giving objective and impartial decisions. "It would not only be illogical but dangerous to submit to an ordinary procedure differences with regard to a change in the rules of law in force." [12] It is very true that courts do not merely "apply" the positive law automatically; it is very true, both in common-law and in civil-law countries, that the judicial activity necessarily is also law-creating, that the courts inevitably bring about a gradual evolution of the law. But the distinction between judicial and legislative functions remains, nevertheless, fundamental. "Judges do and must legislate, but they can do so only interstitially, they are confined from molar to molecular motions." [13] But the degree of change, as between "almost imperceptible" and "drastic change" of the positive law, is not the basic difference between judicial and legislative function; the basic difference is that legislatures create abstract and general, judges concrete and individual norms, that the judge is bound by the hierarchically superior general norms, that not only the procedure but the contents of his decision is to a large extent legally prescribed, that the judge is much less free than the legislator, that the field of judicial, law-creating interpretation, however extended it may be, is always limited, although not entirely determined, by the existing juridical materials, as Justice Cardozo so often underlined. True, the establishment of an international legislature is at this time utopian; that is why quasi-legislative substitutes are necessary, but not decisions by courts. Let us not forget that the necessity for settling disputes, not by courts, but by other procedures, is by no means restricted to the sphere of international law. Modern labor law furnishes analogies, as in the settlement of disputes between employers and workers.

Compulsory international adjudication, says Kelsen, is perhaps the most efficient means of maintaining the positive law. But, apart from the question of the possibility of freezing the status quo against drastic changes in a continuously changing world, the question arises as to whether the positive law deserves to be maintained? Justice under the law is one problem, but justice in law another. Kelsen does not ask what the content of the positive law is nor how it was brought about. But if the positive law is unjust and no other solution is available but judicial decision exactly under this positive law, then either we will see a perpetuation of tyranny or a resort to force.

The goal cannot be to look for the most efficient means of maintaining positive law *à tout prix*, but of maintaining peace, which is itself a dynamic conception. Kelsen's idea that war can be eliminated by compulsory international adjudication alone is based on his unwillingness to recognize the double function of war in the present primitive international legal order. Kelsen is strongly inclined to consider *bellum justum* a positive norm of international law, although he concedes that it cannot be proved to be such. *Bellum justum* never was a legal, but a religious, problem, the problem of making it possible for a Catholic to participate in a war without committing a sin. But not religious, moral, or political, but logical considerations lead Kelsen to this position. Force, he says, can appear in a legal order only as a sanction or as a condition of a sanction (as "illegal act"). War, therefore, is either a primitive sanction to enforce the law, or an illegal act. Consequently the elimination of war is possible through compulsory international adjudication.

But it must not be overlooked that in every legal order, municipal or international, law can be created, either in conformity with or contrary to the positive law prescribing the creation of new law. True, from the point of view of the positive law, revolution can only be conceived as an illegal act; but, nevertheless, a successful revolution creates a new positive law: *ex injuria just fit*.

The situation is exactly the same in international law. War functions either as a primitive sanction to enforce the positive law, comparable to blood-feud, or as a revolutionary means of changing the law. To eliminate war we must find substitutes for both its functions.

In the last analysis Kelsen's position stems from his impatience with emotions: he demands positive law, not "nebulous justice." When Kelsen started his great theoretical work, he found what posed as legal science to be a hodge-podge of subjective, political, ideological considerations. He wanted to create a real science of law. This he did with his first *magnum opus* in 1911. The pure theory of law, *monumentum aere perennius,* overcoming both the factual, sociological, and the ideological *jus naturae* approach, created an objective legal science. Here, in the theory of juridical cognition, in the systematic exposition of the logical a priori elements of all possible positive law, in the realm of the "pure forms of law," values have no place.

But in the realm of the politics of law it is not possible to ban the conception of justice. Whether values are, philosophically speaking, mere illusions, whether there are eternal, objective, self-evident, or merely subjective, relative values, whether justice is a wholly irrational, emotional conception, not accessible to human reason, or not, it is a fact that they do play the greatest role in individual, national, and international life. The greatest internal conflicts, the greatest wars, were not conflicts as to what the law is, but conflicts as to what the law should be. The feeling of injustice is one of the strongest human emotions, and if men or nations see no peaceful way out, they may rise and resort to force, even if they have to perish.

Compulsory international adjudication is of the utmost importance, should be the object of our greatest efforts, would constitute the greatest, the deepest, single advance. But it alone cannot eliminate war; it can decide, but not settle, all conflicts. It is an illusion to believe that it ever will be possible to transform world history into nothing but a court procedure. In the science and application of law there must be objectivity, justice under the law. But in politics, in the politics of law, in the making of law, justice in law cannot be banned. What the Latin verse says of

nature is equally true of justice: *Justitiam expellas furca,
tamen usque recurret.*

[1] Cf. the statement, *The International Law of the Future*, 38 AM.
J.INT'L L. (Supplement) 123, proposal 17 (1944).

[2] LAW AND PEACE IN INTERNATIONAL RELATIONS 145–68 (1942).
See further, 37 AM.J.INT'L L. 397–406 (1943); 46 AM.JUD.SOC'Y,
PROC. 571; *Peace Through Law*, 2 J. LEGAL & POL.SOCIO. 52 (1943);
article in 53 YALE L.J. 207–20; also THE LEGAL PROCESS AND INTER-
NATIONAL ORDER (1935).

[3] Cf. the President's statement: "We are not thinking of a super-
state with its own police force and other paraphernalia of coercive
power"—N.Y. Times, June 16, 1944, p. 12.

[4] THE LEGAL PROCESS 23.

[5] Kelsen's historical argument was made use of by Uruguay at the
Lima Conference in its proposal for international adjudication
("inspirándose en aquel concepto básico que enunciaba Kelsen."—
OCTAVA CONFERENCIA INTERNACIONAL AMERICANA, LIMA, 1938. DIÁRIO
DE SESIONES 141 [1939]).

[6] LAUTERPACHT, THE FUNCTION OF LAW IN THE INTERNATIONAL
COMMUNITY (1933). Also D. Schindler 25 RECUEIL DES COURS 235–364.

[7] Lauterpacht's statement: "De maximis non curat praetor."

[8] Cf. Prime Minister Churchill's speech in the House of Commons
of May 24, 1944, in which he strongly underlined his reliance on superior power and on a "world-controlling Council, comprising the
greatest states which emerge victorious from this war, to prevent
wars and enforce peace."—N.Y. Times, May 25, 1944, pp. 12, 13. Cf.
also the statement by the President of the United States (*ibid.* June
16, 1944, p. 12).

[9] Cf. the proposals by Uruguay and Mexico at the Lima Conference.
DIÁRIO DE SESIONES, 114–40, 140–42 (1939).

[10] The formula of the Taft-Knox Treaties of 1911, characterizing
such conflicts as "justiciable" in their nature "by reason of being
susceptible of decision by the application of the principles of law
and equity," is certainly theoretically untenable. Little can also be
said in favor of the enumeration method. The distinction between
"legal" and "political" conflicts with regard to the importance of the
matter in controversy is equally untenable.

[11] Cf. M. Huber in 33 ANNUAIRE DE L'INSTITUT DE DROIT INTER-
ATIONAL 262.

[12] M. Habicht, THE POWER OF THE INTERNATIONAL JUDGE TO GIVE
A DECISION EX AEQUO ET BONO. 80 (1935).

[13] Justice O. W. Holmes in Southern Pacific Co. v. Jensen, 244
U. S. 205, 221 (1917).

CHAPTER XXXII: *The United Nations and the Rule of Law*

THERE IS NO DOUBT that we are in the present epoch living in a climate of so-called realism; power, not international law, prevails in the thinking of many, whether laymen, scholars, or representatives of governments.[1] True, even in normal times, there are many factors which explain why rules in international law may be twisted for political purposes: the uncertainty of the rules of general international law, a customary law; the different interpretations held, not only by different scholars or schools, but also by different states; the fact that international law, to a great extent, by the very nature of the relations regulated, is a highly political law; the circumstance that this law is a primitive law which has no courts with compulsory jurisdiction to settle conflicts peacefully, authoritatively, and with legally binding force. It is nothing unusual, even in normal times, to see one and the same state interpreting the same norm of international law in a different way under different situations, according to its political interest. It is an ancient observation that powerful states, when *they* are belligerents, impose upon the neutrals the breaking-off of trade relations with their enemy, whereas the same powerful states, when they are neutrals in a war between minor powers, insist in the strictest way on the rule of international law, according to which neutrals have, apart from recognized exceptions, a right to trade with all the belligerents. But in normal times the states have, nevertheless, respect for law. They recognize the place of international law in international relations.

Under the modern "realistic" conception, international law as such is denied; it is held by the preachers of "national self-interest" that in international relations "legal questions are largely irrelevant." This attitude must lead to a lower and lower respect for the rule of law. This attitude is itself the outcome of the deep-seated crisis of our whole Western Christian culture which is now struggling for its very survival. Of that total crisis the crisis of international law is only one facet; and understandably so, because our international law is permeated with and based upon the values of the Western Christian culture, among which respect for the rule of law has held a very high place, at least since the times of Hesiod.

It is also the different attitude toward international law which spells the difference between the two great attempts at international organization on a quasi-universal scale, between the League of Nations and the United Nations. The sponsors of the United Nations flattered themselves with a "realistic" conception of their child. The strong emphasis which was placed upon international law in the League of Nations has been replaced by a subordinate role given to international law in the United Nations. Both the Assembly of the League and the General Assembly of the United Nations had, or has, six main committees. It is, perhaps, symbolic that in the League the first committee dealt with constitutional and legal questions and the last one with political problems, whereas in the United Nations, exactly to the contrary, the first committee handles security and political, and the last committee, legal questions. But even so, the Legal Committee plays no particular role.

The danger inherent in a neglect of legal considerations has not gone unobserved. The British attorney-general, Sir Hartley Shawcross, said in his speech to the sixth committee [2] on October 13, 1949:

> In the United Kingdom we have a great and traditional respect for the Rule of Law. . . . We deplore the fact that some States . . . are unwilling to accord to international law its proper place in the international community.

It was also the British Delegation which took the initiative to put the problem of "consideration of the Assembly's methods and procedures for dealing with legal and drafting questions" on the agenda of the sixth session of the United Nations General Assembly, held in Paris. The Legal Committee dealt with the two British draft resolutions from November 21 to December 4, 1951, and an interesting debate took place. An amended draft by the Netherlands [3] was adopted, recommending that the Assembly establish a special committee of fifteen members from fifteen countries [4] to consider and study the question and report to the seventh session. This recommendation was adopted by the plenary session on December 20, 1951.

The British attorney-general, in a highly interesting speech,[5] developed the reasons and ideas which had inspired the British initiative. The reproaches which he had to make —all well illustrated by numerous concrete examples taken from the practice of the United Nations—were of different kinds. First of all, he attacked the misallocation of items to the particular committees. He especially condemned the practice by which items which clearly were of an entirely legal character were assigned to non-legal committees, never came to a legal committee: "such practice seems to be quite wrong in principle and must result in a complete distortion of the item and of the method of its consideration." This reproach holds equally good for items which were not entirely legal but which had important legal

aspects. Very rightly he complained that, as far as the
Covenant of Human Rights is concerned,

> at no point throughout its consideration or the attempted draft-
> ing of the relevant clauses has the Sixth Committee, or any
> Legal Committee been consulted or invited to undertake the
> framing of any texts on human rights.

He attacked the ignoring of the Legal Committee when
it comes to recommendations that certain matters be referred to the International Law Commission or to requests
to the International Court of Justice for advisory opinions.
All that resulted often in faulty drafting, so that the Court
had in a number of cases "to edit or interpret the question
before it could answer it." The ignoring of the Legal Committee, and, in consequence, faulty drafting, shows itself
in the "undue variety or ambiguity of the operative words
of the Assembly's resolutions." Important drafting questions arise with regard to the Assembly's rules of procedure or amendments to them, with regard to staff and
financial regulations, terms of reference, functions and
powers of fact-finding commissions and similar organs, and
with regard to the drafting of conventions and other
instruments.

It is clear that correct legal drafting is of the utmost
importance, and we may recall Jenks' pleading for an international legislative drafting body. It goes without saying
that legal clarity and precision, the outcome of technically
good drafting, is of the highest importance also for purposes of interpretation.

There is no doubt that interpretations of the United
Nations Charter by the organs of the United Nations cannot always be defended from a legal point of view. The
reason lies, first, in the extremely bad drafting of the
Charter itself. There is, second, the inherent contradiction
in the Charter itself, which, on the one hand, wants col-

lective security, respect for human rights and fundamental
freedoms for all, and, on the other hand, is based on the
sovereignty of the members and on non-intervention in
matters of domestic jurisdiction. It is not possible to eat
one's cake and have it. That is why a French international
lawyer [6] recently could ask whether the revolutionary "purposes" of Article I or the very traditional "principles" of
Article II prevail. And he maintains that this antithesis
allows the governments of the Great Powers to play on two
tables; according to what their political interests demand,
they invoke in one case the "purposes," but, in another case,
the "principles" of the Charter. To all that there must be
added the influence of the East-West split, which has not
only paralyzed the Security Council, but has led to interpretations necessitated by the cold and hot wars, but not
always in accordance with the Charter. The corresponding
Committee of the San Francisco Conference [7] recognized
the inevitability of interpretation of the Charter by the
United Nations organs in the course of operations from
day to day. In case two member states are at variance concerning the correct interpretation of the Charter, it was
said that they or the Assembly or the Security Council can
ask the International Court of Justice for an advisory
opinion. But in the prevailing atmosphere such a request is
more often not made than made. This San Francisco Committee further laid down that "it is to be understood, of
course, that if an interpretation made by any organ is not
generally acceptable, it will be without binding force." The
suggested procedure to embody the authentic interpretation
in an amendment is, because of the veto, also practically
not available.

The British attorney-general speaks of "a sense of dis-
quiet at the attitude of the Assembly to legal questions."
How, he asks, under such circumstances can the rule of law
prevail? And he warns:

Where legal questions are dealt with in a haphazard or ad hoc
manner, sometimes ignored entirely or overlooked, sometimes
deliberately brushed aside, there must be a danger that the
institution will be subordinated to considerations of expediency.
Only upholding the Rule of Law fosters objectivity.

Although in the Dumbarton Oaks Proposals international law was not even mentioned, there can hardly be any
doubt that the creators of the United Nations Charter at
San Francisco wanted to establish the United Nations on
the basis of the rule of law. But, as Dr. Jacob Robinson,
delegate of Israel, stated [8] in the Paris debate of the sixth
committee, "the general development in the last five years
has not gone in the direction of the supremacy of the legal
over the political, but the other way around"; and he
characterized the present situation as the "politicization" of
the United Nations. We see many delegates in the United
Nations growing annoyed and impatient when legal considerations are voiced. Also a handy word is not lacking:
"legalism." But "legalism" is merely a partisan word; correct legal considerations are "legalism" when he who objects to them does not like them from political motives.

One international lawyer, who for a long time has wor-
ried about the rule of law and the United Nations, is
Professor Clyde Eagleton. Once he asked: "Is the United
Nations a legal or a political organization?" And Assistant
Secretary General of the United Nations for Legal Affairs
Ivan Kerno answered: "It is both." But as the question was
not correctly put, the answer is ambiguous. For there can
be no doubt that the United Nations is a *political* organization. "We fully recognize," stated the British attorney-
general, "that the United Nations and the General Assembly
are political institutions in which political considerations
will always predominate." But it is a political organization
based upon the rule of law and operating under a legal constitution, just as the United States Congress is a political

body, but operating under the Constitution of the United States.

The United Nations is a political institution; but its organs are bound by the Charter. Dr. Robinson asked: "Does the Rule of Law prevail, or is simply everything for which a majority can be found, 'law'?" The correct answer has been given by the International Court of Justice:

> The political character of an organ cannot release it from the observance of the treaty provisions established by the Charter when they constitute limitations on its powers or criteria for its judgment. To ascertain whether an organ has freedom of choice for its decisions, reference must be made to the terms of its constitution.

[1] See "The Swing of the Pendulum," above.

[2] Reprinted in 3 INT'L L.Q. 1–8 (1950).

[3] U.N. Doc. No. A/C.6/L. 187.

[4] Belgium, Canada, Chile, Czechoslovakia, Egypt, El Salvador, France, Indonesia, Iran, Israel, Sweden, Soviet Union, United Kingdom, United States, and Venezuela.

[5] Extracts of his speech are reprinted in 1 INT'L & COMP.L.Q. 54–63 (1952).

[6] J. L'Huillier, *Intervention et non-intervention dans la Charte des Nations Unies*, 4 REVUE HELLÉNIQUE DE DROIT INTERNATIONAL 253–60 (1951).

[7] 13 UNCIO DOCUMENTS 700.

[8] See his statement of November 29, 1951.

IT SEEMS LIKELY that the establishment of supranational organs by international treaty as a new experiment in international organization will first be made on a regional level in non-communist Europe. Since 1945, the idea of a European union has made great ideological and a certain practical progress, through private movements as well as by way of intergovernmental organizations.[1] There is, in the economic field, the Benelux [2] Customs Union, the Organization for European Economic Co-operation (OEEC),[3] and, established by the latter, the European Payments Union (EPU).[4] There is, in the military field, the Western European Union,[5] based on the Brussels Treaty of 1948. There is, finally, the Council of Europe at Strasbourg.[6]

These attempts are not aimed at the realization of the old "Pan-Europe" idea; in consequence of the East-West split of the world, of Europe and of Germany in particular, they try to unite "free Europe." But even with this restriction to a part of Europe, "one cannot but be impressed by the organizational confusion." [7] Different groups of European states participate in the different organizations. There is no clarity as to the relationship between them. There is, further, on a quasi-universal scale, the United Nations

Economic Commission for Europe.[8] In all these organizations can be seen the powerful influence of the United States, the dominating power of the "Free World." The OEEC stems from the Marshall Plan; the United States spends billions for the economic rehabilitation and the rearmament of free Europe, promotes the unification of free Europe,[9] and endorses the Council of Europe.

There is, furthermore, a "North Atlantic Community" in the making, of which even a united free Europe, perhaps, will only be a part. A complicated North Atlantic Treaty Organization (NATO) [10] exists with its seat in Paris, perhaps symbolically in the same Palais du Chaillot, which served for the General Assembly of the United Nations. An American general, through NATO, will be the commander-in-chief of a "European Army," if and when created. The military functions of the Brussels Union have already been absorbed by NATO. There was a danger that, after the end of the Marshall Plan, the Council of the OEEC would survive, at the best, only with a very reduced staff and budget.

Finally, the existing regional European organizations have been recognized as inadequate for the task to be performed. Hence new ideas for new European organizations arose. But these same new ideas brought about a further split within free Europe, as Great Britain, followed by the Scandinavian states, disassociated itself from these new ideas. These new ideas center around the Schuman Plan; according to its model, other European organizations [11] are planned, and the machinery of the Schuman Plan will also be used for them.

The so-called Schuman Plan,[12] in reality the brain child of Jean Monnet, was announced to the world in the declaration by the French foreign minister of May 9, 1950.[13] The French government sent invitations to a conference, but the British government kept aloof. On June 20, 1950, the Paris Conference, at which France, West Germany,

Italy, and the Benelux countries were represented, started under the presidency of Jean Monnet. On March 13, 1951, the treaty was ready, but with some articles left open.[14] From April 12 to 18, 1951, there took place at Paris the Conference of the Foreign Ministers and the completed treaty emerged.[15] The treaty consists of four parts: On the European Coal and Steel Community; on the Institutions of the Community; on the economic and social dispositions, containing the substantive law of the Community; and general dispositions, plus three annexes. There are, further, three Protocols: on the privileges and immunities of the Community, on the Statute of the Court, and on the relations with the Council of Europe; there is, finally, attached an exchange of letters between France and Western Germany concerning the Saar Territory.

At the time of writing, the treaty has been ratified by all the treaty states. The members of the High Authority have been appointed; the High Authority, under the presidency of Jean Monnet, has started its work at Luxembourg. The judges of the Court have been appointed. On September 12, 1952, the Assembly, under the presidency of Paul-Henri Spaak, began its deliberations at Strasbourg. The treaty has been bound up with the Treaty for the Creation of a European Defense Community and with the so-called Contractual Agreement between the three Western powers and Western Germany.

The treaty has been compared with the Briand Pan-Europe Memorandum of 1930; but, although more limited, it is more concrete; it tends toward what the French foreign minister called "une solidarité de fait." It has also been compared with the Locarno Treaty of 1925, an earlier attempt at ending Franco-German hostility. But France has now recognized, as was clearly indicated in the speech of the French foreign minister at the San Francisco Peace Conference of 1951, that anti-German alliances and peace treaty efforts to keep Germany demilitarized only lead to the next war. She has, therefore, changed her methods. She tries now direct and intimate co-operation with Germany in the framework of a united free Europe. For while the treaty is naturally based on economic considerations, on a merger of these two key industries, on a single market, common objectives, and common institutions, political considerations were paramount from the beginning. For the French foreign minister the treaty was, first of all, a means to end the centuries-old feud between France and Germany, to make, to quote his own words, a new Franco-German war, so to speak, economically impossible; it was at the same time to be the first step toward a Federation of Free Europe. For Dr. Adenauer, a sincere adherent of European federation, it was a means to integrate the Federal Republic into the Western world, to get rid of Allied controls, to reach for his country at least near-sovereignty. Dr. Adenauer and Robert Schuman, coming from Alsace-Lorraine, speaking German just as well as the German Chancellor, were the right men to carry through the Plan, and that it has been ratified notwithstanding many enemies in France as well as Germany is primarily their merit. Certainly the success of this experiment for fifty years is not yet assured, either economically or politically, the problem of the Saar Territory continues to stand between France and Germany.

The basic new thing in the Schuman Plan is its supranational character.[16] In his declaration of May, 1950, the French foreign minister spoke of "une Haute Autorité, dont les décisions lieront la France et l'Allemagne" and underlined that the decisions of the High Authority, composed of independent personalities, "seront exécutoires en France et Allemagne." It was exactly against this idea that Prime Minister Attlee protested in the debate of the House of Commons of June 26, 1950:

I entirely agree that there is an infringement of the old idea of absolute sovereignty, but in every instance that surrender is

made to a responsible body. It does indicate the difference between what is *international* and what is *supranational*.

And in the meeting of November 3, 1950, of the sixth
committee of the fifth session of the United Nations General
Assembly, the British Crown jurist, Fitzmaurice, voiced his
skepticism toward regarding an individual directly responsible under international law in the same way as a state,
and declared that the relations between states always have
and always will constitute the essence of international law.

Already in the private movement for the union of Europe
we find the difference between the "federalist" [17] and the
"functional" [18] thinking in terms of specialized economic
agencies. This antithesis is also clearly to be seen in the
Council of Europe.

What is the legal difference between "international" and
"supranational" organizations and organs? This difference
has, of course, nothing to do with the distinction between
universal and regional organizations. Neither is "international" identical with "functional." The European Coal and
Steel Community is both regional and functional, yet supranational. It is also clear that the difference does not lie in
the words taken literally. For "international law" is, theoretically speaking, a misnomer; if international law is to
be law at all, it, by necessity, must be supranational; if it
is to be law at all, it cannot be a law "between," but only a
law *above* the states. The difference lies, therefore, in a
different principle of organization. To understand this
difference fully, one must take a look at the nature of general international law and at the attempts, hitherto made,
at international organization.

General international law and the international community constituted by it are, up to the present moment,
"unorganized"; not in the sense that it has no organs, but
in the sense that it has no *special* organs, according to the

principle of the division of labor. In this respect general international law can be said to be a primitive law. It is obvious that primitive general international law is a weak law, a precarious law, a law no longer adequate for the world situation of today, for the atomic age. If the primitiveness of general international law, a consequence of its extreme decentralization, were its only characteristic, then it could be argued that, by analogy to the development of primitive municipal law to an advanced law, the correct method to make general international law a more advanced law is the way of centralization. It should be noted that, up to the present moment, no attempt has been made to transform general international law into a more advanced law, to transform the international community as such into a more centralized community. All attempts at international organization based on treaties created only particular international law and particular international communities, including such "quasi-universal" organizations as the League of Nations and the United Nations. The United Nations notwithstanding, the international community as such remains unorganized and general international law remains a primitive law. And this primitive general law always continues; it is the basis of the United Nations; it always reappears when the particular international law of international organizations disappears, as in the case of the League of Nations, or does not function, as in the case of the United Nations. Thus, military self-help under Article LI becomes, in the case of the paralysis of the Security Council, simply war in the sense of general international law—war limited only by the laws of war.

International law is not only a primitive law, it also has certain peculiarities which distinguish it from municipal law—peculiarities which would remain even if it were less primitive. Its principal persons are sovereign states; international law does not operate directly upon individuals but only through the legal orders of the states. If progress toward a more centralized legal order would go as far as in the development from a primitive to advanced municipal law, it would lead to this type of a relatively highly centralized order which we call a sovereign state; it would act directly upon individuals, the sovereign states would become integral parts of a new, larger state. In a word, while it is recognized that the progress of international law lies in centralization, i.e., in international organization, the latter cannot go so far as to remove completely the particularities of international law without bringing the international law of today to an end, supplanting it by the municipal law of a larger state. A full realization of international organization, if made on a universal scale, must lead to a world state, and, if made on a regional level, to a federal state. In both cases we would no longer have mere restrictions of sovereignties but their disappearance, a transfer of sovereignty, a merger of sovereignties. This is exactly what happens when formerly sovereign states by treaty form a new federal state.

As already stated, no attempt at the organization of the international community as such has yet been made. But also in the attempts at the organization of particular international communities, whether regional or quasi-universal, the limit not to remove completely the particularities of our international law has always been observed, and has to be observed because of the political resistance of the sovereign states to merging and completely giving up their sovereignty. This is true of isolated regional or quasi-functional organizations such as the international river commissions, the international administrative unions; it is true of the quasi-universal political organizations such as the League of Nations and the United Nations; it is true of the specialized organizations of the United Nations; it is true of regional organizations such as the Organization of American States, the Arab League, or the European organizations prior to the Schuman Plan. These very different types of organizations have made great progress, and many competences in many fields have been conferred upon them.[19] But basically they are all "international" organizations: They are based on the "sovereign equality" of their members, on non-intervention in domestic affairs; the sovereignty may be more or less restricted but never transferred by basic treaty which forms their constitution; the organs created by this treaty are "international" in the sense that they cannot *bind* the member states legally,[20] nor can they operate directly against the individuals subjects of the member states; they cannot command; their decisions are not directly executory in the territories of the member states. Even where they can take exceptionally binding decisions, the voting procedure shows the sovereignty of the members, whether there is unanimity of all or unanimity of certain privileged members, as in the United Nations Security Council. The organs are generally composed of diplomatic representatives of the member states which appoint, instruct, and recall them. It is always the sovereign member states which have the last word. These "international" organizations are on an intergovernmental level. This shows how scientifically untenable and practically misleading it is to speak of a "world government" or a "world law." All these organizations are no more than loose associations of sovereign states which have their highest form in the type of union of states which is known as a "confederation of states."

Where, on the other hand, the organization by treaty leads to a merger of formerly sovereign states, we have the creation of a federal state as a new sovereign state, and the only sovereign state which alone becomes a member of the international community. Here the centralization leads to an extinction of international law and its replacement by a new national law. Where, therefore, the international organization leads to a federal state, we have again nothing new.

Now "international" organizations can work excellently in a restricted field where no political problems are involved; where there is not a question of differences and antagonisms between the members but of interests necessary and common to all, as in the Universal Postal Union. But things are vastly different when the attempt is made at "international" organization on a quasi-universal and political scale, as in the League of Nations and the United Nations. Here the political antagonisms and the cultural differences [21] between the members clearly reveal the inherent weakness of merely "international" organizations which are based on treaty, with all the weaknesses inherent in an international treaty, where the business is done on an intergovernmental level. Such loose organizations, however complicated the organization may be, depend in the last analysis on voluntary co-operation, on the good will and bona fides of the members. Where these are lacking in consequence of the unwillingness of the leading members to fulfil the obligations, the organization disappears like the League of Nations; or where these are lacking in consequence of the obstruction of powerful members, the organization is paralyzed, as is the United Nations.

That merely "international" organization is not enough, that the security of the world or of a particular region must be anchored in something more solid than voluntary co-operation and the good will of the members has at last been recognized. It is this insight which led to the new idea of supranational organs. The idea is new because it transcends "international" organization without constituting a federal state. It is based not on a mere restriction, but on a *transfer* of sovereignty, but a transfer of sovereignty in a particular area only. Supranational organs stand, therefore midway between international and federal organs.

The proposed "High Atomic Authority" under the Baruch plan would have been a supranational organ in this sense, and on a quasi-universal scale. The European Coal and Steel Community and its High Authority, as originally announced, would have been purely supranational. But the resistance of the six member states made far-reaching changes necessary. Under the treaty, as now ratified, neither the Community nor its organs are purely supranational; much is international, where the sovereignty of the members reappears. But there remain plenty of features which are clearly supranational.[22] The Community and some of its organs are quasi-federal. The new thing is that these quasi-federal organs are not working within the framework of a federal state, but within the area of international law. This is also indicated by the mixture of supranational and international features in the treaty.[23] Whether such a quasi-federal organization and organs, if it comes into being and functions unhindered by political and economic difficulties, can work *a la longue* without a federal state remains to be seen. Let us not forget that the French foreign minister conceived this Community as the first step toward a federal union of Europe. Even with respect to a confederation of states, history shows that it either leads to a federal state— "the more perfect Union"—as in the case of the United States, Switzerland, Germany, or breaks up into its component sovereign parts, as Bolivar's *Gran Colombia*. If the new Community and its organs can come into being and work, it seems to this writer likely that it either must lead to new antagonisms or, as we all hope, to a much more intimate union of this part of Europe.

[1] See "The Inter-American Treaty of Reciprocal Assistance," below. For a general survey see Schlochauer in 3 ARCHIV DES VÖL-

KERRECHTS No. 2 at 147–90 (1951); Karl Loewenstein in 52 COLUM.
L. REV. No. 1 at 55–99 (1952), and No. 2 at 209–40 (1952); and the
books: OLIVIER PHILIP, LE PROBLÈME DE L'UNION EUROPÉENNE (1950);
EDOUARD BONNEFOUR, L'IDÉE EUROPÉENNE ET SA RÉALISATION (1950).

2 Belgium, Netherlands, Luxembourg.

3 Established in 1948. Seat in Paris. Participating states: Austria,
Belgium, Denmark, France, Greece, Ireland, Iceland, Italy, Luxem-
bourg, Netherlands, Norway, Portugal, Sweden, Switzerland, Turkey,
United Kingdom, plus Western Germany and Trieste.

4 Agreement concerning the foundation of the EPU, signed in Paris
on September 19, 1950. Same members as listed in note 3. Cf. Pierre
Huet, Aspects juridiques de l'Union Européenne de paiements, 78
JOURNAL DE DROIT INTERNATIONAL No. 3 at 770–866 (1951); see also
the article by Louis C. Boochever in 26 DEP'T STATE BULL. No. 672
at 732–36 (1952).

5 Great Britain, France, and the Benelux countries.

6 Established in spring, 1949; members the same as in the OEEC,
minus Austria, Portugal, Switzerland, and Trieste; but with Western
Germany as a full member, and the Saar Territory as an associate
member. See George L. Powell in 3 INT'L L.Q. No. 2 at 164–96 (1950);
Fred L. Schuman in 45 AM.POL.SCI.REV. No. 3 at 724–40 (1951); R.
Oyarzum in POLÍTICA INTERNACIONAL No. 5 at 79–95 (1951); W.
Cornides in 6 EUROPA ARCHIV No. 2; and article in 26 DEP'T STATE
BULL. No. 667 at 523–29 (1952).

7 S.Rep. No. 90, 82nd Cong., 2nd Sess. 13 n. 10.

8 Started work in Geneva, Switzerland, in 1947.

9 The Economic Co-operation Act of 1949 stated it to be the policy
of the people of the United States "to encourage the unification of
Europe." These words were strengthened in 1950 to read: "to encourage the further unification of Europe." And in the Mutual
Security Act of 1951, the phrase reads: "to further encourage the
economic unification and the political federation of Europe."

10 Apart from the United States and Canada, the following Euro-
pean states are members of NATO: Belgium, Denmark, France, Greece,
Iceland, Italy, Luxembourg, the Netherlands, Norway, Portugal,
Turkey, United Kingdom.

11 There is a plan for a European Agricultural Union for a united
European market in wheat, dairy products, sugar, and wine. The
plan was elaborated by French Minister for Agriculture Pflimlin in
1950 and was handled by a special committee of the consultative
assembly of the Council of Europe. An international conference concerning the organization of this union will take place at Paris. See
Susan Strange, A European Agricultural Authority, WORLD AFFAIRS
(October, 1951). There is the Bonnefour Plan for the creation of a
European Transport Union and, finally, the Pleven Plan for the

creation of a European Defense Community and a European army as an integral part of NATO is now embodied in treaties signed but not yet ratified.

12 See Julio H. G. Oliveira, *El Plan Schuman*, 2 REVISTA DEL INSTITUTO DE DERECHO INTERNACIONAL No. 13 at 63–80 (1950); special number of 6 EUROPA ARCHIV Nos. 10–11 at 3615–4113; C. BARCIA TRELLES, EL PACTO DEL ATLÁNTICO 511-59 (1950); F. W. MEYER and A. ZOTTMAN, DER SCHUMAN PLAN UND SEINE PROBLEMATIK; Enrico Serra, *Un problema europeo: la destinazione della Ruhr*, 6 LA COMUNITÁ INTERNAZIONALE 39–53, 278–89, 437–51 (1951); G. Gozard, *Le Pool Charbon-Acier*, REVUE POLITIQUE ET PARLEMENTAIRE (July, (1951); John A. McKesson, *The Schuman Plan*, 68 POL.SCI.Q. No. 1 at 18–35 (1952). There is much interest in the Schuman Plan. Cf. Hans J. Morgenthau's address in PROCEEDINGS OF THE AMERICAN SOCIETY OF INTERNATIONAL LAW 130–34 (1952). At the 1952 Session of the Hague Academy of International Law, F. Dehousse gave a course on "Juridical Problems Arising from the Supranational Organization in Europe," and Max Sorenson lectured on the European Coal and Steel Community.

13 LA DOCUMENTATION FRANCAISE No. 1339 at 651–53 (June 13, 1950).

14 *Ibid.* No. 1460, article entitled *Projet de Traité instituant la Communauté Européenne du Charbon et de l'Acier* at 38; English translation in Department of State Pub. No. 4173 at 126 (European and British Commonwealth Ser. 22, April, 1951); analysis of the Schuman Plan in 24 DEPT. STATE BULL. No. 613 at 523–28 (1951).

15 The treaty is only in one copy and only authentic in French: TRAITÉ INSTITUANT LA COMMUNAUTÉ EUROPÉENNE DU CHARBON ET DE L'ACIER (1951). English text in SEN.EXEC.Q. & REV. 82nd Cong. 2d Sess. at 255; reprinted in 46 AM.J.INT'L L. 107 (1952); official German translation in 3 ARCHIV DES VÖLKERRECHTS No. 2 at 191–236 (1951).

16 For a legal analysis see Schlochauer in JURISTISCHE ZEITUNG, May 20, 1951, pp. 289–90; Carl Bilfinger in 13 ZEITSCHRIFT FÜR AUSLÄNDISCHES ÖFFENTLICHES RECHT UND VÖLKERRECHT No. 3 at 615–59 (1951); Hermann Mosler, 14 *ibid.* Nos. 1–2 at 1–45 (1951); G. Jaenicke, *Die Sicherung des übernationalen Charakters internationaler Organisationen*, *ibid.* at 46–117; E. van Raalte, *The Treaty Constituting the European Coal and Steel Community*, 1 INT'L & COMP.L.Q. No. 7 at 73–85 (1952).

17 See J. F. Köver, *Der Weg sum Neuen Europa*, 50 FRIEDENS-WARTE No. 3 at 193–206 (1951); A. Spinelli, *I movimenti federalisti Europei*, 3 LA COMMUNITÁ INTERNAZIONALE 581–93 (1948); Paul H. Spaak, *L'Europa Unita*, 6 *ibid.* No. 1 at 3–15 (1951).

18 See Dirk U. Stikker, *The Functional Approach to European Integration*, 29 FOREIGN AFFAIRS No. 3 at 436–44 (1951).

19 See "Experience and Technique in International Administration," above.

²⁰ Except *pro foro interno* of the organization. The rules made *pro foro interno* can also directly bind individuals, e.g., the functionaries. These norms are also norms of international law, but of a hierarchically lower level, as they are not based, like the basic treaty, on the norm *pacta sunt servanda* of general international law, but only on the norms of the basic treaty. Such norms show significantly the technique of municipal law: direct validity toward individuals, individual responsibility, punishment and execution as sanctions.

²¹ See F. S. C. Northrop, *Contemporary Jurisprudence and International Law*, 61 YALE L.J. No. 5 at 623–54 (1952).

²² For a clear analysis of what is supranational and what is international, see Van Raalte, *loc. cit.*

²³ Van Raalte calls it "a new structure in the marches between internal and international law."

WHEN THE LEAGUE OF NATIONS came into force on January 10, 1920, it was received with enthusiasm and hope by victors, vanquished, and neutrals. It was the first great experiment of its kind, and the first decade of its functioning was relatively successful. But after 1930, it began rapidly to decline and, after 1940, existed only on paper, disappearing legally in 1946. With the decline of its fortune came indifference, sarcasm, and even hostility. As early as 1935, the Venezuelan international lawyer, Planas-Suárez,[1] wrote a strong anti-League of Nations book as a "Warning to America" and stated: *"La Sociedad de las Naciones es un cadaver —y nada más."* The "failure of the League" became a slogan. And yet it was not the League that had failed, but its members.

This "failure of the League" was also strongly in the minds of those who, at the San Francisco Conference of 1945, drafted the Charter of the United Nations. The wish was create a new quasi-universal international organization, far stronger than the League. Hence, complete prohibition of the "use or threat of force in international relations" (with significant loopholes, it is true), collective security and international sanctions named as the primary goal, great programs of international protection of human rights, power to command and enforce for the Security Council; but all that on the basis of "sovereign equality of all the Members" and non-intervention in matters "which are essentially within the domestic jurisdiction of any State." The makers of the Charter—which is very badly done from the point of view of legal technique—erroneously believed that the strength of a legal order is exclusively determined by the clauses of its constitution, and hoped, unrealistically, that the alliance of the "Big Three" would continue in peace.

The United Nations was perhaps at first officially "oversold" to the public; and highly unfavorable world political conditions in which the United Nations had to operate from the beginning, the cold war, the paralysis of the Security Council, the many failures and frustrations, have brought a part of the general public from early enthusiasm to deep disillusionment. Even the scholars were divided. On the right, there were the ultra-conservatives, opposed to any international organization of this type and longing for a return to "classic" international law. They were matched, on the left, by the 'wishful thinkers." Still more to the left, there were the world government utopians. On the extreme right there were the "neo-realists." If the utopians wanted to do away with international law in order to replace it by "world law," the municipal law of a world federal state, the neo-realists wanted to do away with international law completely, as being a mere fabric of abstractions, a sheer illusion; they proudly concentrated on "power."

The great events of 1956—Suez, Hungary—have brought about a very critical attitude in Europe with regard to the United Nations, particularly in the United Kingdom, and more so in France. Attacks against the voting system, the increasingly large Afro-Asian bloc, the "double morality" of United Nations resolutions, and the wisdom of prohibiting the use of force without international enforcement of the law, are common.

In the present international situation of intensified "cold war," a well-balanced appraisal of the nature and the role of the United Nations, equidistant from utopia and from abysmal pessimism, is obviously very much needed. Such a balanced appraisal has recently been given by Secretary General Dag Hammarskjöld.[2] The Secretary General of the United Nations has a more enhanced legal position than the Secretary General of the League of Nations.[3] He is not only the chief administrative officer of the United Nations, but, under Article XCIX, also has a right of political initiative. The importance of the Secretary General has in recent years very much increased.[4] Dag Hammarskjöld's role as a diplomatic negotiator could already be seen in his mission to Peiping in 1954 and to the Middle East in 1956. But in the Suez crisis of 1956, his position was truly dominating. He had to take responsibility for creating the U.N. Emergency Force (UNEF) in a surprisingly short time, to give orders and instructions to this force, to carry on negotiations with the members contributing forces to UNEF, to propose financial arrangements, to act as chairman of the Advisory Committee, to negotiate with Israel, to negotiate with Egypt as to the deployment of UNEF, and to take care of the problems of the Gaza Strip and the Gulf of Aqaba. He had to make quick reports to the General Assembly and make proposals and give legal interpretations. He was responsible for bringing about compliance with the resolutions of the General Assembly concerning the evacuation of foreign troops from Egypt. He had to take care of the compliance with the old armistice agreement between Israel and the Arab states. At the same time he organized and directed successfully the clearing of the Suez Canal. He was often given very wide discretion. For a time the United States was satisfied in its foreign policy concerning this region to approve, support, and sometimes to accept in advance the decisions and legal opinions of the Secretary General. However, while Secretary General Trygve Lie, through his dutiful behavior in the Korean affair, earned the implacable hostility of the Soviet Union, Secretary General Dag Hammarskjöld was unanimously re-elected by the Security Council and the General Assembly. The strong initiative, the cool Swedish objectivity, the enormous capacity for work, the high diplomatic skill, the strictly legal attitude—in a word, the great talent and achievements of the Secretary General—entitle his opinion on the present role of the United Nations to the greatest respect.[5]

In order to assess the role of the United Nations correctly—critically and yet constructively—it is, first of all, necessary to recognize the United Nations clearly for what it is, both in fact and in law. It is, notwithstanding many differences in detail, essentially a second League of Nations, namely, a loose organization of sovereign states as it corresponds to the occidental idea of international organization.[6] In any such international organization success depends, in the last analysis, on the bona fides and good will of the sovereign members. To this congenital weakness has to be added the facts of the present crisis and transformations, of a deeply divided world, of the renaissance of Asia and the awakening of Africa, and of the coming of the atomic age. All that is reflected by the ever increasing membership in the United Nations. But, as the Secretary General states, these conditions are not created by the United Nations, and they would be worse without the United Nations. The latter is a mirror of the present world situation. But, asks Lester B. Pearson, would it be wise to break the mirror because we do not like the reality which it reflects?

Owing to its constitutional limitations and to present world conditions, the United Nations cannot enforce the law upon nations great and small. There is no doubt that the emphasis on "collective security" and military sanctions is played down. It seems that the Korean action is not to become a precedent, but will rather remain an isolated instance. And even in the Korean action, one could neither speak of a decision of the Security Council—there was only a legally non-binding recommendation—nor of a true United Nations action with United Nations forces. If these ideas of the Secretary General hit the "wishful thinkers," others are directed against the world government utopians. For it is stated that the limitations under the United Nations constitution are not only unavoidable but that far-reaching changes are at this time politically impossible. It is today politically impossible to transform the United Nations into a world authority enforcing the law upon nations. As the Secretary General strongly emphasizes, these weaknesses and limitations "do not derive from the provisions of the Charter, but from facts of international life which are not likely to be by-passed by a different approach or surmounted by attempts at merely constitutional reforms." He is, therefore, against a revision of the Charter at this time.

On the other hand, contrary to the neo-realists, the Secretary General adheres strictly to the principle of the rule of law. United Nations action must be in accordance with international law and valid agreements. The Secretary General should normally take no position in differences between members, but in critical situations he must act as the "servant of the principles of the Charter." He stated in the Suez crisis that it cannot be admitted that the *status juris* may be changed by the use of force. At the same time he states the law of the Charter correctly: Only the Security Council has the power to order the use of force and that only with the concurrent vote of the permanent members and only to maintain or restore international peace and security. The General Assembly "may recommend, investi-

gate, pronounce judgment, but it does not have the power
to compel compliance with its recommendations." The Secretary General states clearly and correctly that the "Uniting for Peace" Resolution did not involve a transfer of the
power of the Security Council. All the General Assembly
can do under Article LIV [7] is to recommend economic sanctions and military aid to the victim of an armed attack, but
the decision rests with the governments of the members.
The majority action in the two crises of 1956 was in conformity with the Charter: political recommendations. There
was compliance in the Suez case, but no compliance in the
Hungarian case. In neither case were sanctions ever proposed, for resolutions of the General Assembly are not
legally binding. It is in the same spirit of legality that the
Secretary General ruled that the deployment of UNEF, created by a resolution of the Assembly, on the territory of a
member needs the consent of that member; consent was
given by Egypt, but not by Israel.

The strong feeling for the rule of law can be seen in the
Secretary General's regret at the decline of acceptance of
the Optional Clause of compulsory jurisdiction and at infre-
quent recourse to the International Court of Justice. The
Secretary General feels that the United Nations has a good
record in the Suez crisis. UNEF, basically different from a
United Nations force created under Article XLI, has, in
spite of its "incomplete presence, temporary duration and
limited authority," made a successful contribution, and
studies relating to the creation of a "Permanent United
Nations Peace Force" are under way.[8]

The United Nations is by no means a super-state and cannot act outside the framework of decisions by its member
governments. Progress toward solutions of problems depends on governments. The United Nations can help, but
it cannot and should not attempt to surmount difficulties
alone. But—and that is the new thing—states alone cannot

do it either. The Secretary General sees an abuse in the use of the United Nations for mere propaganda or for purposes of national power politics. Nations or groups of nations "will never be able to arrogate judgment unto themselves in international affairs in ways which once were a matter of course." Hence, he holds that alliances, maintained side by side with the United Nations, have only a limited value. So-called voting victories are likely to be illusory in a loose organization of sovereign members. The General Assembly is by no means a parliament, but a diplomatic body, consisting of delegates appointed and instructed by governments and representing the policies of their states. The Secretary General defends the principle of "one state—one vote," which recently has been under sharp attack, because it corresponds to the principle of "sovereign equality" and because no system of "weighted voting" is at this time politically possible.

The Secretary General recognizes the value of debate and voting and admits the importance of the United Nations as a world forum, where the hopes and fears of nations in all parts of the world may be freely expressed. But he sees a particularly important, perhaps the principal, role of the United Nations as an "instrument for negotiations among and, to some extent, for governments, as an instrument for concerting action by governments in support of the Charter." There is, apart from public proceedings, much room for "quiet diplomacy," for a policy of reconciliation, for winning consent to peaceful and just settlement of the problem at issue.

Let us not forget that the second task of the United Nations—international co-operation in many so-called non-political fields—is of the greatest importance, too, and that the United Nations, like the League of Nations, is here often far more successful than in the problem of peace. The United Nations already is indispensable, and it would have to be invented, if it did not exist. We must neither exaggerate nor minimize its value and role. These are exactly the paradoxes of the present dynamics of history: International organizations are absolutely necessary and, at the same time, their limitations are unavoidable.

[1] SIMÓN PLANAS-SUÁREZ, LA POLÍTICA EUROPEA, Y LA SOCIEDAD DE LAS NACIONES. UNA ADVERTENCIA A LA AMÉRICA (1935).

[2] Introduction to ANNUAL REPORT ON THE WORK OF THE UNITED NATIONS (reprinted in N.Y. Times, September 5, 1957, pp. 10–11).

[3] See "The Legal Position of the Secretary General of the United Nations," above.

[4] Elmore Jackson, *The Developing Role of the Secretary General*, 11 INT'L ORG. 431–57 (1957).

[5] A very similar appraisal of the role of the U.N. has recently been given by Lester B. Pearson, in 1 INT'L REL. No. 8 at 329–38 (1957).

[6] See W. SCHIFFER, THE LEGAL COMMUNITY OF MANKIND (1954).

[7] This correct construction was made from the beginning by Professor A. Verdross.

[8] See article by Louis B. Sohn, 52 AM.J.INT'L L. 229 (1958). Somewhat different was the "U.N. Guard," proposed by Secretary General Trygve Lie in 1949 as a small police force to protect U.N. missions in the field in troubled areas.

I

La justice sans la force est impuissante . . . parce qu'il y a toujours des méchants.—Pascal, Pensées, Fragment 298.)

Human conduct is regulated by a plurality of normative systems—religious, ethical, conventional, and legal norms. Religious and ethical rules embody higher values and are sometimes more effective than legal rules. Yet, up to now, law has proved to be indispensable to the relatively peaceful living together of human beings,[1] and the relatively peaceful living together of nations is no exception. Law, to speak with Kelsen,[2] is essentially a coercive order, an organization of force, a system of norms providing for sanctions. Legal sanctions constitute the reaction of the legal community against a delict.[3] In contrast to disapproval by the members of a community as a moral sanction, legal sanctions are socially organized measures; in contrast to the transcendental sanctions of religious norms, they are to be applied on this earth;[4] they are to be applied against or without the will of the person against whom they are directed; they are, finally, to be applied by physical force, if necessary.[5]

As sanctions in this sense are indispensable to any legal system,[6] it is not surprising that the problem of sanctions has played at all times an important role in the theory and practice of international law. The alleged absence of sanctions has been and is today the principal argument of those who deny that the rules of international law have the character of legal rules. But general international law *has* sanctions: reprisals and war. This is not a unique feature of international law, but is common to all primitive, highly decentralized legal orders, whether municipal or international. Such legal orders have no central organs either for the making or application of legal rules or for the determination of the delict or the execution of sanctions. All these functions must be left to the members of the legal community; in international law, to the sovereign states. There are no collective but only individual sanctions, carried out by way of self-help; there is no monopoly of force at the disposal of a central law-enforcing organ; there is no distinction between criminal and civil sanctions; the sanctions are based on collective, not on individual responsibility.

The tremendous disadvantages of such a system are clear. Each state is *judex in causa sua,* has a right of auto-interpretation of international law, a right of auto-determination of the delict and of the state guilty of it and must carry out the sanctions itself. Where collective security is absent, the states, for their individual security, follow the policy of armaments, alliances, and the balance of power. Under such a system a weak state can hardly go to war or take reprisals against a more powerful state, whereas the latter may abuse its power.[7] And a greater disadvantage is that this lack of centralization of the judicial function makes peaceful settlement of a conflict only possible by agreement and, in the case of the use of force, makes it impossible to determine with legal authenticity which state is legally right and which is wrong, which state is using force legally and which illegally. But the same impossibility exists in a primitive municipal legal order to state with legal authenticity who is the murderer and who the avenger.

To this it should be added that, whereas reprisals can be conceived as sanctions because they presuppose a delict, even if auto-determined by the state exercising the reprisals, the status of war as a sanction was open to doubt. For under general international law, as it stood up to 1914, any state could at any time and for any reason go to war without committing an international delinquency. The *jus ad bellum* remained unrestricted;[8] only the carrying-on of war was regulated by the legally binding, customary, and treaty norm of the *jus in bello*.[9]

Since 1914, international law has been in a period of crisis and transformation, of flux and change; but one of the greatest differences between the "classic" and the "new" international law is the attitude toward war. In consequence of World War I, the attempt to restrict or abolish war, to distinguish between legal and illegal use of military force, to subject the use of military force to the control of the international community, to maintain international peace and security, to replace the crude individual sanctions by single states with collective measures by a system of "collective security," became the principal task to such an extent that the problem of peace overshadowed and overshadows today the problem of justice. This task implied, of course, the problem of sanctions.

The first attempt was the League of Nations. It was greeted with enthusiasm by victors, vanquished, and neutrals; and the first decade of its existence looked hopeful. But whether the times were ripe, whether the methods chosen were correct, is debatable. For the corresponding norms remained largely on paper, experimental, proved in serious test cases to be ineffective and, finally, an illusion. The thousand years' history in medieval Europe of doing

away with the equally disastrous system of self-help by
Fehde, bellum privatum, shows that it was possible to ban
private war effectively and make it a crime only after the
primitive legal order had developed into an advanced legal
order by way of centralization: centralization of the legislative, judicial, and sanctioning function. In former times
the problem was to ban private war, whereas public, international war was considered inevitable in the primitive,
highly decentralized international community. Since 1920,
the problem has been to ban public war as "the private war"
of single states. May the method to reach this goal effectively not be analogous to that which, after a long time,
did away with private war? But, contrary to the historical
experience in the battle against private war, the drafters of
the League of Nations Covenant were under the impact of
the occidental idea of international organization [10] which
had developed in the Utopian writings on "eternal peace"
from the times of Pierre Dubois (1305) to Kant (1795),
climaxing in Abbé de St. Pierre (1716), taken over by
Simón Bolívar and the first Pan-Americanism [11] and then
by the League of Nations.[12] Like their forerunners, the
drafters of the Covenant believed that, as far as the international community is concerned, no such degree of centralization is necessary or even desirable; they believed that peace
and security can be achieved through a loose union of sovereign states. They superimposed a superstructure of treaty
norms on the unchanged sociological basis, including the
individualistic distribution of power, of the primitive, decentralized international community. Sanctions, as already
in some earlier Utopian writers, played a great role, but the
basis of the new system was very different from the ancient
doctrine of *bellum justum.*[13]

The system of collective military sanctions was opposed
by the United States and by conservative international lawyers like Professor Borchard. But when, with the collapse

of collective security in the thirties in the Far East, South America, and Africa, the illusion on which the League system had been built became obvious, a mass withdrawal of members from the League and a mass flight into classic neutrality started. Neither the League nor the Kellogg Pact was able to prevent the outbreak of the greatest war in history. The noble experiment of the League of Nations itself disappeared in the holocaust of World War II.

Treaty law, including the League of Covenant, is particular international law, always based on general international law. Where the particular treaty norms, created in derogation of general international law, cease to function, they are automatically replaced by the corresponding norms of general international law. The failure of collective security in the League of Nations and in our time has also produced a swing from an attitude favorable to collective sanctions to the opposite attitude in the minds of statesmen as well as of international lawyers. After the collapse of collective security in the League of Nations, even the remaining League members declared that the sanctions article had become, for the time being, only optional. Lord Cranborne's report of September 8, 1937, discussed the ideas of a "coercive" and of a "non-coercive" League. The issue of sanctions *vs.* non-sanctions played a role also in Pan-American developments, and was discussed in the literature in this country.[14]

After the outbreak of World War II, Niemeyer [15] took a decisive and dogmatic stand against sanctions in international law. Starting from the thesis of the "unreality of international law and the unlawfulness of international reality," he came to the conclusion that international law must be a "law without force." His reason was the Hegelian conception of sovereignty states which are "units of supreme government in human society and are by inherent necessity the highest, most powerful and most efficient organizations." International law must be a "law without force," it must be 'functional," "more political"; its rules "must be effectual because of their inherent appeal," they must be "based on non-moral values." He stated: "There is no lawfulness in international relations outside the immanent lawfulness of the individual impulses of statesmen." As a criticism, it is sufficient to state, from a political point of view, that these words were written at a time when Adolf Hitler occupied nearly the whole European continent, and, from a theoretical point of view, that, as law is an organization of force, the postulate of a "law without force" is, to speak with Kelsen, a contradiction in terms.

III

The development which led to the United Nations was certainly not inspired by Niemeyer's "law without force"; sanctions again played a great role. But before considering the actual status of sanctions under the law of the United Nations, mention should be made that there exist today sectors of international law, the rules of which directly obligate individuals and where, therefore, the problem of sanctions takes on an entirely different form. Quite apart from the new and not yet clear and consolidated law of personal responsibility under international law of war criminals, there are cases of direct international administration of territories;[16] there are cases of direct international legislation, binding upon individuals, containing sanctions distinguishing between criminal and civil sanctions, based on individual, not on collective, responsibility, providing machinery, including courts, competent to give a decision with judicial impartiality and able to enforce their decision.

Even prior to 1914, the European Danube Commission had authority to make regulations binding on all who navigate the maritime Danube, and had its own courts. Today a great deal of the internal law of international organizations, particularly the whole law of international officials, as well as a part of the law of the supranational organizations in Europe, belongs here. We have here to deal with international norms, international by their creation, reason of validity, and function; but the internal structure of these norms is not different from that of advanced municipal legal orders. Yet the bulk of international rules providing for sanctions, including those of the United Nations and specialized agencies, whether creating specific [17] or general sanctions, binds only states.

IV

The apocalyptic experiences and consequences of World War II, the "total" character of war, the tremendous power of new weapons of mass destruction, the coming of the atomic age, soon followed by the space age, have created world-wide fear of a third world war—they have tremendously strengthened the conviction, existing since World War I, that war nowadays has become too dangerous; the competence to go to war must, therefore, be taken away from the individual states; the international community itself must control the use of military force in international relations. This is the cardinal purpose of the United Nations, stated in the emotional phrase at the very beginning of the Charter that the intention is "to save succeeding generations from the scourge of war which twice in our lifetime has brought untold sorrow to mankind."

But the method to achieve this end is exactly the same as in 1920: again a loose nation, "based on the principle of the sovereign equality of all its Members"—even if that is not wholly true. In spite of many differences in detail, the United Nations is essentially no more than a second League of Nations. It again fails to offer a complete system of

peaceful procedures for the settlement of international conflicts; it again has no international courts with compulsory
jurisdiction; its provisions for peaceful change are even less
significant than the wholly inadequate Article XIX of the
Covenant. Again it was believed that something can be had
for nothing, that norms, which for their effectivity would
need a centralized legal order, can successfully be superimposed by treaty upon the unchanged sociological basis of
a primitive, highly decentralized international community.
After the experience of the League of Nations, the failure
of the system of collective security of the United Nations
could have been foreseen.

The sanctions of the United Nations are, as far as their
structure is concerned, old-fashioned, just as under general
international law; they are directed against states, are
based on collective responsibility, and do not distinguish
between criminal and civil sanctions. But whereas general
international law knows only individual, and not collective,
sanctions, the Charter knows only collective, and not individual, sanctions; this is clearly shown in the Dumbarton
Oaks Proposals, but remains also true under the Charter,
notwithstanding the addition of Articles LI, LIII, and
CVII.

The scope of collective security is again restricted to
protection against the illegal use of military force; the
United Nations is again an organization for the maintenance and restoration of international peace and security,
but not an organization for enforcing the law against all
other violations of international law. But the scope of
"peace and security" was enlarged considerably. The Covenant did not forbid war, but imposed only certain "obligations" not to resort to war. Although this has been much
criticized, and paper attempts to close these "gaps" were
unsuccessfully made, it was logical; the makers of the
Covenant understood that, before prohibiting resort to war,

substitute measures have to be given to the states; where the Covenant provided such measures, resort to war was prohibited; sanctions were provided against those who "resort to war in disregard of their covenants under Articles XII, XIII or XV"; where the Covenant failed to provide such substitute procedures, war remained legal even between League members.[18] The Kellogg Pact renounced war "as an instrument of national policy," but contained no definitions, no organization, no sanctions, and fully recognized not only the right to go to war in self-defense but also the unhampered auto-determination by the state alone, acting in self-defense, whether the conditions of self-defense exist. Covenant and Kellogg Pact speak only of "war" and do not touch the use of military force in reprisals and "measures short of war."

The U.N. Charter, in a radical and progressive development, replaces the legally ambiguous term "war" by the wider and clear term of the "use of force." Collective sanctions are provided—preventive and repressive sanctions and, in both cases, sanctions not involving the use of military force and military sanctions—against "any threat to the peace, breach of the peace or act of aggression." It is also a progressive development that the determination of the delict and of the guilty state, the decision on non-military and military sanctions, and the execution of the sanctions were radically centralized in the Security Council. For the first time an organ of an international organization, the Security Council, was created with real power; it alone has the sanctioning competence; its decisions are legally binding on all the members of the United Nations. There are also weak points: the centralization of the sanctioning function in a strictly political organ; the extremely bad drafting of the Charter from the point of view of legal technique; the character of the measures under Articles XLI and XLII as sanctions is less clear than under Article

XVI of the Covenant; the vague wording in Article XXXIX, the lack of general abstract definitions, the wide discretion given to the Security Council.

But this wide discretion was intentional; taking their clue in this respect from the Concert of Europe rather than from the League of Nations, the drafters of the Charter tried to create in the permanent members of the Security Council a sort of directorate, which, disposing of effective power and acting in accord, can maintain or restore international peace and security. But here had to be paid the price of the veto, which contained the germ of destroying the whole progress achieved by the radical centralization of the sanctioning function in the Security Council. The Security Council must, first, bindingly determine the delict and the aggressor; after that it may directly decide upon preventive or repressive non-military or military sanctions; it can utilize regional arrangements or agencies for enforcement action under its authority; it shall, in the case of Article LI, "take the measures necessary to maintain" (or rather to restore) "international peace and security." Under all three hypotheses, we have to do with collective sanctions, radically centralized in the Security Council, for the maintenance of international peace and security. Only under Article XCIV, paragraph 2,[19] may the Security Council decide upon sanctions to give effect to the judgment of the International Court of Justice against the state which has failed to perform the obligations incumbent upon it under this judgment. This is the only case where the Security Council may take executive sanctions, where the United Nations is, at least in this one case, a law-enforcing agency in general.

The United Nations system: only collective sanctions, radically centralized in the Security Council, restricted—apart from Article XCIV, paragraph 2—to the maintenance or restoration of international peace and security, has its counterpart in the prohibition of the "threat or use of (military) force in international relations" by the single states—Article II, paragraph 4, with the two exceptions of Article LI and of Articles CVII, and LIII. The replacement of the term "war" by "threat or use of force" has made the baffling problem of a strict division between "war in the sense of international law" and military reprisals less important, but has not abolished this distinction. The economic and diplomatic sanctions under Article XLI constitute non-military reprisals; the measures under Article XLII embrace war and measures short of war. On the other hand, the individual state is not only deprived, to speak with Scelle, of the "compétence de la guerre" even as a method of sanctions but also of any other sanctioning competence by threat or use of military force, whether military reprisals in the strict sense or "measures short of war," such as troop concentrations near the border of another state, mobilization, naval demonstrations, pacific blockade, all involving the threat of force. The Charter knows no individual military sanctions, either for the maintenance or restoration of international peace and security or for the enforcement of international law in general. But the prohibition of Article II, paragraph 4, goes even further. Kelsen has stated that the use of force can, within a legal order, only constitute either a delict or a sanction, and this dictum has been accepted by many writers. But it seems to us that this dichotomy is incomplete. Kelsen himself must admit [20] that there are collective coercive acts, such as the forcible evacuation of inhabitants from houses that threaten to collapse, which are legal but do not constitute sanctions.

Under general international law, states have the right to use military force as sanctions, be it in the form of war or military reprisals; but they are allowed also to use military force in the form of self-protection by way of self-help, where such use of force does not constitute sanctions; [21]

where there is the right of a state to self-protection by using military force on foreign territory—the *Caroline case,* landing of troops on foreign territory for the protection of citizens. If that is done in cases where the foreign state is *unable* to fulfil its international obligations, such acts against an innocent state are not, of course, sanctions. An excellent example is furnished by the law of neutrality; under Article XXV of Hague Convention XIII (1907), a neutral state is under a duty to prevent any violation of its neutrality, but only "as the means at its disposal allow." A neutral state which has used all the means at its disposal to prevent a violation of its neutrality but is *unable* to prevent it has fulfilled its international duty, is not guilty of any violation of international law; hence, no sanctions, no military reprisals against this state are justified. Yet

> when the means at its disposal are clearly inadequate to fulfill its neutral obligations, it is recognized that a belligerent is not forbidden from taking, as an extreme measure, acts of hostility in neutral jurisdiction against an enemy making improper use of that jurisdiction.[22]

Here we have a legal use of force not constituting a sanction. Such use or threat of military force is equally forbidden by Article II, paragraph 4; it is, for instance, clear that states no longer have the right to land troops on foreign territory for the protection of their citizens abroad. Article II, paragraph 4, therefore, deprives individual states, not only of any sanctioning function by threat or use of military force, but also of the right to use a threat or use of military force not constituting a legal sanction under general international law. This follows clearly from the sentence of the preamble "that armed force shall *not* be used, save in the common interest." But from the same sentence it follows equally clear—contrary to the opposite views of some writers—that only the use of *military* force is prohibited. Non-military—economic, financial, diplomatic —sanctions, reprisals not involving the threat or use of military force, remain legal under the U.N. Charter. But the Bogotá Charter of the Organization of American States also expressly forbids the use of coercive measures of an economic or political character to force the sovereign will of another state and obtain from it advantages of any kind.

The statement that the Charter deprives single states of any competence to apply sanctions by the threat or use of military force also remains true with regard to the admitted exceptions. Articles CVII and LIII allow the use of military force as a "transitional security arrangement" against ex-enemy states; this exception is broader than Article LI, less subject to United Nations control, and allows also the preventive use of force. Article LI contains the exception of "individual and collective self-defense." [23] Here we again have a point in which the dichotomy "force as delict or as sanction" is incomplete. Self-defense by military force, under Article LI, is legal, but it certainly does not constitute a sanction. Bowett [24] is right in maintaining that self-defense has the precondition of delictual conduct on the part of him against whom this action is taken, in common with methods of self-help as a sanction, contrary to the right of "self-protection" against an innocent state; not to speak of the case of 'necessity" (*Neptune case*), which gives no right, but only an excuse; but the merely preventive and non-retributive character of self-defense distinguishes it radically from the use of military force by self-help as a sanction. The individual, exercising self-defense against an attacker, merely defends himself; he has neither the intention nor the authority to enforce the law, to punish the attacker; that remains for the criminal court. The right of self-defense, even in an advanced legal order, must be given to the individual because the organized community action would be too late. Hence it is for the indi-

vidual to auto-determine whether the conditions for self-
defense exist and how far he can go in self-defense; the
right of self-defense is exceptional and provisional; he
himself determines, but only for the time being, subject to
the law and later action by a criminal court; he makes the
determination himself, but at his risk; a criminal court and
jury may later find him guilty of having exceeded his right
of self-defense; he himself determines, but possibly at the
risk of his life.

Article LI, as intended, gives the same right of self-
defense, plus the right of defense of others—incorrectly
called "collective self-defense"—as an exceptional and provisional measure until the Security Council acts. Also "collective self-defense" is not a sanction, enforcement of the
law, or "collective security." The Security Council shall
later take the necessary measures to restore international
peace and security. The Security Council may determine
that the state or states against which individual and collective self-defense measures have been taken are the
aggressors, and authorize the states, acting hitherto in self-
defense, to carry on sanctions against the aggressor and/or
also call upon other states. Or the Security Council may
determine that the states, claiming to act in self-defense,
are the aggressors and order sanctions against them. Under
both hypotheses the provisional stage of individual and collective self-defense has come to an end and collective sanctions under the exclusive authority of the Security Council
have begun. The state, acting in self-defense, determines
for the time being whether the conditions for self-defense
are present, whether its action is proportional to the attack,
and so on, but it does so at its own risk and subject to the
law and to the control of the Security Council.

But this right of individual and collective self-defense
under Article LI is strictly limited only to the case of an
armed attack that occurs. No such right is given against
an imminent attack, *no preventive* use of military force is

allowed. Some writers deny that; but it is not possible to deny it if one is interested in the statement of what the law is. Neither the doubtful "inherent right" ("droit naturel"), which certainly is not adequate for the right of "collective self-defense," nor the history of the drafting of Article LI can prevail against the clear wording: *"if* an armed attack *occurs";* the equally authentic Spanish text says: "en caso de ataque armado"; the equally authentic French text puts it even more clearly: "dans le cas où un membre des Nations Unies est l'objet d'une agression militaire." Where the text is so clear and unequivocal, it is not permissible, as the two International Courts have often laid down, for the interpretation to go back to the "travaux préparatoires." It is, of course, an excellent criticism to say that such right could be entirely inadequate in the atomic age; but this is an argument *de lege ferenda;* the Charter was written in the pre-atomic age.. That Article LI is restricted to the case "if an armed attack occurs," has been recognized by many prominent international lawyers;[25] the attitude of a number of governments in the United Nations has been to the same effect; Arab, communist, Latin-American writers strongly insist on it.[26] But where an armed attack occurs, even in a border clash, the right under Article LI exists; it is clear that India has a right of self-defense under Article LI against the invasion of its borders by Chinese troops, even if "only" a few Indians are killed and captured.

The system of sanctions, as under the U.N. Charter, is therefore the following one:

(A) Only collective sanctions under the exclusive authority of the Security Council and only—apart from Article XCIV, paragraph 2—to maintain or restore international peace and security.

(B) No individual military sanction at all, either to maintain or restore international peace and security or to enforce international law in general; only the limited right of using military force under Article LI against an armed attack.

(C) Hence, neither individual nor collective—apart from Article XCIV, paragraph 2—military sanctions for the enforcement of international law in general.

V

Soon after the United Nations had come into existence this system of sanctions was made unworkable in consequence of the actual split among the two Great Powers and their associates. This situation had two impacts on the system of sanctions.

(A) The treaties provided for under Article XLIII have, up to now, not been concluded; in consequence, the Security Council, under Article CVI, is unable to decide on military sanctions, although its capacity to determine the delict and the guilty state and to decide upon sanctions not involving the use of military force is thereby not impaired. The drafters on the Charter expected, of course, that the treaties under Article XLIII would be concluded soon; the "joint action" was provided for in Article CVII as a mere interim measure. But this interim measure would prevail as of today; and, for the same reasons, neither is the joint action by permanent members of the Security Council possible. As the treaties under Article XLIII have not been concluded, Articles XLIII to L of Chapter VII have, as Jiménez de Aréchaga remarks,[27] an unrealistic and purely academic character; the duties of the members under Article XLIII have not come into existence.

(B) The exercise of the veto has paralyzed the whole sanctioning function of the Security Council; we can agree with Jiménez de Aréchaga [28] that a system which makes it a priori impossible to apply sanctions against the permanent members of the Security Council and their client-states "does not deserve the name of a system of collective security."

Up to now, two attempts have been made to remedy the breakdown of the United Nations system of sanctions: the first came from the members, the second from the United Nations itself.

(1) Where there is no collective security, the states must try to protect themselves individually; as always, the forms used under general international law furnish the pattern: armament, alliances leading to counter-alliances, and an armament race—today an atomic, thermonuclear, and missiles armament race. States in general do not like to violate their treaty obligations; a system must, therefore, be found which makes it possible to reconcile these alliances with the basic treaty. When the League of Nations system of collective security could not be relied upon, members concluded old-fashioned alliances under Article XXI of the Covenant, always, of course, "dans le cadre de la Société des Nations." When the United Nations system of collective security broke down, the two escape clauses of Articles CVII, LIII, and LI conveniently offered themselves.

The Soviet bloc preferred Article CVII, which, as stated, is less subject to United Nations control and allows the preventive use of force, but is only temporary. But whereas all Soviet bilateral alliances are based on that article, the first Soviet multilateral treaty—the Warsaw Pact— like the corresponding treaties of the West, is anchored in Article LI.

The West from the beginning chose Article LI, which allows the use of military force without previous authority by the Security Council; it has the further advantage that, in contrast to Article LIV, the Security Council need not at all times be kept informed of activities undertaken or in contemplation for the maintenance of international peace and security. Article LI is in Chapter VII, not in Chapter VIII on "Regional Arrangements." The prototype of these Western alliances is the Inter-American Treaty of Reciprocal Assistance.[29] It was followed by NATO and many similar pacts. They are fully based on Article LI, on the right of individual and collective self-defense; they allow the use of force only against an "armed attack"; they recognize that they can function only "until the Security Council takes the necessary measures to restore international peace and security." The legal change which they bring about consists only in transforming the right of individual and collective self-defense into a duty. They always remain on the level of self-defense; they do not constitute sanctions; they are not measures of "collective security." They do not, as is often stated for political reasons, "strengthen United Nations collective security," but are a substitute, an ersatz for the failure of the collective security system. The Western pacts, such as NATO and so on, are certainly indispensable for the defense and even the survival of the free world; yet they are, as Charles de Visscher [30] has stated, old-fashioned defensive alliances—although even in time of peace highly organized—which emphasize the actual split of the world.

It is exactly this failure of the United Nations system of collective security that has brought about a radical change in the importance and function of Article LII. While it was conceived as a rare and exceptional norm, it has become one of the most important articles of the Charter. While it was conceived as a merely temporal and provisional measure, subject to the authority of the Security Council, to be followed by collective sanctions, it may now lead to old-fashioned war, controlled only by the laws of war. Here we see again that treaty norms, enacted in derogation of general international law, are, if they do not work, re-placed by general international law.

(2) The second reaction came from the United Nations itself, through the "Uniting for Peace Resolution" of 1950. It was an attempt to transfer, to a certain degree, the sanctioning competence from the Security Council to the General Assembly, in order to evade the veto and to revive the task of the United Nations to maintain and restore international peace and security. The constitutionality of this resolution is extensively debated in the literature. But even if we take it to be fully constitutional, its practical effect must not be overestimated. Typical of such overestimation is the enthusiastic treatment of this resolution by Jiménez de Aréchaga.[31] He praises the constitutional flexibility of the Charter; he believes, in a typically Latin American way, that it has "the transcendental consequence to democratize the Charter," "to heal the essential vice of the San Francisco product," by giving to the Assembly, where there is no veto, the competence to decide on the delict and the aggressor and to extend collective sanctions, with the equal right of the medium and small states, even against a permanent member of the Security Council and their client-states, although he must admit that the votes of the Assembly under this resolution have only the legal character of recommendations. All that is, of course, untenable, practically and legally. Practically, the strong and growing Afro-Asian bloc, always helped by the Soviet bloc and some other countries, can now—in contrast to 1950—prevent the reaching of the necessary two-thirds majority. From the point of view of law, the votes under this resolution are not legally binding recommendations; the Assembly cannot bindingly determine the delict and the aggressor, cannot bindingly decide on non-military or military sanctions, cannot bindingly utilize regional arrangements or agencies for

purposes of sanctions, cannot bindingly take the necessary measures under Article LI. All it can do is recommend. The Assembly has no sanctioning competence, which, under the Charter, is solely and exclusively in the Security Council. The Assembly cannot order the use of military force as a sanction, it can only recommend, and in a legally non-binding way, that the members make use of their right of individual and collective self-defense under Article LI. While this has been recognized from the beginning by Professor Alfred Verdross,[32] it has now been also officially recognized by the United Nations itself, in consequence of the 1956 crises concerning the Suez Canal and Hungary. The Secretary General stated in 1957 that *only* the Security Council has the power to order the use of force, and then only to maintain or restore international peace and security. The Uniting for Peace Resolution, he stated, did not involve a transfer of the power of the Security Council. The General Assembly "may recommend, investigate, pronounce judgment, but it does not have the power to compel compliance with its recommendations." In consequence of this resolution, he continued, all that the Assembly can do under Article LI is to recommend economic measures and military aid to the victim of an armed attack. In neither of the two 1956 crises, he stated, were sanctions ever proposed, for resolutions of the General Assembly are not legally binding.

Hence, neither of these two attempts have been able to remedy the failure of collective sanctions; neither constitutes sanctions, but only individual and collective self-defense which, in consequence of the paralysis of the Security Council, may lead us back to general international law: war, restricted by the *jus in bello*.

VI

Although collective sanctions—the only sanctions under the Charter—do not function, and pacts like NATO, as well as recommendations of the General Assembly under the Uniting for Peace Resolution, do not constitute sanctions but only collective self-defense, the absolute prohibition of the threat or use of military force in international relations by single states, a prohibition which deprives them of resort to any threat or use of military force, whether as a sanction or as another means of self-help not constituting a sanction, with the only exception of the limited right of individual and collective self-defense against an armed attack, stands.

Jiménez de Aréchaga [33] is, indeed, emphatic in his statement that Article II, paragraph 4, is the most important article of the Charter, not only from the point of view of collective security, but also from the point of view of general international law. He believes that we have attained for the first time the centralization of the use of military force in international relations, that military force has been subjected to the same regulation as in advanced municipal law; delict or sanction. He insists that the duty under Article II, paragraph 4 continues to be valid in its entire integrity, notwithstanding deficiencies or even the failure which the United Nations mechanism may see; although the Security Council may be unable to make a decision because of the veto or for whatever other reason, this prohibition will always remain in force.

It is interesting to note that most writers [34] who discuss Article II, paragraph 4, think only of the prohibition of the threat or use of military force in order to change the actual law. The same is true of statesmen. Secretary of State Christian A. Herter, in his speech before the United Nations on September 17, 1959,[35] regarded as the major problem the prevention of change through aggressive force; he felt that the way in which change comes about is of overriding importance in the nuclear age; total nuclear war has now become, quite literally, a suicidal enterprise. But he sees also the necessity for accomplishing constructive change through peaceful means, a problem which the

League of Nations did not master and that the United Nations has not yet been able fully to resolve.

Certainly, to prevent changing the status quo through the use of military force, and hence the problem of peaceful change, is particularly important at this time.[36] Yet the use of military force has also had the function of a sanction; under the *bellum justum* doctrine, war only had the function of a sanction. Of this function of the use of military force as a sanction most writers do not speak.[37] But the reaction and, recently, nearly a rebellion against Article II, paragraph 4, from the sanctioning point of veiw, can be seen too, particularly with British writers. Even prior to 1956, assertions are not lacking to show that Article II, paragraph 4, does not prohibit the threat or use of military force by single states for purposes of sanctions to enforce international rights, if their exercise is legally denied. The reaction takes the form of an interpretation of Article II, paragraph 4. Hints at such interpretation can be seen in the writings of Professor Schwarzenberger. Particularly clear is the attitude of Professor Waldock in the *Corfu Channel Case* as well as in his writings.[38] This way of thinking led to the British-French military intervention in Egypt in 1956. This intervention was defended as legitimate by the prime minister of the United Kingdom and by France, and their position was expressed in the British and French vetoes in the Security Council. This military intervention was in fact, a total failure; but after this failure the British also stood firm as far as the legality of the intervention is concerned. They felt, as Professor Stone will say later, that the "extreme" interpretation of Article II, paragraph 4, is an absurdity, that it leaves the law-abiding states helpless whereas the attitude of the United Nations not only saved Egypt from certain defeat, but also made a state, a villain in British eyes, a hero. There was for a long time British and French bitterness and resentment against the United States, against the

United Nations and the Secretary General of the United Nations; this attitude was shared by many countries of free Europe. The literary expression of this bitterness and resentment, the scholarly attempt to justify the intervention in Eygpt, is the recent book by Professor Julius Stone.[39] It is a bid for the legality of the threat or use of military force by single states as a sanction to enforce general international law. Professor Stone tries to show that this corresponds to a true interpretation of Article II, paragraph 4. But it can be easily shown by the clear text of the Charter and by going back to the *travaux préparatoires* that his interpretation is untenable: All threat or use of military force, including that for purposes of sanctions, is prohibited; this is the sense of the *Corfu Channel Judgment*, the practice of the United Nations, the attitude of the Secretary General, and also, overwhelmingly so, the literature.[40]

Stone's scientific error consists in that he tries to present his critque of the positive law as constituting this positive law; but as a *critique* his arguments deserve attention. Such criticism has been and is, indeed, widely voiced. Judge Alvarez [41] criticizes the lack of sanctions for enforcing international law in general. Sir Gerald Fitzmaurice [42] states "that now it is possible to violate a large part of international law in all sorts of different ways, and to commit breaches of treaties, right and left, without ever having recourse to aggression"; "international law is less enforceable to-day than it ever has been in the whole of its history." He continues:

> The Charter frowns on self-help, without, however, as yet, having put aything in its place; it goes far toward rendering unenforceable by direct action the whole of international law, except the breach of peace.

George Scelle [43] has, as his own *advocatus diaboli,* excellently presented all the arguments *contra;* it is this exposé which serves Professor Stone as a starting point. Scelle admits the necessity of sanctions, admits that Article II, paragraph 4, makes it possible for states to violate international law, as long as such violation does not take the form of an armed attack; he even recognizes that the tolerability of a renunciation of the use of military force by the states depends on collective sanctions against the violation of international law in general.

These ideas have recently been strongly voiced again by French writers. In the preparatory work of the twenty-fourth commission of the Institute de Droit International, Emile Giraud [44] stated that Article II, paragraph 4, has had a most unfavorable influence on the progress of arbitral and judicial settlement; the smaller powers, he states, now do what they like, only keeping away from an armed attack; why should they take the risk of losing their case in an international court? [45] He criticizes the U.N. Charter as showing "a dangerous lack of equilibrium." One pretends to forbid the states any recourse to force, whereas one does not give them any means to make their rights respected. And he concludes: "Un tel systéme ne peut être viable à la longue." Also Judge Huber [46] refers to the lacunae of the Charter. Breach of the peace, he states, is far from being the only violation of international law; an organization destined to assure the peace must have a complete system capable of furnishing a peaceful solution to any international conflict. The Resolution on Compulsory Jurisdiction of International Courts and Tribunals, adopted by the Institut de Droit International at its 1959 Session at Nauchâtel, warns in paragraph 2 of the preamble that "the maintenance of justice . . . is an essential complement to renunciation of recourse to force in international relations."

The complete prohibition of the use of military force as a sanction by single states, without collective and effective

sanctions for enforcing international law in general, has
left states against which violations of international law
not constituting an armed attack have been committed
sometimes without any adequate remedy either by self-help
or by collective action under the U.N. Charter. True, states
may, under the Charter, still exercise sanctions not involving the threat or use of military force; that is shown by
the Charter itself, as well as by the fact that Brazil's proposal at San Francisco also to forbid economic reprisals was
rejected. But under the Charter of Bogotá states are rather
helpless in the face of violations of international law by
other states, since economic, financial, or political reprisals
are also expressly forbidden. This situation has further
consequences: it may damage the legal situation of the
aggrieved states in the long run. These states, it is true,
may protest; but it is certain that a protest or even repeated protests, if they remain without effect, do not preserve the rights of the protesting states indefinitely. For
the protest is not a sanction. but a declaration which needs
a sanction in order not to deteriorate into an ineffective
"paper protest." The attitude of international tribunals
shows that in such a case the protesting state must undertake further steps going beyond protest to vindicate its
rights.[47] But, under the Charter of Bogota, neither military
nor non-military reprisals are allowed; an offer to submit
the dispute to an international court will be rejected by the
violating state.[48] Such lack of action by the aggrieved state
may be construed as acquiescence and give the state making
illegal claims a "historical right."

McDougal and Feliciano write:

> The overwhelming interest in basic order, and the exorbitant
> potential costs of exercise of force by contemporary weapons,
> would appear to counter-balance losses states may occasionally
> incur from lesser wrongs left inadequately redressed because of
> deficiencies in available remedial procedures or the limited

ability of a poorly organized community to create effective remedies for all wrongs.[49]

We fully grant the dangerousness of nuclear war. But what is "interest in basic order?" Is everything but use of military force "lesser wrongs or merely tortious conduct?" Such a nonchalant attitude, we believe, cannot be upheld indefinitely. "Even under the most primitive legal order," Kelsen states,[50] "murder was not the only crime." The failure of collective security has led to old-fashioned alliances, leading possibly to old-fashioned war. Is it not to be feared that the complete lack of individual and collective sanctions to enforce international law in general may lead back to the old-fashoned, unorganized sanctions exercised by individual states by way of self-help?

VII

That the collective security system of the United Nations at this time does not work is shown by the fact that the United Nations has, up to now, applied neither non-military nor military sanctions; for the armed action in Korea was not, in a strict legal sense, an enforcement action by the United Nations; it is also probable that this action will not constitute a precedent, but remain rather an isolated event. The creation of the United Nations Emergency Force was certainly successful, but equally certainly it does not constitute a United Nations peace-enforcing force. "Unfortunately, events have shown that the function of war has not yet been replaced by adequately efficiently legal procedures." [51] The peace, such as it is, is based at this time on the actual deadlock and stalemate of the thermonuclear and missiles armament race between the only two truly Great Powers. This armament race, the alliances, and counteralliances prove that everywhere the possibility of war is recognized. It cannot yet be said that the primary intention of the Charter "to save succeeding generations from the scourge of war" has been definitely achieved. The possibility of nuclear war hangs over the world like the sword of Damocles. There is always the possibility of war by miscalculation, by mistake, by the act of an all-powerful and ruthless dictator, by a radical change of the balance of terror in favor of the Soviet Union. We must also take into consideration the rise of the third Great Power, China, which, as Prime Minister Nehru said, does not show the same concern about war as the Soviet Union. Is it not amazing that a man like Prime Minister Nehru could state recently in the Indian Parliament that "if war comes between India and China, it will be a struggle for life and death that will shake the whole Continent of Asia and even the whole world?" History shows that alliances and counteralliances, an armament race, have a tendency to lead toward war. For us who have lived through this whole century and, at the beginning of it, in Europe, it is ominous to recall the split of Europe between the Triple Alliance and the Triple Entente, the naval armament race between Germany and Great Britain, the land armament race between Germany and France, the continuous series of crises, engendered by this split, in Morocco and in the Balkans, a split which finally led to World War I; and at the time, in contrast to the present situation which is somewhat analogous, only on a world-wide level and primarily between two powers, there existed no profound ideological split between the two potentially hostile camps. Naturally, history must not repeat itself; there is today the changed attitude toward war, the fear of much more powerful weapons.

The possibility of war remains; hence, the laws of war retain their importance and their revision is an urgent necessity, as it is more and more recognized. Just as the breakdown of collective security in the League of Nations led to a revival of neutrality, thus the non-functioning of collective security in the United Nations has led back toward the possibility and politics of neutrality. Section 232 of the U. S. Instructions, "Law of Naval Warfare," September, 1955, states: "If the Security Council is unable to fulfill its assigned functions, the members may, in case of war, remain neutral and observe an attitude of strict impartiality"; footnote 19 adds that "recommendations by the General Assembly do not constitute legal obligations" and that "in these circumstances neutrality and complete impartiality both remain distinct possibilities." Nothing is more significant in this respect than the admission of permantly neutral Austria as a member of the United Nations without any objection or any special status, such as was granted to Switzerland in the League of Nations.

After the failure of collective security in the League of Nations, the League considered itself a "non-coercive" League. Thus, today the United Nations itself plays down the emphasis on sanctions. It is also characteristic that present diplomatic activity is carried on, to a very great extent, outside the United Nations. The Secretary General himself [52] feels that the United Nations at this time cannot enforce the law on nations, great and small. He sees a particularly important, perhaps the principal, role of the United Nations as "an instrument for negotiations among, and, to some extent, for governments, as an instrument for concerting action by governments in support of the Charter," and emphasizes the role of "quiet diplomacy," so skillfully carried on by himself. This is, certainly, a United Nations very different from that designed at San Francisco.

This changed situation of the United Nations, the general deterioration of international law—its importance in the League of Nations, the nearly complete ignoring of it in U.N. proceedings [53]—the non-functioning of collective sanctions for the maintenance of peace, the absence of either collective or individual sanctions for the enforcement of international law in general, and, hence, the near non-enforceability of all international law, are of course, reflected in the literature. The neo-realists throw international law away and rely on "power"; the answer is that law has proved indispensable in the whole history of mankind. The other extreme is presented by those who demand a "world state"; at present this demand is Utopian. The adherents of the "realist school," whether American or Scandinvian, sometimes comes close to Niemeyer's "functional law without force." Thus, for instance, Foighel,[54] a disciple of Professor Alf Ross, writes that in consequence of the difficulty of enforcement, the main task of international law must be to prevent clashes between individual power units through exhortation, mediation, persuasion. McDougal and Feliciano state [55] that "the international situation has placed greater emphasis on the function of conciliation and mediation of the United Nations rather than on the coerive function." Even Professor Jessup [56] looks for excuses; he pleads at this time "for a modest objective for international law," for its application "within a selective community of like-minded states," insists on the "fallacy of the great issue test." But is not the maintenance of peace threatened by the non-like-minded states the greatest problem today? Shall international law remain condemned by Judge Lauterpacht's dictum: *De maximis non curat praetor?*

An adherent of the American realist school, Professor McDougal, for whom international law is a dynamic, global process of authoritative decisions, and who, always writing as a politician of law, wants to reconstruct the whole existing international law, believes that "reciprocal patterns of assertions and defense produce a quality of stability that is often sufficient to warrant classification of law." He takes a stand [57] against the primacy of international law, defended by this writer. His ardent follower, Professor Falk,[58] calls present-day international law a "horizontal legal order," an "order between equal centers of authority." He states that the aspects of such horizontal legal order are self-imposed restraint reciprocally exercised, restraint imposed by circumstances, such as insufficiency of power, and adds to that "more formalized horizontal procedures, such as international organizations and agreements." He would at this time "not invest" in the expansion of judicial settlement; he expects more from state than from international organization to state relations. It is correct that states, while no longer the only subjects of international law, are still by far the most important ones. But what he calls a "horizontal" legal order is only another word for old-fashioned formulas that, whereas an advanced municipal law is "a law of subordination," "ein Herrschaftsrecht," actual international law is "a law of co-ordination," a "law *inter pares,*" "ein genossenschaftliches Recht." All these formulas mean no more than that present-day international law, including the law of the United Nations, is still a primitive, highly decentralized legal order in which centralized organs are mostly lacking. But even a "horizontal" law is necessarily *above* the *pares;* otherwise it could not be called law. This necessary supra-ordination of law above those who are bound by the law, even if they are the makers of the law, is all that the primacy of international law means. This latter construction in no way means that statutes enacted by states in contradiction to international law are automatically void; it says nothing about the division of competences between international law and the legal orders of the states; it says nothing as to whether individuals are directly bound by rules of international law. All these are problems of content which can only be answered by analysis of the international law actually in force. But the primacy of international law does mean that international law, although to a great extent created by states, is legally binding upon, and therefore necessarily *above*, the states; in the sense, every legal order is "vertical." Professor McDougal affirms "that the international community has achieved a distribution between permissible and nonpermissible coercion"; *if* he is right, then the corresponding rule of international law must be legally binding, and hence *above* the states, although its enforcement may show all the disadvantages of a primitive legal order.

Rules of an international treaty, negotiated between states as equals and based on their consent, are just as much *above* the contracting parties as a statute of Congress is above those subject to these rules. There is, in this sense, no difference between treaties and contracts. Advanced municipal law also knows "private law-making." A contract is made between equals, between "equal centers of legal authority"; but the rules created by contract are legally binding upon the parties and constitute, in the language of the Code Napoléon, "la loi entre les parties." Contracts as well as treaties can never be based merely on consent. Both contracts as well as treaties have their reason of validity in a superior rule of law which stipulates that, under certain legal conditions, the rules created by contract or treaty be legally binding upon the parties; the rules created are necessarily *above* the parties; their breach constitutes a delict and subjects the parties to the sanctions stipulated by law. But whereas conflicts arising out of contracts can be peacefully settled by courts and sanctions can be executed by central organs, there is uncertainty and often impossibility of judicial settlement in international law; that is nothing else but the difference between an advanced and a primitive legal order. Professor Falk is right when he says that Austin's conception of law, restricted exclusively to advanced municipal legal orders, is unacceptable for international law; primitive law is law, too; but there is still a difference between a legal order, however primitive, and a normative order, which does not constitute law at all.

That even a primitive law must have sanctions was recently nicely affirmed by the immediate reaction, not of writers, but of statesmen, on the occasion of the proposal by the prime minister of the Soviet Union of "total disarmament" without international sanctions. Secretary of State Christian A. Herter immediately criticized the lack of sanctions for maintaining international peace and security; for even totally disarmed nations may fight with arrows or their fists; and Ambassador Henry Cabot Lodge stated at the United Nations: "If all nations lay down their arms, there must be institutions to preserve the peace and security and promote the Rule of Law." [59]

VIII

This study is written from a strictly legal, not a political, point of view. The analysis of the corresponding norms of the United Nations and of their application leads to the conclusion that, at the present time, almost the totality of international law is unenforceable. That shows that international law is even today a very primitive legal order. But this result does not necessarily imply a gloomy picture. If it could be said today as a matter of law that the rules of section VII of the Charter are no longer valid, then general international law with its primitive sanctions would take their place. But such statement, as a matter of law, cannot yet be made. Somewhat over ten years is, after all, a short time in the life of such an institution; it can only be stated that the norms of section VII are momentarily suspended in their validity; but they may very well come again into full force. There are other hopeful signs, both legal and extra-legal.

In contrast to the League of Nations, when, after the breakdown of collective security, a mass withdrawal of members started and the League became more and more powerless and finally disappeared, the prestige of the United Nations remains strong; it has expanded so as to embrace today nearly all sovereign states, and each new state immediately applies for admission. This shows that the United Nations continues to be an institution of the highest importance, not only in the many fields of international co-operation, but also with regard to its main task of maintaining international peace and security; even here the United Nations can still do much, and remains indispensable.

There is the ever-growing number of international and even supranational organizations which, although they have not yet changed the basic structure of the international community, may contain the germs of such change. The expansion of international organizations is not a mere fashion, but corresponds to genuine necessities; it shows the growing recognition by states of whatever ideology and type of government that there are many vital tasks which can no longer be performed by a state alone. All that may make the states gradually more willing to transfer authority to international and even supranational organizations.

There is, further, in the field of international peace, and security, not only the deep longing of all the peoples for peace, but, what is more important, a fear of a new global atomic war among all the governments. This strong concern is shared by the two leading Great Powers. It is extremely significant that the Catholic Church has changed the ancient doctrine of *bellum justum*. Whereas just war was a sanction against a delict, it has been stated by Pope Pius XII that modern weapons have revealed the immorality of any aggressive war, and the doctrine of *bellum justum* can, henceforth, be applied only to a war in self-defense.[60] There is the recent treaty on Antarctica [61] which may constitute a precedent for international controls of outer space.[62]

Present-day international law is still far away from an advanced international legal order; whether it is, as Jenks believes, the "common law of mankind" in an early, imperfect, and precarious stage of its development cannot yet be determined with scientific authority. In the present difficult international situation it is necessary to "muddle through" by all kinds of devices to prevent a third world war. But the goal—and here, we believe, Professors Mc-Dougal and Falk agree—cannot be a "law without force," but an effective international legal order, and that means also enforceable sanctions.

It is not possible here to treat fully the problem of sanctions, which is a fundamental problem of jurisprudence. Only to avoid misunderstandings and unjustified attacks, especially by adherents of different types of "natural law," a few remarks will be made. Legal positivism by no means teaches that law relies only on force; it fully recognizes the fundamental importance of voluntary obedience to the law; in fact the more effective a legal order is the less necessity there is to execute sanctions; sanctions have, it is true, to be applied by physical force but only if necessary. Legal positivism fully recognizes that there are higher values than law; it fully endorses the postulate that the contents of a positive law should correspond to the values of justice. It is not claimed, on the other hand, that even the most advanced municipal legal orders can ever give absolute and full security, for perfection does not belong to this earth. It is fully acknowledged that there are norms without sanctions also in municipal law, and that sanctions cannot be, or are not always, applied.

The importance of self-restraint, of bona fides, the necessity and opportunity of settlements out of court, by negotiation, renunciation, persuasion, and so on, is of the greatest importance also in advanced municipal legal orders. Even in such legal orders situations may arise where the monopoly of force breaks down, and military force also becomes legally decisive, as every revolution and civil war shows; we note the similarity of situations arising under modern labor law with international conflict situations.

But legal positivism does state that legal norms must have validity, that they are prescriptions; that the character of being legally binding means that conduct contrary to that prescribed by the norm is put under a sanction that shall be executed, by physical force if necessary. A condition of the validity of legal norms is that they are, in general, by and large effective. A legal norm must contain a sanction; already the Romans, the greatest jurists of all times, stated that an obligation under the condition, "if you want to fulfil it," *non est obligatio*. But the sanction must also be, where it should be applied, by and large effective. Mere paper rules are not rules of law. All this is true of primitive as well as of advanced legal orders.

The goal for a better international law cannot be a "law without force," but a law with less primitive sanctions. Whereas legal rules are prescriptions, are on the normative level, the *making* of the law belongs to the realm of facts. Hence, such progressive development of international law cannot be brought about merely by further treaties; for such treaties would again be dependent, in the last analysis, on the voluntary co-operation of the contracting parties. Such development can only be brought about by political action, changing the actual sociological conditions on which the present international community is based. In this sense Charles de Visscher has written that the progress of international organization depends on a change of the actual individualistic distribution of power. A more advanced international law must be based on the full recognition by states of the primacy of international law and on enforceable sanctions both for the maintenance of peace and security and for the enforcement of international law in general by organs of the international community. In this sense, M. Henri Spaak, Secretary General of NATO, wrote:

> . . . International organizations will only become fully effective, when it is understood that *over* and *above* the will of a nation there exists an international law, deriving its *sanctions* from the majority and to which all countries, large and small, must submit.[63]

Professor Jennings stated:

> The only mechanism by which a viable international society of states can be created is through effective submission to a developing international law, the sovereignties must recognize its supremacy.[64]

And Sir Hersh Lauterpacht holds: "It is only under the shelter and through such general organization, endowed with *overriding* and *coercive* power for creating, ascertaining and *enforcing* the law, that international law can overcome its present imperfection." [65]

---

[1] Even in the Soviet Union, Marxist prophecies of living together without law and state have now been relegated *ad calendas Graecas*.

[2] HANS KELSEN, GENERAL THEORY OF LAW AND STATE (1945); THE LAW OF THE UNITED NATIONS (1950); COLLECTIVE SECURITY (1957).

[3] Political measures against a state not guilty of an international delinquency may be legal or illegal; but they do not constitute sanctions. A delict is a violation of a legally binding norm; one cannot speak of a sanction against a non-acceptance of the proposals of a mediator or conciliator, of the report of an international commission of inquiry, against the non-fulfillment of a normal, legally-not-binding recommendation of an organ of an international organization. Professor McDougal writes that "the thin line between recommendations, sustained by effective power, and prescriptions becomes continuously

thinner."—4 S.D.L.REV. 41 (1959). This is, of course, a political, not a legal, statement.

4 Eternal condemnation is a religious sanction; but excommunication is a legal sanction, for canon law is a legal order.

5 Hence world public opinion, so often rhetorically invoked, is not a legal sanction. Apart from the fact that often no such opinion exists, or that, at this time, two contrary opinions exist, it is mere disapproval, i.e., a moral, not a legal sanction. For the same reason the Stimson doctrine of non-recognition, although it may have important moral and political value, is not a legal sanction. It may remain without any effect. It is rather, as has been stated, an attitude which *needs* a sanction.

6 "Whatever else legal philosophers have said about law, they have, with rare exceptions, agreed . . . that it is enforced by physical sanctions."—Jerome Hall in 7 BUFFALO L. REV. 384 (1958). "Enforceability is a necessary characteristic of any system of law."—Sir Gerald Fitzmaurice in 19 MODERN L.REV. 1 (1958). In the same sense modern adherents of Catholic natural law; See Jean Dabin on the indispensability of "la contrainte" in THÉORIE GÉNÉRALE DU DROIT 36 (2nd ed. 1953).

7 This state of facts is basic for the Latin American battle against "intervention."

8 The right to go to war or use military force could be restricted only by treaty norms; see, e.g., the Drago-Porter Convention of 1907.

9 The Catholic doctrine of *bellum justum* wanted to make war either a sanction or a delict. It did not aim at abolishing war; to the contrary, it insisted on the necessity of war as a sanction, as long as the international community remained primitive, highly decentralized, and without a superior. But the just war can only be a sanction against a violation of a rule of positive or natural law ("Unica est et sola causa justa inferendi bellum injuria accepta."—Victoria). But the *bellum justum* doctrine was never positive international law; and even if it had been, it would have faced the same difficulties of application as arose under general international law: the prince, even having a very just cause of war, could hardly go to war against a more powerful state; and the "justice" of the war was always self-determined; hence Gentili's doctrine of the "bellum justum ex utraque parte"— and we are back at the free *jus ad bellum* of general international law.

10 WALTER SCHIFFER, THE LEGAL COMMUNITY OF MANKIND (1954).

11 See "The Idea of Collective Security in Pan-American Developments," below.

12 Latin American writers are right if they call Simón Bolívar the forerunner of Woodrow Wilson and of the League of Nations; but to set the historical record straight, it must be added that Bolivar was also the follower of Abbé de St. Pierre.

13 See "Bellum justum and bellum legale," above.

14 Foreign Policy Association, New York, 1932: "Are Sanctions Necessary for International Organization?" Raymond L. Buell: Yes; John Dewey: No.

[15] GERHART NIEMEYER, LAW WITHOUT FORCE (1941).

[16] Saar Territory 1920–35; the possible administration of trusteeship territories by the United Nations itself (Article LXXXI of the U.N. Charter).

[17] Suspension from the rights and privileges of membership (art. V), expulsion (art. VI), suspension from the right of voting in the General Assembly (art. XIX), for nonregistration of treaties (art. CII).

[18] This corresponds, by analogy, to the attempts to eliminate private war in medieval Europe, to the *Constitutio Moguntina* of 1250; only after the full centralization of the legal order could Emperor Maximilian I in 1495 effectively prohibit private war and make it a crime.

[19] For the relation between Article XCIV, para. 2, and Article XXXIX, see EDUARDO JIMÉNEZ DE ARÉCHAGA, DERECHO CONSTITUCIONAL DE LAS NACIONES UNIDAS 555–60 (1958). See also the paper by Oscar Schachter, *The Enforcement of Arbitral and Judicial Decisions against States*, PROCEEDING, Second Summer Conference on International Law, Cornell Law School, 97–103 (1958); 54 AM.J. INT'L L. 1 (1960).

[20] GENERAL THEORY OF LAW AND STATE 278–79.

[21] See the excellent discussion on sanctions under general international law in A. VERDROSS and K. ZEMANEK, VÖLKERRECHT 343 (4th ed. 1959).

[22] Thus U. S. INSTRUCTIONS: LAW OF NAVAL WARFARE, September, 1955, Sec. 441, footnote 21.

[23] See "Individual and Collective Self-Defense in Article LI of the Charter of the United Nations," above.

[24] D. W. BOWETT, SELF-DEFENSE IN INTERNATIONAL LAW (1958).

[25] E.g., Kelsen; Verdross; Jessup, A MODERN LAW OF NATIONS 166–67.

[26] For a full discussion see JIMÉNEZ DE ARÉCHAGA, *op. cit.* at 399–407.

[27] *Ibid.* at 390.

[28] *Ibid.* at 195.

[29] See "The Inter-American Treaty of Reciprocal Assistance," below.

[30] CHARLES DE VISSCHER, THÉORIES ET RÉALITÉS EN DROIT INTERNATIONAL PUBLIC (1953).

[31] *Op. cit.* at 197–209.

[32] First in his study, *The Charter of the United Nations and General International Law*, in LIPSKY (ed.), LAW AND POLITICS IN THE WORLD COMMUNITY 154–61 (1953).

[33] *Op. cit.* at 75–94.

[34] Thus McDougal and Feliciano, *Legal Regulation of Resort to International Coercion: Aggression and Self-Defense in Policy Perspective*," 68 YALE L.J. 1059–1165 (1959).

[35] 41 DEP'T STATE BULL. 467–75 at 467 (1959).

36 BLOOMFIELD, EVOLUTION OR REVOLUTION? THE UNITED NATIONS AND THE PROBLEM OF PEACEFUL TERRITORIAL CHANGE (1957).

37 Some writers do not see that the system of collective security of the U.N. (or the Organization of American States) is only a system for enforcing peace, but not for the enforcement of international law in general. Thus, e.g., THOMAS & THOMAS, NON-INTERVENTION (1956). But see A. J. Thomas, *Non-Intervention and Public Order in the Americas*, AM.SOC'Y INT'L L.PROC. 72–77 (1959).

38 *The Regulation of the Use of Force by Individual States in International Law*, 81 RECUEIL DES COURS No. 2 at 455–517 (1952).

39 JULIUS STONE, AGGRESSION AND WORLD ORDER (1958).

40 Thus, e.g., Kelsen, Verdross; refutation of Stone's interpretation by McDougal and Feliciano (*loc. cit., supra,* note 34); strongly, in the same sense, the Latin American (Jiménez de Aréchaga), Arab (Nasim Hasan Shah, *Discovery by Intervention*, 53 AM.J.INT'L L. 595–612 (1959), and Soviet (K. Skubiszewski, *The Postwar Alliances of Poland and the United Nations Charter, ibid.* at 613–34 writers.

41 A. ALVAREZ, LE DROIT INTERNATIONAL NOUVEAU (1959).

42 *Loc. cit. supra,* note 6.

43 Georges Scelle, *Quelques Réflexions sur l'Abolition de la Compétence de la Guerre,* 58 REVUE GÉNÉRALE DE DROIT INTERNATIONAL PUBLIC 1 (1954).

44 Emile Giraud, ANNUAIRE DE L'INSTITUT DE DROIT INTERNATIONAL No. 1 at 271–72, 277 (1957).

45 Very similar are the statements by the rapporteur, C. Wilfred Jenks, *ibid.* at 167–68.

46 *Ibid.* at 302.

47 I. C. McGibbon, *Some Observations on the Part of Protest in International Law,* 30 BRIT.YB.INT'L L. 293–310 (1953); idem, *The Scope of Acquiescence in International Law,* 31 *ibid.* at 143–86 (1954).

48 Josef L. Kunz, *Continental Shelf and International Law: Confusion and Abuse,* 50 AM.J.INT'L L. 828–53 (1956).

49 *Op. cit.* at 1124–25, footnote 193.

50 COLLECTIVE SECURITY 10.

51 MORRIS GREENSPAN, THE MODERN LAW OF LAND WARFARE vii (1959).

52 See "The Secretary General on the Role of the United Nations," above.

53 See "The United Nations and the Rule of Law," above.

54 ISI FOIGHEL, NATIONALIZATION (1957).

55 *Op. cit.* at 1123 n. 192.

56 PHILIP C. JESSUP, THE USE OF INTERNATIONAL LAW.

57 Myres S. McDougal, *The Impact of International Law upon National Law: A Policy Inspired Perspective,* 4 S.D.L.REV. 25–92 (1959).

58 R. A. Falk, *International Jurisdiction: Horizontal and Vertical Conceptions of Legal Order,* 32 TEMP.L.Q. 295–320 (1959).

[59] N.Y. Times, September 15, 1959, p. 47.

[60] See Verdross and Zemanek, *op. cit.* note 21 above, at 356.

[61] 41 DEP'T STATE BULL. 912 (1959); reprinted in 54 AM.J.INT'L L. 477 (1961).

[62] PHILIP C. JESSUP and HOWARD J. TAUBENFELD, CONTROLS FOR OUTER SPACE AND THE ANTARCTIC ANALOGY (1959).

[63] Henri Spaak, *Problems Facing the West,* 107 VA. L. REV. 1085–97 1095 (1959), Emphasis added by this writer.

[64] R. Y. Jennings, *The Progress of International Law,* 34 BRIT. YB. INT'L L. 334–55, at 355 (1958).

[65] 1 OPPENHEIM-LAUTERPACHT, INTERNATIONAL LAW 370 (8th ed. 1955). Emphasis added.

PART VI

PAN-AMERICA

I

WHILE INTERNATIONAL ARBITRATION is an ancient institution, its modern development dates from the Jay Treaty of 1794. This treaty, the *Alabama Arbitration* (1872), the Hague Peace Conferences of 1899 and 1907, and the establishment of the Permanent Court of International Justice at The Hague, are the outstanding points in the development of the last one hundred fifty years.[1]

The importance of the United States in the recent history of international arbitration is shown by the events of 1794 and 1872. International arbitration has had a long record in this country in practice and in theory.[2] International arbitration has played an equally prominent role in Latin America: many boundary disputes [3] were arbitrated and a great number of arbitration treaties were signed by American nations *inter se* and with extra-continental states.[4] Latin-American writers have also been greatly interested in this subject.[5] While the idea of some defenders of an "American International Law," [6] claiming international arbitration as a characteristic feature of international practice in this hemisphere, cannot be upheld, it is true that international arbitration has occupied a prominent place in the Americas. It is, therefore, pertinent to investigate the role of international arbitration in Pan-American developments.

After a glance at the role of international arbitration in the first Pan-Americanism—that of Simon Bolivar—the historical development of international arbitration in the present Pan-Americanism will be reviewed by periods as a basis for understanding the recent problems involved in relating arbitration to other modes of pacific settlement and in integrating within a single instrument the Pan-American peace system, as now has been done at the ninth International Conference of American States, held in 1948 at Bogota.

II

The first Pan-Americanism, restricted to Spanish-America and inspired by the ideas of Simon Bolivar, gave much attention to international arbitration. Although by no means all the Spanish-American republics participated at the different conferences of this period and although none of the corresponding conventions were ratified, these conventions are interesting for the ideas expressed in them.

The Treaty of Union, League and Perpetual Federation of the Panama Congress (1826) [7] in Article XVI would have obliged the parties to bring their disputes, in case of failure of settlement by direct negotiations, before the Assembly. No special judicial organ was created; the Assembly was also to function as a court. But the Assembly had no compulsory jurisdiction; its power to give a binding judgment depended on the express agreement of the parties that the decision should be binding. Arbitration was, therefore, to be voluntary, with jurisdiction based on the consent of the parties. The Mexican opposition in 1826 had eliminated the important function of the Assembly—

a function insisted upon by Bolivar and laid down in the bilateral Bolivarian treaties of 1822 and 1823—to act as an arbitral judge with compulsory jurisdiction. Then, as now, national sovereignty rebelled against compulsory arbitration.

Of the later congresses,[8] the Treaty of Confederation of Lima of February 8, 1848, took the most advanced position. It established a series of successive amicable procedures— thus linking arbitration with pre-arbitral procedures of peaceful settlement—arriving, in the last resort, at a duty of obligatory arbitration, although not a compulsory juris- diction by a pre-established court. The parties were free to submit the dispute to an arbiter of their choice; but if they could not agree the congress was to give a binding decision. Obligatory arbitration, on the basis of a multipartite treaty, here makes its first appearance. But this obligatory arbitra- tion is not a judicial settlement; the congress was to give a binding decision which, in its opinion, would be the most just. The congress was not to be restricted to the applica- tion of positive international law; it could act as a judge, but it could also act as an amiable compositeur, or as a legislator. Its decision was not to be based on law, but on justice; yet this decision was to be binding upon the parties without special agreement or consent on their part. The advance toward obligatory arbitration is here marred by a confusion between international judicial settlement and the very different procedure of international legislation.

In the Continental Treaty of 1856, the idea of sovereignty forced a retreat from the advanced position of the Lima Treaty of 1848. But the Lima Treaty on the Preservation of Peace of 1865 would again have obliged the conflicting parties to resort to obligatory arbitration if they could not settle the conflict by other peaceful means. Contrary to the Lima Treaty of 1848, the Lima Treaty of 1865 provided obligatory arbitration, not by the congress, but by an arbiter, to be designated by an ordinary or extraordinary meeting of the congress. Again contrary to the Lima Treaty of 1848, the binding and unappealable award was not to be a decision on the basis of justice but a true judicial decision on the basis of international law.

III

The present Pan-Americanism,[9] brought into being by the United States, has in the fifty-eight years of its existence passed through different stages of development. During the period from 1890 to 1923, Pan-Americanism was conceived as a system of "practical," non-political co-operation, contrary to the highly political nature of a confederation and of a system of "collective security" of Bolivar's ideas. But international arbitration [10] played a role from the beginning.

The Act of the United States Congress of 1888 [11] put on the program of the first Pan-American conference: "An agreement upon and recommendation for adoption to their respective Governments of a definite plan of arbitration of all questions, disputes, and differences, that may now or hereafter exist between them, to the end that all difficulties and disputes between such Nations may be peaceably settled and wars prevented." [12]

The discussion of this point at the Washington Conference of 1889-90 showed Argentina, Brazil, the United States, Peru, Columbia, Guatemala, Honduras, and Paraguay in favor of this proposal; Mexico raised objections; Chile was strongly opposed. The outcome of the Conference was a "Plan of Arbitration." [13] Arbitration was adopted as a "principle of American international law" (Article I) and the plan foresaw general and obligatory international arbitration. General: for all controversies whatever may be their origin, nature, or object (Article III), whether pending or hereafter arising, even though they may have originated in occurrences antedating the present treaty (Article V) ; only questions were excepted which, in the judgment of any one of the nations involved in the controversy, may imperil its independence (Article IV) ; further questions were excluded in which a definite agreement had already been reached (Article VI). Obligatory, but not compulsory, arbitration: there is no right for a party to bring the dispute unilaterally before an international court, but merely an obligation to conclude a "compromis" for the concrete case; in every case an *ad hoc* tribunal must be created. The Plan of Arbitration is not a treaty, not even a draft treaty subject to ratification, but merely a model of a multipartite arbitration treaty. Compared with contemporary European arbitration treaties, it shows at many points a progressive tendency: all controversies are included; no distinction is made between legal and political, between justiciable and non-justiciable, disputes; no European clause excluding "les intérêts vitaux, l'indépendance ou l'honneur" but only the exception of independence.[14] But there is no right of unilateral action, no preconstituted court, and no rules of procedure are laid down; finally, the decision as to whether the exception of independence applies is left to the unfettered discretion of any party. The strong opposition of Chile, in 1890 and later, was motivated by her conquests in the Pacific War and the pending Tacna-Arica dispute with Bolivia and Peru.

International arbitration was also prominent on the agenda of the Second Conference held at Mexico City in 1901-02. General obligatory arbitration—"el arbitraje amplio"—was primarily defended by Argentina.[15] Argentina stood for arbitration without restrictions and exceptions,[16] and quoted her arbitration treaties with Italy of June 23, 1898, with Uruguay of June 8, 1899, and with Paraguay of November 6, 1899. The "Argentina formula" embraced all controversies of whatever nature [17] with one,

typically Argentine, exception that the controversies do not
affect the norms of the constitution of the one or the other
country.[18] Argentina contrasted voluntary arbitration as
typically European with general, obligatory arbitration as
characteristically American; she condemned voluntary arbitration as useless and opposed the distinction between
pending and future conflicts.

Chile was, of course, adamant against obligatory arbitration and the inclusion of pre-existing conflicts. But the
United States had shifted from obligatory arbitration, defended in 1890, to optional arbitration. In consequence, the
Commission on Arbitration of the Conference could reach
no agreement and merely a protocol on adherence to the
Convention of The Hague (1899) was adopted.[19] Progress
was made with regard to a particular matter in the Treaty
of Arbitration on Pecuniary Claims.[20] A Treaty on Compulsory Arbitration [21] was signed by ten delegations and
ratified by the Dominican Republic, Guatemala, Mexico,
Peru, San Salvador, and Uruguay.[22] This treaty follows
the Hague Convention of 1899 in many details; it admits
the exceptions of independence and national honor.

The third Pan-American Conference, held at Rio de
Janeiro in 1906, reached no solution of the arbitration problem. Only a resolution on arbitration [23] was adopted and
all the Latin-American republics invited to the second
Hague Peace Conference. At the fourth Pan-American
Conference, held at Buenos Aires in 1910, arbitration had
completely disappeared from the agenda.

But at least regionally progress was achieved. The Central American Peace Conference of 1907 [24] produced also
the Convention of a Central-American Court of Justice.
This Court,[25] which existed from 1908 to 1918 and gave a
number of decisions,[26] had jurisdiction in inter–Central–
American disputes and in disputes between states and private individuals. In this respect this Court, although

otherwise not of great and lasting importance, was unique; at the same time it was the first pre-established international court in the history of the law of nations. Unfortunately, the Court came to an end in 1918. Later efforts were unsuccessful. The convention for the establishment of an International Central-American Court [27] of 1923 was, from all points of view, a step backward. It embraced, it is true, all differences, present and future, but it introduced the exceptions of "sovereignty or independent existence"; it did not foresee a permanent pre-constituted court, but merely a permanent list, a panel of thirty jurists; it would have established the necessity of a "compromis" in each concrete case. Even this proposal never came into force.

IV

The net result of Pan-American efforts from 1899 to 1910 was, therefore, not great. The problem of permanent, general, obligatory arbitration found no solution; the very subject was discarded in the later conferences. Pan-America did not give leadership but followed European leadership as given by the Hague Peace Conferences.

The period of 1922-33 was a period of crisis for Pan-Americanism which reached an all-time low ebb at Havana in 1928. Inspiration came again from Europe, from the League of Nations. In keeping with the Covenant, pre-arbitral measures came into the foreground, as shown by the Gondra Treaty of 1923. The fifth Pan-American Conference, held at Santiago in 1923, recognized the impossibility of solving the arbitration problem and restricted itself to the adoption of a harmless resolution.[28] But during the negotiations, arbitration played an important role. Whereas Chile continued in her habitual attitude, Argentina stood strongly in her proposal [29] for "broad arbitration," according to the "Argentina formula." Argentina was backed by

Uruguay and a number of smaller Latin-American republics; Colombia was equally in favor, but objected against the exception of constitutional questions as being too vague; but, in general, the Argentinian proposal was defeated.

Under the impact of the League of Nations and the Permanent Court of International Justice, proposals for an American League of Nations and for an American Court of International Justice began to appear; e.g., Costa Rica's proposal of 1923,[30] many features of which are borrowed from the Statute of the Permanent Court of International Justice. The proposal was forwarded for study to the International Commission of American Jurists. This Commission proposed at its meeting at Rio de Janeiro in 1927 the Draft Treaty No. XII [31] on peaceful settlement, containing only voluntary arbitration.

The sixth Pan-American Conference, held at Havana in 1928, was for the most part dominated by heated discussions on intervention. The problem of an Inter-American Court of Justice,[32] defended by Costa Rica in 1923, reappeared through a Colombian proposal, drafted by Professor Yepes.[33] In the second commission of the Conference, again no agreement on arbitration could be achieved. But sensing that a solution of this problem which had occupied Pan-America since 1899 could no longer be delayed, the Conference adopted a resolution [34] stating that "the American Republics adopt obligatory arbitration . . . for the pacific solution of their international differences of a juridical character" and convoking within one year a special conference at Washington which should adopt a convention on obligatory arbitration "with the minimum exceptions . . . indispensable to safeguard the independence and sovereignty of the States, as well as matters of domestic concern, and to the exclusion also of matters involving the interest or referring to the action of a State not a party to the Convention."

V

The special International Conference of American States on Conciliation and Arbitration,[35] held in Washington from December 10, 1928, to January 5, 1929, produced the two principal Pan-American instruments on arbitration: the General Treaty of Inter-American Arbitration [36] and the Protocol of Progressive Arbitration.[37] It is extremely significant that Argentina was not represented at this conference. The treaty is one of obligatory arbitration of "all differences of an international character which have arisen or may arise between them by virtue of a claim of right . . . under treaty or otherwise, which it has not been possible to adjust by diplomacy and which are juridical in their nature by reason of being susceptible of decision by the application of the principles of law" (Article I). The only exceptions are "controversies within the domestic jurisdiction of the parties and which are not controlled by international law" and those "which affect the interest or refer to the action of a State not a party to this treaty" (Article II). But Article VIII admits further individual reservations. Such reservations have been made by twelve Latin-American republics. They are of different types: (1) matters which according to the constitution or laws are under the jurisdiction of domestic courts, except in the case of denial of justice (Bolivia, Chile, Colombia, Costa Rica, Dominican Republic, Ecuador, Mexico, San Salvador, Uruguay, Venezuela); (2) matters controlled by international agreements now in force (Ecuador, Guatemala, Venezuela), or settled by arbitral awards (Costa Rica); (3) restriction to subsequent disputes and not having their origin in causes antedating the treaty (Bolivia, Chile, Colombia, Ecuador, Honduras, San Salvador); (4) Bolivia made the reservation that in territorial disputes the zone must be previously determined in the arbitral agreement, whereas Paraguay excluded from arbitration "questions directly or indirectly affecting the integrity of the national territory and not being merely questions of frontier;" these reservations were, of course, formulated with the pending Chaco conflict in view; (5) Guatemala reserved for boundary conflicts the approval of the legislative assembly; (6) San Salvador excluded controversies concerning questions which, according to its constitution, must not be submitted to arbitration. Article IV of the treaty contemplates a "compromis" in every concrete case.

Under the Protocol of Progressive Arbitration, any party to the General Arbitration Treaty may at any time deposit an instrument evidencing "that it has abandoned in whole or in part the exceptions stipulated in the treaty or the reservation or reservations attached by it thereto."

It is clear that this treaty is practically no more than a treaty of voluntary arbitration. It must be added that, notwithstanding many controversies which have arisen, the treaty has, up to now, not yet been applied a single time.

VI

The treaty and the Protocol have remained the only two Pan-American instruments on arbitration. No progress was made in this respect during the new period of "good neighbor policy," starting in 1933. The seventh Pan-American Conference, held at Montevideo in 1933, and otherwise very successful, did not even put the problem of arbitration on its agenda. The first commission, dealing with the "Organization of Peace," produced only a resolution [38] in favor of securing prompt ratification of the Arbitration Treaty of 1929. Also a Resolution on Commercial Arbitration [39] was passed. But San Salvador proposed the creation of an American Court of Justice and Mexico proposed an elaborate "Peace Code:" [40] Articles XXV-LIV deal with international arbitration; Articles LV-CII contain the proposal of an American Court of International Justice. Original is the idea that the Court should consist of one member of each American republic (Article LV), plus a Canadian judge (Article LVI), although its jurisdiction would extend only to disputes between the American republics (Article LXXI); original also is the proposal that by ballot one-half of the judges should form the Tribunal of the First Instance, the other half the Tribunal of Appeal (Article LI). The Conference resolved merely to submit the "Peace Code" to the consideration of the governments.[41]

At the special conference, held at Buenos Aires in 1936, the "Organization of Peace" was the first topic on the program. Guatemala and Uruguay proposed the creation of an Inter-American court. Chile presented a memorandum on obligatory arbitration, without regard as to whether the controversy is juridical or of another nature, but excepted problems of domestic jurisdiction, controversies with states not parties to the convention, controversies under the jurisdiction of domestic courts except in case of denial of justice, controversies already settled by treaties or decisions, and controversies arising out of facts antedating the treaty. Saavedra Lamas for Argentina submitted a draft treaty for the revision of the Arbitration Treaty of 1929 to provide for submission of all differences, not merely juridical ones; no general reservations, and only special reservations of certain categories permitted: namely, questions definitely settled by treaty or judicial decision; questions to be settled by agreement of the parties through another peaceful procedure; problems within the domestic jurisdiction of a party; constitutional questions; controversies affecting the interest or referring to the action of a state not a party to the treaty.

But the Conference, submerged in problems of neutrality and consultation, had no time to consider these proposals; neither could it consider Mexico's revised Peace Code. It adopted resolutions concerning the ratification of the peace instruments [42] and concerning the generalization of the Inter-American juridical system.[43] It entrusted the study of all projects concerning an Inter-American Court of International Justice to the governing board of the Pan-American Union [44] and sent the Mexican Peace Code to the Committee of Experts for the Codification of International Law.[45] The result was postponement. If arbitration had dominated Pan-American conferences prior to 1914 and pre-arbitral measures from then until 1933, since 1936 the procedure of Inter-American consultation—a "pre-pre-arbitral procedure," if one can say so—has held the center of the stage.

The eighth conference, Lima 1938, had the report of the governing board concerning an Inter-American Court of Justice [46] before it. To the Lima conference were submitted projects on arbitration by Venezuela,[47] Uruguay,[48] the report of the Committee of Experts, including the report of Dr. Afranio de Mello Franco,[49] and finally the memorandum on arbitration by Pedro M. Oliveira;[50] further, relating to the co-ordination of procedures of pacific settlement, a project by the United States,[51] the second version of the Mexican Peace Code,[52] and the report and version of the Peace Code by the Committee of Experts, with the report of Dr. Luis Anderson of Costa Rica.[53] The United States project repeated only the text of the Arbitration Treaty of 1929. The Lima conference again merely postponed a solution. Resolution XXV [54] dealt dilatorily with the Inter-American Court of Justice. The Declaration of American Principles [55] does not even mention arbitration specifically. Resolution XV[56] referred the Mexican Peace Code and all other projects submitted to the Pan-American Union for "classification," for transmission to the American governments, and for sending the projects with the opinions of the governments to the International Conference of American Jurists which should then present a detailed report to the ninth Pan American Conference at Bogota.

VII

The Meetings of Foreign Ministers in Panama (1939), Havana (1940), and Rio de Janeiro (1942) were fully occupied with the political, economic and military problems of World War II. The Havana meeting reiterated the necessity of the continuation of the studies for the improvement and co-ordination of Inter-American peace instruments,[57] but international arbitration was not discussed. But the Pan-American Union, in carrying out Resolution XV of the Lima Conference, published an excellent report, written by William Sanders.[58]

The Inter-American conference on problems of war and peace, held in Mexico City in 1945, adopted the Act of Chapultepec,[59] which lists among the American principles "the adoption of unrestricted arbitration or the application of international justice." Resolution IX [60] on the reorganization of the Inter-American system charged the governing board of the Pan-American Union with the preparation of a draft charter for the improvement and strengthening of the Inter-American system, which also "shall take into account the need of accelerating the consolidation and extension of existing Inter-American peace instruments and the simplification and improvement of the Inter-American peace structure," utilizing to this end the services of the Inter-American Juridical Committee.

Chile and Peru had jointly presented to the Mexico City conference a project on Co-ordination of Inter-American Peace Agreements. The conference submitted this project for study to the Pan-American Union.[61] Finally, Resolution XXXIX,[62] insisting on the necessity of co-ordinating the

peace agreements "into an organized and harmonious unified instrument" and calling the Lima Resolution XXV
"a categorical statement in favor of including an Inter-
American Court of International Justice, leaving for later
determination only the date on which that Court might be
established," charged the Inter-American Juridical Committee with the immediate preparation of a co-ordinating
draft of an "Inter-American Peace System." [63]

The special Inter-American Conference for the maintenance of continental peace and security, held in Rio de
Janeiro in 1947, adopted the Inter-American Treaty of
Reciprocal Assistance,[64] which reiterates in the preamble
that the American states propose to conclude a treaty on the
Inter-American Peace System envisaged in Resolutions IX
and XXXIX of the Mexico City Conference. Article II
obligates the American states to submit any controversy
between them to the methods of peaceful settlement. Resolution X of the final act[65] recommends that the Bogotá
Conference study with a view to approval institutions which
may give effectiveness to a pacific system of security and
among them "compulsory arbitration for any dispute which
may entangle peace and which is not of a juridical nature."
The Inter-American Juridical Committee submitted for the
consideration of the Bogotá Conference a "Definitive Project of Inter-American Peace System." [66] Before the results
of the Bogotá Conference of 1948 are considered, the developments prior thereto may be summarized and evaluated,
and the problems facing the Conference indicated.

VIII

International arbitration has thus occupied the present
Pan-Americanism from its beginning in 1889 to the present
day. But while the records of the Pan-American conferences are rich in interesting discussions and contain a

storehouse of information and ideas, not too much has been achieved in creating progressive positive law. Pan-America has not held the leadership, but has remained behind European developments in this field. Already prior to 1914, the Hague conventions dominated in Pan-American arbitration. Since 1920, Europe has achieved progress in international arbitration through bilateral treaties, such as the German-Swiss treaty of 1921 and the Swiss-Italian treaty of September 20, 1924, the League of Nations Covenant, the establishment of the Permanent Court of International Justice, the optional clause, the Locarno Pact, and the General Act of 1928.[67] The only multipartite Pan-American arbitration treaties, apart from the Treaty on Obligatory Arbitration of 1902, ratified only by six states,[68] are the Washington Arbitration Treaty of 1929 and the Protocol of 1929 on Progressive Arbitration. Critiques and reform proposals, mostly inspired by recent European developments, have centered around the Arbitration Treaty of 1929. The reform proposals moved in three directions: modification of or addition to existing treaties, conclusion of additional treaties, and co-ordination of all the procedures of peaceful settlement within a single and comprehensive, harmonious peace instrument.

As the American republics have undertaken to submit every controversy which may arise between them to methods of peaceful settlement [69] and as Resolutions IX and XXXIX of the Mexico City Conference of 1945 order the co-ordination in one instrument of the Inter-American Peace System, a major problem presented was the correlation of international arbitration with other types of peaceful settlement. Article I of the Arbitration Treaty of 1929 makes the obligation to arbitrate only dependent on the failure to adjust the differences by diplomacy. The Project of the Organic Pact of the Inter-American System [70] only enumerates in Articles V-IX the different procedures of peaceful settlement. But the Definitive Project of the Inter-American Peace System, submitted in 1947 by the Inter-American Juridical Committee [71] would make arbitration or juridical settlement obligatory if it has not been possible to settle the controversy by diplomatic means or by the procedures of mediation and investigation and conciliation (Article XVII). On the other hand, the maintenance of peace and security through the methods of consultation and self-defense, in accordance with the Rio de Janeiro Treaty of 1947, does not belong to the peaceful settlement of disputes, although Article VII gives the organ of consultation in Inter-American conflicts the duty to take all the necessary measures for the peaceful settlement of the conflict. Such co-ordination of arbitration within the Inter-American Peace System could serve at the same time the purpose of integrating this regional system within the peace machinery of the United Nations. For under Article II of the Rio de Janeiro Treaty of 1947, the American republics bind themselves to solve all conflicts *inter se* through the procedures in force in the Inter-American System before they refer them to the General Assembly or the Security Council of the United Nations. In the Pact of Bogotá it has been undertaken to solve the problem of integrating arbitration with other procedures and of relating the Inter-American System to the United Nations.[72]

One evidence of progress in arbitration was the development from "isolated" to "institutional" arbitration; in "isolated" arbitration an agreement to arbitrate is reached only after a conflict has arisen and is limited to this conflict, whereas in "institutional" arbitration a treaty to arbitrate all or certain conflicts which may arise is concluded. Pan-American arbitration is institutional. Institutional arbitration may be created by bilateral and by multipartite treaty (Arbitration Treaty of 1929).

But the difference between isolated and institutional arbitration has nothing to do with the other distinction between an *ad hoc* tribunal and a permanent tribunal. Only the Permanent Court of International Justice and its successor, the International Court of Justice, have been permanent and pre-established courts, with a bench of judges, and a pre-established procedure. Within Pan-America, only the Central American Court of Justice was permanent and pre-established. The Arbitration Treaty of 1929, and proposals by Uruguay in 1938, as well as the Mexican Peace Code contemplate *ad hoc* tribunals; Venezuela's proposal of 1938 makes the tribunal permanent in principle. The great advantage of a permanent and pre-established court makes the idea of permanence strong in discussions or proposals. Either a permanent tribunal or the creation of an Inter-American Court of Justice have been proposed by a number of republics since 1923. But, on the one hand, the American republics should be allowed to create *ad hoc* tribunals [73] and on the other hand, the proposals for the creation of an Inter-American Court of Justice, although strongly pressed by several smaller republics, have generally not aroused enthusiasm among the greater states. It is true that Resolution XXXIX of the Mexico City Conference (1945) interpreted Declaration XXV of the Lima Conference (1938) as "a categorical statement in favor of including an Inter-American Court of International Justice, leaving for later determination only the date on which that Court might be established." But neither the Project of an Organic Pact of the Inter-American System nor the Definitive Project of the Inter-American Juridical Committee mention the Inter-American Court. The Juridical Committee said in its report specifically that "no decision was reached with respect to the proposed Inter-American Court of International Justice." The creation of this court seemed, therefore, unlikely even before the Bogotá Conference failed to adopt the idea. Such court is also hardly desirable, all the more as the International Court of Justice, the president of which is at this time a Latin American, is available.

With regard to *ad hoc* tribunals, many problems have to be progressively solved: the administration, the financing, the election of judges, and their full impartiality. It is clear that the decision of the tribunal is binding upon the parties, definitive and without appeal. But norms as to the non-validity of decisions, because of fraud or *exces de pouvoir*, have been lacking until now in Pan-American instruments; also norms concerning the revision of the decision because of the discovery of an essential fact previously existing and unknown to the tribunal.[74] The problem of the execution of the decision arises also. The problem of the procedure of the tribunal is now left to the *compromis*.

But the greatest problems are those of jurisdiction and of the organization of the tribunal, as well as of the applicable law. In this respect it seems to this writer that some grave theoretical errors have crept into the Pan-American proposals.

It seems that these errors, at least in part, stem from the fact that after the establishment of the Permanent Court of International Justice, a distinction has been made between "arbitration" and "judicial settlement." One may, if one wishes to do so, make this distinction, but only in the following sense: In case of arbitration the parties create an *ad hoc* tribunal and may determine the rules of procedure; we speak of "arbitrators," of an "arbitration tribunal," which renders an "award." In case of judicial settlement, there is a pre-established court, with a pre-constituted bench of judges, and a pre-established procedural law; we speak of a "court," of "judges," and of their "judgment." But this difference is wholly one of machinery, of organization, of composition of the tribunal; it is only a technical difference in degree, not a basic difference in kind. The "international court" is a more perfect way of achieving international arbitration; it is the goal to which the development of international arbitration tends. But it is one and the same procedure of settling international conflicts peacefully. An "arbitration tribunal" may have obligatory jurisdiction; on the other hand, even the Permanent Court of International Justice or the present International Court of Justice have obligatory, but no compulsory, jurisdiction. The essential oneness of "arbitration" and "judicial settlement" lies in that both are strictly judicial procedures. "International arbitration" is exclusively a judicial procedure; it is as already correctly defined by Article XXXVII of Convention I of the Hague of 1907 "the settlement of disputes between States by *judges* of their own choice and on *the basis of respect for law*." [75]

The error of the recent proposals lies exactly in that they make of a mere technical difference in degree as regards "arbitration" and "judicial settlement" a basic difference in kind, thus misconceiving the very essence of "international arbitration" as a strictly judicial procedure.

While Article VI of the Project of Organic Pact of the Inter-American System enumerates "arbitration" and "judicial settlement," disputes of a juridical nature should, according to Article IX, "as a general rule, be submitted by the parties to the International Court of Justice." Under Article XVIII of the Definitive Project of the Inter-American Juridical Committee, the parties, "may submit their controversies to the International Court of Justice" and it is added that the "controversies to which this article is applicable" are those referring to the four categories of Article XXXVI, point 2, of the Statute of the International Court of Justice. This is a wholly arbitrary restriction of the jurisdiction of this court. The revised edition of the Mexican Peace Code, Articles XXV-LIV, submits to arbi-

tration only "all the differences of a political character."
The draft of the Mexican Peace Code, made by the Committee of Experts, has excluded the political disputes from
arbitration.

If permanence is one of the main ideas in Pan-American
proposals, another main idea is the extension of international arbitration, the longing for a comprehensive, ample,
broad arbitration. In this respect many proposals have been
and are being made to submit obligatorily to international
arbitration all disputes of whatever nature: thus the Plan
of Arbitration of 1890; Argentina stood for arbitration
without restrictions and exceptions, under the Argentine
formula excluding constitutional questions, in Mexico City
(1902) and at Santiago (1923). Uruguay and Colombia
were in favor. Chile presented a draft in this sense in
Buenos Aires in 1936 and also Argentina. At the Lima
Conference the proposals, submitted by Venezuela and Uruguay, stood for "unrestricted" arbitration. Venezuela wrote
that the "restriction of arbitration to juridical questions is
tending to disappear." Resolution X of the Rio de Janeiro
Conference (1947) stated that the ninth Pan-American
Conference also study, with a view toward approval, "obligatory arbitration for all controversies which may entangle
the peace and which are not a juridical character." Under
the impact of these proposals and the above-quoted Resolution X, the Inter-American Juridical Committee introduced
into Article XVII of its definitive project the obligation
"to submit to arbitration the controversies of any nature,
juridical or non-juridical, which have arisen or may arise
in the future between them."

First of all, it must be remarked that in most proposals
of this type exceptions are added excepting constitutional
questions, or controversies arising out of facts antedating
the treaty, or controversies under the jurisdiction of domestic courts, or controversies settled by treaties or de-

cisions, or excepting problems of domestic jurisdiction, or a number of these exceptions combined. Now it is obvious that most of these "non-juridical" conflicts arise exactly out of facts mentioned in these reservations, e.g., the wish of one party for the revision of a valid treaty, or the complaint against activities of a state which, by positive law, are clearly within the domestic jurisdiction of the other state. It follows that the extension is by no means so sweeping as it would appear, that the exceptions take back most of what the first statement conceded.

But also apart from that, this extension to "non-juridical" conflicts is a theoretical misjudgment of the nature and function of judicial settlement and arbitration and is based on an error as to the possibilities of maintaining peace by means of international adjudication alone. As this writer has fully shown in other studies,[76] such extension is based on a confusion between judicial settlement and international legislation, between decisions *de lege lata* and revision *de lege ferenda*, between static and dynamic conflicts.

The difference between static and dynamic conflicts between states and their different procedure of settlement is fundamental and perfectly analogous to the same distinction in municipal law. A static conflict is a controversy in which the parties are in conflict as to what the positive international law, i.e., the customary general international law, actually in force and the treaty law, binding upon the parties, *is*. Such a conflict is a juridical conflict and eminently appropriate to be decided and settled by an international court on the basis of positive international law.

But a dynamic conflict is a controversy between states where both fully agree as to what the positive law is, but where one party wishes for political, meta-juridical reasons that the law be changed. This is not a juridical, but a political conflict, not a conflict as to what the law *is*, but rather as to what the law *should be*. Naturally, such con-

flicts too can be submitted to an international court and can
be decided by it. But as the court could only give a decision
on the basis of positive international law and, therefore,
reject the one party's wish for a change, such a decision
cannot settle the conflict. For as to what the law is, both
parties were agreed beforehand. The conflict arises here
exactly out of the positive law by which the court is bound.

It is perfectly true that the current distinction between
"legal" and "political" [77] international conflicts, excluding
the latter from international arbitration, is entirely untenable. "Legal" disputes may, at the same time, be highly
political; "political disputes" may contain many legal points.
Equally untenable is the distinction between "justiciable"
and "non-justiciable" disputes. All disputes of whatever
nature can be judicially decided under positive international
law; there are no disputes "not regulated by international
law," in no case would the court have to give a *non liquet*.
At least, the claim of a party, not based on international
law, can be rejected by the court. While all disputes can
thus be judicially *decided*, it is not true that all disputes
can be judicially *settled*.

Article I of the Arbitration Treaty of 1929 subjects to
obligatory arbitration all international disputes "which
have arisen or may arise by virtue of a claim of right and
which are juridical in their nature by reason of being susceptible of decision by the application of the principles of
law." This definition is taken from the Taft-Knox Treaties
of 1911. It is a combination of the subjective and of the
objective method of the definition of disputes. The objective method, contained in the second part of the definition,
is theoretically untenable because there are no "non-justiciable" disputes. Article I of the 1929 Treaty combines with
this method the enumeration method, taken from Article
XIII of the Covenant of the League of Nations and Article
XXXVI of the Statute of the Permanent Court of Interna-

tional Justice. This enumeration method is equally subject to criticism, especially as the second point of the mentioned four categories, namely "any question of international law," covers all the three others.

The real distinction is between what this author calls "static" and "dynamic" conflicts. In the first category, the parties are in conflict as to what law is, in the second as to what the law should be. Only the first category is apt to be settled by judicial decision. The category of arbitrable disputes must, therefore, be subjectively defined, as done in the Locarno Pact, Article III and in Article XVII of the Geneva Act of 1928: "All disputes with regard to which the parties are in conflict as to their rights." It follows that if only one party puts forward a claim beyond positive international law, whereas the other party insists on the positive law, the conflict is a dynamic one.[78]

The proposals, including the Definitive Project of the Inter-American Juridical Committee, extending obligatory arbitration also to dynamic conflicts are theoretically unsound. Obligatory arbitration must be restricted to static conflicts, where the parties are in conflict as to their rights. But within this category the greatest extension of obligatory arbitration should be achieved. The restriction takes two forms: exceptions, stated in the treaty, and the possibility of making reservations of whatever content. The ideal is, of course, no restrictions and no reservations. To approach this ideal within the politically possible limits must be the aim.

It is clear that the older exception of "sovereignty, independence, honor and vital interests" practically annuls the value of the arbitration treaty. While this clause has now generally disappeared, it has been often replaced by restrictions and reservations which amount practically to the same effect as the older clause. Article II of the Arbitration Treaty of 1929 has only two exceptions: "domestic jurisdiction," taken from Article XV, para. 8, of the Covenant of the League of Nations, and "disputes which affect the interest or refer to the action of a State not a Party to this treaty." Article XVII of the Definitive Project of the Inter-American Juridical Committee retains only the exception of "domestic jurisdiction." It is clear that many restrictions as they now appear in the reservations to the 1929 treaty are mostly unacceptable; the exception of existing conflicts or of conflicts arising out of events antedating the treaty tends practically to nullify the effect of the treaty; equally untenable is the exception of matters which are under the jurisdiction of domestic courts; here the rule of international law which prescribes the exhaustion of local remedies and *res judicata* fully suffices; it is untenable to restrict this exception to cases of denial of justice, especially if this concept is so narrowly defined as in most Latin-American republics; untenable is the exception of territorial questions or boundary disputes; untenable is the exception of constitutional questions.

The ideal would be to include all static conflicts with no exceptions; but if exceptions are politically necessary, perhaps the two, now contained in the 1929 treaty, can remain; and perhaps a third exception, concerning disputes definitely settled by treaty or judicial (arbitral) decision.

Reservations are more dangerous than exceptions: they may take any content; their play, if the reservations are numerous and of varied content, completely breaks the unity of the treaty, and it is in every case a problem of research what the law under the treaty is. There could be a limited number of exceptions stated in the treaty and a prohibition of reservations. Or there could be no exceptions, but a permission of reservations. Or it has been proposed to enumerate the reservations which are allowed in the treaty itself; this was done by Article XXXIX of the Geneva Act of 1928 and has been proposed by Mexico. But it is feared

rigidity will keep states from signing and ratify-
strument at all. It is a matter of political possi-
nich method should be adopted and how far one
so that the better may not become the enemy of

with permanence of the tribunal and extension of
of arbitration, the third reform is in making the
ion more and more compulsory. Strictly speaking,
compulsory jurisdiction—very different from obligatory
arbitration—would mean that the court, as in municipal
law, has jurisdiction on the basis of law, regardless of the
consent of the parties. Compulsory jurisdiction in this strict
sense is up to now unknown to international law. All international jurisdiction is exclusively based on the consent of
the parties, whether given in the concrete case or in advance
by treaty. This is also true in the case of the "optional
clause." This clause is optional, the states may adopt it, and
there is no duty to adopt it; and even if they adopt it, they
can limit the adoption in time, they can adopt it with reservations and under the condition of reciprocity.

Compulsory jurisdiction in the usual, less strict sense
exists if an international court has power to decide a case
at the request of a single party. Permanence of the court
will greatly facilitate the achievement of compulsory jurisdiction: the ideas of permanence and of compulsory jurisdiction are closely related. As the Arbitration Treaty of
1929 knows no permanent tribunal, its obligatory arbitration is far from compulsory jurisdiction. To achieve this
latter, at least four reforms are necessary:

(A) To determine whether a concrete dispute is one
which must be arbitrated or not; whether it falls under the
definition of the treaty or under the definition of the restriction, such as domestic jurisdiction, or under the definition of a reservation must not be left to the discretion
of the parties. The phrase added to definitions, "in their

opinion," [79] negatives even obligatory arbitration, so compulsory jurisdiction. For this reason neither XXXVIII of the Hague Convention of 1907, nor XIII of the Covenant of the League of Nations ("any pute which they recognize. . . ."), nor the Charter of United Nations contains an obligation to arbitrate. It is absolutely necessary to confer jurisdiction upon the tribunal to decide its own jurisdiction,[80] to decide whether a concrete dispute is subject to its jurisdiction, to decide the interpretation of the *compromis,* and to decide differences which arise with regard to the interpretation and execution of the decision.

(B) Compulsory jurisdiction further means that the court has jurisdiction at the unilateral request of one party. For this purpose a permanent, preconstituted court is of enormous advantage. But such unilateral right to invoke the tribunal can also be given in case of *ad hoc* tribunals, as shown by modern European arbitration treaties. But to reach this goal, two further conditions are necessary.

(C) Under the 1929 Treaty, Article IV, the parties to the dispute "shall formulate by common accord, in each case, a special agreement which shall clearly define the particular subject-matter of the controversy, the seat of the court, the rules which will be observed in the proceedings, and the other conditions to which the parties may agree." There is a necessity of a special *compromis* in each concrete case. Under this article the "treaty is, in a sense, only an agreement to agree—a pactum de contrahendo. The obligation which it creates falls far short of creating a compulsory jurisdiction," [81] The United States reservation, in ratifying the 1929 Treaty, that the *compromis* in each concrete case needs the advice and consent of two-thirds of the members of the Senate, makes arbitration under this treaty in fact voluntary for the United States. There can be no compulsory jurisdiction if there is not only the necessity of a *compromis* in each concrete case but also if the whole arbitration procedure can be paralyzed by a failure of the parties to agree upon the *compromis*. The German-Swiss Treaty of 1921, therefore, gives the competence to the Permanent Board of Conciliation to determine the *compromis* if the parties have not concluded the *compromis* within six months; the Geneva Act of 1928 gives, in case of failure to agree upon the *compromis*, to each party the right to bring the case directly before the Permanent Court of International Justice.

(D) Article IV, para. 2, of the Arbitration Treaty of 1929 provides, it is true, that in case of failure to agree upon the *compromis* within three months from the date of the installation of the court, the agreement shall be formulated by the court.[82] But this proviso is insufficient, because the very constitution of the court can be paralyzed by the failure of the parties to agree. Article III of the Arbitration Treaty of 1929 fails not only to ensure the greatest impartiability of the judges, as each party nominates two arbitrators, but also to ensure the composition of the tribunal in case of a failure of the parties to agree. Article XIX of the Definitive Project of the Inter-American Juridical Committee seeks to introduces a better procedure.

IX

The ninth International Conference of American States, held at Bogotá from March 30 to April 30, 1948, has, notwithstanding its tragic interruption, concluded its task of completely reorganizing the Inter-American System, of integrating it with the United Nations, and of putting it, finally, on a treaty basis. This treaty, the constitution of what is now called the Organization of the American States, is the Bogotá Charter.[83] Part of this task consisted in reorganizing completely the inter-American peace machinery.

The Bogotá Charter contains in Chapter IV (Articles XX-XXIII) only the guiding principles. Article XX provides that all disputes arising between the American states shall be submitted to peaceful inter-American procedures before being referred to the Security Council of the United Nations. Article XXIII foresees a special treaty for the peaceful settlement of inter-American disputes "in such a manner that it will not be possible for a dispute among American States to fail of definitive settlement within a reasonable period."

In fulfilment of Article XXIII of the Bogotá Charter, a special American Treaty on Pacific Settlement has been concluded on April 30, 1948, known as the Pact of Bogotá.[84]

The Pact of Bogotá shall be ratified (Article LII) and shall come into effect between the contracting parties in the order in which they deposit their respective ratifications (Article LIII). The treaty shall be registered with the Secretariat of the United Nations through the Pan-American Union (Article LVII). It shall remain in force indefinitely, but may be denounced upon one year's notice, continuing in force for the remaining signatories (Article LVI).

The Pact of Bogotá has three aims: integration of the inter-American peace machinery with that of the United Nations; simplification and centralization of the inter-American peace machinery as such; and elaboration of such a peace machinery that any inter-American conflict can be definitely and peacefully settled within a reasonable period.

The integration with the United Nations is reached by different methods: by making use in many ways of the International Court of Justice, a principal organ of the United Nations; by obligation to settle inter-American disputes by regional pacific means before reference of them to the Security Council of the United Nations (Article II); and as the inter-American peace machinery shall be so organized that it will not be possible for a dispute among American states to fail of definitive settlement within a reasonable period, there should logically never exist a possibility of submitting an inter-American dispute to the Security Council. In this way, the pact takes care to preserve the relative autonomy of the Organization of American States within the United Nations.

All the American states solemnly reaffirm their commitments and agree to refrain from the threat or use of force or from any other means of coercion for the settlement of their controversies and to have recourse at all times to pacific procedures only. The centralization of the inter-American peace machinery as such is to be brought about by the proviso that the Pact of Bogotá shall constitute the only instrument of the inter-American peace machinery and that as it comes into effect through the successive ratifications the other inter-American treaties for the peaceful settlement of conflicts, including the General Treaty of Inter-American Arbitration and the Protocol of Progressive Arbitration of 1929, shall cease to be in force (Article LVIII).

For all types of procedures for the settlement of inter-American disputes provided for in the Pact of Bogotá, it is a condition that settlement by direct negotiations through the usual diplomatic channels has failed (Article II). In such a case, the American states are bound to use the procedures provided for in the Pact of Bogotá, or such special procedures as, in their opinion, will permit them to arrive at a solution.

The Pact of Bogotá binds the parties not to apply force and to seek the settlement only by pacific procedures. But they are free to leave their controversies either unsettled or to apply such procedures provided for in the pact, as they wish, or to apply special procedures, not provided for by the pact, on which they can agree. The greatest freedom in the choice of pacific procedure is left to the parties. Nearly all the norms of the pact are only subsidiary, if and insofar as the parties do not agree on other procedures.

In consequence, no attempt has been made to establish a certain binding order in which different pacific procedures must be used successfully. Quite to the contrary, the pact expressly provides that the order of the procedures established in the Pact does not signify that the parties should use all these procedures, or that any of them have preference over others (Article III). Judicial procedures, therefore, must not be preceded by conciliation; on the other hand, judicial procedures have no preference over any other procedure. There is only one binding rule: If any pacific procedure has been initiated, whether by agreement or in fulfilment of the Pact of Bogotá or a previous pact, no other procedure may be commenced until that procedure is concluded (Article IV). It follows that once the procedure of judicial settlement or arbitration is initiated no other procedure can thereafter be commenced, as the two mentioned procedures must lead to a definitive and binding decision.

For our subject, Chapters IV–VII are of particular importance: judicial procedure, arbitration, fulfilment of decisions, and advisory opinions. In all respects three exceptions are laid down in the pact, which also admits reservations. The first exception is as to matters which, by their nature, are within the domestic jurisdiction of the state. The phrasing deserves, certainly, to be criticized. It is well known that no matters are "by their nature" within the domestic jurisdiction. What matters are, at a given time, within the domestic jurisdiction of a state is, as the Permanent Court of International Justice has stated, essentially a relative question which depends on the development of international law. The phrase of the exception stems from Article XV, para. 8, of the Covenant of the League of

Nations, which speaks of "matters which *by international law* are *solely* within the domestic jurisdiction" of a state (italics supplied). But Article V of the pact has made great progress by laying down that in case of disagreement between the parties as to whether the controversy concerns a matter of domestic jurisdiction, "this preliminary question shall be submitted to decision by the International Court of Justice, at the request of any of the parties." But against this part of Article V, Peru and Argentina have made a reservation.

The second exception relates to "matters already settled by arrangement between the parties, or by arbitral award, or by decision of an international Court, or which are governed by agreement or treaties in force." (Article VI). Three states have made reservations to this article: Ecuador in general; Bolivia insists in her reservation that pacific procedures must also be applied to controversies arising from matters settled by arrangement between the parties, when the said arrangements affect the vital interests of a state. Bolivia naturally thinks of the problem of her access to the Pacific. Nicaragua, on the other hand, reserves that her signature of the pact of Bogotá "cannot be alleged as an acceptance of any arbitral decision that Nicaragua has attacked and the validity of which is not certain."

Article VII, finally binds the American states "not to make diplomatic representations in order to protect their nationals or refer a controversy to a court of international jurisdiction, when such nationals have taken steps to place their case before competent domestic courts of the respective State." This article reflects the strong Latin-American attitude against the diplomatic protection of citizens abroad, an attitude which is not in conformity with international law and has never been recognized by the United States. The United States promptly placed a reservation against Article VII, stating at the same time the correct rule of international law: In not accepting Article VII, the United States maintains "the rules of diplomatic protection, including the rule of exhaustion of local remedies, as provided by international law." Argentina, in a reservation also, did not adhere to Article VII.

Of the three procedures which interest us here, one is entirely new: the settlement of conflicts through an advisory opinion of the International Court of Justice (Article LI). While such advisory opinion is not binding in law, it carries *de facto* a nearly-binding prestige. For this entirely optional procedure, it is necessary that the parties agree, and that they petition the General Assembly or the Security Council of the United Nations to request such advisory option. The petition shall be made through the council of the Organization of American States. Such advisory opinion, finally, can be requested only on "any *judicial* question."

The judicial procedure (Articles XXXI–XXXVII) makes use of the International Court of Justice, which in the appropriate cases shall decide, according to the agreement of the parties, either in full court or in special chambers; the parties may also agree to have the controversy decided *ex aequo et bono* (Article XXXVI). The court naturally follows the procedure established in the statute thereof (Article XXXVII). As expected, no new Inter-American Court of Justice was established. The heart of these articles consists in the rule that the American states, by Article XXXI, accept the optional clause concerning the compulsory jurisdiction of the International Court of Justice in relation to any other American state and without necessity of any special agreement in all disputes of a juridical nature concerning any of the four categories,[85] enumerated in Article XXXVI, para. 2, of the Statute of International Court of Justice (Article XXXI). Article XXXIII lays down that in case the parties fail to agree whether the court has jurisdiction over the controversy, the court itself shall first decide that question; this is in harmony with Article XXXVI, para. 6, of the statute of the court. If the court declares itself to be without jurisdiction for the exceptions, contained in Article V, VI, and VII, "such controversy shall be declared ended" (Article XXXIV). Peru has made a reservation against Article XXXIII and the pertinent part of Article XXXIV, holding that the exceptions of *res judicata* (Article VI) "determine the exclusion of the case from the application of every procedure." The United States has made two important reservations: (1) She will not undertake as the complainant state to submit to the International Court of Justice any controversy which is "not considered to be probably within the jurisdiction of the Court." (2) The acceptance of the compulsory jurisdiction of the court (Article XXXI) "is limited by any jurisdictional or other limitations contained in any Declaration deposited by the United States of America under Article 36, paragraph 4, of the Statute of the Court."

In consquence of the principle of the utmost freedom of the American state to choose such procedure as they prefer for the peaceful settlement of their conflicts, it is, of course, open to them also to submit to the court other juridical disputes than those of the categories enumerated in Article XXXVI, para. 2, of the statute of the court; but in such case, an agreement is necessary, whereas in the disputes of Article XXX the compulsory jurisdiction of the court is accepted in advance and a case can be brought before the court by a written application of one party only addressed to the registrar. On the other hand, even in cases of legal disputes concerning a category enumerated in Article XXXVI, para. 2, of the statute of the court, the parties may, if they so agree, submit it to arbitration. There are only two compulsory rules: If a dispute has been submitted under Article XXXI to the International Court of Justice and if this court declares itself without jurisdiction for

any other reason than the exceptions laid down in Articles
V, VI, and VII, then the parties are obligated to submit the
dispute to arbitration (Article XXXV). To this article Peru
has made a reservation in the sense that "before arbitration is resorted to, there may be, at the request of one of
the parties, a meeting of the Organ of Consultation." The
second compulsory rule is: When a previous conciliation
procedure does not lead to a solution and the said parties
have not agreed upon an arbitral procedure, either of them
shall be entitled to have recourse to the International Court
of Justice and the court shall have compulsory jurisdiction
(Article XXXI).

While arbitration has heretofore been a strictly judicial
procedure and whereas the revised Mexican Peace Code
wanted to restrict arbitration solely to non-judicial disputes,
Articles XXXVIII–XLIX of the Pact of Bogotá have now
made of arbitration a mixed thing: "The conflicting parties
may, if they so agree, submit to arbitration differences of
any kind, whether *judicial or not,* that have arisen or may
arise in the future between them" (Article XXXVIII).[86]
The pact contains rules as to the representation of the
parties before the arbitral tribunal (Article XLIV) and
the financial remuneration of the members of the tribunal
(Article XLIX). The award shall be accompanied by a sup-
porting opinion and shall be adopted by a majority vote;
dissenting opinions may be added (Article XLVI). The
award settles the controversy definitively, is not subject
to appeal, and shall be carried out immediately (Article
XLVI). Differences as to the interpretation or execution
of the award shall be submitted to the arbitral tribunal
that rendered the award (Article XLVII). While no appeal
is admissible, there is a review of the award by the same
tribunal within a year if a previously existing fact is discovered, unknown to the tribunal and to the party request-
ing the review, and if the tribunal is of the opinion that

such fact might have a decisive influence on the award (Articles XLV, XLVIII).

But the bulk of these articles is devoted to solve the problem of securing the constitution of an *ad hoc* tribunal and a *compromis,* even if the parties fail to agree. In accordance with the principle of the utmost freedom of the parties, they may, by mutual agreement, establish the tribunal in the manner they deem most appropriate; they may even select a single arbiter, designating in such case a chief of a state, an eminent jurist, or any court of justice in which the parties have mutual confidence (Article XLI). Only "unless there exists an agreement to the contrary," the constitution of the arbitral tribunal is prescribed by Article XL of the Pact of Bogotá in a very elaborate way. Each party shall, within two months, name "an arbiter of recognized competence in questions of international law and of the highest integrity and transmit the designation to the Council of the Organization of the American States." At the same time each party shall present to the council a list of ten jurists chosen from among those on the general panel of the Permanent Court of Arbitration of The Hague who do not belong to its national group and who are willing to serve. Then within a month, the council establishes the tribunal by adding to the two designated national arbiters three others chosen from the lists presented, according to an elaborate procedure (Article XLI, para. 2, a–g). This proviso shall guarantee the prompt constitution of an impartial arbitral tribunal. But it is, of course, possible that one of the parties does not designate an arbiter and does not present its list. Against this circumstance, Article XLV is devised. In such a case, the council gives the delinquent party an additional period of fifteen days to fulfil its obligations after which time the council itself (Article XLV a–d) establishes the tribunal without the concurrence of one party, but binding both parties. Against this point, Peru has made a reservation, holding that "arbitration set up without the participation of one of the parties is in contradiction with the Peruvian Constitution."

In each case the parties shall draw up a *compromis* clearly defining the specific matter that is the subject of the controversy, the seat of the tribunal, the rules of procedure, the period within which the award is to be rendered, and other conditions agreed upon. Naturally even after the constitution of the tribunal, arbitration can be paralyzed by the failure of the parties to agree upon a *compromis*. In that case, if an agreement cannot be reached within three months after the date of the installation of the tribunal, the *compromis* shall be drawn up by the International Court of Justice through summary procedure, and shall be binding upon the parties (Article XLVIII). Against this article Paraguay has made a reservation, insisting on a prior *compromis* of the parties as a prerequisite of arbitration on "questions of a non-juridical nature, affecting national sovereignity and not specifically agreed upon in treaties now in force." The United States has made a reservation making the submission of any controversy to arbitration dependent upon the conclusion of a special *compromis* of the parties.

It is to be noted that Argentina in a reservation has not accepted all of the articles on judicial procedure and on arbitration (Articles XXXI–XLIX), because, although firmly adhering to these procedures, they "should have been established only for controversies arising in the future and not originating in or having any relation to causes, situations or facts existing before the signing of this instrument."

Article L is an innovation, concerning the compulsory execution of decisions of the International Court of Justice and of arbitral awards. In case of non-fulfilment by one party, the other shall, before resorting to the Security Council, propose a meeting of consultation of ministers of foreign affairs to agree upon appropriate measures to ensure the fulfilment of the judicial decision or arbitral award. Argentina, in a reservation, has not accepted this article, because such "compulsory execution is contrary to Argentine traditions."

X

As far as the problem of international arbitration is concerned, the Pact of Bogotá integrates, as shown, the inter-American peace machinery with that of the United Nations. No Inter-American Court of Justice is established, but the International Court of Justice is made use of in many ways. The Pact of Bogotá, if successful, does concentrate the inter-American peace machinery into one document, unifies it, and establishes a link between the different types of procedures for the peaceful settlement of inter-American conflicts. The Pact of Bogotá tries to furnish a peace machinery in such a way that no inter-American conflict whatever shall fail of peaceful settlement within a reasonable time. In the field of arbitration the greatest innovation—and in this writer's opinion a more than questionable one—is to create a barrier between judicial settlement and arbitration, and to make out of arbitration which had developed in the clear sense of a truly judicial procedure, a procedure for the settlement of juridical and non-juridical questions. True, great precautions are taken to assure the constitution of an *ad hoc* tribunal and of a *compromis,* if necessary, without the concurrence of one party. But to entrust to a judicial body the decision of dynamic conflicts which is essentially a legislative function, for which a court is neither competent nor equipped, appears an unhappy idea. Will arbitration of juridical questions also not necessarily be on the basis of the positive international law in force? It is significant that the pact thinks in judicial terms; for Article XL speaks of "arbiters of recognized competence in questions of international law" and of a list "of ten jurists from the panel of the Permanent Court of Arbitration"; Article XLI speaks with regard to a single arbiter of "an eminent jurist" or "any court of justice." But are jurists the competent persons to decide political questions? And is it compatible to call a political decision a "binding award," the fulfilment of which may be enforced? It is amazing to see that the whole Chapter V, dealing with arbitration, does not contain a word about the vital problem of the basis on which the award, whether in static or dynamic conflicts, will be rendered. Or shall the basis also be prescribed in the *compromis*? But here again Article XLIII, dealing with the *compromis*, contains no word as to the basis of the award.

The submission of non-juridical conflicts to arbitration, although, as noted above, compulsory under two hypotheses, nevertheless excludes a great number of such conflicts through the exceptions of Articles V, VI, and VII, not to speak of far-reaching reservations.

The Pact of Bogotá must, first of all, be ratified by all the American republics, and they must show the good will to make it work if a conflict arises. Even so, experience under the system will be necessary to determine whether the system will really prevent any inter-American conflict from failing to be peacefully settled in the light of the exceptions of Articles V, VI, VII, of the reservations, and of what would appear to be a theoretically misconceived treatment of the arbitration procedure.

---

[1] See HUDSON, INTERNATIONAL TRIBUNALS (1944).

By the Jay Treaty of November 19, 1794, concluded between the United States and Great Britain, these "two States submitted for adjudication by mixed commissions important boundary controversies as well as disputes relating to the exercise of belligerent rights at sea by Great Britain and the observance of the duties of neutrality by the

United States." 2 OPPENHEIM-LAUTERPACHT, INTERNATIONAL LAW 32 (6th ed. 1940).

Again it was the settlement by arbitration of a long and rather serious controversy between this country and Great Britain which gave a new impetus to arbitration—the *Alabama Arbitration* of 1872. In 1862, a ship had been built in England for the Confederate States. This ship had left Liverpool unarmed, but was armed at the Azores to prey upon the merchantmen of the United States. In 1865, after the end of the Civil War, the United States claimed damages for the alleged violation of neutrality by Great Britain. After long negotiations the two powers concluded the Treaty of Washington of May 8, 1871, which provided for arbitration. In 1872 the Geneva Alabama Tribunal gave an award, 1 MOORE, ARBITRATIONS 653–59 (1898), deciding that Great Britain should pay to the United States an indemnity of $15,500,000. This payment was made by Great Britain.

2 See BALCH, INTERNATIONAL COURTS OF ARBITRATION (1874); CARLSTON, THE PROCESS OF INTERNATIONAL ARBITRATION (1946); CORY, COMPULSORY ARBITRATION OF INTERNATIONAL DISPUTES (1932); FOSTER, ARBITRATION AND THE HAGUE COURT (1904); HUDSON, *op. cit.;* LINDSEY, HISTORY OF INTERNATIONAL ARBITRATION; MOORE, ARBITRATIONS (1898); MORRIS, INTERNATIONAL ARBITRATION AND PROCEDURE (1911); RALSTON, INTERNATIONAL ARBITRATION FROM ATHENS TO LOCARNO (1924); SCHURZ, ARBITRATION IN INTERNATIONAL DISPUTES (1896); SCOTT, THE HAGUE CONVENTIONS (1918); STATUS OF THE INTERNATIONAL COURT OF JUSTICE (1916); MYERS, *Arbitration and the United States,* 9 WORLD PEACE FOUNDATION 451 (1926).

3 See IRELAND, BOUNDARIES, POSSESSIONS AND CONFLICTS IN SOUTH AMERICA (1938); *idem.,* BOUNDARIES, POSSESSIONS AND CONFLICTS IN CENTRAL AND SOUTH AMERICA (1941).

4 MANNING, ARBITRATION TREATIES AMONG THE AMERICAN NATIONS (1924), reported that 228 inter-American arbitration treaties had been concluded by the end of the year 1910.

5 See BORGES, LOS PROCEDIMIENTOS DE INVESTIGACION, DE CONCILIACION Y DE ARBITRAJE (1933); BRUM, EL ARBITRAJE AMPLIO (1922); J. V. GONZALES, INTERNATIONAL ARBITRATION IN ARGENTINE POLICY (1910); MAURTUA, LA IDEA PAN AMERICANA Y LA CUESTION DEL ARBITRAJE (1910); QUESDA, ARBITRATION IN LATIN AMERICA (1907); SAAVEDRA LAMAS, LA CONCEPTION ARGENTINE DE L'ARBITRAGE ET DE L'INTERVENTION (1928); TORO, NOTAS SOBRE ARBITRAJE INTERNACIONAL EN LAS REPUBLICAS LATINO-AMERICANAS (1898); URRUTIA, LA EVOLUCION DEL PRINCIPIO DE ARBITRAJE EN AMERICA (1920); d'Eca, *Arbitration Agreements in Specific Matters Among Latin American Nations* 1829–1922, 70 BULL. OF THE PAN AMERICAN UNION 500; Rodriquez y Von Sobotka, *La evolucion del arbitraje en America,* 16 REVISTA DE DERECHO INTERNACIONAL HABANA 85 (1929).

6 See ALVAREZ, LE DROIT INTERNATIONAL AMÉRICAIN (1910). For the opposing view see DE SA VIANNA, DE LA NON-EXISTENCE D'UN DROIT INTERNATIONAL AMÉRICAIN (1912).

⁷ 1 ARANDA, CONGRESOS Y CONFERENCIAS EN QUE HA TOMADO PARTE EL PERU 5–81 (1909) ; PORRAS BARRENECHEA, EL CONGRESO DE PANAMA (1930).

⁸ See ULLOA, CONGRESOS AMERICANOS DE LIMA)1938).

⁹ See FRIED, PAN AMERIKA (2d ed. 1818); MORENA QUINTANA, EL SISTEMA INTER-AMERICANO (1927) ; YEPES ET DA SILVA, COMMENTAIRE THÉORIQUE ET PRATIQUE DU PACTE DE LA SOCIÉTÉ DES NATIONS ET DES STATUTS DE L'UNION PAN AMERICAINE (1934–1939); PEPIN, LE PAN AMÉRICANISME (1938); CERETI, PAN AMERICANISMO (1939); HUMPHREY, THE INTER-AMERICAN SYSTEM (1942).

¹⁰ For a study of the Pan-American efforts toward a peaceful settlement of international disputes and arbitration in particular, see BERER, DIE PANAMERIKANISCHEN FRIEDENSSICHERUNGSVERTRAGE (1938); BUCHI, GESCHICHTE DER PANAMERIKANISCHEN BEWEGUNG (1914); MEYER-LINDENBERG, EL PROCEDIMIENTO, INTER-AMERICANO PARA CONSOLIDAR LA PAZ (1941).

¹¹ 25 STAT. 155, §2, 7 (1888); SCOTT (ed.), THE INTERNATIONAL CONFERENCES OF AMERICAN STATES 1889–1928, 3 (1931).

¹² Repeated in the invitation to the Conference of July 13, 1888, SCOTT, op. cit. at 5.

¹³ SCOTT, op. cit. at 40.

¹⁴ Recommendation to European powers, in SCOTT, op. cit. at 44.

¹⁵ ACTAS Y DOCUMENTOS DE LA SEGUNDA CONFERENCIA PAN AMERICANA 181 (1902) : "Que con tratados o sin ellos el Gobierno Argentino está resuelto a terminar todas las cuestiones internacionales por el arbitraje."

¹⁶ Ibid. at 182, n. 15: "Arbitraje en términos amplios y sin trabas meticulares."

¹⁷ Ibid.: 'Todas las controversias de cualquier naturaleza. Nada importa que tales controversias tengan su orígen en hechos anteriores al presente tratado."

¹⁸ Ibid.: ". . . En cuanto no afecto los preceptos de la Constitución de uno u otro país."

¹⁹ SCOTT, op. cit. at 61.

²⁰ SCOTT, op. cit. at 104. See also the Conventions of Rio de Janeiro 1906, ibid. at 132, and of Buenos Aires 1910, ibid. at 183, as well as ¶3(c) of the Declaration of Principles of Inter-American Solidarity and Co-operation of the Buenos Aires Conference 1936.

²¹ SCOTT, op. cit. at 100.

²² See PAN AMERICAN UNION, STATUS OF THE PAN AMERICAN TREATIES AND CONVENTIONS (revised to July 1, 1948).

²³ SCOTT, op. cit. at 124.

²⁴ Conferencia de Paz Centro-Americana, Washington, 1907.

²⁵ CASTRO RAMIREZ, CINCO AÑOS EN LA CORTE DE JUSTICIA CENTRO-AMERICANA (1918) ; EYMA, LA COUR DE JUSTICE CENTRE-AMÉRICAINE (1928) ; Hudson, Central American Court of Justice, 26 AM.J.INT'L L. 759 (1932) ; ibid., THE PERMANENT COURT OF INTERNATIONAL JUSTICE 1920–1942, 22 (1943) ; PLANAS-SUAREZ, LA CORTE DE JUSTICIA CENTRO-

AMERICANA (1909); GUERRERO, *La corte di giustizia Centro-Americana*, RIVISTA DI DIRITTO INTERNAZIONALE 289 (1910).

26 See ANALES DE LA CORTE DE JUSTICIA CENTRO-AMERICANA (1911–17).

27 INT'L CONC. 658, *n* 189 *August*, (1923).

28 SCOTT, *op. cit.* at 283.

29 ACTAS DE LAS SESIONES DE COMISIONES, QUINTA CONFERENCIA INTERNACIONAL AMERICANA (1923).

30 SCOTT, *op. cit.* at 452.

31 PROJECTOS DE CODIFICACAO 61 (Comissão Internacional de Juristas Americanos).

32 PAN-AMERICAN UNION (JURIDICAL DIVISION), INFORMES Y PROYECTOS SOBRE EL ESTABLECIMIENTO DE LA CORTE INTER-AMERICANA DE JUSTICIA; Arrévalo y Carreño, *Corte Inter-Americana de Justicia*, 4 REVISTA PERUANA DE DERECHO INTERNACIONAL 343 (1944); Scott, *Creación de un Tribunal Inter-Americano de Justicia*, 21 REVISTA DE DERECHO INTERNACIONAL, HAVANA 97 (1932); Gomez Reinoso, *El Tribunal de Justicia Inter-Americana y las Conferencias Pan Americanas*, 45 REVISTA DE DERECHO INTERNACIONAL, HAVANA 119 (1944).

33 DIARIO DE LA 6A CONFERENCIA INTERNACIONAL AMERICANA, HAVANA 1928, 107 (1928).

34 SCOTT, *op. cit.* at 437.

35 PROCEEDINGS OF THE INTERNATIONAL CONFERENCE OF AMERICAN STATES ON CONCILIATION AND ARBITRATION (1929).

36 SCOTT, *op. cit.* at 458; 30 L.N.T.S. 136; Pradier-Fodéré, *La question de l'arbitrage devant la Conférence de Washington*, 22 REVUE DE DROIT INTERNATIONAL ET DE LÉGISLATION COMPARÉE; Stone, *The Pan-American Arbitration Treaty*, FOREIGN POLICY REPORTS 313 (1929-30); Whitton and Brewer, *Problems Raised by the General Treaty of Inter-American Arbitration*, 25 AM.J.INT'L L. 447 (1931); Hudson, *International Treaties for Pacific Settlement*, 15 FOREIGN AFFAIRS 170; Maurtua, *Revision de las Convenciones Inter-Americanas de Conciliacion y Arbitraje*. 36 REVISTA DE DERECHO INTERNACIONAL, HAVANA 327 (1939).

37 SCOTT, *op. cit.* at 462.

38 THE INTERNATIONAL CONFERENCE OF AMERICAN STATES 19 (First Supp. 1933–40).

39 *Ibid.* at 68. In 1934 the Inter-American Commercial Arbitration Commission was created. The eighth conference, Lima, 1938, passed also a resolution on commercial arbitration. *Ibid.* at 267.

40 See also: ALVAREZ FALLER, PARTICIPACIÓN DE MÉXICO EN LA ORGANIZACIÓN DE LA PAZ (1936); PUIG CASAURANC, ALGO SOBRE LA POSICIÓN DE MÉXICO EN MONTEVIDEO (1934); SIERRA, MÉXICO Y LA CONFERENCIA DE MONTEVIDEO (1934).

41 Resolution XXXV, CARNEGIE INST., *op. cit. supra* note 38, at 50.

42 *Supra note* 38, at 143.

43 *Supra note* 38, at 144.

44 *Supra* note 38, at 144.

45 *Supra* note 38, at 161.

⁴⁶ PAN-AMERICAN UNION, REPORTS AND PROJECTS ON THE ESTAB-LISHMENT OF THE INTER-AMERICAN COURT OF INTERNATIONAL JUSTICE (1938).

⁴⁷ PAN-AMERICAN UNION (JURIDICAL DIVISION), IMPROVEMENT AND COORDINATION OF INTER-AMERICAN PEACE INSTRUMENTS 29 (mimeo.).

⁴⁸ *Ibid.* at 33.

⁴⁹ *Ibid.* at 37.

⁵⁰ *Ibid.* at 51.

⁵¹ *Ibid.* at 155.

⁵² *Ibid.* at 74.

⁵³ *Ibid.* at 107.

⁵⁴ *Supra* note 38, at 253.

⁵⁵ *Supra* note 38, at 309.

⁵⁶ *Supra* note 38, at 244.

⁵⁷ *Supra* note 38, at 358.

⁵⁸ PAN-AMERICAN UNION (JURIDICAL DIVISION), IMPROVEMENTS AND COORDINATION OF INTER-AMERICAN PEACE INSTRUMENTS (mimeo.); volume 3 gives the texts of the existing inter-American peace instruments.

⁵⁹ PAN-AMERICAN UNION, RESOLUTION VIII (FINAL ACT) 40 (1945).

⁶⁰ *Ibid.* at 44.

⁶¹ *Ibid.* at 77.

⁶² *Ibid.* at 78.

⁶³ The juridical committee submitted the draft on September 4, 1945.

⁶⁴ See Kunz, *The Inter-American Treaty of Reciprocal Assistance*, 42 AM.J.INT'L L. 111 (1948). PAN-AMERICAN UNION, INFORME SOBRE LA CONFERENCIA INTER-AMERICANA PARA EL MANTENIMIENTO DE LA PAZ Y DE LA SEGURIDAD EN CONTINENTE 41 (1947).

⁶⁵ *Ibid.* at 48.

⁶⁶ PAN-AMERICAN UNION (1946) (mimeo.). See also PAN-AMER-ICAN UNION, REPORT ON THE PROVISIONS OF THE PROJECT OF INTER-AMERICAN PEACE SYSTEM RELATIVE TO OBLIGATORY ARBITRATION (1948 (mimeo.).

⁶⁷ For the development of international arbitration in general see FARAGGI, L'ACTE GÉNÉRAL DE GENÈVE (1935); EAVIER, DE LA CLAUSE COMPROMISSOIRE (1910); GOSSWEILER, L'ARBITRAGE INTERNATIONAL AVANT 1914 ET APRÈS 1919 (1923); HABICHT, POSTWAR TREATIES FOR THE PACIFIC SETTLEMENT OF INTERNATIONAL DISPUTES (1937); HAM-MARSKJÖLD, JURISDICTION INTERNATIONALE (1932); HUDSON, INTERNA-TIONAL TRIBUNALS (1944); *idem.,* THE PERMANENT COURT OF INTERNA-TIONAL JUSTICE 1920-1942 (1943); KAUFMANN, DIE FORTBILDUNG DER INTERNATIONALEN SCHIEDSGERICHTSBARKEIT SEIT DEM WELTKRIEG DURCH DEN LOCARNO-PAKT (1927); LAMMASCH, DIE LEHRE VON DER SCHIEDS-GERICHTSBARKEIT (1914); *idem.,* DIE RECHTSKRAFT INTERNATIONALER SCHIEDSSPRUCHE (1913); LANGE, L'ARBITRAGE OBLIGATOIRE EN 1913 (1914); LAUTERPACHT, THE FUNCTION OF LAW IN THE INTERNA-TIONAL COMMUNITY (1933); LORCH, DIE ABGRENZUNG DER INTER-

NATIONALEN STREITIGKEITEN IN DER GENFER GENERALAKTE (1934) ; POLITIS, LA JUSTICE INTERNATIONALE (1924) ; SCHINDLER, DIE SCHIEDS- GERICHTSBARKEIT SEIT 1914 (1938) ; STUYT, SURVEY OF INTERNATIONAL ARBITRATIONS (1939) ; THIEME, DIE FORTBILDUNG DER INTERNATION- ALEN SCHIEDSGERICHTSBARKEIT SEIT DEM WELTKRIEG (1927) ; WITEN- BERG, L'ORGANISATION JUDICIAIRE, LA PROCÉDURE ET LA SENTENCE INTER- NATIONALES (1937) ; WUNDRAM DIE FAKULTATIV KLAUSEL (1933) ; Makowski, *L'organisation actuelle de l'arbirtage international,* 36 RE- CUEIL DES COURS 263 (1931) ; Schindler, *Les progres de l'arbitrage obligatoire depuis la création de la Société des Nations,* 28 RECUEIL DES COURS 235 (1928) ; ARBITRAGE ET SECURITÉ L. N. Doc. No. C. 653 M. 276 (1927).

68 Salvador, Guatemala, Mexico, Peru, Dominican Republic, and Uruguay.

69 Inter-American Treaty of Reciprocal Assistance, art. II.

70 PAN-AMERICAN UNION (1948).

71 *Ibid.*

72 See *infra* at p. .... ff.

73 Art. XIX of the Definitive Project 1947 of the Inter-American Juridical Committee lays down the procedure for the creation of an *ad hoc* tribunal "in the absence of agreement to the contrary," but leaves the parties in controversy full freedom to select a single arbi- trator or "any national court of justice in which they may have mutual confidence."

74 Definitive Project 1947 of the Inter-American Juridical Commit- tee, art. XXII.

75 Italics added.

76 Kunz, *The Problem of Revision in International Law ("Peaceful Change"),* 33 AM. J. INT'L L. 33 (1939). Hans Kelsen has strongly defended compulsory international adjudication of all international conflicts in *Compulsory International Arbitration of International Disputes,* 37 AM. J. INT'L L. 397 (1943) ; for a critique, see "Com- pulsory International Arbitration and Maintenance of Peace," above.

77 Among the rich literature on this topic see: BALCH, LEGAL AND POLITICAL QUESTIONS BETWEEN NATIONS (1924) ; CERETI, LA TUTELA GIURIDICA DEGLI INTERRESSI INTERNAZIONALI (1929) ; Verzijl, *La classi- fication des differends internationaux,* 6 REVUE DE DROIT INTERNA- TIONAL ET DE LÉGISLATION COMPARÉE 732 (1925) ; Hostie, *Differends justiciables et non justiciables,* 9 REVUE DE DROIT INTERNATIONAL ET DE LÉGISLATION COMPARÉE 263, 568 (1928) ; Fischer-Williams, *Justici- able and Other Disputes,* 26 AM. J. INT'L L. 31 (1932) ; MORGENTHAU, LA NOTION DU "POLITIQUE" ET LA THÉORIE DE DIFFÉREND INTERNATION- AUX (1933) ; Bruns, *Politische und Rechtstreitigkeiten,* 3 ZEITSCHRIFT FÜR AUSLÄNDISCHES ÖFFENTLICHES UND VÖLKERRECHT 445 (1933) ; Schiffer, *Über den begriff der politischen Streitigkeiten im Völkerrecht,* 14 ZEITSCHRIFT FÜR ÖFFENTLICHES RECHT 594 (1934).

78 VERDROSS, VÖLKERRECHT 275 (1937).

79 See the United States reservation in accepting the compulsory jurisdiction of the International Court of Justice, concerning questions

within the domestic jurisdiction, "as determined by the United States."
See Wilcox, *The United States Accepts Compulsory Jurisdiction*, 40
AM. J. INT'L L. 699 (1946); Preuss, *The International Court of Justice, the Senate, and Matters of Domestic Jurisdiction*, 40 AM. J.
INT'L L. 720 (1946).

[80] STATUTE OF THE INTERNATIONAL COURT OF JUSTICE, art. 36, 6.

[81] HUDSON, INTERNATIONAL TRIBUNALS 75 (1944).

[82] To the same effect see art. XXI of the Definitive Project of the
Inter-American Juridical Committee.

[83] PAN-AMERICAN UNION, CHARTER OF THE ORGANIZATION OF AMERICAN STATES, BOGOTÁ 20 (1948). See "The Bogotá Charter of the Organization of American States," below.

[84] PAN-AMERICAN UNION, AMERICAN TREATY OF PACIFIC SETTLEMENT 13 (Pact of Bogotá, April 30, 1948).

[85] Legal disputes concerning (a) the interpretation of a treaty;
(b) any question of international law; (c) the existence of any fact
which, if established, would contribute a breach of an international
obligation; (d) the nature or extent of the reparation to be made for
the breach of an international obligation.

[86] Italics added.

"La Sécurité d'abord!" *

I

IN THE HIERARCHY of juridical values security is the lowest, justice the highest value. But exactly for that reason, security is the more basic. Every legal order must first realize security for those subject to it. A state is a community of men, constituted by the national legal order: therefore the state's first goal is security. This internal security has been realized through special organs for the creation and application of legal norms and for the peaceful settlement of conflicts; by the disarmament of citizens; by the prohibition of self-help, except in case of law-regulated self-defense; by the stability of the constitution; and by a monopoly of armed force at the disposal of the government. Between security and justice, stability and change, there is, in the words of Gustav Radbruch, a certain antinomy. Here is the great problem of every legal order: law, as Roscoe Pound puts it, must be stable and yet it cannot stand still. If the tension between security and justice grows too great, security even within the state may break down, as every revolution shows; hence procedures for "peaceful change" through legislation and, in the case of the constitution, through amendments, are necessary. Stability also depends on the fact that the great majority of citizens share the values on which the national legal order is based.

Things are different in general international law: it is yet a primitive law, and there is less cohesion in the international community as far as common values are concerned. Hence the problem of a state's external security is difficult. Security, too, is each state's first goal in foreign policy. The primitive general international law cannot guarantee the security of all the members of the international community, cannot guarantee the peaceful settlement of international conflicts, has no special organs, controls no monopoly of armed force. In consequence, security becomes, as in all primitive law, the individual task of each state. Each tries to get as strong as it can by armaments—and armament policy is, under general international law, a domestic affair. Each has the right of self-help through reprisals and the right to go to war, either to redress—in static conflicts—international wrongs, or—in dynamic conflicts—to change the status quo by force. Security considerations lead to alliances, to the balance-of-power principle, to the "grand coalition" against the preponderant power of the time. But alliances are temporary, shifting, and, as is shown by the struggle over whether the *casus foederis* is given, unreliable. They are directed against a certain state or states according to changing circumstances; hence the amazing *revirements des alliances*. "England," stated a British foreign secretary of the nineteenth century, "has neither eternal friends nor eternal enemies, she has only eternal interests." Armaments, as history has shown, lead to an armament race and, therefore, to war. Alliances lead to counteralliances and thus lessen, not increase, international security. Machiavelli pointed out in his *Il Principe*

the paradox that each state's longing for security con-
tributes to the insecurity of all. That is why sometimes a
policy of conquest is defended as a policy of security.

Since ancient times—in Hellas as well as in ancient
China—dreams of eternal peace have been voiced. The
achievement of advanced municipal legal orders made possible either world-empire—the *Pax Romana*—or, on a regional basis, federation. They reappear today in the form
of the *Pax Sovietica,* or, in democratic countries, in the
ideal of a world federal state, a "world government." They
reappear on a regional basis in the plans of the federation
of "Little Europe."

The shock of World War I led to the recognition that the
old system of individual security by each state had broken
down. The impossibility, perhaps even undesirability, of a
world federal state was recognized. Hence, an attempt was
made to arrive at a new system of collective security by
international organization on a quasi-universal scale; that
is, by norms of particular international law, by a basic
treaty which would adopt some of the features of an advanced municipal legal order and yet remain within the
framework of international law. The end envisaged was a
loose confederation of sovereign states which would accept
by treaty certain restrictions of their sovereignty. The term
"collective security" was coined for this system. The League
of Nations experiment failed, but was renewed under the
present United Nations. Both experiments differ considerably in detail,[1] but are basically identical.

Since 1920, the new concept of collective security has
found enthusiastic supporters among statesmen and writers
and has developed an extensive literature.[2] From a legal
point of view even its definition [3] is by no means settled.
But it is clear that it involves such problems as partial
or total prohibition of war (use of force) in international
relations, apart from admitted exceptions; disarmament;

peaceful settlement of international conflicts; "peaceful
change"; collective sanctions, economic or military; an
"international police force." In the League of Nations, collective security did not function. The fate of collective
security by military action has now been tested in the
Korean War; but it still has to await definitive evaluation.
Uncertainty as to the functioning of quasi-universal collective security under the League of Nations led to old-
fashioned alliances, based on Article XXI of the Covenant,[4]
to a new wave of national neutrality legislation in the
thirties, and to an attempt at regional collective security.[5]
The same uncertainty [6] now has again led to alliances or
treaties aimed at regional collective security, the Soviet
Union making use of escape-clauses LIII and CVII, the
"Free World" of Article LI of the United Nations Charter.[7]

II

The concept of collective security, so much discussed since
1920, is seemingly new. But early Pan-Americanism, a
century before 1920, experimented with just such a system.
In that respect Bolivarian Pan-Americanism was, on a regional scale, the forerunner of the quasi-universal League
of Nations and United Nations, as well as the inspiration
for the most recent development of present-day Pan-Americanism. The Rio Treaty of 1947 has served as a model
for other treaties of regional collective security.

Most of the legal and technical problems, most of the
difficulties which have arisen since 1920 with regard to
a system of collective security, had already been experienced
by the early Pan-Americanism which, therefore, constitutes
a storehouse of ideas and experiments. North American
and European writers mostly neglect these precedents.

It is nowadays often stated that the only way to abolish
war is through federalism. The European Coal and Steel

Community and the proposed European Defense Community are at least partly supranational and, in consequence, "quasi-federal." The principle of federalism played a prominent role in the ideas of Simon Bolivar. Bolivar, it is true, never thought of making liberated Spanish America one single nation, one federal state. "This," he wrote from Kingston, Jamaica, on September 6, 1815,[8] "would be a grandiose idea, but in spite of the same origin, religion, language, and customs this is a utopia, because remote climates, different situations, opposed interests, unequal character divide America." He aimed from the beginning at a Spanish American confederation of independent states. The principle of confederation or federalism on a more restricted regional scale played a role with Bolivar and later. As the successor to the vice-royalty of Nueva Granda, Bolivar created Gran Colombia. This was not even a federal state, but one unitary republic, divided into the three great departments of Colombia, Venezuela, and Ecuador. But Gran Colombia (1822-30) did not survive the life of the Liberator and fell apart into three sovereign republics. Disillusioned and pessimistic after the failure of the Congress of Panama, Bolivar dreamed of the great *Confederación Andina*,[9] which, in addition to Gran Colombia, should include the other two "Bolivarian States," Peru and Bolivia, but which never came into existence. The *Confederación Peru-Boliviana* was realized, although only for a short time (1835-39). Only once, for a limited time (1824-38), did there exist a Federal Republic of Central America. All later attempts at confederation or federation of Central America[10] have failed. These early attempts at regional confederation served as preparation for the Spanish American confederation which was Bolivar's aim.

This ideal was older than the Congress of Panama of 1826, older even than Spanish American independence. Bolivar had forerunners; other men had dreamed of the lib-

eration of Spanish America,[11] its unity and solidarity, and
many plans had been proposed prior to 1826.[12] But it was
Simon Bolivar, "El Libertador," alone who took these
ideas into the realm of practical politics. He envisaged a
Spanish American confederation through a congress of
representatives assembled at Panama. This confederation
should assure victory over Spain and then guarantee independence against any attempt at reconquest by Spain, aided
perhaps by the Holy Alliance. It was to be, first an alliance: but also an organization, a system of collective
security, transcending an old-fashoned alliance. The congress was to be permanent and had the further task of
guarding against the internal dangers of anarchy or dictatorship. The confederation should not merely be a defensive alliance, but a "league of sister nations," deciding
future conflicts between them though an "Amphictyonic
Council." After long diplomatic preparations, he concluded
treaties between Colombia, on the one hand, and Peru,[13]
Chile,[14] Mexico,[15] and Central America,[16] on the other. All
these were treaties of alliances, but also much more. The
contracting parties were bound mutually to support each
other in order to repel in common—collective security—
any attack or invasion which in any way might endanger
their political existence. But the treaties foresaw also the
formation of an assembly which, in Bolivar's words, was
"to serve as a counsellor in the great conflicts, as a point
of contact in common dangers, as a faithful interpreter of
their treaties, and as a conciliator and arbitral judge in
their disputes." The assembly was not to intervene in the
domestic affairs of the states. All these treaties were to be
steppingstones towards the Spanish American confederation. Bolivar was unable to achieve a treaty with Argentina,
then his opponent, as she is now ever the antagonist of the
United States in the present Pan-Americanism. Argentina's
foreign policy was dominated by the political ideas of

Mariano Moreno,[17] the "Apostle of the May Revolution of 1810"; he was decidedly opposed to any plan of American confederation. National sovereignty, resistance to any attempt at hegemony in the Americas, faith in Argentine leadership, American solidarity but no American confederation—these were his ideas.[18]

On December 7, 1824, Bolivar sent from Lima a circular letter of invitation to the Congress of Panama. Meeting in 1826,[19] from June 22 to July 15, it was attended by delegates from Gran Colombia, Mexico, Peru, and Central America (representing eleven of the present-day Latin-American republics), by an agent of England, and by an unofficial observer from Holland. Four draft treaties were signed.[20] The most important was the Treaty of Union, League, and Perpetual Confederation: the other treaties were supplementary to it. Not one was ever ratified. Bolivar was disillusioned. Attempts to revive the Panama Congress at Tacubaya, Mexico, had to be abandoned definitively on October 9, 1828.

From a practical point of view, the Panama Congress was a failure. There was lack of harmony among the delegates. Peru was thinking in terms of the "Amphictyonic Council," Colombia primarily in terms of a war alliance. Mexico successfuly opposed, for reasons of sovereignty, the authority of the congress to decide the conflicts as an arbitral judge with binding force and without appeal. Opposition to a really compulsory international judicial decision was as strong in 1826 as it was in 1945 at the occasion of drafting the statute of the present International Court of Justice. Central America wanted the inclusion of a clause on frontiers, and this wish at once brought nationalistic desires into the foreground. During the struggle for independence there had been real and spontaneous fraternity; but at the time of the Congress of Panama victory had been won and conflicting interests and ambitions appeared which were stronger than the feeling of community. For these very reasons, President Roosevelt convoked the San Francisco Conference for drafting the United Nations Charter while World War II was still going on. But the Panama Congress, notwithstanding its failure, remains of the greatest importance because of its influence on both early and present Pan-Americanism because it was a forerunner of recent quasi-universal experiments, because of its ideas, problems, and methods, its difficulties, and its very reasons for failure.

III

The Panama Congress wanted to establish—like the League of Nations and the United Nations—not a federal state, not a "superstate," but a loose confederation of sovereign states. The principle of what is now called in Article II, paragraph 1, of the United Nations Charter "sovereign equality of all members" was basic, and it has remained fundamental to the whole later history of Pan-Americanism to the present. For that reason, and in order to avoid even an appearance of Colombia's "hegemony," the order of precedence of the delegations was decided by lot, a procedure still followed in the Pan-Americanism of today. For the same reason the presidency was by rotation, a system inspired by the Congress of Vienna of 1815, but this was later abandoned. It was again applied, at Mr. Molotov's insistence, at the San Francisco Conference.

The Treaty of Union, League, and Perpetual Confederation provided that contracting parties should confederate in peace and war. Not all the Spanish American states were represented at Panama; but provision was made for them. The system was one of mere accession, not of admission as in the League of Nations, the United Nations, NATO, and the European Defense Community Treaty. The goal was a

Spanish American confederation, which would have been only a regional organization. But there was in the mind of Bolivar always the idea of a world confederation: he was fundamentally a universalist.

The first object of the treaty was to maintain in common, defensively and offensively, the sovereignty and independence of each state against any foreign domination. It is interesting to compare this treaty with later developments. The parties were bound to defend themselves mutually against any attack which endangered their political existence and to employ all their influence, resources, land and sea forces against the enemy, according to the contingents which each one was bound to contribute to the common cause. These contingents—as in Article XVI of the League of Nations Covenant and in Article XLIII of the United Nations Charter—were to have the right of free passage over the territory of any of the confederate states. The second convention—on contingents—foresaw an army of 60,000 men, organized, equipped, and ready to enter a campaign. According to the fourth convention, the contingents were to be unequal; [21] each ally was to contribute a subsidy of 200,000 pesos. It was a confederate, not a federal, army, just as under the League of Nations and the United Nations, but contrary to the European Defense Community Treaty. Bolivar, like the French in 1920, had wanted an "army independent of the constituent parts and at the order of the Assembly." But under pressure of nationalistic considerations, the treaty provided that the contingents should preserve under their commanders the organization, order, and discipline of their own country. There is nothing corresponding to the Military Staff Committee of Article XLVII of the United Nations Charter; no military command, like the U.N. Command in Korea. Only if it were deemed wise to take the offensive against the enemy beyond the territories of the allies—here the problem of the aim of "military sanctions," mere repelling of aggression or

offensive action, as it arose in Korea in the offensive toward the Yalu River is involved—was strategic unity and
an allied commander in chief foreseen.

Unlike the provision for contingents, the treaty created
a confederate navy. Peru's fleet was to remain independent, but was charged with the protection of the Pacific
Coast of all the allies: but there was to be an Atlantic
confederate navy, composed of the men-of-war of the three
other contracting parties, with unity of service and command. Interestingly, a special organ was provided, the
Board of Directors (*Commisión Directiva*), composed of
three members, each appointed by his government to have
command and direction in the Alantic. Each member had
full diplomatic privileges and immunities—one of the earliest cases of such immunities granted to an international
organ.

Although this treaty contains much of collective security,
it was basically an alliance, directed against a particular
state—Spain and, perhaps, the Holy Alliance—just as there
is an element of defensive alliance against the U.S.S.R. in
the NATO pact. But the treaty was more than an alliance;
it had also to secure permanent peace and to promote
internal harmony among allies. The confederation was to be
permanent. Highly interesting and contrary to the League
of Nations and the United Nations, the treaty was based on
the republican regime of the parties and tried to establish
a strong barrier against a monarchy in Spanish America.
Essential change in government by an ally excluded this
state *ipso facto* from the confederation. More far-reaching
than Article X of the League of Nations Covenant was
the duty of each state to maintain and defend the others'
territorial integrity and, if necessary, to employ in common its forces and resources to this end. They further
guaranteed mutually each other's territorial integrity *inter
se.*

Contrary to later developments, the confederation had only one organ: the congress, which, as in the League of Nations and the United Nations, was to be a permanent institution with periodic meetings. As the only organ, it had wider powers than its counterparts in the League or the United Nations. A system of collective security presupposes machinery for the peaceful settlement of international conflicts, direct negotiation being the first step. If no settlement could be reached, then the parties—as under Article XV of the Covenant and Article XXXVII of the United Nations Charter—were bound to submit the dispute to the congress; but its action, contrary to Bolivar's wish, was not legally binding unless the conflicting parties expressly so agreed. But neither of the conflicting states could declare war or order acts of reprisals without first having submitted the dispute to the conciliatory procedure of the congress. In case any confederate deemed it advisable to declare war or commence hostilities against a foreign power, he had first to solicit the good offices and mediation of the allies. If mediation were unavailing, the congress then was to declare whether it would embrace the cause of the confederate or not; but even in the latter case, it should never ally itself with the enemy of the confederate. Thus, allied solidarity was upheld, even if a confederate started a war of aggression against a foreign power.

As in present-day organization, compulsory arbitration was, at the insistence of Mexico, eliminated. The treaty, like the League of Nations Covenant, did not absolutely forbid resort to war, not even *inter se*. It contains only certain prohibitions, based, as in the Covenant, not on the justice of the cause, but on the fulfilment of procedural duties. But whereas the Covenant and the Pact of Paris use the word "war"—contrary to the term "use of force" in the United Nations Charter—the formula of the 1826 treaty, "war, commencement of hostilities or reprisals," is far superior.

As far as basic problems of a system of collective security are concerned, the Panama congress was a forerunner of later regional and quasi-universal developments. It also set the pattern for many other features—international conciliation procedure, advisory opinions which the congress could give at the demand of a confederate, diplomatic privileges for international organs, and provision in the additional article of the treaty for a later conference for the codification of international law, inviting also "neutral and friendly Powers."

Bolivar may be called a precursor of Woodrow Wilson, the Panama congress a forerunner of the League of Nations.[22] But the arguments advanced by some Latin-American writers that Bolivar had no predecessors are untenable. Although precedents for his ideas do not lay in classic Hellas, despite his "Amphictyonic Council," the Panama congress had precedents in the long series of European proposals for eternal peace, beginning with Pierre Dubois and climaxing in Bolivar's time with the much-read proposal of the Abbé de St. Pierre; between it and the congress of Panama, there are many and great similarities. This writer believes that Bolivar must have known of the proposal by the Abbé de St. Pierre, at least through the extract made by Rousseau, who exercised great influence on Bolivar's ideas. The Panama congress is a link in the chain in the history of ideas; while it had influence on future developments, it was also firmly connected with the past. There is this difference: the earlier European proposals remained merely theoretical; with Bolivar and the Panama congress they entered for the first time into the realm of practical politics, they determined the action of the leading statesmen, were discussed at a diplomatic gathering, and took the shape of draft treaties; but, because of their non-ratification, they never became positive law. The League of Nations Covenant, for the first time, translated these ideas into positive law, even if only for the interwar period.

IV

The Panama congress was practically a failure. With Bolivar's death the leadership of Colombia came to an end, but Bolivar's ideas survived and show historical continuity. In early Pan-Americanism, as today, ideas of collective security held a prominent place in time of stress, but subsided when there was no outside common danger. Mexican attempts to promote Pan-American union in 1831 and 1838 were unsuccessful. But from 1840, Peru [23] took the leadership and kept it until her disaster in the war with Chile in 1879.

It was Peru that sent out the invitation to the first American congress at Lima,[24] which was attended by delegates from Bolivia, Chile, Colombia, Ecuador, and Peru and was, therefore, not only a strictly Spanish American but also—contrary to Panama, 1826—an exclusively Spanish South American congress. It lasted from December 11, 1847, to March 10, 1848, and produced four draft treaties,[25] of which only the first is important here. This *Tratado de Confederación*, signed at Lima on February 8, 1848, does not constitute a full-fledged confederation but rather a combination of an alliance against foreign powers with, in the words of Ullóa, a pact of non-aggression *inter se*, and rules for the pacific settlement of international conflicts. Strong emphasis is put on the sovereignty of the members, against any appearance of a "superstate" —the declarations against a "superstate" were frequent in the early years of the League of Nations—on the prohibition of intervention in domestic affairs. "Noninterven-

tion" has remained a cornerstone of Pan-Americanism up
to the present day, but plays also its role in quasi-universal
organizations, as Article XV, paragraph 8, of the League
of Nations Covenant and the much worse Article II, paragraph 7, of the United Nations Charter show. Nevertheless, this treaty contains far-reaching restrictions on
sovereignty and goes in some points much farther than
either the treaties of Panama of 1826 or modern quasi-
universal treaties.

The first feature of this treaty was an alliance against
foreign powers and each state's duty to help the others
with land and sea forces and other means of defense. The
political situation had changed: victory had been won;
the alliance was, therefore, not in an existing war, but
pro futuro. But the Spanish American republics felt themselves weak; they feared not only armed attack and conquest but also foreign intervention by force; they were
highly sensitive to diplomatic outrages by European nations.
The expedition by Flores, the attempt to place Ecuador
under a Spanish prince, made them aware that their independence might be threatened by intrigues of Latin-
American adventurers. All that is reflected in the four
types of the *casus foederis*: (1) threat to the territory of
any confederate by a foreign power; (2) forceful intervention by a foreign power to change the constitution of
a republic, or to impose upon it demands that were not
in conformity with international law; (3) grave diplomatic
offense; and (4) invasion by adventurers. Great progress
was made, by centralizing—unlike Article XVI of the
League of Nations Covenant—the determination of the
casus foederis: this right was given to the congress. The
offended member had to bring the facts and its inability
to obtain reparations or satisfaction before the congress.
The congress would then first decide whether the demand
of the republic was just. If so, the congress communicated

this decision to all confederates so that each of them might direct itself to the offending foreign power and ask for due reparation or satisfaction. If it were denied by the foreign government without sufficient justification, the congress would declare the existence of the *casus foederis* and communicate its decision to all confederates. Each had to contribute its respective means and contingents. The legal effects of a declaration of the *casus foederis* were: (1) all confederates considered themselves at war with the foreign power in question; (2) there was complete cessation of all relations with that foreign power, economic sanctions being applied in the absolute manner provided in Article XVI of the League of Nations Covenant and contrary to Article XLI of the United Nations Charter; (3) all other confederates were bound to contribute their contingents. Unlike the Panama agreements, there was no convention on contingents: these were to be determined in each case by the congress. Also contrary to Panama, unity of command of the confederate forces was foreseen from the beginning.

In addition to this alliance, there were the norms *inter se*: no confederate was allowed to recruit or organize forces or manufacture arms within its territory for the purpose of disturbing the peace of any other confederate republic— a prohibition which has become a standard feature in Pan-Americanism down to the present. There was, as in the Pact of Paris, or in Article II, paragraph 3, of the United Nations Charter, the duty to settle all conflicts *inter se* only by peaceful means. War between confederates was absolutely forbidden, a norm which goes beyond the Panama Treaty and the League of Nations Covenant. Further, for peaceful settlement of these conflicts, provision was made for direct diplomatic negotiations, the good offices of other confederates, or arbitration. Should no settlement be reached by these means, the Congress would give a

binding decision. Following the Abbé de St. Pierre, and
going far beyond the Treaty of Panama or the League
of Nations Covenant, the treaty established sanctions—
either complete economic or military ones—against a member opening hostilities in violation of its duty to settle
conflicts *inter se* by peaceful means only, or not fulfilling
the decision of the congress.

This treaty of 1848 had its weak points: emphasis on
national sovereignty, and on the prohibition of intervention
in domestic affairs; and there was, as in the Panama
Treaty, only one organ, the congress. This congress—outcome of tendencies against a "superstate"—was weaker
than that provided for by the Panama Treaty, for it had
no periodic meetings. But it was, from many aspects, a very
remarkable treaty, more far-reaching than any prior and
most subsequent agreements. The determination of the
casus foederis even against a foreign power is made dependent on the *justice* of the claim by a confederate; even
if the justice of this claim is recognized, a further attempt
at peaceful solution must be made. Should the foreign
power refuse reparations, justification for the refusal must
be considered. If the congress does not find the confederate
claim just, or if a foreign power cannot obtain reparations
for injury, the congress asks all confederates to mediate; if
mediation fails and war breaks out, the other confederates
have to remain neutral. This is a system very different from
the complete solidarity with a confederate, even if he commits aggression, provided under the Panama treaty.

This treaty of 1848 is also remarkable because of its
system of economic and military sanctions, not only against
a foreign power, if the *casus foederis* is given, but also
against a member guilty of a breach of the treaty in the
relations of the confederates *inter se*. War is here absolutely
prohibited between members, the peaceful settlement of conflicts being obligatory. The League of Nations Covenant

could not forbid war absolutely because it did not guarantee the peaceful settlement of all conflicts. The United Nations Charter forbids the use of force, although it, too, does not guarantee the peaceful settlement of all conflicts. But the treaty of 1848 could logically forbid war between members absolutely because it guaranteed the peaceful settlement of all international conflicts through the decision of congress, binding by the treaty and without special submission by the parties. We see here, for the first time, such binding decision. But it is not the appearance of compulsory arbitration or judicial settlement because this binding decision need not be a judicial one; the congress can act as amiable *compositeur,* as judge or as legislator; its decision need not necessarily be based on law but must be based on justice. Remarkable also—and contrary to the League of Nations Covenant—is the centralization of the determination of the *casus foederis* against a foreign power and of a breach of treaty by a member in the international organ, the congress, which, like the United Nations Security Council, can decide, order, command, and has to be obeyed. What is more, this centralization is not vitiated and nullified by the voting procedure, as in the Security Council through the "veto"; the binding decisions of the Congress need no ratification and are voted—indeed remarkable for a treaty made in 1848—by simple, absolute majority.

V

Early attempts at collective security were aimed, so far as non-Spanish American powers are concerned, primarily at Spain and the Holy Alliance. But times changed. While the first American congress was sitting in Lima, the United States–Mexican War was going on. From 1854 to 1857, the filibustering expedition of William Walker took

place in Nicaragua.[26] Peru again led the protests. Attempts
at collective security, made in 1856, had, therefore, an anti-
United States flavor. Both attempts were not only, from a
practical point of view, unsuccessful, but they also hold a
minor place in the history of ideas. The so-called Washington Treaty [27] of November 18, 1856, was not a treaty, but
an agreement between the representatives of Mexico, Guatemala, Salvador, Costa Rica, Colombia, Venezuela, and
Peru to propose a treaty of alliance and confederation to
their governments. More important was the second attempt,
the so-called Continental Treaty,[28] signed on September 25,
1856, in Santiago de Chile by representatives of Chile, Peru,
and Ecuador, but not ratified. This treaty proposed a Hispanic-American confederation, including Brazil. But the
proposed confederation was much looser than the one proposed by the Lima Treaty of 1848, and showed also, with
regard to the peaceful settlement of international conflicts,
a marked retrogression.

Again the international situation changed completely.
The outbreak of the American Civil War removed, for the
time being, any danger from the United States, but exactly
for that reason new dangers appeared from Europe: the
reincorporation of Santo Domingo in Spain (1861-65), the
French invasion of Mexico, and the Spanish occupation of
the Chincha Islands, Peru (1864). In this situation Peru
sent out invitations to the second American congress in
Lima,[29] which lasted from November 14, 1864, to March
13, 1865. There were represented Bolivia, Chile, Ecuador,
Colombia, Peru, Salvador, Guatemala, and Venezuela.
Argentina did not participate, although the Argentinian
minister, D. F. Sarmiento, sat in the congress, probably up
to February 15, 1865, *ad referendum*. The congress signed
four draft treaties, of which the first two are here interesting; the Treaty on Union and Alliance, and the Treaty on
Preservation of Peace, both signed on January 23, 1865:
they were not ratified.

What the Lima congress of 1848 had put into one treaty was here put into two. In both, the parties bind themselves to solicit the adherence of the other American states. Even the title of the first treaty shows that it does not go so far as did the treaties of 1826, 1848, and 1856. The concept of "perpetual league and confederation" had dwindled to "union and alliance," to the concept of the "great American family of nations." A confederation is no longer even mentioned, while the idea of a "superstate" is more remote than ever. The parties unite to provide for their external security and to affirm peace between themselves. They mutually guarantee independence, sovereignty, and territorial integrity, and obligate themselves to defend each other against any aggressor seeking to deprive them of these rights. There are three types of *casus foederis*: aggression by a foreign power, by one of the contracting powers, or by foreign forces which do not obey a recognized government, the echo of the "filibustering expeditions." Especially mentioned as acts of aggression are those aimed at depriving a party of its territory, changing the form of its government or establishing a protectorate, or seeking cessions or purchases of territory. National sovereignty led, contrary to the Lima Treaty of 1848, again to the decentralization of the determination of the *casus foederis*. Each party must make this decision for itself; if affirmative, it is then bound to break off all relations with the aggressor. Delegates will then be appointed to conclude conventions on contingents, although the parties obligate themselves to give to the attacked party any means of defense at their disposal, if urgently needed, even if the stipulations for contingents have not taken place. This is similar to the "collective self-defense" provision under Article LI of the United Nations Charter.

It is interesting to note that here, as in modern developments, a strict dichotomy is made between aggression and the peaceful settlement of international conflicts *inter se*.

Acts of agression *inter se* are dealt with under the first treaty; here the same norms prevail as in case of aggression by a foreign power. The second treaty deals with peaceful settlement of conflicts *inter se*, where, therefore, no *casus foederis* arises. This second treaty returns to the norms of the Lima Treaty of 1848: absolute prohibition of war among the members, compulsory international arbitration. If they cannot settle the conflicts directly between themselves, they are bound to submit them, including boundary disputes, to the unappealable award of an arbiter; if they cannot agree on an arbiter, the appointment will be made by a special assembly of plenipotentiaries, or by the regular congress, if it is assembled.

In this respect the system is different from that provided by the Lima treaty; the binding decision is not given by the congress, but an arbiter, chosen by the parties or appointed by the congress. On the other hand, this binding decision is not on the basis of justice, but a strictly judicial decision on the basis of law.

VI

Having reviewed the precedents of a system of collective security in early Pan-Americanism, it remains to sketch the further development of this idea to the present day. In all these early developments, neither Brazil nor the United States participated. Although well-disposed toward Latin-American independence, the United States was the protagonist of neutrality. In the early nineteenth century, she showed some interest in Latin-American trade and cultural relations. Her strongest protagonist of Pan-Americanism was Henry Clay.[30] Colombia had invited the United States to the Congress of Panama of 1826. Following the bitter debate in the Senate, the invitation was accepted; and Richard C. Anderson and John Sergeant were appointed delegates, but they never reached Panama. Anderson died en route, Sergeant came too late. The instructions of Henry Clay to these two delegates serve to emphasize the position taken by the United States: that the Panama conference was to be regarded as diplomatic, not legislative; anything adopted would need ratification; all notion of an "Amphictyonic Council" invested with power to regulate the conduct or finally to decide controversies between the American states was to be rejected, as well as any idea of an alliance; strict United States neutrality was to be observed. Nothing could have been farther from what is today called a system of collective security than this United States attitude.

In later decades interest in Latin America declined; but by 1880, the now powerful and industrialized United States again became concerned with its neighbors to the south. This renewed interest centered on relations in trade and commerce. A new movement for Pan-Americanism started in the early eighties, led by James G. Blaine.[31] In this respect Blaine was the heir of Henry Clay and the founder of the present Pan-Americanism, which was created by the initiative of the United States. But this new Pan-Americanism was entirely different from that conceived by Bolivar. It was restricted to non-political co-operation, primarily in economic relations. This new "pragmatist" Pan-Americanism, entirely unrelated to the idea of collective security, was not without precedents. Even the congresses of Panama and Lima, and particularly the Continental Treaty, in addition to a system of collective security, dealt also with problems of non-political co-operation. There was a direct precedent in the first Pan-Americanism. With the second congress of Lima the Spanish American political congresses had come to an end. The reason was a growing conviction— consequence of bitter experience with these experiments since 1826—that the ideal of Spanish American union had failed, had proved incapable of political realization. In this

second period, the conferences [32] no longer tried to achieve
a Spanish American confederation but to prepare for political union by the establishment of common juridical norms
and Spanish American co-operation in non-political fields.
Finally, the Argentinian Juan Bautista Alberdi, protagonist
of progress and prosperity, had published a memorandum
in 1844 on the convenience and objects of a general American congress [33] containing proposals for a "practical Pan-
Americanism" not very different from the ideas expressed
forty years later by James G. Blaine.

During the first period of the present Pan-Americanism
(1889-1910), this non-political tendency dominated. Co-
operation was extended from the economic to many other
fields. Problems of international arbitration were discussed.
Latin-American wishes were reflected in the treaty of arbitration for pecuniary claims at the Second Conference of
American States (Mexico City, 1901-02); in the recommendation of the First Conference (Washington, 1889-90)
opposing the recognition of conquest—an idea which dominated the early Spanish American congresses; in the
recommendation of the First Conference concerning diplomatic intervention, to which the United States submitted
a minority report voting in the negative.

Then followed the "great gap" (1910-23) as a consequence of World War I. The unilateral Monroe Doctrine,
isolationism, and neutrality of the United States had barred
any return to the ideas of Bolivar. To these had been added
imperialism under Presidents McKinley and Theodore
Roosevelt, which brought about violent attacks against the
United States by Latin-American agitators, writers, and
poets. There followed a period of crises (1923-28), which
climaxed in the Latin-American attacks against intervention at the Sixth Conference of American States at Havana
in 1928. This Latin-American attitude explains Article VI
of the proposed, but not ratified, Convention on the Pan-

American Union, which forbids the Union and the governing board to exercise any function of a political character. Thus, the non-political character was strongly affirmed. A crisis was averted in Havana by the brilliant speech of the leader of the American delegation, Charles Evans Hughes, who developed the theory, not of intervention, but of "interposition"; but the United States became aware that Pan-Americanism was in danger. Hence, the new policy of President Herbert Hoover (1928-32),[34] followed by the "good neighbor" policy of President Franklin D. Roosevelt, Secretary of State Cordell Hull, and Assistant Secretary Sumner Welles.[35] The principle of non-intervention was recognized by the United States, and the last vestiges of "imperialism" were eradicated. The doors were open for a vigorous development of the present Pan-Americanism and for a return to Bolivar's ideas.

But another development of the greatest importance had occured: the coming into force of the League of Nations in 1920. Here a system of collective security was for the first time tried in positive law. Latin America adhered enthusiastically; it had voiced universalist ideas since the first conference in 1889. It saw in Wilson a follower of Bolivar; in the League of Nations with its partial prohibition of war, with its provisions for peaceful settlement of conflicts, with its ideology of "self-determination of nations," with its system of collective security through economic and military sanctions, a realization of Bolivar's ideas. All Latin-American republics were, at least at one time, members of the League.[36] But, prior to the "good neighbor" policy, their adherence to the League was also motivated by the political wish to enhance Latin-American prestige on the international stage and to balance Washington with Geneva. The influence of the League was felt in the twenties, as can be seen from the so-called Gondra Treaty, adopted at the fifth conference in 1923 at Santiago, which introduced the new procedure of international conciliation into Pan-Americanism.

But even after the coming into force of the "good neighbor" policy, the universalism of the League of Nations and the regionalism of Pan-America [37] created difficulties of many types. On the one hand, Pan-America was, during the whole life of the League, a regional organization, legally fully independent of Geneva; and necessarily so, as the United States never became a member of the League, nor of the Permanent Court of International Justice. The United States was strongly opposed to the collective security system of the Covenant. Isolationism was still strong, and the period from 1935 to 1939 saw a new wave of United States neutrality acts. The contradiction between Article XVI of the League of Nations Covenant and United States neutrality policy made many Pan-American treaties, especially those promulgated at the Buenos Aires Conference (1936), with their clauses in favor of Article XVI, of highly doubtful value. The unsatisfactory status of the Pan-American peace machinery made it possible for Bolivia and Paraguay in the Chaco War to play one system against the other. Although in the exodus of Latin-American republics from the League took place and sometimes harsh words were written against it,[38] Argentina, outside the League since its beginnings, appeared at Buenos Aires in 1936 as its great champion in her eternal role as opponent of the United States. Álvarez [39] wanted to integrate Pan-America into the League of Nations by decentralizing the League on a continental basis. But many wanted, to the contrary, to make Pan-America completely independent.[40] Hence, during the thirties, many proposals were made, especially by the smaller Latin-American states, for an American League of Nations,[41] and for an Inter-American Court of Justice,[42] and these were discussed at Buenos Aires (1936) and at Lima (1938). But these ideas were strongly opposed by the larger Latin-American republics and by the United States. The latter, in the midst of the new neutrality acts, and never a member of the League of Nations, was not ready for a system of collective security.

A return to Bolivar's ideas took place, however, insofar as Pan-American solidarity was concerned. The United States definitively wanted to transform Pan-America into an organization vigorously political. Under the shadow of the approaching World War II, Pan-American solidarity— politically, economically, militarily, and ideologically—assumed a greater importance, and therefore became a necessary aim of United States foreign policy. Already the seventh conference, at Montevideo in 1933, had adopted Resolution XXII, authorizing the Pan-American Union to prepare a compilation of the ideas of Bolivar, "such as the Pact of the American Confederation." At the same conference, the Mexican Peace Code was submitted.

To foster Pan-American solidarity in the light of deteriorating political conditions in Europe, the United States proposed a special conference, which was held in Buenos Aires in 1936. Here the "Declaration of Principles of Inter-American Solidarity and Co-operation" (Resolution XXVII) was adopted. But the United States abstained from voting on "Co-ordination of Pacific Instruments with the Covenant of the League of Nations" (Resolution XXIX). The United States policy was one of Pan-American solidarity, of Pan-American neutrality in the event of an international war outside America." It wanted a policy of consultation, a duty to consult, but one which would leave the United States free to decide what, if any, measures it should take on the basis of such consultation. The new system of consultation [43] was established in 1936 by the "Convention for the Maintenance, Preservation and Reestablishment of Peace." Although the procedure of consultation was not institutionalized in Buenos Aires in 1936, this end was achieved by Resolution CVII of the eighth conference, Lima, 1938. Pan-American solidarity was re-affirmed by the "Declaration of the Principles of the Solidarity of America" (Resolution CIX). This resolution takes into consideration only non-American intervention. All the republics "reaffirm their decision to maintain [the principles] and defend them against all foreign intervention or activity that may threaten them." But they will make effective their solidarity only by "co-ordinating their sovereign wills by means of the procedure of consultation" and "it is understood that the Governments will act independently, in their individual capacity." This is still far from a system of collective security. But a special procedure of consultation, a special organ, the Meeting of Foreign Ministers, was established.

At the first Meeting of Foreign Ministers, Panama, 1939, after the outbreak of World War II, the United States policy of Pan-American neutrality dominated. But economic co-operation (Resolution III) and the protection of the American ideal of democracy against subversive ideologies (Resolution XI) were stressed. In the "Joint Declaration of Continental Solidarity" (Resolution IV), it is stated that these principles "are free from any selfish purpose of isolation, but are rather inspired by a deep sense of universal co-operation," and that the American republics "will endeavor to maintain and strengthen peace and harmony" *inter se* "as an indispensable requirement" for their world-wide duties.

At the second Meeting of Foreign Ministers, which was held at Havana in 1940, after the fall of France, the policy of Pan-American neutrality was changed to a policy of Pan-American defense. Hence the many resolutions for combating subversive activities; the "Act of Habana," concerning the provisional administration of European colonies and possessions in the Americas; the resolutions for the peaceful solution of conflicts and the maintenance of peace and union among the American republics. Most outstanding was Resolution XV on reciprocal assistance for the defense of the nations of the Americas. For the first time a system of collective security is aimed at in the declaration: "That any attempt on the part of a non-American State against the integrity or inviolability of the territory, the sovereignty or the political independence of an American State, shall be considered an act of aggression against the States which sign this declaration." While there is, in case of such aggression, merely a duty to consult, there is also a proviso that "all the signatory nations, or two or more of them, shall proceed to negotiate the necessary complementary agreements so as to organize co-operation for defense and the assistance that they shall lend each other in the event of aggressions." Here the return to the ideas of Bolivar, but on a truly hemispheric, Pan-American scale, is evident.

When, with the Japanese attack on Pearl Harbor, such agression against an American state had occurred, the third Meeting of Foreign Ministers was held at Rio de Janiero from January 15 to 28, 1942. On the basis of Resolution XV of 1940, Pan-American belligerency was due. But the weak Resolution I, while paying lip service to the words of Resolution XV of 1940, speaks only of rupture of diplomatic relations with Japan, Germany, and Italy. This is a legally non-binding recommendation, further crippled by the proviso that even such rupture of diplomatic relations should take place only at the discretion and within the position and circumstances of each country. This weak text was the only one to which all the republics could consent: Argentina, which at Buenos Aires had stood against the United States as the protagonist of the League's system of collective security, in 1942 as the protagonist of neutrality opposed the collective security promoted by the

United States. This resolution is, no doubt, a step backward, as compared with Resolution XV of 1940.

While nearly all the American republics wholeheartedly
co-operated with the United States in World War II, there
was a lessening of direct contacts through Pan-American
organs after 1942. Tension with Argentina was one reason:
but, more important, the United States was fully engaged
on a world-wide scale, as the leader in the battle against
the Axis, and as the leader in creating, after the war, a
new quasi-universal organization, including what was
hoped would be an effective system of collective security.
The Dumbarton Oaks Proposals gave the first outline of the
United Nations Charter. Latin-American criticism was
strong. From February 21 to March 8, 1945, there took
place in Mexico City the Inter-American Conference on
Problems of War and Peace, Argentina being absent. This
conference made far-reaching proposals for the reorganization of the inter-American system,[44] including its integration into the quasi-universal organization. This conference
also adopted Resolution VIII on "Reciprocal Assistance and
American Solidarity," known as the Act of Chapultepec.[45]
Here the return to the ideas of Resolution XV of 1940, and,
hence, to the ideas of Bolivar, is evident; a system of hemispheric collective security is outlined. This act was only
valid for the duration of the war, but a permanent treaty
after the war was recommended and promised.

The Act of Chapultepec led to the so-called Latin-American crisis at the San Francisco Conference. Here was a
real dilemma: how to strengthen the inter-American system
and keep it relatively autonomous, even within the United
Nations, without weakening the world-wide authority of
the Security Council; how to make the coming permanent
treaty legally compatible with the United Nations Charter;
and how to assure the working of inter-American collective
security even in the event that the Security Council should
be paralyzed by the veto. The solution was found in a pro-

posal made by the United States, which was embodied in Article LI of the Charter "on individual and collective self-defense." [46]

In 1947, at a conference in Rio de Janiero, the Inter-American Treaty of Reciprocal Assistance [47] was concluded. The heart of this treaty is the obligation of mutual defense, the fulfilment of the ideas contained in Resolution XV of 1940, and of the Act of Chapultepec; but it goes much farther than these two previous agreements. It is not restricted to aggression by non-American states; it contains more than a duty to consult: it is a legally binding treaty, whereas Resolution XV was only a recommendation. A resolution adopted calls for a new codification of the inter-American peace machinery, which, at that time, was entirely inadequate. The treaty is wholly based on Article LI of the United Nations Charter. While it constitutes in fact a hemispheric system of collective security, it is technically a treaty for individual and collective self-defense.

The ninth International Conference of American States adopted the Bogota Charter,[48] the constitution of the Organization of American States. Articles XXIV and XXV give the basic principles on collective security as laid down by the Rio Treaty of 1947. As one prerequisite to a system of collective security, the Pact of Bogotá [49] tries to set up peace machinery which should guarantee the peaceful settlement of all inter-American conflicts.

The Organization of the American States has developed from an independent body into a "regional agency within the U. N." [50] But Article LI of the Charter, inserted in consequence of Latin-American insistence, has become the means for the conclusion of treaties of regional collective security. The Rio Treaty of 1947 is not only the first of these treaties, but it also inspired the subsequent Brussels (1948) and NATO (1949) agreements.

On the other hand, quasi-universal collective security, as tested since 1950 in Korea, had little echo in Latin America.

Although Resolutions I and II of the fourth Meeting of Foreign Ministers, held in Washington from March 26 to April 7, 1951,[51] are in favor of strong support of the United Nations, and pledge not only positive support for the collective defense of the hemisphere, but also for the prevention and suppression of aggression in other parts of the world, many representatives of Latin-American republics looked at the Organization of American States primarily as a regional organization. Hemispheric, not global, aspects interested them; they were rather unhappy to see this regional system involved in United Nations affairs and the representatives of Guatemala, Mexico, and Argentina said so openly. Their own pressing problems make those of Asia and Europe look very remote indeed to many Latin-Americans. Only Colombia sent troops to fight in Korea.

The United States has turned from isolationism and neutrality at the time of Bolivar and of the League of Nations to become the protagonist of quasi-universal and regional international organization and of a system of collective security. Pan-America, starting with Bolivar, abandoning his ideas after 1865 and in the first more than forty years of the present Pan-Americanism, has clearly returned to his ideas. Latin America, starting under Bolivar in the spirit of universalism, but preoccupied with defense against external aggression or revolution within, has, while retaining a universalist spirit, returned to the ideas of Bolivar, the first to defend this hemisphere against aggression whether by a non-American or an American state. This idea of collective security in Pan-American developments has thus formed a complete circle, starting with and returning to the ideas of Bolivar.

* The French slogan during the interwar period.
1 For a comparison, see 2 OPPENHEIM-LAUTERPACHT, INTERNATIONAL LAW: A TREATISE 161 (7th ed. 1952) ; and HANS KELSEN, PRINCIPLES OF INTERNATIONAL LAW 39 (1952).

[2] See for the League of Nations, M. Bourquin, *Le problème de la sécurité internationale*, 3 RECUEIL DES COURS 473–542 (1934) ; JULES BASDEVANT, L'ORGANIZATION DE LA PAIX (1936). See for the present time, ANDREW MARTIN, COLLECTIVE SECURITY: A PROGRESS REPORT (1952).

[3] Martin, *op cit.* at 14, defines it as "a state of affairs in which attempts to change the status quo by violence are unlawful and doomed to frustration through opposition in overwhelming force."

[4] French-Belgian alliance; "Little Entente"; Balkan Entente; Soviet "neutrality and non-aggression' 'treaties.

[5] Locarno, 1925.

[6] R. G. Mackay, Annals 123 (July, 1953), states: "As long as the Soviet Union remains a member of the United Nations, it will be impossible for any military organization at the headquarters of the UN . . . to take any effective action of any sort. One cannot make defensive plans in the presence of the representative of the potential aggressor against whom the plans are directed. . . . It follows that in these troublous times most of Chapter VII of the Charter is dead and cannot be revived."

[7] Rio Treaty, 1947 Brussels Treaty, 1948; NATO Treaty, 1949.

[8] Reprinted in SIMÓN BOLIVAR, PENSADORES DE AMÉRICA 57–83 (1943).

[9] See V. A. Belaúnde, *La Fédération des Andes*, REVUE DE L'AMÉRIQUE LATINE 20–86 (January, 1928) ; *ibid.* at 132–51 (February, 1928).

[10] See L. BATRES, LA CUESTIÓN DE UNIÓN CENTRO-AMERICANA; JOSÉ BETETA, LA UNIÓN DE CENTRO-AMERICA (1885) ; JOSÉ BETETA, MORAZÁN Y LA FEDERACIÓN (1888) ; LAUDELINO MORENO, HISTORIA DE LAS RELACIONES INTERESTATUALES DE CENTRO-AMÉRICA (1928).

[11] E.g., General Francisco de Miranda, the "Presursor," born in Caracas in 1750.

[12] See MARTINEZ DE ROSAS, CATECISMO POLÍTICO-CRISTIANO (1810) ; JUNA EGAÑA, MEMORIA SOBRE LA FEDERACIÓN EN GENERAL Y CON RELACIÓN A CHILE (1825) ; BERNARDO MONTEAGUDO, ENSAYO SOBRE LA NECESIDAD DE UNA FEDERACIÓN EN GENERAL ENTRE LOS ESTADOS HÍSPANO-AMERICANOS Y PLAN DE SU ORGANIZACIÓN (1825). Particularly the plan of the famous Central American José Cecilio del Valle published in his newspaper *El Amigo de la Patria* in Guatemala City on February 22, 1822, independently from Bolivar, is far-reachingly analogous to the ideas of Bolivar and of the Panama congress; see Pedro de Alba, *Simón Bolivar y José Cecilio del Valle*, REPERTORIO AMERICANO Nos. 39–40.

[13] *Tratado de Unión, Liga y Confederación Perpetua, July 6, 1822*, 1 TRATADOS PÚBLICOS Y ACUERDOS INTERNACIONALES DE VENEZUELA 11–15 (1820–1900). 11 BRITISH AND FOREIGN STATE PAPERS 105–12, 115–20.

[14] *Tratado de Unión, Liga y Confederación, October 21, 1823, op. cit.* at 19–24.

[15] *Tratado de Unión, Liga y Confederación, October 3, 1823, op. cit.* at 26–31. 11 BRITISH AND FOREIGN STATE PAPERS 784⁴92.

¹⁶ *Tratado de Unión, Liga y Confederación, March 51, 1825, op. cit.*, 43–49.

¹⁷ See RICARDO LEVENE, ENSAYO HISTÓRICO SOBRE LA REVOLUCIÓN DE MAYO Y MARIANO MORENO (2 vols. 1920, 1921); LEVENE, SIGNIFICACIÓN HISTÓRICA DE MARIANO MORENO (1937); G. F. ELORDI, MARIANO MORENO, CIUDADANO ILUSTRE (1943).

¹⁸ He published these in an article in the *Gaceta de Buenos Aires* on November 28, 1810. This article is reprinted in LA POLÍTICA EXTERIOR DE LA REPUBLICA ARGENTINA 13–20 (1937).

¹⁹ Out of the immense literature of the congress, we mention here M. DE PRADT, CONGRÈS DE PANAMA (1825); F. A. ZUBIETA, CONGRESOS DE PANAMA Y TACUBAYA (1912); RICARDO ARANDA, CONGRESOS Y CONFERENCIAS EN QUE HA TOMADO PARTE EL PERÚ 5–81; J. B. LOCKEY, PAN-AMERICANISM: ITS BEGINNINGS 288–467 (1920); Frances L. Reinhold, *New Research on the First Pan-American Congress*, 18 HISPANIC-AMERICAN HISTORICAL REVIEW 342–83 (1938); and the carefully edited documentary material in 1 RAÚL PORRAS BARRANECHEA, EL CONGRESO DE PANAMÁ (1930).

²⁰ The four treaties are often reprinted. In Spanish: ZUBIETA, *op. cit.* at 96–109, 109–118; PORRAS BARRENECHEA, *op. cit.* at 405–31; CONFERENCIAS INTERNACIONALES AMERICANAS 1889–1936, Supplements XXVIII–XXXIII (1938). In English: INTERNATIONAL CONFERENCES 1889–1928, xxiv–xxix (1931).

²¹ Mexico, 32,750; Colombia, 15,250; Central America, 6,750; Peru, 5,250 men.

²² See J. M. Yepes, *Bolívar et Wilson, Le Traité de Panama de 1826 et la Pacte de la Société des Nations*, 40 DIE FRIEDENSWARTE Nos. 1–2 at 37–46.

²³ See P. UGARTECHE, EL PERÚ EN LA VIDA INTERNACIONAL AMERICANA, 1826–1879 (1927). ALBERTO ULLÓA, POSICIÓN INTERNACIONAL DEL PERÚ (1941).

²⁴ 2 & 3 ALBERTO ULLÓA, CONGRESOS AMERICANOS DE LIMA (1938).

²⁵ Text in *ibid.* at 301–33.

²⁶ WILLIAM O. SCROGGS, FILIBUSTERS AND FINANCIERS: THE STORY OF WILLIAM WALKER AND HIS ASSOCIATES (1916); Isidoro Fabela, *El filibusterismo americano en Centro-América*, 3 REVISTA MEXICANA DE DERECHO INTERNACIONAL No. 1 (1921).

²⁷ 1 ULLÓA, CONGRESOS AMERICANOS DE LIMA 628–35.

²⁸ *Ibid.* at 579–627, 637–80 (documents), 613–20 (text).

²⁹ ARANDA, *op. cit.* at 333–442; UGARTECHE, *op. cit.* at 22–30; 1 ULLÓA, CONGRESOS AMERICANOS DE LIMA 337–575; D. F. SARMIENTO, EL CONGRESO AMERICANO DE 1864 (1865); BARTOLOMÉ MITRE, CORRESPONDENCIA CON D. F. SARMIENTO SOBRE EL CONGRESO AMERICANO DE LIMA. 1864–1865.

³⁰ See CALVIN COLTON, LIFE AND TIMES OF H. CLAY (1846); CARL SCHURZ, LIFE OF H. CLAY (1909), J. B. MOORE, *(Henry Clay) and Pan-Americanism*, COLUMBIA UNIVERSITY QUARTERLY 346–82 (September, 1915); H. L. Hoskins, *Hispanic-American Policy of Henry Clay 1816–1828*, HISPANIC-AMERICAN HISTORICAL REVIEW 460–76 (November, 1927); James Brown Scott, *Clay el americano, un pan-americano*,

18 REVISTA DE DERECHO INTERNACIONAL 275–83 (1930); E. Barton, *Henry Clay*, in 4 S. F. BEMAS, THE AMERICAN SECRETARIES OF STATE AND THEIR DIPLOMACY 115–58, 352–57 (1930); Enrique Gil, *Henry Clay*, 7 REVISTA ARGENTINA DE DERECHO INTERNACIONAL (2nd ser.) 40–57.

31 See J. B. Lockey, *J. G. Blaine*, in 8 BEMIS, *op. cit.* at 263–97, 323–26, 109–84; G. HAMILTON, BIOGRAPHY OF JAMES G. BLAINE (1895); EDWARD STANWOOD, JAMES GILLESPIE BLAINE (1917); A. Curtis Wilgus, *Blaine and the Pan-American Movement*, 5 HISPANIC-AMERICAN HISTORICAL REVIEW No. 4 (1922); A. F. TYLER, THE FOREIGN POLICY OF JAMES G. BLAINE (1927); DAVID S. MUZZEY, JAMES G. BLAINE (1934); Sumner Welles's address in 8 BULLETIN PAN-AMERICAN UNION No. 188 at 104–7 (1943).

32 Sanitary congresses, pedagogical congresses, American Congress of Jurists at Lima, 1877–1879, and the successful Montevideo Congress on Private International Law, 1888–1889.

33 J. B. ALBERDI, MEMORIA SOBRE LA CONVENIENCIA Y OBJETOS DE UN CONGRESO GENERAL AMERICANO (1844). See Jose N. Matienzo, *La política americana de Alberdi*, 1 REVISTA ARGENTINA DE CIENCIAS POLITICAS 28, 42 (1910).

34 A. DE CONDE, HERBERT HOOVER'S LATIN AMERICAN POLICY (1951).

35 E. O. GUERRANT, ROOSEVELT'S GOOD NEIGHBOR POLICY (1950); Sumner Welles, *La política de buena vecindad*, 5 REVISTE DE LA HABANA 35–48 (September, 1949); JOSÉ DE LA VEGA, EL BUEN VECINO; WADE C. BARCLAY, GREATER GOOD NEIGHBOR POLICY (1945).

36 Of the great literature, we mention R. Fernández, *L'Amérique du Sud et la Société des Nations*, in 2 MUNCH, ORIGINES ET L'OEUVRE DE LA SOCIÉTÉ DES NATIONS 141 (1924); P. A. Martin, *Latin America and the League of Nations*, AMERICAN POLITICAL SCIENCE REVIEW 14–30 (February, 1926); V. B. Galleano, L'Amérique Latine, les Etats-Unis et la Société des Nations (unpublished thesis, Paris, 1927); 12 W. H. KELNER, LATIN-AMERICAN RELATIONS WITH THE LEAGUE OF NATIONS No. 6 (1927); José Matos, *L'Amérique latine et al Société des Nations*, 3 RECUEIL DES COURS 5–103 (1929); H. VAN LEISEN, L'AMÉRIQUE LATINE ET LA SOCIÉTÉ DES NATIONS (1934); M. PEREZ-GUERRERO, LES RELATIONS DES ETATS DE L'AMÉRIQUE LATINE AVEC LA SOCIÉTÉ DES NATIONS (1936).

37 For a detailed discussion, see Josef L. Kunz, *The Inter-American System and the U. N. Organization*, 39 AM.J.INT'L L. 758–67 (1945).

38 See S. PLANAS-SUÁREZ, LA POLÍTICA EUROPEA Y LA SOCIEDAD DE LAS NACIONES (1935).

39 Alejandro Alvarez, *La réforme du Pacte sur des bases régionales et continentales*, RAPPORT À LA Vᵉ SESSION DE L'UNION JURIDIQUE INTERNATIONALE.

40 These ideas stem from the proposal by the president of Uruguay, Baltasar Brum, *Estatutos de la Asociación de los paises americanos*, BOLETIN DEL MINISTERIO DE RELACIONES EXTERIORES 174–95 (1923).

41 See RICARDO ALFARO, *Toward an American Association of Nations*, 1 INTER-AMERICAN QUARTERLY 25–36 (1923); JESÚS MARIA YEPES, LA SOCIEDAD DE LAS NACIONES AMERICANAS (1936).

42 See PAN-AMERICAN UNION (JURIDICAL DIVISION), INFORMES Y PROYECTOS SOBRE EL ESTABLECIMIENTO DE LA CORTE INTER-AMERICANA DE JUSTICIA INTERNACIONAL.

43 Josef L. Kunz, *Consultation*, DIE FRIEDENS-WARTE 21–28 (1939).

44 See Josef L. Kunz, *Inter-American Conference on Problems of Peace and War and the Problem of the Reorganization of the Inter-American System*, 39 AM.J.INT'L L. 527–33 (1945).

45 See Manuel S. Canyes, *The Inter-American System and the Conference of Chapultepec*, 39 AM.J.INT'L L. 504-17 (1945).

46 See "Individual and Collective Self-defense in Article LI of the Charter of the United Nations," above.

47 See 'The Inter-American Treaty of Reciprocal Assistance," below.

48 For an analysis see "The Bogotá Charter of the Organization of American States," below.

49 For a full analysis and critique, see Josef L. Kunz, *Interamerikanische Streitschlichtung unter dem Pakt von Bogotá*, 2 OSTERREICHESCHE ZEITSCHRIFT FÜR ÖFFENTLICHES RECHT 486–519 (1950); and "International Arbitration in Pan-American Developments," above.

50 Bogotá Charter, 1948, art. I.

51 See Josef L. Kunz, *Fourth Meeting of Consultation of Ministers of Foreign Affairs*, 45 AM.J.INT'L L. 740–45 (1951).

THE IDEA of Pan-American solidarity, always inherent in Pan-Americanism, has steadily gained since the inauguration of the "good neighbor policy" and became of paramount importance with the outbreak of World War II. The development can be observed very clearly in the relevant resolutions adopted at Buenos Aires in 1936, at Lima in 1938, and at Panama in 1939. A first climax was reached in resolution XV of the Havana Meeting of Foreign Ministers.[1] Resolution I of the Rio de Janeiro meeting of 1942, called after the Japanese attack on Pearl Harbor, constitutes, it is true, a step backward. But the Mexico City conference of 1945 produced the Act of Chapultepec [2] which, for the first time, went so far as to stipulate the "use of armed force to prevent or repel aggression." This act, binding only "during the war," provided for the conclusion of a permanent inter-American treaty to replace the Act of Chapultepec "following the establishment of peace."

The conclusion of this treaty should have taken place at a special conference, to be held at Rio de Janeiro in the fall of 1945. Two obstacles arose. The first was the problem of the legality of the Act of Chapultepec and the new treaty under the Charter of the U.N. This problem was solved by the insertion of Article LI [3] in the Charter at the San Francisco Conference. The second obstacle was the long political tension between this country and Argentina. Twice the date for the Rio Conference was fixed [4] by the governing board of the Pan-American Union, but twice it had to be postponed, the first time at the request of the United States, the second time at the request of Uruguay. It was only in the spring of 1947 that this long feud came to an end. In his speech before the Pan-American Union on Pan-American Day, April 14, 1947, Senator Vandenberg[5] emphasized that "all" the American republics must collaborate with each other to promote unity in this hemisphere and urged Canada to join also. The way had, at last, been cleared for the Rio Conference.

Already during the first months of 1946 eight American governments [6] had proposed projects for the Rio treaty and a special committee of the governing board submitted, on May 15, 1946, a report [7] containing an analysis and a comparison of the projects submitted; they all start from the Act of Chapultepec and make full use of Article LI of the Charter of the U.N. On June 27, 1947, the governing board resolved to undertake a consultation among the American governments on the principal points to be incorporated in the Rio treaty and, on July 14, 1947, a committee submited to the board its report on this consultation.[8]

The conference took place from August 15 to September 2, 1947, at Rio de Janeiro or rather at the Hotel Quitadinha at Petropolis, forty-four miles from the capital. It adopted the treaty [9] and fifteen resolutions.[10] The conference, well prepared [11] and well organized,[12] was a complete success.[13] Twenty American republics were represented,[14] many by their foreign ministers;[15] the United States delegation [16] was likewise led by the secretary of state. Two interesting and important problems as to representation [17] arose. The first one concerned the failure to invite Nicaragua, the *de facto* government of which had not been recognized by a majority of the American republics. It seems that the rule of law is—as confirmed by the procedure applied by Chile at the time of the invitations for the Santiago Conference of 1923—that every American republic has a constitutional right to be represented at every Inter-American conference, regardless of whether its *de facto* government is or is not recognized by the inviting state. Failure to invite would, therefore, constitute a violation of law and would deprive the conference of its inter-American character. A special procedure, concerning the recognition of *de facto* governments through inter-American consultation, was adopted during the recent war. Is this only an emergency measure or a basic new rule of inter-American law? The director-general rightly emphasizes that the inviting state has no right of discrimination and points out that Brazil laid the problem of the invitation of Nicaragua before the governing board. It was the governing board which, after consultation of the governments, decided, in its session of July 28, 1947, not to invite Nicaragua. Brazil, moreover, left the sending out of invitations in general to the governing board.

Ecuador had, of course, been invited and has participated at the conference. But while the conference was in session, a *coup d'etat* occurred in Ecuador and the central commission decided that the Ecuadorian delegate could not sign the treaty on behalf of his country. The problem calls for a permanent solution in the very constitution of the Inter-American System, a constitution to be made by the Bogotá Conference in 1948. It is certainly surprising to see Nicaragua and Ecuador excluded from an Inter-American gathering when they are normally represented at the General Assembly of the U.N.

The Rio conference was to be restricted to the working out of the treaty. Nevertheless a few other issues arose, including the adoption of a resolution concerning the Para-

guayan civil war.[18] The most important extraneous issue
consisted of the battle over the inclusion of inter-American
economic co-operation; Mexico, Argentina, Chile, and Cuba
had insisted on this topic while the United States wanted
to see the Rio conference restricted to inter-American defense.[19] Mexico had proposed the shelving of the economic
problem but Cuba asked the inclusion in the treaty of
provisions prohibiting "threats and aggressions of an economic character," thus linking the economic problem with
that of security. A compromise resolution [20] was adopted
providing for a basic draft agreement on inter-American
economic co-operation to be prepared by the Inter-American
Economic and Social Council and submitted to the Bogotá
Conference; the latter has to act upon the draft and to fix
the date for a special Inter-American Economic Conference,
to be held, probably at Buenos Aires, in the second half
of 1948.

The Inter-American Treaty of Reciprocal Assistance is
an inter-governmental treaty; the formula "in the name
of their peoples" in the preamble has, as in the U.N.
Charter, an ideological, but no legal, significance. The treaty
consists of a preamble and twenty-six articles; it has been
signed by nineteen republics, but is open for signature—
and not merely for adhesion—at Rio by the "American
States." [21] Nicaragua and Ecuador will thus be enabled to
become original signatories of the treaty. Could Canada
sign under this article? The treaty is subject to ratification
and will come into force as soon as the ratifications of two-
thirds of the signatory states have been deposited with the
Pan-American Union.[22] It is then to be registered with the
Secretariat of the U.N. through the Pan-American Union.[23]
The treaty is to remain in force indefinitely, but can be
denounced by any contracting party by a written notification to the Pan-American Union; after the expiration of
two years from the receipt of such notification, the treaty

ceases to be binding with respect to such state, but remains in force for all the other contracting parties.[24] It seems that this procedure has been borrowed from Article I, paragraph 3, of the Covenant of the League of Nations.

The treaty formally condemns war, and the contracting parties undertake in Article I not to resort to the threat or use of force in any manner inconsistent with the U.N. Charter. They obligate themselves to submit every controversy *inter se* to the inter-American peace machinery before referring it to the General Assembly or the Security Council of the U.N. The heart of the treaty is the obligation of mutual defense. It is, in this respect, the fulfilment of the ideas contained in the Havana Resolution XV and in the Act of Chapultepec, but goes much further than these two previous agreements. Contrary to the Havana Resolution, it is not restricted to aggression by non-American states; it contains more than the mere duty to consult; it is, finally, a treaty, clearly binding in law, whereas the legally binding validity of inter-American resolutions is, to say the least, highly controversial. On the other hand, the Havana resolution had provided that all the signatories or two or more of them should proceed to negotiate the necessary complementary agreements so as to organize co-operation for defense and assistance. Contrary to the Act of Chapultepec, the treaty is permanent in character; the duties undertaken go beyond mere consultation; the Act of Chapultepec speaks only of the measures "it may be advisable" to take after consultation and contains nothing as to the binding character of measures agreed upon.

Contrary to the Act of Chapultepec, the treaty, making full use of Article LI of the U.N. Charter, distinguishes "armed attack" from other forms of aggression. It distinguishes aggressions on American states by non-American and by American states.[25] It further distinguishes between aggressions within and outside of the "region" defined in

Article IV. A combination of these different distinctions gives the following picture as to the legal situation under the different hypotheses: (1) Armed attack within the region of Article IV by a non-American or by an American state;[26] (2) Armed attack outside of the region of Article IV but within the territory of an American state;[26] (3) Armed attack outside the region of Article IV and outside the territory of an American state;[27] (4) Aggressions which are not armed attacks, whether inside or outside the region of Article IV;[28] (5) Threats of aggression, extra-continental or intercontinental conflicts, or any other fact or situation which might endanger the peace of the Americas.[28]

Under hypotheses one and two an armed attack by any state against an American state is to be considered as an attack against all the American states. The state or states attacked have, under Article LI of the Charter, the right, but no duty, of individual self-defense. The other American states which have ratified the Rio Treaty have, under Article LI of the Charter, the right of collective self-defense; but this right is also made a duty by Article III, para. 2, of the Rio Treaty. The treaty imposes in these cases a double duty: that of individual assistance to the state attacked and that of consultation. Whereas the consultation can be initiated at the request, addressed to the governing board, by any American state which has ratified the treaty,[29] individual assistance can legally be given only at the request of the state or states directly attacked.[30] But when such request is made there arises the legal duty to give individual assistance; until the decision of the organ of consultation, each contracting party determines itself the immediate measures which it may individually take in fulfilment of its obligation. The organ of consultation is to meet immediately for the purpose of examining the individual measures taken and of agreeing upon the measures of a collective character; such collective measures must be taken, but they need not be of the same type and nature for all the American states. Hypotheses one and two cover the cases of armed attack against an American state within the region of Article IV, of armed attack against an American state outside of this region, but within the territory of an American state (as Hawaii), and of armed attack within the region of Article IV, although not against a member state of the Inter-American System (European colonies, Canada, Greenland).

The "region" set up by Article IV as a security zone [31] runs, in the words of Senator Vandenberg,[32] "from pole to pole. It is a gigantic ellipse—a great oval—encompassing North, Central, and South America and their surrounding seas." It includes not only the continental territories of all the twenty-one American republics, but also parts of the Artic Ocean and of Antarctica, and territories outside of the Inter-American System: European colonies, Canada, Greenland, but not Iceland. Are we to see in this "region" the present determination of the concept of the "Western Hemisphere"? It should also be noted that the "region" of Article IV is not identical with the "Neutrality Zone" of the Panama Declaration of 1939 which, devised for other purposes, began only at the terminus of the United States— Canada boundary. With regard to this "region," several "Statements" [33] were made: by Guatemala, concerning Belice; by Argentina, concerning the Falkland Islands; by Argentina and Chile, renewing the claims of sovereignty over their respective "Antarctic Zones." [34] But it is clear, as the United States expressly stated, that the Rio Treaty "has no effect upon the sovereignty or national or international status of any of the territories included in the region defined in Article 4 of the Treaty."

Hypotheses one and two refer to armed attack against an American state by any state, non-American or American, and thus make the treaty not a mere alliance, but an instrument of reaction against aggression, whoever the agressor may be. Nevertheless a special procedure is provided for in the case of armed attack by an American state.[35] In this case, too, there is not only the right of the victim to resort to individual self-defense but, at the request of the victim, also the duty of the other American states individually to assist in collective self-defense and the duty of consultation. But the organ of consultation may call upon the contending parties to suspend hostilities and restore matters to the status quo *ante bellum,* and then take the necessary measures for the peaceful settlement of the conflict. Only if one of the contending parties rejects these calls may collective measures be agreed upon; the rejection will be considered in the determination of the aggressor. This is the only contribution which the treaty makes to the vital problem of the determination of the aggressor. Also the very different problem of the definition of aggression is avoided.[36]

Armed attack[37] against an American state outside of the region of Article IV and not within the territory of an American state—hypothesis three—constitutes equally an attack against all the American states. But in this case only the duty to consult arises: the organ of consultation, however, must take collective measures to assist the victim of aggression.

In the case of aggressions which are not an armed attack[38]—hypothesis four—but which affect the sovereignty, independence, or territorial integrity of any American state, it is irrelevant whether such aggression has taken place within or outside of the region of Article IV. In any case there is only the duty to consult, but the organ of consultation must meet immediately and must take collective measures. In all of these cases, therefore, the treaty excludes the attitude of neutrality. In the cases of threats of aggression—hypothesis five—there is also a duty to consult; the organ of consultation must meet immediately and agree upon the measures that "should" be taken; the taking of such measures is here optional.

The measures which each state may take individually or which may be agreed upon as collective measures are, in conformity with the Act of Chapultepec and with Articles XLI and XLII of the U.N. Charter, either diplomatic or economic measures [39] or the use of force. As the organ of consultation, the governing board can act provisionally until the regular organ of consultation meets.[40] This regular organ is the meeting of the foreign ministers of the American republics which have ratified the treaty.[41] As the director-general points out,[42] this is not the established organ of the Inter-American System, but a special meeting, restricted to the foreign ministers of the republics that have ratified the treaty, whereas the governing board, as the provisional organ of consultation, is composed of representatives of all the American republics. But the states which have not ratified the treaty are excluded from voting;[43] equally excluded from voting are the interested parties in the case of an inter-American conflict.[44] All organs of consultation take decisions by a vote of two-thirds of the states which have ratified the treaty.[45] The decisions concerning collective measures are binding upon all the states which have ratified the treaty, whether they have concurred in them or not, with the sole exception that no state shall be required to use armed force without its consent:[46] "a combination of these two provisions may provide a workable substitute for the UN veto." [47]

The Rio Treaty needs further implementation. Apart from the problem of inter-American economic co-operation and an American Educational Charter for Peace,[48] the resolution [49] calling for a new codification of the inter-American peace machinery is of particular importance. It is a matter of record that this peace machinery is actually, for many

reasons, entirely inadequate.[50] Another resolution [51] bars
any excessive rearmament as a consequence of the Rio
Treaty. Also the military implementation,[52] the creation of
a Permanent Military Inter-American Staff, envisaged in
Resolution IX of the Mexico City Conference 1945, will
come up at the Bogotá Conference. The treaty itself refers
in Articles XI and XXI to "existing organs or those which
may in the future be established," for the consultation and
for the execution of measures agreed upon by consultation.
The treaty itself gives new political functions to the governing board which is made an organ of liaison between the
American republics, the provisional organ of consultation,
and the organ of liaison with the U.N.[53] From all of these
points of view, the Bogotá Conference, charged with the
complete reorganization of the Inter-American System,
will have to act.

The Rio Treaty, probably the most important and most
far-reaching treaty ever signed by the American states,
points not only to future Pan-American developments and
relates back to the Havana Resolution and the Act of
Chapultepec: it constitutes a return to the ideas of Bolivar.
It is very interesting to compare the treaty with early
Latin-American projects,[54] with the early bilateral Bolivarian alliances,[55] and with the treaties of Panama of
1826,[56] Lima (1848), the Continental Treaty, the Washington Treaty of 1856, and the Treaty of Lima of 1865.[57] In
varying degrees we find in these treaties the same ideas
which inspire the Rio Treaty of 1947.

But the Rio Treaty has also a character entirely different from all previous inter-American treaties. Whereas the
latter were treaties of an independent regional system—
independent also vis-à-vis the League of Nations—the Rio
Treaty is a regional treaty within the system of the United
Nations. The references to the U.N. Charter are frequent
in the treaty.[58] The treaty is based on the strictly legal obli-

gation of solidarity against aggression, but this solidarity is built upon the exercise of the right of individual and collective self-defense under Article LI of the U.N. Charter; one of the purposes of Article LI is exactly to guarantee Pan-America a relatively autonomous position within the U.N. The Rio Treaty is the first regional treaty for the implementation of Article LI. It is, in the words of Senator Vandenberg, "not a substitute for the UN, but a supplement to the UN and part of its machinery." But the treaty certainly had in view the fact that the Security Council is paralyzed by the veto; here, as in the U.N. as a whole, Article LI is being used more and more as a substitute, as ersatz for the non-existing general collective security and sanctions. But, self-defense and Article LI gain, under such conditions, a very different meaning and become a technique pretty near to the old-fashioned right to resort to war, especially as there is no judicial control over the exercise of self-defense. True, under Article V of the treaty the American states are bound, in conformity with Articles LI and LIV of the Charter of the U.N., to send immediately to the Security Council complete information concerning the activities undertaken under Article LI; true, under Article III, para. 4, of the treaty such measures of self-defense can be taken only until the Security Council has taken the necessary measures to maintain international peace and security. But if the Council, paralyzed by the veto, cannot act? For good reasons Senator Vandenberg has in his radio address underlined the word "necessary," when speaking of the necessary measures to be taken by the Security Council.

The Rio Treaty is built entirely upon Article LI of the Charter and on the conception of "armed attack." It can, therefore, only be a system of self-defense, not a system of sanctions. The monopoly of the use of force is in the hands of the Security Council; the member states can resort to force only under Article LI and only against an armed attack. It follows that the organ of consultation can agree upon the use of force only under the above-named hypotheses one to three, but not under the hypotheses four and five. The Rio Treaty, which the Secretary of State has called a "significant example" for the whole U.N., has, in consequence of its basis, nothing to do with collective security and sanctions, but only with self-defense. It makes use of the "collective self-defense" in two stages: collective self-defense individually exercised,[59] and collective self-defense on, so to speak, the second level, through collective measures agreed upon in consultation by states already exercising, if one can say so, the right of "individual collective self-defense." In an independent Inter-American System the collective measures would constitute sanctions; but in the Rio Treaty they constitute only later "collective self-defense." This necessary construction leads naturally still further away from the concept of self-defense in municipal law.

[1] THE INTERNATIONAL CONFERENCE OF AMERICAN STATES, 1st Supplement 1933–40 at 360–61 (1940).

[2] INTER-AMERICAN CONFERENCE ON PBORLEMS OF WAR AND PEACE. Final Act. Pan-American Union, Res. VIII at 40–44 (1945).

[3] See "Individual and Collective Self-defense in Article LI of the Charter of the United Nations," above.

[4] Original date: October 20, 1945; first postponed to March, 1956; then postponed *sine die*.

[6] Bolivia, Brazil, Chile, Ecuador, Mexico, Panama, United States, Uruguay.

[7] PAN-AMERICAN UNION, INTER-AMERICAN CONFERENCE FOR THE MAINTENANCE OF CONTINENTAL PEACE AND SECURITY 143 (1946) (mimeo.).

[8] CONSULTATION OF THE PRINCIPAL POINTS OF THE TREATY TO BE SIGNED AT RIO DE JANEIRO 37 (1947) (mimeo.).

[9] INTER-AMERICAN TREATY OF RECIPROCAL ASSISTANCE 7 (1947) (mimeo.). The text is also reprinted in 17 DEP'T STATE BULL. No. 429 at 565–72 (1947); N.Y. Times, August 31, 1947, p. 26; A.B.A.J. 1058–60 (October, 1947); CURRENT HISTORY 229–31 (October, 1947).

[10] Final Act 7 (1947) (mimeo.).

11 The governing board had also—in 1945—prepared a handbook for the use of delegates.

12 The president of the conference was the foreign minister of Brazil, Raúl Fernandes. Apart from a central commission, composed of the chairmen of all the delegations, a credentials commission and a commission of redaction and co-ordination, the conference was organized in three commissions: I (preamble, principles, general articles), chairman, Mateo Marquez Castro (Uruguay); II (measures to be taken in case of threat or acts of aggression), chairman, Ricardo J. Alfaro (Panama); III (procedures and organs), chairman, Luis Anderson (Costa Rica).

13 CONFERENCIA INTER-AMERICANA PARA EL MANTENIMIENTO DE LA PAZ Y DE LA SEGURIDAD DEL CONTINENTE. INFORME SOBRE LOS RESULTADOS DE LA CONFERENCIA PRESENTADO AL CONSEJO DIRECTIVO DE LA UNIÓN PAN AMERICANA POR EL DIRECTOR GENERAL 83 (1947) (mimeo.), hereafter cited as INFORME. This report by the director-general, Alberto Lleras Camargo, is unusual for a document of this type. It is a most excellent and interesting report, giving a detailed legal analysis of the treaty. Fine legal investigation is combined with blunt critique, where necessary, and courageous leadership for future developments.

14 List of delegations in INFORME 74–79.

15 Yet the Rio Conference was not a reunion of the permanent organ, known as the Meeting of Foreign Ministers of the American Republics, but a special inter-American conference.

16 17 DEP'T STATE BULL. *No.* 424 *at* 325–26 (1947).

17 INFORME 5–8.

18 For months prior to the Rio Conference a serious civil war had been going on in Paraguay; and just at the time of the opening of the conference, the insurgents were beseiging Asunción. But they were, while the conference was still in session, defeated and fled. Another issue, Santo Domingo's charge that armed Communists were being trained in Cuba for the purpose of invading Santo Domingo and overthrowing the Trujillo regime, was not brought before the conference.

19 See 17 DEP'T STATE BULL. *No.* 424 at 324–25 (1947), and Secretary of State Marshall's speech at Petropolis on August 20, 1947 (17 DEP'T STATE BULL. *No.* 426 at 414–15 [1947]).

20 Final Act, Res. IX.

21 Article XXII.

22 Article XXIII.

23 Article XXIV.

24 Article XXV.

25 Venezuela stood originally for two different instruments, the one covering aggressions by non-American, the other by American states. Argentina's move at Rio to bar collective actions between American states was defeated.

26 Article III, para. 3.

27 Article III, para. 3 and 6.

[28] Article VI.

[29] Article III.

[30] Article III, para. 2.

[31] A map of this zone is to be found in N.Y. Times, August 30, 1947, p. 7.

[32] 17 DEP'T STATE BULL. No. 428 at 504 (1947).

[33] Final Act 7.

[34] See Philip C. Jessup in 41 AM.J.I.NT'L L. 117–19 (1947).

[35] Article VII.

[36] The INFORME (at 44–45) speaks of the *descripción del agresor*, whereas it means the different problem of the definition of aggression.

[37] Armed attack constitutes aggression. As in Article LI of the Charter, it should, therefore, read: "unlawful armed attack." Article IX gives only examples of armed attack and leaves the determination of other aggressions to the organ of consultation. Article IX (a) speaks also of unprovoked armed attack "against the land, sea or air forces" of an American state. If such attack is made within the region of Article IV or within the territory of an American state (as at Pearl Harbor), the case falls under hypotheses one and two and leads to the double duty of immediate assistance and consultation; if made outside of these areas (as against the American fleet in the Mediterranean), only the duty of consultation arises.

[38] Article VI.

[39] Recall of chiefs of diplomatic missions, breaking of diplomatic relations, breaking of consular relations, complete or partial interruption of economic relations or of rail, sea, air, postal, telegraphic, telephonic and radio-telephonic or radiotelegraphic communications (Article VIII).

[40] Article XII.

[41] Article XI.

[42] INFORME at 45–46.

[43] Article XIV.

[44] Article XVIII.

[45] Article XVII. This norm was, after debate, adopted. Argentina had stood for unanimity. Uruguay had originally proposed a mere absolute majority. Contrary to some voting norms of the U.N. Charter, the two-thirds majority is here that of the states that have ratified the treaty, whether they are present at the consulation meeing or not. Article XIX lays down the necessary quorum.

[46] Article XX. This norm was also adopted after debate. In their earlier proposals Brazil, Chile, Mexico, Panama, and the United States suggested that the decisions be binding only upon those states which had concurred in them. The United States modified its original position in the sense of the present Article XX (in DEP'T STATE BULL. No. 425 at 367 [1947]).

[47] L. Sohn in A.B.A.J. 1058 (October, 1947).

[48] Final Act, Res. XIII.

[49] Final Act. Res. X; see also the preamble of the treaty.

50 See the sharp critique by the director general and his telling remark that failure of such improvement would lead to the paradoxical situation of a system of sanctions without peace machinery. (INFORME at 25–27).

51 Final Act, Res. XI.

52 The problem of U. S. help for the armament of the Latin-American republics and for standardizing equipment is also pending, since the Congress has not yet acted upon the respective proposals of the President of the United States.

53 Article XV.

54 MARTÍNEZ DE ROSAS, CATECISMO POLÍTICO-CRISTIANO (1810); JUAN EGAÑA, PROYECTO DE UNA DECLARACIÓN DE LOS DERECHOS DEL PUEBLO DE CHILE (1810), reprinted in RAMÓN BRICENO, MEMORIA HISTÓRICO-CRÍTICA DEL DERECHO PÚBLICO CHILENO (1849). The proposals of José Cecilio del Valle can be found in JOSÉ RODRÍGUEZ CERNA, CENTRAL AMÉRICA EN EL CONGRESO DE BOLÍVAR (1938). BERNARDO MONTEAGUDO, ENSAYO SOBRE LA NECESIDAD DE UNA FEDERACIÓN GENERAL ENTRE LOS ESTADOS HISPANO-AMERICANOS Y PLAN DE SU ORGANIZACIÓN (1825).

55 Colombia-Peru, July 6, 1822 (1 TRATADOS PÚBLICOS Y ACUERDOS INTERNACIONALES DE VENEZUELA 11–18 [1820-1900]). Colombia-Chile, Santiago, October 29, 1822 (*ibid.* at 19–24). Colombia-Mexico, October 3, 1823 (*ibid.* at 26–37). Colombia–Central America, Bogotá, March 15, 1825 (*ibid.* at 43–49). Peru-Chile, December 23, 1822 (1 RICARDO, CONGRESOS Y CONFERENCIAS EN QUE HA TOMADO PARTE LE PERÚ 167–92 (1909).

56 RAÚL PARRAS BARRENECHEA, EL CONGRESO DE PANAMÁ. ARCHIVOS DIPLOMÁTICOS PERUANOS (1930).

57 See 1 ALBERTO ULLÓA, CONGRESOS AMERICANOS DE LIMA (1938). On the Lima treaties and the Washington Treaty, see also 1 ARRANDA, *op. cit.;* on the Washington Treaty, also CERNA, *op. cit.* at 306–23.

58 Articles, I, II, III, V, VII, X, XV, XXIV.

59 The director-general points out (INFORME at 32) that the "collective" quality of "collective self-defense" does not lie in the application of collective measures previously agreed upon, but in the right and duty to take individual measures of assistance by states which have not been the direct object of attack.

CHAPTER XXXIX: *The Bogotá Charter of the Organization of American States*

CONTRARY TO MOST international organizations, the Inter-American System lacked, up to now, a treaty basis. It was based merely on resolutions. Among them the famous resolution of April 14, 1890, which created the "International Union of the American Republics," has a particular character and importance. This resolution needed ratification which was given, but by the American governments only. By this ratification the American republics bound themselves legally and consented to be bound for ten years—and still longer if nothing to the contrary was done—and consented to the making of modifications and amendments concerning the organization by majority vote. Generally resolutions of the international conferences of American states and other such meetings constitute only recommendations and are not legally binding; but resolutions concerning organization are legally binding at once on the basis of point 16 of the ratified resolution of April 14, 1890;[1] the latter is, up to now, in a strictly legal sense, the constitution, the fundamental norm, of the Inter-American System.[2]

The reasons why no treaty was adopted on this subject were several times discussed at Pan-American conferences.

They were primarily pragmatic reasons, especially the wish to avoid the necessity of ratification of a treaty. Positive arguments also were made to the same effect: resolutions better fit the empirical character of Pan-America, they render its gradual development more practicable, make easier its revision, its adaptation to circumstances, its evolution according to the broadening of the Pan-American movement; Anglo-American examples, the British constitution, the common law were cited to the same effect.

Yet, already in 1910, the director-general of the Pan-American Union (PAU) proposed to base it on an international convention,[3] a proposal repeated in the report to the Santiago Conference of 1923.[4] Finally at the sixth conference at Havana, in 1928, a convention on the Pan-American Union was signed.[5] But this convention had never been ratified by all the members and had never come into force. Later developments made this convention appear to be out of date.

The International Union of American Republics had been created in 1890 as an international administrative union, originally only for one, later for more, purposes, but always for purposes of non-political co-operation. The Havana Resolution of 1928[6] specifically forbade the exercise of political functions by the Pan-American Union and its governing board. Yet out of humble beginnings, after a long period of non-political co-operation and after a period of serious crisis in the twenties, the Inter-American System has since 1933 grown immensely. It was no longer restricted to relations of the American republics among themselves; it became more and more also a political organization.

The constant creation, shifting, and fading away of Pan-American organs—many only of temporary character —and their growing number and complexity led to uncertainty, confusion, duplication, vague definition of competences, inadequate financial foundation, inefficiency, and, in some cases, to an existence on paper only. There was, further, a complete lack of interrelation, co-ordination, integration, and centralization. The need for a complete reorganization made itself strongly felt in recent years.[7]

The Mexico City Conference of 1945 adopted Resolution IX [8] on the reorganization, consolidation, and strengthening of the Inter-American System,[9] to be carried out by the Bogotá Conference. A special committee of the governing board [10] prepared the Project of the Organic Pact of the Inter-American System [11] which was, in a new version,[12] before the Bogotá Conference.[13] These projects also had to integrate the Inter-American System with the United Nations.[14]

Of the five topics on the agenda of the Bogotá Conference,[15] the first two deal directly with the problem of reorganization. The Bogotá Conference, notwithstanding its tragic interruption, has in the main solved the problem before it.

The basic treaty on which the Inter-American System will rest from now on is known as the "Bogotá Charter" (Carta de Bogotá).[16] The Inter-American System, itself a name of recent date as compared with the original "Union of American Republics" and the popular "Pan-America," will be officially called the Organization of the American States (OAS).[17] The Bogotá Charter consists of three parts in eighteen chapters and one hundred and twelve articles.

II

The first fundamental change brought about by the Charter consists in creating, at last, a treaty-basis for Pan-America. Article I of the English text says that the American states "establish" in this charter the international organization that they have developed. But the word "establish" cannot have the sense of founding, as the word "consagran" in the equally authentic Spanish text clearly shows. The fact that the OAS will now be treaty-based ends, of course, the possibility of changes or modifications by mere resolutions. Such changes will have now to be brought about by an amendment procedure. Only an inter-American conference, specially convened for that purpose, can adopt amendments (Article CXI). Amendments will enter into force among the ratifying states when two-thirds of the signatory states have deposited their ratification, and with respect to the remaining states in the order of their deposit of ratification (Article CIX). This procedure is very different from the amendment procedure of the League of Nations or of the United Nations. It does not bind the states which have not consented, nor are they forced to leave the OAS. But if a far-reaching amendment has come into force, it may be difficult to retain the unamended charter in operation with regard to the "remaining states."

As up to now the OAS has been a strictly regional or continental organization, only American states can be members. "All American states that ratify the present Charter are members of the Organization" (Article II). The charter needs, of course, ratification, and the instruments of ratification have to be deposited with the PAU (Article CVIII). It will enter into force with the deposit of ratification by two-thirds of the signatory states (Article CIX). Article II, concerning membership, is interesting. Up to now every American state was a member "as of right." [18] But now ratification of the charter is necessary. The question arises: what will be the legal position of the seven or less than seven American states which do not ratify or, at least, have not yet ratified the charter? Article II speaks of "all American states." Membership is, in consequence, open only to "states," that is, to sovereign states in the sense of international law, not to states of a federal union,[19] not to

European colonies in the Americas.[20] But there is no restriction to the present signatory twenty-one American republics. Article II would allow Canada as an "American State" [21] to become a member by ratification. "All" American states clearly includes sovereign states which may newly come into existence in the Americas.[22] It is to be noted that there is no "admission" into the OAS. If an entity is a sovereign American state, it has a right to become a member by ratification. The charter remains permanently open for signature, not merely for accession, by the American states.[23] Article III—an innovation—foresees membership for any new political entity that arises from the union of several member states, whereas the states that constitute the new entity lose their membership. One may think of a possible "Central American Republic."

Up to now, each republic was free to leave the Inter-American System at its pleasure. The charter too, contrary to the dubious legal situation in the U.N.,[24] gives a right of withdrawal by denunciation (Article CXII), but after two years notice and "after having fulfilled the obligations arising from the present Charter," a norm clearly taken from the League Covenant.

III

The second great change brought about by the Bogotá Charter is the reorganization and centralization of the OAS. This can already be seen in the shorter reformulation of the basic principles, in the preamble,[25] and Articles IV-XXXI.

Article IV names as purposes of the OAS: the strengthening of the peace and security of the continent, the pacific settlement of inter-American disputes, group action in the event of aggression, political and non-political co-operation, and promotion of inter-American welfare.

Article V states the basic principles: international law as the standard of conduct of states, respect for sovereignty and independence of states, faithful fulfilment of international obligations, good faith, effective exercise of representative democracy, condemnation of wars of aggression, individual and collective self-defense, peaceful settlement of disputes, social justice, economic co-operation, fundamental rights of the individual without any discrimination, respect of cultural values, and importance of education. These basic principles [26] contain nothing new and are taken from earlier Pan-American declarations and conventions.[27] From a legal point of view, it must be said that these principles as such constitute only a program, not legally binding norms. They are general expressions of policy for erecting legal norms which shall contain concrete obligations and providing sanctions for their violation.

Articles VI-XIX contain the "fundamental rights and duties of states." The principal features: juridical equality, jurisdiction over citizens and aliens, inviolability of territory, and strictest non-intervention are taken from the corresponding Montevideo Convention of 1933. Interesting are the articles dealing with the recognition of states; further norms, concerning recognition of *de facto* governments, will have to follow. The Mexico City Conference of 1945 had charged the governing board not only to prepare a declaration of the rights and duties of states, but also to include a "Declaration of Rights and Duties of Man," the text of which was to be formulated by the Inter-American Juridical Committee. This declaration has now been adopted in Resolution XXX [28] of the Bogotá Conference. It is of particular interest that Resolution XXXI [29] charges the Inter-American Juridical Committee to prepare a statute for an inter-American court for the protection of the rights of man; this statute shall be submitted to the tenth inter-American conference "for deliberation."

Articles XX-XXIII contain the fundamental norms for the pacific settlement of disputes. The urgent necessity of a complete reorganization of the inter-American peace machinery had been strongly felt for a long time. The Mexico City Conference of 1945 recommended in Resolution XXXIX the immediate elaboration by the Inter-American Juridical Committee of a project of an "Inter-American Peace System." [30] Article XXIII of the charter refers to a special treaty which was concluded at the ninth inter-American conference and will be known as the "Pact of Bogotá." [31]

Articles XXIV-XXV give the basic principles on collective security, as laid down by the Rio treaty of 1947.[32]

Articles XXVI-XXVII contain the basic principles concerning economic standards as they were developed especially since 1936. The conference adopted also the "Economic Convention of Bogotá." [33] As legally interesting, we quote Article VIII of this convention which forbids the application of coercive means of an economic and political character in order to force the sovereign will of another state, and Article XXV, which prescribes the payment of prompt, adequate, and effective indemnity in case of expropriation, an issue which was so prominent at the occasion of the Mexican expropriations.[34] Resolution VIII [35] of the Bogotá Conference convokes a specialized inter-American economic conference for the end of 1948 to Buenos Aires.

Articles XXVIII-XXIX contain the basic principles concerning social,[36] and Articles XXX-XXXI concerning cultural, standards.

IV

The Bogotá Charter carries out the complete reorganization with which the Mexico City Conference had charged it; Resolution IX, 1945, gave some specific instructions, but also a sweeping authority to create or confirm the various organs, to create new or to adapt or eliminate old ones.[37]

(A) The supreme organ, up to now, is the inter-American conference (formerly the International Conference of American States). It decides upon the general action and policy of the OAS, determines the structure and functions of its organs, and has the authority to consider any matter relating to friendly relations among the American states (Article XXXIII). It shall convene every five years (Article XXXV). The system of rotation remains in force, each conference fixes the place of meeting of the next conference (Article XXXVI). In addition, there are special inter-American conferences [38] which may be held in special circumstances and with the approval of two-thirds of the American governments. These special conferences must be carefully distinguished from the specialized conferences which deal only with certain technical matters.

All member states have the right to be represented at the inter-American conferences (Article XXXIV). This seems to re-establish the legal rule that the right to be represented does not depend on whether the *de facto* government of a member state is or is not recognized at the time in question. According to the equality principle of the OAS, each state has the right to one vote (Article XXXIV). While an effort is always made to reach unanimity, it seems that resolutions can be taken with a simple majority vote, except where otherwise provided,[39] but the charter contains no express norm. Another lacuna of great importance is that the charter contains nothing about the controversial question of the legal nature of resolutions.

While the inter-American conference is the supreme organ of the OAS, it is a diplomatic conference; true, a diplomatic conference as an organ within the framework of a constitution, but by no means a parliament or a legislative organ.

(B) The Meeting of Consultation of Ministers of Foreign Affairs, envisaged by the Buenos Aires Conference of 1936, and made an institution by the Lima Conference of 1938, is to be held in order to consider problems of an urgent nature and of common interest to the American states (Article XXXIX). As already laid down by Resolution IX of the Mexico City Conference of 1945, they are regular organs with particular competences, clearly distinguished from regular as well as special inter-American conferences; they are emergency meetings. But whereas Resolution IX of 1945 recognized ordinary meetings, to be held annually—except in years of an inter-American conference—and extraordinary meetings, the ordinary meetings have now been dropped. The calling of a meeting may be requested by any member state and the meeting will be held if the council so decides by an absolute majority (Article XL). On the other hand, the meetings now have a new function, namely as an organ of consultation under Article XI of the Rio Treaty of 1947 (Article XLIII). But there is an interesting discrepancy, unsolved, between Article XLIII of the charter and Article XI of the Rio Treaty, as the latter foresees a different organ, namely the Meeting of Foreign Ministers of the American republics which have ratified the Rio Treaty. Let us hope that all the twenty-one republics will ratify the charter and the Rio Treaty; then the legal discrepancy will be of no importance practically.

The meetings, in their capacity as organs of consultation, have at their disposal the Advisory Defense Committee (Articles XLIV-XLVII). The Inter-American Defense Board [40] had been created by the Rio de Janeiro meeting of 1942 as a temporary organ and was sitting in Washington. Resolution IV of the Mexico City Conference of 1945 recommended the prompt establishment of a permanent military organization. The *Project of an Organic Pact of the Inter-*

American System had foreseen an "Inter-American Defense Council" as one of the four dependent organs of the governing board. But at Bogotá objections of sovereignty were made against putting this organ under the council and it was put directly under the meetings of consultation of foreign ministers.

The new Advisory Defense Committee is to be established to advise the organs of consultation on problems of military co-operation in connection with collective security (Article XLIV), and to be convoked under the same conditions as the organ of consultation (Article XLVI). But it is also to meet when the conference or the meeting or the governments, by a two-thirds majority, assign to it technical studies or reports on specific subjects (Article XLVII). In the meantime, the Inter-American Defense Board will continue to work until the American governments, by a two-thirds majority, resolve to end its work.[41]

(C) The council as created by the Bogotá Charter is a far-reaching innovation, not only with regard to the law as it has existed up to now, but also with regard to the proposed organic pact. The governing board had only been the governing board of the PAU. But the council, as this organ is now called, is the council of the OAS,[42] a central organ with wide competence. To a certain extent it has the position of the League of Nations Council, but with far more restricted competence. It does not correspond to the Security Council of the U.N., as the functions of the latter are, to a certain extent, exercised by the organ of consultation. On the other hand, it is superior to the other U.N. councils.

The composition of the council (Articles XLVIII-XLIX), which functions in Washington, D.C. (Article LVI), remains the same as that of the former governing board, as recognized by Resolution IX, point 3, of the Mexico City Conference of 1945.

The powers and duties of the council are: (1) to be responsible for the proper performance of the duties assigned to the PAU (Article LV); (2) to draft its own regulations (Article LV); (3) to establish the bases for fixing the quotas of contributions (Article LIV); (4) to fix the time for the inter-American conferences (Article XXXV); (5) to prepare the programs and regulations of the inter-American conferences (Article XXXVIII) and of the meetings of consultation (Article XL); (6) to decide by simple majority whether a meeting of consultation should be held (Article XL); (7) the chairman of the council immediately calls a meeting of consultation in case of an armed attack within the region of security, defined by Article IV of the Rio Treaty of 1947 (Article XLIII); (8) to serve provisionally as organ of consultation, in accordance with Article XII of the Rio Treaty of 1947 (Article LIII); (9) to take cognizance, under a general clause—within the limits of the charter and of inter-American treaties and agreements— of any matter referred to by the council by inter-American conferences or meetings of consultation (Article L); (10) to make the final decision concerning studies to be prepared by the Committee for Cultural Action (Article LXXVII); (11) to elect the secretary general (Article LXXXXV); (12) to remove, by a two-thirds majority vote of its members, the secretary general or the assistant secretary general (Article LXXXVII); (13) to lay down the general standards as to the officers of the PAU, their powers and duties, and their compensation (Article LXXXIV, b). The assistant secretary general is the secretary of the council (Article LXXXVI). The council has important functions with regard to specialized conferences and specialized organizations (Article LIII).

The council thus has far-reaching competences, also of a political character. But the latter, dubiously framed at the Mexico City Conference of 1945, remain restricted.

The council has three organs (Article LVII) which have technical autonomy within the limits of the charter (Article LVIII). They are composed of representatives of all the member states of the OAS (Article LIX). They are to render to the governments, as far as possible, such technical services as the latter request and to advise the council (Article LX). The council is, with the advice of the appropriate bodies and after consultation with the governments, to draft the statutes of such of its organs as are in process of formation (Article LXII).

These organs are:

(1) The Inter-American Economic and Social Council at Washington (Articles LXIII-LXVI). The Panama Meeting of Consultation of 1939 had created the temporary Inter-American Financial and Economic Advisory Committee.[43] Resolution IX, point 7, of 1945 substituted a permanent Inter-American Economic and Social Council subsidiary to the governing board as the co-ordinating agency for all official inter-American economic and social activities, and authorized the board to organize this council provisionally. It is now to be organized permanently. Under Article XI of the Economic Convention of Bogotá, this council is to organize a permanent technical body.

(2) The Inter-American Council of Jurists (Articles LXVII-LXXI).[44] This body is to serve as an advisory body in juridical matters and to promote the development and codification of public and private international law and to study the possibility of making uniform the laws of the American countries (Article LXVII). This council replaces the multitude of hitherto existing and ineffective codification agencies.[45] The Inter-American Juridical Committee,[46] originally created as the Inter-American Neutrality Committee by the consultative meeting of Panama, 1939, and re-baptized by the consultative meeting of Rio de Janeiro, 1942, is the permanent committee of the Inter-American

Council of Jurists (Article LXVIII). As hitherto, it will be an organ composed, not of representatives of all of the American republics, but only of some of them, but representing all the member states of the OAS. The number of members and their method of appointment is changed. Instead of seven, it will be composed of jurists of nine countries. The selection is to be made by the Inter-American Council of Jurists from a panel submitted by each of the countries chosen by the conferences (Article LXIX). The juridical committee is to undertake such studies and preparatory work as are assigned to it by the inter-American conferences, the meetings of consultation or the council and may also undertake studies and projects on its own initiative (Article LXX). As long as the reorganization is not carried out, the inter-American juridical committee will continue to function in its actual organization.[47]

(3) The Inter-American Cultural Council (Articles LXXIII-LXXVII), a new organ. It is the central organ for promoting education, scientific, and cultural exchange and friendly relations and mutual understanding.[48] The Committee of Cultural Action, composed of members of five states, selected by the council from a panel submitted by each country chosen by the conferences, will act as the permanent committee of the council.

(D) The Pan-American Union [49] (Articles LXXVII-XCII), at Washington (Article XCII), is the central permanent organ of the OAS and its general secretariat (Article LXXVII). The title of the two leading officers is now secretary general and assistant secretary general. The first is elected by the council for a ten-year term, may not be reelected or succeeded by a person of the same nationality (Article LXXIX). He directs the PAU and is the legal representative thereof (Article LXXX). He participates with voice, but without vote, at all types of inter-American conferences, at the meetings of the council and its organs

(Article LXXXI). The PAU will, as up to now, be organized into technical and information offices (Article LXXXII). These will be established, with the approval of the council, by the secretary general, who also appoints the necessary officers, regulates their powers and duties, and fixes their compensation (Article LXXXIV). The assistant secretary general is elected by the council for a ten-year term and is eligible for re-election (Article LXXXV); he is the secretary of the council and serves as advisory officer to the secretary general (Article LXXXVI). Both leading officers may, whenever the proper functioning of the OAS so demands, be removed by the council by a two-thirds vote of its members (Article LXXXVII). The present functionaries who have to take the new titles are confirmed in their appointments.[50]

The functions of the PAU (Article LXXXII) remain essentially the same. It is definitely made the custodian of the documents and archives of the inter-American conferences and meetings of consultation and serves as a depository of ratifications of inter-American agreements. The chiefs of the respective departments of the PAU are executive secretaries of the three organs of the council (Article LXXXVIII).

(E) The OAS is to enjoy in the territory of each member such legal capacity, privileges, and immunities as are necessary for the exercise of its functions and the accomplishment of its purposes (Article CIII). The representatives of the governments on the council, and on the organs of the council, the secretary general, and the assistant secretary general are to enjoy the privileges and immunities necessary for the independent exercise of their duties (Article CIV). Correspondence of the OAS—not only of the PAU—when bearing the frank thereof, shall be carried post-free in the mails of the member states (Article CVI). The representatives in the conference, the meeting of consultation, and the council are diplomatic representatives, appointed by their governments; all member states are represented. The members of the organs of the council and Defense Committee, are composed of specialized delegates appointed by the governments; here, too, every member state is represented. The Inter-American Juridical Committee and the committee for cultural action are committees of experts, selected by inter-American organs, and are composed only of men of nine or five American republics, but representing all of them. Men and women are equally eligible to participate in the activities of the various organs and hold positions therein (Article CVII).

The officers of the PAU are strictly international officials; in the performance of their duties they may not seek or receive instructions from any government or from any other authority outside the PAU. They must refrain from any action that might reflect upon their position as international officials responsible only to the Union (Article LXXXIX). The member states pledge themselves to respect the exclusively international character of the staff and not to seek to influence them in the discharge of their duties (Article XC). While efficiency, competence, and probity are primarily to determine the selection of the personnel of the PAU, importance is to be given to recruiting personnel on as broad a geographical basis as possible (Article XCI).

(F) The financing of international organizations is of fundamental importance for their effective and successful functioning. Up to now, the financing of the PAU has been entirely inadequate. Under so small a budget the PAU is hampered in many ways; it does not have enough competent officials, it is scandalously limited in its publications. Point 12 of Resolution IX of the Mexico City Conference of 1945 charged the governing board also to include the problem of financing in its proposals. Two main problems must be solved: adequate financing and just distribution of quotas among the member states. The governing board submitted to the Bogotá Conference a report on the plan of financing.[51] The Bogotá Charter gives the competence to fix the quotas of each government to the council. The budget must be approved by the council and transmitted to the governments at least six months before the first day of the fiscal year. Decisions on budgetary matters require the approval of two-thirds of the members of the council (Article LIV). The budget includes the costs of the PAU, of the council, of the organs of the council and of the Secretariat of the Inter-American Defense Board.[52] The Bogotá Conference charged the council to develop the continued technical perfection of the bases of financing the PAU, in order to guarantee an equitable repartition.[53] In fixing the quotas, the council has under Article LIV to take into consideration two factors: first, the capacity to pay of each country, and, second, "the willingness of each country to contribute a fair share." This last phrase must be severely criticized. To contribute a fair share is a strictly legal duty of the members of an international organization, not a matter of grace or discretion. Contrary to the U.N. Charter,[54] the Bogotá Charter provides no sanctions for the non-fulfilment of the financial obligations of the members.

V

(G) Among the hundreds of inter-American "technical conferences" [55] as they have been called up to now, we must distinguish strictly between three different types: official (intergovernmental), semi-official, and private. It is clear that private inter-American specialized conferences are no part of the OAS. But official conferences also are often in little or no contact with the PAU. They are often convoked by single governments, in consequence of a resolution of an inter-American conference, or of a resolution of a previous technical conference, or on the initiative of a government. The matter of their regulations is often left entirely to them. Their proceedings are sometimes extremely difficult to obtain, if available at all. Some of these technical conferences meet only once, others have become periodic. Here, too, the Bogotá Charter seeks to introduce order, centralization, relation with the council and the PAU.

The specialized conferences meet to deal with special technical matters; but, from now on, they are to be clearly connected with the OAS and its central organs. They meet (A) when it is so decided by the inter-American conferences or the meetings of consultation; (B) when inter-American agreements so provide; (C) when the council considers it necessary, either on its own initiative or at the request of one of its organs or at the request of one of the specialized organizations (Article XCIII). Their programs and regulations are to be prepared by the organs of the council or by the specialized agencies concerned and shall be transmitted to the council for its information (Article XCIV). The Secretary General of the PAU participates with voice, but without vote, also at the specialized conferences (Article LXXXI). The PAU is, in so far as possible, also the custodian of the documents and archives of the specialized conferences (Article LXXXIII, d). The Bogotá Conference has resolved to call two specialized conferences: the Inter-American Economic Conference,[56] already mentioned, and the Inter-American Conference for the conservation of renewable natural resources.[57]

Some of the specialized conferences stand by themselves; others create specialized organizations, others are the general conferences of existing specialized organizations.

(H) Specialized Organizations (Articles XCV-CI). The Mexico City Conference of 1945 had specifically charged the governing board "to provide for the strengthening of the Inter-American System by the creation of new organs or the elimination or adaption of existing organs, dovetailing their functions between the several agencies and with the world organization."

The governing board has, by resolution of October 20, 1947, submitted a special *Report on Specialized Inter-American Organizations* [58] to the Bogotá Conference. The Bogotá Charter merely lays down general norms. It has made a necessary clear-cut distinction between inter-governmental, semi-official, and private organization. It is clear that the private (unofficial) inter-American organizations [59] do not and cannot form a part of the OAS. That says, of course, nothing against their importance or the advisability of collaboration and close relations with them. As the report, adopted on October 20, 1947, states: "Such organizations may be very useful in contributing to the carrying out of the purposes of the Inter-American System" and "the Council might be authorized to enter into agreements with these bodies." Article LIII, d makes it the duty of the council "to conclude agreements or special arrangements for co-operation with other American organizations of recognized international standing." Such co-operation is even prescribed with national organizations. [60]

The semi-official organizations have a membership, partly official and partly private; some are also supported partly by official and partly by private funds. There is no uniformity in their organization and structure. Article LIII, d applies here too. The most important organizations of this type are: (A) The Inter-American Statistical Institute, [61] which had already expressed a desire for closer affiliation with the PAU. Resolution IV [62] recommends that the council examine the possibility of a special agreement establishing relations between the OAS and the Institute, including the bases of financing. (B) The Pan-American Coffee Bureau, New York, [63] with which the council may also conclude an agreement for co-operative relationship. (C) Pan-American Commission of Inter-Municipal Co-operation, Havana,[64] which itself has proposed closer relations with the PAU. (D) Pan-American Congress of Railways, Permanent Commission, Buenos Aires,[65] and (E) Inter-American Development Commission, Washington,[66] an emergency creation of World War II. Its position in relation to the OAS has never been clearly defined. Its future position is now the object of a study of the Inter-American Economic and Social Council.

The Bogotá Charter deals primarily with the official specialized organizations. They are "intergovernmental organizations established by multilateral agreements and having specific functions with respect to technical matters" (Article XCVI). In determining their geographic location, the interests of all the American states are to be taken into account (Article CI). Other norms provide for their integration into the OAS. The council has the duty (Article LIII) to draft and submit to the governments and the inter-American conferences proposals for the creation of new specialized organizations or for the combination, adaptation, or elimination of existing ones; further, to draft recommendations to the governments, the inter-American conferences, the specialized conferences, or the specialized organizations for the co-ordination of activities and programs of such organizations, after consultation with them; to conclude agreements with them and determine their relations with the OAS. The specialized organizations enjoy the fullest technical autonomy and are to take into account the recommendations of the council (Article XCVII). The council is to maintain a register of these organizations (Article XCVI). They are to submit to the council periodic reports on the progress of their work (Article XCVIII).

The specialized organizations must be strictly distinguished from the organs of the council and the Advisory Defense Committee which are integral parts of the OAS.

They supersede in certain cases hitherto existing specialized agencies.

The problem of financing the specialized organization is of great importance; the budgets of some of them are utterly inadequate. The report on financing of March 8, 1948[67], dealt also with this problem. It considered the two possibilities, a single budget for the whole OAS and separate budgets. It inclined rather to the second solution, in view of the differences among those organizations and the fact that not all the twenty-one republics participate in all of them. The Bogotá Charter merely lays down that the council may draft and submit proposals including the financing and support of the specialized organizations (Article LIII, a). They must submit to the council also periodic reports on their annual budgets and expenses (Article XCVIII). Agreements between them and the council may provide that they transmit their budgets to the council for approval; arrangements may be made for the PAU to receive the quotas of the contributing countries and distribute them in accordance with pertinent agreements (Article XCIX).

The whole rearrangement of the specialized organizations has still to be made. Resolution VI [68] lays down that the council open the register, provided for in Article XCVI, conclude the agreements (Article LIII) and make, as soon as possible, a complete examination of the situation and activities of the existing specialized organizations, in order to adopt, with the authorization of the governments, the necessary measures for the abolition of those the maintenance of which is not advisable and for the strengthening, adaptation, or fusion of the others.

In this impending reorganization, we may distinguish:[69]

(1) Specialized organizations, now existing, which may be abolished. To these belong (a) in all probability, the Inter-American Trade Mark Bureau (Havana),[70] as the Protocol of 1929 has been denounced by all ratifying states

except Cuba, as there is a lack of interest and no business to transact, and (b), probably, the Pan-American Railway Committee.[71]

(2) Existing specialized organizations which may be maintained. Their eventual reorganization can be done by resolution, if they have been created by resolution of international conferences of American states, of consultative meetings, or of technical conferences. But others exist by virtue of conventions. Some are permanent, some temporary, some of an emergency character. This group includes: (a) Emergency Advisory Committee for Political Defense, Montevideo;[72] but it may be continued in view of the anticommunist resolution adopted by the Bogotá Conference.[72] (b) American International Institute for the Protection of Childhood, Montevideo,[74] it needs a greater budget; (c) Inter-American Coffee Board,[75] Washington, an agency created during the war emergency; (d) Inter-American Indian Institute,[76] Washington; (e) Inter-American Institute of Agricultural Sciences, Turrialba, Costa Rica;[77] (f) Inter-American Telecommunications Office,[78] Havana; (g) Pan-American Highway Congresses,[79] Buenos Aires; (h) Pan-American Institute of Geography and History,[80] Mexico City; (i) Permanent American Aeronautical Commission;[81] (j) Postal Union of the Americas and Spain, International Office,[82] Montevideo; (k) Pan-American Bureau of Eugenics and Homiculture,[83] Havana; (l) Pan-American Sanitary Bureau,[84] Washington; (m) Inter-American Commission of Women,[85] Washington. Resolution XXIII of the Lima Conference, 1938, charged the governing board with a study of the statute of the commission. Resolution IX of the Mexico City Conference, 1945, provided specifically the inclusion of the commission "among the organs which form the PAU." A subcommittee of the governing board prepared the organic statute which the governing board adopted on February 4, 1948.[86] Resolution XXVIII of the Bogotá

Conference [87] approved the resolution of the governing board by which the Secretary General is authorized to organize the Secretariat of the Commission. Resolution XXI [88] adopted the organic statute of the commission. Contrary to the proposal of the governing board of 1948, the commission is not a specialized organization but a permanent entity which functions attached to the Secretariat General of the OAS.[89]

Will the Inter-American Commission for Territorial Administration,[80] which has never met, continue? If so, is it a specialized organization? The same question may be asked with regard to the newly created American Commission of Dependent Territories,[91] to be established at Havana.

C. Specialized organizations, newly to be created. The Bogotá Conference has made recommendations (a) to include the Inter-American Institute of Musicology, Montevideo, in the study on the situation and activities of specialized organizations;[92] (b) to charge the Inter-American Economic and Social Council to study the possibility and convenience of creating an Inter-American Institute of Immigration,[93] proposed by Peru; (c) to study the possibility of an Inter-American Institute of Commerce [94] and (d) an Inter-American Bank,[95] and eventually to revise the corresponding convention of May 10, 1940. All these three studies and proposals shall be submitted to the specialized economic conference, to be held at Buenos Aires.

VI

The third great change brought about by the Bogotá Charter is to transform the OAS which had hitherto been an independent organization, independent particularly with reference to the League of Nations, into a regional system within the U.N. and in conformity with the provisions of the U.N. Charter.[96] Already in the preamble of the Bogotá

Charter, the principles and purposes of the U.N. are
solemnly reaffirmed. Article I declares expressly: "The
OAS is a regional agency within the U.N." Under Article
IV, the OAS has "to fulfil its regional obligations under the
Charter of the U.N." No provisions of the Bogotá Charter
are to be construed as impairing the rights and obligations
of the member states under the Charter of the U.N. (Article CII). The Bogotá Charter is to be registered with the
Secretariat of the U.N. through the PAU (Article CX). The
council is to promote and facilitate collaboration between
the OAS and the U.N. as well as between the inter-American
specialized organizations and similar international ones
(Article LIII, e). The organs of the council shall establish
co-operative relations with the corresponding organs of the
U.N. (Article LXI). The specialized organizations shall
establish co-operative relations with world agencies. Resolution X [97] provides for the division of functions between
the Inter-American Economic and Social Council and the
Latin-American Economic Commission of the U.N. to avoid
duplication. The Economic Convention of Bogotá foresees
co-operation with the U.N. Economic and Social Council,
with the International Monetary Fund, and the International Bank of Reconstruction. Resolution XXXIX [98] provides for the participation of the U.N. in the inter-American
conferences and meetings of consultation and for the participation of U.N. organs in the conferences of inter-
American specialized organizations.

   Just as the complete reorganization of inter-American
specialized organizations and the creation of some organs
which are integral parts of the OAS are still in the stage of
formation, so the integration with the U.N. is also in a
formative period. Such integration may take very different
forms, from mere co-operation via a relationship based on
agreement, to a form of collaboration so close as to lead
to the performance of regional functions, as will be the case

with the Pan-American Sanitary Bureau with regard to the World Health Organization (WHO).

The Bogotá Charter is also in its structural aspects deeply influenced by the U.N. Charter. Thus the names of the OAS; of the council; of the Secretary General; the names and structures of the different councils; the names of the specialized organizations; their position outside of the OAS, but to be "brought into relationship with the Organization"; the formulas for defining the legal capacity of the OAS; and the privileges and immunities are under the strong influence of the U.N. Charter. On the other hand, the differences are also pronounced. Somewhat different rules are established concerning privileges and immunities; there is only one council; the other councils are not co-ordinated as in the U.N. but are organs of the council. There are even basic differences: absolute equality, sovereignty, non-intervention, no preferred position for any member state, no veto, express right of withdrawal.

While the Bogotá Charter transforms the OAS into a regional organization of the U.N., it takes good care, at the same time, to preserve its identity and relative independence. Thus Article XX prescribes that all inter-American disputes shall be submitted to inter-American peace procedures before being referred to the Security Council of the U.N.; and as Article XXIII lays down that the special treaty on pacific settlement of disputes shall make provisos in such a manner that it will not be possible for an inter-American dispute to fail of definitive settlement within a reasonable time, a submission to the Security Council of the U.N. can hardly arise. Thus Article C, in a particularly interesting way, states that "Inter-American Specialized Organizations, in concluding agreements with international agencies of a world-wide character, should preserve their identity and status as integral parts of the OAS, even when they perform regional functions of international agencies."

By incorporating the Rio Treaty of 1947, the OAS not only preserves its identity and relative independence, but transcends the U.N., although remaining in full conformity with the U.N. Charter, by achieving "collective security," in spite of the U.N. veto. True, legally, this is not collective security, but a system of individual and collective self-defense, based on Article LI of the U.N. Charter.

VII

The Bogotá Charter can, as a whole, be welcomed.[99] The drafting is, from the point of view of legal technique, generally good. There are a few important omissions, particularly as concerns the legal nature of resolutions of inter-American assemblies. It is also interesting to note that the charter contains no norms on Pan-American sub-regional developments, such as Central America or the Inter-American Caribbean Union. As in the U.N. Charter, so in the Bogotá Charter, it would be appropriate to allow specifically such sub-regional organizations, conferences, and organs, but, at the same time, to lay down guiding principles and rules to which such sub-regional developments must conform.

The Bogotá Charter gives Pan-America a treaty basis and a constitution, makes it a regional organization within the U.N., strengthens it by the inclusion of the principles embodied in the Rio Treaty of 1947. With the Bogotá Charter, Pan-America's long period of a mere empirical evolution has, perhaps, come to an end. Pan-America has now reached a remarkable organization, more closely knitted, better organized than any other existing regional or continental organization. Yet, it does not constitute a real innovation in international law. It by no means leads to a super-government; in some respects it is more conservative than the U.N. Pan-America, under the Bogotá

Charter, is a remarkable achievement, but basically, no more than a loose association of sovereign states based on voluntary-co-operation.

The charter must, first of all, be ratified. It needs implementation, some already existent, such as the Rio Treaty, the Pact of Bogotá, the Declaration of the Rights and Duties of Man. The reorganization, strengthening, or transformation has, to a great extent, still to be done. Much remains, for the moment, still in a stage of transition or formation. Thus some of the newly created organs of the council and the Advisory Defense Committee are in formation or transformation. The whole reorganization of the specialized organizations has to be carried out.

Pan-America will, with the ratification of the Bogotá Charter, have a constitution. Such constitutional foundation is of the very greatest importance. But it is further necessary that the constitution functions. For that purpose, the faith in this constitution by all the members, their willingness to co-operate, good, neighborly relations between all the twenty-one American republics, and between this country and Latin America are indispensable. In the last analysis, it is the spirit which decides.

[1] Thus correctly Señor Berméjo (Argentina) in 1902 (ACTAS Y DOCUMENTOS DE LA 2ª CONFERENCIA PAN-AMERICANA 243–49 [1902]).

[2] See "The Pan-American Union," above.

[3] Report of the director to the fourth Pan-American conference, Washington, 1910. Also in CUARTA CONFERENCIA INTERNACIONAL AMERICANA 12–60 (1910).

[4] INFORME A LOS GOBIERNOS MIEMBROS DE LA UNIÓN PAN-AMERICANA (1923).

[5] THE INTERNATIONAL CONFERENCES OF AMERICAN STATES, 1889–1928 at 398–403 (1931).

[6] *Ibid.* at 397–98.

[7] See JOHN P. HUMPHREY, THE INTER-AMERICAN SYSTEM (1942). MARGARET BALL, THE PROBLEM OF INTER-AMERICAN ORGANIZATION (1944). RUTH D. MASTERS, HANDBOOK OF INTERNATIONAL ORGANIZATIONS IN THE AMERICAS (1945) (hereafter cited as MASTERS).

[8] Final Act at 44–48.

[9] See this writer's editorial comment in 39 AM.J.INT'L L. 527–33 (1945).

[10] See already the earlier REPORT AND PROJECT OF THE EXECUTIVE COMMITTEE ON POST-WAR PROBLEMS OF THE GOVERNING BOARDS PAN-AMERICAN POST-WAR ORGANIZATION 71 (1944) (mimeo.).

[11] PROJECT OF ORGANIC PACT OF THE INTER-AMERICAN SYSTEM (1946) (mimeo.).

[12] PROJECT OF ORGANIC PACT OF THE INTER-AMERICAN SYSTEM. Submitted to the Bogotá Conference by resolution of the governing board of February 4, 1948, PAU, Washington, 1948 (mimeo.).

[13] On the Inter-American System, as it existed prior to the Bogotá Conference and the changes envisaged, see the extensive article by William Sanders, *Sovereignty and Interdependence in the New World*, 18 DEP'T STATE BULL. No. 449 at 155–84 (1948).

[14] See this writer's editorial comment in 39 AM.J.INT'L L. No. 4 at 758–67 (1945).

[15] For excellent information on all the topics and for the corresponding documents see HANDBOOK FOR DELEGATES TO THE 9TH INTERNATIONAL CONFERENCE OF AMERICAN STATES (1947).

[16] CHARTER OF THE ORGANIZATION OF THE AMERICAN STATES (1948) (mimeo.). Also printed in 18 DEP'T STATE BULL. No. 464 at 666–73 (1948).

[17] Resolution I, adopted at the Bogotá Conference (ACTA FINAL at 10 [1948] [mimeo.]), calls on the American states to take measures for making the Bogotá Charter widely known. Resolution XL (*ibid.* at 56) orders that the organs of the OAS immediately adopt the new nomenclature and the régimes established by the charter.

[18] Thus still the PROJECT OF AN ORGANIC PACT OF THE INTER-AMERICAN SYSTEM.

[19] See the membership of the Ukraine and of Byelo-Russia in the U.N.

[20] The constitution adopted by the twelfth Pan-American Sanitary Conference (Caracas, January 12–24, 1947) for the Pan-American Sanitary Organization gives membership by right to all "self-governing nations of the Western Hemisphere." But territories within the relations shall have the right to be represented and to participate in the Organization. The nature and extent of their rights and obligations shall be determined in each case by the Directing Council."

[21] Contrary to the earlier formula "American Republic."

[22] As an independent Puerto Rico. See the earlier cases of Cuba and Panama.

[23] This feature is taken from Article XXIII of the Rio Treaty of 1947.

[24] See Hans Kelsen, *Withdrawal from the United Nations*, Western Political Quarterly 29–43 (March, 1948).

[25] The Charter is an intergovernmental treaty. The beginning "In the name of their peoples" has political, but no juridical, significance; it is a modern *phrase diplomatique* which seems on the way to replace the beginning "In the name of the Holy Trinity" of earlier treaties.

[26] See earlier, EXECUTIVE COMMITTEE ON POST-WAR PROBLEMS OF THE GOVERNING BOARD, THE BASIC PRINCIPLES OF THE INTER-AMERICAN SYSTEM (1943).

[27] Especially from CONVENTION ON THE RIGHTS AND DUTIES OF STATES (1933); DECLARATION OF PRINCIPLES OF INTER-AMERICAN SOLIDARITY AND CO-OPERATION (1936); PROTOCOL RELATIVE TO NON-INTERVENTION (1936); DECLARATION OF AMERICAN PRINCIPLES (1938); DECLARATION OF LIMA (1938); and declarations of the three consultative meetings of 1939, 1940, and 1942; finally from the Rio Treaty, 1947.

[28] ACTA FINAL at 41–49.

[29] *Ibid.* at 49.

[30] See PROJECT OF INTER-AMERICAN PEACE SYSTEM (1948) (mimeo.), and REPORT ON THE PROJECT OF INTER-AMERICAN PEACE SYSTEM, RELATIVE TO OBLIGATORY ARBITRATION (1948) (mimeo.).

[31] IXa CONFERENCIA INTERNACIONAL AMERICANA, TRATADA AMERICANA DE SOLUCIONES PACIFICAS, PACTO DE BOGOTÁ (1948) (mimeo.). With the coming into force of the Pact of Bogota all earlier peace instruments will cease to be in force including the Gondra Treaty (1923), Washington Treaties of Conciliation and Arbitration (1929), Additional Protocol on Concilation (1933), Anti-War Treaty (1933), and the corresponding treaties of Buenos Aires (1936). Here, too, we see simplification, unification, and civilization.

[32] See "The Inter-American Treaty of Reciprocal Assistence," above.

[33] IXa CONFERENCIA INTERNACIONAL AMERICANA, CONVENIA ECONOMICO DE BOGOTÁ (1948) (mimeo.),

[34] See JOSEF L. KUNZ, THE MEXICAN EXPROPRIATIONS (1940).

[35] ACTA FINAL at 14–15.

[36] See also Res. XXIX (ACTA FINAL at 33–40), containing the International American Charter Guarantees; Res. XX (*ibid.* at 22–24), concerning services of social assistance; Res. XIX (*ibid.* at 21–22), on conditions of work; and Res. XXII (*ibid.* at 29–30), on the economic condition of women workers.

[37] This is the table of organs of the OAS under the Bogotá Charter.

Inter-American Conferences
(Arts. XXXIII–XXXVIII)

Regular   Special (Art. XXXVI)

Meetings of Consultation of
Ministers of Foreign Affairs (Arts. XXXIX–XLVII)

Advisory Defense Committee
(Arts. XLIV–XLVI)

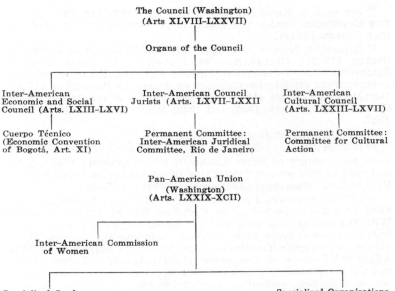

The Council (Washington)
(Arts XLVIII–LXXVII)

Organs of the Council

Inter-American
Economic and Social
Council (Arts. LXIII–LXVI)

Inter-American Council
Jurists (Arts. LXVII–LXXII

Inter-American
Cultural Council
(Arts. LXXIII–LXVII)

Cuerpo Técnico
(Economic Convention
of Bogotá, Art. XI)

Permanent Committee:
Inter-American Juridical
Committee, Rio de Janeiro

Permanent Committee:
Committee for Cultural
Action

Pan-American Union
(Washington)
(Arts. LXXIX–XCII)

Inter-American Commission
of Women

Specialized Conference
(Arts. XCIII–XCIV)

Specialized Organizations
(Arts. XCV–CI)

38 Up to now, Buenos Aires (1936), Mexico City (1945), Rio de Janeiro (1947).

39 A two-thirds majority is required (A) of the governments—(1) for the coming into force of the Bogotá Charter (Article CIX), (2) for the coming into force of amendments (Article CXI), (3) for the convocation of a special inter-American conference Article XXXV), (4) for the convocation of the Advisory Defense Committee (Article XLVII)—(B) of the organ of consultation under Article XVII of the Rio Treaty of 1947, (C) of the council—(1) for approval of decisions on budgetary matters (Articles LIV), (2) for removal of the secretary general or assistant secretary general (Article LXXXVII).

40 See MASTERS at 123–26.

41 Resolution XXXIV, ACTA FINAL at 53.

42 Whereas Humphrey (op. cit. at 199) could write in 1942 that the "Union of American Republics is a purely theoretical body without constitution or officers," the OAS is now treaty-based and all inter-American organs are organs of the OAS.

43 See MASTERS at 139–46.

44 See REPORT OF THE COMMITTEE ON THE ORGANIZATION OF THE IN-TER-AMERICAN SYSTEM RELATIVE TO THE ESTABLISHMENT OF AN INTER-AMERICAN COUNCIL OF JURISTS, approved by the governing board, December 4, 1949.

45 See INTER-AMERICAN AGENCIES FOR THE CODIFICATION, UNIFICA-TION OF LAW IN THE AMERICAS (5th ed. 1944) (mimeo.).

46 MASTERS at 163–69.

47 Resolution II, ACTA FINAL at 10–11.

48 See Resolution XXIV (ACTA FINAL at 30–31) on the porgram and activities of the cultural council.

49 See Joseph L. Kunz, 31 IOWA L. REV. No. 1 at 58–89 (1945).

50 Resolution XLI (ACTA FINAL at 57).

51 INFORME SOBRE EL PLAN FINANCIACIÓN DE LA UNION PAN AMERI-CANA Y LOS ORGANISMOS ESPECIALIZADOS (1948) (mimeo.). The budget of the PAU for the fiscal year of 1948–49, as prepared by the director-general, was $2,130,000.

52 Resolution VII (ACTA FINAL at 12–14).

53 Resolution VI (ACTA FINAL at 13).

54 Article XIX.

55 THE INTERNATIONAL CONFERENCES OF AMERICAN STATES, FIRST SUPPLEMENT, 1933–1940, Apendix A at 381–452 (1940).

56 Resolution VIII (ACTA FINAL at 14–15).

57 Resolution IX (ACTA FINAL at 15–16).

58 PAU (1847) (mimeo.).

59 See the American Institute of International Law, the Inter-American Bar Association, the Association of American Writers and Artists (Havana), the Inter-American Bibliographical and Library Association (Washington), the Inter-American Commercial Arbitration Commission (New York), the International Institute of Ibero-American Literature, the Pan-American Institute of Mining Engineering and Geology (Santiago, Chile), the Pan-American Medical Association (New York), and many others.

60 Article: "The Inter-American Council of Jurists and the Juridical Committee should seek to obtain the cooperation of national committees for the codification of international law, institutes of international and comparative law." Res. XXIV (ACTA FINAL at 30), provides: "Colaboración con las comisiones nacionales de cooperación intelectual y con otros organimos culturales nacionales."

61 Organized in 1940 during the sessions of the eight American Scientific Congress (MASTERS at 177–181; (REPORT,) cited above, n. 58, at 28–30).

62 ACTA FINAL at 12.

63 MASTERS at 287–91.

64 Created by resolution of the first Pan-American Congress of Municipalities (Havana, 1938), under a resolution of the sixth International Conference of American States (MASTERS at 115–23).

65 Organized originally in 1910 as the South American Congress of Railways and broadened in 1941 to include all the twenty-one American republics.

66 Originated in Resolution XIII of January 15, 1940, of the Inter-American Financial Economic Advisory Committee.

67 See above, n. 51.

68 ACTA FINAL at 11–12.

69 See the proposals in the REPORT, cited above, n. 58.

[70] Established originally under the Trade Mark Convention of the Fourth International Conference 1910), continued by the convention of 1923 and the Protocol of 1929 (MASTERS at 182–87).

[71] Created originally in 1890 (MASTERS at 320–24).

[72] Establihed by a resolution of the Third Consultative Meeting, Rio de Janeiro, 1942; composed of seven members, apointed by seven of the American republics designated by the governing board, but representing all the American republics: in structure and function an unusual and interesting organ. See its first report, published in Monevideo, 1943. SECOND ANNUAL REPORT (1944). See PAU, BULLETIN 489, 693 (1942). J. F. Pimentel in REVISTA DE DERECHO INTERNACIONAL 116–18 (1943); Carl B. Spaeth and W. Sanders in 38 AM.J.INT'L L. 218–41 (1944).

[73] Resolution XXXII, ACTA FINAL at 49–50.

[74] Established in 1927 (MASTERS at 8–12).

[75] Created pursuant to the Inter-American Coffee Agreement of 1941 (MASTERS at 93–98).

[76] Established by terms of a convention, Mexico City, November 1, 1940 (MASTERS at 150–56).

[77] Established in accordance with a convention of January 15, 1944.

[78] This office will supersede the Inter-American Radio Office (on it, MASTERS at 170–75), when the Convention of September 27, 1945, signed at Rio de Janeiro, is ratified by five governments.

[70] The report proposes the maintenance, but considers it desirable that the central committee be made more truly inter-American in character.

[80] Established in 1929 (MASTERS at 307–10).

[81] Provided for in a resolution of the Inter-American Technical Aviation Conference, Lima, 1937 (MASTERS at 357–59); hitherto inactive.

[82] Established 1921. Members: the twenty-one American republics, Canada, and Spain, International Transfer Office in Panama City (MASTERS at 379–89).

[83] MASTERS at 25–36.

[84] Created by the Second International Conference of American States, 1902 (MASTERS at 324–31). The twelfth Pan-American Saniization plan. The organization will consist of (A) The Pan-American Sanitary Conferences, to be held four years; (B) the directing council, meeting annually; (C) the Executive Committee, and (D) the Pan-American Sanitary Bureau in Washington (see article by James A. Doull in 18 DEP'T STATE BULL. No. 452 at 283–85 [1948]).

[85] Created by resolution of the sixth International Conference of American States, Havana, 1928 (MASTERS at 106–10).

[86] PROJECTO DE ESTATUTO ORGÁNICO DE LA COMISIÓN INTER-AMERICANA DE MUJERES (1948) (mimeo.).

[87] ACTA FINAL at 32.

[88] ACTA FINAL at 24–28.

89 UNA ENTIDAD PERMANENTE QUE FUNCIONA ADSCRITA A LA SECRE-
TARÍA GENERAL (art. I).

90 Created by the Act of Havana, 1940 (MASTERS at 103–6).

91 Resolution XXXIII, ACTA FINAL at 51–52 (Reservation by Brazil; the United States abstained from approving this resolution).

92 Resolution V, ACTA FINAL at 13.

93 Resolution XIV, *ibid.* at 19.

94 Resolution XVI, *ibid.* at 20.

95 Resolution XV, *ibid.* at 20.

96 United Nations Charter, arts. LII–LIV, XXXIII, XXXVII, LI.

97 ACTA FINAL at 16.

98 ACTA FINAL at 55–56.

99 See the remarks by Assistant Secretary for Political Affairs Nor-
man Armour on the achievements of the Bogotá Conference, 18 DEP'T
STATE BULL. No. 465 at 714–15 (1948).

PART VII

LAWS OF WAR

AT THE BEGINNING of the war the belligerents, of course, set up prize courts. Germany enacted a new Prize Law Code [1] and a new Prize Court Code.[2] But no belligerent, with the exception of Great Britain, has yet published reports of prize cases. True, compared with the enormous amount of prize cases during the war of 1914–18 [3] in Great Britain,[4] France,[5] Germany,[6] and Italy,[7] the number of British prize cases so far reported [8] is comparatively very small.[9] Yet it seems important to investigate these cases to which the science of international law has paid no attention up to now. It is proposed to give here a systematic study of these prize cases, from the points of view of substantive and formal prize law, and of the law of prize procedure.

THE LAW OF PRIZE PROCEDURE

1. Toute prise doit être jugée.

This norm of international law has always been observed by Great Britain.[10] At the time of the outbreak of the war, Great Britain enacted the Prize Act, 1939.[11] This act has only the character of an amendment to the Naval Prize Act,

1864,[12] the Prize Courts (Procedure) Act, 1914,[13] and the Prize Courts Act, 1915.[14] The most important, and a very significant and far-reaching amendment, consists in the proviso that "the law relating to prize shall apply in relation to aircraft and goods carried therein as it applies in relation to ships and goods carried therein, and shall so apply notwithstanding that the aircraft is on or over land." The other important clause of the Prize Act, 1939, relates to the establishment of prize courts not only in Great Britain, the Dominions, India, and the colonies,[15] but also "outside of H. M. Dominions," namely, in any British protectorate, any League of Nations mandate, and "any other country or territory in which for the time being H. M. has jurisdiction in matters of prize." [16] For the procedure in prize cases the Prize Rules, 1939,[17] were published.[18]

2. *Stare decisis*

The British Prize Court in London sat for the first time in the present war on November 2, 1939. The prize judge of the war was Sir Boyd Merriman (later Lord Merriman). When the first prize case—The Pomona [19]—came up, the prize judge pledged to do his best to follow the example of his predecessors and uphold the tradition of the British prize court. Notwithstanding all dicta to the effect that British prize courts apply international law directly in complete independence of municipal law,[20] British prize courts apply in fact British prize law, which may or may not be in conformity with international law. British prize law is formed by a body of precedents. The prize decisions of Lord Stowell have, to a great extent, created British prize law, and during World War I "the law as interpreted in British prize courts has received, under the familiar guise of decisions in particular cases, a new body of doctrine." [21] The rule, *stare decisis* applies in prize courts.[22]

This rule has come into prominence in the decisions of the present war, whereas, on other occasions, the prize judge, in dealing with precedents, has "distinguished" these cases from the actual ones.

3. *Jurisdiction ratione materiae*

This jurisdiction, it may be said, covers all matters relating to captures at sea, and now also relating to aircraft on land or sea. "The chief function of a court of prize is to determine the question: prize or no prize." [23] But British prize courts exercise jurisdiction also over all problems connected with prizes. This jurisdiction embraces also the competence of the prize court to decide on its own jurisdiction, if this jurisdiction is challenged. A novel problem presented itself in the case of the "Astoria" [24] where the commonwealth government of Australia moved for the requisition of this Danish vessel pending a decision of the court as to the condemnation of the ship as a prize of war. The Danish vessel was, at the time of the German occupation of Denmark, off the coast of New South Wales. The Naval Board sent a message to the captain directing him to proceed to Sydney. The master consulted with the Danish consul-general in Sydney and decided to follow his advice. The representative for master and vessel objected to the ship being requisitioned without appraisement, and challenged the jurisdiction of the prize court because "it would have to be established that a state of war existed between Britain and Denmark." The representative of the Crown tendered proclamations by the Commonwealth "as to the state of war" and a certificate by the minister for external affairs "as to the present condition of Denmark." The judge agreed that he had jurisdiction for the purpose of requisition and granted an order to this effect, but stated that he would not be able to make a final order until it was established in the suit for condemnation that the vessel was an enemy ship. We will come back to this case later.

The jurisdiction of the prize court covers also problems of prize procedure and problems concerning trading with the enemy.[25] The prize court has to apply strict law and cannot introduce considerations of equity, e.g., as far as national or neutral mortgagees are concerned. "Under the existing practice," said Sir Boyd Merriman,[26] "it is quite plain that this court does not deal with bounty. Sir Samuel Evans said in the plainest words that he had nothing whatever to do with bounty."

4. Jurisdiction ratione loci

This jurisdiction is determined by the port into which the captured ship is brought or where the goods have been seized. But under Section 1 of the Prize Courts Act, 1915, a prize court has power to transfer proceedings to another prize court on application by the proper officer of the Crown, if the court is satisfied that the proceedings would be more conveniently conducted in this other prize court. In the case of the "Gabbiano," [27] proceedings started in the Prize Court of Gibraltar but were remitted to the London Prize Court.

Prize procedure overrides admiralty action. In the case of the "Pomona" [28] the British time-charterers prior to the outbreak of the war had put this German vessel under arrest in a procedure in the admiralty court in which they were the plaintiffs. On September 3, 1939, the "Pomona" was seized and requisition by the Crown was granted by the prize court. In the case of the "Prins Knud," [29] a British firm, which had rendered very valuable salvage services to this Danish ship prior to the German occupation of Denmark, had obtained from the admiralty court a salvage award of £6,500; but the admiralty court directed that the judgment for the sum assessed should stand over until after prize proceedings.[30]

5. *Parties, Claims*

Prize procedure is an action *in rem,* brought by the captor state against the captured *res.* The suit is, therefore, initiated [31] by the representative of the capturing state.[32] Apart from the proper representative of the Crown, the interested parties may be represented. Such interested parties are, first of all, the owners. Even enemy owners have *personna standi in judicio,* not in general as alien enemies under common law are *ex lege*—and this refers to prize courts, too—but *pro hac vice.* In World War I prize cases, "enemy claimants have been repeatedly recognized to assert rights under international conventions, or to contest condemnation of their goods, if shipped or carried under circumstances which gave immunity from capture." [33] These precedents were followed in the case of the "Pomona." [34] In addition to owners, there appeared as interested parties in the prize cases of the war, national time-charterers of a seized enemy vessel,[35] national and neutral mortgages,[36] national claimants for brokerage and dispatch money,[37] a national firm as seller claiming proceeds of sale,[38] the master of the vessel,[39] the salvors.[40]

6. *No appearance, no claims: six-months rule*

Since "a claimant in a prize court is not in a position analogous to that of defendant, but rather to that of plaintiff," [41] the *onus probandi* is, generally speaking, on the shoulders of the claimant.[42] Absence of any appearance or of any claim does not hinder the prize procedure, nor does it necessarily lead to condemnation. In the case of the "Benmacdhui" (*cargo ex*)[43] where the Crown asked for

condemnation of parcels of cargo in a British vessel, no
appearance was made; motion was made less than six
months from service of writ. Prize Court Rules, 1939,
Order 15, Rule 9,[44] is as follows:

> No ship (or cargo) shall be condemned at the hearing in the
> absence of an appearance or claim until six months have elapsed
> from the service of the writ . . . unless there be on the ship
> papers . . . and on the evidence, if any, of the witnesses from
> the captured ship . . sufficient proof that such ship . . . be-
> longs to the enemy or is otherwise liable to condemnation.

The prize judge interpreted this rule to mean, as to evidence,
that the ship or cargo must stand "self-condemned," [45] that
so-called extrinsic evidence is here excluded. The judge
decided that in this case the cargo stood self-condemned.

In the *Alwaki and other vessels* (*cargo ex*),[46] the Crown
asked for the condemnation of the cargo of four Dutch
vessels and one Norwegian vessel as contraband after six
months from the service of the writ, no claims having been
made in the meantime. The problem arising in this case was
as to the right of the Crown to invoke the six-months rule
and whether this rule is absolute. The attorney-general
acknowledged that, prior to the Prize Court Rules, 1939,
the general usage of nations fixed a period of one year and
one day but pointed out that Sir Samuel Evans had substituted in many cases the six-months rule. The prize judge
asked why, if this rule is absolute, evidence should be given
the court after the lapse of six months? The attorney-
general admitted that seizure and lack of claim for six
months is to be shown *prima facie,* and that if it were
affirmatively shown to the satisfaction of the court that the
goods were not contraband, or not condemnable, the six-
months rule should not apply. The judgment laid down that
"it is not for the Crown, as a matter of pleading, to plead
an affirmative case; the capture may be presumed to be in

order until some claimant comes forward and establishes his claim." Enemy ownership is presumed after the lapse of a year and a day, if no claimant comes forward.[47] But the judge went into the question whether a municipal rule of procedure can legally substitute six months for a period recognized by the usage of nations. Relying not only on Sir Samuel Evans' decision in the *Antilla*,[48] but also on Lord Sterndale's decision in the *Frogner*,[49] the judge decided that the six-months rule is not an absolute rule, the decision being based on the judicial interpretation of the municipal law.

7. Costs

The determination of costs is in the discretion of the judge under the Prize Court Rules, 1939, Order 18, Rule 1.[50] An interesting problem arose in the case of the "Gabbiano," in which the decision as to proceeds of sale was in favor of the claimants, and claim for costs against the Crown was made.[51] That in a proper case both damages and costs may be awarded against the Crown was laid down by the Privy Council in the *Zamora*.[52] That the discretion of the judge in determining costs is to be exercised judicially was laid down in the *Stanton*.[53] The representative of the Crown argued that costs are never awarded in prize courts against the Crown, except in cases where the court also awards damages, quoting Sir Samuel Evans' decision in the *Kronprins Gustav Adolf* [54] and the Privy Council's decision in the *Baron Stjernblad*.[55] The theoretical problem involved in the discussion before the judge between the representative of the Crown and the representative of the claimants was whether a precedent as to the exercise of the prize judge's discretion as to costs is binding on a later judge. Counsel for claimants argued that the judge "could get assistance from the manner in which discretion has been exercised in the past, but that no court has the power to lay down a rule binding a judge to exercise his discretion only according to certain conditions." The representative of the Crown, on the other hand, argued that the judge's discretion as to costs has not only to be exercised judicially, but that "the way in which discretion had been exercised had been sanctioned by practice." The judge made no order as to costs, considering himself bound by the decision in the *Baron Stjernblad*, notwithstanding his discretion, holding that the decision in the *Baron Stjernblad* did not involve the manner in which discretion had been exercised, but constituted a rule of law.

8. Appeal

From any order or decree of a prize court an appeal lies to the Privy Council, as of right in cases of a final decree and in other cases with the leave of the court making the order or decree.[56] In the case of the "Prins Knud," [57] the claimants wanted to take the legal issue presented by this case to the Privy Council. In conformity with the Prize Court Rules, 1939, Order 44, Rule 3, the judge gave them leave and fixed £150 as security for the due prosecution of the appeal and the payment of all costs.

FORMAL PRIZE LAW

1. Capture of ships

British prize law uses the terms "capture" and "seizure" as identical. The prize cases hitherto decided in British prize courts during the war show capture of German ships at sea [58] as well as in British ports,[59] seizure of Italian ships in a British port,[60] and seizure of Danish ships in British ports.[61] The problem of destroying certain ships' papers or throwing them overboard before seizure arose incidentally in the case of the "Cap Norte." [62] The problem of a false flag arose in the case of the "Konsul Hendrik Fisser," [63] a German vessel sailing under the Norwegian flag and having the Norwegian colors painted on her sides and on a hatch.

2. Seizure of goods

Seizure of goods as enemy property at sea or in a British port on board British ships is upheld in many of the decided cases.[64] Seizure of goods as contraband on board neutral ships is upheld in other cases.[65]

3. Requisition pendente lite

Capture must be distinguished from condemnation, on the one hand, and, on the other, from measures affecting ships which do not come under prize law, such as the exercise of the *jus angariae*, sequestration of ships under economic war measures, "protective sequestration" for police reasons, "taking over" ships under municipal law—e.g., for violation of an anti-sabotage statute—or as a measure of reprisal. "Detention" under Article II of the sixth Hague Convention of 1907 is also of a different character. Of particular importance is the requisition [66] of enemy ships. Here again two possibilities arise: the requisition of captured ships or goods prior to the opening of proceedings in a prize court,[67] and the requisition of captured ships or goods during the prize court procedure, i.e., requisition *pendente lite*.

As we have seen,[68] the rules of international law that the prize must be brought into a prize court and that capture does not affect the ownership of the thing seized,[69] have always been fully recognized by British prize courts; but under the Prize Court Rules, 1914, Order 29, as amended by

the Order in Council of April 29, 1915,[70] the prize judge
shall "when it is made to appear to the judge on the application of the proper officer of the Crown that it is desired to
requisition on behalf of H. M. a ship (or goods) in respect
of which no final decree of condemnation has been made,
order that the ship be appraised and that upon an undertaking being given in accordance with Rule 5,[71] the ship
shall be released and delivered to the Crown." In case of
urgency, requisition can be made without appraisement.

In the famous case of the "Zamora," [72] Sir Samuel Evans
laid down that "the prize court has inherent powers to deal
with the property brought within its jurisdiction as it may
deem fit in the exercise of its discretion," that claimants
have no right under international law to demand that the
property be preserved in kind until the final decree determines whether it is to be released or condemned, and that,
apart from the inherent powers of the prize court, the
practice is prescribed by the Prize Court Rules, which
violate no acknowledged and settled principle of international law because they deal only with a matter affecting
procedure and practice of the court. The decision of the
Privy Council,[73] reversing the decision of Sir Samuel Evans,
denied this "inherent power" of the prize court. It said:

> The primary duty of a prize court is to preserve the *res*. . . .
> The inherent power of the court as to sale or realization is con-
> fined to cases where this cannot be done. . . . Such a limited
> power would not justify the court in directing a sale of the *res*
> merely because it thought fit to do so, or merely because one of
> the parties desired the sale.

And with regard to requisition *pendente lite,* the same decision laid down that

> a belligerent Power has by international law the right of requi-
> sitioning vessels or goods in the custody of its prize court pend-
> ing a decision whether they should be condemned or released,

but such right is subject to certain limitations: (1) The vessel or goods must be urgently required for use in connection with the defense of the realm . . . ; (2) There must be a real question to be tried so that it would be improper to order an immediate release; (3) The right must be enforced by application to the prize court, which must determine judicially whether, under the particular circumstances of the case, the right is exercisable.[74]

Requisitioning does not divest the property in captured vessels from the owners thereof.[75] Requisition *pendente lite* in the present war is prescribed in the same sense by Order 29 of the Prize Court Rules, 1939. In the first prize case of the present war, the "Pomona," [76] a motion was made by the procurator-general for requisition without appraisement of this seized German motor vessel. The prize judge granted the requisition, closely following the *Zamora* decision of the Privy Council, having found that the three conditions were fulfilled. And he allowed requisition without appraisement,[77] but under an undertaking by the representative of the Crown to pay the value of the ship into court "at such time as the court shall declare by order that the same or any part thereof is required for the purpose of payment out of court," an undertaking which "will be available to meet any possible question which may arise out of the later history of this vessel in the hands of the Crown."

Requisition without appraisement was also granted in the case of the German ship "Hannah Boge." [78] This requisitioned ship was later condemned as a good and lawful prize.[79] Requisition of the Italian (enemy) ships "Remo" [80] and "Sistiana" [81] was granted; in the first case, after appraisement; in the second for reasons of urgency without an order for appraisement. The cases of requisition *pendente lite* of the Danish ships "Gudrun Maersk," [82] "Astoria," [83] and "Kalo" [84] were exceptional for reasons to be now examined.

SUBSTANTIVE PRIZE LAW

1. Existence of a state of war as precondition for the exercise of the right of prize—Danish ships

The exercise of the right of prize is legal from the beginning of the existence of a state of war. Whereas Britain's formal declaration of war on Germany on September 3, 1939, and Italy's declaration of war on Britain on June 10, 1940, created a legally clear situation in this respect, questions of the existence of a state of war [85] between Britain and Denmark arose later.

Up to April 9, 1940, Denmark was unquestionably a neutral state; but on April 10, 1940, she was, with her consent, occupied by Germany. Although Denmark made no declaration of war and in no way participated in hostilities, she was, as an enemy-occupied country, open to British attack; but was there a state of war between Britain and Denmark? Britain did not declare war on Denmark. The fate of Danish vessels on the high seas or in British ports was uncertain. Up to the time of this article, four such cases [86] had come up in British prize courts.

The first case was that of the "Gudrun Maersk," [87] a Danish ship which entered Bombay harbor on April 13, 1940. On April 15, a notification was published in the Bombay government *Gazette Extraordinary* that the central government had decided that all Danish vessels entering port in the Province of Bombay should be seized; and the vessel was seized. The court granted the motion for requisition by the Crown.

The "Kalo," [88] a Danish vessel entered Durban and was taken into the custody of the South Africa (Natal) Supreme Court (In Prize). The court granted an order for requisition, after appraisement, by the Crown, but held that it would not be justified in granting the immediate release of the ship "in regard to the contention that the ship was not an enemy ship, in view of the unusual circumstances created by the action of the German Government in over-running Denmark" and that "argument that the ship was not an enemy ship could be addressed to the court in the contemplated proceedings for the condemnation of the ship as prize."

In the case of the "Astoria," [89] the representative of the master and the vessel challenged, as reported above, the jurisdiction of the prize court. He referred to the Danish Shipping Commission in New York, which sought to establish control of all Danish ships outside occupied territory. The judge, going first into the question of jurisdiction, said he would have to be satisfied "that the ship came within the definition of a prize of war." The representative of the Crown, insisting on requisition, not on chartering, tendered proclamations by the Commonwealth Government "as to the state of war between Britain and Denmark." Counsel for the master objected on the ground that the statement was inadmissible. "The ordinary procedure of proving military occupation of a country by hostile forces was to give evidence of that fact." He insisted that, in order to give the court jurisdiction, "it would have to be established that a state of war existed between Britain and Denmark." The representative of the Crown stated it would have to be determined at the hearing of condemnation whether the ship was a prize of war or not. The judge, in granting requisition, held that he could not make a final order until it was established in the suit for condemnation that the vessel was an enemy ship. "The question will arise as to whether this vessel, by reason of the occupation of Denmark, has assumed an enemy character or is simply a homeless wanderer."

In both cases, therefore, the question whether Danish ships were enemy ships was left for the suit for condemnation. The problem entered into a new phase with the case of the "Prins Knud," [90] a real test case. This vessel had been arrested in prize on April 11, 1940, the day after the invasion of Denmark. On April 12, the writ in prize was issued and the arrest withdrawn, and on April 20, the Registrar, in appropriate procedure, permitted the Crown to requisition the ship. Counsel for the British salvors asked for an order that the Crown "do forthwith proceed to adjudication in this cause for condemnation." The procurator-general handed to the judge a statement of the position of H. M. Government to the following effect: (1) After the German occupation of Denmark, assurances were given that, speaking generally, Danish vessels seized as prize would be handed back to their owners after the war, and that, therefore (2) the present policy of H. M. Government is to refrain from seeking decrees of condemnation of Danish vessels seized as prize.

Counsel for salvors argued that the fact that the government had adopted this policy does not affect the court in the exercise of its prize jurisdiction, and that the government's procedure was contrary to the accepted rules of international law which governed the court's jurisdiction in prize. The Crown, he said, was not entitled to depart from the ordinary procedure and to act in a way contrary to the accepted canons of prize procedure: it was for the Crown to proceed to proper adjudication. A novel problem was thus raised: can the Crown be compelled by order of the court to continue the suit for condemnation of a prize, especially if the Crown asks for requisition of the thing seized *pendente lite*. There is, as far as this writer knows, no precedent available.[91]

The prize judge accepted the statement of the government's policy as "a matter of high interest to the realm," and said in an *obiter dictum* that "Denmark had become an enemy country" and that "here the vessel in question is, beyond doubt, within the meaning of prize law, an enemy vessel." As to the decision of the novel problem, he admitted that he was "at one time in some doubt whether the action taken to requisition the vessel, while at the same time saying that there was no intention to seek condemnation, was consistent with the decision of the Privy Council in *The Zamora,* but that he has been satisfied that there is really no conflict," for the *Zamora* decision forbade requisition merely by executive order and insisted on requisition in prize and in advance by condemnation. In this case the government had undertaken that there would be no release to owners without application to the prize court, and then only upon proper notice to claimants, and that, finally, the same undertaking applied to any sum brought into court in lieu of the ship in the event of her loss. "The mere fact that the Government have expressed a unilateral intention of taking a course which will not involve condemnation, ultimately does not seem to me really to affect the matter one way or the other. I think I should be doing wrong if I made an order compelling the Crown to bring this case to adjudication," as such decision would, "in effect, reverse the decision on policy at which the Government has arrived."

The four Danish ships cases are, therefore, inconclusive as far as the topic of this paragraph is concerned. The question before the court was only that of requisition *pendente lite.* The prize judges agreed that the right of prize against these Danish vessels could legally have been exercised only if the Crown could prove that they were enemy vessels. This issue has to be decided in the proceedings for the condemnation of these ships as prize. While the rule of international law, according to which the existence of a state of war is a necessary pre-condition for the legal exercise of the right of prize, is unquestioned, the only question to be decided is whether this condition was fulfilled;

whether, in other words, a state of war existed in law between Britain and Denmark, whether these ships have "by
reason of the German occupation of Denmark assumed an
enemy character." On this question the prize judges made
no decision, for the above-quoted words of the prize judge
in the Prins Knud Case constitute merely an *obiter dictum*.
But not only have, up to now, such proceedings for condemnation not taken place, but, in consequence of the British policy as to Danish ships, it is unlikely that they ever
will take place. The statement of this British policy by the
procurator-general is legally open to attack; for the formula
to hand these ships "seized as prize" after the war back to
the owners contains a *petitio principii;* the words "seized
as prize" beg the question which is exactly the question to
be decided by the prize court.

2. Seizure of land

As in World War I, during the war, the right of prize
had been exercised not only on the high seas and in ports,
but sometimes even on land,[92] and captures have been made
not only by men-of-war, but also by port authorities, contraband control officers, customs officers, and so on. In the
case of the "Glenearn" [93] the ship had arrived at London
harbor about August 24, 1939; the goods had been unloaded
and placed in a Port of London Authority's warehouse on
September 1; and on September 12 they were received into
the British firm's own warehouse, where they were seized
as prize on October 9, 1939. But the court, as we shall see
later, gave judgment in favor of claimants.

3. Enemy character of vessels

Enemy merchant vessels, apart from the exceptions recognized by international law, are always subject to capture

and condemnation; but the question, What is a merchant vessel?, can lead to difficulties.

Is purpose or ownership the criterion? [94] Are, therefore, merchant vessels in the sense of prize law all ships which are not state-owned, so that the merchant vessel would be identified with the privately-owned ship, or only those privately-owned vessels that are destined for trade? The problem arose in World War I, particularly with regard to pleasure yachts, and especially under the sixth Hague Convention of 1907. German, British, and French prize courts condemned pleasure yachts in World War I. Whereas German prize courts, in cases in which the sixth Hague Convention of 1907, was not involved, condemned them as being merchant vessels,[95] British [96] and French [97] prize courts, in order to deprive them of the benefit of the sixth Hague Convention, condemned pleasure yachts as not being merchant vessels. But in the war with the sixth Hague Convention denounced by Britain, the prize court did not go into the question of the benefit of this convention and condemned the small pleasure yacht "Elvira III" [98] simply as German owned. The flag [99] is of great importance also under British prize law, and the flying of an enemy flag, in fact, creates a non-rebuttable presumption of enemy character.[100] Enemy character is determined by legal ownership [101] at the date of capture, a principle often applied in the prize cases of this war. "British prize courts have made ownership the criterion of national character." [102]

4. Neutral, national, or allied rights in or against enemy vessels.

Such rights are equally subject to condemnation.[103] The following problems arose in the British prize cases of the war:

A) *British time charterers of a captured German vessel.*
The "Pomona," [104] a German vessel, was under time charter
(for seven months every year, the charter to run until 1946)
to the Jamaica Banana Producers' Association Ltd., a British firm. The conduct of the master and the owners was
such that the association treated it as a repudiation of the
charter party and, on its motion, the vessel was arrested in
admiralty on August 25, 1939. On September 3, the vessel
was seized. The representative of the Crown stated that
"seizure overrode all mortgages, liens and all other rights
of every kind," and the representative of the time charterers, not opposing the motion for requisition, agreed
entirely that "the rights of the Crown took precedence
over the charterer's rights as plaintiffs in the action mentioned" in the admiralty court.

(B) *Neutral charters of captured German vessel.* The
"Bianca," [105] a German vessel, chartered by a Portugese
company under a prewar charter party, was condemned as
good and lawful prize.

(C) *Mortgagees not in possession.* The "Konsul Hendrik
Fisser," [106] originally a British vessel, was sold in 1937 to a
German company, the money being advanced by a British
firm on mortgage. At the date of seizure a sum of £30,000
was outstanding. Apart from these national mortgages,
there was a second, a neutral (Dutch) mortgage. Counsel
for the national and neutral first and second mortgagees
pleaded, first, that the right of the mortgagees ought to
prevent the Crown from obtaining condemnation at all, and,
alternatively, if the ship be condemned, it should be subject
to a charge on her value to protect the mortgagees' security.
Both mortgages were undisputed and perfectly valid in law.
The British contract provided further that the mortgagees
were to hold the ship as security by way of first mortgage,
were to be permitted to collect all freights in respect of the
vessel, and were authorized to act as chartering agents,

ship brokers, and otherwise. The court was satisfied that the mortgagees exercised not only in law but in fact a very strict control over the movements of the vessel. The mortgagees were further entitled to take immediate possession of the ship and register her as a British vessel in case of default or of impossibility to renew insurances except at a rate of premium exorbitant in their opinion. At the outbreak of war the ship was on a voyage from Newfoundland to Antwerp and Bordeaux, but because of the war she put into Vigo and later tried to go back to Germany, when she was captured. The mortgagees intended, when the ship arrived at Bordeaux, to take steps to obtain possession of the vessel and register her as a British ship, and had instructed their solicitors to this effect. Because of the right of control and of possession, counsel for mortgagees tried to distinguish this case from the precedent of the "Marie Glaeser," [107] but the judgment followed the precedent of that case, according to which mortgagees, British or neutral, not in possession of a ship captured as prize, can not only not prevent condemnation but are not entitled to have the mortgage debt paid to them out of the proceeds thereof. The ship was condemned and the claims of the two mortgagees dismissed with costs; for, as the judge said, there is a great difference "between instructing solicitors to take steps to enforce rights to take possession and taking possession."

(D) *Mortgagees in possession.* Mortgagees not in possession have no *locus standi,* as held in the *Konsul Hendrik Fisser Case.* The case of the "Christoph von Doorum" [108] was very similar. A captured German vessel had, in 1937, been sold from England to Germany, indeed to the same firm as the "Konsul Hendrik Fisser" under a mortgage by the same London firm, the mortgage deed being identical. But in this case the mortgagees had enforced their right to take possession; the vessel had been arrested on August

26, 1939, seized on September 3, 1939, later chartered by
the Crown and was, during a voyage to England, torpedoed
and beached, becoming a total loss. Counsel for British
mortgagees resisted condemnation, claiming that they were
the true and lawful owners of the vessel as mortgagees in
possession. But the court, relying on the decisions in the
cases of the "Marie Glaeser" and the "Odessa," and quoting
the American case of the "Hampton" [109] as well as the
"Konsul Hendrik Fisser," condemned the ship and dismissed
the claim of the mortgagees. "If they had taken proceedings in the nature of foreclosure and had transferred the
ship to British registry, the position might possibly be
different."

(E) *Brokerage, dispatch money.* In the case of the
"Rheingold" [110] the Crown asked for the condemnation of
this German vessel and of the freight. The vessel was, at the
time of capture, time chartered to another German Company, and they had chartered her to a British firm in
Durban. The time charter had been negotiated by British
brokers in London; the voyage charter to the British firm
in South Africa had been effected by their British brokers.
Brokerage was claimed by the London firm which acted as
agents for the German time-charterers, and for another
London firm which acted as agents for the South African
charterers and which also claimed dispatch money. Counsel
for claimants argued that the brokers were entitled to be
paid out of the freight the commissions they had earned.
The vessel was captured on a voyage from Durban to Dunkirk and brought into an optional port under the voyage
charter; the freight was paid by British consignees. The
prize judge, relying again on the decision in the case of
the "Marie Glaeser,[111] condemned the ship and the freight,
and dismissed the claims with costs. For brokers, in respect
of their brokerage on freight, cannot be in a better position
than mortgagees who have a charge on the ship itself.

(F) *Salvage.* In the case of the "Prins Knud," [112] an English firm had by tugs rendered important salvage services in February and March, 1940, and the admiralty court assessed the salvage award at £6500, but directed the judgment to stand over until after prize proceedings,[113] for, after the German occupation of Denmark, this Danish ship was seized. As mentioned above, the principal problem of the case dealt with the question whether the Crown could be compelled to continue the condemnation proceedings. The court decided that the rights of the salvors should be postponed for determination and satisfaction until the end of the war, but should be safeguarded by registration.

5. *Enemy or non-enemy character of cargo*

(A) *Cargo on board an enemy ship is presumed to be of enemy character.* This presumption is rebuttable, but the *onus probandi* is on the claimants.[114] In the case of the "Pomona," [115] this German vessel was on time charter to a British firm, and their counsel stated that there were on board the vessel about five hundred tons of bunker oil; the question arose whether to condemn it as part of the ship's furniture, or not to condemn it on the ground that it was of British ownership. This question was not decided, but the representative of the Crown was willing to pay the value of the fuel oil if it turned out that the oil, which, under the charter, was provided and paid by the charterers, ought not to be condemned.[116]

In the case of the "Bianca," [117] the Crown asked for condemnation of this German vessel and cargo on the presumption that all goods on board an enemy ship were prima facie enemy property. The ship, with a cargo of coal was captured on a voyage from Rotterdam to Lisbon. The judge, condemning the vessel, held over the question of the cargo, as it was a prewar charter party, a prewar shipment in a

ship chartered by a Portuguese company, and as the shipment, on the face of documents, was to a named consignee
in Portugal. The representative of the Crown relied on the
presumption mentioned, and on the fact that no appearance
had been entered by the consignee or any other claiman,
but admitted the possibility that under the contract for
sale the property in the coal had passed to the neutral consignee at the date of seizure.

In the case of the "Gloria," [118] a motion for the condemnation of this German ship and part of her cargo was granted.
The contraband issue did not come up, only the presumption
"enemy ship, enemy goods" until the contrary is shown, a
presumption valid regardless of the destination of the
ship.[119]

(B) *Passing of property—Ante bellum contracts.* In the
case of the "Benmacdhui," [120] application by the Crown for
condemnation of parcels of cargo in a British ship was
granted. The goods were consigned before the war to the
order of German firms at Hamburg. The Crown asserted
that evidence on the papers showed that these goods belonged to the enemy, that property had passed to the
consignees and was enemy-owned at the crucial date of
capture. The judge followed a decision of Sir Samuel
Evans [121] by accepting as prima facie evidence of enemy
property the consignment to, or to the order of, an enemy
firm in an enemy port.

In the interesting case of the "Gabbiano,"[122] the Crown
asked for the condemnation of a cargo of nine thousand
tons of manganiferous ore, or the proceeds thereof, shipped
by the Sinai Mining Company, Ltd., a British company, in
an Italian ship from a port in Egypt to Stettin on August
27, 1939, under an *ante bellum* contract of sale of December 23, 1938, made between the claimants as sellers and a
Czechoslovakian company as buyers. By letter of April 11,

1939, after the establishment of the German "protectorate of Bohemia and Moravia," the buyers exercised their option to receive the goods at Stettin. On July 11, 1939, full payment was made in sterling as a voluntary payment in advance. The "Gabbiano" was chartered on July 14, 1939. At the time of the outbreak of war this neutral Italian vessel was bunkering at Messina. Claimants arranged that the ship should proceed with the cargo to England. She was seized at Gibraltar and brought under a prize crew to Cardiff. Soon after arrival the cargo was sold.

The question was whether the property had remained in the claimants at the date of seizure. The Crown argued on these lines: the contract is expressed to be a c.i.f. contract; under such a contract it is customary to take the bills of lading to seller's order because payment is to be made against tender of the shipping documents. In such cases the prima facie presumption of the reservation of the right of disposal, under Section 19/2 of the Sale of Goods Act, 1893, is invoked, with the result that the property in the goods does not pass. In this case payment had been made in advance of shipment, and, therefore, the property passed to the enemy buyers at the date of shipment. The Crown asked the court to treat the contract as an f.o.b. contract [123] and relied on the decision in the "Parchim." [124]

This case is disinguishable from that of the "Parchim," for in the case of the "Gabbiano" the contract contained a clause according to which in case of loss of the ship or inability to deliver the cargo or any part thereof, "the quantity of ore so undelivered shall be written off the contract." The judge went into the question of what is a c.i.f. contract under English commercial law.[125] While the mentioned clause is inappropriate to a c.i.f. contract proper, the contract may remain a c.i.f. contract, but with variations. The judge came to the conclusion that in taking the

bills of lading to their own order, the British sellers did not
do so as the agents or on behalf of the buyers, but intended
to reserve the right of disposal and thus to retain the property in the goods. Judgment was, therefore, in favor of
claimants who had established their right to the release to
them of the proceeds of this cargo.

(C) *Transfer in transitu. Contract made imminente bello.*
Trading with the enemy. The "Gabbiano" is a case of a
bona fide *ante bellum* contract; in consequence, English
commercial law is to be applied, and if under this law,
property remained in the British sellers at the moment of
seizure by the Crown, the goods were not subject to condemnation, notwithstanding their enemy destination. The
question is very different in cases of *post bellum* contracts
or contracts made *imminente bello*. This question was involved in the interesting and complicated case of the "Glenearn." [126] The facts were as follows: A British company on
April 18, 1939, entered into an agreement with a German
company for the sale of latex rubber by the British company. The "Glenearn" sailed with the rubber about July 24,
1939, from Shanghai to Hamburg; she arrived in London
on August 23, 1939, and the voyage to Hamburg was abandoned. In the ordinary course of business two other cargoes
of latex rubber were also on their way to this German firm
on board German ships, and had been landed at Genoa. The
claimants had not been paid in respect of the Genoa cargoes,
whereas they had handed over, on August 16, the documents
of the "Glenearn" cargo against acceptance of a bill of
exchange for the price named in the provisional invoice. On
August 25, when the claimants learned of the abandonment
of the ship's voyage from London to Hamburg, they were
the sellers of the London cargo, who had parted with the
documents of title and had been paid, and were in respect of
the Genoa cargoes unpaid sellers who had not parted with
the documents.

On August 28, the British and the German firms agreed to exchange the Genoa for the London cargo which at that time was discharged into the Port of London Authority's letter of the German firm dated August 30. The shipping documents were exchanged through a banking firm in Amsterdam. The claimants were paid for the Genoa cargo and had to pay as buyers for the London cargo. Under the Sale of Goods Act, 1893, Section 18, property in the London cargo had re-passed to the claimants before the outbreak of war. On September 1, 1939, the claimants instructed their usual warehousemen to clear the goods and take them to store as soon as possible. The warehousemen took delivery from the Port of London Authority's warehouse on September 11, and the goods were received in their own warehouse on September 12, where they were seized as prize on October 9, 1939.

The representative of the Crown insisted that "the English company lent itself to a scheme by which the risk of capture was taken off the shoulders of the German company." The exchange agreement as a contract made *imminente bello* in fraud of belligerent rights cannot be recognized in a prize court, is against public policy, and is void under municipal and under common law, as well as under the Trading with the Enemy Act, 1939.[127] Counsel for the claimants argued that the sale was valid under municipal law, as the common law allows entering into any transaction with a person who may, in the future, become an enemy; nor was there anything illegal under the Trading with the Enemy Act merely because, for a brief period, the goods had belonged to someone who was not then, but subsequently became, an enemy. The judgment decided first that the doctrine of public policy could not be invoked because the purchase of the cargo of the "Glenearn" did not offend any existing legislation, and because the common law and the Trading with the Enemy Act forbidding any form of

commerce with the enemy applied only to transactions after
the outbreak of war, not to transactions completed before
the outbreak of war with a potential enemy.

The judgment then considered the case in prize law. The
contract was made bona fide in the sense that there was no
secret clause or collusive understanding that it was to be dis-
regarded should war not break out; but it was certainly also
a contract made *imminente bello.* Quoting decisions [128] to
this effect, the judge held in the case of a bona fide contract made *imminente bello,* the buyer cannot establish his
claim to the goods unless he has taken actual delivery
before seizure. The present case offered two novel features:

(1) The buyer was not a neutral but a national. The
difference is that no considerations of the comity of nations
can apply and that a British claimant is subject to the
municipal law concerning trading with the enemy. Therefore, nothing less than actual delivery would avail the claimants.

(2) Does the term "transit" in prize law apply only to
goods which at the outbreak of war were at sea? [129]
Without expressing a final opinion on this point, the judge
assumed that in the Port of London Authority's warehouse
the goods were still in transit. As they were not seized
there, but in the claimant's own warehouse, the claimants
had taken actual delivery, contrary to the opinion of the
representative of the Crown,[131] and judgment was in favor
of claimants.

6. Declaration of Paris, 1856, Article II

"All enemy property—ships and cargoes—may, after
the outbreak of war, be captured *jure belli* on the sea or
in rivers, ports and harbors of this country," [132] as far as
there is no recognized exception under international law.
One of these exceptions is enemy cargo on board neutral

ships, except contraband of war, under Article II of the
Paris Declaration of 1856.[133] But enemy goods on board
British ships are subject to capture and condemnation.[134]
Whereas in World War I, Great Britain and France openly
violated Article II of the Declaration of Paris by their
Reprisal Orders,[135] British prize cases in the war showed
respect for this rule [136] by implication. In the case of the
"Benmacdhui," [137] the prize judge referred to the fact that
the enemy goods were on board British ships, "because,
if these goods had been in a neutral ship, the Declaration
of Paris would have applied, unless it could be shown that
they were contraband of war."

7. *Property of master and crew*

Property of master and crew of an enemy vessel is often
held to be exempt from condemnation.[138] In the case of the
"Pomona," [139] the Crown gave an undertaking to hand back
the personal effects of master and crew, and the judge,
quoting the practice prevailing during World War I "approved, for all other cases, of the release of the effects
of master and crew of any vessel."

8. *Sixth Hague Convention of 1907*

Another well-established exception was the "days of
grace" under the sixth Hague Convention of 1907.[140] Such
days of grace were often granted in World War I. While
the granting of such days of grace was not a legal duty
even under this convention, the ships could not, under Article II, be confiscated, but only requisitioned against indemnity or detained under duty to restore them without
indemnity. In the first prize case of World War I, the
"Chile," [141] the so-called Chile order—"detention until further order"—was made.[142]

But as Great Britain had denounced [143] the sixth Hague Convention of 1907, no days of grace were granted in the war and vessels seized in port at the outbreak of war were simply condemned as good and lawful prize.[144] The "Christoph von Doornum" [145] was seized on September 3, 1939, while being arrested and under *Vis major* in port, but this aspect of the case was not even mentioned. Exactly the same situation existed in the case of the "Pomona,"[146] the representative of the Crown pointed to the fact that the sixth Hague Convention had been denounced by Britain. The judgment said that the owners appeared to raise the question whether the vessel, having been detained in an English port at the outbreak of war by *force majeure,* should be subject to an order for detention until the end of the war in the form of the Chile order. But since the Crown was applying for requisition, not for condemnation, this question was reserved for a later stage of the procedure.

9. Equipment of ship

Objects which are part of the equipment of an enemy ship are subject to condemnation. In the "Biscaya," [147] not only the ship but also her wireless installation which had been removed was condemned as good and lawful prize.[148]

10. Neutral goods on enemy ships

That neutral goods on board enemy ships are free, with the exception of contraband of war, has been recognized in World Wars I and II. In the *Bianca* case,[149] the vessel was condemned, but the question of the cargo—coal shipped to a named neutral consignee in Portugal—was held over, as "it was difficult for the court to draw the inference that the cargo was enemy property." [150] In the case of the "Gloria," [151] the Crown asked for the condemnation of this German vessel and part of the cargo. There was a question between the judge and the representative of the Crown concerning 10,875 bags of wheat. The latter relied on the presumption of enemy character of goods found in an enemy ship until the contrary is shown, regardless of the destination of the ship. The judge said that these goods were consigned under bills of lading by an Argentine neutral to a range of ports which might include Hamburg. "The moment documents were produced which showed a neutral, did not the Declaration of Paris arise?" The judge said that the presumption "enemy ship, enemy goods" does not arise in the face of the Declaration of Paris, as it appeared that the bill of lading on its face indicated the property of a neutral. Nevertheless, and without further reasoning, the judge made an order for the condemnation of this part of the cargo, or rather, as it had been sold, against the proceeds.

11. Contraband of war

Contraband of war is always subject to seizure and condemnation, whether on board enemy ships, on board British ships, or on board neutral ships. In order that goods may be classified as contraband of war they must have a certain character and show hostile destination; they must, further, have been declared contraband by the belligerent in question. Whereas in World War I the long-established distinction between absolute and conditional contraband was nearly wholly abolished in fact, and, in some countries, even in law, it is interesting to see that in the war this distinction was made again. According to the British Contraband Proclamation,[152] Schedule I, the following articles are absolute contraband: all kinds of arms, ammunitions, etc., fuel of all kinds, all articles useful as means of communications, etc., coin, bullion, currency, evidence of debt, metals, etc. Schedule II enumerates as conditional contraband all kinds of foods and foodstuffs, feed, forage, clothing and articles and materials used in their production.

In most cases in which cargo on board British ships was condemned it was condemned as enemy property and the contraband issue was not mentioned. But in the case of the Benmacdhui,[153] the Crown asked for condemnation of the cargo as enemy property and as contraband: 497 bags of wolfram ore and 250 cases of antimony regulus were claimed to be absolute, and 330 bales of cassia to be conditional contraband, although the Crown admitted that the case concerning cassia "was not very strong." The judge condemned the goods as enemy property, but held that the evidence was insufficient to decide whether they should be condemned as contraband of war. In the case of the "Newfoundland," [154] on the other hand, the cargo on board this British ship, consisting of 90 cases and 26 cases of canned lobster and 310 bags of lead ore, was condemned as enemy property and as contraband.

In the case of the "Egret," [155] the cargo on board this British ship consisted of 40 cases of peg wood consigned to Frankfort-am-Main. The representative of the Crown said that peg wood was used in the manufacture of boots: "he could not say whether it was used in connection with boots for the German Army, but it might be used for auxiliary forces." The goods were condemned.

In the case of the "Hawnby," [156] condemnation was asked of 18 pieces of poplar logs on board this British ship, consigned to Rotterdam. Generally speaking, it is the captor who has to prove before the prize court the hostile destination of goods seized as contraband.[157] During World War I this proof was facilitated by the introduction of new presumptions, both legal and judicial, of hostile destination,[158] In this case the representative of the Crown relied on the absence of claims [159] and on the judicial presumption of hostile destination.[160] The bills of lading showed that, although the goods were consigned to Rotterdam, arrival of the cargo was to be notified to a firm in Düsseldorf, and he suggested that Rotterdam was a convenient port for Düsseldorf. But the prize judge adjourned consideration of the application, holding that proof of hostile destination was insufficient.

In the case of the "Inge Maersk," [161] condemnation of a cargo of petrol on board this Danish neutral vessel was asked prior to German occupation of Denmark. The ship's papers showed consignment to Hamburg to a "Foreign Tankship Corporation" with directions to notify an enemy, but did not indicate whether the corporation was an enemy or neutral. The cargo was condemned as absolute contraband, as the destination was Hamburg, and in the case of absolute contraband, documentary evidence of shipment to an enemy port constitutes a non-rebuttable legal presumption of hostile destination.[162]

Finally, in the case of the *Alwaki and other vessels*, [163] condemnation was asked of parts of the cargo of four Dutch and one Norwegian vessels, all neutral, as contraband of war. The representative of the Crown claimed some parts of the cargo to constitute absolute, others conditional, contraband, and relied (1) upon the absence of claims; (2) on consignment to German ports or to Rotterdam, "and Rotterdam is a recognized port for German imports"; and (3) on the judicial presumption of central control in Germany over the articles in question,[164] analyzing various German decrees bringing many imports under control and requiring persons importing such articles to report them to a principal association set up by the German government. The prize judge condemned the goods claimed to be absolute contraband on the evidence of affidavits by witnesses of authority, but stated twice that,

while a large consignment of manganese ore was clearly
absolute contraband, there were several parcels which "un-
enlightened, I should never have dreamed were absolute
contraband, but which on the evidence I am convinced are
such." He condemned the other goods as conditional contraband, following the decision of the "Håkan," "on the
clearest possible evidence of German decrees which impose
government control on all these articles and prescribe that
they are automatically seized at the moment of coming
into the customs house."

¹ Prisen-Ordnung of Aug. 28, 1939, 1 R.G.Bl. No. 161 [1939];
English translation, 3 C.C.H. WAR LAW SERVICE (foreign supp.)
65, 569–576.

² Prisen-Gerichts-Ordnung of Aug. 28, 1939, 1 R.G.Bl. No. 161
[1939]; English translation, 3 C.C.H. WAR LAW SERVICE (foreign
supp.) 65,576–581.

3 See particularly the fundamental work by J.H.W. VERUIJL, LE
DROIT DE PRISES DE LA GRANDE GUERRE (1924). For a brief digest of
British prize cases, see H. HULL, DIGEST OF CASES DECIDED IN BRITISH
PRIZE COURTS 1914–1927 (1937).

⁴ LLOYD'S REPORTS OF PRIZE CASES 1914–1924; TREHERN and GRANT,
BRITISH and COLONIAL PRIZE CASES.

⁵ 1 DÉCISIONS DU CONSEIL DES PRISES (1916); 2 ibid. (1923).

⁶ 1 ENTSCHEIDUNGEN DES OBERPRISENGERICHTES IN BERLIN (1918);
2 ibid. (1921).

⁷ SENTENZE DELLA COMMISSIONE DELLE PREDE, 1915–1918 (1927).

⁸ 1 LLOYD'S PR. CAS. (2nd ser.) No. 1 at 1–10; ibid. No. 2 at 11–26;
ibid. No. 3 at 27–42 ibid. No. 4 at 43–56; ibid. No. 5 at 57–72.

⁹ They are not more than thirty-four, of which twenty-eight were
decided in the British Prize Court in London, one in India, one in
Newfoundland, two in Australia, and two in South Africa.

¹⁰ Cf. "Seizure . . . does not affect the ownership of the thing
seized. Before that can happen, the thing seized, be it ship or goods,
must be brought into the possession of a lawfully constituted court
of prize, and the captor must ask and obtain its condemnation as
price."—Odessa, [1915] 2 Lloyd's Pr. Cas. 405. "The obligation is
unquestioned to bring the prize in for condemnation."—Oscar II,
[1920] A.C. 748.

¹¹ 2 & 3 Geo. 6, c. 65. Reprinted in J. BURKE, LOOSE-LEAF WAR
LEGISLATION 25–29 (1939).

¹² 27 & 28 Vict. c. 25.

¹³ 4 & 5 Geo. 5, c. 13.

¹⁴ 5 & 6 Geo. 5, c. 57.

15 A schedule of British prize courts overseas during World War I is to be found in VERZIJL, *op. cit.* annex to 8. Prize courts had been set up also in Zanzibar and Egypt. See Prize Courts Act, 1894, 57 & 58 Vict. c. 39.

16 Cf. The North Borneo Prize Court Order in Council (S.R. & O., 1939, No. 1136); Zanzibar (Prize Court) Order in Council (S.R. & O., No. 1137); Zanzibar (Prize Court) Order in Council (S.R. & O., No. 1138).

17 S.R. & O, 1939, No. 1466.

18 During World War I, the Prize Court Rules, 1914, were in force.

19 1 Lloyd's Pr.Cas. (2nd ser.) No. 1 at 4.

20 See The Zamora, 4 Lloyd's Pr.Cas. 62. For a fuller discussion see KUNZ, KRIEGSRECHT UND NEUTRALITÄTSRECHT 183-86 (1935), and the literature there quoted.

21 HULL, *op. cit.* at iv.

22 "This decision [in The Franciska, 10 Moo.P.C 73] is, of course, binding upon their Lordships."—The Dusseldorf, [1920] 9 Lloyd's Pr.Cas. 12. "Their Lordships are bound by the decisions of their predecessors, which, consistent as they are, it is too late to overrule and impracticable to distinguish."—The Kronprinsessan Margareta, [1920] 8 Lloyd's Pr.Cas. 241.

23 The Roumanian, [1915] 2 Lloyd's Pr.Cas. 378.

24 1 Lloyd's Pr.Cas. (2nd ser.) 53-54 (1940).

25 The Glenearn, [1940] *ibid.* at 63.

26 The Konsul Hendrik Fisser, [1940] *ibid.* at 24.

27 *Ibid.* at 27.

28 *Ibid.* at 1.

29 The Konsul Hendrik Frisser, *ibid.* at 57.

30 See The Chataeubriand, [1916] 5 *ibid.* at 24.

31 See The Odessa, [1916] 1 A.C. 145 at 153-54.

32 In Great Britain by the procurator-general.

33 The Vesta [1921] 10 Lloyd's Pr.Cas. 106 at 139. Cf. also The Möwe, 2 *ibid.* 70; The Marie Glaeser, 1 *ibid.* 56; The Hakan, [1917] 5 *ibid.* 186; The Gutenfels, [1915] 1 Br. & Col.Pr.Cas. No. 1 at 102 (Egypt).

34 I Lloyd's Pr.Cas. (2nd ser.) 1 at 2, 5.

35 The Pomona, *ibid* at 1.

36 The Konsul Hendrik Fisser, *ibid.* at 16; The Christoph von Doornum, *ibid.* at 49.

37 The Rheingold, *ibid.* at 19.

38 The Gabbiano, *ibid.* at 27.

39 The Astoria, *ibid.* at 53.

40 The Prins Knud, *ibid.* at 57.

41 The Möwe, [1915] 2 Lloyd's Pr.Cas. 70.

42 The Alwaki, [1940] 1 Lloyd's Pr.Cas. (2nd ser.) 43.

43 *Ibid.* at 6.

44 Cf. Prize Court Rules, 1914, Order 15, Rule 7.

⁴⁵ Cf. for the "out of the ship's mouth" doctrine, DEÁK and JESSUP, NEUTRALITY: I—THE ORIGINS 217–24; the case, Dos Hermanos, 1817 (7 MOORE, *Digest* 611–12); T. BATY, BRITAIN AND SEA LAW 60–70 (1911); KUNZ, *op. cit.* at 187.

⁴⁶ I Lloyd's Pr.Cas. (2nd ser.) 43 (1940).

⁴⁷ Quoting Justice Story in The Harrison, 1 Wheat. 298.

⁴⁸ 7 Lloyd's Pr.Cas. 401 at 408.

⁴⁹ 8 Lloyd's Pr.Cas. 382 at 388.

⁵⁰ In the same sense, Prize Court Rules, 1914, Order 18, Rule 1.

⁵¹ 1 Lloyd's Pr.Cas. (2nd ser.) 34–41.

⁵² 4 Lloyd's Pr.Cas. 1 at 114.

⁵³ 6 Lloyd's Pr.Cas. 121 (1917).

⁵⁴ 6 Lloyd's Pr.Cas. 245 at 254.

⁵⁵ 6 Lloyd's Pr.Cas. 89 at 101: "If there were suspicious circumstances justifying the seizure, the claimant is not entitled to either costs or damages." Cf. also the résumé of the practice of the London Prize Court as to costs, in The Australia [1916] 2 Br. & Col.Pr.Cas. 315 (Ceylon).

⁵⁶ Naval Prize Act, 1864, art. V.

⁵⁷ 1 Lloyd's Pr.Cas. (2nd ser.) 57.

⁵⁸ The "Hannah Boge" (1 Lloyd's Pr.Cas. [2nd ser.] 5, 8) was captured at sea, while on a voyage to Germany; the "Cap Norte" (*ibid.* at 8), on a voyage from Buenos Aires to Hamburg, was seized by a contraband control official; the "Bianca" (*ibid.* at 9) was captured on a voyage from Rotterdam to Lisbon; the "Gloria" (*ibid.* at 11), bound from Buenos Aires to Antwerp and Hamburg, was "seized near a contraband control station"; the "Biscaya" (*ibid.* at 12) was "arrested and taken to a contraband control port"; the "Henning Oldendorff" (*ibid.* at 12) and the "Eilbeck" (*ibid.* at 13) were captured; the "Konsul Hendrik Fisser" (*ibid.* at 16) was stopped on the high seas while en route from Vigo to Germany, captured, and brought into a British port under orders from the warship; the "Rheingold" (*ibid.* at 18) was seized while on a voyage from Durban to Dunkirk; the "Leander" (*ibid.* at 26) was captured.

⁵⁹ The Pomona, *ibid.* at 52; The Elvira III, *ibid.* at 8; The Christoph von Doornum, *ibid.* at 49.

⁶⁰ The Remo, *ibid.* at 52; The Sistiana, *ibid.* at 55.

⁶¹ The Gundrun Maersk, *ibid.* at 42; The Astoria, *ibid.* at 53; The Kalo, *ibid.* at 56; The Prins Knud, *ibid.* at 57

⁶² 1 Lloyd's Pr.Cas. (2nd ser.) 8. So-called spoliation of documents which constitutes sufficient ground for capture. See The Ophelia, [1915] 3 Lloyd's Pr.Cas. 13; Dr. Lushington's decision in The Johanna Emilie, [1854] Spinks 12.

⁶³ I Lloyd's Pr.Cas. (2nd ser.) 16.

⁶⁴ The Benmacdhui, 1 Lloyd's Pr.Cas. (2nd ser.) 6; The Newfoundland, *ibid.* at 10; The Egret, *ibid.* at 10; The Hawnby, *ibid.* at 10, 14; The Bassa, *ibid.* at 13; The Glengarry, *ibid.* at 13; The Soudan, *ibid.* at 13; The Glenroy, *ibid.* at 13; The Warwick Castle, *ibid* at 14; The Mataroa, *ibid.* at 14; The Glearn, *ibid* at 63.

[65] The Alwaki and other vessels, *ibid.* at 43. The neutral Italian ship, "Gabbiano," was captured for carriage of contraband, had a prize crew put on board at Gibraltar, and so arrived at Cardiff. Cargo from a neutral Danish vessel, the "Inge Maersk" (*ibid.* at 15), was seized at a contraband control station as absolute contraband.

[66] Other than under the right of angary, and under other hypotheses mentioned in the previous paragraph.

[67] Cf. German Prize Law Code of August 28, 1939, arts. LXX, LXXI.

[68] *Supra*, note 10.

[69] Cf. also: "The effect of a condemnation is to divest the enemy subject of his ownership . . . and to transfer it to the Sovereign."— The Odessa, [1916] 1 A.C. 145 at 154. "Subject to condemnation in prize, the capture is for the Crown's benefit."—The Oscar II, [1920] A.C. 748. Se also the Südmark, [1918] 6 Lloyd's Pr.Cas. 352.

[70] S.R. & O., 1918, No. 387.

[71] Namely, an undertaking in writing by the proper officer of the Crown for payment into court on behalf of the Crown of the appraised value of the ship.

[72] 4 Lloyd's Pr.Cas. 1 (1915).

[73] 4 Lloyd's Pr.Cas. 62 (1916).

[74] See also The Canton, [1916] 2 Lloyd's Pr. Cas. 264.

[75] The Pellworm, 9 Lloyd's Pr.Cas. 170 (P.C. 1922), overruling the contrary holding by the prize court in The Pellworm, [1920] 9 Lloyd's Pr. Cas. 158.

[76] 1 Lloyd's Pr.Cas. (2nd ser.) 1.

[77] Cf. the case of The Marie Leonhardt, [1920] 3 Br. & Col. Pr.Cas. 761.

[78] 1 Lloyd's Pr.Cas. (2nd ser.) 6.

[79] *Ibid.* at 8. Thus also The Biscaya, ibid. at 12.

[80] 1 Lloyd's Pr.Cas. (2nd ser.) 52.

[81] *Ibid.* at 55.

[82] *Ibid.* at 42: Without appraisement, the Crown filing an undertaking for payment into court of the appraised value of the ship.

[83] *Ibid.* at 53: Requisition and payment into court of appraised value.

[84] *Ibid.* at 56: Requisition, appraisement of vessels and stores; undertaking by Crown for payment into court.

[85] See The Nicolae (1920), where the Rumanian Prize Court in the case of a Bolshevist vessel captrued by Rumania in the Black Sea, on July 2, 1919, had to deal with the question whether a state of war existed between Rumania and Soviet Russia (VERZIJL, *op. cit.* at 239–41).

[86] The Inge Maersk, [1940] 1 Lloyd's Pr.Cas. (2nd ser.) 15, was still the case of a *neutral* Danish vessel.

[87] 1 Lloyd's Pr.Cas. (2nd ser.) 42.

[88] *Ibid.* at 56.

[89] *Ibid.* at 53.

[90] 1 Lloyd's Pr.Cas. (2nd ser.) 57.

[91] In *The Zamora*, [1916] 2 A.C. 77 at 108, the Privy Council laid down only the captor's duty to bring in promptly the property seized for adjudication: "If the captors do not promptly bring in the property seized for adjudication, the court will, at the insistence of any party aggrieved, compel them to do so." The *Zamora* decision further laid down as one condition for the requisition of the thing seized *pendente lite* that the right of requisition must be enforced by application to the prize court. It is further well settled in British prize law, contrary to the practice of other states, that the release by the organs of the captor, during or after prize procedure, must be sanctioned by the prize court. See *The Birkenfels and Cargo* (1915), CASES DECIDED IN THE PRIZE COURTS OF SOUTH AFRICA, 1914-1918 at 39 (1925).

[92] See, The Roumanian, [1914] 1 Lloyd's Pr.Cas. 191; and [1915] 2 Lloyd's Pr.Cas. 387.

[93] 1 Lloyd's Pr.Cas. (2nd ser.) 63.

[94] Cf. KUNZ, *op. cit.*, *supra*, note 20, at 114.

[95] The Primavera, [1916] Entsch. I, 194.

[96] The Germania No. 1, [1917] 4 Lloyd's Pr.Cas. 263; The Oriental, [1915] 1 Lloyd's Pr.Cas. 575.

[97] *The Tolna, 1920*, REVUE GÉNÉRALE DE DROIT INTERNATIONAL PUBLIC 90 (1920).

[98] 1 Lloyd's Pr.Cas. (2nd ser.) 8.

[99] Declaration of London, 1909, art LVII. The Order in Council of October 20, 1915, replaced the London Declaration, Article LVII, in British prize courts by the principles and rules observed by these courts prior to 1909.

[100] "She was flying the German flag at the time of capture."—The Henning Oldendorff, 1 Lloyd's Pr. Cas. (2nd ser.) 12.

[101] See The Odessa, [1915] 2 Lloyd's Pr.Cas. 405.

[102] The Christoph von Doornum, 1 Lloyd's Pr. Cas. (2nd ser.) 49 at 51.

[103] So already Lord Stowell in The Tobajo, 1804 5 C.Rob. 218.

[104] 1 Lloyd's Pr.Cas. (2nd ser.) 1.

[105] *Ibid.* at 9.

[106] *Ibid.* at 16.

[107] 1 Lloyd's Pr.Cas. 56: "The court has no hesitation in pronouncing upon the authorities, upon principle, and upon grounds of convenience and practice, the claim of the neutral mortgagees of this captured vessel must be rejected. The same conclusion would be arrived at, if the claims were by British subjects." See also *The Odessa*, 2 Lloyd's Pr.Cas. 405, where it was held that legal ownership, as the criterion of enemy character, means the property as opposed to any special rights created by contract, whether this contract was made before or after the outbreak of war, but that the power of the Crown to redress hardship caused to subjects by decrees of the prize court by the grant of bounty is unimpaired. But, as Sir Samuel Evans

stated in *The Marie Glaeser,* "The prerogative of bounty is another matter; I have nothing to do with that; I am here merely to administer the law."

[108] 1 Lloyd's Pr.Cas. (2nd ser.) 49.

[109] 5 Wall. 372: "In proceedings in prize and under principles of international law, mortgages on vessels captured *jure belli* are to be treated only as liens, subject to being overridden by the capture."

[110] 1 Lloyd's Pr.Cas. (2nd ser.) 78.

[111] 1 Lloyd's Pr.Cas. 111: "What I have said as to the shareholders applied with greater force to those who have advanced sums of money, or rendered services, such as brokerage. As judge of the Prize Court, I cannot allow such claims."

[112] 1 Lloyd's Pr.Cas. (2nd ser.) 57.

[113] See The Chateaubriand, [1916] 5 Lloyd's Pr.Cas. 24.

[114] See the cases: The Roland, [1915] 2 Lloyd's Pr.Cas. 253; The Palm Branch, 6 Lloyd's Pr.Cas. 1; The Australia, [1916] 2 Br. & Col.Pr.Cas. 315 (Ceylon.

[115] 1 Lloyd's Pr.Cas. (2nd ser.) 1.

[116] See The Hamborn, [1919] 7 Lloyd's Pr.Cas. 67: Condemnation of an enemy vessel; bunker coal being the property of the American time-charterers did not pass as part of the vessel.

[117] 1 Lloyd's Pr.Cas. (2nd ser.) 9.

[118] 1 Lloyd's Pr.Cas. (2nd ser.) 11.

[119] In the *Roland,* Sir Samuel Evans stated: "According to prize law, property upon an enemy ship consigned to an enemy port is *prima facie* enemy property." But in the *Australia,* the court held in a case where the cargo was not consigned to an enemy port that "Sir Samuel Evans did not intend to engraft any such limitation upon the principle he was affirming."

[120] 1 Lloyd's Pr.Cas. (2nd ser.) 6.

[121] In the unreported case of the "Durham Castle," September 16, 1914.

[122] 1 Lloyd's Pr.Cas. (2nd ser.) 27.

[123] Contrary to the prize courts of other states, British prize courts distinguish among *ante bellum* contracts, contracts made *imminente bello,* and *post bellum* contracts. Equally contrary to the practice of prize courts of other states, British prize courts, in deciding the question of ownership of captured cargo in cases of bona fide *ante bellum* contracts, apply the English municipal law. See particularly The Miramichi, [1914] 1 Lloyd's Pr.Cas. 157. As to taking into account the Sale of Goods Act, 1893, see the Marquis Bacquehem, [1915] 2 Br. & Col.Pr.Cas. 96 (Egypt); on the f.o.b. clause, see The Sörfareren, [1915] 4 Lloyd's Pr.Cas. 174; on the c.i.f. clause, see The Miramichi; The Derfflinger, [1918] 7 Lloyd's Pr.Cas. 394; The Parchim, [1915, 1917] 4 Lloyd's Pr.Cas. 375, 388; and The Australia, [1916] 2 Br. & Col.Pr.Cas. (Ceylon); "The effect of the shipment of goods f.o.b. is undoubtedly, as a general rule, to transfer the risk of loss of the property from the seller to the buyer and to put an

end to the right of stoppage in transitu"; in a c.i.f. shipment, "the goods are at the risk of the purchaser." On the clause "no arrival, no sale," see The Derfflinger, No. 2 [1915] 1 Br. & Col.Pr.Cas. 398 (Egypt).

124 4 Lloyd's Pr.Cas. 388 (1918).

125 Relying on the authority of Johnson v. Taylor Bros. & Co., [1920] A.C. 144 at 155–56.

126 1 Loyd's Pr.Cas. (2nd ser.) 63.

127 2 & 3 Geo. 6, c. 89 (sec. 89 gives the definition of an enemy), reprinted in J. BURKE, LOOSE-LEAF WAR LEGISLATION 213–22 (1939). Trading with the Enemy (Custodian) Order, 1939 (S.R. & O., 1939, No. 1198), *ibid.* at 26. Cf. alsoKRUSIN and ROGERS, THE SOLICITOR'S HANDBOOK OF WAR LEGISLATION 236–64 (1940), and *ibid.* 1st Supplement at 19–23 (1940).

128 Older cases: The Jan Frederik, [1804] 5 C. Rob. 128; The Baltica, [1857] 11 Moore P.C. 141. World War I cases: The Southfield, [1915] 3 Lloyd's Pr.Cas. 404; The Daksa, [1917] 5 Lloyd's Pr.Cas. 317. See The Kronprinsessan Margareta, [1917] 6 Lloyd's Pr.Cas. 222: "It is well established as a principle of prize law that during . . . imminent danger of hostilities, the property in cargoes of belligerent parties cannot change its national character *in transitu;* and that if neutrals purchase goods *in transitu* during a state of impending danger of war, the contract of purchase is held invalid." The Kronprinsessan Margareta, [1920] 8 Lloyd's Pr.Cas. 241 at 257: "The law of prize . . . refuses to recognize transfers of the ownership of movables afloat from an enemy transferor to a neutral transferee when unaccompanied by actual delivery of the goods." Cf. also The Vrow Margareta, [1799] 1 C.Rob. 336.

129 Thus counsel for claimants, quoting The Roumanian, 2 Lloyd's Pr. Cas. 378 at 394, the words "while at sea" in the *Kronprinsessan Margareta* at 257; he could also have quoted the words "transfer of goods at sea" in the *Daksa.*

130 Thus the representative of the Crown quoting *the Roumanian,* at 403, and the words "so long as the original transitus is deemed to continue" in The Vesta, [1920] 10 Lloyd's Pr.Cas. 106 at 127.

131 Invoking The Bawean, [1918] 7 Lloyd's Pr.Cas. 113.

132 The Roumanian, [1914] 1 Lloyd's Pr.Cas. 197.

133 *Le pavillon couvre la marchandise.*

134 See The Aldworth, [1914] 1 Lloyd's Pr.Cas. 137; The Miramichi, [1914] 1 Lloyd's Pr.Cas. 157; The Roumanian, [1915] 2 Lloyd's Pr.Cas. 378; and in World War II cases: The Benmacdhui, 1 Lloyd's Pr.Cas. (2nd ser.) 6; The Newfoundland, *ibid.* at 10; The Egret, *ibid.* at 10; The Bassa, *ibid.* at 13; The Glengarry, *ibid.* at 13; The Soudan, *ibid.* at 13; The Glenroy, *ibid* at 14; The Warwick Castle, *ibid.* at 14; The Mataroa, *ibid.* at 14.

135 British Orders in Council of March 11, 1915, and February 16, 1917; French Decree of March 13, 1915. See KUNZ, *op. cit. supra,* note 20, at 255–56.

136 Thus also the decision in The Dirigo and other vessels, [1919] 8 Lloyd's Pr. Cas. 395.

137 1 Lloyd's Pr. Cas. (2nd ser.) 6 at 7.

138 See The Schlesien No. 1, [1914] 2 Lloyd's Pr.Cas. 92.

139 I Lloyd's Pr. Cas. (2nd ser.) 1.

140 Cf. KUNZ, *op. cit., supra*, note 20, at 167–68.

141 1 Lloyd's Pr.Cas. 8 (1914); "I pronounce The Chile to have belonged at the time of seizure to enemies of the Crown, and to have been properly seized; and on the application of the Crown, I order that the ship be detained by the marshal until a further order is issued by the court."

142 Still after World War I, judgments concerning the sixth Hague Convention of 1907 were rendered. In the case of The Tibor (Ann. Dig.P.I.L.C. 1931–1932, at 440–41 [1938]), a Hungarian vessel, seized by the French naval authorities on August 1, 1914, on her arrival at the port of Bordeaux, requisitioned by France, and lost during the war, compensation under Article II of the sixth Hague Convention of 1907 was granted. *Contra*, The Minna: Reinhold v. Belgian State, Ann.Dig.P.I.L.C. 1923–1924, at 452–54 (1933); and The Neckar: L. Littlejohn & Co. v. U.S., [1926] 270 U.S. 215 (Ann. Dig.P.I.L.C. 1925–1926, at 483–84 [1929]).

143 Miscellaneous Documents, No. 19, Cmd. 2654 (1925).

144 German yacht Elvira III, 1 Lloyd's Pr.Cas. (2nd ser.) 8; the Italian ships "Remo" (*ibid.* at 52) and "Sistiana" (*ibid.* at 55).

145 *Ibid.* at 49.

146 *Ibid.* at 1.

147 *Ibid.* at 12.

148 See The Schlesien, [1914] 2 Lloyd's Pr.Cas. 92.

149 1 Lloyd's Pr.Cas. (2nd ser.) 9.

150 The question of cargo was held over also in the case of The Henning Oldendorff, 1 Lloyd's Pr.Cas. (2nd ser.) 12.

152 *London Gazette* of September 4, 1939, p. 6051, reprinted in 3 C.C.H. WAR LAW SERVICE (foreign supp.) 65–552. Identical: Contraband proclamations of New Zealand (*ibid.* at 65,555 and 65,605), Canada (*ibid.* at 65,588), but also of France (*ibid.* at 65,554). For Germany, cf. Articles XXII–XXVII of the Prize Law Code, August 28, 1939 (September 3, 1939, 1 R.Ges.Bl. No. 161); but the amendment (3 C.C.H. WAR LAW SERVICE [foreign supp.] 65,553) follows closely the British contraband proclamation. Britain again instituted the system of "black lists," of the "navicert," and so on, as in World War I. For later developments, see the seizure of German exports (S.R. & O., 1939, No. 1709; 3 C.C.H. WAR LAW SERVICE [foreign supp.] 65,557–588; French decree of November 28, 1939, *ibid. at* 65,559; Canadian proclamation of December 8, 1939, *ibid.* at 65,585), and the British Extension of Blockade Order in Council, August 1, 1940 (*ibid.* at 65,587–588) (so-called All-Europe blockade).

153 I Lloyd's Pr.Cas. (2nd ser.) 6.

154 *Ibid.* at 10.

155 *Ibid.* at 10.

156 I Lloyd's Pr.Cas. (2nd ser.) 14.

157 See the Kim and other vessels, [1915] 3 Lloyd's Pr.Cas. 167: "It is, no doubt, incumbent upon the captor in the first instance to prove facts from which a reasonable inference of hostile destination can be drawn, subject to rebuttal by the claimants."

158 It is typical of the British conception of prize law to hold: (1) that the "procedure and practice of the prize court is a domestic affair, in which no foreign neutral or enemy has any voice or right to interfere."—The Zamora, [1915] 4 Lloyd's Pr.Cas. 1; and (2) that "as to the modifications and onus of proof . . . these are matters really affecting rules of evidence and methods of proof in this court, and I fail to see how it is possible to contend that they are violations of any rule of international law."—The Kim [1915] 3 Lloyd's Pr.Cas. 167. But as the rules of evidence concerning hostile destination and burden of proof are most intimately connected with substantive prize law, the recognition of new legal presumptions by British prize courts and the setting up, by these courts, of new judicial presumptions, constitute, in fact, a change of substantive prize law to the detriment of the claimants. Against this practice are KUNZ *op. cit.* at 187; VERZIJL, *op. cit.* §§ 30, 111, 451; 2 C.C. HYDE, INTERNATIONAL LAW CHIEFLY AS INTERPRETED AND APPLIED BY THE UNITED STATES 815–17 (1922).

159 An appearance had been entered by the National City Bank of New York, but was withdrawn.

160 See The Kim, *loc. cit.*: "The convenience of Copenhagen for transporting goods of Germany need hardly be mentioned."

161 1 Lloyd's Pr.Cas. (2nd ser.) 15.

162 Thus, already, the London Declaration of 1909, art. XXXI.

163 1 Lloyd's Pr.Cas. (2nd ser.) 43.

164 This judicial presumption of hostile destination was established during World War I. See The Kim, The Esrom, [1919] 8 Lloyd's Pr. Cas. 492; The Håkan, [1916] 5 Lloyd's Pr.Cas. 161.

Law is the Lord of All.—Pindar.

ONCE MORE, as he did sixteen years ago,[1] this writer
wants to raise his voice in order to point at the actual
chaotic status of the laws of war, at the grave inherent
dangers, and at the urgent necessity for the revision of
this part of international law. The problem involves the
very survival of our western Christian civilization, if not
of mankind. Under these circumstances, it becomes the
duty of an international lawyer to treat this subject, notwithstanding its "unpopularity" since 1920. It was Grotius
who, under the impression of the "total war" of thirty
years, urged upon men the necessity of the "temperamenta
belli." It is amazing to see that the men of this generation,
living under a more terrible total war, turn their backs
upon the laws of war. This neglect is the outcome of different and often contradictory ideologies: indifference, apathy, over-optimistic wishful thinking, political wishes to
keep one's hands free in the next war, and pessimistic
fatalism. All the arguments for this neglect are untenable,
are in contradiction with the law as well as the facts; and
yet, strong drives by writers and statesmen have nearly
succeeded in putting over men a veil of voluntary blind-
ness in adopting a policy of the ostrich which may lead

to disaster, to the return of new and more terrible "dark ages." A full exposé would need a book, not an article. But while no full picture can be given here, it will be attempted to give, at least, a complete sketch, dealing with the law and the facts, with the arguments *pro* and *con*.

I

From medieval times on and, later, from Grotius to 1914, the laws of war were studied and occupied a prominent place in the literature and teaching of international law as well as in the practice of states. From the middle of the nineteenth to the first decade of the present century, this oldest part of international law [2] was also the first to be partially codified. These codifications had been preceded and were followed, up to World War I, by municipal regulations. A rich literature on the laws of war in general and on every detailed problem sprang up in the principal languages. This codification had been helped by semi-official conferences and by studies of learned societies.

The codification of the laws of war was by no means complete. Some of the most important and, at the same time, most controversial problems, such as the problems of hostages and reprisals, were simply passed over under diplomatic silence. The Hague conventions lack logical and systematic arrangement; are vitiated by the *clausula si omnes,* by the insertion in many places of the formula "if military circumstances permit"; are weakened by numerous and very different reservations and by sometimes vague and unprecise formulations. Contrary to the rules of war on land, "the agreements reached about war at sea were of less importance and subsequent experience has shown them to be of little practical value." [3] The Hague conventions could, of course, not regulate methods of warfare unknown at that time.

The belligerents again enacted municipal regulations in World War I, but it was not surprising that the laws of war proved inadequate. The international law of World War I has, up to now, not yet been fully studied.[4] Both groups tried to defend acts, illegal *per se,* either by such arguments as the use of "new weapons," or existence of "changed circumstances," or by the ever-expanding argument of reprisals—all arguments apt to uproot the whole laws of war, so that, finally, "each side felt free to decide for itself to what extent it would consider itself bound by the laws of war." [5]

II

The World War I had shown abundantly the insufficiency of the laws of war in force. Their revision was urgently needed. But the reaction was their complete neglect. This neglect of the laws of war since 1920—the paralyzation of their revision, the hostility toward the whole subject, the fashion simply to ignore the problem, the fact that the very mentioning became, so to speak, taboo—all that was fully deliberate. It was part and parcel of an officially created illusion of wishful thinking fostered by statesmen and utopian writers. This dominating attitude created a wholly unreal atmosphere in the face of existing realities; it was in open contradiction with the practice of states both as to facts and as to the law. But this attitude was part of a policy and was often highly praised as a great conquest of our time, as important progress, as a decisive step on the road toward the elimination of war. The result of this much-praised attitude was the manner in which World War II was fought.

Two opposite tendencies are responsible for this new, unreal, and unsound trend: the ideology of extreme pacifists, well intentioned, good, but utterly utopian and the thinking of hard and shrewd people, who did not, like the first group, believe that war has been "abolished," but who wanted to keep their hands free as to the conduct of the next war.

As early as 1920, an anonymous article [6] had given a nearly complete list of arguments against the possibility and the desirability of any study and revision of the laws of war by the League of Nations. The practice of states and the science of international law followed these ideas. The movement for the codification and revision of the laws of war nearly came to an end in the inter-war period. Even the existing Hague conventions were ignored by most of its newly established states. The Washington Convention of 1922 concerning submarine and chemical warfare never came into force. The Committee of Jurists for the elaboration of a plan for the Permanent Court of International Justice adopted, on July 23, 1920, a *voeu* recommending the revision of the laws of war and a new Hague conference. But the League did nothing about it. The Committee of Jurists, created by the Washington Conference of 1922 for the purpose of revising the laws of war, elaborated in 1923 at The Hague an excellent general report, and presented two draft conventions on control of radio in time of war and on aerial warfare. But the states ignored them.

The same neglect of laws of war was shown by the science of international law. The Institut de Droit International, which, prior to 1914, had given so much attention to the laws of war, has not once prior to 1920 treated a problem of the laws of war. The Interparliamentary Union adopted at its twenty-fourth session, held in Paris in 1927, a resolution according to which any attempt to codify the laws of war should be abandoned in the future. The Hague Academy of International Law banned, until the end of the twenties, any course on the laws of war. The proposal put forward by Senator Borah to convoke a conference in 1928 for the codification of maritime warfare was lost. The League of Nations would have nothing to do with the laws of war. Even the teaching of the laws of war was opposed by many.

III

As early as 1934, this writer warned against this mistaken belief, warned that this neglect, the policy adopted since 1920, may lead to wars without any laws of war, to battles in which the great progress brought about by the laws of war may be lost to barbaric methods which one had hoped are banned forever. The fears voiced by this writer in 1934 were more than fully justified by what happened in World War II, in which the neglect of the laws of war in the inter-war period was coupled with the full appearance of "total war."

The religious wars of the sixteenth and seventeenth centuries had been fought in a barbaric and ruthless way. The Thirty Years' War can be called a total war and shows that total war is not dependent on the astounding progress of natural sciences of today. But from 1648 to 1914, notwithstanding technological progress, wars were, in general, fought in a more civilized, less cruel way. Why is it that we see since 1914, and particularly since 1939, this disastrous decline of civilization in the conduct of war?

It has been stated that the Hague conventions were, even in 1907, incomplete and had many defects and limitations. The inadequacy of the laws of war in the two great wars was, further, a consequence of the radical change of general conditions as compared with those prevailing in 1899 and 1907. These codifications presupposed the doctrines of

democracy, capitalism, economic liberalism, the principle
of the sanctity of private property, the strict distinction
between private enterprise and economic activities by the
states, the Rousseau-Portalès doctrine, and the strict distinction between armed forces and civilian population. The
appearance of state socialism, even in democracies, and of
totalitarian régimes has changed these conditions basically. They paved the way for the modern "total war,"
which made its first limited appearance in World War I.
While statesmen and scholars indulged in the neglect of
the laws of war, total war was studied by strategists, and
made its full appearance in World War II. At the present
time, it seems that we are in for bigger and better things,
where modern developments may lead to the possibility
that human culture has available a means to commit suicide.

Total war as it exists today is not a consequence of
totalitarian régimes; democracies, too, are forced to prepare for and to wage total war. Total war [7] is the result
of the combination of technological progress in arms with
a changed manner of waging war, of the combination of
unlimited use of highly destructive weapons for unlimited
war aims. Since World War I, we have seen a continuous
trend toward mechanized warfare: long-range artillery,
submarines, aerial warfare, chemical warfare, tanks made
their appearance. Many of these new weapons and methods
made it for the first time technically possible to attack
the hinterland and the civilian population. Economic warfare, too, acquired a world-wide aspect. Yet at the end of
World War I defensive strategy in a war of trenches seemed
superior to the offensive, thanks particularly to machine-
guns and mortars.

After 1920, the theoretical study of the use of tanks
and of aerial warfare tried to regain the supremacy of
the offensive. The new theory was put into practice in

World War II by the Germans: "blitzkrieg," massing of tanks, armored divisions; great progress in mechanized transportation of troops and weapons; more and more ruthless development of aerial warfare, more and more unrestricted submarine warfare. Against the new technique, the Maginot Line proved to be an anachronism. The Allies followed and brought these techniques, thanks to overwhelming industrial capacity, to heights compared with which the early German techniques seemed to be those of beginners. The climax came in the last days of the war against Japan, with the atomic bombs, delivered by man-piloted planes.

But even before the atomic bombs had been dropped over Hiroshima and Nagasaki, the Germans had sent V-1, and later V-2, bombs to England; the V-2 bombs made use of the stratosphere and traveled faster than sound, so that no warning and hardly an interception was possible. These developments are, perhaps, more significant than the atomic bombs of 1945. Pilotless planes directed by remote control, radar-controlled glide-bombs, "guided missiles" open the way for a new phase of total war: from mechanized to automatic warfare.

These new techniques lent themselves to more and more inhuman warfare, to wholesale devastation, and fostered the adoption of unlimited war aims. It is fundamental to understand that technological developments makes total war only technically possible, but not inevitable. In very ancient times wars were often fought with primitive weapons in the most inhuman way; later times with very advanced weapons saw much more human and civilized warfare. Weapons, however terrible, however destructive, however automatic, are in themselves dead machines; everything depends on the heart of men who use them. It is not alone, and even not primarily, the technological development in arms, the replacement of small professional armies by the "nations-in-arms" and the subsequent transformation of the whole economy and science, the mobilization of the whole civilian population for war purposes, which explains total war. It is the wish of men to make use of these technical possibilities for unlimited war aims which is decisive. War has been considered as the *ultima ratio* for deciding international conflicts; the aims were limited. The new thing is the unlimited war aims: the possibly total destruction of the enemy's economy, greater and greater devastation. Such type of total war makes it necessary on all sides to indoctrinate each belligerent nation with a deadly hatred of the enemy, to make the enemy infamous down to the roots of his national, historical, and cultural character and history. Total war must be fought in ideological terms; it is no hazard that the word "crusade" is again fashionable; no more limited wars for limited objectives: world-wide wars of annihilation, where nothing but unconditional surrender, total conquest, economic ruin, permanent crippling of the enemy will do. Naturally there is no road to peace from total war, because total war is fought ruthlessly, without regard to postwar consequences.

Total war must necessarily lead all around to a decline of moral feeling, must undermine the respect for the rule of law. And this reversion to barbarism naturally will make itself felt, too, in times of so-called peace which, at the present time, is labeled with a new word as no better than "cold war." Total war is thus one of the forms in which the total crisis of our western Christian culture, a crisis which threatens the very survival of our civilization, manifests itself. It is, so to speak, a form of visual education to teach us that the pessimism, the feeling that the cultured man of the twentieth century is no more than a barbarian under a very superficial veneer of civilization, that the fear of new and more terrible "dark ages" is, perhaps, unfortunately hardly exaggerated.

IV

Total war as waged during World War II saw a continued violation of the laws of war by all belligerents. The laws of war are, at the present time, in a chaotic status, as will be shown later. This chaotic status concerns not only single problems, but the very foundations of the laws of war. Their revision is of the most urgent necessity. But, strangely enough, the same neglect, indifference, and apathy, the same hostility toward this subject, which so disastrously prevailed during the interwar period, prevails again since the actual end of fighting in 1945. All the old arguments—the impossibility and futility of a revision of the laws of war, the "abolition" of war and, hence, the non-existence of the laws of war, the idea that any occupation with the laws of war could make "a bad impression on public opinion"—are repeated again. To that comes the new pessimistic resignation, the fatalism toward the inevitability of lawless wars.

The United Nations, like the League of Nations, is again leading in this policy of the ostrich. Although Article XXX (1) (a) of the Charter of the United Nations makes it the task of the General Assembly to initiate studies and make recommendations for encouraging the progressive development of international law and its codification, and although the International Law Commission has been created for this purpose and has held its first two sessions, the whole topic of the laws of war is carefully avoided. If one only mentions this subject as a possible topic for codification to Dr. Yuen-Li Liang, he shakes his head negatively, with the most friendly smile. In the memorandum, *Survey of International Law,*[8] in which Professor Lauterpacht surveys "the whole field of international law," in accordance with Article XVIII of the Statute of the International Law

Commission, the laws of war do not appear. Is it because they do not belong to the "whole field of international law" or because they need no revision?

At the first session of the International Law Commission, held from April 12 to June 9, 1949, the commission reviewed the laws of war as topic 25, the last one. But

> it was suggested that, war having been outlawed, the regulation of its conduct had ceased to be relevant. The majority of the Commission declared itself opposed to the study of the problem at the present stage . . . It was considered that . . . public opinion might interpret its action as showing lack of confidence in the efficiency of the means at the disposal of the U.N. for maintaining peace.

We find in these few lines nearly all the arguments fashionable since 1920 and the same result, nothing is to be done. When the Chinese member, who knows something about the existence of fighting in China from 1911 to the present day, proposed an additional article to the Draft Declaration on Rights and Duties of States to the effect that it is the duty of states to condition military necessity by the principle of humanity in the employment of armed force, legitimate or illegitimate, "some members objected. The Commission did not accept the proposed addition."

The science of international law again shows, to a great extent, the indifference and hostility adopted since 1920.[9] Learned societies do not like the topic of the laws of war. When Major Downey at the forty-second annual meeting of the American Society of International Law [10] made a "brief plea for some constructive thought concerning the development of the international law of war," particularly with regard to aerial warfare, he knew very well that he was speaking for an "unpopular cause"; the echo of his words was exactly zero.

In the following year the topic "Revision of the Rules of Warfare" was put on the program.[11] We heard many excellent remarks and, at least, one very good speech; but, in general, the impression was exceedingly disappointing. Many speakers took a negative attitude, but the strongest attack against the revision of the laws of war came from our distinguished and esteemed friend, Professor Fenwick. His speech was obviously the expression of a strongly-felt and deep-rooted, genuine conviction. And he made it perfectly plain that he does not belong to the wishful thinkers, that he does not join their belief that war has been "abolished," that he does not look forward to a pacific future. But he resigned himself to the fatalistic pessimism of the inevitability of lawless wars. He deplored, therefore, the waste of time spent even in an attempt at the revision of the laws of war; we must keep our hands free for the great problems of self-defense.

V

Having shown the methodical neglect of, and hostility to, the laws of war and their revision since 1920, it is pertinent to discuss the arguments brought forward in defense of this attitude. The anonymous article, mentioned earlier, published in the *British Yearbook of International Law* of 1920-21, contains nearly all these arguments. They are of two types. The first group of arguments consists in saying that laws of war are impossible; war can only be abolished, not regulated. Further, they are valueless for they will be broken. These arguments are not only entirely untenable theoretically, but also highly dangerous practically, because they undermine any constructive effort at revision in advance.

These arguments are based on a whole chain of theoretical and factual errors. First, it is said that war in itself is brutal force, contrary to law; one must eliminate war by "replacing force by law." The fundamental error of this argument is not to see that all law, primitive and advanced, is a coercive normative order and rests, in the last analysis, on the application of physical force, if necessary. One must distinguish legal and illegal use of force. A primitive legal order, as general international law still is, has to entrust the execution of the law to the members of the legal community. War in primitive international law has, therefore, a necessary function. This function is a double one: as a procedure to redress a wrong, analogous to *Fehde* and *vendetta* in primitive municipal law, in view of the lack of compulsory international courts, police, and sheriffs; and as a revolutionary procedure to change the law, in view of the absence of an international legislature, analogous to revolution in municipal law; in both cases it is not necessarily the right, but the greater force which decides. To eliminate war is not to replace "force by law," but to replace a primitive by an advanced procedure of law. Private war could be successfully forbidden in the Holy Roman Empire only in 1492, when compulsory courts with sheriffs and a legislature had been firmly established. The elimination of war, in order to be successful, presupposes that general international law has developed from a primitive to a highly advanced legal order. To forbid a revolution by law is no adequate means to prevent a revolution. To forbid war by pact is, as the history of the last decades has demonstrated *ad oculos,* no adequate means to prevent war.

The argument, sometimes advanced, that the lack of laws of war would lead war *ad absurdum* and thus be an advantage does, in the light of the experience of the first two world wars, not even deserve a refutation. The argument that the laws of war are no laws because they are violated, that it, therefore, would be idle to revise them, is untenable theoretically and in fact. Theoretically it must be borne in mind that the possibility of its own violation is inherent in every legal norm, primitive or advanced, municipal or international. The fundamental structure of every legal norm consists precisely in prescribing a sanction under the condition of a behavior contrary to that ordered by the norm. If a legal norm could not be violated physically, it would not be a legal norm but a law of natural sciences. Law deals with liberty, not with necessity. If, on the other hand, a legal norm, although it could be violated physically, would never be violated in fact because of the high ethical standard of the members of the legal community, then we would need no legal norms at all but could do with ethical norms only. But, notwithstanding the existence of other normative systems—religion, ethics, conventional norms— law is indispensable as a means of social control to regulate the coexistence of men. Everybody knows that the criminal municipal law is constantly being violated and that in some cases the criminals escape punishment. But has anyone concluded that criminal law is no law; has anyone proposed to abolish criminal law because it certainly will be violated and is therefore "futile"?

Furthermore, there are many other errors in the same argument. There is, first, what may be called the error of ignorance. People often speak of the violations of the laws of war because they simply do not know what is the law actually in force. There is the error produced by propaganda. Violations of the laws of war are sometimes fabricated for propaganda purposes or invented or exaggerated under the spell of war hysteria. There is, finally, what may be called the optical error. The real violations of the laws of war are often sensational, make front-page news. The man in the street thus gets a totally wrong impression; he hears only of the sensational violations but knows nothing as far as their observation is concerned, for their observation does not make "news." This writer has given many years to the study of the laws of war, but he also served for more than four years as an officer at the front in World War I. We who know the laws of war, not only from desk

study, but from actual experience on the field of battle,
know that there certainly were violations, and grave violations, of the laws of war; but we know also that in an
overwhelming number of cases they were well observed.

True, the situation was much worse in World War II. But
even so, that millions of prisoners of war from all camps,
notwithstanding the holocaust, did return is due exclusively
to the observance of the Geneva Prisoners of War Convention of 1929, that is, to the observance of the laws of war.
It should also be noted that not a single belligerent pretended not to be bound by the laws of war; the very
argument of reprisals is an admission that the acts committed are in themselves contrary to the laws of war. The
fact that the violations of the laws of war in World War
II were more sweeping is an additional incentive for their
revision. When a great wave of crimes sweeps a country,
people give more time to the revision of criminal law rather
than to advise its abandonment.

VI

The arguments against the laws of war and their revision,
discussed and refuted in the preceding chapter, are older
than the League of Nations. They have remained the same
since 1920. To these pessimistic arguments has, since 1920,
been added another group of over-optimistic arguments:
war has been "outlawed," "abolished"; in consequence,
there are no more, there can be no more laws of war. This
argument also takes the form that, as war has been outlawed, any occupation with the laws of war would not only
be futile, but illogical; would, at the same time, be a sign
of mistrust in the great progress, already realized, on the
road toward the elimination of war; and would "make a
disagreeable impression" on the public.

First of all, it must be clearly stated that the position of
war in general international law has not changed until
today. All attempts to restrict or even to forbid the right
to go to war were, until now, based on treaties, that is, on
particular international law, binding on the parties only.
But even these treaties have by no means abolished war,
neither in law nor in fact. As the League of Nations no
longer exists, it will be sufficient to point out in a few words
that the Covenant by no means abolished or outlawed war.
There were under the Covenant cases of legal wars, not
only between non-members, but even between members. The
much-praised collective security never did exist, and even
the illusion of collective security broke down completely in
the thirties. Economic sanctions were tried once and failed,
common military action was never undertaken. Let us add
that the League of Nations, further, fully recognized at all
times that even illegal wars are, nevertheless, wars, and,
therefore, under the laws of war, that the "action commune" under Article XVI was even in the theoretical discussions always treated as constituting, for all practical
purposes, war.

This argument that war has been outlawed was made
more strongly after the conclusion of the Pact of Paris in
1928. As this pact is still in force, the argument deserves
closer scrutiny here. After so many fancy interpretations,
it is at last necessary to treat the problem in a lawyer-like
fashion. The Pact of Paris does not "outlaw" or "abolish"
war; it only contains a "renunciation of war as an instrument of national policy," a phrase which never has been
interpretated satisfactorily. War clearly remains as an
instrument of international policy. But there is more to it.
Mr. Kellogg's circular letter forms an integral part of the
pact: Every state retains the inherent right of self-defense
and is itself the only judge to decide whether there is a

given case of self-defense. As the pact leaves to every signatory the ascertainment of the presuppositions of a legal
war, it does not constitute an advance over general international law.[12] Lauterpacht,[13] a strong adherent of the Pact
of Paris, states correctly:

> The effect of the Pact of Paris is not to abolish, even for its
> signatories the institution of war as such. War remains lawful:
> a) as a means of a legally permissible self-defense; b) as a
> measure of collective action; c) as between signatories of the
> pact and non-signatories; d) as against a signatory who has
> broken the Pact by resorting to war in violation of its provisions.

In a subcommittee meeting of the United Nations War
Crimes Commission in 1944, Sir Arnold McNair, now judge
of the International Court of Justice, declared correctly that
the state cannot be the subject of criminal liability and that
this position had not been altered by the Pact of Paris which
"has not abolished war as an institution regulated by
law." [14]

Let us add that even an illegal war under the Pact of
Paris is, nevertheless, a war under the rules of the laws
of war.

The practice of states from 1920 to 1939 abundantly
proves that war continued to exist in fact and to be recognized as an institution of international law, and that the
laws of war continued to be recognized as valid law. Innumerable collective treaties, concluded since 1919, many of
them under the auspices of the League of Nations, contain
special rules "in case of war."

The interwar period was filled with wars, civil wars, and
fighting: The Russo-Polish War and the Greco-Turkish
War were recognized as wars by the practice of states.
The *Wimbledon Case* turned on Germany's neutrality,
which presupposes the existence of war. In the Greco-
Turkish War, the Allies made a strict declaration of neu-

trality and insisted, contrary to their own practice in World War I, on the neutrals' right to trade. There was the Fiume coup of d'Annunzio and his "war" with Italy; fighting in the Burgenland; there was Zeligowski's coup in Wilna, fighting between Poles and Ukrainians in East Galicia. On this continent we had the Leticia Affair, the long and bloody Chaco War, in which all neighboring South American nations made declarations of neutrality. Bolivia protested in 1932 to all nations that Paraguay had put prisoners of war at the front and continued: "This fact constitutes a monstrous violation of all the conventions and principles with regard to warfare." There was the Manchuria Affair of 1931-33 and the "China Incident" since 1937. There was the German armed reoccupation of the Rhineland, the annexation of Austria, Sudetenland, Czechoslovakia, Memel, and Danzig; the Italian armed annexation of Albania. There was the Ethiopian War leading to the conquest of Ethiopia by Italy. There were the civil wars in the Soviet Union with foreign intervention. There was the long and cruel Spanish Civil War with foreign intervention on both sides. Armies, navies, and air forces were built and trained. Alliances were concluded. In the Pan-American orbit, the sixth Conference of American States, held at Havana in 1928, adopted the Convention on Maritime Neutrality. In the thirties Belgium rushed back to traditional neutrality. The United States adopted the Neutrality Laws of 1935, 1936, 1937, and 1939. The Scandinavian Neutrality Rules were promulgated on May 27, 1938. Switzerland, in 1938, had already laid the foundations for her economic survival in case of another general war. Italy enacted war and neutrality rules in 1938.

Notwithstanding the general neglect of the laws of war in this period, English and American treatises on international law continued to devote full attention to them. From the end of the twenties more monographs on the laws of war begin to appear in the different languages. At that time courses on this subject made their appearance even at the Hague Academy of International Law. There were also in this period scholars who insisted on the importance of the laws of war and on the necessity for their revision; but their voices were not heard.

Even new laws of war were enacted: the Geneva Protocol of June 27, 1925, on the Prohibition of Chemical and Bacteriological Warfare; the new Geneva Convention of July 27, 1929, for the Amelioration of the Condition of the Wounded and Sick of the Armies in the Field; the new Geneva Convention of the same date, giving us the highly important Prisoners of War Code; the Roerich Pact, signed at Washington on April 15, 1935, for the Protection of Artistic and Scientific Institutions and Historical Monuments; the London Protocol of November 6, 1936, concerning the rules of international law regulating the action of submarines toward merchant vessels. In addition, further attempts were made by the International Red Cross and by a conference convoked by the Prince of Monaco.[15] It should not be overlooked also that the Disarmament Conference of the League of Nations occupied itself to a far-reaching degree with problems of the laws of war.

VII

That the fancy interpretations of the Pact of Paris, in contrast to its real value,[16] do not correspond to the international law actually in force was clearly shown by the unanimous practice of states which treated World War II and its component wars as wars under the rules of war. Declarations of war and declarations of neutrality were made. Every belligerent insisted vis-à-vis his enemies on the observance of the laws of war; protests against their violation were made, diplomatic correspondence through neutral channels took place. In the Pan-American orbit, the Panama Consultative Meeting of the Foreign Ministers of the American Republics passed Resolution I of October 3, 1939, containing a general Declaration of Neutrality and set up the Inter-American Neutrality Committee at Rio de Janeiro. Resolution VI of the same day dealt with the humanization of war and appealed to European nations to abstain from the use of poisonous gases and other chemical methods of warfare; from bombarding open cities, objects, and places without any military value; from employing inflammable liquids; from poisoning water and disseminating bacteria; from employing offensive weapons which increase the suffering of the wounded; from imposing unnecessarily rigorous measures upon civilian populations; from sinking merchant vessels without having first placed the passengers, crew, and ship papers in a place of safety; and condemned the unrestricted application of measures causing unnecessary and inhuman suffering in injuring the enemy. All that shows that the American state practice regarded the laws of war as valid. On the same day, Resolution VII on contraband of war was adopted.

The belligerents made regulations concerning the laws of war. Prize courts were set up, and prize decisions rendered. That the laws of war are valid law was again confirmed in the Judgment of the Nuremberg Trial.[17] The accused were indicted for violations of the laws of war; they include, but are not limited to, murder, ill-treatment, or deportation to slave labor or for any other purposes of civilian population of or in occupied territories; murder or ill-treatment of prisoners of war or persons on the seas; killing of hostages, plunder of public or private property; wanton destruction of cities, towns, or villages, or devastations not justified by military necessity.[18]

VIII

In World War II the laws of war "were regularly and on a mass scale violated by all the belligerents." [19] Most bel-

ligerents forgot the rule of Article XXII of the Hague
Regulations (Convention IV) that the belligerents have *not*
an unlimited right as to the means they adopt for injuring
the enemy. The consequence has been an absolutely chaotic
status of the laws of war at the present time. A full study
on World War II and the laws of war has not yet even been
attempted. Here only a list of the problems can be given.
As to land warfare, such problems as the legality of particular weapons, e.g., flame-throwers, chemical warfare, the
treatment of the sick and wounded, of prisoners of war, the
taking and killing of hostages, devastation, status of civilian
population, of public and private enemy property, requisitions and contributions, destruction of enemy property,
bombardment, are to be mentioned. The whole law of *occupatio bellica*, guerilla warfare, resistance underground
movements, of espionage and war treason, of war crimes, of
the plea of superior orders is in a chaotic status. Also
chaotic is the status of the whole law regarding maritime
warfare: the distinction between men-of-war and merchant
vessels, the law of mines and of "war-zones" on the high
seas, the law of capture and of immunity from capture, of
hospital ships, the destruction of enemy merchant vessels,
prize procedure, visit and search, deviation of vessels for
visit and search, the whole law of submarine warfare, the
whole law of contraband, blockade, and unneutral assistance. Chaotic is the status of air warfare as well as of
economic warfare.

To put a few questions: Is it legal to take hostages and,
if so, what must be their treatment? [20] What is the law of
guerilla warfare? [21] What is the law of war booty? [22] Is the
use of the atomic bomb legal? [23] The list of such questions
could be prolonged indefinitely.

World War II has not only shown the inadequacy of many
existing laws of war, e.g., concerning prisoners of war,
belligerent occupation, and so on; it has not only demon-

strated the disastrous result of the complete lack of regulation with regard to such problems as reprisals, hostages, economic warfare, aerial warfare. It has shown the necessity of regulating new methods of warfare, such as use of magnetic mines, atomic bombs, guided missiles, and so on. But there are even more fundamental reasons for the chaotic status of the laws of war. It is often not possible to decide whether certain methods of conducting warfare, violative of the rules of war, are to be justified only as reprisals, so that the violated rules of war survive. The incomplete and often imprecisely formulated laws of war make it relatively easy to charge the enemy with a breach of the rules of war and to resort to reprisals, especially as there are no rules of war regulating reprisals. Violations of the rules of war have often been justified by "new weapons" or "changed circumstances." Now the legal situation is that these arguments can make necessary an adjustment or abolition of the existing rules of war or the enactment of new ones, but they cannot justify the breach of the existing laws of war by one belligerent. The valid laws of war, like all legal rules, survive their violation intact. Violation of the laws of war by one belligerent, and even analagous conduct by the enemy on the basis of reprisals, has no law-creating faculty. But if valid rules of war are violated continuously by all the belligerents and go unprotested and unpunished, have new rules of war come into force by a revolutionary and accepted practice of states? Have we here, as so often in international law, a case of *ex injuria jus oritur?* Where is the dividing line between mere violations of the valid laws of war and creation of new rules of war? Or are certain methods of conduct to be interpreted as not yet constituting new valid laws of war, but merely as trends in this direction, as new rules of war in *fieri?*

Here is the basis of the present chaotic status of the laws of war, so well presented by Morgenthau [24] and H. A.

Smith.[25] That is why different writers are so divided as to what is the law actually in force on a particular problem. If we compare Sumner Welles's statement of June 3, 1938, against indiscriminate aerial bombardment, the protests against Soviet bombardment, against German bombardment of Rotterdam and England, and pass on to the later Allied bombardment of Germany and the dropping of the atomic bombs, we see the change. Hyde [26] stated in 1945 that "it cannot be admitted that aerial bombardment for the purpose of terrorizing the civilian population of the enemy, or of destroying private property, not of military character, or of producing harm to non-combatants . . . is lawful." But Jessup [27] writes that indiscriminate civilian aerial bombardment must be anticipated. What does "anticipated," by the way, mean: as an illegal practice, or as the new law?

Let us remember the horror which German unrestricted submarine warfare in World War I, the phrase "spurlos versenkt," created here, and pass to the adoption of the same conduct by the Allies in World War II. By the Nuremberg Judgment,[28] Dönitz and Raeder were acquitted of the indictment of waging unrestricted submarine warfare,

> in view of all the facts proved and in particular of an order of the British Admiralty announced on 8 May 1940, according to which all vessels should be sunk at night in the Skagerrak, and to answers to interrogatories by Admiral Nimitz stating that unrestricted submarine warfare was carried on in the Pacific Ocean from the first day that Nation entered the war.

What is the legal value of this judgment? Is unrestricted submarine warfare now legal, or, in spite of all that, is the London Protocol of November 6, 1936, to which forty-eight states, including Germany, Italy, and Japan, had adhered by the end of August, 1939, and which forbids it, still the valid law as Colombos [29] affirms?

At the beginning of the war, Charles Warren [30] attacked the methods of a "lawless, maritime warfare"; he attacked, for instance, the diversion of neutral vessels into a belligerent's ports for purposes of search; but Colombos [31] asserts that "altered circumstances . . . have introduced a change in the rules hitherto accepted," and says that the legality of the new practice was affirmed as early as 1916 by the British Prize Court. What about the methods of "blacklists," of "rationing neutrals"? What about the "long-distance blockade"? Garner [32] had stated in 1925 that "these measures constituted clear violations of the freedom of the seas and severe encroachments on the long-established rights of neutrals." Grob [33] states today that "the operation of long-distance blockade is a question not of right but of might." But Colombos,[34] although admitting that the "blockade" of Germany 1914-18 "departed from the accepted principles of international law" and could not be based on the law of contraband, reaches the conclusion that under modern warfare "blockades are now impracticable" and that "long-range blockades must be accepted under modern conditions."

The chaotic status of the laws of war at the present time is a fact which cannot be challenged. It is also fully recognized, and, therefore, the urgent necessity of their revision is pressed by serious writers on the subject.[35] Notwithstanding the general attitude of neglect of the laws of war, treatises and monographs on problems of the laws of war are being published again in greater number; voices are being heard in favor of the revision of particular rules of war or of the whole laws of war. We mention Hyde's and Oppenheim-Lauterpacht's treatises, many monographs on the necessity of the revision of the law of belligerent occupation;[36] revision of the laws of maritime warfare has been urged recently by Colombos and Smith, who asked the basic

question: Has new practice made new law? Smith warned
that "unless the civilized order of states disintegrates entirely, the present anarchy is bound to end some time."
Downey [37] insisted on a new code of aerial warfare and
warned that indiscriminate bombing of cities, which, in his
opinion and on the basis of his experience in Europe, serves
no useful purpose, threatens to wipe out our whole western
civilization. Mossup [38] studied the problem of hospital ships
and concluded that there is an urgent need for revision of
the tenth Hague Convention in the light of modern experience. Raja Gabaglia [39] has written a large volume to the
effect that, as war is still always possible, the knowledge
and dissemination of the laws of war as well as their
revision is an urgent task. The discussion of the revision
of the laws of war at the 1949 annual meeting of the
American Society of International Law, although disappointing because of the dominance of opponents of such
revision, nevertheless brought valuable contributions to the
problem. George A. McDonough [40] stated that, as a prosecutor and defense counsel in the war crimes program in
Europe, he "was alarmed to realize that in nine problems
out of ten the authorities and textbooks had no answer." He
particularly refers to the problem of the defense of superior command" and concludes that there is "a pressing
necessity for a codification of the laws of war."

IX

That the laws of war are actually in a chaotic state and
urgently need revision is a fact which cannot be challenged.
Is the argument of the opponents of revision that there are
no more laws of war because war has been "abolished,"
"outlawed," any stronger since 1945 than it was during the
interwar period?

The experience under the League of Nations and the Pact
of Paris that the word "war" used in these instruments is

of uncertain meaning has led to great technical progress in the Charter of the United Nations. Here the term "war" has been replaced by the broader and less ambiguous phrase "threat or use of force." Does Article II, paragraph 4, "abolish" wars? It certainly does not. First of all, the Charter is, probably, binding only on members. Second, Article II, paragraph 4, prohibits the "threat or use of force against the territorial integrity or political independence of any state," i.e., whether a member or not. True, it is added, "or in any other manner inconsistent with the Purposes of the United Nations." This latter phrase may exclude armed reprisals, armed intervention, or armed interference for the protection of nationals abroad. But the Charter gives the members a right to use force under Article CVII (against enemy states), Article LIII (enforcement action through regional arrangements or agencies under the authority of the Security Council) and Article LI (individual and collective self-defense). To these exceptions must be added, probably, the right of self-defense under general international law which is broader than the right granted under Article LI. The latter avails only "if an armed attack occurs against a Member of the United Nations," whereas the right of self-defense under general international law is also given against an "imminent attack." It is further clear that armed action is legal in the case of action by air, sea, or land forces at the direction of the Security Council with the assistance of the Military Staff Committee (Article XLVI). Finally, there must be considered large-scale fighting in the case of civil wars which are not illegal either under general international law or under the United Nations Charter.

It follows that even if the United Nations could function in an ideal way, the use of legal force has to be regulated, if applied under Articles CVII, LIII LI, or XLII. Even if, in the case of Article LI, the Security Council were able to "take the measures necessary to maintain international peace and security" very rapidly, fighting might go on for some time in which both parties claim to act under Article LI. Fighting on a great scale in the case of civil wars also needs regulation. Military action under the direction of the Security Council obviously needs regulation, too, just as municipal police forces are not allowed to act as they like, but are restrained by rules of law. That is why Professor Scelle said at the first session of the International Law Commission that regulation of the use of force by the United Nations should have a high priority. Of course, it makes no difference whether such fighting on a great scale is technically called war or not.[41] That is why Philip C. Jessup, writing wholly *de lege ferenda,* insists nevertheless on the necessity of regulating the legal or illegal use of force.[42] The fact that in civil wars the rules of war apply is also an excellent argument against those who find rules of war illogical after war has been outlawed. People engaged in civil war are, from the point of view of the municipal law in force, criminals, rebels, traitors; yet the rules of war are often applied which, for example, make of the captured insurgents prisoners of war, not traitors. This is, as Jessup aptly remarks, not a matter of sentiment, but of military necessity. The same is true as concerns a military action by the United Nations [43] and in case of the illegal use of force.

It is of the utmost importance to keep in mind that even a war, illegal under the Pact of Paris, or a use of force, illegal under the United Nations Charter, is, nevertheless, a war or large-scale fighting regulated by the laws of war. This rule of international law is firmly established and recognized by all leading international lawyers.[44]

The laws of war, therefore, do by no means "belong to the past," as far as the law is concerned. What are the facts? What is the practice of states? Again, since 1945, fighting on a large scale goes on in many places, whether called war in the technical sense or not. There have been or are civil wars in Iran, Korea, Burma, and, sporadically, in the Philippines; the long civil war in Greece with foreign intervention, the colossal Chinese civil war; armed action by India against Hyderabad; fighting between India and Pakistan in Kashmir; the British war in Malaya; the Dutch-Indonesian war; the French war in Indo-China; the Palestine war between Jews and Arabs. And the laws of war are invoked by the states.[45]

War is recognized as possible in recent constitutions;[46] hints at possible war are found in declarations of statesmen. Article LI of the United Nations Charter is the basis of regional treaties for defense, such as the Pan-American Treaty of Rio de Janeiro, the Western European Treaty, and the North Atlantic Pact. There is not the slightest doubt that these alliances are purely defensive. This writer is in full agreement with the North Atlantic Pact and the policies taken thereunder, in view of the very real Soviet menace; but it must be recognized that even the most defensive alliance is an alliance, having, in the last analysis, common fighting in view. The goal of the North Atlantic Treaty is, first, to prevent war with the Soviet Union, but also, in case of failure, to win this war. The rearmament of Europe with American aid is under way; strategic plans are being set up, giving to every country of the North Atlantic Pact its strategic role. The Soviet Union has an enormous army, is engaged in enlarging its air force, even its navy, and in building up the armies of the eastern European states under her domination, apparently also giving military help to China. An armament race, from atomic and other weapons of mass destruction to all weapons of "conventional armament," is in full swing.

American and probably Russian studies and productions in atomic bombs are being continued; the United States is preparing the superweapon of the hydrogen bomb, and there is little doubt that the Soviet Union will try to do the same. A race for new weapons is on:[47] submarines, equipped with German "schnorkels," even atomic-powered submarines; guided-missiles ships; submarine troop-carrier-cargo ships; anti-submarine bombs; a tremendous research is going on with regard to guided missiles and new jet-propelled aircraft. The developments in the field related to nuclear physics must not blind us to the fact that other and perhaps more terrible forms of combat are under full study and experimentation: radio-active dusts, enormously powerful and lethal gases,[48] bacteriological and biological warfare.[49] Many special agencies and experimental stations have been set up for the study and development of all these new forms of warfare.

Men, especially in Europe, are afraid of World War III. States in this country are creating civil-defense agencies with power to prepare now for meeting possible atomic bomb or bacterial warfare attacks on the United States. Secretary of State Dean Acheson has warned recently that a "total cold war" is raging, that the world situation is very tense, that "total diplomacy" is needed. George F. Kennan [50] recently answered his question "Is war possible?" by saying: "Of course it is, and we must unfortunately always think of it as possible as long as we have the sort of world we have today." That is why "the laws of war retain more than academic interest"; that is "why the laws of war must continue to be a legitimate object of the science of international law." [52]

There is nothing illogical in trying to eliminate war and to regulate its conduct. Civil war is a crime under municipal law, yet often the rules of war are applied. It is not true that we have only the alternative of either forbidding the resort to force or not forbidding and regulating it. The whole career and scientific work of this writer proves that he is fully averse to resort to war, that he wholeheartedly stands for the restriction and final elimination of the crude and primitive method of war through the development of international law from a primitive into an advanced legal order. He has been an enthusiastic supporter of the League of Nations. He also stands by the United Nations which, in spite of its shortcomings, is the best type of international organization we can have today, the only bridge which today leads from the East to the West. He is, by no means, fatalistically resigned to the inevitability of World War III; he believes and fervently hopes that it can be avoided. But there is no contradiction between the utmost effort, not only to prevent the outbreak of an actual war by means of diplomacy, but also to resist resort to war by general rules and regulating large-scale fighting by rules. The one effort by no means excludes the other. Just as there is no contradiction in enacting and revising criminal laws and the superior effort so to shape social conditions that less and less crimes will be committed. But "we must face the facts . . . we must carry water on both shoulders at the same time." [53]

X

As war or use of force has not been abolished in law and is possible in fact, the laws of war, actually in a chaotic condition, urgently need revision. This revision certainly poses many problems. Writers have asked whether the revised rules of war should make a distinction between "small" and "major" wars.[54] Clearly not every possible war must be a world war; and one is not justified in thinking only in terms of a new world war and not being interested in "little wars." After all, the law of contracts applies not only to contracts which involve hundreds of millions of dollars.

Laws of war involve not only combat operations. They touch nearly every department of life. What the laws of war regarding private persons or private property in enemy country are will influence migrations, investments, and many other things in time of peace. There are, further, laws of war for the protection of the victims of war. Even opponents of revision are agreed that they should be upheld and revised; in this sense Nicolas Politis spoke in the League of Nations. Dr. Kulski [55] also declared himself in favor of this type of rules of war, making a distinction between rules which are compatible with total war and rules concerning combat operations which are not.

Indeed, revision of this type of rules of war is already under way. The Prince of Monaco again called a conference of experts on this topic in 1950. Already the four new Geneva conventions of 1949 have been signed by forty-four states.[56] This great achievement is primarily due to the efforts of the International Red Cross, which took the initiative in 1945, and to the Swiss government. The United States actively supported the initiative of the International Red Cross in 1945. The International Red Cross [57] was inspired by the rich experience it gained in World War II and in the experience gained by the National Red Cross Societies which were convoked in a preliminary conference held from June to August, 1946. In 1947, a Conference of Government Experts was held, in which the United States participated and at which a report [58] was elaborated. Then followed the seventeenth International Conference of the Red Cross at Stockholm in 1948, in which the United States also participated, at which Draft Conventions I-IV [59] were approved. Finally, the Swiss government convoked a diplomatic conference which took place from April 21 to August 12, 1949, in Geneva, at which fifty-nine states, including the United States and the Soviet Union, took part. Although there was unanimous agreement to conclude these conventions, some doubted the wisdom of the action, because of the impression on public opinion. But the Swiss foreign minister stated that it is necessary and an imperative duty to establish such conventions in time of peace; that it is of the utmost urgency to do so to prevent the repetition of the terrible horrors perpetrated in World War II. And at the time of signature, on December 8, 1949, he said that the conventions were signed "on the unhappy assumption that a new war is not impossible."

The new Geneva Conventions of August 12, 1949,[60] deal only with the protection of the victims of war. Convention II is a revision of the tenth Hague Convention (Hospital-Ship Convention). Conventions I and III are revisions of the two Geneva Conventions of 1929. Convention III (Prisoners of War) contains a new and somewhat controversial rule, which, it seems, was adopted under strong insistence by the Soviet Union; this new rule, corresponding to a pressing problem appearing in World War II and hitherto unregulated, gives to members of underground resistance movements in occupied territory under certain conditions the status of prisoners of war. All three conventions constitute strong improvements. Convention IV deals with a new, hitherto unregulated problem urgently in need of regulation, namely, the treatment of civilians in wartime. It is a great step forward in the development of international law. All the conventions are based, as they should be, on practical and realistic considerations, striking, in the words of the Swiss foreign minister, Max Petitpierre, an equilibrium between the cruel necessities of war and humanitarian ideals.

Rules of war, including rules of combat, are essential, as said earlier, even in time of peace. They are essential to protect soldiers and civilians in war; they are essential in these times to guarantee the survival of our whole civilization, if not of mankind itself. They are essential, representing, in the words of Jessup, not a matter of sentiment, but of military necessity. An army, as distinguished from a savage horde, must know what to expect, must know under

what rules fighting is to be carried on. They are essential
for the law of war crimes. A situation cannot be called
legal in which both belligerent groups will do what they
like, and then the victors "will try the vanquished for having committed crimes determined unilaterally and with
retroactive force by the victors." [61] That is why rules of
war for the actual conduct of fighting are indispensable.
If the United Nations is unwilling or unable to draft such
rules, it must be done outside of the organization,[62] just as
were the four new Geneva conventions. But just as the
efforts at disarmament by the League of Nations dealt in
effect to a great degree with the laws of war, so do the
efforts of the United Nations Commission for Conventional
Armaments and the Atomic Energy Commission. The envisaged prohibition of the use of the atomic bomb pertains
to the rules of war and shows that even in the United
Nations large-scale fighting, whether legal or illegal, is
considered possible; otherwise why try to enact this prohibition? This commission has, further, to deal with all
other weapons of mass destruction. Secretary General
Trygve Lie suggested even in 1948 that the United Nations
forbid chemical and bacteriological warfare,[63] and he suggested in 1950 that the United Nations begin the study of
controlling germ warfare,[64] and that the hydrogen bomb
is a United Nations topic.[65] The International Committee
of the Red Cross has recently appealed to all signatories
of the new Geneva conventions to take appropriate steps
to reach agreement on a prohibition of atomic weapons and
of all weapons of non-directed mass-death-missiles.

We have already answered the arguments of those op-
timists who believe that war is "abolished" and, therefore,
laws of war do not and cannot exist. Let us state once more
that naturally all must be done to prevent wars diplomatically and to restrict, and ultimately eliminate, war
legally. This is the higher goal. But this does not exclude

the necessity of regulating large-scale fighting, legal or illegal, as long as the first goal is not reached. That the first goal has not yet been reached and is not likely to be reached within the near future is clear. To abandon the smaller progress achieved through the laws of war in favor of a higher goal not reached would be folly. It is indeed paradoxical that, in the words of Erich Hula,[66] "though men despaired of being able to attain the comparatively modest goal of regulating war, they entertained strangely enough, the more excessive hope of being able to eliminate war altogether." Such an attitude "is unfortunately rather the symptom of grim prospects for the future conduct of wars than a guarantee of the elimination of war as such."

It must also be stressed that the laws of war pertain rather to the law of peace, that they are "a part of human rights." [67]

One word has still to be said to answer the arguments of the fatalistic pessimists who resign themselves to total war, because "laws of war, as to combat, are incompatible with total war." Such fatalistic pessimism is a confession of utmost determinism, a belief that men are in no way the masters of their destiny, but the slaves of inexorable developments, a negation of the possibility of creative human effort. The real problem is not whether such laws of war are incompatible with total war, but whether total war is compatible with the survival of human culture. How can the pessimistic fatalists at the same time be firm believers in such developments as international courts for the protection of human rights? It is also clear that total war will make illusory even such laws of war as are considered "compatible with total war," such as rules concerning prisoners of war, sick and wounded, and so on, a consequence strongly emphasized in the recent appeal made by the International Committee of the Red Cross.

The movement for laws of war, Summer Maine has stated, owes less to professors, statesmen, or moralists than to military commanders. Today, too, the revision of the laws of war is particularly endorsed by military men.[68] For the laws of war are not exclusively and not even primarily a matter of humanitarian sentiment, but of military necessity.

Large-scale fighting does and will occur, whether called war or not. It is obvious that more and more terrible weapons do not guarantee the much longed-for security, but rather increase insecurity. It is also clear that the progress of natural science in producing more and more terrible weapons is endless. A continuance on the road of neglect of the laws of war, while at the same time the higher goal of abolition of war remains unsolved, must necessarily lead to greater and greater catastrophes.

True, the present world climate makes the revision of the laws of war difficult. But does it make the abolition of war less difficult? If men do not want to return to the dark ages in a new and more terrible form, the moral courage, the revival of reason to do away with total war must be found. And ethical and humanitarian considerations are powerfully aided by considerations of military necessity and by healthy anticipation of retaliation in a world where no group of states holds a monopoly of weapons of mass destruction. The time to revise the laws of war so as to eliminate the fear of total war is now. Later it may be too late. *Caveant consules!*

[1] See Josef L. Kunz, *Plus de lois de la guerre?*, in REVUE GÉNÉRALE DE DROIT INTERNATIONAL PUBLIC 22–57 (1934). This article has gained wide attention. See, e.g., LA PRADELLE, VONCKEN, and DEHOUSSE, LA RECONSTRUCTION DU DROIT DE LA GUERRE 87 (1936); Sidney H. Brown, *Les lois de la guerre selon la doctrine du droit international depuis 1914 (à propos de l'article de M. Jos. L. Kunz)*, in 16 REVUE INTERNATIONALE DE LA CROIX ROUGE 367–87 (1934). See also J. L. KUNZ, KRIEGSRECHT UND NEUTRALITÄTSRECHT (1935).

[2] Prior to Grotius "seul le droit de la guerre se développe sérieusement; il forme le noyeau du droit international."—ERNEST NYS, LE

DROIT DE LA GUERRE ET LES PRÉCURSEURS DE GROTIUS 7 (1882); "The most important as well as the first to spring into existence was that [part of international law] which occupied itself with the laws of war."—T. E. HOLLAND, STUDIES IN INTERNATIONAL LAW 45 (1898).

3 H. A. SMITH, THE LAW AND CUSTOM OF THE SEA 65 (1948).

4 By far the best work is still J. W. GARNER, INTERNATIONAL LAW AND THE WORLD WAR (1920).

5 SMITH, *op. cit.* at 67.

6 *The League of Nations and the Laws of War*, BRIT. YB. INT'L L. 109–24.

7 See B. H. LIDDELL HART, THE REVOLUTION IN WARFARE (1947).

8 U.N. Doc. No. A/CN.4/1 at 70 (1948).

9 See CHARLES G. FENWICK, INTERNATIONAL LAW (3rd ed. New York, 1948). This author never speaks of the laws of war, but only of the "laws of war" which, he feels, have no future. He puts them in his treatise "in the past tense."

10 PROCEEDINGS OF THE AMERICAN SOCIETY OF INTERNATIONAL LAW 32–33 (1948).

11 The paper and discussion are printed *ibid.*, at 102–14, 117–22, 123–26, 128 (1949).

12 In this sense also 2 P. GUGGENHEIM, LEHRBUCH DES VÖLKER-RECHTS 593 (1949).

13 2 OPPENHEIM-LAUTERPACHT, INTERNATIONAL LAW, para. 52j; at 149–50 (6th ed. 1947).

14 HISTORY OF THE UNITED NATIONS WAR CRIMES COMMISSION AND THE DEVELOPMENT OF THE LAWS OF WAR (London, 1948), p. 181; reviewed in 44 AM.J.INT'L L. 431 (1950).

15 See RENE CLEMENS, LE PROJET DE MONACO. LE DROIT DE LA GUERRE (1838); Beinhauer, *Monaco-Konferenz, Neugestaltung des Kriegsrechts*, 21 ZEITSCHRIFT FÜR VÖLKERRECHT No. 1 at 115–25.

16 See 3 CHARLES CENEY HYDE, INTERNATIONAL LAW CHIEFLY AS INTERPRETED AND APPLIED BY THE U.S. 1683–84 (2nd ed. 1945).

17 41 AM.J.INT'L L. 174, 218–19, 225–49, (1947).

18 All these rules of the Nuremburg Charter, the Nuremberg Judgment stated, "are merely declaratory of the existing laws of war."

19 HANS J. MORGENTHAU, POLITICS AMONG NATIONS 218 (1948); reviewed in 44 AM.J.INT'L L. 219 (1950).

20 See, e.g., A. C. Melen, *La Question des otages à la lumière du droit*, REVUE DE DROIT INTERNATIONAL (January-March, 1946); A. K. Kuhn, *The Execution of Hostages*, 36 AM.J.INT'L L. 271–74 (1942); E. Hammer & M. Salvin, *The Taking of Hostages in Theory and Practice*, 38 *ibid.* 20–33 (1944); VAN NISPEN TOT SEVENAER, LA PRISE D'OTAGES (1949), reviewed in 44 AM.J.INT'L L. 219 (1950).

21 See, e.g., L. P. Trainin, *Questions of Guerrilla Warfare in the Laws of War*, 40 AM.J.INT'L L. 534–62 (1946); L. Nurick & R. W. Barrett, *Legality of Guerrilla Forces under the Laws of War*, *ibid.* at 563–83.

22 See H. A. Smith, *Booty of War*, 23 BRIT.YB.INT'L L. 227–39 (1946); A. V. Freeman, *General Note on the Law of War Booty*, 40

AM.J.INT'L L. 795–803 (1946); W. G. Downey, Jr., *Captured Enemy Property*: *Booty of War and Seized Enemy Property*, 44 AM.J.INT'L L. 488 (1950).

[23] In the third edition of his treatise (p. 559) Professor Fenwick speaks of the "doubtful legality of the atomic bomb." The British expert J. M. Spaight declared himself against the legality of the atomic bomb (AIR POWER AND WAR RIGHTS 273–76 [3rd ed. 1947]).

[24] *Op. cit.* at 219.

[25] *Op. cit.* at 69.

[26] 3 HYDE, *op. cit.* at 1829–30.

[27] A MODERN LAW OF NATIONS 215 (1948).

[28] 41 AM.J.INT'L L. 303–5, 308 (1947).

[29] C. JOHN COLOMBOS, A TREATISE ON THE LAW OF PRIZE 28–29, 299–300 (3rd ed. 1949); reviewed in 44 AM.J.INT'L L. 788 (1950).

[30] *Lawless Maritime Warfare*, 18 FOREIGN AFFAIRS 424–41 (1940).

[31] *Op. cit.* at 287–88.

[32] J. W. GARNER, RECENT DEVELOPMENTS IN INTERNATIONAL LAW 356 (1925).

[33] THE RELATIVITY OF WAR AND PEACE 266 (1949); reviewed in 44 AM.J.INT'L L. 429 (1950).

[34] *Op. cit.* at 266–70.

[35] See, e.g., G. Vedovato: "Il diritto bellico . . . si trova actualmente in uno stato caotico; le guerre 1914–1918 e 1939–1945 hanno messo in discussione le basi stesse della sua existenza. Ricostruire, oggi, orientamenti e prassi della vita reale bellica è di eccezionale interesse."—DIRITTO INTERNAZIONALE BELLICO 7 1946).

[36] See the excellent study by ERNST H. FEILCHENFELD, THE INTERNATIONAL ECONOMIC LAW OF BELLIGERENT OCCUPATION (1942). The author starts from the fact that Articles XLII–LVI of the Hague Regulations, 1907, "have survived all historical changes since 1914" (p. 5).

[37] PROCEEDINGS OF THE AMERICAN SOCIETY OF INTERNATIONAL LAW 32–33 (1948).

[38] J. C. Mossop, *Hospital Ships in the Second World War*, 24 BRIT.YB.INT'L L. 398–406 (1947).

[39] A. C. RAJA GABAGLIA, GUERRA E DIREITO INTERNACIONAL (1949); reviewed in 44 AM.J.INT'L L. 800 (1950).

[40] "Codifying laws of war," letter to the editor, N.Y. Times, October 31, 1948, p. 8E.

[41] It is a mistake to assume that the acceptance of the concept of an international police force . . . with its subsequent abolition of the concept of 'war' in a legal sense, eliminates the necessity for the legal regulation of the rights and duties of those who are active participants in the struggle. We may cease to call it war, but there will be fighting and people will be killed."—P. C. JESSUP, A MODERN LAW OF NATIONS 188–89 (1948).

[42] See the full discussion in *ibid.* at 188–221.

43 The *action commune* under Article XVI of the League of Nations Covenant was always practically considered as war. In the committee charged to put the Covenant into harmony with the Pact of Paris (League of Nations Doc. No. C. 16.O.M.69.1930.V), it was clearly stated that in case of aggression or international police measures, "les normes du droit de la guerre conservent leur valeur, quel que soit le nom de telles opérations." This manuscript had been finished before the outbreak of the Korean war, which shows that military action, based on a resolution which the Security Council (because of the absence of the Soviet Union) was able to adopt, constitutes, for all practical purposes, war, and that the observation of the laws of war is essential.

44 "The fact of the existence of war is a matter unrelated to the question concerning the propriety of the mode by which it is brought about."—C. C. HYDE, INTERNATIONAL LAW 1693 (2nd ed. 1945). In conformity with the view which has remained unchallenged . . . Grotius lays down that the question of the justice or injustice of the war is irrelevant for the purpose of observing the rules of warfare as between the belligerents."—Lauterpacht, *The Grotian Tradition in International Law*, 28 BRIT.YB.INT'L L. 1-53 at 39 (1946). "A war thus undertaken (against the provisions of the Pact of Paris) would be illegal, but it would still be war regulated by the accepted rules of warefare."—2 OPPENHEIM-LAUTERPACHT, INTERNATIONAL LAW 150 (6th ed. 1940). "Whatever may be the cause of a war that has broken out . . . the same rules of international law are valid. . . . This is so even if the declaration of war is ipso facto a violation of international law. The rules of international law apply to war from whatever cause it originates."—*Ibid.* at 174. The last-quoted words were cited by the Maritime and Commercial Court of Copenhagen, in the decision of the *Adelaide Star case of October* 24, 1947 (1 Jus Gentium 117-25 1949). "Even an unlawful war will undoubtedly have the same legal effects as any other war."—Alf Ross, *Denmark's Legal Status during the Occupation, ibid.* at 6; see also *ibid.* at 8-9.

45 Jews and Arabs agreed that the laws of war should apply to their fighting. Egypt recognized this fighting as war, promulgated war legislation (5 REVUE EGYPTIENNE DE DROIT INTERNATIONAL 73-81 (1949), and established a prize court in Alexandria (*ibid.* at 28-33) which rendered prize decisions (*ibid.* at 139-51.

46 French constitution of October 13, 1946, art. VII: "La guerre ne peut être déclarée sans un vote de l'Assemblée Nationale et avec l'avis préalable du Conseil de la République."

47 See Hanson W. Baldwin's article in N.Y. Times, May 7, 1950, p. 5E.

48 See CURT WACHTEL, CHEMICAL WARFARE (1941); VANNEVAR BUSH, MODERN ARMS AND FREE MEN (1949).

49 See THEODOR ROSEBURY, PEACE OR PESTILENCE (REPORT ON BIOLOGICAL WARFARE (1949).

50 22 DEP'T STATE BÜLL. No. 555 at 269 (1950).

⁵¹ 3 HYDE, *op. cit.* at 1679.

⁵² 2 OPPENHEIM-LAUTERPACHT, *op. cit.* at 150, note 4.

⁵³ W. J. Bivens, in PROCEEDINGS OF THE AMERICAN SOCIETY OF IN-TERNATIONAL LAW 117–18 (1949).

⁵⁴ Thus already G. Schwarzenberger, *Problems of Peace and War* 37 TRANSACT. GROT. SOC'Y 1 (1942). The question is also put by H. A. SMITH, THE LAW AND CUSTOM OF THE SEA 71 (1948).

⁵⁵ PROCEEDINGS OF THE AMERICAN SOCIETY OF INTERNATIONAL LAW 124–26 (1949).

⁵⁶ Official notes can be found in DEP'T STATE BULL. No. 26 at 1205 (1947), and *ibid.* at 404 (October 30, 1949), as well as the brief article by William H. McCahon, 21 *ibid.* No. 531 at 339–40 (1949). The texts are not yet available here. No studies on those conventions have yet been published. The four new conventions are already fully worked in by A. C. RAJA GABAGLIA, *op. cit.*

⁵⁷ MAX HUBER, PRINCIPLES, TASKS AND PROBLEMS OF THE RED CROSS IN INTERNATIONAL LAW (1946).

⁵⁸ COMMISSION D'EXPERTS GOUVERNEMENTAUX POUR L'ÉTUDE DES CON-VENTIONS PROTEGEANT LES VICTIMES DE LA GUERRE. . . . RAPPORT SUR LES TRAVAUX (1947).

⁵⁹ PROJETS DE CONVENTIONS . . . XVIIᵉ CONFÉRENCE INTERNATION-ALE DE LA CROIX ROUGE (1948). See also volumes for 1948 and 1949 of the REVUE INTERNATIONALE DE LA CROIX ROUGE (Geneva).

⁶⁰ LES CONVENTIONES DE GENÈVE DU 12 AOÛT 1949, at 251 (1949).

⁶¹ H. Kelsen, *Will the Nuremberg Trial Constitute a Precedent,* 2 INT'L L. Q. No. 2 at 171 (1947).

⁶² Last year there was some information as to a private interna-tional conference on the revision of the laws of war at Buenos Aires. The Hague Conference of the International Bar Association, 1948, asked the Executive Council and the House of Deputies to take appro-priate steps to promote the setting up of a committee to study the adaptation of prize law to modern conditions and its unification (*ibid.* No. 4 at 638 [1948]49).

⁶³ N.Y. Times, August 9, 1948, p. 3.

⁶⁴ *Ibid., January* 3, 1950, p. 12.

⁶⁵ *Ibid.,* March 31, 1950, p. 22.

⁶⁶ Erich Hula, *The Revival of the Idea of Punitive War,* 21 THOUGHT No. 82 at 411, 434 (1946).

⁶⁷ W. B. Cowles in PROCEEDINGS OF THE AMERICAN SOCIETY OF INTERNATIONAL LAW 121 (1949).

⁶⁸ See H. W. Baldwin's article in N.Y. Times, Dec. 7, 1949, p. 14.

I

IT SEEMS that the development of the laws of war from the beginnings of our international law to the present day has completed a full circle. With the definitive decentralization of the medieval *communitas Christiana* and the coming into existence of the national sovereign state, wars appeared in which new methods for the conduct of war—armies of mercenaries on foot, invention of gunpowder—were combined with the deep ideological split between Catholics and Protestants. The wars of that time were conducted with the greatest cruelty and inhumanity, reaching their climax with the terrible Thirty Years' War, which may be called a total war. At that time, as today, the problem arose: Will the nations continue to conduct their wars in such a way? Will there be a permanent return to barbarism? For this reason the fathers of international law dedicated their primary attention to the laws of war; that is why Grotius, in protest against the practice of states in his time, appealed to the princes of Europe to observe the *temperamenta belli*. And indeed the wave toward barbarism was stopped. The laws of war in the modern sense were created, a tendency which reached a climax in the partial codification of the

laws of war in 1907. After 1914, however, a new retrogressive movement set in which reached its present climax
in the terrible conduct of World War II threatening a new
"advance to barbarism." [1] We have arrived where we
started, in the sixteenth century, at the threat of total,
lawless war, but this time with weapons which may ruin
all human civilization, and even threaten the survival of
mankind on this planet.

This writer in earlier studies [2] warning against the
neglect of the laws of war has given the reasons for this
retrogressive movement; he has emphasized that war has
not been abolished and that the laws of war remain an
important part of international law. He has shown that
the laws of war are today in a chaotic condition and that
their revision is an urgent necessity. He has shown the
fallacy of the tendency, so fashionable since 1920, to neglect
and to ignore the laws of war.

Fortunately, this complete neglect of the laws of war has
come to an end in recent years. The tendency to put the
laws of war "into the past tense" has largely disappeared.
The laws of war are again fully treated in recent treatises
on international law,[3] and appear on the agenda of learned
societies. Articles and monographs on the laws of war are,
in an increasing number, being published in all languages.
Colombos [4] fully treats the law of naval warfare. Very important treatises on the law of war have recently been
published by Lauterpacht,[5] Balladore Pallieri,[6] Stone,[7] and
Castrén.[8] Many of these writers agree that war has not
been abolished, that the laws of war are still a necessity,
and that, in their present chaotic condition, they urgently
need revision. As long as war has not been abolished,
writes Balladore Pallieri, it is much better for international law, being aware of this reality, to try at least to
discipline the conduct of war. Castrén, like this writer,

considers the negative attitude toward the subject since
1920 regrettable and puts emphasis on the urgent need
for objective scrutiny and development of the laws of war.
Stone calls the neglect of the laws of war since 1920 a
grave disservice to humanity.

The Institut de Droit International, which had not once
since 1920 treated a problem of the laws of war has
attacked the problem of their revision; a preliminary report [9] was presented at its session at Aix-en-Provence in
1954, and a fuller report is being prepared by Professor
François.

The United States and the United Kingdom are preparing new manuals of land warfare; in May, 1953, an
Anglo-America conference took place at Cambridge, England. [10] The United States has recently issued a new manual on naval warfare. When this writer, in December, 1953,
conducted a series of seminars on the law of naval warfare at the U. S. Naval War College at Newport, he was
greatly impressed by the strong and genuine desire of the
three hundred officers of higher rank of the U. S. Navy
to be told—to know what is the law of naval warfare
actually in force. UNESCO, at its seventh session at Paris
on September 30, 1952, adopted a Draft International Convention for the Protection of Monuments, Collections, and
Other Cultural Property in the event of armed conflict. The
United Nations for years has been discussing the problem
of atomic weapons and other weapons of mass destruction.
Nearly all the states of the world participated in the Geneva
diplomatic conference which produced the four new Geneva
conventions of August 12, 1949.[11] The latter have come into
force, and, at the end of 1954,[12] had received eight acces-
sions (including Japan and West Germany) and thirty-six
ratifications, including France and the Soviet Union; they
were ratified by the United States on July 6, 1955.[13] The

International Committee of the Red Cross is preparing new draft rules for the protection of the civilian population from the dangers of indiscriminate warfare.

II

Much of the present discussion on the laws of war [14] is dedicated to their revision. A first point relates to the *procedure* of such revision. Opinion is divided, apart from municipal legislation such as the enactment of new war manuals, between a unilateral statement by a certain group of states [15] or for certain military operations [16] and a general revision; as to the latter, we see proposals regarding official and private codification and revision. The failure of the League of Nations Conference on Codification of International Law at The Hague in 1930 has produced a strong tendency in favor of private codification by means of a "restatement." [17] Professor (now Judge) Lauterpacht,[18] on the other hand, strongly favors official codification by international treaties. "Unless," he writes, "the work of codification is thought of in terms of eventual acceptance by governments, it has little meaning." With this opinion this writer fully concurs. Scientific restatement at best has only persuasive authority, and is not legally binding. There can be no doubt that a revision of the laws of war must take the form of international treaties, signed and ratified so as to constitute legally binding rules.

Lauterpacht, writing on codification of international law in general, states that codification need not be conceived as universal codification whose *raison d'être* lies in acceptance by all governments. But, as far as the revision of the laws of war is concerned, the participation and ratification by the greatest possible number of states, and especially by *all* militarily important states, is essential. Phillips rightly insists that a revision of the laws of war is only meaningful if it can be honestly and unequivocally accepted by at least all the important states.

Certain fundamental principles must be observed in a treaty on the revision of the laws of war, apart from its acceptability to all the important states. In order to be acceptable to all the important states, such revision, while taking humanitarian interests into account to the highest possible degree, must at the same time be adapted to the necessities of war. Laws of war, to be accepted and to be applied in practice, must strike the correct and just balance between, on the one hand, the principles of humanity and chivalry and, on the other hand, military interests. The laws of war are in essence a reconciliation between these contradictory interests, just as the reconciliation between the contradictory interests of the belligerents and the neutrals is the essence of the law of neutrality. It is therefore likely that the revised laws of war will be stiffer than the rules of 1907. It will not be possible, for instance, to exclude aerial warfare. The fact that the drafters of the Hague Air Warfare Rules of 1923, which Phillips calls a "juridical fantasy," did not take military necessities sufficiently into account has prevented their acceptance by states. It is probable that the protection of the civilian population will have to be restricted. But taking military necessities into account does not at all mean the acceptance of all the inhuman excesses of the last great war. Military authorities stand particularly in favor of the laws of war. Many military experts have, for instance, voiced their conviction that indiscriminate aerial bombardment during World War II had no military value comparable to the expenses incurred, the efforts required, and the sufferings caused. Military experts are of opinion that the ruthless conduct of the last great war, rather than having broken the resistance of the enemy, strengthened the will

to resist and lengthened the war. Military experts know—
and this writer has not only studied the laws of war for
many years but has, as a front officer during World War
I gained the only real experience of the laws of war, not
in the armchair, but on the battlefield—that the laws of
war, however imbued with the spirit of humanity, are at
the same time a matter of military necessity. The revised
laws of war must have a realistic basis; on the other hand,
they must be far removed from the present trend toward
savage inhumanity and barbarian lawlessness.

Finally, the revised rules must be free from any ambiguity. Judge Max Huber has recently rightly insisted that
there is no part of international law where entire clarity and
precision are more necessary than in the laws of war.

While, therefore, a valuable revision of the laws of war
must be made by treaties, based on the above-mentioned
principles and ratified at least all militarily important
states, the *preparation* of such revision is a task of private scholars and associations. Lauterpacht, while insisting
on international treaties, also insists on the independence
of the codifying agency from governments. It is significant that the Report of the Three states that it cannot
be the task of the Institut de Droit International to proceed to a restatement of the laws of war, that the Institut
can only "déblayer le terrain," and can only examine certain principles which might serve as a starting point for
such revision. But the preparatory task includes not only
the examinations of these principles, which will be treated
in the next chapters, but also the enormous work of in-
vestigating and clarifying the present status of the laws
of war. For such task a revived Harvard Research in International Law, whose earlier restatements have been recognized everywhere as being of great value, would be
competent. This reactivated research could be charged, *inter alia*, with the preparation of the revision of the laws

of war by a body composed of the leading international lawyers of the whole world in this field.

III

In treating *substantive* problems of the revision of the laws of war, we start from the question: When do or should the laws of war apply? The answer was always: in times of war. But the definition of "war in the sense of international law" was uncertain and ambiguous. Today the situation is much clearer in this respect. Article II, paragraph 4, of the United Nations Charter contains the obligation of the members not resort to the use or threat of *force* in their international relations. The laws of war apply, therefore, in any situation of large-scale international fighting, whether or not it is called war, whether or not the fighting groups are states in the sense of international law. They often apply also in civil wars. This widest application of the laws of war is confirmed by the recent practice of states, in the fighting between the Arab states and the Jews (prior to the establishment of the State of Israel), in the war in Indo-China against the Viet-Minh, in the armed conflict in Korea. It is also specially sanctioned by the rules of the Geneva conventions of August 12, 1949, which make a minimum of these norms binding even in civil wars, apart from agreements and from the recognition of insurgents as a belligerent party.

While the applicability of the laws of war has thus been widely extended, new ideas have been voiced to the effect that the same laws of war should not be valid for all belligerents; the revised laws of war should be discriminatory. This new idea has appeared in two forms: The first form is the postulate that the laws of war should discriminate between the legal and the illegal belligerent. It has been positive international law since the time of

Grotius that the laws of war apply equally to just and unjust, legal and illegal wars. This principle was strongly reaffirmed after World War I by Rolin; [19] and recently by Hyde [20] and Lauterpacht.[21] Recently, however, the doctrine of different laws of war for the legal and the illegal belligerent has been defended by a number of writers, e.g., Yepes,[22] Scelle,[23] Quincy Wright,[24] and Lauterpacht.[25]

Quincy Wright believes that the laws of war are still important; but since, according to him, war has been outlawed, the international community stands toward the illegal belligerent in a relation analogous to that of the national state towards the rebels in a civil war. This analogy is self-defeating; for when the laws of war apply in a civil war, they apply equally and without discrimination to the troops of the government and to the troops of the rebels. The illegal belligerent has, according to Wright, no more powers than in time of peace. He has no rights as a belligerent occupant, no right to destroy foreign armed forces, no right to confiscate foreign property, no right to capture merchant vessels on the high seas. The illegal belligerent must pay reparations for all damages to life and property which have resulted from his military operations, whereas the legal belligerent owes only reparations for acts done in violation of the laws of war. He admits that the "humanitarian" laws of war are valid for the legal and illegal belligerent and that both have a right to punish individuals guilty of violation of such laws.

It is obvious that these statements are in clear contradiction with the present practice of states; nor can they have much practical value as proposals *de lege ferenda.* War has not been "abolished." The present primitive state of international law makes any analogy with an advanced municipal law futile. Even a more advanced international law, as a law will be very different from municipal law, which is essentially a law among individuals. Even in municipal law, situations arise where negotiations, as in the case of great strikes, or fighting, as in the case of civil wars, must be resorted to. There is, moreover, the military impossibility of such a distinction, which would seriously endanger the troops and the civilian population of the legal belligerent. Wright must admit that the proposed distinction can only be applied after the end of hostilities—but the laws of war apply primarily *durante bello*—and under the supposition that the illegal belligerent has been vanquished, a supposition which is not warranted by history.

Lauterpacht stated in 1952, contrary to his former writings, that the equal application of the laws of war to the legal and illegal belligerent can no longer be upheld, and, in 1953, made some specific proposals *de lege ferenda*. He says, for instance, that a peace treaty imposed by a victorious illegal belligerent has no juridical validity. But what about the Treaty of Moscow of 1940? He states that title by conquest has no juridical validity in favor of an illegal belligerent. Great Britain recognized *de jure* the illegal conquest of Ethiopia. Thirdly, he proposes that an illegal belligerent should assume all reparations for all damages he has caused by his conduct of an illegal war. Fourth, an illegal belligerent cannot derive rights from his illegal action; he derives no title and cannot transfer title to property acquired in connection with the conduct of war, as by requisitions, certain confiscations, or condemnations by a prize court. He fully recognizes that this is not a statement of the law actually in force, but only proposals *de lege ferenda*. He also recognizes that all these questions are of minor importance, that they all refer rather to the liquidation than to the conduct of war, and that they all necessarily depend on the final defeat of the illegal belligerent.

The overwhelming majority of recent writers on this topic reaffirm, like this writer, not only the validity of the equal application of the laws of war to all belligerents, but also the necessity—for practical reasons—that this non-discrimination should be also fundamental to the revision of those laws; see, for instance, Rousseau, Balladore Pallieri, Castrén, Schätzel,[26] Ford,[27] Alf Ross,[28] and Verdross,[29] as well as the recent practice of states and decisions of national and international courts.[30]

Lauterpacht himself fully recognizes in his study of 1953 that *durante bello* the laws of war must apply identically to the legal and to the illegal belligerent. The illegal belligerent during warfare has the same rights as the legal belligerent. Lauterpacht mentions particularly that the illegal belligerent also has all the rights of a belligerent occupant, e.g., to the obedience of the civilian population. He recognizes, as the Nuremberg Trials do, the untenability of the "logic" that an illegal belligerent has not a single belligerent right. It follows that even a vanquished illegal belligerent cannot be held guilty of war acts as such, but only of violations of the laws of war. With these statements we fully concur.

The Report of the Three of the Institut de Droit International again mentions the discriminatory character of the laws of war as a preliminary problem which must be solved before a real revision is undertaken. It is clear that the solution of this problem must be against such discriminatory character *durante bello*.

The second form of discrimination presently discussed in the literature stands for special laws of war in favor of the troops acting under a military sanction by the United Nations. Such military sanction no doubt constitutes a legal use of force; but it is certainly use of force in international relations. Early some voices were heard arguing that United Nations troops should not be bound by any laws of war. But Philip C. Jessup [31] has insisted with great energy that such troops must be bound by legal norms just as are police officers under municipal law. The present discussion turns only on the question whether there should be special laws of war in this case.

Quincy Wright[32] proposes to give to United Nations troops even more rights than the legal belligerent, although he recognizes that those rights must not be unlimited; for, he states, while even a legal belligerent fights primarily in the interest of a single state, an international military sanction has a higher dignity, as it represents the interests of the international community. Proposals to codify the laws of war for United Nations troops have been made several times. We have already mentioned Bivens' proposal. Professor Georges Scelle, as a member of the International Law Commission of the United Nations insisted—although unsucessfully—that a high priority should be given to the elaboration of a code of rules of war for the military forces employed in an international military action. Such a proposal, in the form of a "restatement," has recently been made again by Sir Arnold D. McNair.[33]

This writer is of opinion that these proposals neither state the law actually in force nor have much practical value. The first presupposition is that so-called collective security would normally function and lead to the speedy defeat of the aggressor. It is not necessary to go into details in order to show that this presupposition may not be fulfilled. Even in the armed conflict in Korea, there were no "forces of the United Nations engaged in pursuance of a decision of the Security Council";[34] these forces, as Baxter[35] correctly states, were "not in a strict legal sense, execution forces of the United Nations, because they were only, in consequence of a recommendation of the Security Council, created to be at the disposal of a Supreme Command of the United States. These military forces were neither controlled nor directed by the United Nations."

The second reason against special laws of war for United Nations forces is a military reason. The operation of laws of war presupposes uniformity and identity for all belligerents and full reciprocity. Lauterpacht[36] correctly states

that even in the case of a higher integration of the international community, including the effective legal capacity
of its organs to determine the fact of aggression and to
enforce the peace collectively, there will remain the necessity of regulating the conduct of hostilities, regardless of
whether such collective enforcement is described as war
or not. And he further states:

> Unless the force at the disposal of the international community
> is so overwhelming as to approach rapid police action permitting
> of no organized resistance, it is doubtful whether such special
> rules can differ appreciably from those governing the principal
> aspects of the relations of belligerents in an ordinary war.

With these statements we fully concur. The preliminary
problem of the discriminatory character of the revised laws
of war in this second form must therefore also be answered
negatively. To this negative solution Judge Max Huber [37]
recently lent his high authority, when he stated:

> It seems to me that this idea of discrimination must be totally
> avoided. For it would change nothing in the deplorable situation
> which hostilities, contrary to the regime of collective security,
> would constitute, but could only make them more atrocious. A
> minimum of humanity must be guaranteed even in hostilities con-
> trary to international law. If the law is violated, at least the
> spirit of humanity should not be sacrificed.

IV

The preliminary problems dealt with in the preceding
section turn on the discriminatory character of the revised
laws of war. Other preliminary proposals would make the
laws of war equally applicable to all belligerents, but en-
visage either different laws of war applicable to different
kinds of wars, or a distinction within the laws of war.
The first idea, which needs only to be mentioned briefly,

is contained in the question [38] whether the laws of war should not distinguish between "small" and "big" wars, between limited wars and world or total wars. It is clear that international law has hitherto made no such distinction. It is true that many authors writing today on the laws of war think primarily in terms of a third world war, whereas there have been, and may also be, small wars. But the laws of war must be the same for all wars.

Much more important is the other preliminary problem discussed today, namely, the distinction within the laws of war between the so-called humanitarian law and the law for the conduct (methods and weapons) of war. If this distinction is meant especially in the sense that the "Geneva" laws of war should be upheld and developed whereas the "Hague" laws of war should be abandoned, this preliminary problem goes to the very essence of the laws of war and their revision and, therefore, requires a fuller discussion.

There is universal agreement that the so-called humanitarian principles of the laws of war remain valid and must be developed; even those who, as Nicolas Politis, took an absolutely negative stand as far as the laws of war are concerned. Today it is also agreed that this part of the laws of war is apt to be revised. And, indeed, new positive law has been created in this field by the Geneva conventions of August 12, 1949. But doubts are voiced as to whether the laws of war dealing with the actual conduct of war—methods and weapons—have any value at this juncture of history and whether there is any chance for their revision. It is sometimes said [39] that these rules, contrary to the humanitarian norms, are not compatible with total war. But the answer is that the real problem is whether total war is compatible with the survival of civilization or even with the survival of mankind. The most serious argument *contra* is the ineffectiveness [40] of rules concerning the actual conduct of war. There is no doubt that a revision of this part of the laws of war presents great difficulties, particularly today; we will come back to this problem in the last section. Yet rules for the actual conduct of war are absolutely necessary, even in time of peace, because they correspond not only to humanitarian sentiments but to military necessity; they are a requisite pre-condition for the punishment of war crimes, and are needed today to guarantee the survival of civilization and even, perhaps, the physical survival of humanity.

It seems to us, furthermore, that it is hardly possible to draw distinctions in the laws of war between the humanitarian rules and those regulating the actual conduct of war. First of all, it must be emphasized that the whole law of war, including the norms regulating its actual conduct, is humanitarian in character; it is in the truest sense a part of the law for the protection of human rights. On the other hand, the *whole* law of war, including the humanitarian rules, also corresponds to military necessity.

Second, it is obvious that a complete neglect of the law regulating the actual conduct of war endangers the whole so-called humanitarian law and must lead to its ineffectiveness. "The provisions, or some of the provisions of the four Geneva Conventions," writes Lauterpacht [41] in one of his tortured phrases, "*may*—and that is sufficient—be capable of application even if humanity is subjected to the ordeal of atomic warfare and even if the conduct of war should again be characterized by lawlessness rather than by scrupulous observance of the law." But the answer is that even this "may" is doubtful and in any case insufficient. The International Committee of the Red Cross years ago warned against the disastrous effects of lawless warfare upon the whole humanitarian law.

Third, it is not possible to draw a clear dividing line between the humanitarian rules and the norms governing the actual conduct of war. Nothing is more instructive in this sense than the Geneva conventions of 1949.[42] The Geneva Diplomatic Conference emphasized again and again its lack of competence as to the laws concerning the actual conduct of war; many rules of the conventions were inspired by experience in the conduct of World War II and show the impression of the atrocities perpetrated during that war and the influence of modern conditions of warfare, without taking any stand as to their legality. The influence of total war—the vanishing dividing line between armed forces and civilian population—can be seen in a number of principles of the Geneva conventions. On the other hand, there are nevertheless many norms which deeply influence the law concerning the actual conduct of war: the prohibition of reprisals against protected persons; the prohibition against taking hostages; the prohibition of individual or mass forcible transfer, as well as deportations of protected persons from occupied territory regardless of the motive; prisoner-of-war status for members of organized resistance movements under certain conditions, even in occupied territory. There can be no doubt that these norms have the most far-reaching influence on the law of belligerent occupation, an important part of the rules governing warfare.

These second and third considerations have recently been strongly emphasized. Max Huber writes:

The present laws of war present considerable and very dangerous lacunae. If this abyss is not filled out and if one continues to exploit for warlike purposes the available technical possibilities, as, unfortunately has been the case since 1907, the value and very existence of all that remains of the laws of war and, even of the law of nations in general, will become problematical.[43]

Spaight writes:

The historians of the future will be puzzled by or will wax cynical about, the conclusion of the new Geneva Conventions in

1949, and the failure of the Powers who agreed to them to do anything to regulate also those methods of war which, if continued, will make the humanitarian Conventions read like hypocritical nonsense.[44]

The second and third considerations have recently been strongly stressed by the International Committee of the Red Cross in its elaboration of new rules for the protection of the civilian population. Whereas the first three Geneva conventions are revisions, the fourth convention, relative to the protection of the civilian population, creates new international law. This fourth convention applies only in Articles XIII to XXVI to the *whole* population of the countries in conflict. Articles XXXV to XLVI apply only to protected persons in the territory of a party to the conflict; articles XLVII-XLVIII apply only to protected persons in occupied territories; articles XXVII-XXXIV are common to both groups of persons. This convention does not deal with the methods and weapons of warfare. Thus no convention concerning the protection of the whole civilian population in all circumstances, nor a convention concerning protection against aerial bombardment, was enacted. The "general protection" of the civilian population found no expression in rules, but only in the recommendation of "sanitary and security zones," which is not legally binding.

The second and third considerations, discussed above, have now forced the International Committee of the Red Cross to elaborate new proposals which tend toward a new creation of the whole laws of war with special reference to the protection of the civilian population.[45] In the introduction to the Draft Rules [46] the International Committee begins by saying: "The whole world is longing for peace, but living in fear of war." "The developments in the means of war would, if they were to continue completely unchecked, make any new conflict a catastrophe out of all proportion to the objects which those responsible for start-

ing it wish to attain," and "there would be a danger that
all of the Geneva Conventions, however complete they may
be, might remain inoperative, if the belligerents were not
limited in any way in their choice of methods and weapons
of war." "Scientific progress leads to nothing but ruin and
death, if it is not controlled by reason. It is therefore war
which must give way to the demands of humanity." For this
reason the committee had to go beyond the "Geneva" into
the "Hague" laws of war. The field covered by the Draft
Rules is rather different from that covered by the Geneva
conventions.

The idea of the committe was to "re-affirm permanent
principles," to establish "ultimate barriers beyond which
armed conflicts would end in extermination pure and
simple," but to "reaffirm them in closer conformity with
present-day facts." The committee convoked a commission
of experts, consisting of fifteen persons,[47] which met at
Geneva from April 6 to 13, 1954.[48] The experts confirmed
that certain basic principles of the laws of war established
before aviation existed, such as those prohibiting direct
attack on noncombatants or the causing of unnecessary
harm, were still in force. They agreed that a code of rules
for aerial warfare was most needed; they recognized also
that military necessities must in certain cases give way to
those of humanity. Finally, they agreed that attempts to
produce a code of rules would be all the more effective if
states would agree to renounce the use of weapons of mass
destruction. After these preparations, the committee has
worked out Draft Rules consisting of five "general principles" and sixteen articles containing rules of application.
While it is not possible here to give a full analysis of all the
draft rules proposed, some fundamental principles should
be emphasized: acts of violence are only justified if their
object is the destruction, or placing out of action, of the
enemy armed forces, whereas acts *directed* against the

civilian population are prohibited. The Draft Rules contain proposals as to the concept of the "civilian population" and propose a list of "military objectives." The principle of *proportionality* is strongly emphasized. The use of weapons which, even if directed against the enemy armed forces, would, by their nature or effect, cause considerable losses among the civilian population, is excluded. These principles, imposing imperative limits determined in accordance with the requirements of humanity to the necessities of war, are applicable under all circumstances, whatever the means or weapons employed. Hence, for instance, not only machine-gunning of civilians at point-blank range from aircraft, but also bombardments by rockets and guided missiles should be prohibited. No fundamental difference between the persons whom a member of the armed forces is authorized to attack on the ground and those he is authorized to attack from the air can be recognized. International bombardment of civilian populations, as such, is forbidden; attacks for the terrorization of the civilian population are prohibited. A recognized military objective is an objective the military importance of which in times of armed conflict is generally acknowledged; an annex enumerates the following categories: armed forces, their equipment, communications, and stores; industries engaged in the production of arms and military supplies, but not in the manufacture of food products; installations, positions, or constructions occupied by the armed forces, as well as combat objectives; stores of arms or military supplies; airfields and naval base installations; railways, roads, and canals of definitive military importance or of a strategic character; plants of broadcasting and television stations; telephone and telegraph exchanges of definite military importance; industries concerned with national defense and the plants of power-producing centers feeding them; experimental and scientific research installations the nature or purpose of which is clearly military. Indiscriminate bombing from the air is prohibited; weapons of unpredictable and uncontrolled effects are forbidden, especially the use of asphyxiating, poisonous, or other gases, bacteriological methods of warfare, and all similar liquids, as well as the use of substances which, when disseminated by the deflagration of a projectile or by any other means, are dangerous to human beings by reason of their radioactivity or other similar effect.

The Draft Rules are now open for study, discussion, and improvement; they will be presented to the next International Red Cross Conference which will meet at New Delhi in October, 1956. After that the time may have come for the convocation of a new diplomatic conference to prepare a new international convention.

V

Discussion of the "preliminary problems" of the revision of the laws of war seems to have led to the following conclusions: The revised laws of war must apply in all cases of armed international conflict, and even in civil wars; they must apply *durante bello* equally to the legal and the illegal belligerent, to the "aggressor" and to United Nations troops engaged in an international military action; they must apply to all wars, small or big; they must embrace, not only the humanitarian rules, but also those regulating the actual conduct of war—methods and weapons. As to the procedure for the revision of the laws of war, it must be done ultimately by international treaties, although the preparation of this revision is a task for the science of international law.

It seems to this writer that, while the so-called preliminary problems of revising the laws of war are resolved, the principal task is a correct investigation as to what are the laws of war actually in force. For their revision does not start *ab nihilo,* but from a development which is at least three centuries old. In this respect a primary problem arises: Is it convenient or is it even possible to attack the problem of revising the laws of war without at the same time doing something about the law of neutrality? True, while the law of neutrality presupposes war, the laws of war can apply even if there were no law of neutrality. In fact, the law of neutrality was developed relatively late. It could, therefore, be argued that the law of neutrality should be left alone in order to concentrate fully on revision of the laws of war. But since the law of neutrality, as partially codified in 1907, is intricately linked with the laws of war, it seems difficult to revise the latter without at the same time giving some attention to the law of neutrality, especially since that law is actually in an even more chaotic condition than the laws of war.

Whereas, prior to 1920, neutrality was recognized as a benevolent institution, serving to limit the conduct of war and to localize wars, a very different estimate of neutrality prevailed at the time of the foundation of the League of Nations and the conclusion of the Kellogg Pact. There were many writers who told us that the law of neutrality, "being incompatible with the League of Nations Covenant," had been abolished like the laws of war, and neutrality was looked upon as something immoral, if not criminal. Naturally these ideas were completely contradictory to the law and practice of states. There were many strictly neutral states in the wars between 1920 and 1930 and there was a strong movement toward neutrality after 1930 up to the first part of World War II. It was again asserted, in connection with the United Nations Charter, that the last traces of neutrality had disappeared. Yet the problem of neutrality remains in law, in the practice of states, and in politics. "The law of neutrality," writes Stone,[49] "is not visibly more obsolete in the mid-twentieth century than it was in the ill-fated League of Nations." Neutrality is far from dead, and the problem of neutrality is far from disappearing.[50] It is clear that the neutrality of certain states like Ireland or Sweden during World War II was not illegal. Even if the United Nations Charter worked normally, there are possibilities of neutrality, as, e.g., in the case of a legal war under Article LI before the Security Council has reached a decision. Much more important, all of Chapter VII of the Charter is practically dead; there is no definition of aggression; there are no treaties concluded under Article XLIII; the Security Council is paralyzed by the veto in a world split by an abyss. Only decisions of the Security Council under Article XXXIX, which the members under Article XXV are bound to accept and to apply, exclude neutrality. Even recommendations of the Security Council under Article XXXIX are not legally binding and do not absolutely exclude neutrality. This was seen in the armed conflict in Korea where there were commissions of "Neutrals," composed, apart from Switzerland, entirely of members of the United Nations. Equally, recommendations by the General Assembly under the "Uniting for Peace" resolution—and it is doubtful whether such recommendations, in the present world situation, could be made—are not legally binding and do not absolutely exclude neutrality. The Geneva Conventions of 1949 definitely presuppose neutrality, and it holds a very important place in these conventions.[51] Switzerland has remained, Austria has become, a permanently neutral state. The loss of the power of the United Nations to enforce peace, and the deep split between the free and the communistic worlds have, as Verdross [52] recently stated, led to a re-evaluation of neutrality, in contrast to the attitude prevailing after 1920. Neutrality, writes Castrén, remains a subject of importance. The terrible power of new weapons of mass destruction has produced a widespread longing for neutrality.

On the other hand, there can be no doubt that the law of neutrality has entered a new phase of its development since 1920, that there is a contemporary crisis of neutrality, that the coming of general international organizations and the ideas, although not realized, of the abolition of war and of collective security have had a profound influence on the classic law of neutrality. Violations of the law of neutrality by belligerent states, retreat of neutrals by renunciation of rights, and violation of neutral duties in the form of so-called non-belligerency—a purely political, not a legal concept—have brought about a chaotic condition, have produced a constant oscillation between a pretended abolition and a strong reaffirmation of neutrality, and have rendered the law of neutrality at present one of the most uncertain parts of international law.

Wishful thinkers, closing their eyes to the non-existence of collective security in the United Nations, are therefore strongly inclined to leave the subject in this uncertainty which at the same time can help political expediency, since it permits, according to political motives, insistence upon the law of neutrality at one time and invocation of its non-existence at another time. That is the reason why there is much more opposition to the revision of the law of neutrality than to the revision of the laws of war. Lauterpacht [53] has stated the consequences of the oscillation mentioned in these words:

> The traditional law of neutrality has undergone a profound change. It may be too early to translate that change into precise legal rules. It is probably too late . . . to attempt to give more precision and vitality to the old law of neutrality.

Hence:

> From a wider point of view there may be weighty objection to a renewed attempt at codification of the law of neutrality, on the traditional basis of the absolute equality of the belligerents.

The Report of the Three of the Institut de Droit International—and this report clearly shows the hand of Lauterpacht—touches the law of neutrality only in one short sentence in the form of a question and knows no more neutrals at all, but only "neutrals." Stone,[54] fully recognizing the contemporary crisis of neutrality, is much more realistic:

> Neutrality and its traditional rules are destined for a period of travail, in which these rules remain legally relevant, if often merely as a measure of the deviation of practice. . . . But the law of neutrality will escape the effort to displace it by a modern version of the just war doctrine: neutrality and its rules are not likely to disappear or to be replaced.

As the law of neutrality remains of great importance, a clear statement and revision of the law are also important. Modern treatises fully deal with it. A restatement of the law actually in force must examine "qualified" neutrality, must examine whether and, if so, in what way the liberty of action of neutrals and their duties under the regime of classic neutrality are affected by their membership in the United Nations. But the classic law of neutrality is also of importance in the case of non-members of the United Nations, in the case of permanently neutral states such as Switzerland and Austria, and, moreover, in cases where the Security Council does not or cannot make a decision under Article XXXIX. It is this latter, certainly very possible, eventuality which leads Colombos[55] to state that the discussion of classic neutrality is also of practical interest, as in such case "the British Commonwealth and the United States may well decide to maintain a strict neutrality in the traditional sense of the doctrine." As the law of neutrality is so closely connected with the laws of war in the air, on land, and especially as far as concerns contraband, blockade, and unneutral service, which embrace the totality of economic relations between neutrals and belligerents, Max

Huber [56] considers it advisable to include the revision of
the law of neutrality in the revision of the laws of war.

VI

The practice of states and the overwhelming majority of
writers are agreed that international fighting does and may
take place and that, therefore, the laws of war continue to
be important. On the other hand, there is also agreement
that the actual laws of war are inadequate. The U. S. Military Tribunal in the I. G. Farben trial stated:

> It must be admitted that there exist many areas of grave un-
> certainty concerning the laws and customs of war. Technical
> advances in weapons and tactics used may have made obsolete,
> in some respects, or may have rendered inapplicable, some of the
> provisions of the Hague Regulations, having to do with the
> actual conduct of hostilities.

Castrén [57] admits that "only a few of the laws of war and
neutrality now in force are suited to present-day conditions,
and belligerents do not pay much regard to them."

It follows that a revision of the laws of war—land, air,
naval, economic, psychological warfare—is urgently necessary. The urgent necessity, which this writer has insisted
upon, is now upheld by most writers; Max Huber emphasizes this necessity to the utmost; the Commission of Experts of the International Committee of the Red Cross
agreed; the new Draft Rules take this urgent necessity as
their starting point. But the preliminary task of the revision
is an objective, scientific, and full investigation as to what
the laws of war actually are. Here the jurist has to function
as a jurist *de lege lata;* he has to find the law as it is without deforming it, regardless of whether he likes it or not.
Only such objective statement can be the basis from which
the jurist and others can operate *de lege ferenda.* This
investigation has not yet been made. The laws of war have

not yet been fully studied in their operation during World
War I, even less so for World War II and the period since
1945. An enormous body of material, hitherto hardly
touched and certainly not yet scientifically scrutinized, is
awaiting the investigator: the practice of states during
and since the two great wars, the instructions of the high
commands, national, international, and prize-court decisions,
diplomatic negotiations, proceedings of the United Nations,
of regional organizations, treaties, attitudes of states at
diplomatic conferences, and scrutiny of the Geneva Conventions of 1949 and many other documents. The question is
to determine, objectively and equally far removed from
wishful thinking and from prejudiced proposals *de lege
ferenda*, to what extent the traditional law is still binding.
As Max Huber [58] states, it is necessary to determine the
degree of validity of the Hague Conventions: Which states
are actually bound by them? This question is of particular
importance, because of the *si omnes* clause; for the same
reason it is necessary to determine how far the content of
these conventions is binding as customary general international law. It is necessary to determine whether certain
norms, even if still valid, are considered as obsolete or as
inapplicable because of total war and of new weapons of
mass destruction. Max Huber himself states that "the great
question is whether it is possible to return to the concepts
of former times," and he bluntly asks: Is it now the law
that terrorization pure and simple is allowed?

The most serious problem is to investigate whether violations of the laws of war constitute merely violations or
are, at the best, justifiable as reprisals, or whether, by
revolutionary procedure, they have created new law. It is
still more important to inquire whether the fundamental
principles underlying the whole law of war are still in force.

There can be no doubt that "the laws of war were regularly and on a mass scale violated by all the belligerents,
in the Second World War." [59] But some writers take the

comfortable although hardly tenable stand that there were violations only by the enemy, whereas "British and U. S. practice corresponded with previous practice, subject to the modifications which changes in modern warfare have rendered necessary"; they were only "adaptations of some of the principles which have been rendered necessary by the modern conditions of war at sea, but which have never infringed the laws of humanity and the basic rules of international law." [60] Hence, Colombos stands against the idea that the laws of war were exploded during the two great wars. He insists that war must be waged in accordance with humanitarian principles and that it is necessary to conform belligerent rights with the rules of neutrality. Hence his stand against unrestricted submarine warfare and in favor of the continuing validity of the London Protocol of 1936. On the other hand, revision of the laws of war at sea will have to adopt the new "adaptations": belligerent right of visit and search in port, use of the economic weapon against the finances and trade of the enemy, establishment of long-distance blockades, defensively armed merchant vessels, which all are now in accord with "accepted principles of the law of nations." Opinions are by no means unanimous. According to Castrén,[61] for example, "violation of existing rules does not create new ones and the importance of changed conditions has been widely exaggerated." He agrees with Colombos that the London Protocol of 1936 is today actually in force and that unrestricted submarine warfare—a violation of the law of humanity, of neutrality, and of the freedom of the high seas—is strictly illegal.[62] But, according to him, the arming of merchant vessels even for defensive purposes ought not to be allowed, and the establishment of war zones on the high seas is illegal *de lege lata* and *de lege ferenda*.[63] The idea that the long-distance blockade may be a revolutionary creation of new law has also been hinted at by Stone.[64]

Lauterpacht also, in his seventh edition (1952) of Oppenheim's second volume, starts like Colombos from the idea that "the Second World War witnessed war crimes on a scale, unprecedented in history, on the part of Germany, and, to a lesser part, of some of her Allies," and bases his analysis of the new developments as to the rules of war "to a considerable extent on the record of the violations of the laws of war by Germany and her allies, and on the decisions of the various war crime tribunals." [65] Hence, he considered unrestricted submarine warfare by Germany— the "American practice" is only mentioned in a footnote —as illegal "in disregard of the London Protocol of 1936." [66] But even here he doubts whether atomic bombing can be considered as illegal in law, and expresses a suspicion that the dividing line between combatants and noncombatants has ceased to exist. In an extremely curious sentence [67] he justifies, in 1952, atomic bombing of Germany during World War II under a hypothesis which has not risen, at a time when it was notorious that the first atomic bombs had been dropped on Japan. But in his study published in 1953,[68] Lauterpacht goes much farther. He states "that it may be unprofitable to inquire whether the practice of aerial bombing [at the end of World War II] was in accordance with international law." He comes to the conclusion that in the matter of aerial bombardment and atomic warfare

> there is little that legal principle as deduced from generally acknowledged law and practice can supply as a reason for prohibiting or drastically limiting the use of these instruments of war.

He denies not only that there is any law in force but teaches also that "probably there are at present no overriding, universally or generally agreed, juridical principles of the laws of war." He states that the "continental doctrine" has not been accepted in Anglo-American countries. But such a statement, pure and simple, is misleading.[69] The true difference between the continental and the Anglo-American doctrine concerns only economic warfare; but with regard to the principle that *military* acts are not allowed to be *directed* against the civilian population, both doctrines are identical. "All members of the enemy," wrote Wheaton, "may be lawfully treated as enemies in a public war, but it does *not* follow that all these enemies may be lawfully treated alike." That "the continental doctrine [in *this* sense] is now a relic of the past," that total war has reduced the distinction between armed forces and the civilian population [70] "to a hollow phrase," is, to say the least, certainly exaggerated. The equally pessimistic Phillips [71] also speaks of the functionally non-existent distinction between combatants and non-combatants."

According to Lauterpacht the only principle which remains unchallenged is that the civilian population must not be made the object of attack unrelated to military operations and directed exclusively against them; bombing for mere purposes of terrorization is equally unlawful. But he must admit that the practical importance of this exception is of limited value. The fact that at the end of World War II the protection of the civilian population became largely nominal, is, according to him, "*not* due merely to reciprocal adoption of reprisals." He considers that the legality of the atomic weapon "is not capable of a categorical answer." As to unrestricted submarine warfare "the problem involved is deeper than that raised by the arming of merchant vessels and by the interplay of the operations of reprisals. It touches upon the reality of any solution grounded *previously* in the distinction between combatants and non-combatants." Hence the Germans with their "illegal practice" are now the creators of the new law? Whereas he recorded in 1952 that the Nuremberg Tribunal upheld the

validity of the London Protocol of 1936, he now writes that
"it has remained a dead letter." But he who takes such a
"realistic" attitude would also have to know that Chapter
VII of the United Nations Charter has remained a dead
letter. He accepts total war. "The possibility must be envisaged that total war has *irrevocably* removed the foundation of a substantial part of this branch of the law"
(contraband, blockade) and that "juristic—or even political
—efforts to give it a new lease of life may be in vain."

Naturally, after having made *tabula rasa* not only of the
laws of war, but also of the underlying fundamental principles, there is nothing to revise:

> The law on the subject must be shaped—so far as it can be
> shaped at all—by reference not to existing law, but to more
> compelling considerations of humanity, of the survival of civil-
> ization, and of the sanctity of the individual human being.

Exactly in the same pessimistic sense is the Report of the
Three, which tells us that it is not a question simply of
adapting general and universally recognized principles to
new conditions, but that one must look for a wholly new
system of rules. It must, particularly, be established to
what extent the humanitarian principles will be able to
continue to limit the rights of belligerents.

Fortunately, this gloomy view is not shared by the majority of writers, nor does it find expression in the present new
law or in the present practice of states. The Nuremberg
Military Tribunal laid down that "the rules of land warfare
as expressed in the Hague Convention were recognized by
all civilized nations and were regarded as being declaratory
of the laws and customs of war." Schätzel [72] states that
those who say that the Hague Rules are no longer valid
have the burden of proving it; he refers to the whole literature, to the practice of states during World War II invoking

this law, to the War Crimes Trials, to the armed conflict in
Korea. Verdross [73] insists on the validity of the Hague law,
on the continued validity of the fundamental underlying
principles: military acts of war must be aimed directly
only against combatants and military objectives; all means
of war are forbidden which cause superfluous suffering;
perfidy is prohibited. Also in air warfare the *armed* enemy
alone is a legitimate target of acts of combat. Hence, a
direct bombardment of noncombatants and of private houses
is contrary to international law. The use of guided missiles,
which *cannot* be directed against *military* objectives is contrary to international law. The validity of these norms,
Verdross writes, cannot be shaken by the circumstances
that they were violated in World War II by all belligerents
because these measures violate fundamental principles of
the laws of war. Ford [74] emphasizes the importance of the
distinction between armed forces and civilian population
which, even if gradually blurred, may not, in spite of total
and ruthless warfare, simply be dropped. In the Geneva
conventions the states have recognized that certain norms
are only "complementary to Hague Convention IV." These
Geneva conventions of 1949 presuppose the validity of the
Hague conventions and operate within their framework.
The rule of Article XXII of the Fourth Hague Convention
that the right of belligerents to adopt measures for injuring
the enemy is *not* unlimited is still the law. It is still the law
that

> in cases not included in these Regulations the inhabitants and
> the belligerents remain under the protection and the rule of the
> priciple of the law of nations, as they result from the usages
> established among civilized peoples, from the laws of human-
> ity, and the dictates of the public conscience.

There *is* still some law of war. That is why the new Draft
Rules of the International Committee of the Red Cross state

that "they are *not* embarking completely on virgin territory," that the prohibition of acts of violence against the civilian population is "firmly established in international law," and that the experts, as shown in the fourth chapter, have agreed on the continued validity of certain basic principles of the laws of war. Hence the Draft Rules have "to reaffirm the law and make it more precise, but *not* to create it entirely." For this reason Max Huber [75] emphasizes the necessity of revising particularly the Fourth Hague Convention. Much is to be revised, e.g., the whole law of belligerent occupation which Stone has called a "twilight-zone," and many other norms; the *si omnes* clauses have to be deleted; first of all, establishment of the basic principles of the distinction between armed forces and civilian population and re-establishment of the fundamental notion of the military objective are necessary. The prohibition of "armes aveugles," he states, is a necessity.

This brings us to the problem of modern weapons.[76] It is an interesting parallelism that after each world war there was an attempt to prohibit by treaty that new weapon which seemed to be the most dangerous one: gas warfare after the first, atomic warfare [77] after the second. As to the latter, its legality *de lege lata* was hardly discussed; only Spaight [78] came out against its legality. The reason for this silence seems to be the fact that atomic bombs were first used by the United States; most international lawyers condemned the V_1 and V_2 rockets used by Germany as illegal, because they could be directed against specified military objectives. Hence, the problem of atomic warfare was from the beginning mostly studied *de lege ferenda*. But all attempts to prohibit atomic and hydrogen warfare have hitherto remained unsuccessful. The reasons are clear: (1) At the time of the American monopoly of atom bombs, the Baruch Plan, offered by the United States, was rejected by the Soviet Union, which insisted on previous prohibition and was vague on inspection and control, emphasizing the role of the U. N. Security Council, where the veto applies. (2) Later, when the Soviet Union had atomic and hydrogen weapons, her policy remained the same, a policy fully unacceptable to the United States. (3) At the present time, somewhat like an atomic and hydrogen stalemate between East and West has been reached. (4) The necessity of defending the free world has led to the well-founded fear that a renunciation of modern weapons in which we are superior, without a real guarantee, may lead to an inferior position in view of the vast manpower and conventional weapons of the Communist world. (5) Finally, even on our side doubts have been voiced whether absolutely reliable international inspection and control are today—as distinguished from the time of the presentation of the Baruch Plan—technically possible.

Vast experimental tests are going on on both sides; whole "families" of atomic and hydrogen weapons, both for strategic and tactical use, are being developed. The destructive power of hydrogen bombs is continuously increased and ranges in megatons. Added to that is an armaments race in guided missiles with atomic or hydrogen war-heads anticipated for the future, finally to lead to the Inter-Continental Ballistic Missile, sometimes referred to as the "ultimate weapon." NATO has declared it will rely for defense on atomic weapons in case of aggression. The immense danger of large-scale atomic and hydrogen warfare must by now be clear to everybody. It is not necessary to be an expert in nuclear physics in order to understand what we have been told officially about the dangers of radio-active fallout. We know from Admiral Strauss, chairman of the U. S. Atomic Energy Commission, that one large and well-placed hydrogen bomb might destroy or seriously cripple even the biggest city. It is the realization on all sides of this immense danger which led to the tacit understanding at the

Geneva Summit Conference that a hydrogen war would be a tremendous disaster for everybody that must not be permitted to occur. In his Christmas message of 1955,[79] the Pope proposed to the world a three-point program of putting a check on experimentation in nuclear weapons, a convention renouncing the use of these weapons, and the subjection of all states to an effective control; but the Pope made it crystal clear that all three proposals form one whole and that a mere adoption of only the first two proposals cannot be considered; which corresponds exactly to the attitude taken by the United States.

In view of the reasons given, it seems hardly possible that a prohibition of nuclear weapons can be achieved in the forseeable future. The present precarious peace and security are only, in the words of Field Marshal Viscount Montgomery, a "Pax Atomica," i.e., rather a consequence of the atomic deadlock between East and West. It is, in the words of Mr. Richard Sandler, Swedish representative at the United Nations,[80] "only security guranteed by the balance of terror." That is why he proposed, since control of nuclear weapons cannot be realized, to adjourn all atomic disarmament, perhaps indefinitely. This situation is fully recognized by the new Draft Rules proposed by the International Committee of the Red Cross. They do not propose to prohibit nuclear weapons, but propose, from the point of view of protection of the civilian population against indiscriminate warfare, principles and rules constituting imperative barriers in the conduct of war, whatever the weapons or means employed.

The Swedish representative at the United Nations proposed, in view of the hopelessness of atomic disarmament, that the United Nations take up the prohibition of chemical and bacteriological warfare. While attention, as far as weapons of mass destruction are concerned, is now mostly concentrated on nuclear weapons, it must be borne

in mind that other and perhaps more terrible weapons
of mass destruction in the fields of chemical, bacteriological, and biological warfare [81] are being tremendously per-
fected. There is, indeed, the Geneva Protocol of 1925
prohibiting gas and bacteriological warfare.[82] It is also
true that this prohibition was violated only once—by Italy
in the war against Ethiopia—and was violated by no belligerent during World War II. But it has been ratified by
Japan and the United States, and the latter recently declined to ratify it, considering it as obsolete, since it contains nothing about international inspection and control.
The American secretary of the army recently approved a
report [83] made by a committee of civilians urging the development of a complete family of chemical, biological, and
radiological weapons for actual use if necessary. Hence
the Geneva Protocol of 1925 also stands in need of revision.

Even a pessimistic writer like Phillips [84] is not wholly
against revision of the laws of war. Lauterpacht also recognized certain fields where revision is possible on the
basis of existing law. We have emphasized that a revision
of the whole traditional law of war must be started from
an investigation of the validity of present rules and underlying principles. But there are further fields for revision in the traditional as well as in the new law of war.

First, there are many problems of existing law which
need revision and clarification, apart from nearly every
aspect of the law of belligerent occupation: non-hostile
relations (flag of truce, parliamentaries, capitulations, unconditional surrender, armistices); the problem of spies;
the dividing line between ruses and perfidy; certain weapons: flame-throwers, incendiary bombs, napalm bombs.

There is, second, necessity for a critical study of the
war crimes trials; we have to take into consideration here
only that aspect of these trials which deal with punishment for violations of the laws of war, a topic into which

no features of *ex post facto* law enter. Such critical study may lead to revisions. As far as reprisals are concerned, there is a contradiction between the attempt of the trials to regulate reprisals normatively and the prohibition of reprisals against protected persons in the Geneva Conventions of 1949.[85] There is a necessity for clarification of the law concerning the international responsibility of higher commanders for violations of the laws of war by troops at least nominally under their command.[86] There is the necessity of clarifying the problem of the plea of superior orders.

Third, it is necessary to study in a detailed and critical way the new law of the Geneva conventions of 1949. While this new law is, generally speaking, a great progress, we agree with Lauterpacht that there are also "gaps, compromises, obscurities and somewhat nominal provisions." The rules granting prisoner-of-war status, under certain conditions, to members of resistance movements even in occupied territory seem, on the one hand, to go farther than military necessity would allow,[87] and are, on the other hand, perhaps nominal, because the surreptitious tactics of resistance movements will make more or less impossible the fulfilment of the conditions on which the privileged status depends. As to revisions, it has been remarked that the Geneva conventions of 1949 contain too many express reservations of military necessity.[88] The problem of voltary repatriation of prisoners of war as it arose in the armed conflict in Korea [89] points to the necessity of a revision of Article CXVIII of the third Geneva Convention of 1949.

The highest goal is the greater and greater restriction by law, and final abolition, of recourse to force in international relations. But we are still far from having reached this goal. The present world situation makes it likely that there will sometimes be international fighting.

Hence the laws of war and their revision are of the greatest importance. What is needed, first, is an objective statement of what are the laws of war actually in force. In this respect the *tabula rasa* doctrine that nothing of the traditional law of war, not even the underlying fundamental principles, survives is untenable *de lege lata*. It is equally clear that much of this law is antiquated. From this basis, as well as from a critical study of the new law of the war crimes trials and of the Geneva conventions of 1949, proposals *de lege ferenda* can start. Such proposals must take into consideration military necessity and changed conditions; they must reaffirm the fundamental principles and rules in closer conformity with present-day facts. Like all proposals *de lege ferenda*, they must have a political chance of being adopted and applied; they must be clear and unambiguous. For reasons explained, there is at this time little hope that a prohibition of nuclear weapons can be adopted; that is the reason why the Draft Rules of the International Committee of the Red Cross make no such proposals. But the application of any weapons whatsoever must not go beyond certain imperative barriers laid down by the law. While the statement of the law actually in force must closely follow the practice of states objectively determined, the proposals *de lege ferenda* must, as in the time of Grotius, be made in opposition to the recent practice of states. Total war in the sense of limitless and absolutely lawless war must be overcome. Total war stands like a symbol of the total crisis of our culture which, like every genuine crisis, is not only a matter of technical problems which are only on the surface; its real roots are philosophical, ethical, and religious. If it should not be possible to overcome total war, there is little hope for our culture. It is impossible to accept fatalistic resignation to the ordeal of an atomic and lawless war, and to hope at the same time for the "progress" of humanity, for greater and greater success of international organization, for greater and greater international protection of human rights. If it should become true that destruction of millions of men in one city by one hydrogen bomb is "perfectly legal," there is little hope for the international law of peace. In the atomic age, to paraphrase a sentence of Sir Winston Churchill, we stand either at the gates of an epoch of the greatest progress or at the portals of the Inferno. But we cannot go in the two opposite directions at the same time.

That is why international lawyers have at this time a duty to fulfil. The late Mr. Coudert, in sending to this writer a copy of the Report of the Three, wrote that he felt that something had to be done regardless of success, that international lawyers in this situation cannot simply fold their arms. For international lawyers to sit idly by and let the world perish would, as the great idealist Georges Scelle wrote in another connection, constitute the crime of the "trahison des clercs." For, as the old master of international law Max Huber [90] has warned:

One must ask oneself, whether the revolution in the nature of war by the new weapons of mass destruction will not only mean the disappearance of the laws of war, but, in its consequences, a rapid fall of the whole law of nations.

[1] J. F. P. VEALE, ADVANCE TO BARBARISM (1953).

[2] Josef L. Kunz, *Plus de lois de la guerre?*, REVUE GÉNÉRALE DE DROIT INTERNATIONAL PUBLIC 22–57 (1934); and "The Chaotic Status of the Laws of War," above. See also *idem*, KRIEGSRECHT UND NEUTRALITÄTSRECHT (1935).

[3] See e.g., C. *Rousseau*, DROIT INTERNATIONAL PUBLIC (1953); 2 P. GUGGENHEIM, TRAITÉ DE DROIT INTERNATIONAL PUBLIC (1954); A. VERDROSS, VÖLKERRECHT (3rd ed. 1955).

[4] C. JOHN COLOMBOS, THE INTERNATIONAL LAW OF THE SEA 359–695 (3rd ed. 1954).

[5] 2 OPPENHEIM-LAUTERPACHT, INTERNATIONAL LAW. A TREATISE (7th ed. 1952).

[6] G. BALLADORE PALLIERI, DIRITTO BELLICO (2nd ed. 1954).

7 J. STONE, LEGAL CONTROLS OF INTERNATIONAL CONFLICT 286–32 (1954).

8 CASTREN, THE PRESENT LAW OF WAR AND NEUTRALITY (1954).

9 Institut de Droit International, *La Révision du Droit de la Guerre. Rapport des Trois (Coudert, Francois, Lauterpacht)*, 45 ANNUAIRE DE L'INSTITUT DE DROIT INTERNATIONAL 555 (I) (1954).

10 See R. R. Baxter in 47 AM. J. INT'L L. 702–3 (1953).

11 See Josef L. Kunz, *The Geneva Conventions of August 12, 1949*, in LAW AND POLITICS IN THE WORLD COMMUNITY 279–316, 368–73 (1953).

12 See the REPORT OF 1954 OF THE INTERNATIONAL COMMITTEE OF THE RED CROSS (1955) (in German).

13 33 DEP'T STATE BULL. 69–79 (1955). See R. R. Baxter in 49 AM.J. INT'L L. 548–55 (1955).

14 See also this writer's Spanish lectures, held in 1954 at the Cursos Francisco a Vitoria in Spain, now published as a book, LA PROBLEMÁTICA ACTUAL DE LAS LEYES DE LA GUERRA (1955).

15 Thus a unilateral restatement of the laws of war by the states of the free world is suggested by C. P. Phillips, *Air Warfare and Law*, in 21 GEO. WASH. L. REV. 311–35, 395–422 (1952–53).

16 Thus Bivens, in 48 AM.J.INT'L L. 140–45 (1954), proposes the revision in the form of a restatement of the laws of war for the armed forces of collective security organizations.

17 See Sir Cecil Hurst in 32 TRANSACT. GROT. SOC'Y 135–53 (1946); see also recently Sir ARNOLD D. MCNAIR, THE DEVELOPMENT OF INTERNATIONAL JUSTICE (1954).

18 H. Lauterpacht, *Codification and Development of International Law*, 49 AM.J.INT'L L. 16–43, esp. at 31–35 (1955).

19 A. ROLIN, LE DROIT MODERNE DE LA GUERRE 10 (1920).

20 CHARLES CHENEY HYDE, INTERNATIONAL LAW 1693 (2nd ed. 1945).

21 *The Grotius Tradition in International Law*, 23 BRIT. YB. INT'L L. 1–53, at 39 (1946); 2 OPPENHEIM-LAUTERPACHT, INTERNATIONAL LAW 150 (6th ed. 1940).

22 PHILOSOPHIE DU PANAMÉRICANISME 46 (1945).

23 In 58 REVUE GÉNÉRALE DU DROIT INTERNATIONAL PUBLIC 58 (1954).

24 *The Outlawry of War and the Laws of War*, 47 AM.J.INT'L L. 365–76 (1953).

25 OPPENHEIM-LAUTERPACHT, *op. cit.* at 217–23;H. Lauterpacht, *Rules of Warfare in Unlawful War*, in LAW AND POLITICS IN THE WORLD COMMUNITY 89–113.

26 W. Schätzel, *Agressionskrieg und Haager Kriegsrecht*, 24 NORDISK TIDSSKRIFT FOR INTERNATIONAL RET 17–31 (1954).

27 W. J. FORD, DE VOLKENRECHTELIJKE POSITIE VAN VERZETSLIEDERN 299, 300 (1955).

28 *Denmark's Legal Position during the Occupation*, 1 JUS GENTIUM 2–21 (1949).

29 *Op. cit.* at 361.

30 See, e.g., U. S. v. List, XI War Trials 1247; *The Adelaide Star* case, decided in Denmark, 1 JUS GENTIUM 117–228 (1949).

31 A MODERN LAW OF NATIONS (1948).

32 *Loc. cit., supra*, note 24.

34 *Op. cit.* at 224.

35 PROCEEDINGS OF THE AMERICAN SOCIETY OF INTERNATIONAL LAW 97 (1953).

36 *Op. cit.* at 99.

37 *Quelques considérations sur une révision éventuelle des Conventions de La Haye relatives à la guerre*, 37 REVUE INTERNATIONALE DE LA CROIX ROUGE 417–33, at 433 (1955).

38 See, e.g., G. Schwarzenberger, in 37 TRANSACT. GROT SOC'Y 1 (1952); also H. A. Smith.

39 E.g., Kulski, in PROCEEDINGS OF THE AMERICAN SOCIETY OF INTERNATIONAL LAW 124–26 (1949).

40 See, e.g., R. R. Baxter, *ibid.* at 90–98 (1953).

41 *The Revision of the Laws of War*, 29 BRIT. YB. INT'L L. 360–82, at 372 (1952).

42 See Josef L. Kunz, *The Geneva Conventions of August 12, 1949*, at 291–98, 301–04.

43 *Op. cit.* at 432.

44 JOURNAL OF THE ROYAL UNITED SERVICE INSTITUTION 61 (1954).

45 This writer is indebted to the International Committee of the Red Cross for sending him the text of the proposed Draft Rules in English and French, as well as the accompanying materials. See also Erik Castrén, *La Protection juridique de la population civile dans la guerre moderne*, 59 REVUE GÉNÉRALE DE DROIT INTERNATIONAL PUBLIC 121–36 (1955).

46 International Committee of the Red Cross: Draft Rules for the Protection of the Civilian Population from the Dangers of Indiscriminate Warfare (D 386 b) with Commentary (1955) (mimeo).

47 Among them two Americans, Major R. R. Baxter and Mr. Raymund T. Yingling.

48 See Commission of Experts, Summary of Opinions (D 347 b) (1954) (mimeo.).

49 *Op. cit., supra* Note 7, at 382.

50 See W. Schätzel, *Neutralität*, 53 DIE FRIEDENS-WARTE 28–36 (1955).

51 Kunz, *The Geneva Conventions of August 12, 1949*, at 288–90.

52 See his article in 50 AM.J.INT'L L. 61–68 (1956).

53 *The Revision of the Laws of War*, 378, 377.

54 LEGAL CONTROL OF INTERNATIONAL CONFLICT, 407.

55 THE INTERNATIONAL LAW OF THE SEA, 500.

56 *Op. cit., supra*, note 37, at 426–28.

57 THE PRESENT LAW OF WAR AND NEUTRALITY, 5.

58 *Loc. cit., supra*, note 37.

59 HANS J. MORGENTHAU, POLITICS AMONG NATIONS 218 (1948).

60 COLOMBOS, *op. cit.*, at 360, 370, 381.

61 *Op. cit.* at 245.

62 *Ibid.* at 289.

63 Heinz-Gerhard Helm in a doctor's thesis sent to this writer, Das Operationsgebiet im Seekriegsrecht 250–64 (Munich), holds that war zones are now legal under certain conditions, and unrestricted submarine warfare is legal within these zones, but not on the high seas in general.

64 "The British retaliatory system in the two wars had to justify itself (if at all) as retaliation. In policy, however, that system may as well and more significantly justify itself de lege ferenda."— *Op. cit.* at 500.

65 OPPENHEIM-LAUTERPACHT, *op. cit.* at 576.

66 *Ibid.* at 491–93.

67 *Ibid.* at 351, also note 1; see the discussion on aerial bombardment in World War II, *ibid.* at 527–30.

68 *The Revision of the Laws of War.* At the time of writing, this writer had not yet received the 1953 *British Year Book of International Law* and thus could not make use of Judge Lauterpacht's latest study on "The Limits of the Operation of the Laws of War."

69 See KUNZ, KRIEGSRECHT UND NEUTRALITÄTSRECHT 2–4.

70 *That* is the correct distinction, not between "combatants and noncombatants"; the latter is a distinction *within* the armed forces.

71 C. P. Phillips, *loc cit., supra*, note 15.

72 *Agressionskrieg und Haager Kriegerecht*, 17–31.

73 VÖLKERECHT, 361–97.

74 DE VOLKENRECHTELIJKE POSITIE VAN VERZETALIEDERN, 299, 300.

75 *Loc. cit., supra*, note 37.

76 BUSH, MODERN ARMS AND FREE MEN (1950); H. A. Smith, *Modern Weapons and Modern War*, YEARBOOK OF WORLD AFFAIRS 222–47 (1955).

77 See Josef L. Kunz, *Atombombe und Völkerrecht*, 2 ÖSTERREICHISCHE ZEITSCHRIFT FÜR ÖFFENTLICHES RECHT 414–36 (1950).

78 AIR POWER AND WAR RIGHTS (3rd ed. 1947).

79 N.Y. Times, December 25, 1955, p. 40.

80 *Ibid.*, December 2, 1955, p. 6.

81 ROSEBURY, PEACE OR PESTILENCE (1949); J. Voncken, *Devant la guerre biologique*, REVUE GÉNÉRALE BELGE, 786–95 (1953).

82 See JOSEF L. KUNZ, GASKRIEG UND VÖLKERRECHT (Vienna, 1927).

83 N.Y. Times, November 7, 1955, p. 13.

84 "Codify convenience, where convenience can undisputably be demonstrated; leave military effectiveness alone, so long as military effectiveness remains the direct shield of the free world and no reciprocal advantage can be gained by its merely formal limitation."— *Air Warfare and Law*, 423.

85 See Albrecht in 47 AM.J.INT'L L. 590–614 (1953).

86 Cf. A. F. REEL, THE CASE OF GENERAL YAMASHITA (1949).

87 "Unprivileged members of resistance movements may be punished by the enemy after they have been captured. In no other way can an army guard and protect itself from the gadfly tactics of such armed resistance," stated the U. S. Military Tribunal in the *Hostage Case*. In the 7th ed. of Oppenheim's second volume, Lauterpacht argues in highly complicated sentences in favor of this new norm; but in the 6th ed. (1940, p. 456) he had written: "Beyond the limits of these concessions [Hague Convention IV, Regulations, Articles I and II] belligerents will *never* be able to go without the greatest danger to their troops." (Emphasis supplied.)

88 N. H. C. Dunbar, *The significance of Military Necessity in the Laws of War*, 68 JURID. REV. 201–12 (1955).

89 See Josef L. Kunz, *Die Koreanische Kriegsgefangenenfrage*, 4 ARCHIV DES VÖLKERRECHTS 408–23 (1954), and in PROCEEDINGS OF THE AMERICAN SOCIETY OF INTERNATIONAL LAW 99–111 (1953). See also Lt. Col. Frederick W. Hess, *A Post-Korea Look at the Geneva Conventions*," 35 MILITARY REVIEW 52–58 (1955).

90 Max Huber, *Wandlungen des Völkerrechts*, 52 DIE FRIEDENS-WARTE 297–310, at 308 (1955).

CHAPTER XLIII: The New U.S. Army Field Manual of
the Law of Land Warfare

THE TIMES of ignoring the laws of war are over: new
treaties have been concluded concerning the laws of war,
there is a considerable literature, and states are again is-
suing instructions to their armed forces on the laws of war
and neutrality. The United States has recently published
new instructions on the *Law of Naval Warfare* [1] and now
a field manual on the law of land warfare.[2]

The manual is, generally speaking, restricted to the conduct of warfare on land and to relationships between belligerent and neutral states; but it also governs naval forces
operating on land.[3] The manual is in every point, and particularly with regard to fundamental problems, in harmony
with the Law of Naval Warfare. Although the manual is
an official publication of the U. S. Army, its provisions
are neither statute nor treaty and should not be considered
binding upon courts and tribunals applying the laws of
war, although such provisions are of evidentiary value.[4]

The manual is based on the firm conviction that there
are laws of war, binding upon states and individuals. Their
purpose is to protect both combatants and noncombatants
from unnecessary suffering, to safeguard certain fundamental human rights of persons who fall into the hands

of the enemy, and to facilitate the restoration of peace. Laws of war are prohibitory; they place limits on the exercise of belligerent power, they are pervaded with the principles of humanity and chivalry. Hence, as the manual lays down clearly,[5] military necessity, where not expressly foreseen in the laws of war, is no defense for acts forbidden by the customary and conventional laws of war, because the latter have been developed and framed with consideration for the concept of military necessity.[6] The laws of war have their sources in custom and treaties. The manual, by incorporating the third, fourth, ninth, and tenth Hague conventions (with the Hague Regulations on the Laws and Customs of War on Land)[7] proves that these conventions are still the law. The four Geneva conventions of August 12, 1949,[8] are fully incorporated.[9] The manual states[10] that the customary law of war, being part of the law of the United States, will be strictly observed by the United States; treaties must be observed by both military and civilian personnel with the same strict regard for both the letter and the spirit of the law which is required with respect to the Constitution and statutes. As treaty provisions "are in large part but formal and specific applications of general principles of the unwritten law," the treaty provisions quoted will be strictly observed and enforced by the United States forces without regard to whether they are legally binding upon this country.

It is fundamental that the laws of war, notwithstanding the prohibition of the use of force in the United Nations Charter, are fully reaffirmed. The application of the laws of war is, in conformity with Article II of all four Geneva conventions of 1949, greatly expanded. They apply not only to declared wars but to any other international armed conflict, and, in a restricted sense, to civil war, even when the insurgents are not recognized as a belligerent party. They apply particularly to the exercise of armed force pursuant to a recommendation, decision, or call by the United Nations, to the exercise of the inherent right of individual and collective self-defense against armed attack, or in the performance of enforcement measures through a regional arrangement; and they apply equally to all belligerents.[11]

Equally clear is the standpoint of the manual toward the law of neutrality. The latter plays, indeed, a very important role in the Geneva conventions of 1949.[12] The manual [13] states that, if a United Nations member is called upon under Articles XLII and XLIII of the Charter, it loses its neutrality only to the extent that it complies with the direction of the Security Council.[14] There is, therefore, room for classic neutrality and a "military commander in the field is obliged to respect the neutrality of third States." Chapter IX [15] enumerates the rights and duties of neutral states, quoting the Fifth Hague convention.

Some chapters of the manual largely repeat the corresponding rules of the Geneva conventions of 1949 in bold print. This is the case concerning protecting powers,[16] concerning the wounded and sick,[17] and concerning civilian persons.[18] The same is true with regard to prisoners of war;[19] but here a number of interesting explanations with regard to certain points of the laws of war as currently interpreted can be seen. Paragraph 63 states that:

> commando forces and airborne troops, although operating by highly trained methods of surprise and violent combat, are entitled, as long as they are members of the organized armed forces of the enemy and wear uniform, to be treated as prisoners of war upon capture, even if they operate singly.[20]

Under Article V of the Geneva convention of 1949 concerning prisoners of war, prisoners of war are under the protection of the convention "from the time they fall into the power of the enemy until their final release and repatriation." But the moment of the beginning of captivity has often presented difficult problems. The manual [21] now defines the phrase "fall into the power of the enemy" as "having been captured by, or surrendered to members of the military forces, the civilian police, or local civilian defense organizations or enemy civilians who have taken him into custody." Also of interest is the attitude with regard to Article CXVIII of the Geneva convention of 1949 on prisoners of war concerning the release and repatriation of prisoners without delay after the cessation of active hostilities. This article, as is well known, led to considerable difficulties in the negotiations for an armistice in Korea and to an ad hoc settlement. Paragraph 199 states:

> A Detaining Power may, in its discretion, lawfully grant aslyum to prisoners of war who do not desire to be repatriated.

But there is no doubt that Article CXVIII stands in need of revision.[22]

Of greatest interest is the treatment of the problem of spies, a topic which for a long time has needed clarification and revision. The manual [23] gives the definition of spies according to Article XXIX of the Hague Regulations of 1907, and according to Article CVI of the United States Uniform Code of Military Justice; where these two definitions are not in conflict, they will be applied and construed together; otherwise Article CVI governs American practice. The problem of espionage has long been somewhat like a legal puzzle.[24] Every writer has had to concede that the employment of spies by belligerents is perfectly lawful. But, it has been argued, "espionage has a twofold character": the employment of spies is lawful, but the spy is a war criminal,[25] an obviously untenable construction. This writer,[26] as early as 1935, developed the theory that espionage is not illegal but a "risky" act. Espionage is lawful under international law; but as it is particularly dangerous to the enemy, international law authorizes a belligerent as an exception to treat a spy caught *in flagranti*, not as a prisoner of war, but as punishable. It is not a question of punishment for a crime, but of a repressive measure against a dangerous although lawful act. This construction has been accepted by Walter Schätzel and Erik Castrén.[27] The manual has now adopted the "risky" act theory. Paragraph 77 reads:

> Resort to that practice (employing spies) involves no offense against international law. Spies are punished, not as violators of the laws of war, but to render that method of obtaining information as dangerous, difficult and ineffective as possible.

As to sanctions for the violation of the laws of war,[28] the manual deals in detail with reprisals and recognizes crimes against peace and against humanity, but deals primarily with war crimes, defined as "violations of the laws of war by any person or persons, military or civilian." The Geneva conventions of 1949 avoid the term "war crimes" and speak rather of "grave breaches." The manual, among newest developments, states[29] that in some cases, "military commanders may be responsible for war crimes committed by subordinate members of the armed forces, or other persons subject to their control." Such responsibility arises, of course, when such acts have been committed in pursuance of an order of the commander concerned. But he is also responsible if he has actual knowledge, or should have knowledge, and if he fails to take the necessary and reasonable steps to insure compliance with the laws of war or to punish violations thereof. The defense of superior orders[30] "does not lie unless the accused did not know and could not reasonably have been expected to know that the act ordered was unlawful." But superior orders may be considered in mitigation of punishment. To strike a correct balance it is added:

> In considering the question whether a superior order consti-
> tutes a valid defense, the court shall take into consideration the
> fact that obedience to lawful military orders is the duty of every
> member of the armed forces; that the latter cannot be expected,
> in conditions of war discipline, to weigh scrupulously the legal
> merits of the orders received; that certain rules of warfare may
> be controversial; or that an act otherwise amounting to a war
> crime may be done in obedience to orders conceived as a measure
> of reprisal.[31]

It is most important to note that paragraph 506 of the
manual expressly states that the belligerents are under an
obligation to take measures for the punishment of war
crimes committed by all persons, including members of a
belligerent's own armed forces.

Certain parts of the laws of warfare on land are particularly in need of revision, either because the treaty law of
1907 is incomplete or now inadequate, or because of new
developments. These parts concern the non-hostile relations
of belligerents, nearly every point of the law of belligerent
occupation, and vital problems as to the actual conduct
of war. A real revision of these parts of the law can, of
course, only be brought about by international procedures
of law-making and not by a field manual of one state. But
the manual gives the present status of these problems,
either deduced from general principles of the laws of war
or from a consensus of nations, formed as a consequence
of two world wars, or at least expressing the attitude which
the United States is now taking pending an international
revision of the problem in question.

As to non-hostile relations of belligerents,[32] the manual
reprints the few rules of the Hague Regulations of 1907
concerning envoys to negotiate a truce, capitulations, and
armistices, and supplements them with many paragraphs
summarizing the usage of nations. Paragraph 476 speaks
of unconditional surrender as one "in which a body of
troops gives itself up to the enemy without condition; it

need not be effected on the basis of an instrument signed by both parties." But that is rather what Oppenheim-Lauterpacht[33] calls a "simple surrender" without capitulation; for capitulation is a convention stipulating special terms of surrender. Such simple surrenders by some soldiers of a man-of-war or a fortress have always occurred. But the new concept of "unconditional surrender" at the end of World War II is something different and new. This new "unconditional surrender" terminates hostilities without any agreement—it is neither a capitulation nor an armistice—and may be followed by the assumption of supreme authority which also, in spite of continued occupation of the vanquished country, terminates the technical status of belligerent occupation.[34]

The problem of belligerent occupation is dealt with by the manual in a detailed way.[35] It prints the corresponding norms of the 1907 Hague Regulations and of the Geneva Convention of 1949 on Protection of Civilians, which, in its own words, is supplementary to the Hague Regulations. Respect for human rights; the prohibition of deportations, transfers, evacuation; care for children; hygiene and public health; relief services of inhabitants; measures of security for the occupant; protection of civilian populations in occupied territory; prohibition of reprisals against protected civilians and against taking hostages are all incorporated. There can be no doubt that the fourth Geneva convention represents great progress, inspired by excesses, particularly by Germany as a belligerent occupant in World War II. Yet many problems concerning the legal position of the belligerent occupant, his rights and duties, and the corresponding rights and duties of the civilian population stand in need of revision as a consequence of the change in the conduct of war, the enormous importance of economic warfare, and the far-reaching change in general conditions. The manual clearly distinguishes belligerent occupation from both mere invasion and conquest and sub-jugation. It reflects modern war conditions, paragraph 352 states that "an invader may attack with naval or air forces or troops may push rapidly through a large portion of enemy territory without establishing that effective control which is essential to the status of occupation." For "oc-cupation is invasion plus taking firm possession of enemy territory for the purpose of holding it." [36] Occupation pre-supposes legal effectiveness, which therefore must not only be established but also be maintained. It corresponds to experiences of the last war that military goverment can also be established over allied or neutral territory, recovered or liberated from the enemy, when that territory has not been made the subject of a civil-affairs administration agreement.

As belligerent occupation does not transfer sovereignty, it is unlawful for a belligerent occupant to annex occupied territory or to create a new state therein while hostilities are still in progress.[37] In conformity also with experiences of the last war, paragraph 366 lays down the law that

the restrictions placed upon a belligerent government cannot be avoided by a system of using a puppet government, central or local, to carry out acts which would be unlawful if performed directly by the occupant. Acts induced or compelled by the occu-pant are nonetheless its acts.

Difficulties appear, however, in the paragraphs dealing with the determination whether property is public or private,[38] and with the problem of currency and exchange controls.[39]

Julius Stone [40] has, in a detailed investigation of the present status of the law of belligerent occupation, directed attention to the fact that the corresponding rules of the Hague Regulations, even if their text stands, are no longer adequate because they are based on nineteenth-century as-sumptions of a laissez-faire economy in the states of both the occupant and the occupied. With the great expansion of governmental functions and techniques, with such basic state functions as assuring minimum living standards or functions of currency, banking. debt, exchange, import and export control, with the shifting boundaries of public and private property, the rules based on entirely different conditions are out of harmony. He speaks, therefore, of "the twilight of occupation law" and concludes that

> before the law of belligerent occupation can emerge from this twilight, a rethinking is required going far beyond mere revision and which (despite its advances in other respects) the relevant Geneva Convention of 1949 has not provided.[41]

As to the rules concerning the actual conduct of hostilities,[42] the manual strongly opposes those who would keep only the "humanitarian" laws of war and drop all rules concerning the actual conduct of war.[43] The right of belligerents to adopt means of injuring the enemy is *not* unlimited—a rule which remains the law. But there is no doubt that these norms, incomplete or antiquated as they are, are greatly in need of revision. For instance, the problem of the dividing line between permissible ruses of war and forbidden treachery is, as paragraph 50 states, sometimes indistinct. The manual states that absolute good faith must be observed as a rule of conduct. It would, therefore,

> be an improper practice to secure an advantage of the enemy by deliberate lying or misleading conduct which involves a breach of faith, or when there is a moral obligation to speak the truth.

But the employment of spies, encouraging defection or insurrection among the enemy civilian population, corrupting enemy civilians or soldiers by bribes, or inducing the enemy's soldiers to desert, surrender, or rebel are not prohibited.[44] Legitimate war ruses also include ambushes, dummy mines, and psychological-warfare activities.[45] Use of national flags, insignia, and uniforms as a disguise is taken to be authorized, although to employ them during combat is certainly forbidden.[46] Devastation as an end in itself or as a separate measure of war is not sanctioned by the laws of war. The measure of permissible devastation is found in the strict necessities of war.[47] As to persons desending by parachute, it is laid down, in conformity with modern usage, that such persons, when they are trying to escape from a disabled aircraft, may not be fired upon.[48] Weapons employing fire, such as tracer ammunition, flamethrowers, napalm, and other incendiary agents against targets requiring their use are not violative of international law; but they must not be employed in such a way as to cause unnecessary suffering to individuals.[49] Paragraph 42 lays down that "there is no prohibition of general application against bombardment from the air of combatant troops, defended places, or other legitimate military objectives." As to gas and bacteriological warfare, paragraph 38 states that

> the United States is not a party to any treaty, now in force, that prohibits or restricts the use in warfare of toxic or non-toxic gases, of smoke or incendiary materials, or of bacteriological warfare. The Geneva Protocol of 1925 has not been ratified by the United States and is not binding on this country.[50]

Paragraph 35 states that

> the use of explosive atomic weapons, whether by air, sea, or land forces, cannot as such be regarded as violative of international law in the absence of any customary rule of international law or international convention restricting their employment.[51]

It is obvious that a restriction or prohibition of chemical, bacteriological, and atomic war is only possible by international agreement to which at least all militarily import-

ant states are parties. Negotiations for such agreement
have been under way since the end of World War II, but
in a world which is lacking confidence, have not yet led
to positive results.

1 U.S. DEPARTMENT OF THE NAVY, LAW OF NAVAL WARFARE (1955).

2 U.S. DEPARTMENT OF THE ARMY, ARMY FIELD MANUAL: THE LAW
OF LAND WARFARE (1956) (hereafter cited as MANUAL). It super-
sedes the field manual of October 1, 1940, including C 1, November
15, 1944. The new manual consists of 552 paragraphs, arranged in
nine chapters.

3 LAW OF NAVAL WARFARE § 240.

4 MANUAL, para. 1. In the same sense, LAW OF NAVAL WARFARE
§ 110.

5 MANUAL, para. 3.

6 In exactly the same sense, JOSEF L. KUNZ, KRIEGSRECHT UND
NEUTRALITÄTSRECHT 26–28 (1935).

7 The texts of the Hague conventions and regulations referred to
are reprinted in 2 AM.J.INT'L L. (supplement) 85, 90, 146, 153 (1908).

8 French texts, LES CONVENTIONS DE GENÈVE DU 12 AOÛT 1949
(1950); English texts in T.I.A.S. Nos. 3362, 3363, 3364, 3365; Department of State Pub. No. 3938 (General Foreign Policy Series 34,
August, 1950). On pp. 233–55 of the last-named publication are
printed the reservations; the United States has made only one reservation, namely, with respect to Article LXVIII of the fourth convention (ibid. at 239). The Geneva conventions were ratified by the
United States on July 6, 1955, and came into force for this country on
February 2, 1956. The texts of the Convention on Prisoners of War
and the Convention on Protection of Civilians are reprinted in 47
AM.J.INT'L L. (supplement) 119 (1953), and 50 ibid. at 724 (1956),
respectively.

The following commentaries have, up to now, been published by
the International Committee of the Red Cross: JEAN S. PICTET, COM-
MENTAIRE À LA PREMIÈRE CONVENTION DE GENÈVE DE 1949 (1952);
JEAN DE PREUX, ETUDE SUR LA TROISIÈME CONVENTION DE GENÈVE DE
1949 (1954); LA CONVENTION DE GENÈVE RELATIVE À LA PROTECTION
DES PERSONNES CIVILES EN TEMPS DE GUERRE (1956). See also J. VERGES,
LA 4e CONVENTION DE GENÈVE DE 1949. EXPOSÉ DOCUMENTAIRE (1952);
FROTIN, LA 4e CONVENTION DE GENÈVE, PROTECTION CIVILE (1953);
Ginnane and Yingling, The Geneva Conventions of 1949, 46 AM.J.
INT'L L. 383 (1952); and Pictet, The New Geneva Conventions for the
Protection of War Victims, 45 ibid. at 462 (1951).

9 The MANUAL (para. 57) also incorporates the so-called Roerich
Pact of April 15, 1935 (49 Stat. 3267, T.S. No. 899; 30 AM.J.INT'L L.
[supplement] 195 [1936]), although only the United States and a
number of the American republics are parties to this treaty. See the
corresponding UNESCO treaty signed at Paris on September 30, 1953.

10 MANUAL, para. 7.

11 MANUAL, para. 8a. This corresponds perfectly with the practice of states in the Korean conflict and shows the untenability of the proposals for "discriminatory" laws of war; see "The Laws of War," above. The same idea is thus expressed in LAW OF NAVAL WARFARE § 200: "Distinction must be made between the resort to war and the conduct of war. Whether the resort to war is lawful or unlawful, the conduct of war is regulated by the laws of war."

12 See Josef L. Kunz, *The Geneva Conventions of August 12, 1949* in LAW AND POLITICS IN THE WORLD COMMUNITY 279–316, 368–73 (1953).

13 Para. 513.

14 LAW OF NAVAL WARFARE § 232, states equally that there may not only be qualified neutrality, but classic neutrality: "The obligations of the member States, incompatible with neutrality, come into existence only if the Security Council fulfills the functions delegated to it by the Charter. If the Security Council is unable to fulfill its assigned functions, the members may, in case of a war, remain neutral and observe an attitude of strict impartiality."

15 Paras. 512–52.

16 Paras. 15–19.

17 Chap. IV, paras. 208–45, embodying the second Geneva Convention. This chapter deals also with the Red Cross emblem.

18 Chap. V, paras. 246–350, incorporating the fourth Geneva convention, apart from the rules dealing with civilian persons in belligerent occupied territory.

19 Chap. III, paras. 60–207, incorporating the third Geneva Convention.

20 This paragraph is taken textually from 2 OPPENHEIM-LAUTERPACHT, INTERNATIONAL LAW 259 (7th ed. 1952).

21 Para. 84b.

22 See Josef L. Kunz, *Die Koreanische Kriegsgefangenenfrage*, 4 ARCHIV DES VÖLKERRECHTS 408–23 (1954).

23 Para. 75.

24 JULIUS STONE, LEGAL CONTROLS OF INTERNATIONAL CONFLICT 563 (1954).

25 Thus, OPPENHEIM-LAUTERPACHT, *op. cit.* at 422.

26 KRIEGSRECHT UND NEUTRALITÄTSRECHT 67–69.

27 ERIK CASTRÉN, THE PRESENT LAW OF WAR AND NEUTRALITY 154 (1954).

28 Chap. VIII, paras. 495–511.

29 Para. 501.

30 Para. 509.

31 This paragraph is taken from OPPENHEIM-LAUTERPACHT, *op. cit.* at 569. LAW OF NAVAL WARFARE § 330b (1) adds: "If an act, though known to the person to be unlawful at the time of commission, is performed under duress, this circumstance may be taken into consideration either by way of defense or in mitigation of punishment."

[32] Chap. VII, paras. 449–94.

[33] *Op. cit.* at 543, 545.

[34] In this sense "unconditional surrender" was only applied to Germany. All the other enemy states were also required to surrender unconditionally, but the same term had a different legal meaning. Thus Japan's unconditional surrender was preceded by negotiations in which the Allies accepted Japan's condition of the continuance of Japan's emperor. In the case of Italy, notwithstanding her unconditional surrender, an ordinary armistice agreement was concluded.

[35] Chap. VI, paras. 351–448.

[36] This definition is taken from 2 OPPENHEIM-LAUTERPACHT, *op. cit.,* at 434.

[37] Para. 358.

[38] Under modern conditions, the distinction between public and private property is not always easy to draw. . . . It is often necessary to look beyond strict legal title and to ascertain the character of the property on the basis of the beneficial ownership thereof."—Para. 394.

[39] The occupying power is also "authorized to introduce its own currency or to issue special currency for use only in the occupied area, should the introduction or issuance of such currency become necessary. The occupant may also institute exchange controls, including clearing arrangements." But such measures must not be utilized to enrich the occupant or to circumvent restrictions; debasement of currency by fictitious valuations or exchange rates, as well as failure to take reasonable steps to prevent inflation, are violative of international law (Para. 430).

[40] *Op. cit.* at 693–732.

[41] *Ibid.* at 732.

[42] Chap. II, paras. 20–59.

[43] See "The Laws of War," above.

[44] Para. 49.

[45] Para. 51.

[46] Para. 54. Because Article XXIII(f) of the Hague Regulations forbids only their "improper use."

[47] MANUAL, para. 56. KUNZ, KRIEGSRECHT UND NEUTRALITÄTSRECHT 84–85.

[48] Para. 30. Thus also SPAIGHT, AIR POWER AND WAR RIGHTS (3rd ed. 1947); OPPENHEIM-LAUTERPACHT, *op. cit.* at 521; and the proposed Hague Air Warfare Rules, 1923; doubtful: ERIK CASTRÉN, *op. cit.* at 400.

[49] Para. 36.

[50] Para. 38 is restricted to this negative statement. LAW OF NAVAL WARFARE § 612 states that the U.S. is not a party to any treaty forbidding or restricting these methods of warfare and that it, therefore, "remains doubtful that, in the absence of a specific restriction established by treaty, a State legally is prohibited at present from resorting to their use." Footnote 8 adds that poisonous gases and

bacteriological weapons may be used only if and when authorized by the President.

[51] In the same sense, LAW OF NAVAL WARFARE § 613. Footnote 9 adds that nuclear weapons may be used by U.S. forces only if and when directed by the President.

THE WORLD-WIDE International Red Cross (IRC) [1] consists today of the National Red Cross Societies; the League of National Red Cross Societies, founded in 1919 on American initiative, with the Board of Governors as its deliberative organ; and the International Committee of the Red Cross (ICRC), founded by Henry Dunant at Geneva in 1863. About every four years the international conferences of the Red Cross are held. The national societies, as well as the League, are private organizations, created under municipal law. The International Committee of the Red Cross, too, although strictly international in character, is legally a juridical person under Swiss municipal law and consists entirely of Swiss citizens; but it exercises functions recognized by or conferred upon it by international treaty law. It negotiates with governments, sends appeals directly to them, concludes agreements, and fits out vessels. It acts independently, without the authority of any state, and on its own initiative sends delegates and even supervises the actions of states. It is recognized by the United Nations as one of the non-governmental international organizations with which the United Nations may consult. The violation of its distinctive sign is an illegal act under international law; its delegates have inviolability. The International Conferences of the Red Cross are mixed conferences, attended by unofficial Red Cross delegates and by official delegates of the states. The international position of the International Committee of the Red Cross, already previously recognized by international law, has been greatly strengthened by the Geneva conventions of August 12, 1949. That is why Werner and Schätzel ask whether, in spite of its creation under municipal law and its composition, the time has not come to recognize it as a person in international law. Guggenheim and Verdross see in it already a particular subject of international law.

The fundamental principles of the International Committee of the Red Cross, as strongly restated in 1949 by its former president, Judge Max Huber, are its non-political character, political independence, and absolute neutrality, universality, and humanitarianism. Wherever men suffer through fighting, the ICRC seeks to help. No distinction is made between guilty and non-guilty states; it matters not whether a state or government is or is not recognized, or whether the fighting is "war," reprisals, measures of United Nations execution, or even civil war. The ICRC tried to help both sides in the armed conflict in Korea; it has sent observers to Algeria. At the International Conferences of the Red Cross, delegates of all states are admitted. It is exactly this universal and non-political character, only moved by humanitarian considerations, which gives to the International Red Cross its unique status and makes it the voice of the public conscience of the world.

Of particular importance is the role of the ICRC in the making of new international treaty law, dealing with what is called the "Geneva" laws of war or the "humanitarian" laws of war, as distinguished from the "Hague" laws of war, which deal with norms concerning the actual conduct of war. Within the Geneva laws of war, the role of the International Committee of the Red Cross always was to take the initiative, to direct appeals to the states, to make legal studies, to prepare drafts, to convoke commissions of experts, to have these drafts approved by the International Conferences of the Red Cross, to submit these approved drafts to the states, and to urge them to have these drafts become rules of international law: for this purpose the Swiss government convokes diplomatic conferences, producing on the basis of these drafts, international conventions to be ratified by the states. Thus, the Red Cross conventions of 1864, 1906, and 1907 came into being. Even during the long period after 1920, when the laws of war were neglected by governments and scholars with disastrous consequences, the ICRC took the initiative which led to the two Geneva conventions of 1929. Since that time, the ICRC has been working continuously for better protection of the civilian population in time of war.[2]

After World War II, the national Red Cross Societies held a preliminary conference at Geneva in 1946, followed by a meeting of governmental experts at Geneva in 1947. A draft, prepared by the ICRC, had been sent to the national Red Cross societies and governments. The four new draft conventions were approved at the seventeenth International Conference of the Red Cross (Stockholm, 1948). Then followed the Geneva Diplomatic Conference of 1949, convoked by the Swiss government. This conference produced the four Geneva conventions in 1949.[3]

The fourth Geneva convention of 1949 creates new international law and constitutes important progress, but is not complete.[4] That is why the ICRC in April, 1950, sent an appeal concerning atomic weapons and non-directed missiles to the signatories of the Geneva conventions of 1949. Resolution XXIV of the Stockholm Conference (1948) had earnestly requested the Powers solemnly to undertake to prohibit absolutely all recourse to such weapons (which cannot be aimed with precision or which devastate large areas indiscriminately) and to the use of atomic energy for purposes of warfare.

The Board of Governors of the League, at its twenty-third session (Oslo, May, 1954), requested the ICRC "to make a thorough examination and propose at the next International Conference of the Red Cross the necessary additions to the Conventions in force in order to protect civilian populations from the dangers of atomic, chemical and bacteriological warfare."

The ICRC had, in 1952, resumed the studies started before 1939. It convoked a commission of non-governmental experts which met at Geneva from April 6 to 15, 1954. It worked out the "Draft Rules 1955," [5] which were designed to "reaffirm permanent principles in close conformity with present-day facts." [6] The Draft Rules, 1955, were sent in July, 1955, to all the national Red Cross societies. As in the opinion of some societies there was the risk of going beyond the bounds of the IRC and encroaching upon the province of governments, whereas others urged a joint study prior to the New Delhi Conference, the ICRC invited them to appoint private experts to an advisory working party which met at Geneva, May 14–19, 1956. [7] On that basis, the ICRC prepared a new draft: the Draft Rules, 1956, for the limitation of the dangers incurred by the civilian population in time of war. [8] They are not a draft convention, but a code of fundamental rules and principles; the text is somewhat different, and perhaps less far-reaching, than the Draft Rules, 1955. The Draft Rules, 1956, consist of a preamble and six chapters in twenty articles. The Draft Rules, 1956, were sent in October, 1956, to all the national Red Cross societies and to the governments and were before the nineteenth International Conference of the Red Cross which took place at New Delhi, India, October 16–November 7, 1957.[9]

This conference dealt with the Draft Rules, 1956, in its International Humanitarian Law Commission.[10] Its chairman was Mr. John MacAulay, vice-president of the Canadian Red Cross; Mr. Henrik Beer, secretary general of the Swedish Red Cross, was *rapporteur*. As always, the New Delhi Conference was a mixed conference; [11] all types of countries were represented.[12] The Draft Rules, 1956, were discussed in five meetings of the above-named commission and two plenary sessions. Sixty-two delegates from forty-seven countries spoke on the Draft Rules, some several times and in great detail.

A careful study of the verbatim record reveals strong differences of opinion on procedural and substantive questions which, in spite of all banning of political considerations, often clearly reflected the split between the "two worlds." The ICRC had, at the beginning, submitted a draft resolution for the conference. The draft suggests that (1) "a set of rules revising and extending those previously accepted is desirable"; (2) "deems that the underlying principles of the draft are in conformity with Red Cross ideals and the requirements of humanity"; (3) "requests the ICRC to continue its efforts and prepare the ground for an international agreement"; and (4) "resolves that the record of the discussions and the text of the proposals shall be appended to the Draft Rules." M. Siordet, vice-president of the ICRC, took the position that no discussion, article by article, should take place, but only a discussion leading to general approval; he insisted that only governments and their specialists can draw up international conventions in their ultimate form, that the Draft Rules, 1956, are not a draft convention. The chairman, who conducted the discussions with a firm hand, had ruled that the ICRC draft resolution and amendments to it were before the commission;

and if the resolution was adopted, resolutions dealing with particular articles would not be discussed. But he had also to rule that each speaker was free to discuss particular rules and to propose amendments thereto. It is certainly not a mere accident that the delegates of the communist countries [13] preferred article-by-article debate whereas the delegates of the free world [14] insisted on a more general debate. In fact, amendments to the preamble and to each of the twenty articles were proposed.[15] It is interesting to note that the amendment to Article XIX, proposed by Japan, was based on the conviction "that there must be war criminals also in the victor countries and that it is truly an injustice that war criminals are found only among the vanquished countries." [16]

But the greatest split of opinion, in a matter of substance, concerned Article XIV, dealing with atomic and other weapons of mass destruction. All the communist delegates [17] stood in strongest terms for total and absolute prohibition without any conditions, and mostly also for a total ban of nuclear tests; the delegates of the free world were opposed. This matter was held inopportune [18] and strictly political,[19] forming a part of the problem of disarmament and belonging to the competence of the United Nations.[20] The keynote was given by the delegate of the government of the Philippines,[21] who not only stressed the political character of the problem and the competence of the United Nations, but referred to the antagonism between the "two schools." He insisted that everything depended on the conditions attached to the proposal of banning nuclear weapons, and that his government demanded the right to use nuclear weapons for self-defense. He urged adequate and effective safeguards, including full inspection and control. The same ideas were voiced, in a very restrained form, by General A. M. Gruenther,[22] speaking in his capacity as president of the American National Red Cross, by the delegate of the government

of the United Kingdom,[23] and by the delegates of the French
Red Cross [24] and of the French government.[25] The delegates
of the French Red Cross openly spoke of the danger that
an absolute and unconditional prohibition of atomic weapons would create by weakening some countries and strengthening others, which have great superiority in so-called
conventional weapons, but do not possess such superiority
in nuclear weapons. The strongest warning, the greatest
urge for a "realistic approach," came from General J. D.
Shepers, speaking on behalf of the Netherlands Red Cross.[26]

As to the draft resolution submitted by the ICRC, Judge
Sandström (Swedish Red Cross),[27] stressing the lack of
competence of the IRC, proposed an amendment to delete
the paragraph asking the ICRC to continue its efforts and to
replace the last paragraph by a simple request to transmit
the draft rules to the governments for their consideration.
This amendment was strongly endorsed by many delegations. On the other hand, the Netherlands delegate proposed
an amendment to the amendment, according to which the
ICRC should continue its efforts, and that was also accepted
by many delegations. After the chairman had appointed
special drafting committees, a final resolution was proposed to the last meeting of the commission. First, a
U.S.S.R. amendment, asking the ICRC to prepare a more
complete draft within the shortest time possible, was rejected by vote of 24 in favor, 51 against, and 8 abstentions.
Then the resolution in its final form was adopted by 115
votes in favor, none against, and 2 abstentions. At the
plenary session the resolution was unanimously adopted
with no abstentions. This resolution, as adopted, retains the
first two paragraphs of the draft resolution and, further,
"urges the ICRC to continue its efforts"; and "requests the
ICRC to transmit the Draft Rules, the record of the discussions, the text of the proposals, and the submitted amendments, to the governments for their consideration." In

carrying out this mandate, the ICRC published the verbatim record and sent it, together with a memorandum, to the governments, emphasizing that it now remains with the governments to draft the rules recommended by the New Delhi Conference, and stating its intention of continuing to seek, and possibly to propose, the means for developing the progress of these legal studies in order to reach an international agreement, which is the logical conclusion of this work.

If we look at the unanimous adoption of the resolution, the New Delhi Conference appears prima facie to have been successful. And yet, looking deeper into the matter, doubts as to this success arise. There were good reasons behind the statement of the Yugoslav delegate,[28] who said that

> we did not find a satisfactory common language; we did not progress, but have virtually let the thing go out of the hands of the IRC. What have we done? We are returning again these rules to the governments, to which they were sent before; we do not foresee what other action is to be taken.

Much stronger criticism was voiced by the delegate of the Swiss government, who, during the discussions, called the proposed resolution, "not a step forward, but rather two steps backward," and asked that a basis be provided for the work of the ICRC "with a view to setting up an international instrument, binding upon states, whether it is based on 'Hague' law or on 'Geneva' law." [29] And again, at the plenary session, he urged that "all steps should be taken to enable these rules to become in due course an instrument of international law." [30]

After the 1948 International Conference of the Red Cross, the diplomatic conference of 1949 took place, working wholly on the basis of drafts prepared by the ICRC and producing the new Geneva conventions of 1949. The representative of the ICRC pointed out that this time, at New Delhi, the situation was entirely different. The Draft Rules, 1956, are not yet a draft convention; in 1949, the draft convention had been approved beforehand by the governments, whereas this time everything proposed was the work of the Red Cross only. That is, of course, true; but it is not only a question of more time and of more studies. The New Delhi discussions have shown the present cleavage of the world and the unlikelihood of achieving a new international convention for the protection of the civilian population as long as the problem of disarmament — including also conventional weapons—control, and inspection is not on the way to solution and as long as the heavy tension between the "two worlds" continues. The work of the ICRC is humanitarian, but not Utopian; it is practical and has as its goal the creation of new international law. In the final analysis, time will decide the question whether the New Delhi Conference was successful as an important step leading to a new convention, or whether it was no more than a polite burial of the Draft Rules, 1956.

---

¹ See R. WERNER, LA CROIX ROUGE ET LES CONVENTIONS DE GENÈVE (1943) ; Max Huber, in 1 ANNUAIRE SUISSE DE DROIT INTERNATONAL 11–57 (1944) ; Pictet, *Les Nouvelles Conventions de Genève et la Croix Rouge*, REVUE INTERNATIONALE DE LA CROIX ROUGE, 655 (1949) ; 1 P. GUGGENHEIM, TRAITÉ DE DROIT INTERNATIONAL PUBLIC 288–89 (1953) ; 2 *ibid* at 337–44 (1954) ; A. VERDROSS, VÖLKERRECHT 110–11 (3rd ed. 1955) ; W. Schätzel, *La Croix Rouge et les Nations Unies*, ANNUAIRE DE L'ASSOCIATION DES AUDITEURS ET ANCIENS AUDITEURS DE L'ACADÉMIE DE DROIT INTERNATIONAL DE LA HAYE No. 28, 166–76 (1958).

² The Geneva conference of 1929 had previously recommended unanimously that a careful study be made in preparation for a convention concerning the protection of the civilian population. The idea of "security zones" appeared in 1929 and 1931. On December 22, 1931, the *ICRC* sent its circular No. 300, concerning the legal protection of the civilian population from the dangers of aerial and chemical warfare, to all the national Red Cross societies. The so-called Tokyo Draft on the same subject was submitted to the International Conference of the Red Cross. A revised draft of the 1929 conventions was considered by the sixteenth conference (London, 1938). All these studies were

submitted to the Swiss government which had intended to convoke a diplomatic conference at Geneva in 1940.

[3] See Josef L. Kunz, *The Geneva Conventions of August 12, 1949,* in LIPSKY (ed.), LAW AND POLITICS IN THE WORLD COMMUNITY 279–316, 368–73 (1953).

[4] Articles XXXV–XLVII apply only to protected civilian persons in the territory to the conflict; Articles XLVII–LXXVIII apply only to protected civilian persons in occupied territories; the "general protection" of the civilian population found no expression in rules of law.

[5] Draft Rules for the Protection of the Civilian Population from the Dangers of Indiscriminate Warfare. With Commentary (1955) (mimeo.).

[6] On the Draft Rules, 1955, see "The Laws of War," above.

[7] The report on this meeting was published by the *ICRC* as Doc. No. 347b.

[8] Published with commentary by the *ICRC* (1955).

[9] *ICRC*, Nineteenth International Conference of the Red Cross, New Delhi, October-November, 1957. Final Record Concerning the Draft Rules for the Limitation of Dangers Incurred by the Civilian Population in Time of War (1955) (mimeo.) (hereafter cited as Final Record).

[10] We have already referred to the dividing line: "Geneva" and "Hague" laws of war. This writer has in his study, *op. cit., supra,* note 6, pointed out the reasons why such a complete division is hardly possible. The Geneva Diplomatic Conference of 1949 continuously emphasized its lack of competence within the realm of the Hague laws of war; yet it is clear that such rules as the prohibition of reprisals, prohibition of taking hostages, prisoner-of-war status (under certain conditions) of members of resistance movements, even in occupied territories, profoundly influence the rules concerning the actual conduct of warfare. In 1955, the *ICRC* itself had stated that it had to go beyond the Geneva into the Hague laws of war, that the field covered by the 1955 draft rules is rather different from that covered by the Geneva conventions. But the 1956 draft rules try to restrict themselves to the Geneva laws of war: hence the title of the corresponding commission at the New Delhi Conference. The dividing line between Geneva and Hague laws of war was one of the arguments in the discussions.

[11] Some countries were represented only by Red Cross, others only by governmental delegates; some had two different delegates; in some cases the same person acted in a dual capacity, as representative of the Red Cross and of the government.

[12] All communist countries were represented; there were also delegates of the Federal Republic of Germany and of the "Democratic Republic of Germany," of the Republic of Korea and of the "Democratic Republic of Korea," and of North Viet-Nam.

[13] U.S.S.R., Bulgaria, Hungary, Poland, North Korea, Rumania.

[14] Argentina, Brazil, Belgium, Denmark, Ireland, Sweden, Uruguay proposed to hold a general debate first, followed by a discussion

article by article. Chile proposed a general debate, followed by a discission only of such articles on which there was no general agreement.

[15] See the List of Proposals and Amendments Concerning the Draft Rules, Final Record 175–84.

[16] Final Record 33–34.

[17] Albania, China, Czecholovakia, German Democratic Republic, Hungary, North Viet-Nam, Poland, Rumania, U.S.S.R. The Yugoslav delegation always took a completely independent stand. Burma and Syria took the same position as that taken by the communist delegates.

[18] Brazil, Final Record 20.

[19] Peru, *ibid.* at 25.

[20] Austria, *ibid.* at 43; Belgium, *ibid.* at 34–35; Canada, *ibid.* at 67–68; El Salvador, *ibid.* at 77–78; Mexico, *ibid.* at 40; Pakistan, *ibid.* at 83–84.

[21] *Ibid.* at 21–22.

[22] *Ibid.* at 37–38. He also stated: "I personally wish that atomic weapons had never been invented."

[23] *Ibid.* at 44–45.

[24] *Ibid.* at 47–48.

[25] *Ibid.* at 56–57.

[26] *Ibid.* at 29–37, 62–66. "Do you believe that governments which possess atomic weapons are convinced that the use of those weapons is a moral sin, a proof of wicked men? So far, I have seen no signs in this direction" (p. 65). "Can you believe that if a conflict should break out, and people's vital interests were at stake, that governments would hesitate, on moral grounds, to make use of such weapons? No." (p. 66).

[27] *Ibid.* at 36–37.

[28] *Ibid.* at 112–13.

[29] *Ibid.* at 70–71.

[30] *Ibid.* at 113–15.

DATE DUE

GAYLORD

PRINTED IN U.S.A.